THE COLLAPSE OF THE SOVIET MILITARY

To General Andrew Goodpaster,
who has long been a model
to me and scores of others
as a military leader, statesman,
and intellectual.

As a former SACEUR,
you will, I believe, find
this account of your old
adversary of more than
passing interest.

With great respect,

Bill Odom

7 Sep 98

WILLIAM E. ODOM

The Collapse of the Soviet Military

Yale University Press   New Haven & London

Published with assistance from the foundation established in memory of Philip Hamilton McMillan of the Class of 1894, Yale College.

Designed by James J. Johnson and set in Ehrhardt Roman type by Tseng Information Systems.
Printed in the United States of America.

Library of Congress Cataloging-in-Publication Data

Odom, William E.
The collapse of the Soviet military / William E. Odom.
   p.   cm.
Includes bibliographical references and index.
ISBN 0-300-07469-7 (cloth : alk. paper)
1. Soviet Union—History, Military.   I. Title.
DK54.O36   1998
355'.00947—dc21   98-17588

A catalogue record for this book is available from the British Library.

The paper in this book meets the guidelines for permanence and durability of the Committee on Production Guidelines for Book Longevity of the Council on Library Resources.

10   9   8   7   6   5   4   3   2

Contents

Illustrations

Acknowledgments

My professional life has largely coincided with the Cold War, and my concern with the Soviet military dates to my days as a cadet at West Point, when Soviet military power and political intentions were the most troubling questions for American strategy. Most of the rest of my career has been connected in one way or another with these.

I cannot say that I believed I would live to see the Soviet Armed Forces collapse in peace, but I did fear, on more than one occasion, that the U.S. military might be forced to defeat them in war. It is therefore with a sense of relief and humility that I have been allowed to try to explain what the Soviet military was and how and why it ended.

Much of the first part of the book derives from a seminar on Soviet military policy at Yale University that I taught for several years. My students consistently surprised me with their sophisticated interest in what I thought they would find an arcane and boring subject. They will find the first five chapters familiar because they helped shape them.

For the latter part of the book, I am grateful to the many former Soviet military officers, party leaders, and government officials who answered my questions, discussed the issues I raised, and tried to enlighten me on their realities and experiences. While I am not sad to see the passing of the Soviet Union, I do sympathize with those professional military officers who saw political power and authority collapse around them, leaving them confused about what their duty was and to whom they owed their loyalty. As a fellow professional officer, I have been spared this terrifying experience, which, in some ways, is as horrible as war itself. I hope this book conveys to readers a sense of the trauma of their predicament.

Among other debts, a grant from the Smith Richardson Foundation made most of my research possible, and the Hudson Institute has supported my writing over three years. My colleague at Hudson, Robert Dujarric, commented usefully on an early draft. Nathan O'Brien Hodge was helpful as my research assistant for several months, and both Mary FitzGerald and Robert Arnett lent a hand at critical times in tracking down sources. Eva Grace's secretarial assistance was invaluable. At Yale University Press, Jonathan Brent provided excellent advice, and Dan Heaton's remarkable editing skills earned my deep respect. Finally, my wife Anne is as delighted as I am to see this project ended—finally.

Introduction

In a mere six years, the world's largest and arguably most powerful military melted like the spring ice in Russia's arctic rivers as it breaks up, drifts in floes, and slowly disappears. The Soviet military was not destroyed by invading armies. It did not attempt to seize political power from the disintegrating Communist Party and Soviet state, not even as a desperate act of self-preservation. Nor did it launch a foreign war to rally domestic support for the imperiled regime. Sitting on the largest nuclear weapons arsenal in the world, it made no threats to use them. Instead, the Soviet Armed Forces went complaining but passively into the dustbin of history, to use Trotsky's phrase.

How did this happen? Why? No one expected it. It seemed so improbable that even knowledgeable Western observers discounted the prospect in the face of mounting evidence that the Soviet state was teetering toward an abyss. Some expected the military to drag the regime back to safety, but it did not. Arm-in-arm, the Communist Party and the generals went to their demise together.

Perhaps this failure in understanding should not be astonishing. The Soviet military wrapped itself in secrecy. Scholars were forced to study it like archaeologists investigating vanished civilizations, inferring what they could from fragmentary evidence they dug out of the voluminous, propaganda-filled, heavily censored Soviet literature on the military. Western intelligence services penetrated its veil of secrecy more effectively, but their evidence, though extensive by the late 1970s, was always incomplete. Even after much of that information was declassified and made available to scholars, the Soviet military remained a mystery in many ways.

Part of the reason was cultural. Garrison states are not readily understood by people who grow up in liberal political systems. This was especially true of the Soviet Union, whose ideology and organizational character were both so fundamentally alien to most Westerners. Ethnocentric biases were not easy to overcome, even for scholars and intelligence analysts, and Soviet secrecy deepened the difficulties.

During Gorbachev's rule, secrecy about Soviet military affairs began to be relaxed, and since the dissolution of the Soviet Union in December 1991, a vast amount of new evidence has become available, making it possible to reveal much of the drama of the demise of the Soviet Armed Forces. Some scenes of this play are filled with fascinating scheming and action. In others, arcane organizational developments crowd center stage. And all the while, the main action occurs against a backdrop of the complex organizational arrangements of the military, the party, the economy, and the state.

Thus anyone who wants to raise the curtain on this drama faces a difficult challenge. Only if the bureaucratic stage sets are made comprehensible can the central spectacle of the organizational developments emerge, as the leading characters struggle to control and direct them. This is not an easy effect to achieve. Yet it must be attempted because the discoveries are worth the risks.

Accordingly, the book begins with these "stage sets" of policy-making and bureaucratic arrangements. The first five chapters are devoted to explaining what the Soviet military was in the mid-1980s and how it became what it was. Because the Soviet Armed Forces were so unlike Western militaries, mirror imaging simply will not suffice; such shortcuts both distort and omit key realities.

Chapter 1 explains Marxism as a theory of war and shows why Lenin found it so compatible with Clausewitz's theorizing. Students of Marxism will react to it variously. Those who see it mainly, even affectionately, as a theory of socialism and economic equality may object. More detached readers, though, should find that it clarifies a great deal in later chapters about Gorbachev's "new thinking" in foreign and military policy.

Chapters 2, 3, and 4 describe the "stage sets." Although they were fairly well understood by the 1980s, they are described here with some new evidence. Several books and monographs on these topics provide far more detail, but none treats all three—organizational structures, manpower policies, and military-industrial arrangements—in a coherently related fashion. Impatient readers may be tempted to skip over these chapters, but they will probably find themselves returning to them for clarifications.

In the final backdrop description, Chapter 5, I attempt to put the reader in the minds of Soviet political and military leaders in order to understand what they thought they were doing with their huge military forces in peacetime and how they intended to use them in wartime. The chapter deals with some contentious issues. Although most of what is presented was known previously, some things were not, and several issues were hotly disputed—and not just among specialists but also among journalists, editors, opinion makers, and

Western political leaders. Based on new and old evidence, this chapter represents my attempt to resolve old debates about the Soviet view of nuclear war, arms control objectives, consequences of arms control agreements, and the interaction of U.S. and Soviet strategy and doctrine for war in Europe.

In Chapter 6, the main players enter, and all that follows in succeeding chapters needs little introduction. These actors take us into the most secret circles of Soviet policy making—the Politburo, the Central Committee, and the Ministry of Defense—as well as into military-industrial circles, the public debates, factional struggles in the new parliament, into the military barracks to see how the army lived, and into the streets, as army units tried to repress the new political forces unleashed by glasnost and perestroika. The crisis of 18–21 August 1991 naturally demands intensive examination, but the last months of the Soviet military's existence had less conspicuous but equally critical moments as well—for example, when Gorbachev secretly invited the military to seize power in order to preempt the imminent dissolution of the Soviet Union.

Although this is a study of the Soviet military, it is also a political, and to some extent an economic, analysis. The eminent military historian Peter Paret has observed that "in reality, political, economic, and military power are not easily separated," and that the study of any one separately requires an isolation from which "misinterpretations often follow . . . most often in the historical literature on military power."[1] That has certainly been true of much of the literature on Soviet military power, but no less so in the literature on Soviet politics and economics. It is also reflected in the occasional observation after the collapse of the Soviet Union that the U.S. government must have vastly overrated the Soviet military's capacity for conducting war against NATO. Putting the military in the context of Soviet political and economic power provides a much better basis for judging the validity of that charge. It also lets us see that the centrality of the "military question" for the political and economic foundations of the regime, not only in the Soviet Union, but in Imperial Russia as well, has tended to be overlooked. Taking that question into account suggests that today Russia has its first real opportunity in modern times to break out of a cycle of structural conditions that have kept it from the path of liberal political and economic development. Thus the larger meaning of the collapse of the Soviet military would surely be missed if the political and economic dimensions of the Soviet regime were not an integral part of the story.

Abbreviations

ABM	Antiballistic missile
ADD	Long-range aviation
CC	Central Committee
CP	Communist Party
CPSU	Communist Party of the Soviet Union
DOSAAF	Society for Assistance to the Army, Aviation, and the Fleet
FYP	Five-year plan
GF	Ground forces
GKChP	State Committee for an Emergency in the USSR
GKNT	State Committee for Science and Technology
GKO	State Committee for Defense (World War II)
GOSPLAN	State Planning Commission
GOSSNAB	State Supply Committee
GOSTsEN	State Committee for Prices
GPU	Main Political Administration (also MPA)
GRU	Main Intelligence Administration (military intelligence)
ICBM	Intercontinental Ballistic Missile
INF	Intermediate-range nuclear forces
KGB	Committee for State Security (intelligence, counterintelligence, and several other functions)
MD	Military district
MFA	Ministry of Foreign Affairs
MoD	Ministry of Defense
MPA	Main Political Administration (also GPU)
MVD	Ministry of Internal Affairs
NEP	New Economic Policy, 1921–27

OO	Special section; KGB organ within a military unit
Politburo	Political bureau of the CPSU
PVO	Air defense forces
RSFSR	Russian Soviet Federated Socialist Republic
RVSN	Rocket forces for strategic purposes
SSBN	Nuclear submarine armed with nuclear armed ballistic missiles
Stavka	The "high command" in Moscow during World War II
STO	Council of Labor and Defense, 1919–34
TVD	Theater of military operations
VDV	Airborne forces
VPK	Military industrial commission
VTA	Military transport aviation
VVS	Air forces

ONE

The Soviet Philosophy of War

Marx and Engels can be rightly called the fathers of modern total war.

SIGMUND NEUMAN

The more deeply political a war, the more "military" it seems; the less deeply political it is, the more "political" it seems.

V. I. LENIN

Few issues divided Western observers as sharply during the Cold War as how to explain the intellectual basis of Soviet military thought. Opinion varied from an overly mechanistic view that Marxism-Leninism explained almost everything to an excessively ethnocentric view that it explained nothing. The character of modern military technology, in this latter view, removed the ideological factor; moreover, Soviet military forces could be explained primarily as a reaction to U.S. military programs. A third view, a "political culture" explanation, was occasionally invoked to explain Soviet behavior that was inconsistent with the second view: frequent foreign invasions over the centuries had imbued Soviet military thinking with defensive paranoia. The first view held sway in U.S. policy-making circles during the 1950s but gave way to the second and third views during the late 1960s and through the 1970s.[1]

By the early 1980s, the Soviet Armed Forces were the largest in the world by every measure—in manpower, in numbers of weapons, in varieties of weapons, in mobilization potential, and in the size of their military-industrial base. To be sure, they lagged behind the U.S. armed forces and several NATO militaries in the quality of many categories of weapons, equipment, and manpower, but they were ahead in a few qualitative categories and equal in several others. The vast quantitative advantages held by the Soviet military cannot be explained as the result of a simple action-reaction U.S.-Soviet arms race. Nor is

1

the "political culture" explanation, which imputes only defensive motives to Russia's obsession with large forces, an adequate rationalization. In fact, the Imperial General Staff proudly reported to the tsar that between 1700 and 1870 the army had fought thirty-eight wars, all but two of them offensive.[2] Both explanations may account for aspects of the Soviet military buildup, but ideology has to be reintroduced as a critical determinant, though not in the mechanistic sense that it was too often understood. Marxism-Leninism, as the official basis for Soviet military policy, identified the "threat"—the probable enemy against which Soviet forces were sized and designed to fight. It provided a prism through which military policy was consistently refracted. It also was claimed to provide a scientific explanation of war as a social phenomenon, its purpose, its necessity, its essence, and finally, a view of how it could eventually be banished from human relations.

The truth or falsity of this official ideological view of war is finally beside the point. Its importance lies in the intellectual hegemony it held within the highest ranks of the Soviet political and military leadership. In the course of a few years, from 1985 to 1992, the dramatic changes in Soviet military policy were fundamentally at odds with all these ideological precepts. The psychological dissonance they created in the minds of the senior military leaders is difficult to exaggerate. The Marxist-Leninist philosophy of war formed the dominant cognitive system through which the generals perceived the rapid changes being thrust upon them, and their reactions and policy arguments are only partially comprehensible without an understanding of that system. A look at the intellectual roots of that philosophy of war, therefore, is the essential point of departure for an account of the demise of the Soviet military.

Soviet Thinking About War

Marxism is itself a theory of war. The foundation of the theory was already maturely developed in Marx's early manuscript *The German Ideology*, jointly written with Frederick Engels in 1846.[3] In this short treatise Marx articulates his concept of "alienation," the key to his theory of class struggle. Man's alienation from man is the consequence of "private ownership of the means of production," a material relation determined by the economic system of each historical epoch: the master versus the slave, the feudal lord versus the peasant, the bourgeois capitalist versus the propertyless urban worker. In the epoch of slave-labor economies, the "exploitation" by the owner of the slave produced a relationship in which the two were alienated from one another, one knowing only the fruits of production without the experience of labor, the other knowing only the labor while being denied its fruits. Both were unfulfilled, condemned to alienation inherent in the economic relationship that bound them together. In the feudal epoch, alienation was perpetuated because private ownership of the means of production survived in a new form. And it survives into the capitalist epoch as well. This objective economic reality, alienating man from man, forms the basis for "class interests" and the motivation for "class struggle." Class struggle, of course, leads to violent revolution, and revolutions are a form of warfare, which eventually brings the collapse of each historical epoch, distinctive in its methods of production and its level of technology. War, in Marx's theory of historical development, is a vehicle of change—the phenomenon that propels history—and the objective source of all war is found in the private ownership of the means of production. *The Communist Manifesto* of 1849 has this theory of war deeply embedded in its text.

Later, in his history of the civil war in France, 1870–71, Marx offered a further elaboration of the theory as it applied to the bourgeois epoch in which nation states fought wars against each other.[4] This conflict demonstrated, as Marx saw, that wars do not always have a progressive outcome. The decisions of leaders of classes play a key role in determining whether or not they are progressive or reactionary in their consequences. Marx chided French revolutionary leaders of the Paris commune for nationalist patriotic sentiments and their failure to recognize that the bourgeois governments of France and Germany were merely defending the class interests of their ruling capitalist classes. The interests of the working class transcended national boundaries, and for a truly socialist revolution to occur, the war had to be expanded across state boundaries so that the working classes could join in defending their shared interests in ending exploitation. The French workers should have made common cause with German workers to defeat bourgeois regimes in both countries, but their leaders in Paris, lacking Marx's "scientific" understanding of the historical process, made erroneous decisions that brought about the defeat of the Paris commune.

Lenin went beyond Marx, however, by adding the concept of alliances between the working class and other oppressed classes in a common struggle against the ruling class. In his 1905 essay *Two Tactics of Social Democracy in the Democratic Revolution* (1905), he called for joining the Russian peasantry in an alliance with the working class.[5] The Russian working class was too small to expect to win a revolution alone in the feudal Russian empire. Lenin considered the Russian bourgeoisie both too small and too weak to be worthy of a revolutionary alliance. Moreover, they showed no inclination to play their proper historical role by overthrowing the tsar and establishing a bourgeois regime.

The very large Russian peasantry, by contrast, was in a revolutionary mood, and although it was what the Marxists termed a "petty bourgeois" class in the sense that peasants wanted private ownership of their land as the reward for revolution, it was historically progressive in that it opposed the oppressive feudal landowning class. This reality made it possible, Lenin argued, for the workers and peasants to ally against the regime, and if they did, they certainly possessed the strength to win a revolution. Moreover, they could shunt aside the Russian bourgeoisie, skipping over the capitalist epoch. A victorious revolution in Russia was bound, in Lenin's judgment, to be accompanied by a revolution in Europe, particularly in Germany, France, and Britain, where the working classes were large and most advanced. The two revolutions could then be united, the European working class joining with the Russian working class, making a union that would outweigh the political power of the Russian peasantry after the revolution, when it would show its bourgeois character and demand private ownership of land.

Lenin later generalized this tactic of class alliances on a global scale. In his 1916 essay "Imperialism: The Highest Stage of Capitalism," he explained colonial wars as struggles among the leading capitalist states for markets in the rest of the world.[6] In the process, capitalism had reached a new stage, transcending the bourgeois nation state, consisting of a single global economic system. Capitalism's objective nature required war; its dynamic character propelled the ruling capitalist classes of nation states into violent struggles over colonial markets extending into the backward regions of the world. The resulting global integration of the capitalist economic system demanded, in Lenin's view, a broader interpretation of the international class struggle, one that exposed the revolutionary potential not just in Europe's large working class but also in the progressive classes in the colonial countries.

Thus Lenin's theory of imperialism provided the seeds of a future Bolshevik strategy for the "international class struggle," going beyond Marx's concern for a scientifically informed consciousness within a single worldwide class of propertyless workers of its objective common interest in a political revolution, searching for other classes and groups as tactical allies of the working class. Colonial countries had not yet experienced bourgeois revolutions. Local national liberation movements, notwithstanding their bourgeois character, could, by fighting for their independence, become objective allies of the weak local working classes in those countries. In the context of colonialism these nationalists were objectively "progressive" political forces. Furthermore, because capitalism had become a world imperialist system, revolutions in the colonies might well break the "weakest link" in imperialism's chain of colonies, enabling a war in the colonies to bring down the whole imperialist structure and to spread revolution to imperialism's center in Europe. With this ideological arrow in his quiver, Lenin could call for Social Democratic support of so-called "national liberation wars" in colonial countries.[7] And he could justify his assertion that a world socialist revolution could begin in backward Russia, where the working class was extremely weak. He could cogently argue that he had not abandoned Marxism but was developing it creatively to identify "objective" revolutionary potential, not just in Europe but more widely, by appreciating the "law of uneven historical development," which explained that different countries and societies could be at different levels of economic development and therefore in different historical epochs at the same time.

The complexities confronting this global application of Marxism were enormous—especially how to deal with allied "progressive" classes when they turned "reactionary" after a revolution—but Lenin's unlimited faith in the scientific nature of Marxism convinced him that there were solutions if Marxism were properly used to discover them. Most important for our purposes here is that all of this theorizing centered on wars, wars of several kinds, wars throughout the world. Lenin had not missed the key feature of Marxism: it was, at root, a theory of war.

All theories have their epistemological and philosophical grounds. Obviously, Marx's philosophy of war is first of all eschatological. War has an immanent character, carrying mankind toward an ultimate goal. For both Marx and Lenin, war provides the motor for historical progress because it is an expression of class struggle. It is not something to be prevented before the socialist epoch has been reached. Moreover, man cannot avoid war in the capitalist and earlier stages of history, where private ownership of the means of production is the foundation of economic relations, ensuring man's alienation from man and class struggle. In fact, wars that advance societies through the various stages of development are "progressive," that is, "just wars." Unjust wars are those fought by ruling classes to prevent progressive development. While he was explicitly claiming that he held a scientific view of war, Marx was also implicitly taking a moral view. Although war is materialistically determined, it has both moral and immoral sides. In other words, war serves the inexorable laws of historical development and at the same time confronts man with moral choices, but not in the bourgeois sense of allowing *all* individuals to make morally correct choices in choosing sides. Marx's moral choices are open only to those who comprehend his scientific explanation of war, allowing them to distinguish between progressive wars, which are just, and reactionary wars, which are unjust. Those who are scientifically enlightened acquire an obligation both to promote progressive wars and to work for the achievement of scientifically based peace, the end of all war. How is that to be accomplished?

As Lenin put it forcefully in "What Is to Be Done?" Social Democratic self-consciousness allows the working class to understand that private ownership of means of production is the cause of class conflict, of exploitation, and of war.[8] Armed with this scientific insight, the international working class and its leadership vanguard, a Marxist revolutionary party, could carry through a political revolution, end the system of private ownership, and create genuine socialism and the permanent peace that would come through the elimination of the private. Scientifically based peace, therefore, requires the end of capitalism and its foundation, private property. By ideological definition, "peace-loving forces," as later Soviet rhetoric would label them, are political groups determined to use violent revolution to destroy economic systems based on private ownership. This choice of terms, of course, had the tactical advantage of deceiving the politically naïve in capitalist countries who understood "peace-loving" to mean something quite different, utopian in nature — like the utopian socialism upon which Marx heaped such scorn.

The inherent determinism in this eschatological philosophy of war appears to make unnecessary the voluntarism that Lenin proclaimed essential for revolutionary leadership. Precisely this ideological paradox confronted the Russian Marxists at the turn of the twentieth century. What role should their party play within the feudal conditions of the Russian empire to be? Should they let the laws of history work their predetermined progressive ways? Or should they exercise voluntarist leadership to advance historical development more effectively? This well-known dilemma, of which the Menshevik and Bolshevik factions chose opposite horns, has been the subject of a vast literature, but here it is noteworthy only in connection with the later official Soviet Marxist-Leninist philosophy of war. Lenin insisted on a strong voluntarist component in his Marxism, while his opponents were less convinced that so much voluntarism was compatible with historical materialism. Although the party's split into Bolshevik and Menshevik factions involved more than the issue of voluntarism versus determinism alone, it did play a significant role. It would incline most Social Democrats in 1917 to believe that a socialist revolution was impossible in Russia. Russia first had to go through a bourgeois-capitalist epoch. For them the collapse of the old regime was the dawn of a long bourgeois epoch. Lenin took the opposite view, holding that a socialist revolution was entirely possible in Russia if the working class leadership exercised its free will to take power based on a two-class alliance of workers and peasants.

Lenin could offer a strong a justification for his political voluntarism in

Marx's writings. *The Communist Manifesto* itself described the socialist revolution as a conscious human act, one possible only when the working class possessed a scientific understanding of the laws of history, not something that it would carry through mindlessly, propelled by material conditions alone. Moreover, Marx's work distinguishes "Communists" as the leaders, "the most advanced and resolute section of the working class parties of every country that pushes forward all others."[9] In his history of the civil war in France, he again emphasized the role of leadership, blaming the leaders of the Paris commune for making the wrong choices. A rigid determinist could not logically make such charges. It is difficult to fault Lenin's reading of Marx on this point. Indeed, Marx provided an unambiguous role for human voluntarism in making revolutions and conducting class warfare. Lenin, however, went beyond Marx to buttress this voluntarist component with the ideas of Germany's best-known military theorist, Carl von Clausewitz.

Clausewitz treats war epistemologically as an instrument in the hands of the leaders of states. They try to use it purposefully, to achieve political goals, though they often fail. War, therefore, is not some phenomenon apart from man, like stormy weather or disease, a destructive affair against which man can only try to limit harm to himself. Nor does it serve some divine purpose, leading man toward heaven or utopia. It is man's creation, his policy instrument, and its purposes are his political purposes. This strongly voluntarist aspect of Clausewitz's philosophy, however, is not unconstrained. Leaders can choose to start wars for strategic purposes, but they are never fully in control of all the variables affecting the course and outcomes of wars. The imponderables in war are numerous, making it a very difficult policy instrument to use effectively.

Lenin openly acknowledged Clausewitz's profound influence on him. He read *On War* in 1915 while living in Switzerland, and his lengthy and approving notes on the book indicate the intellectual seriousness with which he treated Clausewitz's ideas.[10] At the time, Lenin was involved in quarrels over the essence of Marxism and its relationship to Hegel. He was also smarting with anger at the European Social Democrats who sided with their national governments in the war instead of leading the workers against those governments and making it the class war that, in his view, it already was. Thus several things in *On War* appealed to him, not least that Clausewitz was influenced by Hegel and had adopted Hegelian affectations in his style of thinking. Most important for Lenin, though, was a correct Marxist understanding of World War I. He was convinced that the war was objectively a conflict between the international working class and international capitalism, even if most of his fellow Social Democrats accepted the bourgeois view that it was a struggle among nations.[11]

Lenin enthusiastically agreed with Clausewitz's view of war as politics, as an instrument of policy for imposing one's will on an opponent. Although he did not himself put it so explicitly, Lenin effectively adopted Clausewitz's "paradoxical trinity" for characterizing the major components in a state's use of war. In Clausewitz's words,[12] "As a total phenomenon its dominant tendencies always make war a paradoxical trinity—composed of primordial violence, hatred, and enmity, which are regarded as a blind natural force; of the play of chance and probability within which the creative spirit is free to roam; and of its element of subordination, as an instrument of policy, which makes it subject to reason alone. The first of these three aspects mainly concerns the people; the second the commander and his army; the third the government."

Put another way, Clausewitz's "trinity" consists of (1) the popular emotions of the "nation" (as peoples were more often calling themselves in nineteenth-century Europe); (2) "the fog of war" (Clausewitz's better-known term for chance and probability) surrounding the army on the battlefield; and (3) the attempt of government (the cabinet and the general staff, as he defines it elsewhere) to impose rationality on war for its own political purposes. The nation provides the psychological energy for combat. The fog of war is the physical context of armed struggle, signifying that war's dynamics are highly problematic, not subject to the simple mechanical laws that Henri de Jomini, Clausewitz's contemporary, tried to devise. The cabinet and the general staff impose purpose and rationality on the nation's passion through strategic direction for achieving political aims with war. The weather metaphor, "fog," when viewed from the perspective of modern meteorological science, suggests probability theory, not Newtonian laws of mechanics, as the appropriate concept for understanding what commanders face on the battlefield. Precisely Clausewitz's resort to the mathematics of probabilities—"the play of chance and probability"—reveals the fundamental difference between Clausewitz and other military theorists of his day.[13] Victory in war cannot be achieved by applying geometry and mechanical "laws of solids," as a civil engineer does in building a bridge. Rather it is more like anticipating and dealing effectively with weather that interferes with or facilitates one's purposes, something that can be partially understood by rational analysis and mitigated by human judgments, yet remains fraught with uncertainties and surprises.

In Lenin's view, all politics is a vast battlefield of class struggle and revolution. It is messy and often unpredictable, involving setbacks, yet guided by comprehensible scientific processes—not simple propositions like those of Euclidian geometry and Newtonian physics, but more analogous to large numbers of apparently random events which can be comprehended approximately by theories of statistics and subjected to human rational action informed by conceptually appropriate theories and analysis.[14]

In Clausewitz, Lenin found a theory that combined the role of leadership with the vast and problematic forces of political struggle. Those forces have an internal logic uncovered in Marx's dialectical materialist interpretation of history, but that logic is not purely mechanistic in the sense of engineering principles. Random variables and human choice are also part of it. Humans who understand the general logic of these forces, however, can act in rational ways to achieve preferred outcomes. Lenin recognized that Clausewitz was onto something with his tough-minded empirical observations, coupled with his Hegelianism, even if he did not have the benefit of Marx's scientific insights.

Clausewitz's trinity was easily adaptable to Lenin's own scheme of war and politics. Lenin's concept of the Bolshevik party's leadership role fit neatly into the role Clausewitz gave to the government for the rational pursuit of political objectives with military means. The revolutionary party provided the working-class movement with rational leadership, based on its knowledge of Marx's scientific theory of history and on its shrewd exercise of the political free will that Marx envisioned for those carrying through a socialist revolution—that is, a war to end all wars. Certainly Lenin's vision of politics fit Clausewitz's fog-of-war metaphor with its "play of chance and probability." Lenin's *"Left-Wing" Communism: An Infantile Disorder* (1920)[15] was aimed at European Social Democrats who interpreted Marxism in a purely mechanistic fashion, just as Clausewitz implicitly criticized the excessively mechanistic character of thinking by Jomini and other contemporary military theorists.[16] Although the problematic component of the trinity would appear to be "the people," because Clausewitz's did not distinguish among classes, Lenin could manage the omission. Clausewitz lived in the very time when the modern nation state was maturing in Europe, and logically, he assumed that warring opponents are states. He could not be expected to realize that "transnational" warfare between classes would soon transcend "international" warfare between states.[17] Lenin merely had to substitute "class" for "the people" and the "party" for the "government" to adapt Clausewitz's trinity to a Marxist framework. Lenin's actions after he took power in Russia can be effectively explained with this trinity—propagandizing and agitating the international working class (primordial violence, hatred, and enmity), recognizing the vicissitudes of class conflicts (the play of chance and probability), and founding communist parties worldwide under Moscow's leadership to lead the international working class in revolution (subordination as an instrument of policy).

In light of this remarkable overlap of theories of war and revolution, Clausewitz's canonization in the church of Soviet military theory is not surprising, but his status as a saint always remained conditional, as a basic text used for educating Soviet officers on ideological matters makes clear:

> "With reference to wars," Lenin wrote, "the main thesis of dialectics . . . is that *'war is simply the continuation of politics by other* (i.e., violent) *means.'* Such is the formula of Clausewitz, one of the greatest writers on the history of war. . . . And it was always the standpoint of Marx and Engels, who regard *any* war as the *continuation* of the politics of the powers concerned — and the *various classes* within these countries. . . .
>
> "We see that in expounding the essence of war, Lenin refers to Clausewitz. . . . And this is only logical, for Clausewitz's research into the relation of wars to politics and his formula about war being a continuation of politics by violent means were an indubitable contribution to the development of military thought at the time.
>
> "It would, however, be a gross error to think that the views on the essence of war held by Marxism-Leninism are identical with those propounded by Clausewitz. On the contrary, there is a fundamental difference between them . . . in their understanding of politics, of its class nature." [18]

As the Soviet military entered its last six years of existence, its leaders were steeped in this philosophy of war. They were imbued with both an eschatological and an instrumental view of war. Yet they were not unique in appropriating a seemingly contradictory amalgam of theoretical viewpoints. As Michael Howard has cogently explained, liberalism has always been torn between incompatible theories of war, far less compatible then those held by the Soviet leadership.[19] From Erasmus to the present, liberal thinkers have viewed war as evil, a thing to be banished through pacifism, arms control, or an appeal to human morality. Yet at times liberals have resorted to war for political aims, in the Clausewitzian tradition, clothing such wars in the garb of crusades for higher moral purposes. Much Western analysis of Soviet military policy has dismissed the eschatological component of the Soviet theory of war, assuming that Soviet generals do not really believe their own ideological propositions. The same can be said of Western military leaders. Do they really believe in Western liberalism's antipathy for war as an instrument of policy? Perhaps many do not, but the hegemony of that idea remains operational for military policy making in Western democracies. For practical purposes Western generals most often act as though they do believe the liberal assumptions about war, even if they do not consciously consider the matter in philosophical terms. The same must said for Soviet military leaders. When I interviewed several of them, most could not easily articulate the theoretical propositions of Marxism-Leninism on war, but a few could, particularly those who worked at the General Staff level.[20] Political officers, of course, were the most articulate on these matters. The compelling conclusion, therefore, seems to be that the propositions of the official ideology held hegemony over their thought whether or not every one of them was conscious of it.

Although Western scholars have too often denied or ignored it, Marxism-Leninism is indeed a significant factor in any explanation of why the Soviet Union built such large military forces and why they devised the kinds of war plans they did.[21] Based on a class analysis, the General Staff could easily identify the "threat" against which it had to plan for war. The "probable enemy" included all countries in which private ownership of the means of production existed. The number of such countries was quite large, forming a great encircling ring around the Soviet Union, its Warsaw Pact allies, and other socialist states.

Moreover, the Communist Party consistently emphasized such class analysis in its strategic guidance to the military, and its practical articulation was fairly consistent throughout Soviet history. Lenin first devised the ideological basis for formal diplomatic relations with imperialist states shortly after the end of the civil war. In 1919 he had founded the Communist International (Comintern), an organization controlling all foreign communist parties.[22] The Comintern became his mechanism for coordinating the revolutionary work of the international working class through a network of responsive communist parties on a transnational basis. Parallel to this linkage, he sought peace with the imperialist states through formal diplomatic ties, realizing his first success with the establishment of diplomatic relations with Germany at Rapallo in 1922. Within the context of peaceful state-to-state relations with the West, he sought economic assistance for the Soviet state. Within the context of party-to-party relations, he sought revolution, foremost in Germany. In the colonial areas, communist parties were instructed to seek political alliances with local nationalist bourgeois parties for the purpose of inspiring revolts against the European empires. All these policies flow consistently from his development of Marxism in his own thinking before the revolution. They make sense as a strategy only in that context; otherwise they are not only incomprehensible but also look contradictory, even absurd.

This strategy, of course, was designed to gain a so-called "breathing space" during which the Soviet Union could prepare for the inevitable military showdown with the imperialist states of the world and the complete victory of socialism. Although Lenin used the term "peaceful cohabitation," the strategy soon became known as peaceful coexistence, and it was continued actively until 1928, when Stalin, without renouncing it, created a war scare, essentially letting the strategy lapse until after Hitler took power in Germany.[23] The Nazi-Soviet Pact of 1939 has generally been seen as a second abandonment of this strategy, but a strong case can be made that the alliance with Germany was the product of Stalin's adaptation of this well-established ideological formula.[24] In the immediate postwar period, Stalin's formula was a "two camp struggle," the socialist camp versus the imperialist camp, but by the mid-1950s, Khrushchev, as part of his de-Stalinization campaign, revived "Leninist norms" in Soviet foreign policy, making peaceful coexistence once more its "general line." In substance it involved most of the same components as in the interwar period, but the Comintern, abolished in 1943 by Stalin, was no longer the vehicle for controlling foreign communist parties, and "polycentricism"—the Western description of competing centers of communist orthodoxy—began to emerge, as Yugoslavia and China challenged Moscow's leadership of the international communist movement.[25]

In the Third Party Program, promulgated at the Twenty-second Congress of the Communist Party of the Soviet Union (CPSU) in 1961, peaceful coexistence was defined as "a specific form of the international class struggle." This formulation made clear to any properly trained communist that "peace" meant the final victory of the socialist camp—not a "bourgeois peace," but rather scientifically based peace in the Marxist-Leninist sense. In other words, the prospect of a military showdown with imperialism was not to be discounted. Khrushchev had revised Lenin's assertion that a war with imperialism was inevitable, based on the advent of nuclear weapons, but that revision did not wholly discount the possibility. War might be avoided, however, as the Soviet military changed the "correlation" of military forces between the socialist and imperialist camps to provide an edge so large that imperialist leaders would not dare resort to use of nuclear weapons. We shall return to the issue of the role of nuclear weapons, but here it must suffice to note Khrushchev's ideological revision. Otherwise, "peaceful coexistence as a specific form of international class struggle" became once again the policy context for Soviet military planning, and it remained so until Gorbachev's radical revision of the concept of peaceful coexistence in 1987.

The Programmatic Implications of the Soviet Philosophy of War

In the postwar period, therefore, especially after Brezhnev came to power, Soviet military planning was based on the assumption that a world war could break out, and if it did, the Soviet Union and its communist allies, especially those in the Warsaw Pact, would confront the entire capitalist world as one great hostile coalition. Such planning was also based on a firm commitment to taking the offensive at the very outbreak of hostilities. This belief in the primacy of the offensive form of warfare goes back to the formulation of a specifically Marxist military doctrine sponsored by Mikhail Frunze, briefly the commissar of war in the mid-1920s. Stalin's lapse from this orthodoxy between 1938 and 1941, to be sure, was an embarrassment explained away by the gross distortions of official Soviet historiography, but after World War II, the primacy of the offensive was once again asserted in Marshal V. D. Sokolovskii's volume *Military Strategy,* taking into account the advent of nuclear weapons, rocketry, and cybernetics and their revolutionary impact on the nature of warfare.[26] Given such a doctrinal outlook, the General Staff saw as its war planning task the design of swift offensives into Europe, into Northeast Asia, and possibly, but with a much lower priority, into Southwest Asia and the Middle East. The plan also required being able to survive a U.S. nuclear attack on the Soviet homeland, as well as to deliver a nuclear attack on the United States. Finally, it meant coping with and eventually defeating the U.S. Navy in the Atlantic and the Pacific.

These were huge tasks, much larger than a traditional "balance of power" strategy would have demanded and many times larger than a realistic assessment of the actual military threats to Soviet territory would have dictated. They required huge forces, forces structured quite differently from U.S. and NATO forces, which were designed to defend initially and to depend on mobilization of large ground forces after the outbreak of hostilities. Apparently the initial Soviet aim was to match the United States and NATO in particular types of weapons and forces—for example, bombers, ballistic missiles, and submarines—but in numbers of weapons and forces, mere equity was obviously considered inadequate. Soviet inventories of new tanks, artillery, air defense missiles, tactical ballistic missiles, tactical combat aircraft, and others soon exceeded U.S. and NATO inventories by very large margins. Difficult additional questions arose. How long would a third world war last? What phase of the war and what specific operations would be decisive? What kinds of forces would be most critical? Different answers to these questions would yield different Soviet force requirements. Ideologically based answers generated requirements for staggeringly large and modern forces.

Clearly the ideology, as it defined the socialist and imperialist camps, dictated the number and location of the likely opponents and allies. It also dictated the preference for the offensive after Frunze won the debate over the issue in the 1920s, resting his case heavily on ideological grounds. At the same time, new technologies were influencing force requirements, both in quantity and in quality. The U.S. lead in the new technologies gave the military force–building competition an "action-reaction" character, but it explains only limited features of the profile of Soviet forces. The eighteen active and ten reserve U.S. divisions hardly prompted a Soviet ground force structure capable of rapidly deploying more than two hundred divisions. And the extremely modest U.S. and NATO air defense structure cannot explain the thousands of Soviet surface-to-air missile systems. Geographic differences and offensive versus defensive planning must be taken into account, but only the official ideology provided an adequate rationale for the whole of the Soviet force structure.

Some Western analysts have tried to explain the unusually large Soviet force structure as the consequence of interservice bureaucratic rivalries.[27] Interviews of former Soviet officers and party officials reveal a complex and strong bureaucratic dynamic, but it was not analogous to the mirror-image inferences of bureaucratic politics in the U.S. defense establishment. In the 1950s the Ministry of Defense appears to have driven the military-industrial sector to meet its newly devised weapons requirements. By the late 1970s, however, the military-industrial sector was pushing its products on an often reluctant Ministry of Defense. Certain important aspects of the Soviet military buildup can be explained as the result of bureaucratic dynamics, but the ideology was the rationale for creating the bureaucratic structures in the first place.

A combination of all the traditional hypotheses is needed to explain the size of Soviet forces, but the least relevant of them is that Russians remained obsessed with insecurity based on a long history of frequent foreign invasions. The experience of Hitler's surprise attack in World War II undoubtedly remains etched on the Russian public mind, but the earlier historical record does not support this popular proposition.[28] Russian invasions of neighboring states were far more numerous than were invasions of Russia.

In sum, a unique philosophy of war took strong roots early in the Soviet regime. Marxism provided its eschatological component, a pseudoscientific theory of historical development. Marx admitted borrowing heavily from Hegel but insisted that he had turned Hegel on his head by basing his theory on "materialism" rather than "idealism," as Hegel had done. Lenin formalized the voluntarist component of theory by underscoring Marx's own assumptions that a socialist revolution depended on the proletariat's class consciousness and understanding of the laws of history. Most important, Lenin devised the theory of a revolutionary party for inducing such class consciousness in the proletariat and leading it to victory by using violence in a purposeful fashion. In borrowing from Clausewitz, Lenin actually inverted Clausewitz's theory—turned him on his head, just as Marx claimed to have done to Hegel, by basing politics on war (revolution) instead of war on politics. War, for Lenin, was not just the continuation of politics by other means; it was the essence of politics, domestic and international, because it was the product of class struggle. Politics could only be warfare of a greater or lesser intensity of class struggle until the final victory of socialism. At that point, war would disappear from human relations.

This understanding of Leninism, though not traced to Lenin's fascination with Clausewitz and to its roots in Marxism, was obvious to Lenin's contemporary and fellow revolutionary Victor Chernov, the theoretician of the Social Revolutionary Party (a powerful rival to the Bolshevik Party in 1917). He wrote in the newly launched American journal *Foreign Affairs,* on the occasion of Lenin's death in 1924, "It has been said that war is a continuation of politics by other means. Lenin would undoubtedly have reversed this dictum and said that politics is the continuation of war under another guise." [29]

When Gorbachev came to power, he faced a party and a military leadership that had deeply internalized this philosophy of war, not always fully conscious of the degree of internalization. His new "defensive doctrine," therefore, clashed both with the subconscious hegemony of this philosophy and with its conscious articulation in the education of military and party.

Party, State, and Military Structure

The question is always who controls the existing bureaucratic machinery.

MAX WEBER

F ormal structures constrain, regularize, and to some extent determine the policy making of governments, militaries, and business corporations. Understanding them is analogous to knowing the rules for football, baseball, or cricket. This is especially true for comprehending Gorbachev's military policies. A leader asserting his own free will in policy making—and Gorbachev certainly asserted his in surprising ways—can confound predictions of his policy choices, but his capacity to implement radically new policies is critically limited by the institutional context in which he operates. A central question, therefore, is how organizational structure both enabled and constrained Gorbachev.

Figure 1 provides a map of Soviet state and party organizations that played significant roles in military affairs as they stood in the mid-1980s. How they operated in the policy-making process requires elaboration.

The Party-State Distinction

The vertical double line marks the formal distinction between party and state structures.[1] On the left is the party structure, and to its right is the state structure. In reality the two were inextricably intertwined through party committees and cells located in virtually every state unit at all but the very lowest levels. Many incumbents in the topmost party positions simultaneously held posts in state organizations. The full-time professional party workers held posts only in the party structure. The incumbents in state organizations, except at the very highest state level, also predominantly held only state positions. They were, of course, party members, belonging to party organizations within their state institutions.

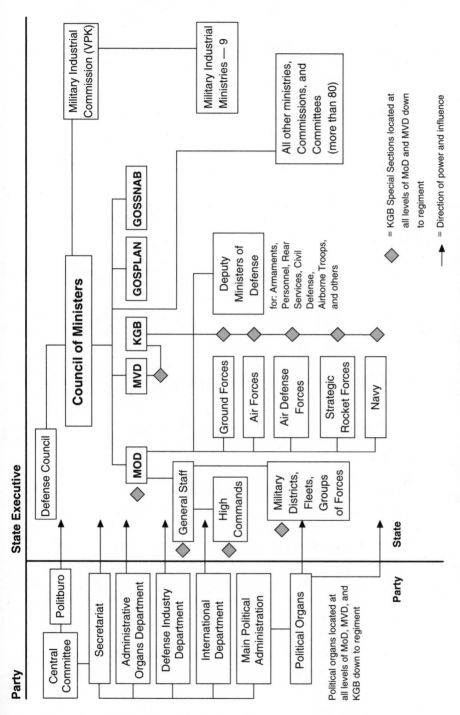

Party   **State Executive**

Military Industrial Commission (VPK)

Military Industrial Ministries — 9

Defense Council

Central Committee

Politburo

Council of Ministers

GOSSNAB

GOSPLAN

KGB

MVD

MOD

All other ministries, Commissions, and Committees (more than 80)

Secretariat

Administrative Organs Department

Defense Industry Department

International Department

Main Political Administration

Political Organs

General Staff

High Commands

Military Districts, Fleets, Groups of Forces

Deputy Ministers of Defense

for: Armaments, Personnel, Rear Services, Civil Defense, Airborne Troops, and others

Ground Forces

Air Forces

Air Defense Forces

Strategic Rocket Forces

Navy

◆ = KGB Special Sections located at all levels of MoD and MVD down to regiment

⟶ = Direction of power and influence

Political organs located at all levels of MoD, MVD, and KGB down to regiment

Party   **State**

Figure 1. Party and state executive structures

Party members within Soviet state structures, therefore, received two sources of direction, formal direction from their state bureaucratic superiors and informal direction from their party organizations. The informal party direction, of course, was more important, and when the party was functioning properly, that direction was so strong and uniformly understood that the two sources of direction seldom conflicted. Over time—months and years—an inevitable diffusion of central party control occurred. Individuals and small cliques of officials at every lower organizational level soon put their local interests and goals ahead of the center's. Numerous mechanisms, such as censorship, informer networks, and state monopoly of the means of production, limited the size of such groups and prevented them from becoming what might be properly called interest groups. Instead they became local cliques of conspirators seeking personal advantages, and in some cases they grew into larger "mafias"—networks of ambitious schemers trying to advance up the party ladder. In most cases, they used the bureaucratic system itself, and even while violating its rules, they retained a personal stake in it because it imposed some predictability on the actions of others and provided resources and power.

Periodic party purges—designed to reinstill ideological commitment and responsiveness to the party's instructions—were the instruments for recentralizing this chronic diffusion of bureaucratic power. Lenin launched the first major purge in 1922, and Stalin's subsequent purges are well known. Khrushchev, although he ended Stalin's practice of blood purges, retained administrative purges, using periodic reassignment of party and state officials to keep them uncertain about their futures and to disrupt "localism" at each organizational level. Under Brezhnev, even administrative purges were largely eliminated. Thus the diffusion of bureaucratic power continued unabated throughout his entire eighteen years of rule, which thus became known as "the era of stagnation."

On the right side of the chart's vertical dividing lines are found the state organizations responsible for military, military-industrial, police, and intelligence functions. Only the executive branch of the state, Council of Ministers, and some of its subunits are shown. The Soviet state also had a legislative branch (the Supreme Soviet) and a judicial branch (the Supreme Court). It possessed several other institutions—for example, the People's Control Commission and the Procuracy—but they can be ignored for our purposes here. The legislative and judicial branches can also be set aside because they played no significant role in military policy making, but they do deserve brief commentary.

The judiciary was not independent, primarily because the party held itself above the law. A party member could not be tried by the courts until he was expelled from the party. This occasionally created special problems in imposing discipline within the military. The legislature—the Supreme Soviet—was also devoid of independent influence on policy and resource allocations. Although it passed laws required to formalize rules for the state bureaucracy and individuals, it met only a few days each year to put its rubber stamp on legislation drafted in advance by executive branch officials.

Resource Allocation and Control

Where, then, was the "power of the purse" in the Soviet system? It rested primarily within Politburo, based on the Central Committee Secretariat's staff review of what the Council of Ministers proposed. Why "primarily" and not entirely? Resources allocated to the military and military industries were managed by the huge bureaucracies of these departments, so considerable informal power over resource allocations rested with these hierarchies. Even with Stalinist discipline, the heads of departments could not prevent their subunits from exercising some discretion in the use of resources. Moreover, the Politburo depended on these bureaucracies to formulate budgets, allowing them opportunities to misrepresent resource realities. As bureaucracies grew, and as purges ceased to be used to restore party discipline, the Politburo slowly lost much of its control over resource distribution for defense.

The power of the Politburo was still enormous. One formal point above all others accounted for the highly centralized control over resource allocations: the state owned all of the means of production. That was the foundation for the centrally planned "command economy." Pockets of nonplanned economic activity existed, to be sure, but state control over the industrial, commercial, and agricultural sectors of the economy was staggeringly large. In its last decade, the Council of Ministers had more than one hundred ministries, committees, and commissions, the majority of which dealt with the economy. The business of the Soviet government, therefore, was primarily business.

Key among the council's ministries was the State Planning Commission (GOSPLAN). It constructed the annual and five-year plans that directed the state economy. In spite of its best efforts, GOSPLAN could never ensure that every firm's input requirements would be available in adequate supply; shortages were endemic. The determination of which firms would get first priority and which would stand at the end of the queue, failing to receive the resources assigned in the plan, was the task of the State Supply Committee (GOSS-NAB). Its authority as the manager of the queue provided the leadership with a powerful instrument for assigning priorities. The military-industrial sector, of course, was a consistent beneficiary of both GOSPLAN's and GOSSNAB's authority. Money and prices in this system played a secondary role, largely serving as accounting devices, managed by the State Bank for dispensing credits, by the Ministry of Finance for accounting of the state budget, and by the State Committee for Prices (GOSTsEN) for establishing prices.

The main part of the industrial sector resided in nine ministries.[2] Many other industrial ministries were entangled with the military-industrial sector through plans for wartime industrial mobilization. Several also supplied products to military-industrial ministries in peacetime. Fear of shortages, nonetheless, encouraged ministry and firm autarky to the extent possible. Thus the military-industrial sector kept its outside dependency as limited as it could, defending its enclave status. Its annual and five-year plans, however, were handled by GOSPLAN as integral to the overall state economic plan.

Moreover, it had its own central management body, the Military Industrial Commission (*Voennaya promyshlennaya kommissiya*, or VPK).[3] The VPK was actually an inner circle of the Council of Ministers, and the first deputy chairman of the council headed it. With its own staff to support its chairman, the VPK occupied a very strong position among the economic bodies, and its primary function was to facilitate plan fulfillment by all military firms through easing bottlenecks, enforcing interministerial cooperation, and overseeing the availability of resources.

How did the Politburo ensure its influence on this distribution of control over resources? In the first place, Politburo members occupied the top posts in the state economic, military-industrial, and military departments. And they also held the top posts in the Committee for State Security (KGB) and the foreign ministry. In 1973, when Brezhnev promoted Marshal Andrei Grechko (minister of defense), Andrei Gromyko (minister of foreign affairs), and Yurii Andropov (chairman of the KGB) to the Politburo, they joined A. N. Kosygin (chairman of the Council of Ministers).[4] Together with the party general secretary, Brezhnev, they held the most significant top posts in the state structure. Marshal Dmitrii Ustinov, who became minister of defense when Grechko died, was already a Politburo member. Gorbachev's 1985 Politburo had essentially the same arrangement.

The Defense Council was a state body actually transcending all three state branches—executive, legislative, and judicial—in which military policy issues could be formally handled with unlimited directive powers. Presumably, it could resolve resource and policy disputes between the military and military-industrial sectors and with any other state sector. The Defense Council was the lineal descendant of the Council of Labor and Defense (STO), established during the civil war as the supreme combination of state civil and military authority.[5] Stalin disbanded it in 1935, but when German invasion caught him by surprise in 1941, he re-created it as the State Committee for Defense (GKO) for the duration of the war, disbanding it in September 1945.[6] The GKO took control of military operations through the so-called Stavka, or supreme high command, with Stalin as supreme commander in chief.[7] On the civil side, it stood above and could override the Council of Commissars.[8] The GKO's scope of formal authority was reflected in its assumed legal powers, requiring every citizen to comply with its directives. Its successor, the Defense Council, was kept secret until it was mentioned in the 1977 constitution of the USSR, but it was apparently established in the 1950s by Khrushchev, not with the full powers of the old GKO, but evidently in a position to assume them in a crisis. The experience of the difficult transition to war in 1941 combined with the implications of a surprise attack in the nuclear age probably dictated the Defense Council's peacetime existence.

Its workings had become largely pro forma by the 1980s, a matter of giving whatever had been decided by the Politburo the status of formal state policy. Its membership included the general secretary (as its chairman), the minister of defense, the minister of foreign affairs, the chairman of the KGB, the chairman of the Council of Ministers or the chairman of the VPK (sometimes both), the chief of the General Staff, and normally some one from the Central Committee Secretariat. The formal membership core apparently was augmented with officials appropriate to the agenda of a particular meeting. The Defense Council had no permanent staff and met only five or six times annually.[9] Marshal Akhromeev was appointed as "the secretary" of the Defense Council in 1984, a new position, and although he tried to revitalize the council, he failed.[10] Gorbachev showed little interest in it but reportedly held a couple of meetings of the Defense Council in 1988.[11]

The chairmanship of the Defense Council was Gorbachev's only state post, one that provided him no state bureaucracy for staff support. The other four Politburo members on the Defense Council, of course, had large staffs in their state posts. Gorbachev depended on the party apparatus, primarily the secretariat, for such support. Figure 1 shows four of the twenty-three departments in the secretariat, those concerned with military, military-industrial, security, and intelligence affairs. The Administrative Organs Department approved all senior military, KGB, and Ministry of Internal Affairs (MVD) personnel appointments, a second political reliability check after the approval of the Organizational Party Work Department. The Defense Industries Department dealt primarily with the VPK, approving its top personnel appointments. The International Department handled foreign policy, relations with foreign communist parties, and some aspect of intelligence work. Finally, the Main Political Administration, holding the status of a department, headed a vast structure of "political organs" throughout all military, MVD, and KGB organizations.[12]

These secretariat departments traditionally served as a kind of "general staff" for the party leader and his fellow secretaries. They prepared papers for Politburo and Central Committee meetings. They kept their noses in the everyday affairs of the state ministries and departments. As often as not, they had competitive relations with their corresponding state organs.[13] Their great strength lay in their direct access to the general secretary and their influence on personnel assignments, but being somewhat removed for policy implementation in the ministries, they sometimes were faced with accomplished facts before they could prevent them. At the same time, the relationship was symbiotic. Ministry officials received fuller interpretations of Politburo decisions from them, and in turn they depended on ministries and departments to provide information and analysis. They could reach down through regional and functional party committees at the lower levels of the ministries for additional information and influence. This is not to say, of course, that they always used all of these channels effectively. Still, they sat at the center of the system with all the burdens and advantages that conveyed. They were for the most part the general secretary's people, although the other party secretaries each normally supervised one or more of the departments.

The overall picture is one of a military-industrial economy within the state-command economy, positioned to dominate any competitor for resources as long as it received the approval of the Politburo. No outsider could penetrate this high-level closed circle controlling allocations to Soviet defense. The legislature had no access. The media had no access, and in any case was subject to systematic censorship. There were, however, occasional exceptions. Distinguished scientists and designers sometimes enjoyed a personal connection with the general secretary, who called them in for technical advice on weapons and program issues.

In liberal democratic states with market economies, many points of public access to the policy-making processes are available as defense ministries submit their budget to the legislatures largely in unclassified form. Lobbyists are legion, and pundits, opinion makers, and many others participate, creating a very complex process. In the Soviet system, the defense resource–allocation process was no less complex, but it was extraordinarily different.

Access to information and policy makers was extremely limited. The Politburo defined strategic aims that served as policy guidance for the military. The Ministry of Defense and the General Staff responded to Politburo directions, using their military academies and military theorists to develop military science and military doctrine, and designing war plans and the related manpower and weaponry requirements. Their resource claims for implementing Politburo directions were submitted to GOSPLAN, which gave them high priority in the state economic plan and passed them for fulfillment to GOSSNAB, the VPK and its economic planners, managers, engineers, and scientists. Ordinary citizens and social groups had no legitimate way to participate in the decision processes, but it could and did exercise influence on resource allocations through deviant behavior (slothful work habits, theft, drunkenness, fraud, and so on). Defense resources were often squandered, not through legislative pork but rather through organizational politics. Behind the scenes, civilian bureaucrats and military officers bent the rules; some even engaged in such criminal activities as theft and misappropriation.[14]

The Ministry of Defense

The Ministry of Defense (MoD) and its General Staff stood at the top of the entire military structure, though the internal troops of the MVD, the KGB's border troops, and a few other KGB military formations were outside the administration of the MoD. The formal term Soviet Armed Forces was defined as comprising all these military formations. It had more than a nominative function: the General Staff, in the event of war, would exercise operational direction of the Soviet Armed Forces as a whole. The designation also gave the General Staff some operational control over the armed forces in peacetime. This practice apparently began in World War II. When the GKO took charge of the war in 1941, the Stavka was the nominal high command for military affairs. But the General Staff became its working arm, coordinating all aspects of uniformed military activities, not just those in the Commissariat of War (renamed Ministry of Defense at the end of World War II). The concept of the Soviet Armed Forces, like the concept of the Defense Council, provided the organizational authority and structure for a rapid transition to war, precluding another crisis like that of 1941, when the German attack caught Stalin without such structures. In the nuclear age Soviet leaders were even more concerned with preparations for a smooth and swift transition to a wartime footing.

In peacetime, the MoD had to perform two major functions (see fig. 2). First, it had to design, equip, and staff the branches of services. In other words, it designed and built forces as well as developed doctrine for their operational

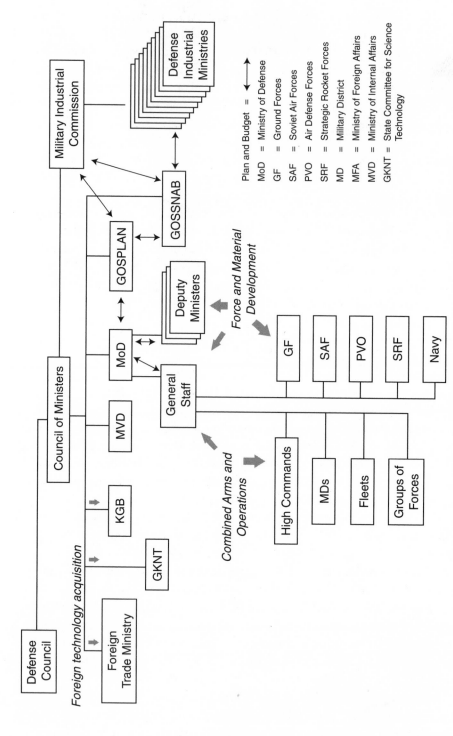

Figure 2. Military command, policy, and industrial organizations

Plan and Budget = ⟷
MoD = Ministry of Defense
GF = Ground Forces
SAF = Soviet Air Forces
PVO = Air Defense Forces
SRF = Strategic Rocket Forces
MD = Military District
MFA = Ministry of Foreign Affairs
MVD = Ministry of Internal Affairs
GKNT = State Committee for Science Technology

Defense Council

Council of Ministers

Military Industrial Commission

Defense Industrial Ministries

GOSSNAB

GOSPLAN

Deputy Ministers

MoD

MVD

KGB

GKNT

Foreign Trade Ministry

Foreign technology acquisition

General Staff

Force and Material Development

GF

SAF

PVO

SRF

Navy

Combined Arms and Operations

High Commands

MDs

Fleets

Groups of Forces

employment. Second, its General Staff managed the operations of extant forces deployed for war contingencies. This involved designing war plans and training exercises, planning mobilization, overseeing training and combat readiness, and developing operational and strategic doctrine for the employment of "combined arms" — that is, making units of all branches of service work in a coordinated fashion above "tactical" levels, at "operational" and "strategic" levels.[15]

The first function was performed by the MoD subunits, including the five military branches of services as well as the deputy minister of defense for armaments (whose apparatus handled procurement of weapons and related equipment), the deputy minister of defense for the rear (whose apparatus managed logistics and supply), and the deputy ministers of defense for personnel, finance, and a few other functions. The commanders of the military services were also double-hatted as deputy ministers of defense. The defense minister, however, depended mainly on the Organization and Mobilization Directorate of the General Staff for overseeing and managing this force-building function. The second function rested entirely with the General Staff and its chief, who was also a first deputy minister of defense. The distinction between the two types of military responsibilities should not be conceived as excessively rigid. Such a division characterizes most Western military establishments, though the two roles overlap at some points.

The Soviet MoD and its higher subunits and field commands each had an associated military collegium. The military collegium as an organizational concept has no exact Western counterpart, nor has it been well studied in the West. Soviet memoirs and other accounts give a fairly clear picture of the MoD military collegium.[16] It consisted of the minister of defense, all of his deputies, and a few other officers. It met frequently and dealt with a wide range of issues, from fairly petty matters to major policy issues and crisis matters.[17] Such military councils, or collectives, were not a purely Soviet invention but had antecedents in the Imperial Russian Army.[18]

The MoD and the General Staff naturally had under their control considerable capacity for analysis and studies. Beyond their staff sections they could call on military academies and institutes. In addition to the General Staff Academy, each military service had one or more such academies that could complete studies, including practical field tests. In technical fields, the MoD had within its jurisdiction a few "design buros" (or "bureaux") staffed with technicians and engineers. Virtually all the analytic work done by these staffs, academies, institutes, and design buros was classified secret. Thus nonmilitary institutes and analysts had no access to the results or the data necessary to do such analysis themselves. Nor did the legislative branch, the Supreme Soviet, have analytic capabilities. Although the Central Committee Secretariat departments could certainly take selective looks for the Politburo's use, they could not perform competing analyses. This left the MoD with an unchallenged monopoly on all matters concerning military requirements and operations, as well as on many technology issues. The rest of the management structure for military policy at the top of the Soviet system, therefore, depended on the MoD for analysis of military policy issues, a reality that would have serious political consequences during 1988–91, as military policy became a publicly debated issue.

Leaving the technical analysis to the military was also codified in the Soviet definition of military doctrine. As the doctrinal formula put it, military doctrine has two aspects, a political-social side and a military-technical side. The uniformed military monopolized the latter and depended on the party, namely the Politburo, for the former.

In the age of modern military technology, of course, military-technical issues greatly exceed the skills of the officer corps. Building nuclear weapons, aircraft, tanks, and ships requires the technical contributions of a large number of highly trained scientists and engineers. In the Soviet system, these people were mainly within the boundaries of the VPK-managed ministries and classified institutes of the Academy of Sciences. To say that the Soviet uniformed military enjoyed a complete monopoly on all the technical aspects of military affairs, therefore, is not the whole truth. Scientists and engineers in the VPK had technical knowledge that was often relevant to high-level military policy making. And they used it for policy influence, if not always successfully.[19]

The General Staff

The General Staff's role deserves some elaboration because legend and even mythology surround the idea of a military "general" staff. The rise of general staffs occurred in European armies during the nineteenth century, most notably in Germany but also in Austria, France, Russia, and, toward the end of the century, also Britain.

Why did general staffs emerge? The key cause was the increasing complexity of modern militaries: proliferation of specialized types of forces, varieties of weapons, increasing training requirements, complex logistics, and so on. Military leadership demanded both higher levels of training and greater specialization. Analogous complexities confronted the simultaneous rise of modern civil government in Europe, and they were met with the development of the modern "ministry."[20] The growing scale and complexities of armies demanded their greater bureaucratization not only to manage their internal affairs but also to handle their relations with industry and civil society. Expertise in managing the military affairs began to compete with other criteria for promotion and assignments of military officers. Modern military professionalism came into being.[21]

Stalin authorized the creation of the Soviet General Staff only in 1935, after thwarting earlier demands for it.[22] During World War II it became Stalin's main organ for operational direction of all military forces. After the war it became the most powerful center for virtually all aspects of military planning, operations, and determination of resource requirements. The minister of defense had only a limited staff for his own support, leaving him heavily dependent on the General Staff. It was also distinct for its unprecedented control of the navy, something no other general staff (or "joint" or "defense" staff) has been able to achieve in modern Western militaries. This was true both for operational control and resource allocations. Within the Ministry of Defense, all the resource allocation issues were normally resolved by the chief of the General Staff before going to the minister and finally, after coordination with GOSPLAN, to the Politburo.[23] A few resource issues, however, were left to be decided by the minister and occasionally even by the Politburo or the Defense Council.

In sum, the Soviet General Staff without the MoD is conceivable, but the MoD without the General Staff is not. The General Staff was the key organization for handling technical military affairs, without parallel in Western military establishments.

The Military Services and Related Structures

As we have seen, the military services and other functional branches of the MoD were responsible for building, manning, equipping, training, and supplying the military fighting forces. While most Western militaries have only three services—army, navy, and air force—the Soviet military had five.

The navy retained its status as a single service after World War II, and the Red Army experienced considerable reorganization. The ground forces became a separate service, inheriting the main combat branches—armor, artillery, infantry, and so on.[24] The air forces were a separate service but in a plural form, as the military air forces, including long-range aviation, military-transport aviation, and frontal aviation.[25] Naval aviation, however, belonged to the navy. In the early 1950s, a new service, the air defense forces or PVO, was formed in response to the U.S. strategic bombing capabilities.[26] The PVO included both surface-to-air missiles and fighter-interceptor aircraft. A fifth military service, the rocket forces, was created in 1960, reflecting Khrushchev's emphasis on nuclear weapons for intercontinental attacks.[27]

Seven airborne divisions were under a separate command, which was directly controlled by the General Staff. There was also a deputy minister of defense for the airborne forces. Their organizational autonomy reflected their mission as a "strategic reserve" force that could be rapidly committed in any strategic sector because of their air mobility.

As indicated in figures 1 and 2, there were deputy ministers of defense for personnel, rear services (logistics), armaments, procurement, training, airborne troops, civil defense, and a number of other support functions. While they managed their functional areas at the center, most had counterparts at the military district level.

A network of military commissariats *(voennye kommissariaty,* or *voenkomaty,* singular *voenkomat)* existed down to the district *(raion)* level in the state territorial administrative structure, roughly the county level in the United States. Their tasks were conducting military conscription, monitoring training of reservists, and managing mobilization. They were deeply involved in elementary, secondary, and college-level schools because most of all they provided preservice military training courses, which were required for all males; some voenkomaty trained females as well. Face-to-face with the public, the voenkomaty became the focal points of confrontation, especially in the national republics, during the last two years of Gorbachev's rule.

Finally, a mass voluntary organization, the largest in the Soviet Union, the Voluntary Society for Assistance to the Army, Aviation, and the Fleet *(Dobrovol'noe obshchestvo sodeistviya armii, aviatsii, i flotu,* or DOSAAF), worked with youth, providing preservice training in a wide range of military and military-related specialties. Especially during the 1970s and 1980s, DOSAAF's contributions to the Soviet Armed Forces' training needs grew in significance. They also came at no cost to the military budget because DOSAAF financed its operations entirely from members' dues and its many small-business activities.

Operational Command and Control

The second major function of the MoD was the operational command and control of force deployments in peace and war. The guiding principle in operations, be they at the strategic, operational, or tactical level, was combined arms. Soviet military leaders incessantly affirmed their commitment to a combined-arms approach to warfare, insisting that no single service or weapons system could win a war. Victory was possible only through the properly orchestrated combination of all kinds of weapons and forces.

Beneath the General Staff, four high commands were established, beginning in the late 1970s and continuing into the 1980s. In order of importance they were the Western High Command and the Southwestern High Command in Europe; the Far East High Command, which was actually the first established; and the Southern High Command, oriented toward the Middle East and southwest Asia. These commands were established as part of the program begun in 1978 to improve theater operational capabilities, especially in Europe.[28]

The General Staff exercised direct operation control over a number of other components on a functional rather than a territorial basis, primarily the rocket forces, parts of the air forces, the PVO, the navy, and the airborne divisions. Their operations were coordinated with the operations of high commands and fronts, though their forces were not put directly under those commands in peacetime.

A few other less significant components also could be controlled by the General Staff. Railroad troops and construction troops were normally assigned to various military district commands, but the General Staff could assert control and move them to other commands when necessary. Civil defense troops were anomalous in that their control line, below the deputy minister of defense for civil defense, followed the administrative-territorial state organization.

Military districts (MDs) deserve special attention (see map 1). To a considerable degree they were small ministries of defense with "main staffs" analogous to the General Staff in Moscow. Thus they had parallel peacetime and wartime functions like the MoD and the General Staff. They controlled the voenkomaty, supply functions, training functions, some of the military schools, and numerous other peacetime functions. At the same time, the military district headquarters on the western frontier had to be prepared to become front headquarters and move off to war. In their place, "second generation" headquarters would replace them to manage the residual military district functions and to mobilize and train second-generation divisions.

A rather confusing aspect of Soviet command and control is the concept of a theater of military operations—*teatr voennykh deistvii,* or TVD. These were territorial areas, marked by flank boundaries in most cases. Maps 2 and 3 show them marked by radial lines from Moscow. Actually, the General Staff divided the entire world into TVDs. North America, Australia, and various oceans were defined as TVDs. Large forces might be deployed within a TVD, or only

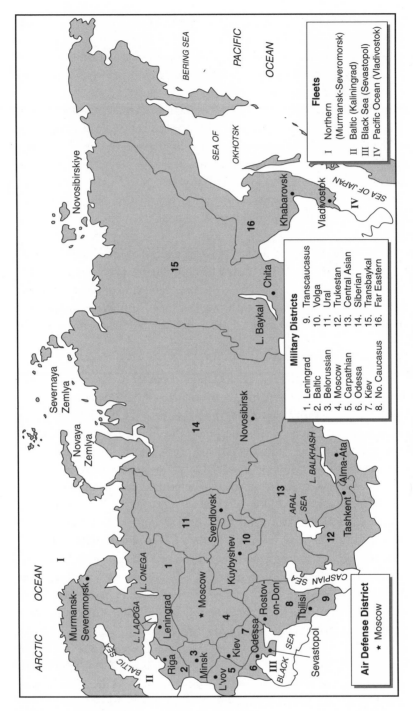

Fleets

I   Northern (Murmansk-Severomorsk)
II Baltic (Kaliningrad)
III Black Sea (Sevastopol)
IV Pacific Ocean (Vladivostok)

Military Districts

1. Leningrad
2. Baltic
3. Belorussian
4. Moscow
5. Carpathian
6. Odessa
7. Kiev
8. No. Caucasus
9. Transcaucasus
10. Volga
11. Ural
12. Trukestan
13. Central Asian
14. Siberian
15. Transbaykal
16. Far Eastern

Air Defense District

★ Moscow

Map 1. Military districts of the Soviet Union
(U.S. Government Printing Office)

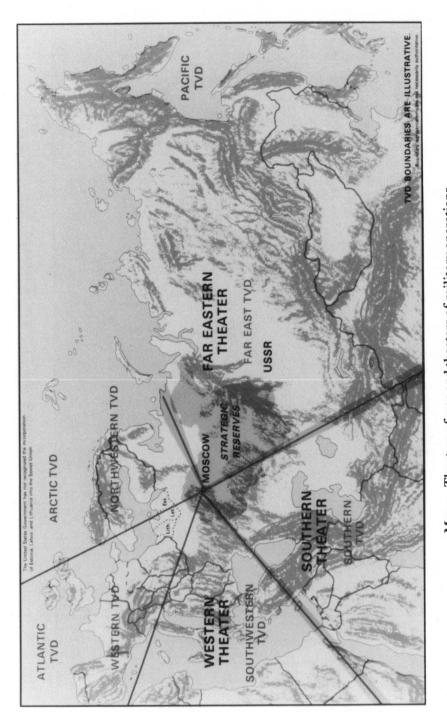

Map 2. Theaters of war and theaters of military operations
(U.S. Government Printing Office)

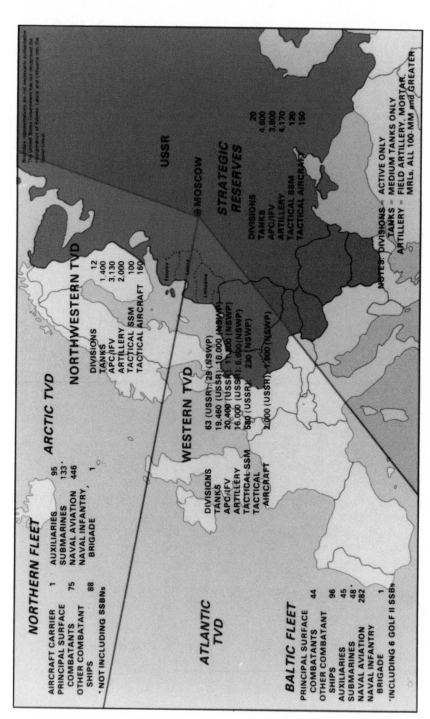

Map 3. Force deployments in the European Theater and TVDs
(U.S. Government Printing Office)

small forces, or no forces at all. The three TVDs projecting into Europe contained forces of greatly varying size, ranging from sixty-three divisions in the Western TVD to twelve divisions in the Northwestern TVD. Two of them, the Western and Southwestern TVDs, had high commands to control their much larger forces. The Southern TVD had thirty divisions (map 4), and the Far East TVD had fifty-seven divisions (map 5).

A "theater of war" was also a Soviet military category, and Europe was the most important one in the view of the General Staff. The Far Eastern and the southern theaters received lower priority.

The KGB and the MVD

Both the KGB and the MVD had their own military formations. The KGB's border troops numbered about 250,000.[29] They manned the entire Soviet border, controlling all entrances and exits. The KGB also possessed other military units, including the Kremlin guards, special guards units, communications units, and signals intelligence units.

The MVD had about 350,000 troops organized in approximately thirty divisions.[30] These forces performed a number of duties, including maintenance of internal order, management of the penal labor camp system, and serving as convoy guards for transporting prisoners. Because both the MVD forces and the KGB military units were part of the Soviet Armed Forces, the General Staff coordinated their wartime operations as well as some of their peacetime activities.[31]

The KGB's "third directorate" played a highly important role in the control of all the Soviet Armed Forces. It placed "special sections" (*osobye otdely,* or OOs,) at all command levels down to the regiment (see fig. 1).[32] Special sections were very small, usually one officer at the regimental level, attached to the commander's staff, dressed in regular army uniforms, but responsible only to the KGB command line, wholly independent of military commanders. Their function was counterintelligence and assurance of the political reliability of personnel. They recruited networks of informers from among the soldiers and officers in the units to which they were assigned. Their operations were notoriously unconstrained, and they could strike fear into all with whom they dealt, no matter what their rank. In the last decades of the Soviet Union, however, corruption and bribery greatly weakened the special sections as their officers increasingly struck deals with local commanders for their mutual private gain.

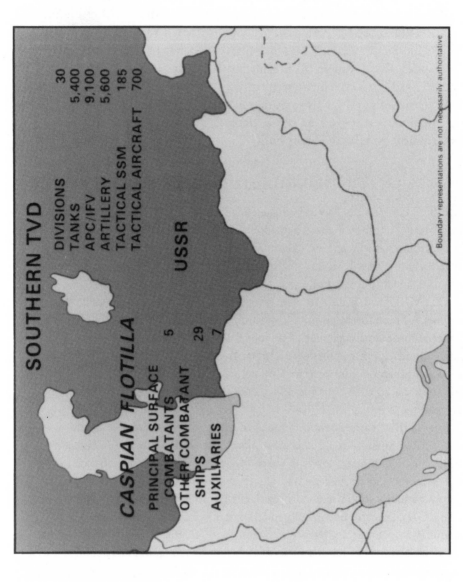

Map 4. Force deployments in the Southern TVD

(U.S. Government Printing Office)

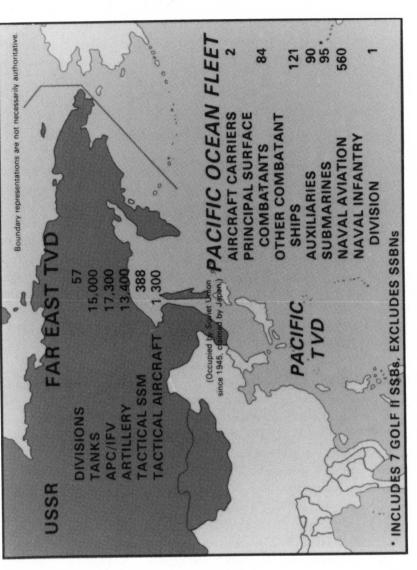

Boundary representations are not necessarily authoritative.

USSR

FAR EAST TVD

DIVISIONS	57
TANKS	15,000
APC/IFV	17,300
ARTILLERY	13,400
TACTICAL SSM	388
TACTICAL AIRCRAFT	1,300

(Occupied by Soviet Union since 1945, claimed by Japan.)

PACIFIC OCEAN FLEET

AIRCRAFT CARRIERS	2
PRINCIPAL SURFACE COMBATANTS	84
OTHER COMBATANT SHIPS	121
AUXILIARIES	90
SUBMARINES	95 *
NAVAL AVIATION	560
NAVAL INFANTRY DIVISION	1

PACIFIC TVD

* INCLUDES 7 GOLF II SSBs, EXCLUDES SSBNs

Map 5. Force deployments in the Far East TVD
(U.S. Government Printing Office)

The Main Political Administration

Another unique structure in the Soviet Armed Forces was the system of "political organs." It derived from the system of Bolshevik Party's commissars established in 1918 to ensure the political loyalty of the officer corps in the new Red Army. Over the several decades after the civil war, the Main Political Administration (MPA) went through many reorganizations, but its basic structure and functions remained more or less the same.[33] Each command level down to regiment, at times down to battalion, had a deputy for political affairs, or *zampolit*. The zampolit's small staff was known as the political organ. This party apparatus was responsible for the political indoctrination of the officers and troops. Political organs were allotted regular training periods for propaganda lectures each week, and in principle they were responsible for troop morale.[34]

Like the KGB special sections, the political organs were answerable to a separate command line. It led up to the chief of the MPA, a four-star general. The MPA was formally located within the Central Committee Secretariat as a department. Thus it cut across the party-state boundary as a hybrid organization. Its officers were trained in military skills only to a limited degree, leaving them unprepared for command at levels above battalion.[35]

The party's presence in the military ranks went far beyond the MPA. More than 95 percent of all officers were party members, and at field-grade and general-officer levels the figure was 100 percent. Thus military units at all levels, including the MoD and the General Staff, had party primary organizations and party committees. The same was true of MVD and KGB officers. No other state institution had more than 10–15 percent party membership in its ranks. Thus the Soviet Armed Forces—MoD, MVD, and KGB—were unique, formally state organizations but staffed almost entirely by party members in their officer ranks. Even in the enlisted ranks, party members were present in about the same percentages as in other state organizations, and membership among soldiers in the Leninist Youth League (the Communist Party's youth organization, the *Komsomol*) was considerably higher than elsewhere.

Finally, the party and KGB roles in officer promotions and assignments additionally strengthened the party-military amalgam. Not only did each officer have a military personnel file; each also had a party record and a KGB record. Promotions were based on reviews of all three. As an officer achieved higher rank and the possibility for more sensitive and important postings, his assignments depended more heavily on his party and KGB records. Soviet military officers therefore had to compete in two career paths, party and military. A blemished party record was severely disqualifying, according to one former Soviet colonel, more so than a blemish on one's military record.[36]

The Policy-Making Dynamic

No Western political leader could bring a mere dozen of his close associates into a closed room, deliberate with them based only on materials prepared by the staff of his military department and reviewed only by his own political staff, and then push through his preferred policy (occasionally over the objections of a disgruntled fellow official), a policy sometimes involving scores of billions of dollars, at a cost not even known by himself in terms of the market value of the resources involved. Yet this is precisely how the general secretary of party made military policy in the Politburo.

This system was by no means static. From the time of the Russian civil war through the First Five-Year Plan in 1933, it changed rapidly and radically. World War II brought extreme centralization at the top, huge increases in the size of the forces, and rapid expansion of military industries. In the postwar period, change continued but assumed a different character. Organizational structure settled down by the 1960s, but the scale and complexity of military and military-industrial affairs became too great for Stalin's style of micro-control to be continued. Increasingly, the details of implementation were so complex that more latitude in execution devolved to lower levels of the bureaucracy, and the Politburo became more dependent on expert advice and analysis from the MoD and VPK.

As the size of the MoD and the VPK ministries grew, changing directions in military policy became extremely difficult. Changes in force structure and industrial production were difficult to consider and virtually impossible to implement. New programs could be introduced, but reducing weapons production and forces was unthinkable. Such was the system that Gorbachev had to use to implement his radically new military policies.

THREE

How the Military Was Manned

The significance of national conscription . . . has been passed over by modern political and historical scholars with incredible frivolity or incredible blindness.

LEWIS MUMFORD

The unique way the Red Army manned its forces goes far in explaining how it won both the Russian civil war and World War II.[1] Manpower politics also goes far in explaining the Soviet military's collapse. By the 1980s, it had become the military's Achilles' heal.

The Soviet Armed Forces were nearly six million strong in 1985, larger than any other military in the world.[2] Because all males were subject to military service until they reached age fifty, an estimated twenty-five million reserves were available for wartime mobilization.[3] In sum, the trained military manpower base was large, very large. As in the case of most other aspects of Soviet military affairs, the roots of manpower policy are found in Marxism-Leninism. The troops for the socialist revolution, as Marx emphasized, were workers, and in a capitalist society ripe for revolution, workers would be the overwhelming majority. Military service for the revolution, therefore, would involve most of the population in order to assure the victory of the working class.

European Social Democrats emphasized this point in the program of the Second International, insisting that a "workers' militia" would be its army and that after the revolution, "barracks-type" armies, characteristic of the capitalist epoch, would be abolished. Separated from society, such armies could be indoctrinated to repress the exploited classes. A workers' militia would be synonymous with the working class and therefore unable to repress itself. Several of Lenin's senior fellow Bolsheviks subscribed to this doctrine, causing considerable intraparty strife during and after the civil war.[4] A regular barracks-type army, Lenin and Trotsky argued, was imperative during the civil war while the White Army was still trying to defeat the young socialist regime. Trotsky's recruitment of large numbers of ex-tsarist officers, however, prompted a strong reaction at the Eighth Party Congress in 1919. A faction at the congress, the so-called military opposition, worried that this military manpower policy would lead to a regular army after the civil war. They were temporarily overridden, but with the Red Army's victory in 1921, the issue surfaced again. Mikhail V. Frunze, who led the faction of Red Army commanders demanding the party's adoption of a Marxist military doctrine, quickly reached the pragmatic conclusion that as long as imperialism had not been wholly vanquished, a regular army was essential. But the regime's economic destitution eventually convinced Frunze that it could afford only a very small one. A small cadre army, he argued, could be supplemented by a large militia system, thus preserving something of the original Social Democratic doctrine that the entire working class had to be trained for military service, while accommodating economic constraints and political realities.[5]

The resulting system served the Red Army very well during its modernization during the interwar period and World War II. It could accommodate both radical reductions and rapid expansions. Two very large demobilizations and one smaller one occurred during its seventy-year history. The first took place at the end of the civil war. From approximately 5 million in 1921, the number was dropped to about 562,000 in 1923, rising slightly by 1927 to 586,000, where it remained until 1937. By 1941 it rose to 4.2 million and by 1945 to 11.3 million. The second demobilization came between 1945 and 1948, when the troop level dropped to 2.8 million. That decline was shortly followed by a slow but steady increase, to 5.7 million by 1955. Khrushchev initiated the third demobilization in that year, and the troop level dropped to 3.6 million by 1960.[6] Beginning in the mid-1960s it began to rise again, peaking in 1985.[7]

Although it shared common features with the manning systems in Western militaries, the Soviet system had significant differences in the way it recruited, trained, promoted, and managed both officers and troops. The early claim that the Red Army was "a new type," therefore, had some justification.

The Officer Corps

The officer corps reportedly made up one-fourth of the total personnel in 1978. Extrapolating to the 1985 figure of 5.3 million, the officers numbered approximately 1.3 million. Of those, about 7,600 were generals and admirals, a ratio of one for 169 lower-ranking officers and 530 soldiers and seamen.[8] Thus, of every 700 military personnel of all ranks, one was a general or admiral. By comparison, in the U.S. Army there were only 419 authorized general-officer positions in 1989, when the total force was 770,000, a ratio of about one general for every 1,835 personnel. In other words, for the same troop level, the Soviet military had more than 2.5 times the number of generals than the U.S. Army. In the entire U.S. Armed Forces in 1989, there were 1,003 U.S. generals and admirals, compared with 7,600 in the Soviet military, almost a 1:8 ratio in the aggregate.[9] The total manpower ratio, 2.1 million U.S. forces to 5.3 million Soviet, was 1:2.5, but that only brings down the comparative ratio of generals and admirals in the two militaries to about 1:3. For all officer ranks the ratio was slightly lower, but by any measure, the Soviet rank structure was extremely top-heavy.

There was an objective reason for this "leader-to-led" ratio. The relatively low education level of the military manpower base, especially during the first five decades of the Soviet regime, had to be offset in some fashion.[10] In part, that was done through rigidity in command, control, and tactical doctrine, but a higher percentage of officers in each military unit also provided compensation. A Soviet rifle platoon, led by one officer, a lieutenant, had fewer than twenty soldiers, compared with a U.S. rifle platoon, also led by a lieutenant, with about forty soldiers. One U.S. officer led a platoon of five tanks, while one Soviet officer led a platoon of three tanks. Higher up the organizational ladder, roughly the same ratios held and sometimes diverged more widely.

Another reason for the high percentage of officers in the Soviet military was the absence of a professional noncommissioned officer (NCO) corps. At the lowest command levels, the lack of professional NCOs required junior officers to fill the leadership gap. This justification was missing at higher levels, but the top-heavy rank structure prevailed nonetheless. Yet another source of this pattern is found in the large number of military-academy faculty posts occupied by colonels and generals, unlike in U.S. military schools. Finally, as time passed, more and more generals continued to serve beyond retirement age. By the late 1970s, the cumulative effect of these practices was an excessively large, rank-heavy, and aging senior officer corps.

The Soviet officer corps experienced a steady transformation after World War II. The Russian Imperial Army had never enjoyed an abundance of well-educated officers, and the Red Army was so destitute of military expertise that Trotsky and Lenin resorted to inducting about 45,000 ex-imperial officers. In the 1920s and 1930s a major effort was undertaken to recruit and train a competent officer corps. That endeavor yielded considerable success, a success largely reversed by Stalin's ruthless purge of the officer corps in 1937–38.[11] The war, of course, provided a practical school that left the Soviet army (the name Red Army was changed by Stalin at the end of the war) with a large and combat-experienced officer corps but not a sophisticated one. Its sociological roots were still mainly in the peasantry, and virtually all had been commissioned after very short training courses—one year, sometimes two years in length. Thus they lacked a postsecondary education as well as training for command and staff duty.

The significant upgrading of the education of the officer corps began in the 1950s and accelerated in the early 1960s.[12] Two- and three-year officer commissioning schools, which provided only a secondary-level education, were expanded to four- and five-year courses with college-level programs. The number of commissioning schools also grew, reaching approximately 140 by the late 1970s.[13] Military academies and advanced technical institutes, about thirty in number, also grew in sophistication of programs, many granting postgraduate degrees, including the doctor of sciences degree, usually in military sciences. In all, officer education schools, academies, and institutes numbered about 170 by the 1980s.[14] Military institutions represented about 30 percent of the total college and postgraduate educational capacity by the mid-1970s.[15] Lack of information on the numbers of students for both civilian and military schools prevents a more accurate picture of the actual share of education dedicated to military science, but it was vastly larger than in any Western country.

Two points about the officer education system are important. First, its extraordinary size would become a problem for military reform in the Gorbachev years and later. Second, it produced unprecedented social change in the Soviet officer corps. For the first time in both Russian and Soviet history, officers with a postsecondary education were sufficiently abundant to staff a full mobilization of the armed forces. More particularly, the semiliterate officer from peasant origins became a thing of the past. Not only was the new Soviet officer literate and reasonably well trained in his military specialty, even receiving midcareer schooling for higher command and staff duties, but he was also far more likely to have grown up in an urban industrial environment and to have had a much higher technical-cultural level—that is, familiarity with motor vehicles, machinery, aircraft, telephones, radios, and many other technologies of twentieth-century industrial society—than did his predecessor.

Another kind of change began in the late 1960s and continued for a time into the 1970s. When Marshal Viktor Kulikov replaced Marshal Matvei Zakharov as chief of the General Staff in 1971, Kulikov was fifty-one years old. Zakharov was in his seventies. About the same time, most of the highest posts began to change hands, incumbents in their seventies turning over their duties to officers two decades younger. This youth movement was a conscious policy aimed at rejuvenating the officer corps at the top and several levels lower. The age of all commanders of military districts, groups of forces, down to army and division levels, dropped significantly. To the foreign observer who had even the most cursory dealings with the Soviet high command at the time, the change was conspicuous. Serving as an assistant army attaché in Moscow between 1972 and 1974, I occasionally had brief chats with officers of both the older and younger generations during diplomatic receptions. The differences were palpable when talking, for example, to Marshal of Aviation Konstantin Vershinin, an elderly World War II veteran, and then to Marshals Nikolai Ogarkov and Viktor Kulikov and Colonel Generals Vladimir Govorov and Aleksandr Altunin. The younger officers were clearly better educated and more sophisticated.

By the late 1970s, however, the youth movement slowed down, and by the mid-1980s, most incumbents in senior posts were approaching seventy years of age, and some were older. Marshal Yevgenii Shaposhnikov, confronted this aging problem when he became minister of defense in fall 1991, bitterly complaining about the large numbers of colonels and generals who evaded the mandatory retirement age in one way or another to remain on active duty.[16]

A less conspicuous problem was corruption. Troops were often used for hired labor from which senior officers received the benefit. Authorized benefits and privileges grew; according to former high ranking party officials, some officers were likelier than senior party members to receive special dachas, estates, hunting areas, sanatoriums, and personal servants. Sometimes scandals were so gross that the Central Committee Secretariat became involved in the investigations, but culprits suffered little, and the affairs were covered up "in order not to harm the honor of the Soviet Army."[17] Corruption was so blatant and widespread, however, that it became an open secret.[18] Major General Yurii Kirshin casually told me in 1991 that Colonel General Makhmut Gareev enlisted the help of aides to construct a brick dacha at the expense of the state budget while concealing this fact from his fellow General Staff officer, Colonel General Danilevskii, whose integrity—or ineptness—left him to face retirement with only an apartment and no private automobile.

By the 1970s and 1980s, many junior officers were having mixed feelings about their military careers. As one former Soviet colonel explained, they saw their pay as adequate because their former high school mates who had become teachers, doctors, and engineers received roughly the same salaries.[19] At the same time, their lives as company- and battalion-level officers had become a kind of hell. They worked around the clock and normally received only three holidays a month, weekends included. Commanders sometimes threatened to cancel annual vacations because of deficiencies in training and weapons maintenance in the junior officers' units. This capricious pressure from above put enormous stress on the junior officers and their families, and it humiliated them before their troops. Most younger officers, unlike the generals, realized that the Soviet military had many problems in urgent need of attention. Thus a growing divide was emerging between the senior and junior officer ranks.

The Enlisted Ranks

The principle of universal military service was established in 1918, and it was sustained down to the end of the Soviet Union. The size of the forces did not allow for every youth of conscription age to be called to active duty each year, but those who were not were still required to learn basic military skills and remain on the rolls of the voenkomaty for wartime mobilization.[20] Secondary schools provided obligatory courses in basic military training, and DOSAAF sponsored courses for a wide range of specialties, including tank driver–mechanic, truck driver–mechanic, radio operator, parachutist, sniper, and many others. The DOSAAF courses were voluntary in principle, but the officers of the local voenkomaty received advanced quota numbers for each specialty and then urged the required number of youths to take the appropriate courses. Civil defense training began even earlier, in elementary schools, and all students received it. Thus virtually all youth reached the conscription age, eighteen, with a modicum of military training.[21] Once trained, even if they were not drafted for a period of active duty service, they were enrolled in the reserves, subject to mobilization until the age of fifty.[22]

This preservice military training allowed the conscript to enter active duty without a lengthy period of basic training as is the practice in the U.S. military. Naturally, remedial training had to be conducted by units receiving these recruits, but a separate organizational structure for basic training did not exist within the MoD. This meant that basic training and some of the specialty training was not paid for by the MoD. The costs fell on the individual for DOSAAF courses and on the Ministry of Education for the 140 hours of military instruction given in secondary schools.

Another peculiarity concerns noncommissioned officers (NCOs). There was only a very small corps of professional NCOs, the majority of NCO positions being held by conscript sergeants.[23] Upon induction of a new cohort of conscripts, a few were selected for NCO rank and given short courses to prepare them, then returned to their units to become squad leaders, platoon sergeants, and the like. As the variety of skills required for modern weaponry expanded in the 1960s, this conscript-NCO system proved inadequate and was supplemented by the creation of a warrant officer rank (*praporshchik* in all services but the navy, which used *michman*, both terms taken from the Russian

Imperial Army and Navy.) Warrant officers received training in various specialties, and by the 1970s they became a professional stratum between the officer
and NCO ranks.[24]

A complex system of deferments allowed youths with family and health
problems to postpone military service. Students who had not finished secondary school by age eighteen and those who were attending college-level educational institutes could also be deferred until they graduated, when they again
were subject to conscription. Many of those attending civilian college-level
schools enrolled in reserve officer programs conducted in many but not all of
those institutions. Upon receiving their commissions, they might be called to
active duty or left on reserve status.[25] In practice only a very small percentage
were called to active duty, making a reserve commission tantamount to a deferment for most students who earned them.

Military pay for enlisted personnel was meager—roughly equivalent to
seven or eight dollars a month.[26] Additional allowances were provided for soldiers with needy families and a few other conditions, but the total wage bill for
pay of the enlisted ranks was a trivial sum by any Western standard. Conscript
soldiers were essentially unpaid labor, a fact that helps account for the apparently low level of official military budget figures. Food was notoriously poor as
well, prompting most regiments to cultivate garden plots and pigsties to supplement the regular troop diet. The MoD also had a network of state farms
dedicated to providing food for the troops.[27] The physical aspects of the soldier's life in all regards were austere, demanding, and generally unhealthy, both
physically and psychologically.

Although assignment policies for conscripts were never made public, and
they were probably not all written down, some of the more conspicuous ones
are easy to infer. First of all, soldiers never served on their home territory.[28]
Conscripts from the Baltic republics were sent to the Transcaucasus, Central
Asia, and the Far East. Conscripts from the Transcaucasus were sent to units
in the Baltic region, Eastern Europe, Russia, Belorussia, and Siberia. These,
of course, are merely illustrative examples of the principle of "extraterritoriality" for place of service. To a significant degree it was unavoidable. Military
units located on the Chinese border—more than fifty divisions—could hardly
have been filled with recruits from the thinly populated regions of Siberia.
Nor could the Northern and Pacific Fleets be manned by recruits from regions
around the naval bases. Other factors, however, also apparently played a role.
The party leadership remembered "localism" on the part of units of the Red
Army during the civil war, and it did not want similar sympathies to exist between Soviet military units and the local population in the event those units

had to assist in maintaining local order.[29] Just such a duty had arisen in 1962 in the southern Russian city of Novocherkassk, when workers demonstrating against increasing food prices marched on the local party headquarters and army troops were used to repress them, leaving twenty-four dead and thirty-nine wounded.[30] For similar reasons, the number of soldiers from the Baltic states serving in East Germany was negligible because of close relations people of these republics had with the Germans before and during World War II.

Russian-language fluency also played a role in assignment policies. Non-Slavic ethnic groups were, as a rule, scantly represented in such technical branches as the strategic rocket, naval, and air defense units. They went to the Ground Forces, on the other hand, in significant numbers. Central Asians were predominantly assigned to military construction units. Russian fluency— or lack of it—was clearly a factor in this assignment pattern.

Related to the criteria of extraterritoriality and Russian fluency was the nationality issue.[31] For most of the first four decades of Soviet rule, some military units were unavoidably recruited on a national ethnic basis. Otherwise, because fluency in Russian varied widely, large pools of non-Russian manpower would have been unavailable for military service. Although national military formations diminished in number after the civil war, they grew rapidly during World War II. After the war, they persisted until the mid-1950s.[32] Thereafter, they ceased to exist, and in line with the official Soviet nationality policy of the "nearing" *(blizhenie)* and "melding" *(sliyanie)* of all Soviet peoples into one, all military units were officially required to contain a mix of national minorities. In fact, military service was hailed as an especially effective mechanism for contributing to the eradication of ethnic and national consciousness in favor of a Soviet identity. Occasionally, émigrés and defectors reported serious problems between ethnic groups within Soviet military units. Indeed, although some Western analysts attributed moderate success to multinational integration, it was in fact a failure.[33]

The ethnic composition of the officer corps was predominantly Slavic. Central Asian, Azerbaijani, Georgian, and Moldavian officers were rare. Armenian, Tatar, and Baltic officers were found in noticeable numbers, but Russians, Ukrainians, and Belorussians, in that order, made up the overwhelming majority. General Igor Rodionov asserted publicly in 1990 that 97 percent of the officer corps was Russian, Belorussian, Ukrainian, and Tatar.[34]

A potential therefore remained for the fragmentation of the military enlisted ranks along ethnic lines; yet the leadership seems to have remained oblivious to this danger until 1988–89, when it became undeniably manifest. Although the officer corps enjoyed a Slavic solidarity, it had also alienated ethnic minority officers within its ranks. A Chechen, Major General Dzhokar Dudaev, later became president of the republic of Chechnya and organized the remarkably effective resistance to the Russian army's invasion of his country in 1994. Even some Slavic officers became disaffected. A Ukrainian, Lieutenant General Ivan Bizhan, was deputy head of the operations directorate of the General Staff in 1991. After the August crisis, he threw his lot in with the Ukrainian independence leadership in Kiev. The turning point for him came immediately after his graduation from the General Staff Academy in the early 1980s, when his assignment to command a division was held up for several months by the Central Committee Administrative Organs Department because he was Ukrainian. Thus he awoke to the reality that all Soviet officers were not politically equal, not even all Slavic officers.[35]

As varying ethnic birth rates changed the demographics among various Soviet nationalities in the 1960s and later, slowing population growth in Slavic republics and increasing it in the Muslim republics, some observers began to predict a manpower crisis for the Soviet military. More non-Russians, especially Muslims, would have to be drafted, and this would adversely affect the average education and technical-cultural level, as well as the Russian fluency, of active-duty personnel.[36] In fact, more conscripts were taken from Central Asia, adding to the problem of Russian-language fluency, but the anticipated drop in Slavic conscripts was partially offset by the elimination of student deferments beginning in 1982.

Not so obvious to Western observers was another aspect of demographic data. Environmental pollution, alcoholism, and poor diets were adversely affecting the health of the youth.[37] Urban life in particular took a heavy toll on young people's health, yielding fewer medically fit and physically strong young men for conscription. In the later glasnost years this problem received attention in the Soviet media with surprising intensity and frequency.

Overall, the social background of the Soviet soldier changed fairly dramatically during the postwar decades. The soldier in World War II was most likely to be from a peasant family. By the 1970s, well over half came from urban backgrounds and families working in industry.[38] Many more had completed a secondary education or worked at some industrial job. In other words, the technical-cultural level of the average conscript was moving upward. Motor vehicles and other machines were less mysterious to him, and teaching him to drive a tank or truck, or to operate a radio or fire artillery pieces and launch ballistic missiles, was not as difficult and time-consuming as during the interwar period and the first postwar decades.

A profound change in the patterns of barracks life in the enlisted ranks came with the promulgation in 1967 of a new military service law.[39] The previous law, promulgated in 1938, required four years of active duty for conscripts in the navy, three years in all other branches. One call-up was conducted each year. The 1967 law reduced active duty by one year and introduced semiannual call-ups, one in the late spring and a second in the late fall. For the bulk of the forces, this change meant that every six months about one-fourth of the enlisted component was replaced with fresh conscripts. The consequence was added turmoil and difficulties in maintaining training standards. Under the old system, only one-third of the enlisted personnel changed each year. Conscripts had longer periods to master their jobs, and conscript NCOs had more time to learn leadership skills, attending regimental NCO schools for six-month training courses at the beginning of their service.

Why was the new conscription law deemed necessary? Most Western government analysts saw it as a "civilian-directed" policy overriding the desires of the MoD and the General Staff.[40] Actually, the senior military leadership appears to have favored the new law, and that stance makes sense in light of the emerging Soviet military doctrine in the early 1960s.[41] According to that doctrine, military manpower needs in a nuclear war would be vastly greater than in any previous war. Initial losses could be enormous, and reserves for mobilization would have to be as large as Soviet society could physically provide. Building up huge reserves of trained manpower for all military specialties was thus an urgent task. The old conscription system apparently did not create trained reserves in the numbers the military leadership believed it might need. By increasing the amount of preservice military training in secondary schools, DOSAAF, and factory and collective farm military training points, conscripts could start their service better prepared, making a reduction of a year in active duty service more manageable.[42] The 1967 military service law appears to have been designed for increasing the pool of trained reserves for mobilization in the event of nuclear war.[43]

With the new conscription system also came a change in the sociology of barracks life. Second-year soldiers began to gain a social coherence as the "seniors" in the barracks. First-year soldiers became somewhat like American college fraternity pledges, to be hazed and treated as servants. Lacking a professional NCO corps to prevent such behavior, the senior cohort took over the barracks and much of the duty life of the ordinary soldier. The resulting cohort solidarity among conscripts increased the brutality of military life. The effect on the psyche of first-year soldiers was to convince them not that such practices should be eliminated but rather that they should survive until they got the chance to treat the next first-year cohort with equal brutality.[44] Junior

officers—platoon leaders, company commanders, and battalion commanders—
effectively lost control of barracks life. In return for autonomy in the barracks,
the senior cohort forced the junior soldiers to carry out most of the tasks assigned by the officers, forging a perverse mutual dependency between the officer and enlisted ranks.[45]

Ethnic groupings also existed within the bifurcated senior-junior cohort
social structure. The abuse of a minority soldier often inspired the wrath and
revenge of his fellow nationals. National groups banded together in fights,
thievery, and other kinds of disorderly behavior.[46] As became widely known
through glasnost in the late 1980s, deaths frequently resulted both from fights
among ethnic gangs and from senior soldiers hazing new conscripts.[47]

Life in the Soviet military was grim and dangerous. In all my interviews
with former Soviet officers on this issue, when they were asked why it could
be that way, most of them answered, in effect, "We do not value human life."
They did not see this as a desirable attitude, and they readily admitted that it
undercut military effectiveness; yet they took it as an enduring feature of Soviet
society. Was Soviet barracks life always such? Or did it become worse after the
promulgation of the 1967 military service law? Here again the evidence is impressionistic, but in my informal discussions with more than a dozen Soviet
émigrés in the United States, all of whom had served before 1967, none recalled the phenomenon of *dedovshchina*—the hazing of first-year soldiers by
second-year soldiers.[48] That feature of Soviet military life, therefore, seems attributable to the system of a two-year service term. Likewise, the humiliation
of junior officers in the eyes of the troops by senior officers was not remembered as common practice by these émigrés. Rifts between Slavs and non-Slav
ethnic minorities, however, were something they had witnessed.

Although Soviet military leaders improved their personnel system in significant ways during the postwar decades, they fatally ignored its accumulating
signs of decay. They could contain some problems within the military's ranks,
but they could not prevent the political impact on the civilian society made by
tales of the horrors of life in the military brought home by veterans. Here was
the military's Achilles' heel.

FOUR

The Permanent War Economy

State socialism has been the economy of the most warlike of all societies.

QUINCY WRIGHT

The military-industrial sector was part of the Soviet military iceberg, largely concealed below the bureaucratic waters of military secrecy but a weighty factor in any calculation to alter military policy. It was much larger than generally realized in the West, notwithstanding the large efforts devoted by Western intelligence services and scholars to estimating its size.[1] The well-known large quantity of weaponry and matériel it was producing, however, had long revealed its enormity. Table 1 provides a conservative estimate of the Soviet military's "order of battle" for weapons and major equipment items in 1985–86, and although it makes no distinctions for quality and technological level of weapons, all were produced in the postwar period.

Gorbachev's perestroika policies for the economy would crash against the iceberg of the military-industrial sector. Apparently Gorbachev believed that he could avoid a direct collision with it, that he might turn it gently, placing some of its mass behind his economic reform policies. The inevitability of his failure becomes clear if the nature and size of the military-industrial sector is fully appreciated. To that end let us examine more closely its organization and formal processes, put it into a comparative perspective within the Soviet command economy and other economic systems, and, finally, consider its dynamic behavior within the overall economy.

The Structure of the Military-Industrial Sector

The place of Soviet military industries within the overall Soviet system has been outlined, but some elaboration is helpful. Figure 3 shows top state organs concerned with the military-industrial sector. The core of military industry

Table 1 Comparison of Soviet and U.S. Forces, 1985–86

Weapons	Number Soviet	Number U.S.
Strategic Forces		
Ballistic missiles		
ICBM	1,418	1,000
SLBM	928	640
IRBM	553	150
Bombers		
Long-range	165	317
Medium-range	567	56
Short-range	450	
Reconnaissance		
Strategic	108	68
Tactical	89	
ECM	160	
Tankers	50	690
Ground Forces		
Tanks	53,000	13,300
Armored fighting vehicles	64,700	26,000
Artillery	29,000	5,740
SS missile launchers	1,510	50
Antiaircraft guns	12,000	
Tactical mobile SAMs	5,000	808
Helicopters	4,600	8,650
Air Defense		
ABM launchers	32	0
Interceptor aircraft	1,760	294
SAMs	9,000	
Warning systems (radars and satellites)	10,000	
Air surveillance systems	7,000	
Air Forces		
Fighter-bombers	2,460	
Fighters	2,000	
Reconnaissance	390	
Transport aircraft	610	
		4,885 (total)
Navy		
Attack submarines	360	96
Carriers	6	15
Cruisers	37	36
Destroyers	63	68
Destroyer escorts	168	115

Table 1 Continued

Weapons	Number	
	Soviet	*U.S.*
Minor combatants	757	
Principal auxiliaries	382	
Amphibious	190	
Naval aviation		
Aircraft	964	
Helicopters	335	

Source: Military Balance 1987–88.
Note: Some numbers have been rounded down and several smaller or older systems have been omitted to make the estimates conservative.

rested in the nine ministries supervised and managed by the Military Industrial Commission (VPK), which was directly under and part of the Council of Ministers, but eight additional industrial ministries were also heavily committed to supporting the VPK ministries.

The military-industrial ministries themselves, though grouped under the VPK for special management, were in principle no different from other industrial ministries. Nor did they produce only military weapons and equipment. Most military-industrial firms maintained production lines for civilian goods as well. Radar factories, for example, produced televisions sets. And naval shipyards produced fishing trawlers as well as naval combatants. The idea behind the dual production stemmed from the 1920s, when there was great concern about shifting from peacetime production to wartime status. It was called the militia approach to industry: factories were designed to be primarily devoted to military production but also capable of producing consumer goods when high levels of military production were not needed. Likewise, most civilian industrial firms were required to maintain standby tools and equipment for a rapid shift to military production.

Thus the line between military and civilian industry was initially quite porous, and it remained so, to a lesser degree, until the end of the Soviet Union. At the same time, modern military production requirements tended to make dual-production lines difficult to maintain, causing the boundary between them and civilian industry to become much less flexible. Security requirements for secrecy in production also contributed to the growing isolation of the military-industrial sector. And its priority treatment in the allocation of resources also gave it an increasingly separate status.

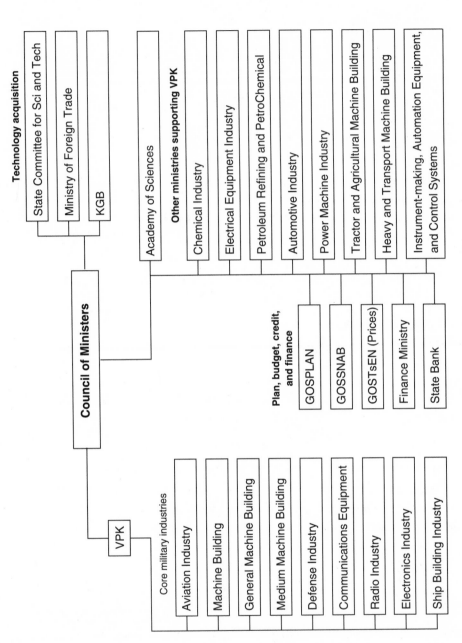

Figure 3. Military industries

The full portion of Soviet industry devoted to military production is not fully reflected in the nine ministries. As shown in figure 3, eight other ministries worked primarily in support of the VPK, making a total of seventeen ministries heavily involved in military production. Given that about fifty industrial and commercial ministries existed by the early 1980s, the seventeen military and supporting ministries made up a large share of the total, but even that figure may not capture the actual portion of the industrial sector devoted to the military.[2] The size of individual ministries varied widely, and the military-industrial ministries were among the largest. Moreover, they drew heavily, directly and indirectly, on the output of civilian ministries—those for coal and steel production, transportation, chemical, construction, and several others.

The linkages between the military-industrial sector and its main customer, the MoD, were extensive. The military had a network of representatives present throughout the thousands of military-industrial firms, in GOSPLAN, the VPK, GOSSNAB, the GKNT, and the USSR Academy of Sciences. Likewise, military-industrial personnel had liaison within the various military branches of service and the MoD. At the apex of this set of linkages, managing and coordinating the execution of procurement and research plans within directives and guidelines formulated in GOSPLAN, were the MoD (mainly through its deputy minister for armaments, deputy minister for rear services, and the General Staff) and the VPK. GOSPLAN, of course, received its guidance directly from the Council of Ministers, but only after the Politburo had reviewed and approved it. It has generally been assumed that the Defense Industries Department of the Central Committee Secretariat acted as the Politburo's staff organ in overseeing the MoD-VPK relation, but a former official from the Defense Industries Department said that it was mainly concerned with approving personnel assignments within the VPK and its ministries.[3]

The decision-making cycle of this system was extremely complex, though generally the same as in the rest of the economy. The five-year plan (FYP) formed the basic guidance. Within the FYP, the annual plan was the working focus, establishing a cycle wherein the industrial firms submitted proposals upward through intermediate bureaucratic levels to the ministries, which then submitted them through the VPK to GOSPLAN. The modified and approved results were then sent back down to firms for execution.

In practice, a great deal of informal communication and bureaucratic bargaining was necessary to make this planning-directive cycle work. Because the military customers were seldom happy with industrial managers' responsiveness, tensions were virtually constant. Relations were especially strained during the First Five-Year Plan (1927/28–32).[4] During World War II and in the early postwar period the MoD was in a strong buyer's position, but by the late 1970s it often had to accept weapons it did not want.

Parallel to the process within the military-industrial sector, the MoD, the General Staff, and the branches of military service had their own internal processes, as we have seen, based on war plans. The General Staff submitted its aggregate requirements to GOSPLAN, not, as was sometimes assumed in Western literature, the VPK.

Determining military procurement requirements is difficult enough when technology is static. When it is dynamic, creating new opportunities to have more effective weapons, the challenge is so great that is often causes temporary breakdowns and serious organizational perturbations. The military and the VPK constantly confronted the more demanding environment of changing technology.

The General Staff had to state its requirements in this dynamic context, but most of the knowledge about new technological possibilities resided within the VPK and the Academy of Sciences. The most advanced technologies were always first developed in the West, where military intelligence operatives and the KGB agents learned about them. Thus the formal cycle, in which military research and development (R&D) and procurement requirements were generated by the military and then levied through GOSPLAN on the VPK, captures only part of the reality. Initiation in the process came from many places and not always in an orderly fashion—from within the MoD, from within the VPK, from the Academy of Sciences, and, not least of all, from the Politburo itself. As messy and erratic as the process was, it remained within the context of the formal state bodies, but it was guided, watched, and enveloped by the party, with its ubiquitous apparatus and membership, including the incumbents for all the military posts and the important military-industrial and scientific posts. Although the military and the military-industrial sector were distinct organizational entities, the party was not separate in the same fashion. It not only penetrated and enveloped both the MoD and VPK as organizations; it also determined the lives and careers of most of the MoD and VPK incumbents. Neither the VPK nor the MoD could do these things to the other.

The Origins and Growth of the Military-Industrial System

The roots of this system reach back to the Russian mobilization economy during World War I and the civil war. During the New Economic Policy (NEP, 1921–28), military industries were put into a single state trust and given low priority.[5] The NEP therefore marked a radical shift of resource allocations away from traditional weapons production but not from the basic profile of the industrial sector resulting from war mobilization. That is, developments in metallurgy, machine building, aviation, energy, the chemical industry, and radio communications that occurred during World War I were preserved during NEP.

Investments for changing the industrial base would begin during the first three five-year plans (1927/28–41), but not so much for reshaping as for incorporating technological change while keeping the emphasis on metallurgy, machine building, chemicals, and energy—that is, the sectors most needed for a modern military-industrial base. The Western literature on the interwar FYPs pays surprisingly little attention to military considerations in their design.[6] Only in the last years of Gorbachev's perestroika did Western economists begin an upward reestimation of size of the military sector.[7] A major reason is that early military considerations were manifest not in the size of military production but rather in the organization of structures of control and their connections to the Red Army. A military five-year modernization plan developed by the commissariat of military and naval affairs in parallel with the first FYP proved a dismal failure.[8] Neither Stalin nor his economic and military advisers seem to have understood initially that expansion of the industrial base had to come before significant modern armaments production was possible. The abject failure of the first plan for military modernization taught them this elementary truth. An industrial base that could produce reasonably modern weaponry in significant quantity did not exist until the mid-1930s.

In 1928, both Klimentii Voroshilov, commissar of military and naval affairs, and Mikhail Tukhachevskii, chief of the Red Army staff, favored an early and rapid rearmament of the army, providing it with tanks, improved artillery, motor transport, and advanced aircraft. Stalin did not share their enthusiasm, provoking Voroshilov to complain in a note to Sergo Ordzhonikidze that the military budget was being cut in half while "the entire world [was] arming itself to the teeth, and against us." Although Stalin approved rather modest military production goals for the first FYP, even they proved impossible for the military-industrial sector to meet.[9] The logical progression for a broad military modernization program had to follow the course charted by Trotsky in the early 1920s: first, general industrialization, then, military modernization.[10]

The inchoate outlines of the future military-industrial system are most visible in the design of the central planning and management institutions of the first FYP.[11] GOSPLAN had a military section already in 1927.[12] A secret Defense Commission was soon created, comprising a small circle of key top leaders and chaired by Stalin. The members of this behind-the-scenes organ personally supervised all military procurement and outlays to military industry, much as the VPK did years later.[13]

The military itself was given a critical mechanism for extracting its demands from military industries. The Commissariat of Military and Naval Affairs (the Ministry of Defense after World War II) placed military engineers and specialists, known as military representatives *(voenpredy)*, within the military-industrial firms. The voenpredy could check any part of the production process, and they had to sign an acceptance document for each weapon or piece of equipment before the military department considered it delivered and before the factory was given credit in the state plan for having produced it.[14] In other words, unlike any other consumer in the Soviet system, the voenpredy could demand quality products. All others had to take what was produced, and the firms received production credit before an item was actually sold. Henceforth, right down to the end of the Soviet Union, this military-buyer control over the military-industrial producer was retained, although it lost some of its clout during the late postwar period. In turn, military-industrial firms retained priority within GOSPLAN's domain and within the GOSSNAB allocation system, allowing them to foist lower quality materials onto civilian industrial production. The bureaucratic effect was an informal siphoning of the higher quality raw materials and intermediate products into military production at the expense of all other sectors, causing a large, hidden, and nonbudgetary contribution to the military that no accounting system could capture in prices or percentages.

Although numerous organizational changes occurred in the military-industrial system over the years, its structural outlines were created in the late 1920s and well established by the end of the second FYP in 1938.[15] The system was not yet devouring the lion's share of industrial production, but during World War II, it came to encompass most of the economy, as more than half the annual national income went to military expenditures.[16]

Was it merely accidental that the command economic system embodied the capacity to make the military sector its central priority? Was it the unintended consequences of bureaucratization that Trotsky and others did not foresee and later complained about? It seems unlikely.

Frunze, shortly after he replaced Trotsky as commissar of military and naval affairs, outlined principles for military-industrial policy, emphasizing the advantages of socialism in "militarizing" the whole civil apparatus of the state for modern warfare. In a short but prophetic essay about the nature of future war, Frunze provided a fairly accurate, though highly general, characterization of how new technology was changing the nature of warfare and of how another world war would require total societal and industrial mobilization.[17] He considered calling for the military to take industrial development into its own hands but dismissed that approach as "utopian." Instead, he asked for a linkage of the military apparatus with the civil economy that would allow it "not just to be aware of what is going on there but to influence the very character of production based on the demands of defense." He also wanted the military to maintain an "organic mutual bond with the industrial sphere of the country, and equally, with the scientific-technical sphere of the country. This connection must not be limited to the central organs; it must also be introduced at the local levels."[18]

The STO, until 1937, and the GKO, which Stalin created in July 1941, provided such a "mutual bond" between the central organs. The postwar Defense Council continued this function. The Defense Commission (later the Defense Committee and finally, in the postwar period, the VPK) with support from GOSPLAN, the Cheka, and the Commissariat of Foreign Trade (and in the postwar period, also GOSSNAB, the GKNT, and the Academy of Sciences), and the network of voenpredy provided both central and local mechanisms that allowed the military to "influence the very character of production based on the demands of defense." In more recent times, the MoD could levy its requirements on the VPK through GOSPLAN, and it could exert direct pressure for their fulfillment through the network of voenpredy inside the industrial firms. The scientific-technical community, including the Academy of Sciences and the design buros in industry and the MoD, was tied by an "organic bond" to industry and the military.

The military-industrial system existing in the mid-1980s, therefore, was an integral part of the evolution of command economic system developed in the first three FYPs. Lenin provided its ideological justification by asserting that a military showdown with the imperialist West was inevitable, and Frunze anticipated the administrative arrangements essential to prepare for that future war.

Comparative Perspectives

Unique though the Soviet economic system was, some of its aspects were not entirely unprecedented. They were characteristic of twentieth-century wartime mobilization economies of the advanced industrial states—Britain, Germany, France, Russia, Japan, and the United States. This is best illustrated by a comparative view of (*a*) command economies, (*b*) market economies, and (*c*) economies with a mix of market and state planning. The triaxial diagram in figure 4 provides a conceptual graphic for relating these three types. No actual economy is a pure type. Most modern industrial economies combine some de-

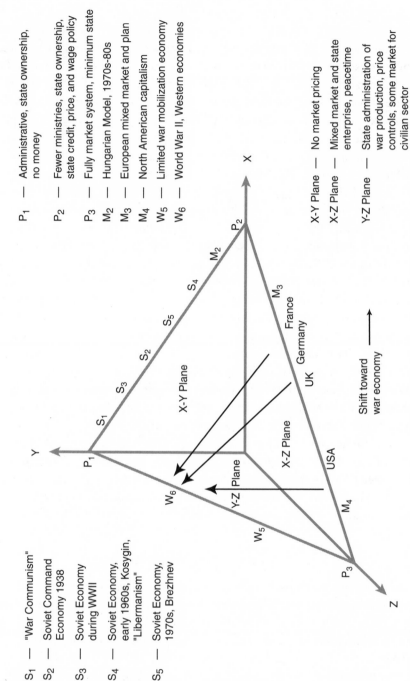

P₁ — Administrative, state ownership, no money

P₂ — Fewer ministries, state ownership, state credit, price, and wage policy

P₃ — Fully market system, minimum state

M₂ — Hungarian Model, 1970s-80s

M₃ — European mixed market and plan

M₄ — North American capitalism

W₅ — Limited war mobilization economy

W₆ — World War II, Western economies

X-Y Plane — No market pricing

X-Z Plane — Mixed market and state enterprise, peacetime

Y-Z Plane — State administration of war production, price controls, some market for civilian sector

S₁ — "War Communism"

S₂ — Soviet Command Economy 1938

S₃ — Soviet Economy during WWII

S₄ — Soviet Economy, early 1960s, Kosygin, "Libermanism"

S₅ — Soviet Economy, 1970s, Brezhnev

Figure 4. **Market, mixed, command, and war economies**

gree of planning and market, but the Soviet system had the most extreme case of central planning. Because it essentially left no significant market sector uncontrolled, it could have a significant impact on price formation.[19] Thus Soviet prices were essentially immune to the information about "relative scarcities" of goods and labor that is reflected in prices formed through free-market transactions. The same was largely true of the planned economies of the Soviet-type regimes in Eastern Europe.

In figure 4, the X, Y, and Z axes indicate three different methods of organizing and controlling an economy. The higher the value on any of the three axes, the larger the physical size of an economy, but because we shall not be concerned here with size, that variable can be disregarded through the simplifying assumption that all the economies are on the lines P_1–P_2, P_2–P_3, or P_3–P_1. Each of these lines reflects a general type of economy, and different positions on a line reflect additional refinements in the type, or methods of organizing and controlling an economy. Absolutely critical to grasp is that in any economy located on the X–Y plane, that is, on the P_1–P_2 line, the state owns all enterprises, all significant "means of production." X and Y indicate two different methods of economic control and direction in fully state-owned economies.

The Y method proceeds purely by administrative direction, requiring no money, no credits, no wages, and so on. To issue instructions and monitor their implementation for an entire economy, even a small one, would require a very large bureaucracy. The large number of ministries in the Soviet system—two or three scores of them—reflects the degree to which the Y method was employed. In reality, no economy has operated entirely with this method because it turns out to be impractical.

The X method involves the use of credit policy, pricing policy, tax policy, and so on for constraining and directing all business enterprises. In principle, if only the X method were employed, the entire economy could be owned by one ministry, greatly reducing the size of the state economic bureaucracy. A central planning agency would determine the general directions desired for economic performance, and then the State Bank and a few other state offices would devise the appropriate credit, wage, tax, and other policies to compel enterprise directors to produce the economic performance outcomes desired by central planners. Far less control is afforded over individual enterprises with this method than with the administrative method, and if managers are not firmly dedicated to achieving the state's goals when they conflict with their own firms' goals, actual economic performance can diverge rather widely from the goals in the state plan.

The Z axis represents a third method for operating an economy, the competitive market. It denotes the extreme form of private ownership and market competition, with virtually no state involvement except to provide the legal and monetary institutions necessary for maintaining property rights and preventing the market's destruction through monopoly behavior. In practice, of course, no market economy is wholly without some state guidance, planning, or ownership. Such mixed economies vary dramatically in the degree and nature of state involvement. The P2–P3 line indicates a range of possible mixed economies, reflecting more or less dependency on markets or state controls and direction. (For the full range, one would have to envision the plane created by P1–P2–P3, or an X–Y–Z plane, mixing all three methods, but for our purposes here, that refinement is not really necessary.)

No economy on the P2–P3 line, however, could operate without legal institutions for defining ownership authority over land and capital as well as legal institutions for litigating disputes over contracts and other matters of free market commerce. For an economy to have a significant Z dimension, it must have legal and other institutions required for defining private property, litigating disputes, and monitoring and managing markets to ensure that monopolies do not destroy them. Economies in the X–Y plane, it should be reemphasized, do not have these institutions. They do not permit private ownership of land and capital except on the most trivial scale, such as in gardening and petty crafts and trade involving no hired labor.

Placing actual examples of market economies on the P2–P3 line, France, with its *dirigisme*, has more state-dictated price, credit, and wage policies and a stronger state hand in directing the economy than does the United Kingdom, for example, placing the French economy closer to P2. One could debate where the German and the U.K. economies stand compared with each other. Germany probably had less state control in the 1960s than Britain but certainly more in the 1990s. The U.S. economy has always had less state involvement and direction than most Western European economies, putting it much closer to P3.

During the twentieth century, when major industrial states have gone to war, they have employed some of the control methods of the X and Y type. In other words, war mobilization economies interfere with the market by using administrative direction in some industrial sectors and by resort to credit, wage, and price controls in others. They do not, however, fully abandon private property and market relations. Thus they never move onto the X–Y plan, either at P1 or P2 or in between. Instead, they move toward the P3–P1 line, increasing administrative direction—the Y method—and also greater use of price and wages controls, credit policy, and so on—the X method. Economies on the P1–P2 line, of course, have a much easier time of war mobilization because they need not make structure and organizational changes but rather must only issue different directions concerning what is produced and for whom.

This scheme for comparing various types of economies can help clarify the complexities and also expose the misconceptions of what effective economic reform required in the Soviet case. Let us use it to reflect on the record of economic reforms and change in both the Soviet Union and Eastern Europe before Gorbachev came to power so that we can see why they failed to prevent increasing economic stagnation.

The point S_1 approximates the location of the Soviet system under War Communism in 1919–20. Money was little used, and virtually all allocations of resources were made by administrative means. M_2 approximates the location of the so-called Hungarian model of the 1970s and early 1980s. It involved a considerable reduction in the economic administrative bureaucracy and greater dependency on price, credit, and wage policies for central control. Economic reforms in other Eastern European economies in the 1960s and 1970s, often wrongly hailed as evolution toward a market system, involved moving toward point P_2, reducing the number of economic ministries and implementing the state economic plan through other than direct administrative means.[20]

In the Soviet case, War Communism was quickly abandoned, and after the seven-year NEP interval, centralization was again introduced. By 1938, after the completion of the first two FYPs, the Soviet command economy was in place (S_2). Although extremely centralized, it did not return to the War Communism model. Price, credit, and wage policies were used, and individual consumers and a few "public" organizations outside the state economic plan depended on money for economic exchange. Small pockets of market activities also persisted—collective farmers' private plots and free marketing of their produce, for example, as well as the labor market, which allowed considerable mobility in response to wage differentials.

During World War II, the Soviet economy moved back toward P_1 to S_3. Administrative controls were increased, and the consumer sector was allowed to suffer huge shortages as GOSPLAN directed most resources to war production. A much larger part of the labor force—in the military, for example—came under administrative control, disallowing most of the earlier discretion left to individuals to seek higher wages. After the war, the economy shifted back to S_2 during Stalin's last years. Khrushchev's industrial reforms in 1957 greatly reduced the ministerial bureaucracies in Moscow, and in this regard, they represent a modest shift toward P_2. When Brezhnev replaced Khrushchev, he began asserting more administrative control. The reforms considered by Aleksei Kosygin during Brezhnev's first years were based on "Libermanism," ideas named for a Soviet economist who called for less administrative direction over firms by the ministries and the introduction of a profit motive. They were meant to shift the Soviet economy toward P2. They were never fully implemented (S4), and to the degree that they were, they were soon reversed.

As a rule, all the Soviet and Eastern European economic reforms tended to move toward P2 and then retreat toward P1. Enterprise managers used their increased discretion to deviate from the state plan, and central planners soon responded by restoring bureaucratic controls. In reality, these reforms seem to have had more to do with politics than with economics. They allowed a new leader to stir up the bureaucracies through cuts, ousting political opponents, then to restore the cuts, appointing their supporters as incumbents.[21] Private ownership of firms was never part of such reforms; nor were market-determined prices, although Czechoslovak leaders in 1967–68 considered letting prices for some goods vary between state-set limits as a minor concession to market forces.

To move an economy off the X–Y plane, genuine market pricing has to be allowed, and that requires a legal basis for private property and a civil-law system for contracts and business litigation. This requirement is not trivial, and to introduce it requires major institutional changes. Much of the Western anticipation of "creeping capitalism" arising from the Kosygin reforms and the reforms in Eastern Europe in the 1960s and 1970s was disappointed. Why such anticipation was unjustified is clear in retrospect. None of these reforms moved any of the economies off the X–Y plane and toward the Z axis. Every reform involved only a shift along the P1–P2 line on the X–Y axis. Only when Gorbachev began to try to introduce limited market activity was such a bold departure even contemplated. And we now can see from Russia's experience in introducing a market sector that the institutional reform requirements for such a departure are indeed dramatic, systemic in nature, even revolutionary.

Let us again consider the P3–P1 line connecting the Z and Y axes. Market economies, when they mobilize for war, begin to move toward P1, or more accurately, toward the P1–P3 line. The German, French, British, Russian, and U.S. economies in World War I all moved a considerable distance toward point P1. And in World War II, the same thing happened, except in the Soviet Union. The Soviet system was already on the P1–P2 line, and not far from P1. Thus in 1941 Stalin already had at his disposal the administration for shifting the Soviet economy rapidly toward P1.

After World Wars I and II, all the Western economies moved back toward the P3–P2 line, letting the market play a bigger role—that is, letting consumers have more impact on price formation, which in turn affected investment patterns and production. In the Soviet case, only for a brief time during the NEP were consumers allowed to play such a role, and with the advent of the first FYP, central planners' preferences again took priority as they had during War Communism. Thus the Soviet Union retained a permanent wartime mobilization system.

A Permanent Wartime Economy During a Technology Revolution

A war mobilization economy, especially in such extreme form that it puts the economy on the X–Y plane of figure 4, denies itself market prices and all the consequences thereby entailed. Lacking "scarcity price" information, the state planners have no way to maintain, much less increase, the efficiency of capital allocations. Systemic incentives for technological innovation are virtually nonexistent among managers, and new technology must therefore be introduced by central directives. Inherent bureaucratic incentives for both managers and workers become increasingly perverse for economic growth because they impede increases in the productivity of labor and capital. These realities, of course, are well-known and have been the topic of a vast literature.[22] The long-term performance of such a system, therefore, should be predictably much poorer than that of a market system.[23]

That prediction is borne out by some of the specific problems that Soviet military industry confronted, especially in its last couple of decades. Even during the interwar decades, when the Soviet economy was relatively small and when Stalin and a few of his fellow Bolsheviks could find time to manage the details of technological innovation, the military-industrial sector yielded a mixed, though generally positive, result.[24] In the postwar period, Soviet R&D faced a set of new challenges. Nuclear weapons had appeared, and U.S. aircraft design and production was driven by a surge in technological innovation. The revolution in electronics, stimulated by the semiconductor development, soon brought the computer age. Computers made possible "computational science" for research, industrial design, industrial production, and many other applications.

Soviet R&D was institutionally ill-designed to cope with such dynamism. The bureaucratic obstacles to Soviet technological innovation have long been noted by virtually all Western studies of the topic. Eminent Soviet weapons designers complained publicly about it. Intervention by top party leaders overcame it in specific instances but not consistently. Not surprisingly, then, the Soviet military was forced to resort to borrowing and stealing Western technological innovations, a strategy that played a major role. Throughout Soviet history, when trade and economic interaction with the Western industrial states did not produce adequate technology transfer, Soviet intelligence operatives strove to fill the gaps. The degree of Soviet dependency on espionage as a source of foreign technology proved to be much higher than was generally appreciated when American intelligence obtained a secret report to the Soviet leadership cataloguing the contributions in the 1970s and 1980s. An unclassified CIA assessment of the report asserts that in 1980 well over five thousand Soviet research projects benefited directly from Western technology, some acquired legally through trade, much more obtained through espionage.[25]

The key economic issue for the Politburo in the 1980s was whether or not a permanent wartime mobilization economic system could continue to meet their aims. If so, then it was necessary only to improve it. If not, then systemic change was necessary. In that case, dismantling the VPK was a sine qua non for systemic reform.

FIVE

Military Strategy

*Everything in strategy is very simple, but that does not mean that
everything is very easy.*

CARL VON CLAUSEWITZ

"Peaceful coexistence" was the Soviet grand strategy for advancing the socialist revolution from the early 1920s and into the 1930s. It was dropped by Stalin as World War II approached, revived by Khrushchev in the mid-1950s, written into the Third Party Program in 1961, and retained right up until Gorbachev's time. Soviet military strategy was designed to support it. Although military strategy is concerned with the conduct of war, it also involves peacetime uses of military power for political influence, as well as arms control negotiations. We therefore must look at all three components.

Strategy for Wartime in the 1980s

A country's initial wartime strategy is normally reflected in war plans. Moscow's war plans can be roughly inferred from the structure of Soviet forces, their regional deployments, and Soviet open-source literature on strategy, operations, and tactics.

The General Staff's war planning was the culmination of a long and sometimes erratic process that began in the late 1950s. By the late 1970s the senior military leadership believed that the Soviet Union had attained strategic parity with the United States, and thus it shifted emphasis to theater capabilities.[1] For the next half-dozen years, improvement in capabilities for theater warfare continued, primarily in Europe, but also in the Far East and in the south on the borders with Turkey and Iran.

The big question, of course, was how to deal with the advent of nuclear weapons. The answer would dictate strategy, operations, and tactics for conventional forces. It would also provide the parameters for arms control strategy.

Nuclear Weapons Forces

Two sharply divergent schools of thought arose in the 1960s among Western analysts over how the Soviet General Staff planned to use nuclear weapons. Those in the first believed that the Soviet military was inexorably bound by the logic of Western deterrence theory—that by the late 1960s both sides had the capability to destroy each other, that both understood this, and that they were inescapably and mutually vulnerable to near total destruction in a nuclear war.[2] "Defense" in nuclear war had no practical meaning. This group pointed to statements by various Soviet political leaders that seemed to imply the acceptance of deterrence theory and that described nuclear war as suicidal. Those in the second school insisted that Soviet leaders intended to use nuclear weapons to wage a war, not just to deter one, that nuclear effects would make war extremely destructive but still winnable in some sense of the word. Some in this school were also skeptical of the logic of deterrence theory, finding Soviet military writings on nuclear weapons more realistic.[3] These skeptics pointed to aspects of Soviet force design, emphasis on civil defense, deployment of an ABM system around Moscow, deep underground command centers, and to the writings of Soviet military theorists as evidence that Soviet leaders were preparing to fight nuclear war, not just deter it. Although a great deal of ink has been spilled debating this issue, a critical review of it is not the most productive way to proceed here.[4] It is better to look at what is known about Soviet strategy as it emerged in the mid-1980s and at the doctrinal assumptions on which it was based.

According to Western historiography, Stalin froze thought about nuclear weapons, refusing to believe that they had changed the nature of war as Western theorists insisted. Although Stalin did dismiss the Western assessment as absurd, it is not true that he failed to see nuclear weapons as capable of changing the strategic balance between the socialist and imperialist camps. On the contrary, he demanded that his scientists and engineers meet impossibly short schedules in building nuclear weapons and bombers capable of dropping them on targets in the continental United States.[5] He also ordered his military to develop tactics for nuclear weapons, and General Ivan Petrov, although he knew nothing about nuclear weapons effects, was directed to conduct an exercise to explore methods of nuclear weapons employment in 1951.[6] In first considering nuclear weapons, therefore, Soviet military leaders had to assume that they were just another new weapon, not an innovation that made winning a war against the United States impossible.

As David Holloway observes in his excellent history of Soviet nuclear weapons development, Stalin's successors, Malenkov and Khrushchev, were awed by the destructiveness of these new weapons.[7] Khrushchev emphasized them as a means of cutting expenditures on more costly conventional forces, but that confronted him with a fundamental ideological problem because it appeared to incorporate acceptance of a permanent nuclear standoff. Did Khrushchev believe, as Chinese Marxist-Leninists chided him, that Lenin and Stalin were wrong about an inevitable military showdown with imperialism? Or did he believe that the socialist camp could not win a nuclear war and that reactionary political forces would prevail? If so, that made mockery of the Marxist-Leninist doctrine on just and unjust wars.[8] These were difficult questions, and Khrushchev's ambiguous answers never fully convinced some of his own generals and party colleagues, much less the Chinese.

Brezhnev allowed the military to develop the following formula to deal with this troublesome problem: although nuclear war would be terrible and should be avoided if possible, one could not be sure that the imperialists would not unleash it, and if they did, the growing Soviet nuclear capabilities would ensure that the social camp would prevail and that imperialism would meet its demise.[9] Although occasional public statements by Brezhnev and other Politburo members created ambiguity about this formula, its logic remained the basis for Soviet military planning right down to Gorbachev's rule.

Much more than ideological tenets, of course, determined the evolution of Soviet strategy for nuclear weapons use. First, because Soviet leaders acquired nuclear weapons later than their U.S. counterparts, they felt insecure in face of the frightening American advantage. Second, the technological lag vis-à-vis the United States adversely affected the Soviet aviation industry, leaving the air forces without the means to deliver a nuclear attack directly on the United States. In fact, they found it easier to develop long-range ballistic missiles than to build modern bombers. Although they built bombers, land-based intercontinental ballistic missiles (ICBMs) became and remained the major component of their nuclear forces. Third, they knew much about early U.S. nuclear war plans, which did not accord with deterrence theory.[10] Finally, building large, high-yield nuclear weapons was easier than designing low-yield warheads to support tactical operations. The United States led in all of these areas (except, for a short time, in rocketry), including tactical nuclear weapons. These arms, in fact, were deployed to U.S. Army units in Germany in the late 1950s, an action that gave the strong impression that the United States took nuclear war fighting seriously.[11] Thus Soviet leaders had more than their own military views and ideological considerations to convince them that nuclear war, though it would entail much greater firepower and destruction, would be fought in the traditional way.

Marshal Vasilii Sokolovskii's *Military Strategy,* which appeared in 1962, was a collective work that summarized the previous decade of internal Soviet military thinking about nuclear weapons and future war.[12] The key to its message about nuclear weapons is Sokolovskii's treatment of the "principle of the objective" in war.[13] In the past, he observed, the primary objective of military strategy had been the destruction of the enemy's forces (as opposed to taking territory), but with nuclear weapons and intercontinental delivery means, it was now possible to strike the enemy's "rear," that is, his economy and its military potential. Did this capability change the objective for nuclear war to the destruction of the enemy's rear? Sokolovskii's answer was largely determined by a related issue: how to apply "surprise," another principle of war, one Stalin had disparaged after World War II.[14] Surprise in launching a nuclear war, Sokolovskii and his fellow theorists reasoned, could make the "initial period" decisive for the outcome in subsequent periods. In the 1950s, the "initial period" became almost an obsession among Soviet military theorists. The Soviet Union had suffered "surprise" at the strategic level in 1941, but that did not determine the war's eventual outcome. For obvious political reasons, Stalin refused to admit that it could be decisive in the nuclear age. After his death, Soviet military theorists began to reach a different conclusion. Still, Sokolovskii did not give a simple "yes" answer to his question about the principle of the objective. Rather, he concluded, the objective would have be the destruction of both the enemy's conventional theater forces and targets in his home economy as combined and simultaneous operations in the war's initial period. That would require both conventional-force operations supported by nuclear strikes in theater campaigns and strikes on the United States with nuclear weapons from the war's very beginning.

This was a tall order, but it guided Soviet force development for the next two decades. Design and production of ICBMs, long-range bombers, and submarine launched ballistic missiles (SLBMs) proceeded in parallel with design and production of shorter-range delivery systems and smaller-yield nuclear weapons, eventually including artillery-delivered nuclear warheads. The Soviet military began building the full panoply of nuclear forces required for their wartime use at each level — strategic, operational, and tactical.

Once the Soviet Union had built up its ICBM forces, proponents of U.S. deterrence theory considered the vulnerability of both the U.S. and the Soviet homelands as a permanent and unchangeable fact. They were puzzled that Soviet leaders expected to evade it. Paul Warnke, as director of the Arms Control and Disarmament agency (1977–79), scoffed that Soviet views on fighting a nuclear war were primitive and insisted that the United States had to reeducate the Soviets.[15] Such an attitude precluded the detached empathy that David Holloway shows in describing Stalin's view of fighting nuclear war.[16] Stalin was not about to let the Americans scare him, or at least he would not admit it. Given his life experience and ideological outlook, it would have been strange indeed for him to admit that he would have to accept the permanent existence of the bourgeois world order. Instead, he bluffed with a show of disdain for Western claims about the nature of nuclear war while pressing ahead with his own nuclear weapons program. He also conveyed that bluff to his generals and scientists, who were allowed no opportunity for critical reflection and doubt. Their reluctance to challenge Stalin's estimate of nuclear weapons persisted after his death, and although Khrushchev may have been more frightened by them than Stalin, he never fundamentally changed the military's attitude on the matter. The military buildup under Brezhnev had the effect of getting the United States to plead for negotiations, probably interpreted by the Soviet side as weak nerves.

How did Soviet military leaders believe they could actually avoid vulnerability? They turned to practical experience. Reflecting in 1995, General Anatolii Gribkov, a former deputy chief of the General Staff and chief of staff for Warsaw Pact forces, said that the Cuban missile crisis left Soviet leaders with the impression that neither side would resort to an all-out exchange, and therefore that the use of nuclear weapons would remain restricted to the theater level, leaving both homelands inviolate.[17] This concept of regionally limited nuclear use differed fundamentally from the U.S. concept of "limited nuclear options" for homeland to homeland strikes intended to control escalation, which was embraced in National Security Decision Memorandum 242 in 1974.

General Gribkov, who believed that nuclear weapons might facilitate the speedy conquest of Europe, went on to describe a 1978 Warsaw Pact exercise. When Marshal Dmitrii Ustinov, director of the exercise, asked Gribkov, its designer, who initiated use of nuclear weapons in the exercise scenario, Gribkov replied that it was a "political decision," not his to make. Warsaw Pact forces were prepared to use nuclear weapons either first or second, whichever the political leaders preferred.[18] Soviet forces, however, did not possess sufficient numbers of nuclear warheads deliverable by short-range rockets and artillery to meet war planning requirements until the early 1980s. At that time, nuclear-capable 152 millimeter guns began to appear in the Group of Soviet Forces in

Germany. Short-range ballistic missiles and intermediate-range bombers were available earlier, but nuclear-capable artillery allowed a considerable refinement in employment at the tactical level.[19]

The General Staff's view of nuclear weapons use is revealed not only by General Gribkov's testimony, by inferences based on Soviet weapons systems' capabilities, and in doctrinal writings, but more definitively by East German war plans recovered after the fall of the Berlin Wall. They dictated first use of tactical nuclear weapons during the early days of a war. In one plan, forty nuclear weapons were to be dropped on Hamburg on the second day of hostilities.[20] As for Soviet war plans, a former Soviet colonel, Igor Shmeshko, told me that he could not recall participating in a single military exercise that did not include nuclear weapons use.[21]

Much additional corroborating evidence has become available. In 1992, Colonel General Igor Rodionov, head of the General Staff Academy at the time and appointed minister of defense in July 1996, wrote that in the 1950s and 1960s the political leaders concluded "that a future war would be nuclear, with massed use of nuclear weapons. . . . And military science, striving to justify this thesis, proved that combat actions, using conventional weapons, had virtually become extinct, and that victory could be achieved in a world nuclear war."[22] Rodionov, of course, was complaining about Khrushchev's policy of putting primary emphasis on the rocket forces while cutting the ground forces sharply in the late 1950s. Also in 1992, Major General Valentin Larionov, a contributor to Sokolovskii's *Military Strategy*, said that the 1960s were considered by some as the "romantic period" because nuclear weapons would "achieve any political or military objective, even the most extreme ones. Strategic planning organs did not even give thought to what form a mass Soviet missile strike would take, whether it would be a first strike or a retaliatory strike. The U.S. 'missile gap' solved every problem for us." "Ideological and psychological considerations" played a major role in planning, and "typically, all calculations at that time were based on the assumption that nuclear weapons would be used." This attitude did not change, he added, until the late 1980s.[23] Even before the end of the Soviet Union, open source publications claimed that Soviet nuclear strategy was based on the belief that nuclear war was winnable and that nuclear use made good military sense. One essay reviewed the history of all Soviet literature on nuclear weapons employment and concluded that although a few voices had tried to cast doubt on the wartime utility of such weapons, the prevailing view treated them as just another type of battlefield capability.[24]

Rodionov and Larionov, of course, were not speaking about nuclear weapons employment limited to the theater, because Soviet forces were not well equipped for it in the 1960s. They appear to be referring to use of intercontinental nuclear weapons, and much less is known about Soviet planning at that level, certainly much less than is known about theater nuclear use. Larionov's brief characterization suggests that intercontinental targeting was not terribly refined. Presumably, it became more so as the large and accurate ICBM forces were fielded in the 1970s.

Colonel General Nikolai Detinov, who was deeply involved in the Soviet arms-control staffing process from its inception to near the end of the Soviet Union, reports that the notion of winning a nuclear war was both ideologically and psychologically rooted in the views of the "political-military leadership," although a few scientists cautiously expressed doubts to Soviet diplomats but to no effect. Detinov also reports that Soviet leaders in the 1960s saw an ABM program as absolutely essential to limit damage from any U.S. nuclear attack. Initially convinced of the technical feasibility of an ABM system, they did not initiate a program for two reasons. First, their own technology was not yet adequate; second, it would draw resources away from and disrupt ICBM programs, which were proceeding smoothly. The U.S. proposal for an ABM treaty, therefore, came as a pleasant surprise. By ending the U.S. ABM program, it would free the Soviets from engaging in simultaneous competition in both strategic offensive and defensive systems and permit Soviet ICBM programs to move ahead on schedule. Thus the ABM treaty appeared to have allowed a considerably larger number of offensive nuclear weapons in the Soviet arsenal than there would have been without it. According to Detinov, the logic of U.S. views on the winnability of a nuclear war and how to achieve strategic "stability" played no role at all in the Soviet acceptance of the ABM treaty.[25]

By the mid-1980s Soviet nuclear strategy appeared to have involved a highly complex set of employment plans for use at the theater and lower levels. Moreover, the Soviet military leadership was deadly serious about implementing these plans. If the party leaders were less serious, they did not rein in the generals, although they occasionally made public statements, such as Brezhnev's so-called "Tula line" speech in 1977, which kept their public position ambiguous.[26] At the intercontinental level, their seriousness about nuclear use also seems to have been genuine, inspired in the 1950s and 1960s as much by ideological and psychological factors as by careful analysis of the likely consequence. As the Soviet arsenal approached parity with the U.S. arsenal, however, Soviet military leaders experienced a change of mood, emerging from the psychological position of nuclear inferiority to see a stalemate of mutual homeland vulnerability leading not to strategic stability but rather to a condition in which regionally limited nuclear use was an acceptable risk.

Conventional Forces

The Eastern Front in World War II conditioned Soviet views on conventional-force operations. The Red Army's deep frontal offensives during 1944–45 re-established the primacy of the offense in Soviet military thought. The huge front-level operations, sometimes involving multiple fronts, became the empirical basis for all Soviet postwar thinking about strategy, operations, and tactics for conventional forces.

The new challenge was how to conduct such operations under nuclear conditions. Soviet officers probably soon learned from nuclear weapons tests what U.S. officers already knew: that armor protection mitigates all three major effects of nuclear weapons—blast, heat, and radiation. In 1960, for example, U.S. officers were taught that if a ten-kiloton nuclear weapons hit a battalion of thirty-some tanks marching in column at one hundred–yard intervals, only six or seven would be destroyed, and the crews inside all the other tanks would avoid serious radiation exposure.[27] Soviet officers certainly realized that nuclear weapons could tear large gaps in an enemy's defenses, opening the way to deep offensive penetrations. Thus the task for ground forces was to exploit those openings before the enemy could reorganize to close them. That put a premium on mobility, and here again, mechanized forces appeared to provide the answer.

Soviet force developments in the 1960s began to reflect exploitation of these elementary truths. Not only were large tank formations required, but also infantry and artillery in armored vehicles capable of cross-country mobility. Tactics and operations would be much the same as in World War II, only faster and deeper. Not surprisingly, then, Soviet tank modernization programs went into full swing, and all infantry units were motorized in armored vehicles.[28] Motorized and armor-protected infantry could better keep up with tank formations and withstand the effects of nuclear weapons. Armor-protected artillery also appeared, though later and in smaller quantities; towed artillery remained abundant. Artillery was supplemented with short-range ballistic missiles at the division and army levels capable of delivering battlefield nuclear weapons. Nuclear-capable tube artillery came somewhat later, in the early 1980s. Modernization of "frontal aviation"—that is, aircraft for interdiction bombing and close air support—proceeded in step with these ground-force developments. Tactical aircraft were designed to operate on grass runways in order to use improvised landing strips, keeping up with the swift offensive. Attack and transport helicopters also began to appear in considerable numbers in the 1960s and 1970s. Improved combat engineer units, communications, and logistical support for high-speed deep offensive operations were also part of the buildup, though the logistics capacity lagged somewhat behind the deployment of combat forces.[29] Moving massive amounts of munitions and other supplies forward with sufficient speed remained a major obstacle until the late 1970s, when Soviet motor transport industry began to benefit from technology transfers from the West during détente.[30]

The scheme for using this vast array of conventional forces was outlined in principle in Sokolovskii's *Military Strategy*. In the simplest terms, it addressed two basic problems. First, because the great mobility of supporting firepower provided by nuclear weapons allowed it to be massed quickly at any point over great distances, maneuver forces had to be dispersed in order to limit the effects of enemy nuclear attacks. Second, maneuver forces themselves had to mass in order to exploit the gaps created by their own nuclear fire support. In past operations, massing of ground forces for a breakthrough took days and weeks, and it was done at preselected forward assembly areas near the point of the main attack. Now such assembly areas would be vulnerable to preemptive nuclear strikes. The requirements to disperse and mass at the same time appeared to be mutually exclusive. How were both to be achieved at once?

The Soviet answer was simple but effective. To achieve dispersal, forces would be deployed rearward in echelons, distributed thinly from the line of contact with NATO forces eastward into the western military districts of the Soviet Union. Thus dispersed, they were less vulnerable to nuclear attacks. When the offensive started, they would all move forward at rates of fifty to one hundred kilometers a day. The units would accumulate at the line of contact with the enemy, too close to afford the NATO forces easy tactical nuclear targeting. This strategy would also bring Soviet forces onto the field in places where the enemy's defenses had been destroyed by Soviet nuclear strikes. The first-echelon forces could open gaps at these points, and following echelons could move rapidly through the gaps, striking deep into the enemy's rear before he could react. That would cause an early collapse of the entire NATO defensive front, allowing the Soviet offensive to sweep to the Atlantic coast in a couple of months.

Figure 5 sketches this Soviet concept in graphic form. Gone is the requirement for choosing a point of the main attack and massing forces near that point before operations begin. Wherever breakthroughs occur, the following echelons are rapidly moving forward, accumulating necessary mass to exploit the openings. This was how Soviet theorists planned to overcome the apparently mutually exclusive requirements for both dispersal and massing of forces on the nuclear battlefield.

Although the solution for theater battlefield in Europe (and in the Far East

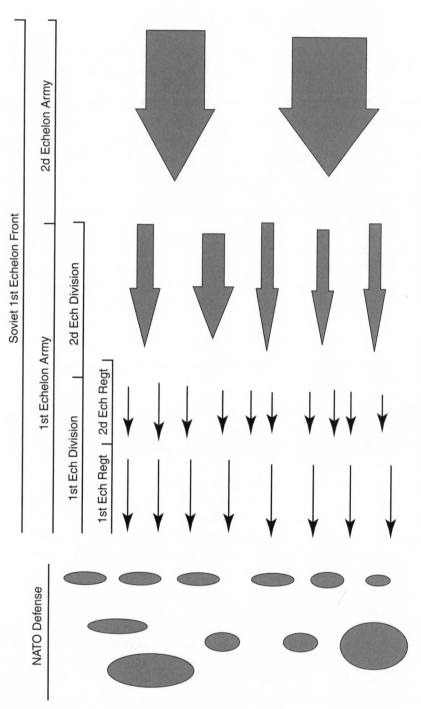

Figure 5. Soviet concept of echelonment for offensive operations

and toward Turkey and Iran in the Middle East as well) was designed for nuclear weapons use, it did not necessarily require them.[31] If the correlation of military forces vis-à-vis NATO favored the Soviet side sufficiently, Soviet forces could succeed without nuclear weapons. In this regard, the Soviet approach was a significant achievement, a quite rational response to the advent of nuclear weapons, yet not wholly dependent on those weapons. The problem for the Soviet side was producing and deploying adequate numbers of new conventional weapons and equipment; the economy was strained to its limits in meeting these requirements. Thus the Soviet military leadership never felt confident about winning without nuclear weapons until the late 1970s, perhaps not even then, although real U.S. defense spending steadily declined from 1968 through 1977, and priority was given to U.S. forces in Vietnam.

Soviet military leaders, however, faced a new challenge as the U.S. military withdrew from Vietnam and turned its attention to the central front in Europe, neglected for nearly two decades. Two concomitant developments on the U.S. side produced the change. The first was technology. Microcircuitry, computers, and lasers were beginning to make possible a whole set of new conventional weapons and delivery means. Small computers could be put into warheads, and lasers allowed new targeting and guidance means. U.S. forces began to use these new "smart weapons" in Vietnam, but after 1975 the weaponry was deployed in Europe.

The second was a change in U.S. operational and tactical doctrine. As U.S. Army leaders began to pay closer attention to Soviet operations and capabilities in Europe, and as they awoke to the Soviet technique of echelonment of forces combined with a high-speed offensive, they realized that NATO defenses could not stand up to it. The U.S. Army's response (with cooperation from the U.S. Air Force) was a "deep attack" doctrine known officially as Air-Land Battle.[32] It rested on the conclusion that follow-on echelons of Soviet ground forces had to be slowed or stopped before they arrived at the line of contact. Attacking them, disrupting their movement or destroying them, and degrading their command and control became the pressing aim for U.S. Army operational art, tactics, and weapons development. "Deep attack" took two forms. First, deep strikes by highly accurate smart weapons would disrupt the follow-on forces. This required both improved tactical air support and more accurate and longer-ranged U.S. artillery. Second, most U.S. Army divisions were upgraded. These "heavy" divisions were mechanized and equipped with M-1 tanks and Bradley infantry fighting vehicles, which could move off roads in open fields at up to forty miles per hour (compared with a top speed of fifteen miles per hour for the tanks and infantry carriers of the 1960s). These new ground forces could do more than defend. They could launch tactical counterattacks 15 to 30 kilometers deep into the oncoming Soviet forces, disrupting their offensive. In principle, such counteroffensives could have been conducted at the operational level, going 100 to 150 kilometers deep, but both political and practical limitations prevented planning for them. Thus Air-Land Battle envisioned attacking the Soviet echelonment both with indirect supporting fires (artillery and air) and with offensive ground operations. NATO political leaders never accepted Air-Land Battle because of the political implications of its offensive character. The Bonn government was terrified of the Soviet diplomatic and propaganda reactions that German approval of Air-Land Battle might bring, but NATO did accept part of the concept, specifically, deep attack of follow-on echelons by NATO air forces and artillery. It was called "follow-on forces attack," or FOFA, in NATO circles in the 1980s. (See figure 6 for a graphic interpretation of Air-Land Battle and FOFA.)

Soviet military leaders obviously never took seriously NATO's political distinctions between "tactical" offense and defense, and they probably anticipated counteroffensive ground attacks to "operational" depths of more than 100 kilometers. They feared that the Warsaw Pact forces would soon face the full measure of Air-Land Battle, especially as U.S. ground forces were modernized in the early 1980s. The Soviet response brought significant changes, most of which can be gleaned from Marshal N. V. Ogarkov's writings in the early 1980s.[33] General Gribkov probably had them in mind when he spoke of the General Staff's shifting its focus to improving theater war–fighting capabilities in 1979.

The task was to neutralize Air-Land Battle, if possible without using nuclear weapons. The chosen solution was to speed up the Soviet offensive by pushing more forces forward in selected sectors before hostilities began in order to make deeper penetrations through NATO defenses much earlier, thereby destroying FOFA and Air-Land Battle capabilities before they could frustrate the Soviet echeloned offensive. The schedule for the Soviet offensive to reach the Atlantic coast was reduced by more than half, to two or three weeks from two months. This was to be done by a complex set of operations involving so-called operational maneuver groups, air-assault operations, and early destruction of NATO's air bases. The echelon approach was retained but modified. Operational maneuver groups were to deploy forward before the outbreak of hostilities where they would pass through gaps in NATO defenses on the very first days of combat, moving 150 to 300 kilometers deep into NATO territory in less than a week. They would link up with air-assault operations that placed Soviet forces on the ground 150 and 300 kilometers deep in NATO's

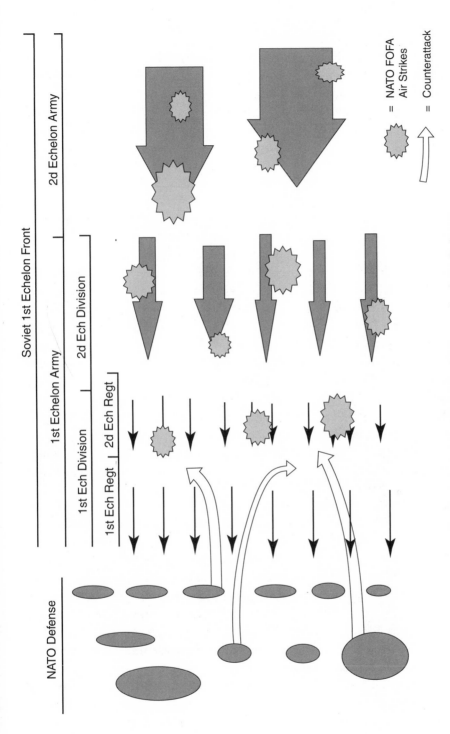

Figure 6. Air-Land Battle response to Soviet echelonment

rear, reaching the objectives of the first-echelon army. The second-echelon army was to repeat this operation to advance another 300 kilometers, which would complete the first-echelon front's objective, up to 600 kilometers deep.

As shown in figure 7, a subsequent frontal operation was to follow immediately, striking another 600 kilometers deep. These doctrinal depths and frontages were not new, but the timing was. The reduction in time was to be achieved by omitting the normal pause of several days or even weeks between the completion of the first-echelon front's operation and the beginning of the second-echelon front's attack.

Two or three fronts would advance abreast, giving the offensive a 500- to 750-kilometer frontage. The entire offensive was considered to overlap the boundary between operational and strategic levels. It was a set of operations, conducted simultaneously, within one theater of military operations (TVD), which would have a strategic consequence for a theater of war: hence it was called a theater strategic operation, or TSO.

Managing TSOs would place huge demands on Soviet command and control structures. In a TVD, not only would two or three fronts have to work in close coordination to keep the offensive on schedule, but when they had reached their objectives about 600 kilometers deep, the first-echelon fronts would have to facilitate the passage forward of the second-echelon fronts, which would sustain the offensive without a pause for another 600-kilometer offensive operation. Only by crowding the echelons forward and giving up the pause of a week or two could the schedule of the overall offensive be shortened significantly. At the same time, counter–air offensives were envisioned to blunt any surviving NATO air capability. Moreover, in the European theater, two theater strategic operations could conceivably be in progress at the same time, one in the Western TVD (the central front) and one in the Southwestern TVD (through the Balkans and south of the Alps through Italy; see map 3). Also, an operation of army or front level could be in progress in the Northwestern TVD, involving the invasion of Norway, and possibly another front moving into Sweden. To provide adequate command and control for TSOs, the General Staff created a new command level, a "high command," between fronts and the General Staff.[34] As we have seen, four such high commands existed by the mid-1980s, one in the Far East, two in the European theater, and one in the Southern Theater facing Iran and Turkey.[35]

Overall Soviet planning for conventional-forces operations in the early 1980s was undergoing a second round of changes, this time in response to further technological innovation and a U.S. revision of its approach to war in Europe. The General Staff always put first priority on the European theater,

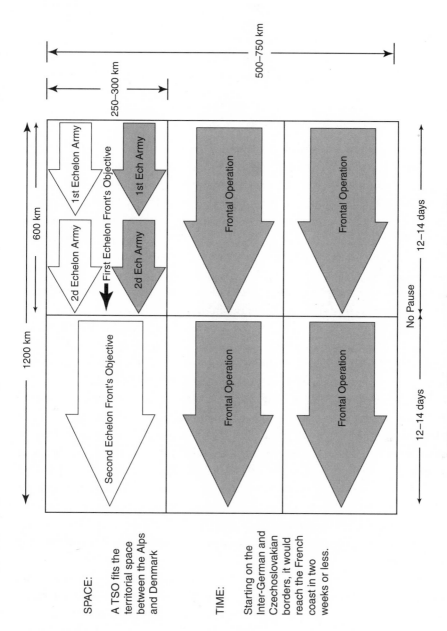

Figure 7. Theater strategic operation—TSO

but remarkably ambitious offensives were also planned for the Southern TVD and the Far Eastern Theater (see maps 4 and 5).[36] The force requirements for them all together not only exceeded the already huge accumulation of weaponry but also involved another technological revolution. Right down to 1985, therefore, the General Staff still lacked all the forces its war plans demanded.

Soviet Naval Strategy

Stalin had an early interest in naval forces, and after World War II he decided to expand his own navy.[37] Admiral Sergei Gorshkov presided over the naval buildup in subsequent decades, and his writings have been examined in great detail in search of the key to Soviet naval strategy.[38] Coastal protection was clearly an early and primary naval mission, but by the 1970s, the Soviet fleet was much larger than that mission demanded, and its ships were sailing around the world, making port calls and practicing operational activities. Still, it had no real capability to engage the U.S. Navy in the open oceans. In some exercises it supported ground offensives into northern Norway, along the Baltic Sea coast, and against Turkey. Its operations in the Third World were primarily diplomatic—"showing the flag," to use U.S. naval parlance. Some analysts saw the navy's rapid growth as a response to the U.S. Navy, an intention to challenge it in the open oceans.[39] Although there is evidence for each of these views, they all miss the most conspicuous aspect of Soviet naval force structure.

The core of the Soviet Navy became the more than sixty submarines equipped with nuclear-armed ballistic missiles, SSBNs. Another roughly three hundred submarines and more than four hundred surface combat vessels, including six small aircraft carriers, constituted a significant force, but not one capable of operations in the central Atlantic or Pacific oceans.[40] The SSBNs were deployed only in the Northern and Pacific Fleets. Neither the Black Sea Fleet nor the Baltic Sea Fleet had these vessels, nor were their surface ships the most modern. The predominant power of the Soviet Navy was in the Northern and Pacific Fleets to defend the SSBNs with their intercontinental nuclear striking power.

Certainly Admiral Gorshkov and his supporters in the Soviet leadership would have liked a navy capable of fighting the U.S. Navy on equal or better terms. But as the SSBNs grew in number and capabilities, becoming a significant part of the Soviet strategic nuclear forces, so too did the U.S. Navy's capabilities to sink them. Thus the more important mission for most of the rest of the Soviet Navy was protection of the SSBNs. That required keeping the U.S. attack submarine fleet and U.S. aircraft carriers away from the Barents

Sea and the Sea of Japan, where the SSBNs operated. No small challenge, it was more feasible than defeating the U.S. fleet in open waters of the Atlantic and Pacific oceans. It also kept the navy integrated within the overall "combined arms" strategy that Soviet military theorists repeatedly emphasized. The primary role of the Soviet Navy, therefore, was as a key part of Soviet strategic nuclear forces, and its secondary role was in supporting theater ground operations into the flanks of Europe. There is no evidence that the Soviet Navy had plans for a naval war only, or for an independent naval strategy of the kind so popular among Western naval strategists. Its "show the flag" operations in the Third World were independent, but not as combat operations.[41]

Soviet Strategy for Air Power

Soviet air forces were closely integrated with ground forces, strategic nuclear forces, air defense, and naval forces. The idea of an independent air war had no support in Soviet military circles. When the Italian theorist Giulio Douhet advanced his concept of victory through air power alone in 1921, it had little impact in Red Army circles, failing to stir the enthusiasm it evoked in Europe and America. His futuristic treatise *Air War 19 . . .*, which appeared in 1930, prompted an anonymous Soviet reviewer to approve of strategic bombing but to reject outright Douhet's claim that bombing alone could decide the outcome of a war.[42] Such ideas did not fit with the Red Army's concept of "combined arms" operations. In fact, Soviet aircraft designers moved ahead of the military theorists, producing the world's first all-metal large bomber in the 1930s, while the Red Army envisioned aviation only as support to ground operations.[43]

After the war, technological constraints limited the role of aviation in military strategy. As David Holloway shows, Stalin initially demanded an intercontinental bomber force to deliver nuclear weapons, but the Soviet lag in technology made it impossible.[44] Soviet long-range aviation forces always took second priority to ballistic missiles, although they did provide a modest bomber component to Soviet nuclear forces.[45]

Land-based naval aviation also played a role in Soviet strategy for defending against the U.S. aircraft carrier fleet. The TU-122M bomber, which became a matter of dispute during the SALT II negotiations, was designed for attacking U.S. naval forces, not for the intercontinental role suspected by some U.S. negotiators.[46]

The General Staff built up the airborne forces to seven divisions by the 1980s, but kept these forces under direct control as a strategic reserve.[47] Their strategic reach, of course, was limited to the capacity of the Soviet air transport fleet, which by the early 1980s could lift only one full division at a time. Still, this marked a large increase in airlift capacity, which was beginning to have international implications.

Soviet Strategy for Force Projection to the Third World

Until the 1970s, the projection of Soviet military power beyond Soviet and Warsaw Pact borders was extremely limited. Various crises in the Middle East brought the presence of the Soviet Navy into play, and Soviet air transport was important for supplying weapons to its Arab clients. The big change came in Angola in 1975 and in Ethiopia in 1978.[48] Soviet air- and sealift capabilities in these two cases moved Cuban combat troops to Africa. Previously, only weapons and supplies had been moved over such distances. Finally, in December 1979, Soviet airborne forces led the invasion of Afghanistan by landing early in Kabul while ground forces were beginning to cross the Soviet-Afghan border.[49]

The deployment of Soviet nuclear weapons and missiles to Cuba in 1962, of course, is a special case, related more to strategy for nuclear weapons than for force projection into the Third World.

Provision of Soviet military advisers and arms to Third World countries played a growing role in Soviet overall strategy in those states, especially as the Vietnam War continued and the Soviet Union found wealthy customers in the Middle East and gave away arms to Marxist-Leninist-led insurgencies in Africa and Latin America. The Soviet record in these commitments is mixed at best, but they did generate markets for Soviet weapons sales and concomitant corruption.[50] Officers in foreign military missions apparently used the opportunity as much for personal profit as for advancing Soviet strategic goals.[51] An increasing number of diplomats, officers, and military industrialists gained a personal pecuniary interest in perpetuating and expanding these Soviet military activities in the Third World. They could easily justify their activities with the strategy of "peaceful coexistence" because it specifically emphasized pursuing the "international class struggle" through "national liberation movements."[52]

The validity of this ideological rationale, however, was always suspect. So-called "class analysis" applied to the politics of Third World countries distorted as much as it explained. Comintern policy guidance to the Communist Party in China in the 1920s led to its decimation by Chiang Kai-shek and to Mao Zedong's decision to follow his own strategy, disregarding Moscow's directions. Thereafter, Stalin avoided direct involvement in the Third World. Khrushchev, as part of reviving "Leninist norms" of peaceful coexistence, began to show interest in the Third World but limited the effort to propaganda, diplomatic activity, and modest economic and military assistance programs.

Brezhnev's activism in the Third World involved far greater resources and commitments. It brought the Soviet Union close to a major crisis with the United States during the 1973 October War in the Middle East. It intensified the competition with the Chinese communists for influence over leftist political forces throughout Africa, Latin America, and Southeast Asia. Soviet material support for North Vietnam was costly and also a sore point in Sino-Soviet relations, but it paid off in dissipating U.S. military power in Europe and creating a crisis in U.S. self-confidence.[53] Finally, in Afghanistan, Third World activism entangled the Soviet military in a disastrous civil war. The question inevitably arises as to why the Politburo pursued this strategy in light of its growing costs and mixed results. Its ideological lenses for viewing the Third World do not explain it fully, but they obviously played a significant role. Lenin had ground those lenses, shaping them to see the socialist and capitalist camps in a state of temporary "peaceful coexistence—a specific form of the international class struggle," and also sharpening their focus on the critical role that Third World national liberation movements could play. How vivid that ideological vision remained was revealed in Aleksei Kosygin's telephone conversation with the Afghan communist leader N. M. Taraki in the spring of 1979.[54] Hafizullah Amin, prime minister after the 1978 coup, had pleaded for the Soviet military to come to his support against opposition forces in the city of Herat. Kosygin responded with questions about the size of the Afghan working class and encouraged Amin to rally workers and students against this anticommunist opposition.

Soviet Arms Control Strategy

In principle, arms control negotiations are supposed to replace or reduce military competition, allowing both sides to maintain their relative military power while reducing the likelihood of war. In reality, negotiations are inherently competitive affairs, as participants seek what they believe enhances their own security. Each participant's military potential is at stake. Mutually advantageous outcomes are not impossible, but they are more probable among states that share basic principles about maintaining international order. Given the fundamental incompatibility of Soviet and Western views on world order, Western negotiators assumed that the realities of nuclear weapons transcended this ideological divide. Accordingly, mutually advantageous treaties should have been possible to negotiate, but whether or not the treaties actually signed were based on a common recognition of the realities has been hotly debated in the United States.

Before Gorbachev came to power and removed the fundamental ideological obstacles, five agreements were reached—the agreement to cease open-air nuclear testing, a threshold test ban, SALT I, the ABM treaty, and SALT II (which was observed in practice but never ratified by the U.S. Senate). Why were they reached? The first nuclear testing ban seems to have been inspired by mutual recognition that open-air testing created dangers that were not really worth accepting, especially when weapons designers could learn about design reliability from underground tests. Moreover, Khrushchev found it useful as propaganda to support the Soviet campaign to rally the "peace-loving forces" all around the world against imperialism. He claimed that it showed a genuine Soviet desire for avoiding the dangers of the arms race. Although the other treaties also offered propaganda advantages, that does not explain the sustained Soviet commitment to the arms control process until 1983, when Soviet diplomats broke off the INF and START negotiations.

Given what is known of the Soviet view of nuclear war, of the psychological impact of the Cuban missile affair, of the design of Soviet forces of all types to fight on a nuclear battlefield, and of the role that the official ideology continued to play in the outlook of the Soviet leaders, their general arms control objectives are reasonably transparent in retrospect. Soviet negotiators were trying to facilitate the Soviet military buildup at least to the point of equality (the term they preferred over "parity" or "stability"), superiority if possible. The treaty limits imposed by SALT I and SALT II appear consistent with this inference. SALT II allowed levels of nuclear weapons in the aggregate much higher than either side possessed when the treaty was signed. A skeptic on the U.S. side could say with considerable justification that the treaties were merely ratifying the continuing expansion of the Soviet offensive arsenal. The ABM treaty could not be dismissed so easily. While placing severe limits on ABM systems, it did allow the continuation of research and development and the deployment of one so-called national site. Still, it blocked deployment of a countrywide defense, consistent with the U.S. view that stability depended on mutual vulnerability.

Colonel General Detinov's account of the Soviet negotiating process throws some light on the behind-the-scenes Soviet thinking about their objectives for the negotiations. Already in the mid-1960s, according to Detinov, the economic burden of the military buildup was acutely recognized. Moreover, technological backwardness placed serious constraints on the Soviet ABM program. Soviet leaders, therefore, decided to enter the SALT negotiations because SALT "promised to slow the burden of the arms race and promised the attainment of some advantages over the United States. The realization of this goal was to be achieved . . . by the formulation of a clearly one-sided negotiating position and a tenacious adherence to it during the negotiations."[55] Specifically at the beginning of the process, he added, "The Soviet Union's goal . . . was clear: to end the uncertainty in the accelerating arms race, to perfect the strategic balance, and, not least, to attempt to keep some of the advantage that the Soviet military leadership believed the nation had obtained in certain military areas."[56]

This description of Soviet goals is not without ambiguities. Did "to perfect the strategic balance" mean codifying parity in offensive weapons and mutual vulnerability? Or did it mean achieving an edge for the Soviet side? In light of Detinov's repeated characterization of the Soviet leaders' view of nuclear war and their struggle with the imperialist camp, the latter inference is more compelling. What was a "clearly one-sided negotiating position"? At face value, it seems to mean a position that favored a Soviet edge in the strategic balance. "To end the uncertainty in the accelerating arms race" apparently meant to put some constraints on U.S. strategic programs so that they would at least be predictable, limited if possible. Finally, "to keep some of the advantage . . . in certain military areas" is clear, and it reinforces the straightforward interpretation of the "one-sided negotiating position."

Detinov's account of Soviet negotiating strategy shows a fairly consistent adherence to these initial goals. Marshal Andrei Grechko sought Soviet military advantages more consistently than other Politburo members, but he repeatedly obtained support from Ustinov and Andropov. At the same time, diplomatic interaction with the United States had an educational effect on some Soviet negotiators, especially concerning the details of weapons capabilities. It also seems to have infected a few members of the Soviet military-industrial community and the foreign ministry with an empathetic, sometimes sympathetic, reaction to U.S. concepts of deterrence theory, but that process had no noticeable impact on the so-called Big Five—the top leaders who made the final decisions. Instructive in this regard are two occasions for which Detinov clarifies the Politburo's thinking about its goals and strategy in arms control negotiations.

First, their interest in the ABM treaty arose from their concern with catching up and overtaking the U.S. arsenal of strategic offensive systems, not from an understanding of the U.S. view that outlawing ABMs would promote strategic stability. They wanted to avoid a simultaneous race in both ICBMs and ABMs because such a competition would slow down their own ICBM production.

Second, they entered the negotiations over intermediate-range nuclear forces (INF) to prevent the deployment of U.S. INF in Europe, not to rectify an imbalance caused by their SS-20 deployments. Because they coupled the INF negotiations with the antinuclear movement in Europe, they faced a dilemma when U.S. Ambassador Paul Nitze offered a compromise position during his "walk in the woods" with his Soviet counterpart in 1983. Nitze sought to discover what the Soviet reaction would be if the United States abandoned its "zero-zero" position (elimination by both sides of all INF). Although getting the United States to abandon its zero-zero position would have been a significant Soviet achievement, it also would have betrayed Western European communist parties, which supported the antinuclear movement.[57] Forced to choose, they refused to explore Nitze's proposal. When it became apparent that the antinuclear movement would not prevail against U.S. deployment of INF, the Soviet side walked out of the negotiations rather than undercut the Western communist parties.

Both examples suggest that the Soviet goal in arms control negotiations before Gorbachev's time was not to ensure strategic stability but rather to mitigate Soviet economic constraints and to retain or increase military advantages. Perhaps new evidence will emerge that significantly alters General Detinov's understanding of the Soviet arms control strategy, but Soviet behavior both in military programs and in negotiations corroborates it. Western students of the subject have differed over Soviet arms control objectives and strategy. Some have insisted that Soviet party leaders, although not necessarily military leaders, came to accept U.S. concepts of strategic stability, parity, and deterrence theory as an implicitly shared basis for negotiations.[58] Others have rejected this interpretation, insisting that Soviet leaders never seriously entertained these concepts as guides to their own negotiating objectives.[59] This divide, of course, is the lineal descendant to the earlier split among Western analysts on the Soviet view of nuclear war, a decade before nuclear arms control began. The former group appears to have erred when it imputed to Soviet leaders an acceptance of U.S. concepts of strategic nuclear stability. The latter group, while closer to the truth, has not always understood either why or the way in which Soviet leadership views of nuclear arms control changed from the mid-1960s through the early 1980s.

Soviet grand strategy in the years leading up to Gorbachev's reforms largely retained its early Marxist-Leninist foundations. The ideological lenses through which the top leaders viewed the world and framed their goals limited their pragmatism and encrusted their thinking. By the mid-1980s, Soviet strategy was in crisis. The large gains of the past two decades had come at great cost, and the expected advantages proved illusory because two parallel dialectical processes were undermining them.

First, the correlation of forces between the socialist and imperialist camps was not shifting inexorably in favor of socialism, as Soviet leaders had been forecasting since the early 1970s. On the contrary, a program of U.S. military modernization based on new technologies confronted the Soviet military with another challenge it could not hope to meet. Political trends were also turning negative for Moscow. The United States stepped up the ideological struggle with President Carter's human rights policy and President Reagan's "evil empire" speech, throwing Moscow on the defensive. The war in Afghanistan was going badly, and Soviet influence elsewhere in the Third World had peaked and was receding.

The second dialectical process was occurring within the Soviet economy and society. The military burden was a growing brake on the economy, and the economic system itself simply could not cope with "information age" technology. Health and ecological problems were becoming too large to ignore indefinitely. Bureaucratic decay had long since destroyed the élan of the Communist Party, undermining its capacity to address any of these problems effectively. As a result, the political leadership and the society as a whole were in a malaise.

SIX

Deciding to Change Course

No man rises so high as he knows not whither he goes.

OLIVER CROMWELL

We need economic reform and political reform. The central question is with which to start.

YURII ANDROPOV

Gorbachev took the fateful decision to reverse seven decades of Soviet military policy cautiously, almost by stealth, as a necessary step for political and economic change. There was no clearly developed credo or manifesto for general reform behind which a coalition of political forces had been mobilized. Most of the senior party leaders understood that a change in military policy was necessary, but they apparently never discussed the details, or even the broad outlines, during the first years of Gorbachev's rule. And not surprisingly. The military question could not initially be analyzed in this way without raising basic questions about the Soviet system itself. The economic question took first place on Gorbachev's agenda in 1985, and as he achieved little progress in improving the economy, he shifted his emphasis to political reform. Because neither kind of reform could proceed far without addressing the military question, it inexorably made its way onto his reform agenda.

Pinpointing a specific time and a definitive decision to pursue a new military policy is therefore difficult. Rather, the decision arose gradually out of the overall context of Gorbachev's shaping of his perestroika policy. The way Moscow viewed the outer world had to be altered before a radical change in military affairs was conceivable, and that required ideological revisions and favorable political alignments within the Politburo and the party apparatus. Gorbachev may have taken a more direct approach rather early in the Politburo and the Defense Council. Marshal Sergei Akhromeev, chief of the General Staff, said that not long after Gorbachev became the chairman of the Defense Council, he directed it to frame a new military doctrine, a "defensive doctrine." The Defense Council debated the matter for about two years, reaching a final decision in 1987.[1] Both circumstantial evidence and the subsequent evolution of the new military doctrine throw grave doubt on the tidy process reported by Akhromeev. Gorbachev appears instead to have approached the military question hesitantly, hinting at it in speeches, introducing new ideas in ambiguous terminology, failing to follow through, then acting abruptly on specific military issues, almost randomly setting the context for a radical change before facing it head on.

This policy-making process does not lend itself to a sharply focused account. A mix of narrative and thematic treatments of selected issues and events over the first two years of Gorbachev's rule creates a more accurate and textured picture of how it took place. Four distinct issues, however, do tie the story together: *a*) the rationale for a radical change in military policy, *b*) personnel changes in the party and the military, *c*) radical revision of the ideology to justify a new military doctrine, and *d*) surprising foreign policy initiatives.

The Aims of Perestroika

Precisely what Gorbachev intended when he introduced "new thinking," "glasnost," and "perestroika" will probably remain indefinitely a matter of speculation, reports by close witnesses and his own post facto testimony notwithstanding. By contrast, his motivations for pushing through major policy changes are less mysterious; they were shared widely within the Politburo and the Central Committee apparatus. Behind the scenes, corruption and drift during Brezhnev's rule deeply disturbed second-level officials. The sniveling behavior by regional party leaders toward Brezhnev and his entourage angered them because it allowed him to ignore urgent problems. In public the Brezhnev gerontocracy was outright embarrassing to these officials.[2] More important, they knew that the economy was in trouble and that environmental, social, and health problems were burgeoning. Gorbachev was acutely aware of these realities. He expressed his feelings succinctly in a remark to his wife, Raisa, the evening before he was elected general secretary, "We cannot go on living like this."[3]

How not to go on living like that, of course, was another matter. Would it require only a reform of the old Soviet system? Or would it demand systemic change, replacement of the Soviet system with a qualitatively different regime? Gorbachev apparently did not see the question in this light. According to one of his close assistants, Georgii Shakhnazarov, Gorbachev initially thought that reform could be limited to the economic sector, keeping the political system intact; he changed his mind only 1987.[4] Gorbachev's strongest Politburo allies, Aleksandr Yakovlev and Eduard Shevardnadze, saw things quite differently. Looking back after the collapse of the Soviet Union, both told me that in 1985 they believed that systemic change would be necessary, including the breakup of the Soviet Union, and they understood that perestroika would bring that result if carried through.[5] Neither apparently shied from these implications from the very beginning, though they could not afford to voice such views openly, or even between themselves—if, indeed, they truly held them in 1985. Yakovlev revealed the depth of his alienation from Marxism in a book on that subject after the collapse of the Soviet Union.[6] Few if any Western anti-Marxists could match his denunciation of the Soviet official ideology.

Although the primary stimulus for perestroika was the system's poor economic performance, what constituted an effective reform program and where it would lead were unanswered questions. Political liberalization, apparently, was of little concern to Gorbachev in the beginning. For Yakovlev and Shevardnadze it was critical. Ligachev's views on reform were initially very close to Gorbachev's; they focused on the economy, not the political system. The rest of the Politburo in 1985–86 included no strong proponent of reform, political or economic, although most of them knew that the country needed change to escape its malaise.

New Cadres

Both the intelligentsia and much of the party bureaucracy, far beyond Gorbachev's circle, desperately wanted change.[7] They saw glimmers that it was beginning under Yurii Andropov's rule in 1983, and they were sorely disappointed to see it stopped by Konstantin Chernenko when he succeeded Andropov as general secretary in February 1984. The most important initial step for change, as Gorbachev and his supporters saw it, was not the working out of a reform program but rather purging the party in an effort to revitalize it, sweeping out the aging and corrupt incompetent officials, particularly in the intermediate and upper levels. Until that was accomplished, candid debate on a reform program simply was not possible. Andropov understood the need for a party purge during his brief tenure as general secretary, and, at the urging of Gorbachev, he accordingly picked Yegor Ligachev to head the Party Organization Department of the secretariat in April 1983, and directed him to continue the "renewal of party cadres" that had just begun.[8] After the Chernenko interregnum, Gorbachev and Ligachev revived the purge, but one of Gorbachev's future aides thought at the time that it was not nearly sweeping enough.[9]

Renewing cadres was the traditional Bolshevik method of preparing for changes in policies and for reinforcing old policies—for restoring "ideological hardness" in Stalin's day and for restoring "Leninist norms" in Khrushchev's day. Brezhnev gave up purges for a policy of "stability of cadres," a policy that produced stagnation during his eighteen-year rule. Purges always required a public rationale and fairly specific criteria for identifying those to be eliminated from the party's ranks. What would the rationale be in 1985? Andropov cited anticorruption, and Gorbachev endorsed that principle and added anti-alcoholism (which proved to be both an economic and a political disaster), but these purposes lacked the ideological inspiration of the rationales for purges past.[10] If the party leaders wanted reform, the nature and aims of reform had to be related to the criteria of cadre renewals. And if the aims included systemic change in the regime itself, then a party purge confronted a paradox: how could a Leninist party that had long led the country on the socialist path toward communism be converted into a force for taking it off that course and onto some radically new direction, possibly a return to a market economy? How was this to be explained ideologically? And what did it involve programmatically?

Gorbachev's answers were as vague as his slogan, "new thinking." He probably had no clear answers in his own mind at that time, but a more charitable interpretation is that he believed that he could not reveal a great deal more without frightening conservative party forces into open resistance. Indeed, ambiguity became his primary means for anesthetizing potential opposition.[11] During his first year, however, the danger of resistance was not so great. In the first half of the 1980s a rather wide and informal consensus was taking shape among all sectors of the party that much was wrong and change was sorely needed. Party officials throughout the country knew that the economy was in serious trouble, that social problems were acute, and that dramatic action, particularly reductions in military spending, was imperative to deal with the impending crises. The officer corps shared this view with party conservatives and reformers alike. Nine former Soviet officers, ranging from Marshal Yevgenii Shaposhnikov to a dissident lieutenant colonel, Aleksandr Rodin, said in retrospect that they believed at the time that the economy was in serious trouble and something had to be done about it, including significant cuts in military spending.[12] They expected Gorbachev to deal with both the economy and the backlog of social problems. Even General Valentin Varennikov, who detests Gorbachev as a traitor, and Lieutenant General Leonid Ivashov, who favored a military coup to oust him out long before the attempt in August 1991, said that economic reform and social problems had to be urgently addressed. Ligachev put it thus: "After April 1985 we faced the task of curtailing military spending. Without this, large-scale social programs could not have been implemented: the economy could not breathe normally with a military budget that comprised 18 percent of the national income."[13]

At the same time, Ligachev did not consider previous military expenditures a mistake; they had been "dictated by the need to achieve strategic parity with the United States."[14] Here was the essence of the difference that would eventually surface between Ligachev and Gorbachev. Ligachev wanted reform but not at the expense of the Soviet Union's international military status, and certainly not if it threatened to undermine the socialist system. Gorbachev was willing to set the Soviet Union's military status aside if that proved necessary for effective reform.[15]

Gorbachev and Ligachev had been close colleagues, even coconspirators, since 1983, when Ligachev came to Moscow from Siberia to take charge of cadre policy in the Central Committee Secretariat. He schemed to promote Gorbachev as Konstantin Chernenko's successor, even to the point of organizing a group of oblast party secretaries to voice opposition at the Central Committee Plenum if Gorbachev were not selected. Andrei Gromyko, longtime foreign minister and very senior Politburo member, turned not to the candidate himself but to Ligachev with an offer to put Gorbachev's name forward to the Politburo as the new general secretary.[16] Thus Ligachev was by no means an opponent of perestroika in its early days. On the contrary, it was to facilitate perestroika that he supervised a huge turnover of regional party secretaries between 1985 and 1987. He believed that reform was impossible within the legacy of corrupt incumbents from Brezhnev's rule. Ligachev stood shoulder to shoulder with Gorbachev against such regional party leaders as the notoriously corrupt Uzbek party chief Sharaf Rashidov. They not only removed him from the Politburo but methodically destroyed his "mafia" in Uzbekistan. They did the same to Dinmukhamed Kunaev, the party chief in Kazakhstan.

But Ligachev did not share Gorbachev's view on the sources of new leading cadres, a seemingly minor matter that would later acquire major importance. A decree issued during Chernenko's rule dictated that new personnel for the central apparatus had to be selected from regional and local party committees. This meant that party members who were engineers, diplomats, scientists, as well as others who had not made careers in the regional party apparatus, could not be brought directly into the Central Committee apparatus. When Gorbachev insisted on exceptions, Ligachev stood by the decree. Georgii Shakhnazarov is undoubtedly correct in seeing Gorbachev's failure to overrule Ligachev on this issue as a serious mistake.[17] The decree excluded party intelligentsia—Gorbachev's strongest base of party support for reforms—from appointments in the central party apparatus, which Ligachev was able to fill with conservative bureaucrats from regional organizations.

How did Gorbachev's reform aims differ fundamentally with Ligachev's aims and those of other top party officials? Ligachev argues in his memoirs that they were in concert until Yakovlev dragged Gorbachev onto a radical "right wing" path.[18] Ligachev blamed the party for the country's mess, which could be overcome only after a revitalization of the party. The economy was in trouble because local party officials interfered in the management of production processes, not a new problem, but a more disruptive one in the 1980s because corruption and localism had become so rampant. Holding down military expenditures to make capital available for the civilian economy, especially for technological innovation, was essential, but introducing market forces was never Ligachev's intent. That idea, he insisted, was never seriously considered in the Politburo until 1989 (a dubious claim in light of laws on the firm promulgated in 1987 and implemented in 1988), and by then he realized that he could no longer compromise with Gorbachev.

Reflecting on his disagreements with Gorbachev in a dinner conversation in 1991, Ligachev added some points. Gorbachev believed the political split in the party was between reformers and conservatives, while Ligachev believed that it was between the center and the regions, especially the national republics. For some time, the entire Politburo ignored the nationality problem because its members believed that mixing of ethnic groups had gone too far for separatist movements to threaten the regime's stability. Ligachev's earlier awakening to this illusion, he insisted, put him sharply at odds with Gorbachev, who openly acknowledged it only in the fall of 1990.[19] When pressed on economic reform issues, Ligachev revealed that he did not understand that the economic system itself was the problem.

To all appearances, neither did Gorbachev before 1987. But as he contemplated more radical notions about economic reform, he met resistance within the party. Purging the party apparatus was not producing the expected results; another kind of political change would have to be found. At this point Gorbachev was clearly parting ways with Ligachev, a parting with roots in his earlier dispute with Ligachev over the renewal of party cadres in the central apparatus. Ligachev blocked the most reform-minded party officials in Moscow whom Gorbachev wanted to put in the top posts, preferring instead those with regional experience like his own, which made them reluctant to tinker with the basic mechanisms of the Soviet economic system.

Yakovlev anticipated this problem. To get around it, he energetically pressed the media, the intelligentsia, and nonparty people to exercise "glasnost" in hopes of mobilizing broader forces for political *and* economic reform. His success brought bitter clashes with Ligachev throughout 1987–89. Gorbachev refused to side unambiguously with either, encouraging first one, then the other. In the end, Ligachev continued to insist that Yakovlev, not Gorbachev himself, was "the real Judas" betraying the Soviet system.[20]

Gorbachev's Evolving Views on Ideology

The seeds of radical reform were germinating in Gorbachev's mind earlier than Ligachev apparently noticed, and not only from Yakovlev's cultivation. Furthermore, his focus was more on foreign than on domestic issues. Chernyaev, in the year before Gorbachev made him his special assistant, worked under Boris Ponomarev in the secretariat's International Department, allowing him insight into Gorbachev's thinking on Soviet foreign policy and relations with foreign communist parties.

Commenting in his diary about Gorbachev's speech in January 1986 about a nuclear-free world by the year 2000, Chernyaev wrote that it signaled Gorbachev's "determination to end the arms race, no matter what." [21] Gorbachev, he was convinced, realized that even if the Soviet Union disarmed unilaterally, Soviet security would not be at risk. The West would not invade the Soviet Union. To be sure, Chernyaev was speaking for himself, but he revealed a key point that would separate Gorbachev, Shevardnadze, and Yakovlev from Ligachev and his allies. For Gorbachev, military parity with the West was not essential if it stood in the way of the domestic goals of perestroika. For Ligachev, it was essential, even if it meant a much more limited perestroika. Ligachev, however, found himself in a weak position to carry his case against Gorbachev, Yakovlev, and Shevardnadze because he helped undermine his potential allies on this point—the older and more orthodox members of the Politburo. Moreover, Gorbachev kept most Politburo members in the dark on his foreign-policy activities, according to his chief of staff, Valery Boldin, by no longer circulating to them the written accounts of his dealings with foreign leaders.[22]

The first clues to Gorbachev's ideas for reform appeared, not surprisingly, in matters of ideology. The memoir literature makes clear the pervasive role of ideology in framing the issues and policy-making tactics. Shakhnazarov offers numerous examples of his years working directly for Yurii Andropov, whose intellect he respected and who periodically demanded that he express candid views on numerous issues. Andropov would listen patiently and then reject them with ideologically based arguments. *"It was a total ideocracy,"* Shakhnazarov said of the Soviet regime.[23]

Chernyaev often displays bitterness about ideological constraints on policy thinking. He recalls a military training class conducted by Marshal Sergei Akhromeev, then chief of the General Staff, in June 1985 for the International Department.[24] After speaking at length about the "imperialist" NATO threat, he called for even more contributions from all Soviet citizens for defense and then showed a film designed to whip up fear of superior U.S. military technology. Chernyaev reacted with contempt, thinking to himself that Akhromeev would, if he could, turn all of Soviet society into an armed camp. He knew that NATO had no offensive plans. He saw Akhromeev and the Soviet military, not NATO, as the real danger. Nor did he see any necessity of maintaining military parity with NATO. Like Ligachev, Chernyaev believed that the economic crisis and social problems could not be solved without a large reduction in military outlays, but unlike Ligachev, he was willing to make that reduction no matter what NATO spent on military capabilities. The party's ideology, he lamented, precluded such thoughts.

Could the ideology be modified to permit radical thoughts about military policy? Chernyaev began to see signs that it could be in connection with policy toward foreign communist parties. Several times in 1985 he made diary entries recording them. His boss, Ponomarev, had long managed Moscow's "party line" for the international communist movement. Chernyaev conspired behind Ponomarev's back with Vadim Zagladin (also in the International Department) and Andrei Aleksandrov-Agentov (Brezhnev's longtime assistant) to have Gorbachev sent to Italy when the Italian Communist Party leader Enrico Berlinguer died, in June 1984. Relations with the Italian party were strained, and the Soviet ambassador in Rome warned that an appropriate response by Moscow to the funeral was critical. Gorbachev attended, favorably impressed the Italian communists, and was profoundly affected by what he experienced. Upon his return, he told the International Department, "Such a party cannot be thrown away. We must deal with them." To be sure, the crowds cheering Gorbachev had influenced him as much as the reception he received from the Italian communist leadership, but he was also impressed by the vigor in the Italian party, reflected in its openness of expression. If this political energy derived from the party's greater autonomy from Moscow, then Gorbachev saw nothing wrong with autonomy. Chernyaev was delighted, but Ponomarev refused to make any adjustments to the stance toward the Italian party.[25]

One year later, in the summer of 1985, Chernyaev thought that the old line might at last be changed. Gorbachev asked Ponomarev to explain what the international communist movement was all about. Was its claim to being a "movement" just a myth—did it in fact mean mechanically following the Moscow line? Or was it a genuine movement? Ponomarev never responded.[26] Gorbachev increased the pressure on Ponomarev in a television address to the French public during his trip to Paris in October 1985. When French journalists questioned him sharply about the French Communist Party's subservience to Moscow and its rigid ideology, Gorbachev disavowed Moscow's control over French communists, played down ideology, and emphasized the much greater importance of French-Soviet state-to-state relations.[27] Ponomarev brushed off Gorbachev's comments as mere rhetoric for Western audiences.[28] A short time later, speaking at the Warsaw Pact Political Consultative Committee meeting in Bulgaria, Gorbachev called for more autonomy for all communist parties. This could not be so easily dismissed; it was an authoritative rejection of Ponomarev's position, delivered to a communist audience. Although Chernyaev felt vindicated, he noted at the time that Gorbachev put him in the position of a "dissident" caught in a "two-faced regime."[29] Policy discussions remained trapped in the vocabulary of the ideology.

Accordingly Chernyaev tried to exploit that vocabulary when Gorbachev created opportunities. In drafting Gorbachev's report to the Twenty-seventh Party Congress, early in January 1986, Chernyaev insisted to Ponomarev that new language was needed on "peaceful coexistence" to convey Gorbachev's "new thinking" about the international class struggle. An illuminating exchanged followed:

Ponomarev reacted, "What is 'new thinking'? We already have correct thinking. Let the Americans change their thinking."

Chernyaev countered, "But here are Gorbachev's texts, where it is written in black and white that he also has in mind *our* new thinking."

"I don't know! I just don't know. He said that in Paris, in Geneva, only for them, for the West," Ponomarev protested.

"That means you consider it simple demagogy?" retorted Chernyaev.

"We have to be able to conduct our struggle with the imperialists," insisted Ponomarev.

"But Gorbachev has a new idea that first of all we must conduct that struggle through the improvement of our own society," continued Chernyaev.

"Are you telling me about peaceful coexistence? I was already writing about that . . . in preparation for the Nineteenth Party Congress during Stalin's day. What is new?" asked Ponomarev.

Chernyaev stood his ground. "What is new is that it now sounds new. Stalin spoke for peace, against war, and no one believed him. They started to believe Khrushchev. Brezhnev expatiated on peaceful coexistence for nearly twenty years. . . . No one believed him. Now they believe Gorbachev because his word is closer to his deed."

Ponomarev had the last word. "And what are your objections to our foreign policy? Didn't we master space? And build intercontinental rockets? Are you rejecting the role of strength, which is the only thing the imperialists consider?" [30]

The fundamental issue, military policy in ideological garb, came into the open in this exchange. Although Ponomarev's version of the text went forward, Chernyaev went around him to an angry Yakovlev to let him know that an alternative text had been prepared. Offending Ponomarev became less risky a few days later, when Gorbachev moved Chernyaev to his own personal staff, where he served for the next six years.

Gorbachev did nothing to clear up the confusion he was creating by insinuating a few revisionist formulas into basic party documents. On 22 February 1986, a few weeks after leaving the International Department, Chernyaev participated in a small group discussion with Gorbachev on the foreign-policy conception he would present to the upcoming Twenty-seventh Party Congress.[31] Gorbachev set forth his ideas at some length, and Chernyaev summarized them in his diary. Gorbachev began by noting the great diversity in the world and attributing to Lenin "the understanding that society's interests are higher than class interests." Then he declared that peaceful coexistence demands reevaluation at each stage of history, that "new thinking" had to be defined fundamentally, that the pace of reform had not been fast enough over the past year, that a new foreign policy direction had to be chosen with care. Yet saying the right things at the congress would not be enough. "We need likeminded people who can cook the kasha together and are prepared to go to the end." Chernyaev found this encouraging but still ambiguously expressed in old ideological slogans and myths.

Apparently he did not immediately recognize a radical ideological revision that Gorbachev had let slip out: society's interests were higher than class interests. This assertion flatly called into question Marx's conception of historical development and the primacy of class struggle. Gorbachev was to take the primacy of society's interests—or "humankind interests," as he would also call them — to its logical conclusion in another year, but for the moment the point got lost. Chernyaev describes Gorbachev as giving mixed messages at the congress, especially in his private meetings with foreign communist leaders. He told the Greeks one thing, the Cubans another, and he told Gus Hall, the American communist leader, that the "principle strategic goals and tasks of the party remain the same." To others he said, "We do not reject socialism" but declared it possible "to reach agreement on peace, not having changed the character of the two opposing systems."[32] This last point was a fundamental departure from Marxism-Leninism on the scientific bases for war and peace, a departure with radical implications for military policy.

As later became clear, Gorbachev was trying to set the stage ideologically to make major arms reductions possible, primarily through negotiated agreements with the United States. Although his closest supporters, like Chernyaev and Shakhnazarov, expressed frustration with his failure to purge the party apparatus of conservatives at the very beginning, to speak early and plainly about his ideological revisions, and to demand a radical reduction in military spending, it is difficult to imagine that he could have kept the reins of power had he jolted the party with such a devastating blow to both ideology and military strength.

The Consequences of Cadre Policy

Cadre policy is another matter. Perhaps Gorbachev could have brought more like-minded supporters of his radical policies into key party posts much earlier, but beyond the narrow circles of the Moscow intelligentsia, how could he be sure who they were? And without a clear ideological line widely enunciated to guide the renewal policy countrywide, Ligachev and his followers in the regional party committees would have been difficult to defeat. Moreover, as Shakhnazarov points out, the problems of reform went much deeper. The economic managers of the country did not know how to change, did not even recognize the degree to which Soviet technology was lagging, and seldom could give sensible answers to Gorbachev when he confronted them directly and tried to get them to face economic realities.[33] Browbeating them, he soon discovered, achieved nothing.

For all of his retrospective assertions that changing the party apparatus was hopeless, however, Shakhnazarov still saw an effective revitalization of the party as essential to making Gorbachev's initial efforts at economic reform possible. Shakhnazarov recounts earlier debates with Andropov over whether to begin with political or economic reform. Andropov came down for economic reform because he believed that improving economic conditions would make political reform acceptable but not vice versa. Shakhnazarov was never fully convinced, though Gorbachev apparently was. And that was presumably why his initial policy initiatives, the so-called "acceleration" policy, concerned the economy. In 1984 he had tried to get a Central Committee scheduled to deal with a problem long put off—how to address the so-called "scientific-technical revolution" that was propelling western economies.[34] The older Politburo members blocked his every attempt to put it on the Central Committee's agenda. In summer 1985, as part of his emphasis on economic improvement, he was at last able to put the scientific-technical revolution before the Central Committee plenum, but with no visible result. Still, he kept economic reform ahead of political reform until 1987, when he at last conceded that purging the party was not enough. Without basic political change, the managers and bureaucrats would defeat him.

Movement of the Foreign Policy Front

As Shakhnazarov points out, Gorbachev made some real gains in those first two years on the international front in Europe, primarily in convincing Western leaders that he really could be trusted to make major changes in Soviet foreign policy.[35] By first impressing Margaret Thatcher, Giulio Andreotti, François Mitterrand, and Helmut Kohl, he was able to get their help in making a connection with Reagan, the kind he had not made in Geneva in November 1985. That led to meetings in Reykjavik in October 1986 and in Washington to sign the treaty banning intermediate-range nuclear forces in Europe in December 1987. Gorbachev's appointment of Shevardnadze as foreign minister was critical to these achievements. Explaining the appointment to a surprised Shevardnadze, Gorbachev said that no movement in stopping the arms race was possible with Gromyko and his people in control of the foreign ministry. With that understanding, Shevardnadze knew that he had license to follow a radically new course in foreign policy.[36] And follow it he did, sometimes faster than Gorbachev might otherwise have done. He understood that reducing the military burden was the sine qua non for domestic reform. Knowing well how the Politburo operated and how it reacted to reports on negotiations with the United States, he proved extremely skilled in coaxing greater concessions than conservative Politburo members actually wanted to yield.

Shevardnadze's emergence as a strong supporter of perestroika and his unrelenting use of his post as foreign minister first to curb the growth of the Soviet military and then to reduce it surprised most observers, both Soviet and foreign. With no practical experience in either foreign or military policy, and with a reputation as a tough leader of the Georgian Communist Party, he had no history that foretold the radical reform role he would play.[37] Nonetheless, he proved determined to make major changes from his very first days in his new office. Like Gorbachev, he chose young assistants with strong inclinations toward radical reform. Sergei Tarasenko and Andrei Stepanov became his closest aides, and they wasted no time in offering suggestions for new and dramatic initiatives.

On the first of April, 1985, Tarasenko, working for Georgii Kornienko in the American department of the foreign minister, drafted a memo, "On the Possibility of a New Initiative in the Area of Disarmament," suggesting that the foreign ministry propose to Gorbachev a dramatic gesture on the occasion of the fortieth anniversary of the end of World War II or the fortieth anniversary of the United Nations.[38] He noted that U.S. policy had the upper hand because Reagan's Strategic Defense Initiative offered the prospect of a morally preferable alternative to nuclear deterrence. The appeal to people in the West of the "technical" solution, he argued, was great. To undercut it required a Soviet comprehensive strategy. To this end, Tarasenko sketched out a three-phase, fifteen-year plan: the first phase featured deep cuts in the U.S. and Soviet strategic nuclear arsenals over three to five years, as well as a number of conventional arms control agreements; the second called for another series of U.S. and Soviet cuts in strategic forces, combined with a wider U.N.-sponsored effort to bring other countries into the disarmament process; and in the last phase, nuclear weapons would be entirely eliminated. Kornienko and Gromyko, if they even gave this proposal a look, probably did not like it, but it reflected precisely the thinking Shevardnadze would soon be seeking.

Soon after Shevardnadze replaced Gromyko in July 1985, Tarasenko gave him a memorandum arguing that the genuine control that NATO states enjoyed over U.S. forces on their soil contrasted badly with the conspicuous lack of such control by Warsaw Pact states over Soviet troops stationed there. It put the Soviet Union at a great political disadvantage. To overcome it in accordance with "our new political thinking," he proposed a Soviet "review of all the treaties and agreements regulating the legal status of Soviet military bases in other countries." In the process, the principle of genuine sovereignty of those countries could be established. Furthermore, he suggested that some forces could be withdrawn, noting that those in Czechoslovakia and Hungary had a "temporary character." Finally, a review of the status of Soviet forces in "brotherly socialist countries" might also erase the "propaganda" advantage afforded the West by the "Brezhnev doctrine."[39]

Shevardnadze's reaction to the proposal reveals how radical his own thinking was at the time. He wrote on the memorandum, "C[omrade] Tarasenko, S. P., We will return to this question later. Shevardnadze." Tarasenko told me that Shevardnadze repeatedly used this tactic —citing Western political advantages to argue for changing Soviet policies—to prod along the perestroika process, particularly with regard to military policy.[40] The strategically placed functionary, Sergei Tarasenko, was testing the limits of "new thinking" very early, just as Chernyaev and Shakhnazarov were doing in the Central Committee apparatus.

After he won the Politburo's confidence by sounding a hard line at his first meeting with U.S. negotiators in Helsinki, Shevardnadze gradually acted more boldly.[41] At critical junctures he asked for approvals of new positions from Moscow, with the proviso that in the absence of a reply within a given time, he would implement the changes anyway. His aides knew the Moscow staffing process well enough to provide too little time for a negative response.[42] This technique allowed Shevardnadze to make concessions that Gorbachev could not get the Politburo to approve in advance. Shevardnadze heaped flattery on Gorbachev, periodically telling him, for example, that his progress in arms control would surely win him a Nobel Peace Prize. He kept a steady stream of laudatory reports coming into the secretariat and the Politburo about Gorbachev's growing status in the West. Bolstered by this flattery, Gorbachev was more susceptible to basic change in Soviet foreign policy. According to Tarasenko, Shevardnadze repeatedly explained to Gorbachev how "fairness" was on the U.S. side in many of the disputed issues, in light of the Western system of mutual respect for the rights of other states. If the Soviet Union was to establish a truly effective relation with the United States, it would have to play by those rules. Gradually, Shevardnadze was able to change the terms of judging what was acceptable in matters like on-site inspection to verify arms control agreements.[43] The General Staff reacted hostilely to Shevardnadze's tactics, but it failed to meet his standing challenge that it should offer better ideas rather than simply stonewall the general secretary.[44]

This was the way it looked from the foreign ministry. Shevardnadze helped change military policy by using the arms control lever with daring. While Gorbachev and his Politburo colleagues debated military reform, Shevardnadze worked to give them no choice but radical military reductions. He did not wait for full party approval of Gorbachev's ideological revision of "peaceful coexistence" to remove "the international class struggle" so that genuine cooperation with imperialist states would be possible. He simply proceeded as though it were already official Politburo policy. According to Tarasenko, a great deal of his success was also due to the way the Reagan and Bush administrations responded. The United States side set a high price for moving forward, but when Shevardnadze began to show that he would pay the price, U.S. officials gave him enough progress to refute the Politburo and secretariat hard liners' stereotyped predictions of U.S. behavior, yet never too much, so that Shevardnadze could demand more discretion for additional progress.[45] The resulting rise in Gorbachev's prestige abroad made his opponents reluctant to block his foreign policy outright. Eventually, of course, Shevardnadze realized that he had exceeded the political limit with this approach; he resigned his post in December 1990.[46]

To leave the impression that Shevardnadze's tactics on arms control had no support from Gorbachev would be wrong. As already noted, Gorbachev kept most of the Politburo ill informed about foreign policy meetings and negotiations.[47] Thus Shevardnadze had Gorbachev's help as well as Yakovlev's sympathies. Shevardnadze will appear only now and then in this account, but this brief picture of how he played his role should be kept in mind because he and his key aides in the foreign ministry remained an effective bastion through 1990 in support of Gorbachev's military policies. This, of course, includes their cooperation in achieving German reunification in October 1990, which unhinged the Warsaw Pact.

Afghanistan

The first substantive change in military policy concerned not arms control but rather Soviet forces in Afghanistan. As Chernyaev tells it, the war in Afghanistan was placed on Gorbachev's agenda as soon as he became general secretary by a deluge of letters to the Central Committee, the central press, and the International Department, mostly signed, mostly from Russian and Siberian oblasts, written mainly by soldiers and their families, all calling for an immediate end to the war.[48] Chernyaev was probably expressing the general secretary's own reaction when he noted in his diary in March 1985 that Gorbachev needed to end the war quickly before it became "his war" as well as Brezhnev's.

In spite of Marshal Sergei Sokolov's optimistic report in June 1984 to the defense minister, Marshal Dmitrii Ustinov, additional Soviet troops were sent to the 40th Army in Afghanistan by the end of the year.[49] In April 1985, General Igor Rodionov took command and stepped up the pace of operations, but when General Valentin Varennikov, chief of the MoD's operational group in Moscow overseeing the war, made an inspection in June, he reported that although the insurgents had been seriously hurt, the effect would be only temporary because they would soon replace their losses.[50] The war was simply not being won, and among the many reasons, according to Colonel Aleksandr Lyakhovskii, a veteran of many of its campaigns, poor command leadership from the lowest to the highest levels was consistently a problem.[51] Only the airborne and special-operations forces commanders showed genuine competence in adapting to the insurgents' tactics and beating them more often than not. More important, in his view, was the fragmented social and political character of the Afghanis themselves, which made the situation hopeless.

The choices at this point, according to Lyakhovskii, commenting on Varennikov's report, were "either to introduce additional forces, uproot all Afghans, and resettle their lands with different people—because to remake Afghanis, to change their beliefs by force, was impossible—or to withdraw forces from Afghanistan," leaving the government and the opposition to work out a settlement.[52] Lyakhovskii makes this judgment retrospectively on Varennikov's report as well as on his examination of many other secret documents, and Varennikov would later try to slow down the withdrawal by painting a rosier picture than justified. Still, they undoubtedly recognized in 1985 that continuing the war was not promising, certainly not without a radically different approach involving massive deportations and resettlements or genocide.

Gorbachev at first appeared to support both courses as he became directly involved at this point, assigning General Mikhail Zaitsev to run the war, giving him "a year or two" to win, and occasionally talking directly to him in Kabul by secure telephone to receive progress reports.[53] The pace of fighting was increased to the highest level of any year of the war, totaling eighty successful operations by the end of 1985. But Gorbachev did not wait to know the results. At the very time he appointed Zaitsev to command, he also formed a Politburo commission to conduct a close-hold review of the Soviet involvement in the war. By early June, the Central Committee Secretariat issued a secret directive announcing the beginning of a reduction of Soviet forces in Afghanistan.[54]

The Afghan leadership was unaware of this reversal of policy until the Central Committee Plenum in October 1985, when Babrak Karmal was in Moscow. The International Department prepared a point paper for Gorbachev's secret meeting with Karmal, suggesting that Gorbachev tell him bluntly that there was no revolutionary base in Afghanistan, recommending a sharp policy turn to a market economy, emphasis on Afghan Muslim values, sharing power with the opposition, and compromising with the rebels. Gorbachev generally followed the point paper, adding that Karmal must defend himself. Although Soviet arms would be supplied, Soviet troops no longer would. Karmal, as Gorbachev related to the Politburo on October 17, reacted with disbelief. Gorbachev next read aloud to the Politburo from several of the letters from mothers and soldiers, evoking teary-eyed reactions from some of his colleagues, and he submitted a draft message to Karmal for their approval, changing Soviet policy on the war. Marshal Sokolov, minister of defense, spoke first, admitting that he was no longer supportive of the war. Gromyko signaled his approval by asking only for a minor word change.[55]

Although the Soviet troop withdrawal came only on 15 February 1989, after long negotiations in Geneva, the decision in 1985 to abandon the Afghan communist leaders proved relatively easy for Gorbachev.[56] The generals were tired of the war, and as Shakhnazarov observes, the political consequences were marginal compared with other changes in military policy.[57]

Perceptions of the Military Problem

Shakhnazarov, more than any other official providing a written memoir, focuses on the ramification of the military question for reform. The Soviet military had become the "Moloch" to which the economy was methodically sacrificed.[58] How had this come about? In the 1920s and 1930s, he explained, Soviet military power was justified to "protect socialism," but even then, Stalin did not neglect social needs. Although the Soviet Union appeared mainly as a military power on the European scene after World War II, "militarism" has not yet taken hold. The "insane arms race" of the 1970s and 1980s brought militarism to its primacy. For Shakhnazarov, militarism included far more than the uniformed sector. The VPK—embracing so much of the economy—caused him to think about the United States' "military-industrial complex," a term dear to Soviet propagandists. He had accepted that image until he began to compare it with the Soviet case where a fifth, or even two-fifths, of the national income went to defense, compared with 4–6 percent of the gross national product in the United States, even less in European countries.[59] "I began to doubt any substantive difference between our Soviet political-military structure and the American one when I was assigned . . . to work on the Warsaw Pact" and became familiar with armament expenditures.[60]

Shakhnazarov separates Soviet "militarism" phenomenon from the ideology and structure of the Soviet system. He cites Lenin's treatise "State and Revolution," which predicted the withering of the state and its military, a flight of fancy in the context of Lenin's writings.[61] Even in retrospect, Shakhnazarov's considerable intellect apparently did not lead him to question the very capacity of the Soviet system to sustain economic growth. For him, Soviet militarism was not inherent to the system but a disease caught during World War II.

His description of its advanced stage, nonetheless, is illuminating. On Warsaw Pact affairs, his Central Committee department periodically clashed with the General Staff, and because he knew Marshal Akhromeev as a young officer during World War II, he was normally sent to settle disputes with him. On one occasion he asked Akhromeev why the Soviet Union had to sell so many arms to the Warsaw Pact armies.

"They buy exactly as many as they need to maintain the combat readiness of their armies," Akhromeev answered.

"Then why must they have such big armies requiring such a heap of weapons?" asked Shakhnazarov.

"What do you mean 'why'? Every Warsaw Pact state, with its army, fulfills a number of tasks in the defense of our socialist collaboration. In the West it is exactly the same. . . . It is all very logical," insisted the marshal.

Shakhnazarov tried another approach. "But in my view, that is inverted logic. You know better than I that if there is a war, for God's sake, it will not be limited to fighting with the kind of tank and artillery battalions you and I fought with. Inevitably nuclear weapons will be used. So, the significance of small armies without nuclear rockets will be trivial. If somehow nuclear weapons are not used, then there are no guarantees that, say, the Hungarians will unquestionably follow the orders of our staff, will not want to remain neutral or even go over to the side of the West in order to get revenge for 1956. I strongly doubt that the GDR Germans will want to fight on Russia's side against their western kinsmen. Wouldn't it be wiser not to push our allies into a military economy, but on the contrary, say to them: we guarantee your security, and you can cut your defense spending in half or a third, and put the savings into our fund for collective security collaboration?"

"They wouldn't do that. Every state wants its own army," insisted Akhromeev.

The debate continued as Shakhnazarov complained that the military burden was impoverishing the Warsaw Pact states and giving socialism a bad name. "Why should they suffer?"

Akhromeev smiled and answered, "Socialist internationalism." And if Shakhnazarov's disarmament idea were implemented, he added, "What would be done with all the weapons produced by the Soviet Union?" When Shakhnazarov asked why it was necessary to produce so many weapons, Akhromeev got to the core of his argument. "Because at a great cost of many sacrifices we created first-class factories, no worse than the American ones. Would you order them to stop work and begin producing cooking pots? No. That is utopia."

Shakhnazarov tried one last gambit. "Do you believe nuclear war is avoidable?"

Akhromeev responded, "I don't. But if it is avoided, then it will be precisely thanks to the fact that we have surrendered no power to the West. As chief of the General Staff, I also see as my mission that we do not."[62]

This episode clarifies what Gorbachev was up against: "the military-industrial mentality," which was deeply rooted not only in the officer corps but in the entire corps of civilian managers of the VPK. Shakhnazarov called it a "cancerous growth" that had "metastasized" to every sphere of Soviet life.[63] Of all the tasks of perestroika, he considered overcoming it the most difficult. Still, Shakhnazarov denies that Gorbachev's defensive doctrine, an indirect challenge to militarism, was genuinely new. The Warsaw Pact's declaratory policy had always been "defensive" and also coupled with the promise to disarm in step with NATO, when it was ready.[64] Gorbachev meant only to move from words of declaratory policy to the deeds it promised.

New Formulas at the Twenty-Seventh Party Congress

Whatever Gorbachev intended, he made several public statements on military policy during his first year that set the context for expounding a new course in military affairs at the Twenty-seventh Party Congress in February 1986. In July 1985 he told a group of officers in Minsk that they should expect no increase in resources.[65] During his visit to France in late September, he emphasized traditional diplomacy and downplayed the Soviet Union as a supporter of revolution—and by implication, also the French Communist Party. His speech of 15 January 1986, proposing to rid the world of nuclear weapons by the year 2000, hit hard on the necessity to disarm and rejected the very idea of strategic parity between the superpowers.[66]

At the Twenty-seventh Party Congress itself, Gorbachev hardly seemed to offer a new line at first glance, but on closer examination, hints of a radical departure were discernible. Instead of treating "peaceful coexistence" as a "specific form of the international class struggle"—the formula Ponomarev claimed to have crafted decades earlier and did not want changed—Gorbachev spoke of a more traditional approach to international security, "a comprehensive system." Such a system was necessary because "the nature of today's weapons leaves no state any hope of defending itself alone." Furthermore, he insisted that "security cannot be built forever on a fear of retribution," an implicit rejection of the Western concept of mutual deterrence.[67] The term from his speech that would galvanize so much subsequent attention was "reasonable sufficiency" as the basis for sizing Soviet military forces. Less noticed in the West at the time, Gorbachev emphasized peaceful relations at the state-to-state level while virtually ignoring the revolutionary role of international communism. Yet that would prove no less important than "reasonable sufficiency" for future Soviet military policy. As one observer noted about the speech, "All of the new or refurbished buzzwords, formulas, assessments, and debating flourishes developed by Yakovlev for Gorbachev over the previous year and half were in it." [68] Yakovlev's influence may have been strong, but he was scarcely Gorbachev's ventriloquist. Boldin describes their relationship as beset with suspicions, especially on Gorbachev's part. Gorbachev consistently used some of Yakovlev's ideas in his speeches, but he "always found ways of cramping Yakovlev's capacity for initiatives." [69]

More important than Gorbachev's report was the new party program approved by the congress. Its draft version provoked protests from the military leadership in late fall 1985 because it omitted the traditional open-ended party commitment to provide resources to the military, promising instead only to maintain "a level excluding strategic superiority on the part of imperialism's forces." The Ministry of Defense wanted the language to promise "all the modern means for the motherland's defenses." [70] The final version contained compromise language, promising "unremitting attention to reinforcing the USSR's might" and its capacity "to rout any aggressor." [71] The more radical change, however, concerned "peaceful coexistence." No longer was it defined to include the "international class struggle." A much longer definition more in line with Gorbachev's idea of an international security system became the new party line, less a clear formula than a wordy and elastic standard that could be stretched around the emerging differences in the Politburo. The quarrels over these ideological nuances signaled growing tensions over military policy.

The Rust Flight to Moscow

On 28 May 1987, a West German youth named Mathias Rust landed a small Cessna aircraft in Moscow, behind St. Basil's Cathedral, virtually on Red Square. At the time Gorbachev was in Berlin at the meeting of the Warsaw Pact Political Consultative Committee. His chief of staff, Valery Boldin, noticed the low-flying aircraft from his Kremlin office but reacted with utter disbelief when he shortly received a call from the MVD, reporting that a West German "sports plane" had just landed near the Kremlin. [72] The following day the full Politburo met Gorbachev at Vnukovo Airport for a report on his foreign trip, standard procedure for a general secretary's return from abroad. This time, the report was pushed aside for the Rust affair. For the next two days the Politburo heard briefings, discussed investigative reports on how Rust had evaded Soviet air defenses, and considered what to do about it. [73]

This seemingly chance event hit the Politburo like a bombshell, having consequences unappreciated in the West at the time or since. Its impact moved Gorbachev beyond talk to his first significant actions in the military sphere since he reversed Soviet policy in Afghanistan. It permanently defined his personal attitude toward his generals as one of deep distrust. It also catalyzed a palpable change in public attitudes toward the military, replacing its iconlike status in the Soviet popular mind with a sense of betrayal for all the economic sacrifices made to it.

Gorbachev remained furious throughout the Politburo deliberations. Boldin attributes Gorbachev's anger to influence by Raisa, his wife. She believed that the military had staged the affair simply to embarrass her husband, and she convinced him of her conspiracy theory. As Boldin put it, "Previously he had viewed the military with some misgivings, but now he was filled with savage hatred for them and never forgave them their little 'joke.' Long afterwards he had not forgotten; in public and private he did his utmost to denounce the military, creating an atmosphere of animosity and feeding them to the media and the parliamentarians of the Union."[74] Boldin, of course, was writing as an unsympathetic witness, but Chernyaev, Gorbachev's unrelenting admirer, describes him at his airport meeting with the Politburo as "red, mocking, angry."[75] Moreover, Chernyaev vented his own anger in a memo written that evening and given to Gorbachev before the Politburo meeting the next morning.

Railing against the military, Chernyaev declared that the Rust affair turned "a great military power for the moment into a joke. . . . What happened forces one to consider the situation in the army. The event did not occur because of technology problems. Technology from the 1930s is sufficient to intercept this aircraft." The problem, Chernyaev insisted, was more in the area of discipline and the general mood in the army, as evidenced by an event where a soldier killed his officers and sergeants out of desperation from being abused by them. The four decades since World War II had led to moral rot in the army. "The army was a closed zone, beyond any criticism."[76]

What should Gorbachev do about it? Chernyaev reflected that every great military power periodically carries out military reforms. In Russia, he wrote, only two major military reforms had occurred between the time of Peter the Great and the end of the empire, and only two reforms in the Soviet period—in the 1920s and in 1938–40.[77] "The time again is ripe for a cardinal reform. For a beginning, an unavoidable 'detail,' but important: the minister of defense must be a general of a new type. And he should not be a member of the Politburo. Let him always attend its sessions in order *to know what the policy is,* but in the formulation of policy you can go around him and without him." Next is the "vital necessity to abandon the multimillion-man army and its total conscription system. . . . A professional, cadre army is needed—quality, not quantity." Chernyaev admonished Gorbachev that without major change, not just in air defense, there could be no perestroika and the "victory of new thinking."[78]

How Gorbachev reacted to this advice, and how much of it he absorbed, Chernyaev was not sure. That he sketched out these thoughts as if they were wholly new to Gorbachev, however, suggests that Chernyaev had heard no such discussion of radical military reform before the Rust affair. For all of Gorbachev's machinations in setting the policy context for major reductions in the military through arms control, it seems that he had given no thought to how those reductions and concomitant restructuring would be shaped or to how he would compel the military leadership to carry them out. Chernyaev's mention of the military conscription system, the need for a professional cadre army, and for new top military leadership of a "new type" is the earliest evidence foreshadowing the main issues in the public debate about military reform in 1989–91. This memo, combined with Boldin's observation that Gorbachev was "filled with savage hatred" for the military after the Rust affair—that he fed the military to the media and the parliamentarians—helps explain why Gorbachev allowed the public debate on the military question to become so visceral and shrill. It also reveals Gorbachev's alternately groping and impulsive approach to a new military policy.

Endless and inconsistent briefings on the Rust affair by Marshal Sokolov and his aides did more to incite Gorbachev's anger than to calm it. Chernyaev, however, concedes a point to the military: the mood in the Air Defense Forces after the shooting down of the Korean airliner over Kamchatka in 1984 had had its effect; no one thereafter was willing to give an order to destroy an intruding aircraft.[79] The Air Defense Forces were also the victim of their own modernization program. New radars and communications had been installed around Moscow, but the communications and computer systems were not integrated with the old systems nearer the Soviet external border. Thus early tracking data on Rust's plane could not be passed to Moscow systems. Moreover, the VPK had refused to supply spare parts for a number of communications systems involved in tracking the Rust flight.[80]

In reality, Rust's evasion of Soviet air defense surveillance systems is not at all surprising. The radars near the Soviet borders had only the capability to detect bombers flying at high altitudes. Even around Moscow, where the newer systems had the capability to follow Rust's aircraft, losing track of a single aircraft is not surprising. Thus Rust's flight did not prove that Soviet air defenses would have failed miserably against a low-altitude bomber and cruise missile attack, the scenario for which they were designed. These realities, however, were beside the point.

The political impact of Rust's flight simply crowded out such technical understandings. The public wondered how such a breach was possible after all the billions of rubles spent on the Soviet military. Chernyaev notes Gorbachev's keen recognition of this "insult" to the Soviet people. Igor Smeshko, a former Soviet colonel and specialist in air defense, characterized the event's significance simply: "Rust won the strategic competition." [81] Asked to elaborate, he described the change in civilian attitudes toward his uniform when he walked on the streets of the city where he was stationed at the time. He sensed their scorn and feeling of betrayal. After the Rust flight, he declared, few ordinary Soviet citizens continued to believe the official media line about the superiority of the Soviet Armed Forces. Rust had made a mockery of years of that kind of propaganda. Had Gorbachev not acted vigorously in dismissing senior commanders, the colonel argued, his prestige as a leader would have suffered severely among the population. And act he did.

Gorbachev fired Marshal Sokolov as defense minister, replacing him with General Dmitrii Yazov. Gorbachev and Raisa had met and liked Yazov when he was a military district commander in the Far East. About 150 officers were tried in court and removed from their posts, and many of them were retired.[82] Although most were from the PVO, they were only the first in a major purge of the senior officer ranks that followed soon after. By the end of 1988, the minister of defense, all deputy ministers but two, all the first deputy chiefs of the General Staff, the commander and the chief of staff of the Warsaw Pact forces, all the commanders of the groups of forces and fleets, and all of the military district commanders had been changed.[83] Even during Stalin's bloody purge of the Red Army in 1937–38, the percentage of change in top level posts was not as high.

Close observers—Shakhnazarov, Chernyaev, Yakovlev, and especially Boldin—complained about Gorbachev's reluctance to take decisive action, to go beyond proclamations and speeches. His response to the Rust affair was an exception, the only one in the first years of perestroika in Boldin's judgment, and only because he and Raisa considered the whole thing an attempt to damage his standing in the eyes of the Soviet public and foreign leaders.

Chernyaev also notes Gorbachev's abiding anger. At a Politburo meeting a few weeks later, Viktor Chebrikov was giving the KGB's report on Rust's debriefing for a decision about what to do with him. Rust insisted that he came to Moscow because he wanted to meet Gorbachev, and although the KGB interrogators were not psychiatrists, they believed that Rust showed signs of

being mentally unbalanced, "touched in the head," as he put it. Chebrikov
had forbidden a psychiatric examination for Rust because if the word got out,
the notorious reputation of Soviet psychiatry in the West would cause bad
publicity. Instead, Chebrikov recommended that Rust be turned over to the
German court in Hamburg, which had already indicted him. But Lev Zaikov
objected, "If this young lad had landed in front of the White House in Washington, what would they have done with him?" Chebrikov answered, "In the
first place, they would have shot him down," provoking an outburst of laughter. Gorbachev grew furious, delivered the Politburo a lecture for jesting about
such a serious matter, and ordered that Rust be tried.

Although the Rust affair provoked Gorbachev to action regarding the military, its effect was limited to a sweeping purge of the senior ranks. Nor did
Gorbachev use the opportunity to find generals of the "new type," as Chernyaev had suggested. Yazov was a mediocre officer, described by Yakovlev as
fit to command a division but nothing higher. General Mikhail Moiseev, Gorbachev's choice for chief of the General Staff (after Marshal Akhromeev resigned in December 1988), had only completed the General Staff Academy
in 1982. He had neither high-level experience in Moscow nor any intellectual
or other redeeming distinctions. Unlike all previous general secretaries, Gorbachev had neither served in the army nor had any working experience with
the military. Thus he did not know generals who might be of a "new type."
He chose mediocre careerists who would follow orders, any orders. Apparently
that was what qualified Yazov and Moiseev.

Although Gorbachev had intimidated his generals, he had not convinced
them to undertake radical military reform. On the contrary, they became defensive, trying to live with his "new thinking" while keeping it out of their own
ranks, but that became increasingly difficult as Gorbachev confronted them
with ever more radical ideological propositions.

Clarifying Ideological Revisions

More than a year after the Twenty-seventh Party Congress's approval of party
documents revised to accommodate some of Gorbachev's "new thinking," he
published his book *Perestroika and New Thinking*, both in Russian and English.[84] The idea for it came from Western publishers, and although Gorbachev
was at first hesitant, he decided to write it. Chernyaev led a team of assistants
gathering all the memoranda of his conversations with foreigners and from
Politburo meetings, drafting parts of the text in spring 1987. In discussing an
early version with Yakovlev, Boldin, Chernyaev, and Frolov in July, Gorbachev

spelled out what the book had to achieve. It had to show "considerations, clari-fication of ideas, and a demonstration of how we came to perestroika; that it is not the ambition of any personality or groups. . . . The book is about the philosophical foundations of the policy of perestroika. . . . Not everyone agreed with this conception; they presented other variants. . . . But in the end, all con-cluded that a book of *this type* has the right of existence."[85] With this guidance, Gorbachev took his assistants to Livadia for the month of August 1987. There he reworked the text three times and then sent it to a few members of the Polit-buro, receiving almost no response. Only Nikolai Ryzhkov offered a protest on a technical economic point. No one praised it.

Given its radical ideological revisions, the lack of praise is not surprising, but the absence of criticism is. Chernyaev insists that it truly reflected Gor-bachev's "personality, character, nature, peculiarities, his intentions, his readi-ness to go far—he himself did not know how and where."[86] Thus it would seem to be an accurate reflection of Gorbachev's views in 1987. In the chapter dealing with war and foreign policy, he clarified the ideological foundations of the new party program and perestroika:

> Until the most recent times, class struggle was the fulcrum of social de-velopment, and it remains so in class-divided states. Accordingly, in the Marxist world view the class approach dominated . . . the main questions of social being. The concept of humankind interests was looked upon as the function and final result of the struggle of the working class, which, freeing itself, also frees all society from class antagonisms.
>
> But today, with the appearance of weapons of mass destruction . . . the objective limit has arisen for class confrontation in the international arena. For the first time, real, not just academic, contemporary, not to be post-poned, humankind interests have appeared.[87]

In asserting the priority of "humankind interests" over class interests, Gor-bachev excoriated Clausewitz's ideas about war as an instrument of state policy, insisting that this classical theorist, whom even Lenin respected for his contri-bution to the understanding of war, was no longer relevant, and that his ideas had to be put back on "the bookshelf" in the nuclear age. The old party view about the inevitability of war between socialism and capitalism was simply no longer appropriate now that nuclear weapons existed. Only defensive military means for preventing war made sense: "The nucleus of new thinking is the rec-ognition of the priority of humankind values and even more accurately, the sur-vival of mankind." He based this analysis not only on the Twenty-seventh Party Congress but also on the Central Committee plenum of April 1985, his first as general secretary.[88] The new program, however, had formally promulgated it:

The Twenty-seventh Party Congress considered it no longer proper to define the peaceful coexistence of states with different social orders as *a specific form of class struggle.* . . .

In developing our philosophy of peace, we have taken a new look at the interdependence of war and revolution. In the past, war often served to detonate revolution. . . . Hence a forecast, which was long adhered to in our country: a third world war, if unleashed by imperialism, would lead to new social upheavals which would finish off the capitalist system for good, and this would spell global peace. . . . At the Twenty-seventh Party Congress of the CPSU we clearly divorced the revolution and war themes, excluding from the new edition of the party program the following two phrases: "Should the imperialist aggressors nevertheless venture to start a new war, the people will no longer tolerate a system which drags them into war. They will sweep imperialism away and bury it." [89]

It is little wonder that these formulations had met objections during the preparation of the new program. As Gorbachev put it, "New political thinking . . . categorically dictates the character of military doctrines. They must be strictly defensive." [90]

The implications for the MoD and the General Staff were staggering. First, Gorbachev was telling them flatly that their views on the victory in nuclear war were now officially rejected by the party. The compromise language in the new party program was far more ambiguous than Gorbachev's language in his book. There, in black and white, the party's general secretary was bluntly rejecting the traditional party view of fighting a nuclear war.[91] At the same time, Gorbachev was rejecting the American concept of strategic stability maintained through mutual vulnerability. His scorn for Western deterrence theory was no less than for the General Staff's views on strategy and operations for winning a nuclear war. Both were Clausewitzian approaches to the use of nuclear weapons, seeking to make them serve political purposes, though in quite different and incompatible ways.

Second, Gorbachev destroyed the very foundations of the Soviet military's theory of war, based, as it was, on Marx's concept of alienation and class struggle, relating war to revolution and historical progress. Clausewitz's theories, alive and well in the Soviet military since the 1920s and soundly endorsed—with a few modifications—by Lenin, were to be sent back to the library shelf, removed from Soviet military thought.[92]

Third, by eliminating "the international class struggle" from the longstanding strategy of peaceful coexistence, Gorbachev was redefining the foreign military "threat" to the Soviet Union. By the old definition, all nonsocialist states with economies based on "private ownership of the means of production" "objectively" threatened the Soviet Union. Accordingly, Soviet military forces had to be adequate to defeat them all. That was implicit in Ponomarev's debate with Chernyaev over "new thinking" and peaceful coexistence and in Marshal Akhromeev's exchange with Shakhnazarov on arms for Warsaw Pact states. As a criterion for sizing and structuring Soviet military forces, it was a blank check on the bank of Soviet resources. Gorbachev's new definition of peaceful coexistence voided the check.

Fourth, Gorbachev's priority for "humankind" above "class" interests dictated military cooperation with the imperialists in pursuit of humankind interests (or "humankind values," as it was sometimes expressed). Arms control agreements, of course, would be the obvious measure of success for this strategic departure.

Exaggerating the significance of these ideological revisions for Soviet military policy is difficult. To what extent did Soviet military officers actually understand these ideological revisions and what they signified? At the very top, in the narrow circles of the Ministry of Defense and the General Staff, their significance was grasped at once, but with doubts about Gorbachev's seriousness. Lieutenant General Leonid Ivashov, a political officer who served close to Ustinov, Sokolov, and Yazov, three former defense ministers, remembers the revisions keenly. He brought them up in an interview, citing them as total nonsense and the beginning of troubles for the military.[93] In numerous interviews with former Soviet officers and senior party officials conducted about the same time (summer 1995, in Moscow), only Ivashov actually volunteered an opinion on the changes, but they all understood the ideological issues when specifically asked about them. Marshal Shaposhnikov had to be reminded of them, as did several generals and colonels. Marshal Akhromeev's views, as reported above by Shakhnazarov, make obvious that the significance was not lost on him. One is left with the impression that the rank and file of the officer corps neither paid much attention to these ideological revisions nor comprehended them if they did. Except at the very top, the officer corps was impervious to, isolated from, or walled off from these considerations. This situation, however, could only be temporary.

The MPA had to integrate Gorbachev's formulas into regular political education of troops and officers. Over the next two years military and party ideologists alike would wrestle with Gorbachev's revisions, constructing tortured arguments to reconcile Marx's concept of class struggle with "new thinking" and the primacy of "humankind interests."[94] As good communists, they did their best to adjust to these ideological revisions, and as good officers, they strove to do as little damage to the Soviet military as possible, avoiding the implications for resource allocations to the military.

Only Ligachev publicly challenged Gorbachev's radical revisions, although he waited for almost a year before doing so in his Politburo capacity of responsibility for ideology. Speaking to a group of party leaders in Gor'ki in August 1988, he asserted the continuing importance of the international class struggle and warned that talk about the primacy of humankind interests over class struggle was confusing both communists at home and Soviet friends abroad. In his vacation dacha in the Crimea, Gorbachev watched Moscow television evening news coverage of Ligachev's speech.[95] Deeply angered by it, he immediately telephoned Chernyaev, asking him to prepare a memorandum by the next morning assessing the speech, particularly as it concerned international affairs. In spite of Chernyaev's scathing critique and subsequent summaries of foreign press reactions to it, characterizing at as a victory for Ligachev's ideological views, Gorbachev hesitated to reproach Ligachev and even made arguments in his defense. Later in September, however, when he shook up the Politburo and the Central Committee apparatus, he relieved Ligachev of his Politburo responsibility for ideology, giving it to Vadim Medvedev, whose views on ideology were closer to Gorbachev's and Yakovlev's.[96] Although Gorbachev finally defended his revisionist formulas, his hesitation about disciplining Ligachev raises questions about how well he understood them or how deeply committed he was to them. Still, they stood as official dogma with their radical implications for policy.

The most remarkable thing about the beginnings of Gorbachev's new military policy is the lack of a well-developed analytic basis for it, not to mention the absence of a strategy for implementation. Its motive, in contrast, was clear. A surprisingly broad consensus existed among most of the Soviet elite that the Soviet economy was in serious trouble and that the burden of military expenditures was much to blame. To reduce it, Gorbachev turned to disarmament through arms control. That was impossible, he realized, without a fundamental change in the Soviet Union's relationship with the world, both the capitalist world and foreign communist parties.

To set a new course in military policy, therefore, Gorbachev quite logically began by changing Soviet foreign policy. His breakthrough in personal relations with Western political leaders convinced most of them that he was serious. Soviet negotiators returned to Geneva and Vienna, and under Shevardnadze's determined guidance, they surprised Western leaders with major changes in traditional Soviet positions.

Gorbachev's ideological revisions implied truly radical changes in Soviet foreign and military policy, but they were not so clearly understood in the West. American arms control proponents and deterrence theorists failed to grasp Gorbachev's disdain for their philosophical and theoretical assumptions. Likewise, Americans skeptical of Gorbachev's intentions overlooked his abrupt dismissal of the theories of his own military scientists.[97]

Still, Gorbachev lacked a practical scheme for dealing with the implications of success in arms control. Large force reductions would inevitably require significant restructuring of the Soviet military itself. Getting the military leadership to plan for such a basic restructuring was no easier than persuading the party to internalize the implications of "new thinking."

Gorbachev and Ligachev alike realized that the economic problem could not be solved with the same old party cadres in the key leadership positions. Accordingly, cadre turnover began on a remarkably large scale, greater than any time since Khrushchev's rule; in some categories of party, state, and military officials, the turnover was greater than under Khrushchev. Turnover in military leadership was delayed, and without the catalyzing effect of the Rust flight to Moscow, it probably would have been delayed much longer. All of this should have augured well for perestroika and military reform, but the purge of the old cadres failed to advance new cohorts of party members truly committed to "new thinking" and perestroika. In part this was due to Ligachev's differences with Gorbachev on the source of new cadres, but it was also the result of the nature of "new thinking." Although Gorbachev did not realize it, his goals required systemic change, which would destroy the party's traditional leading role. Where were young party cadres to be found who would be enthusiastic about abolishing their privileged positions? In the military this problem was particularly acute. Unable to identify "young Turks" who wanted to transform the military, Gorbachev had to choose new military leaders on the basis of political loyalty and submissiveness.

After more than two years, what had Gorbachev accomplished in setting a new course in military policy? He had persuaded the Politburo to approve the negotiated withdrawal of Soviet troops from Afghanistan. He had carried through a sweeping replacement of senior military leaders and articulated "reasonable sufficiency" (and "defensive sufficiency," as it was sometimes called) as a principle for military restructuring. The Warsaw Pact approved a revision of its formal military doctrine. To rationalize these departures, Gorbachev had induced the Twenty-seventh Party Congress to approve a new party program, which downplayed the role of international class struggle. Finally, and perhaps most important, he had convinced key Western leaders that he was deadly serious about fundamental improvements in East-West relations.

None of these things had seriously affected the day-to-day activities of the Soviet military or convinced its leaders that dramatic change would soon have to be implemented. Other than the turnover of senior military leaders, Gorbachev's changes were still largely rhetorical, and the military saw them as only that. Yazov said as much to a meeting of Soviet commanders in Warsaw in 1988, telling them that Gorbachev was a very clever fellow in advancing slogans that put the imperialists off balance and divided the Soviet Union's enemies.[98]

Gorbachev's progress in changing military policy, however, should be judged against the size of the undertaking. Shakhnazarov did not exaggerate when he said in retrospect, "Of all the tasks that fell to the duty of perestroika, the most complicated was demilitarization of the country."[99] Indeed it was, because it required the destruction of the Soviet system.

SEVEN

Defensive Doctrine and Arms Reductions

*Parallel to ending the Afghan venture began the dismantling of the military production
line through which the national wealth was thrown into the Moloch's gullet.
Here one had to show maximum caution, to engage in some sense
in a diplomatic game of cat and mouse.*

GEORGII SHAKHNAZAROV

The Rust flight affair made it relatively easy for Gorbachev to purge the senior military ranks. Cutting forces and armaments production was another matter indeed, requiring skill not unlike that of a cat enticing mice from their hole, but cat-and-mouse games could not go on indefinitely if real progress was to be made.[1] At some point Gorbachev either had to drop the cozy half-truths about his real intentions or give up the economic strategy of major shifts of resources from the military to civilian sector. He eventually made the choice before the United Nations in December 1988 by announcing a large unilateral cut in Soviet forces. That occasion marked the end of his caution, although not his ambivalence, and the beginning of the unraveling of the Soviet military. It also coincided with his shift of primary emphasis from economic reform to political reform, a change prompted by the belated realization that without mobilizing new political forces in support of perestroika, no real progress was possible in either military or economic reform.

The game of cat and mouse was played around two issues — changes in military doctrine and an aggressive arms control policy. Soviet military doctrine traditionally had two faces, one for internal military guidance, the other for external foreign policy and propaganda purposes. Because Gorbachev genuinely sought arms control agreements that imposed large military reductions, he needed somehow to link the two faces. Not only did a new Soviet military doctrine have to reassure the West that he was serious about moving from confrontation to cooperation, removing military security from the agenda of East-West issues; it also had to compel the generals themselves to accept major reductions in the Soviet Armed Forces. Thus consistency between the two faces of a new military doctrine was imperative for Gorbachev's arms control objectives.[2]

The domestic face also had to apply to military industries—to the VPK, that is, not just the Ministry of Defense. Cutting military forces could free manpower for the civilian economy's workforce, but it would not save significant military expenditures because military pay was abysmally low—five or six rubles per month for conscripts. A very large part of the military budget went to the VPK for constant modernization of weaponry. To be sure, great savings could be achieved by cutting forces, but the key point is that Gorbachev confronted more than the uniformed military in this cat-and-mouse game. Somewhere between 20 and 40 percent of the state economy was tied up in military production. The issue of military reform, therefore, set Gorbachev and his allies against this large and privileged sector of the economy as well as against the conservative elements of the uniformed military leadership.[3]

The New Military Doctrine

Doctrine can mean several different things in military affairs, ranging from routinized organizational procedures to tactics and strategy. "Military doctrine" in the Soviet military lexicon had a very specific definition, distinct from military science, military strategy, and military art, similar to "military policy" in the Western understanding.[4] The Soviet definition divided doctrine into a sociopolitical component and a military-technical component. The sociopolitical component dealt with the nature of a state's society, economy, and geography, as well as its ideology, political aims, and the purpose of its military forces; the military-technical component had to do with the narrower military issues of force structure, weaponry, strategy, tactics, and so on.[5] Although hundreds of books and articles were written about military doctrine, and it was at times a major issue of debate, no single directive document is known to have existed that specified in writing precisely what Soviet military doctrine was at specific times. Both its enduring and changing aspects, however, could be inferred from the vast literature on the subjects. More specifically, party programs, directives, and the party's general policy line provided the substance for the sociopolitical side of the doctrine. The military-technical component was developed within the military and approved by the Politburo. Its substantive details were considered military secrets, although its general outlines could be inferred from military textbooks, journals, senior officers' statements, and also the structure of Soviet military forces. Apparently the General Staff was comfortable with no generalizing, formal statement of the military-technical component, at least not an unclassified one.

Although the offensive form of warfare had always been the Soviet military's doctrinal focus on the military-technical side, the sociopolitical side was ostensibly defensive. That was the crux of "peaceful coexistence." Revolution could not be exported; it had to be the product of class contradictions within capitalist societies.[6] If war broke out, of course, the Soviet military was to defend the socialist camp, though it planned to take the military offensive to aid foreign working classes in the name of international working-class solidarity.[7] Thus when Gorbachev began talking about "new thinking" and war in the nuclear age, calling on all states to assume a purely defensive military posture, he was not breaking new ground on the face of the matter. When he talked about "reasonable sufficiency" and "defensive sufficiency," he was not unambiguously promulgating new doctrinal guidance to the military. To be sure, these terms strongly implied reductions in Soviet force structure, but because they were tied to mutual reductions with the United States, they did not differ essentially from similar platitudes uttered by Brezhnev.

The Warsaw Pact, unlike the Soviet Union, did have a written, public military doctrine, insofar as it concerned the sociopolitical side. Having made some basic changes in the military policy in the new party program at the Twenty-seventh Party Congress in February 1986, Gorbachev next sought a written change in the Warsaw Pact doctrine. The communiqué of the Political Consultative Committee (PCC) meeting in Budapest, 10–11 June 1986, reflected Gorbachev's peace offensive language and readiness to eliminate all nuclear weapons through arms reductions agreements. Although it noted the "defensive character" of Warsaw Pact military doctrine, it offered no change in its formulation.[8] The following year at the PCC meeting in Berlin, Gorbachev pushed through an important change. "Preventing war," not "preparing to fight a war," was to be the main military task. This, of course, was an acknowledgment of the line of military policy that Gorbachev had forced on the General Staff in the party program approved by the Twenty-seventh Party Congress, but unlike the changes in the party program, the announcement at the Warsaw Pact PCC meeting was taken in the West as signaling a significant change in the military-technical aspect of Soviet military doctrine, one that would affect resources.

In the course of the year from summer 1987 to mid-1988, public analysis of the "defensive" aspect of this doctrine became widespread, but its full significance was far from clear, especially its ramifications for Soviet force structure changes.[9] Marshal Akhromeev, still chief of the General Staff, visited the

United States as the guest of the Chairman of the Joint Chiefs of Staff, Admiral William Crowe, and observed a number of U.S. military posts and activities. This was only one of several exchange visits between the highest-level U.S. and Soviet defense officials intended to build mutual trust and clarify both sides' military policies. Akhromeev's rank and stature distinguished him from all other visiting Soviet officials as the one who could be most enlightening about the practical implications of the new Soviet military doctrine, and therefore his comments were closely scrutinized. In addition to many hours of discussions with his U.S. military host, he also spoke to a number of public audiences, selling the new doctrine as something fundamentally new. His heart, however, was not in it, or at least he was not prepared to spell out in a compelling fashion its military-technical implications. Asked at a meeting of the Council on Foreign Relations in New York on 11 July 1988 to clarify how the new doctrine would change Soviet war plans, he drew an analogy with the Japanese attack on Pearl Harbor. The United States was defensive until the Japanese attacked; then it launched a strategic counteroffensive. The Soviet Union, if attacked by NATO, would try to negotiate a peace for about twenty days, but if that effort failed, Soviet forces would likewise launch a counteroffensive. This was the "defensive" aspect of the new doctrine. He explained that the Defense Council had debated the issue for two years before it arrived at a decision on this "defensive doctrine." Therefore, it was not just a cosmetic change. It was substantive, a major new departure.[10]

The audience was hardly convinced, especially when Akhromeev offered the example of Pearl Harbor. If the new doctrine implied a reduction in Soviet military forces, would that not make a counteroffensive more difficult? Losses would be suffered during the few weeks of defense, and then an offense would have to be launched from a less advantageous position. Would that not require more, not fewer forces? This little exchange must have disturbed Akhromeev because he was hearing similar questions from his own political leaders. They, too, had questions about how seriously the General Staff was taking the military-technical aspects of the new doctrine.

In preparation for the annual Warsaw Pact PCC meeting in July 1988, the General Staff submitted material for inclusion in Gorbachev's report. Shakhnazarov, among others, looked it over, finding nothing seriously wrong with it. It was in full accord with Soviet foreign policy, supporting arms control negotiations under way with the United States, expressing readiness to withdraw Soviet troops from Afghanistan, calling for radical reductions in strategic nuclear forces and also reductions in conventional forces between the Atlantic and the Urals, and a number of other points, including emphasis on the defensive character of Warsaw Pact doctrine. Not even the most critical eye, Shakhnazarov, complained, could detect the little "trick" in it.[11]

A short time later, Gorbachev's staff received a copy of the report that the Warsaw Pact commander, Marshal Viktor Kulikov, intended to deliver at the PCC meeting. To Gorbachev's surprise's, it declared that the military danger in Europe had increased so that all branches of forces required new and more modern armaments. Notwithstanding the Soviet Union's widely proclaimed readiness to eliminate all chemical weapons, the report explained that "the role for chemical support of combat operations is growing" and that new equipment for that purpose was needed.[12]

The report, of course, was one thing. It could be changed. On further investigation, however, it turned out that much of the equipment for the modernization plans and greater readiness had already been approved and entered into the state five-year plan. For example, more attention was given to air assault forces, helicopter-borne regiments used in speeding up ground offensive operations. Fuel and ammunition stocks in Hungary and Bulgaria were to be increased. New weapons for reserve mobilization divisions were to be produced, more airfields to be built, and more hardened shelters for forward-based fighter aircraft were to be constructed. Gorbachev changed Marshal Kulikov's report and canceled some but not all of the weapons production and construction programs.[13]

As Shakhnazarov rightly observed, the generals believed that "while the politicians and propagandists blabbed about disarmament, the military must concern itself with its own business." Nor did they fall in line after Gorbachev corrected Kulikov's report. Before every PCC meeting, Shakhnazarov declared, the military had to be pushed on each small step toward real disarmament. Not all officers with whom he dealt in the General Staff personally took this attitude. Many, in his judgment, were intellectually talented and realized that military expenditures were leading the Soviet economy to ruin, but they were kept in line, never challenging their superiors, whose self-interest was analogous to that of the party nomenklatura. Both were enormously corrupt. The generals did not want to give up free access to vacations in Karlovy Vary in Czechoslovakia or their hunting lodges in the forests of eastern Poland.[14]

Throughout 1987 and 1988, discussion of the new military doctrine filled the pages of military and academic journals.[15] Some took the new emphasis on defense quite seriously and tried to develop its logic in light of "new thinking" while others only acknowledged it, expressed skepticism, or simply voiced the old military line. The most sophisticated reaction was to insist that defense and offense as forms of combat were converging as a result of new weapons technology which make the offense-defense distinction increasingly vague.[16] The defense minister, Dmitrii Yazov, published a book in 1987 that supported the defensive emphasis in the new doctrine but also insisted that defense alone cannot win a war; at some point, offense has to become the primary form of combat operations.[17] Like Marshal Akhromeev would do a year later before an American audience in New York, Yazov was suggesting a counteroffensive strategy.

Others would also suggest anchoring the new doctrine in counteroffensive operations. A retired General Staff officer, Major General Valentin Larionov, and a civilian military analyst, Andrei Kokoshin, used the example of the World War II Battle of Kursk as a basis for the military-technical side of a defensive doctrine.[18] The largest tank battle of the war, Kursk began with a German double-envelopment offensive against a large Soviet protrusion into German-held territory. The Red Army anticipated the attack and initially took the defensive, held its position against the German onslaught, and then counterattacked with a huge enveloping operation of its own, destroying most of the German forces. A promising German offensive was thus turned into a major Soviet victory. The authors suggested that this defensive-offensive form of operation held instructive lessons for contemporary military planning under the new defensive doctrine. This concept, of course, shared much with Marshal Akhromeev's explanation, but Akhromeev was speaking of the counteroffensive at the strategic level, not just the operational level. While the Larionov-Kokoshin scheme envisioned restoring the prehostilities territorial boundaries, Akhromeev's version implied much more, certainly a Soviet counteroffensive reaching the Atlantic coast if the U.S. strategy after Pearl Harbor was the analogy, as he suggested.

All of this, to be sure, is speculative, but it is based on the only publicly available evidence of Soviet thinking at the time on the military-technical side of the new doctrine. The General Staff's neglect of the task became painfully apparent in the course of 1989–91, when glasnost permitted an acrimonious public debate about defensive doctrine and its force structure implications. Through 1988, however, the military stood its ground. If defense meant the capacity to carry out a counteroffensive, that could easily justify the same or higher levels of Soviet military capabilities.

Restarting Arms Control

Although the General Staff could hide its war plans and its force-structure developments — even from Soviet political leaders except when they made a determined effort to look into them — playing the same cat-and-mouse game on arms control was more difficult. Both the process and the results were under international media scrutiny. Gorbachev understood quite well the special advantages he had in the arms control game. Although the General Staff could pretend to accept the new slogans—"reasonable sufficiency" and "defensive sufficiency"—in the arms control negotiations, sooner or later it would have to deliver on reductions or reveal to the world that the new military doctrine was a sham. In this way, Gorbachev was enticing the mouse out of its hole onto the international scene where his good personal relations with Western leaders and high hopes of real progress in disarmament afforded him considerable power vis-à-vis both the military and his Politburo opponents.

Managing Arms Control

Some knowledge of the organizational system and process that backstopped Soviet arms control negotiations makes it easier to understand how Gorbachev took control of it. Considerable insight into Soviet staffing process has been provided by Nikolai Detinov, who participated in it throughout the negotiations beginning with SALT (Strategic Arms Limitations Talks) and continuing until the breakup of the Soviet Union.[19]

To manage the talks beginning in Helsinki in November 1969 and leading to the SALT I treaty in 1972, the Politburo formed the Commission of the Politburo CC CPSU for Oversight of the Negotiations on Strategic Arms Limitations in Helsinki.[20] It included six members—Dmitrii Ustinov, Central Committee secretary for defense affairs; Marshal Andrei Grechko, minister of defense; Andrei Gromyko, minister of foreign affairs; Yurii Andropov, chairman of the KGB; Leonid V. Smirnov, deputy prime minister and chairman of the VPK; and finally, Mstislav Keldysh, president of the Academy of Sciences. Keldysh was included because of his personal status, not his institutional position, and he was only temporarily a member. The other five were chosen for organizational representation—the Central Committee secretariat, the MoD, the MFA, the KGB, and the VPK—and soon became known informally as the Big Five. Because of his experience, Ustinov came to dominate the Big Five, especially after Marshal Grechko's death in 1976. Minister (or, at that time, people's commissar) of armaments in 1941 when he was only thirty-two years old and promoted to colonel general in 1944, he eventually became the first deputy chairman of the Council of Ministers (that is, head of the VPK), then party secretary for defense affairs.[21] Replacing Grechko as minister of defense and becoming a full member of the Politburo in 1976, he left his post in the Central Committee. The new secretary for defense affairs, Grigorii Romanov, was excluded from the Big Five, leaving it de facto only "the big four" until the Gorbachev era.[22]

Recalling the structures for military policy making outlined in Chapter 2, one must wonder why the Defense Council did not fill this backstopping role. In fact, that was an issue within the Soviet regime, and on occasions, Big Five questions were taken to the Defense Council for resolution, especially when major disagreements with the United States arose toward the conclusion of SALT I. ABM treaty issues also went to the Defense Council for resolution because they involved complex force-structure questions requiring more extensive analysis. Still, the Big Five was able to establish itself vis-à-vis the Defense Council, gaining something close to permanency.

Although it was a commission of "equals," it did not operate that way most of the time. The standard procedure for the Big Five was for the Ministry of Defense and the Ministry of Foreign Affairs to submit papers for its review and approval. No other agency ever offered an alternative paper. The Ministry of Defense, because of its monopoly of technical military information, provided the substance of the positions, and the Ministry of Foreign Affairs added the international political context, concerning itself with propaganda, ideology, and diplomatic aspects of the negotiations.[23] The KGB was more an observer than a participant in the process, and the VPK looked to Ustinov to defend its interests. Once initial positions were established and the Big Five began to respond to the delegation at the negotiations, Ustinov would have his staff draft up a paper, review it with selected experts, then discuss it individually with Smirnov (VPK) and Andropov (KGB), but rarely would he consult Gromyko (MFA) or Grechko (MoD). Only then would he call a Big Five meeting to consider and approve his prepared agenda for submission to the Politburo which normally "simply rubber-stamped" it.[24]

As the issues in SALT II became more complex, however, Ustinov's modus operandi proved inadequate. To provide the necessary interdepartmental coordination, a second-level interagency body—the "Little Five"—was formed just before the Vladivostok summit in November 1974.[25] It took over the details of technical issues and presented more or less finished positions for the Big Five's approval, often by telephone calls and signatures on the documents rather than by a formal meeting. In time, the Big Five came to accept virtually all of its work without changes, making it the primary mechanism for the backstopping negotiations until the dissolution of the Soviet Union.

The Big Five fell idle after December 1983, when the Soviets broke off the negotiations in Geneva in reaction to the beginning of the NATO deployment of intermediate range forces.[26] Ustinov died in December 1984, leaving the Big Five with a leadership void. Gorbachev began its revitalization during 1985–86 by appointing a new party secretary, Lev Zaikov, as a member. Zaikov had replaced Grigorii Romanov as secretary for defense affairs in 1985. First coming to prominence as the director of a military-industrial firm in Leningrad, he next was mayor of Leningrad and eventually the Leningrad party chief. During a brief encounter in 1985, he impressed Gorbachev with his businesslike manner, speaking in concrete terms, not hiding behind vague generalities. According to Detinov, that won Zaikov a place on Gorbachev's team and vaulted him into the post vacated by Romanov.[27]

Zaikov's membership in the Big Five brought its leadership back under the Central Committee. Detinov was impressed with Zaikov's quick grasp of the reins of power in the defense area. To have significant influence, he not only had to assert his control over VPK, but he also needed a seat at the arms control table, because treaties would have large implications for defense industries. After Zaikov captured the head of the table in the Big Five, people began to call it "the Zaikov Commission."[28]

Zaikov abandoned Ustinov's long-established practice of informally working out the details with Smirnov and Andropov and then confronting the Big Five with a final position ready for the Politburo's rubber stamp. Instead he expanded the number of individuals and departments involved in many of the Big Five deliberations. The International Department of the Central Committee was brought in, and the deputies to the principal members of the Big Five often attended. At the working-group level — the Little Five — vast detail was coordinated, especially during ongoing negotiations. Again at the Big Five level, the principal members and their assistants delved deeply into the substance of the negotiations. The major change, however, was in the Politburo's role. Gorbachev used it to work through major political issues in advance of the negotiating positions, often meeting with Shevardnadze and the defense minister to shape a position for Politburo discussion and approval. The resulting decisions were handed down to the Big Five, leaving to it the task of making the negotiating directives fit the political guidance from above. This was wholly new for both the Big Five and the Little Five; according to Detinov, it produced more thoroughly thought-out positions and much better coordination.[29] More important, however, the change in organizational process greatly enhanced Gorbachev's bureaucratic control.

The "Gorbachev Initiative"

The top military leaders began to realize that Gorbachev was serious about reaching arms control agreements when Gromyko and U.S. Secretary of State George Shultz met in Geneva in January 1985 and issued a joint statement expressing intention to start negotiations in three areas: *a*) INF, *b*) strategic arms reductions talks (START), and *c*) weapons in space. The Big Five agreed to link all three negotiations, insisting on banning space weapons (specifically, blocking the U.S. Strategic Defense Initiative [SDI]) as the sine qua non for progress in START. At the same time, it retained the old Soviet positions at INF, namely that U.S. "forward based systems" (FBS) and French and British nuclear weapons be included and that U.S. Pershing II missiles could not be based in Europe. Negotiations resumed in March 1985; Gorbachev announced a moratorium on additional Soviet SS-20 missile deployments in April, and he declared a five-month moratorium on nuclear testing in August. By fall it was clear to the General Staff that the Soviet negotiating positions could not be sustained if Gorbachev was to have the progress he sought.[30]

In September, Shevardnadze suggested in Washington that a 50 percent reduction of strategic offensive arms could be considered if the United States promised to limit research on SDI, a suggestion that shortly became the formal Soviet position at Geneva. In October, during his speech to the French National Assembly, Gorbachev offered to conclude a separate INF reduction agreement not contingent upon agreement to outlaw weapons in space. This offer, of course, was inconsistent with the Soviet official position that all three negotiations be linked. In November, Gorbachev met Reagan in Geneva, again raising the idea of a separate interim agreement on INF reductions and advancing the goal of 50 percent reductions in strategic offensive arms. Gorbachev also gained some propaganda advantage against SDI by emphasizing that the language in the meeting's joint communiqué about stopping the arms race in space and terminating it on earth was a better formula for security than effective strategic defense.[31]

Gorbachev was building negotiating momentum that would derail some major weapons programs. To curb him, the General Staff employed the old military maxim "an offense is often the best defense," proposing to achieve complete nuclear disarmament within fifteen years. As Detinov describes it, this was not an "improvisation" but rather a well-considered tactic, one that made the military look "eager" to eliminate nuclear weapons while assuring that it "could hardly lead to any practical results in the foreseeable future."[32] The minister of defense, Marshal Sergei Sokolov, found the tactic compelling and presented it to a delighted Gorbachev. He promptly put it to the Big Five, who found problems with this "Gorbachev initiative," as it was known thereafter. At Gorbachev's request, Zaikov refereed the dispute in the Big Five between the MoD and MFA, then submitted the initiative to the Politburo, where it was quickly endorsed.

Ironically, this General Staff proposal not only acquired Gorbachev's name but also became the basis for his famous speech of 15 January 1986, calling for complete nuclear disarmament by the year 2000. Detinov candidly observes that "the real authors of this initiative became entrapped in their own gambit."[33] They handed Gorbachev an instrument for compelling them to make future concessions as well as undercutting all their objections to the "Zero Option" in the INF negotiations—the U.S. proposal that both side give up all intermediate range missiles in Europe. The mouse had dared to come out of its hole, and the cat had snatched off a piece of its tail as it scurried back in.

Still, nearly two years would be required to tie down the INF treaty in December 1987. Throughout 1986 and much of 1987, the negotiations in Geneva appeared to be permanently deadlocked, entangled not just in the earlier problems of 1981–83 but now complicated by SDI. The Soviets still found SDI intolerable, not only because it would initiate another round in the arms race, a concern that worried the Soviet military as well as Gorbachev, but also because the prospect of a U.S. defense against offensive strategic weapons —even an imperfect one—complicated General Staff calculations about how far it would go in reducing strategic offensive force levels to meet the START goals. At the same time, the United States tabled the issue of the Krasnoyarsk radar, citing it as a clear violation of the ABM treaty.[34] The outlook for progress in mutual disarmament was dismal at best. In the final event, however, Gorbachev would be able to use the General Staff's own initiative for elimination of all nuclear weapons to help corral it into acceptance of the INF treaty.

The Road to Reykjavik

As most Western accounts emphasize, although no concrete results were reached at the summit in Reykjavik in October 1986, the meeting marked a major turning point in U.S.-Soviet arms control negotiations.[35] Gorbachev became increasingly aware that his domestic reform programs—which he had always tied to progress in changing the East-West relationship, making domestic reform the precondition that would justify massive reductions in Soviet military spending—were going nowhere. Although he could point to breakthroughs in his personal relations with European leaders, they were inconsequential compared to his relationship with President Reagan where military affairs were concerned.

At a Politburo meeting on 3 April 1986, Gorbachev emphasized precisely this understanding. "The Twenty-seventh Party Congress very correctly defined the course toward America: in face of the contradictions in our relations, the reality is such that without them we can do nothing and without us they can do nothing. . . . We cannot react to American policy on the principle of a tooth for a tooth—say, if we are an 'evil empire,' then you are a such and such. Our realistic policy is stronger than any propaganda. . . . That is why it is important . . . not to retreat from the course set by the congress."[36] This line of thinking reflected a change in Gorbachev's strategy, one that he had been considering since his 15 January call for eliminating all nuclear weapons. Until that time, he believed that he could sell "new thinking" to European leaders, isolating the United States and thereby forcing Reagan to come to share the Europeans' enthusiasm for his new foreign policy. Now he concluded that only a direct approach to Reagan would work.[37] At the same time he realized that his own military and VPK bureaucracies were so unyielding that he had little but words to take to Reagan, words not matched by deeds.

At a Politburo meeting in early May, Gorbachev berated his colleagues on this point, criticizing the "old approach" still manifest in all departments and creating the inertia that was undercutting "new thinking." "We cannot allow the world to consider our political decisions as a bluff. . . . We are creating our own blind alleys which are difficult to explain not only to our negotiating partners but also to our friends."[38] The Chernobyl nuclear power plant accident in the spring of 1986 added to Gorbachev's frustration with the VPK, which held a monopoly over all nuclear affairs. Investigations into the accident revealed to him that not only was confidence in the VPK's competence in these matters unjustified but also that the VPK was hiding much detail about nuclear safety issues from the Politburo.[39] Throughout the spring and summer of 1986, therefore, Gorbachev felt frustrated that he could not make his military and the economy policies conform with his arms control policy. A deal with Reagan was essential if arms control progress was to provide him with the lever to squeeze resources out of the military and the VPK.

To say this, of course, is to overlook a great deal that Gorbachev was doing on the domestic front to gain support for perestroika, particularly its economic side. He was busy in the spring and summer of 1986 promoting new cadres to leadership roles throughout the country—that is, carrying through an administrative purge of the party. He also began courting the Soviet intelligentsia in this period.[40] Traveling outside of Moscow, he jawboned perestroika and "new thinking" to workers and ordinary people in numerous provincial towns and cities. But he soon came back to the foreign-policy component of perestroika and to his problem with Reagan.

Among many foreign visitors he received that summer in Moscow, two of them, according to Chernyaev, contributed critically to his "political and psychological preparation" for the Reykjavik meeting. French President Mitterrand surprised Gorbachev by agreeing that Soviet foreign policy was serious, not a political tactic, and that Reagan was making mischief with SDI. But after criticizing Reagan harshly, Mitterrand added a personal assessment of the American leader, describing him as a man who had an instinct for what was appropriate for the historical moment, no matter what he had said or done in the past. "This is a real live man," Mitterrand insisted. Gorbachev was startled, remarking that "This is very important information . . . another important point in our conversation today." [41] When Richard Nixon visited Moscow a short time later, Gorbachev delivered him a long speech, asserting his readiness to deal with Reagan, even if relations were bad, and assuring Nixon that rumors were untrue that he had given up on Reagan and would wait for a new American president—a tactic that made no sense because the business between the two countries was too important to delay. Nixon acknowledged Gorbachev's points and went on to say that he had known Reagan for more than thirty years, that he knew that Reagan believed that he had established a personal relationship with Gorbachev in their first meeting, and that Reagan considered U.S.-Soviet relations his personal business. Clearly intending a message for Reagan, Gorbachev assured Nixon that he had "no devious intentions" in his diplomacy toward the United States, for that would "lead to nothing." [42]

The idea for the Reykjavik summit occurred to Gorbachev in August, while he was on vacation in the Crimea. After only a few days there he asked the foreign ministry to prepare a concept, providing the rationale for a new visit with Reagan. Unimpressed by it, he suddenly directed Chernyaev to have a letter drafted for Reagan, inviting him to a meeting, "in London, or better, in Reykjavik," because it was a halfway meeting place on neutral ground that would "embarrass neither great power." [43] Because Shevardnadze was also on vacation, his deputy at the foreign ministry was left to draft the invitation. What it proposed can only be inferred from Chernyaev's angry message rejecting it. Not only did it fail to capture Gorbachev's intentions, according to Chernyaev's reply, but it was more like routine instructions to the negotiators than a message from one superpower leader to the other. "Again, we have the cart before the horse. They [the military] can say load the cart with good wares before harnessing the horse. However, Comrade Akhromeev's wares probably have all kinds of variants." Chernyaev was sure that Akhromeev would ask: "In which direction are we going and how far?" Then he complained that the military was describing the United States as if it were preparing for war, precisely the charge that could be made about the Soviet Union's behavior. "Of course the military have their logic, their position obliges them to hold the politicians by the shirttails. But that does not mean that military calculations must define the general policy." Chernyaev continued with detailed objections and warned, "From Reykjavik the world must hear huge, politically grand proposals in the spirit of the program of 15 January." [44]

This little episode reveals something of the military's tactics for constraining both the foreign ministry (when Shevardnadze was not at the helm) and the general secretary's own staff in arms control and diplomacy. On previous occasions, Gorbachev had hesitated when confronted by such tactics, but his patience had worn thin. A letter more to his liking was sent to Reagan, and at the Politburo meeting on 22 September, Shevardnadze announced the good news that Reagan had accepted. Yet there was a condition that could easily have scuttled the whole affair: the response included a list of twenty-five Soviet citizens who were to be allowed to travel abroad, including the well-known dissident, nuclear physicist, and designer of the Soviet hydrogen bomb, Andrei Sakharov. Gorbachev acted adeptly to save the day, lecturing the Politburo that too much was at stake—world peace—to allow this condition to be rejected. Thus he persuaded the Politburo to accept Reagan's condition. [45]

The General Staff, however, did not give up. A few days before the delegation departed for Reykjavik, the Politburo met to approve Gorbachev's negotiating instructions. Marshal Akhromeev and Georgii Kornienko prepared the text in advance, and Chernyaev again reacted negatively, this time with a memo to Gorbachev before the meeting, making three points about the inadequacies of the text:

1. Putting SDI ahead of offensive strategic arms reductions was a mistake. For political effect it was essential to emphasize the complete elimination of nuclear weapons and the 50 percent reductions in the first phase.
2. On INF, the draft offered nothing new, only partial reductions. It was critical to liquidate all INF in Europe, ignoring the British and French weapons and initiating separate INF negotiations for the Far East. The French and the British would not dare launch their weapons against the Soviet Union without American permission in any case.
3. Concerning the ABM, it was important to tie this issue to nuclear testing. Soviet negotiators should start at once to get an agreement to cease testing, in line with the Soviet temporary moratorium. Without testing, there can be no SDI. [46]

Gorbachev followed this advice at the Politburo meeting, accusing those who objected of wanting "to fight a nuclear war." Basing his position consistently on the spirit of his 15 January speech—which, of course, the military had not only agreed to but for which they had provided the basis — Gorbachev carried the day.[47] Obviously Chernyaev is putting himself in the best light in describing these episodes, and it may be that others, especially Shevardnadze, gave Gorbachev effective advice as well, but the evidence of the military's struggle to limit Gorbachev's initiative rings true, and Kornienko, long head of the American department of the foreign ministry, was of the Gromyko school, someone Marshal Akhromeev could count on.

The outcome at Reykjavik, on 11–12 October 1986, is well known and fully recorded in other accounts.[48] No specific progress was made because Reagan refused to yield on SDI, but the meeting marked a major turning point in the arms control process. By Chernyaev's account, Gorbachev and Reagan understood each other from the start. Reagan proved that he was indeed a man with an instinct for the demands of a historical occasion, as Mitterrand had said, very humane, nothing like the popular Soviet image of him. Thereafter Gorbachev never again referred to him as a "fool and a clown" or lamented having such an incompetent man as the leader of a superpower, as he had frequently done in the past. And all the future "good meetings," in Washington and Moscow owed much to this special moment in Reykjavik.[49] On the way back to Moscow, taking stock of the summit, Gorbachev, alone of the entourage, was ebullient. Chernyaev was disappointed but on reflection believed that a corner had been turned. It was now evident that arms control progress was possible and that the Geneva deadlock could be broken.

Detinov gives a similar positive assessment, noting that the lack of concrete agreements did not mean that the summit had achieved nothing and offering significant examples of its positive impact. Specifically, the Zero Option for INF had "become more viable," opening the way to the INF treaty. The Soviet position on strategic offensive weapons "contained most of the parameters of the START Treaty signed in 1991." [50] The Soviet side had signaled a willingness to drop its insistence on including U.S. forward-based systems and the British and French arsenals. These things changed the climate very much to the good at the Geneva negotiations. After Reykjavik, the Big Five also changed because the major issues were now being decided by Gorbachev in consultation with leaders from the foreign ministry and the defense ministry. In Brezhnev's time, the general secretary had given no input and had accepted what Ustinov compelled the Big Five to propose. Gorbachev, though, left the Big Five room for few debates; its task became making Soviet positions conform to the political guidance from on high.

The Long Last Mile to the INF Treaty

Notwithstanding the potential opening made at Reykjavik for reaching an INF agreement, negotiations were deadlocked during the next few months. The MoD had been cajoled into supporting Gorbachev's positions at Reykjavik, and shortly after it secured support from other departments for insisting on compensation from the Americans. Because the Soviets had agreed to drop the inclusion of British and French nuclear weapons in the INF negotiations, it was argued that INF should again be tied to cessation of the SDI program. Such a proposal was worked out among the Big Five departments and presented to the Politburo as an equitable compromise. According to Detinov, the MoD was "the most probable actor" behind this compromise, which undercut the understanding Gorbachev had conveyed to Reagan at Reykjavik and ensured that there would be no progress toward an INF agreement at Geneva.[51] Why Gorbachev accepted the Big Five's proposed position is unclear. Perhaps he felt that he had dragged the military as far as he dared for the moment, but his approval quickly stopped the very movement that he had pushed so hard to achieve.

Whatever the reason, he had regained the initiative by April 1987. Secretary Shultz came to Moscow early in the month to find some common ground, but rather than a narrowing of differences, the meeting left the Soviet officials wondering whether the United States was really serious about its Zero Option. Gorbachev apparently intended to find out. Toward the end of the month, the Soviet side offered a major new proposal in Geneva that called for removing all INF missiles from Europe within five years, permitting only one hundred warheads for such missiles to be located in the United States and east of the Urals, eliminating all medium-range missiles (those with a range of more than five hundred kilometers) in Europe, and establishing a strict verification regime, including on-site inspection if necessary. The American side was clearly astonished at this "double zero," as the Soviet officials called it, not to mention the acceptance of on-site inspection. In fact, it did not respond until early summer, when it insisted on the right to convert Pershing II missiles into the older and shorter-range model, the Pershing IB, and to put conventional warheads on ground-launched cruise missiles already deployed in Europe, among other conditions.[52]

Gorbachev reacted by raising the stakes. The Soviet side next proposed to make its "double zero" apply not just to Europe but globally. The European double zero position had been worked through the Big Five, but this global double zero came down from the Politburo, probably originating as Shevardnadze's initiative with Gorbachev's involvement. The military was simply excluded from the process because, as Detinov reports, it would have blocked that proposal in the Big Five; he also notes that most Soviet officials believed that the Americans would never accept it anyway.[53]

They were surprised, although the U.S. side raised a difficulty by insisting on the inclusion of the Soviet SS-23 missiles in Eastern Europe. U.S. intelligence assessments gave the SS-23 a range of five hundred kilometers, putting it within the treaty's limits for elimination. In fact, the range was only four hundred kilometers, and the Big Five members, categorically rejecting its inclusion, countered with a proposal to drop the INF limit to four hundred kilometers, a figure that could include the U.S. Lance-2 missiles in Germany. In September, when Shevardnadze visited Washington to set the stage for the final stage of the negotiations, he promised Shultz to include the SS-23. Back in Moscow, he persuaded Gorbachev to support this concession but at considerable political cost. Not only were the military and the VPK angry, but Kornienko of the MFA also agreed with Marshal Akhromeev's harsh criticism of Shevardnadze. In recalling these events, Detinov rejects the dissenters' charges that the staffing process was violated, leading to ill-considered and unwarranted concessions to the United States. Although Gorbachev did overrule the Big Five on a few occasions, lack of deliberations was never a fair charge. In retrospect, Detinov sees no basis for believing that the United States got special advantages, and he finds it difficult to see how Soviet military security was harmed in any way. It made no sense "to tie the hands and feet" of the political leadership, and that was what the military and VPK wanted to do. The real source of military and VPK discontent was that they had to destroy "about 240 modern, newly-deployed, and highly mobile missiles." [54]

When the INF treaty was signed in Washington in December 1987, Gorbachev could at last say he had reaped concrete result: 889 medium-range missiles, 654 SS-20s, and 957 shorter-range missiles were eliminated. Yet victory had its political costs. Shevardnadze was now an open target for his political enemies. Marshal Akhromeev formally supported the treaty in public statements but privately viewed it as a mistake. At the same time, retired military officers launched a massive letter-writing campaign not only at the Ministry of Foreign Affairs and the Ministry of Defense but also at the Central Committee and the KGB, hurling sharp criticism at the treaty.[55]

The benefits were probably not what Gorbachev, Shevardnadze, and others expected. Eliminating missiles that had already been produced and deployed did not provide much respite from military spending in the short run. Still, it was a beginning, and the political and psychological effect on the West was enormous. Gorbachev could now cite the INF treaty and the negotiations to withdraw from Afghanistan to the Politburo as deeds that made "new think-ing" more than empty talk in the mind of world opinion. Perhaps equally im-portant for Gorbachev was the change in personal relationships between him and Shevardnadze on the one hand and Reagan and Shultz on the other.

Chernyaev marks Shultz's trip to Moscow on 23 October 1987 as the precise time a fundamental change in U.S.-Soviet relations began. Not only were final details worked out to make the INF treaty possible, but the emer-gence of an informal "unified mechanism" was created between the Soviet and American negotiating teams involving both political and personal trust. She-vardnadze and Gorbachev had come to know and trust Shultz, and similar personal relationships were developing at the second levels on both sides. For Chernyaev, this aspect of the INF treaty accomplishment was no less impor-tant than the positive public statements. It prompted Gorbachev to expatiate to the Politburo at some length about how the human factor in the U.S.-Soviet relationship had transcended traditional political factors. As he put it, Reagan had been, in Soviet eyes, only "an expression of the most conservative part of American capitalism and the chief of the military-industrial complex, but now it was clear that he was a responsible leader, reflecting the interests and hopes of the most ordinary people."[56]

One consequence of the INF treaty, however, was to have a profound psychological effect on the military establishment. On-site verification was introduced for the first time, and that meant that Western observers would in-trude into heretofore sacrosanct military installations where even most Soviet civilian officials were not allowed. For the Soviet military, the VPK, and the KGB, secrecy had long been a barrier not just against foreign intelligence ser-vices but also against the Soviet public and, increasingly, the party leadership as well. The new intrusive verification methods did not open a large flow of information to the Soviet public—and yielded only a trickle of selected infor-mation to the United States—but to be forced to lower the curtain of secrecy even in very limited ways was traumatic for the military.[57]

Political Crisis and Recovery

The end of the cat-and-mouse game between Gorbachev and the military finally came in December of 1988, when he announced to the U.N. General As-sembly in New York that the Soviet military would carry out large unilateral reductions. But arms control did not move as swiftly to the next agreements as Gorbachev envisioned, and his attention was drawn more and more to do-mestic affairs. True, he remained active in foreign policy throughout 1988, but as Chernyaev observes, many of his visitors were from the socialist camp, foreign communist parties, and Third World countries. Here Gorbachev's foreign policy bumped up against resistance abroad to his "new thinking," with foreign communists doing less to encourage it than to impede it, especially in China and Cuba.[58]

Gorbachev nonetheless began the year with an unusual proposal to the Politburo concerning military policy. George Shultz had just visited Moscow, and Gorbachev was reporting on their discussions. He said,

> "Yes, we have achieved military-strategic parity with the United States. And no one knows what it cost us. But to calculate is needed. Now it is clear that without a significant reduction of military expenditures we cannot solve the problems of perestroika. Parity is parity, and we must preserve it. But we also need to disarm. And now that is possible. Because politically we have entered a new situation in our relations with the United States. . . .
>
> "Let's set the task to analyze fundamentally what a strong contemporary army means, what the maintenance of security means, what the qualitative dimension of security means. And when we have calculated all of that, cut all the rest."[59]

This straightforward mandate to the military got no response, and a short time later, Gorbachev took another approach, inviting a group of scientists to brief the Politburo on the state of Soviet computer science and technology. The comparative backwardness and poverty in which these scientists worked was soon painfully clear from their commentaries. After they departed, Gorbachev turned on Oleg Baklanov, chairman of the VPK, "And you, how much money do you devour? What does one stage of one of your rockets cost? You spit once into the cosmos, and billions, look, are flying there. And here they [the computer scientists] ask for crumbs."[60]

Notwithstanding these confrontational remarks to the Politburo, Gorbachev did not succeed in compelling the military and VPK to begin perestroika within their own ranks. In fact, except for implementing the INF treaty, the General Staff was left to its own devices most of the year. Shakhnazarov explains why. In the spring of 1988, although the military and the VPK had come to terms with the INF reductions, Gorbachev saw that limiting strategic nuclear arms, reducing the armed forces, and withdrawing troops from Eastern Europe were beyond his power. He had reached the limits of his personal authority in overriding his military leaders while they continued to drag their feet. "Gorbachev could not overcome that resistance without support from a parliament and public opinion," Shakhnazarov insisted. That meant political reform was imperative in order to begin military reform. "And another thing became clear: just as it was impossible without political reform to escape the monstrous burden of militarism, also without it, all efforts to breathe new life into the economy were doomed to failure." [61] Thus Gorbachev had to undertake political reform to keep perestroika from collapsing.

Perestroika was closer to collapse in 1988 than at any time before and probably any time after.[62] Several notable events mark the crisis, but five were conspicuous at the time and even more critical when reviewed with the retrospective advantage of the testimony of several of the participants. These events were the background for Gorbachev's announcement of unilateral force reductions at the United Nations in December 1988.

First, although Gorbachev had promulgated two new business laws in June 1987, giving firm managers the authority to conduct some of their affairs outside the state economic plan's rigid directions, the laws came into effect only at the beginning of 1988. In practice they created enormous confusion for the old command economic system without really allowing any of the advantages of a market economy. Moreover, Ligachev did not consider them a serious step toward a market system—which is probably why he went along with them.[63] Their very conception was flawed, but they signaled that Gorbachev recognized the failure of the "acceleration" program for the economy during 1985–86. Some of his advisers were trying to drag him to a fundamental break with the command system and a commitment to move toward a genuine market system, but Gorbachev, as was often his habit, looked for a compromise solution, combining competing policy alternatives. In this case, a compromise made no sense. The legal and institutional foundations for even a small market sector did not exist; yet yielding discretion over part of the output of firms to their managers caused serious dislocations in the state plan's fulfillment. Gorbachev's opponents, therefore, could point not just to his failure to produce improvements in the economy but also to the economy's worsening.[64]

Second, Gorbachev began to awake to the lack of positive results from his purge of party cadres. During the first two years of perestroika, he had removed around 60 percent of the oblast and raion party secretaries and replaced them with relatively young people, but as Gorbachev complained to the Politburo in the fall of 1987, they had changed nothing in the party ranks nor shown any capacity to absorb "new thinking." [65] His aides repeatedly underscored the party cadre problem, but there is a naïveté about their conviction that the proper set of new party officials might make a success of the economy. Soviet institutions simply could not accommodate a mixed planned and market economy, and the necessary changes in institutions would inexorably destroy the Soviet system.[66]

Even in retrospect, Shakhnazarov sees the impossibility of finding effective party cadres but is reluctant to admit that there was no way out. He was convinced that political reform offered a solution if it involved building new state structures, based on law, to replace the party structures and their lack of any legal restraints.[67]

Third, Nina Andreeva's infamous epistle, "I Cannot Waive Principles," appeared in *Sovetskaya Rossiya* on 13 March 1988, offering a bitter critique of perestroika, condemning glasnost, and challenging Gorbachev's ideological revisions just as he was leaving on a trip abroad. For a time it was exploited in party circles as a signal that glasnost was at an end. When Gorbachev first glanced over the article, he saw nothing unusual about it, actually sympathizing with its criticism of excesses in the press. Valery Boldin thought at the time that Raisa Gorbachev, "the family ideologist," as he described her, probably liked it very much.[68] Aleksandr Yakovlev, of course, was outraged and did not let its implications escape Gorbachev. Two days of Politburo meetings on the matter opened his eyes to the depth of opposition he faced among its members. Although he convinced its members to condemn Andreeva's piece, he did not force Ligachev to admit responsibility for it. Moreover, the troublemaking did not end, as party organizations in a number of cities continued to distribute the essay for a time for discussion and guidance.[69]

Fourth, the Nineteenth Party Conference, 28 June–1 July 1988, was the instrument Gorbachev used to endorse the political reform that he had belatedly come to believe was imperative. Given the standoff in the Politburo between Ligachev and Yakovlev over the Nina Andreeva affair, he realized that he had to find a way to shift the balance of political power against those who were obstructing perestroika. Chernyaev reveals Gorbachev's frustration in a telephone conversation with him in the early spring. Complaining bitterly about the Council of Ministers' thumb twiddling, about Yakovlev's demands for more aggressive criticism and movement on perestroika, about Ligachev's insistence that economic plans be fulfilled, even if everything should collapse as a result, Gorbachev added, "And look, what are they doing on that side (in the West)? Everything is moving there—and here you have the nationality question, the Tatar question, the Jewish question, and they are trying to set the military against me, and in the leadership they try to play off one against the other."[70] "New thinking" abroad was lurching far ahead of "new thinking" at home. Action on the domestic front was imperative. Already at the February Central Committee Plenum, Gorbachev had raised the idea of the party's renouncing its political monopoly over the state. By giving real policy-making power to "law-based state" structures, he intended to prevent the party apparatus from blocking perestroika. He envisioned himself in a dual role, as "president–general secretary," in charge of both.[71]

This was a risky strategy. It required getting the party leadership to abandon its status outside the constraints of any law but "the revolution." Although Gorbachev spoke candidly to three closed meetings of the top 150 party regional leaders about his aim to make the party responsible before a democratic process and subject to state laws, he showed caution in choice of modalities for achieving it.[72] In early April, he directed a small group, including Yakovlev, Nikolai Slyunkov, Medvedev, Boldin, Shakhnazarov, Chernyaev, and a few others, to work them out.[73] The changes Gorbachev had in mind required more authority than either the Politburo or Central Committee had under the party rules. To convene a party congress might cause alarm. Thus a party conference was chosen—a forum last used by Stalin before World War II—because it enjoyed virtually the same powers as a party congress. It could change the top party leadership and alter the party rules. For a time, Gorbachev considered using the occasion to sweep the Politburo and Central Committee clean of opponents of perestroika, but he dropped the idea.[74]

Astonishingly, the Politburo supported his aims for the Nineteenth Party Conference. According to Shakhnazarov, as its members addressed the conference resolutions on 19 May, they spoke about them "in the most flattering terms"—for example, "the document fully corresponds to the revolutionary course of the party," another was "an enormous contribution to the development of Leninist theory," and so on. Then the Politburo offered "to enrich the theses." Ligachev wanted to add "class interests" to "humankind interests," and Vladimir Shcherbitskii, the Ukrainian party boss, wondered how the party's political power would be saved during the democratization process.[75] Gorbachev made some concessions, dropping the proposal to co-opt new Central Committee members—a mistake, in Shakhnazarov's view, but not as egregious as his failure to purge the Politburo. Looking back on it, Shakhnazarov reasons that Gorbachev must have thought, "If the General Secretary is prepared to risk the infringement of his own unlimited power in order to remove the enormous gap between constitutional principles and political practice, then why suspect that experienced members of the Politburo and the Central Committee will rise against it? If any of them do, it will be easy to deal with them." This "simple-minded belief" about how his colleagues would behave had permitted Gorbachev to push through all his earlier innovations, but in this case, the very monopoly of power by the party was at stake.[76]

The Nineteenth Party Conference convened and approved the theses for political reform, laying the groundwork for the dramatic events in the spring of 1989, when genuinely competitive elections produced the new Congress of People's Deputies. Why did Ligachev and the opposition go along with this scheme, one that would be their undoing in 1989–91? Apparently they believed they could turn it into empty rhetoric. Resolutions about strengthening the "soviets" had been common at party congresses ever since Lenin's time, and now party agitators, ideologists, and journalists were calling "a law-based state," the key idea in the Nineteenth Party Conference theses, "the triumph of socialist legality," putting the reform in "an elementary ideological framework," using the "classical canons" to justify Gorbachev's latest ideas.[77]

Exploitation of glasnost by the media may help explain why Gorbachev could push his formulas through the party conference, although it could be argued that glasnost was inspiring his opponents to resist more strongly. Frequently angered by what he called media excesses, Gorbachev nonetheless backed Yakovlev's relentless encouragement of glasnost. Ligachev's unrelenting hostility toward Yakovlev—and his inspiration, no doubt, for facilitating the publication of Nina Andreeva's letter—derived primarily from Yakovlev's defense of growing radicalism in the media.[78] But Ligachev and his supporters failed to shore up the dam against glasnost. The consequences for military affairs would be decisive, and as we have seen, staff members of the many research institutes in Moscow were already publishing articles in 1987 and 1988 on "defensive doctrine," "reasonable sufficiency," and "new thinking" in foreign policy, elaborating and interpreting these terms for a wider readership. Gorbachev, of course, had intended just such a discourse. The political power for driving through his political reform had to come in large measure from mass public support and intelligentsia activism that would intimidate his party opposition. Not surprisingly, Chernyaev entitles the chapter in his memoir on the year 1988 "Glasnost Finds Force." Indeed, by the end of that year, it was becoming a strong force for military reform.

The fifth significant development of the year was Gorbachev's shake-up of the leadership at the end of September. It will be recalled that Ligachev challenged Gorachev publicly in August 1988, telling an audience in Gor'ki that talk about "humankind interests" transcending the international class struggle was confusing both the Soviet people and Soviet friends abroad.[79] Gorbachev was especially startled that Ligachev would say such things after the decisions of the Nineteenth Party conference. As surmised earlier, this event seems to have been the catalyst for the September leadership changes and Central Committee reorganization.[80] Gorbachev eviscerated the Secretariat, reducing its twenty-three departments to nine and creating six commissions, each headed by a party secretary. He retired Gromyko, Mikhail Solomentsev, Petr Demichev, and Vladimir Dolgykh from the Politburo. Chebrikov lost his KGB post but remained a member of the Politburo and a party secretary. Vitalii Vorotnikov, a conservative appointed by Andropov in 1983, stayed in the Politburo but was moved to the chairmanship of the Supreme Soviet of the RSFSR ("Let him twist there," said Gorbachev). Slyunkov was appointed the head of one of the new commissions in secretariat. Anatolii Dobrynin, former ambassador to the United States, lost his job as a party secretary. (Gorbachev said, "Put him on pension. He did not make it as a secretary. He was an ambassador and remained one.") Although Ligachev was obviously the major target of the shake-up, Yakovlev was also downgraded somewhat, made head of the International Department while losing to Medvedev his responsibility for ideology, which he had shared with Ligachev. Ligachev remained a Politburo member and a party secretary, but he lost his responsibility for ideology and became chairman of the commission on agriculture. Gorbachev at first thought of relegating him to head of the Party Control Commission but then chose Boris Pugo instead for that innocuous post. ("He is honest, smart. In Latvia he didn't make it, was not at home there.")[81]

Although Gorbachev pretended that this sudden change in leadership and the organization of the central party apparatus was merely a logical step in the process of political reform, it was widely seen as his "mini–coup d'état."[82] Chernyaev and Shakhnazarov realized at the time what Gorbachev did not. The sooner he became "president of the Soviet Union" the better, because he had dealt a blow to the party which it would not forgive and from which it would not recover.[83] Yet Gorbachev clung to the idea that the party could be made into an effective instrument for implementing perestroika. His advisers may have been wrong. Precisely this duality in his personality that they wanted to overcome allowed him to keep his party opponents confused, convinced that he would not go too far. And he did confuse them. Ligachev would later call him "an incomprehensible puzzle."[84]

Unilateral Force Reductions

On 3 November, Gorbachev initiated a process for approval of his announcement of force reductions before the United Nations in December. To set the stage in the Politburo, he referred to a recent meeting with Komsomol youth who had asked him, "Why do we need such a large army?" Letters from ordinary citizens, a mass of them, were asking the same question. Moreover, at the Nineteenth Party Conference, "the resolutions said we need quality, not quantity." Also troubling, the U.S. secretary of state, George Shultz, was asking about the contradiction between the new defensive doctrine and actual Soviet weapons and force deployments. Moreover, the Soviet Union had announced its readiness to disclose what it spent on defense. What if it became public information that the Soviet Union spends two and a half times as much on defense as the United States? That would make a mockery of Soviet foreign policy. Then Gorbachev turned on Yazov, saying that the Hungarians were complaining that Soviet troops were stationed on the site of a national monument. Admitting that it was true, Yazov added that the troops were being withdrawn. Next Gorbachev said talks had to begin with the Warsaw Pact states about Soviet force deployments. All these issues, Gorbachev suggested, should be put to the Defense Council for analysis and a report to the Politburo. The entire Politburo nodded in approval. Ryzhkov then spoke, declaring that the standard of living could not be raised without major military cuts. At that point, Gorbachev dropped the shoe: "If we are all agreed and we are coming out for major decisions, including unilateral reductions, . . . then I think I'll announce that at the U.N." The Politburo answered in unison, "Yes, yes." With that decision in his pocket, Gorbachev rephrased the argument, trying to be reassuring. As Ryzhkov had said, perestroika is impossible without some cuts from the VPK and the military. "But there is no question: we must be strong militarily. But that is for security, not to scare people."[85] In his diary entry on this meeting, Chernyaev wrote, "Historic."

This initiative, abrupt though Chernyaev makes it seem from the reactions in the Politburo, was not entirely unexpected. Marshal Akhromeev said that the General Staff had become quite aware of the worsening economic conditions in 1987 and that by the beginning of 1988 it sensed the need for unilateral reductions without any direction from Gorbachev. Akhromeev also declared that the Defense Council, with Gorbachev's participation, had frequently worked over military plans, including research and development work and procurement programs as set forth in the five-year plan (1986–90).[86] Unilateral reductions were discussed to a mixed reception at a conference in the foreign ministry in late July with Akhromeev in attendance.[87] In a journal article published in October, Shevardnadze hinted strongly at unilateral reductions if NATO would not cooperate in mutual reductions.[88] Upcoming preparations of the next five-year plan in 1989 probably made Gorbachev realize that if he did not act soon, he might have to wait another five years.

The precise timing, however, appears to have been chosen rather suddenly, during the week before the 3 November Politburo meeting. Gorbachev had staged the meeting with Komsomol youth two days earlier, talking to them about the size of the military.[89] The day before Gorbachev had discussed his intentions with Shevardnadze, Yakovlev, Valentin Falin, and Dobrynin, and he had directed Chernyaev to begin drafting his U.N. speech to include the unilateral reductions.[90] Shevardnadze may even have suggested the U.N. meeting as the occasion for announcing the unilateral cuts. He certainly had been thinking of reducing Soviet forces in Eastern Europe ever since Tarasenko's memorandum proposing such action in 1985.[91]

A number of events also suggest that anger and growing impatience with the military and the VPK inspired Gorbachev simply to order them to make serious resource concessions. As he told the Politburo, Shultz repeatedly reminded him and Shevardnadze that Soviet military doctrine and military actions were noticeably inconsistent, an accumulating embarrassment to them throughout 1988. To make matters worse, Gorbachev more than once discovered that he was being deceived by both the military and the VPK. The Krasnoyarsk radar was clearly a violation of the ABM treaty, and the Soviet side finally had to admit it. In the aftermath of the Chernobyl accident, Gorbachev learned that the VPK routinely misled the Central Committee about nuclear affairs. A most disturbing event occurred during the late summer, when the American and British ambassadors called on Chernyaev to deliver messages from Bush and Thatcher. Both governments had "fresh evidence" that the Soviet bacteriological weapons program was continuing, violating the international convention against such weaponry and producing much greater quantities for biological material for weapons than were necessary for research. When Chernyaev expressed doubt, they reminded him that the Soviet side had had to reverse its first position on the Krasnoyarsk radar and requested an official answer on this additional violation for their leaders.[92] Chernyaev's written report of this meeting to Gorbachev certainly suggests that Chernyaev did not know of the Soviet bacteriological weapons program. Given that Gorbachev immediately ordered an investigation, he too was apparently ignorant of it.

Soviet arms sales abroad also became a nettlesome issue in 1988 and were part of the Defense Council's discussion on the unilateral force reduction decision. At the end of September, Shevardnadze became so frustrated by his inability to influence Soviet arms exports that he wrote Gorbachev an "official protest," complaining that the VPK was making agreements for arms deliveries that undercut Gorbachev's foreign policy, giving the West reason to doubt its sincerity. Why, he asked, was it necessary to promise to Algeria, Ethiopia, and North Korea, as the VPK had just done, deliveries that would not be complete even by the year 2000? Gorbachev directed an investigation, but nothing of consequence resulted, as Chernyaev noted—even in the 1990s, after the Soviet Union was abolished.[93]

By fall 1988 Gorbachev was obviously fed up with the foot-dragging by the military and the VPK, but it was only after he had gained the Nineteenth Party Conference's approval for political reform, shaken up Politburo, and reorganized the secretariat that he felt strong enough to retake the initiative. Still, he had to push his unilateral reduction plan through the Defense Council.

Precisely how the Defense Council handled its tasks from the 3 November Politburo meeting is not known, but according to Chernyaev—who knew of it only from hearsay afterward—it thoroughly examined the figures Gorbachev announced at the United Nations. The General Staff had only about a month to develop its recommendations and arguments, and given that Marshal Akhromeev resigned as chief of the General Staff immediately following Gorbachev's announcement, the Defense Council deliberations were probably acrimonious. In light of his exchange with Shakhnazarov about the need for such large Warsaw Pact forces, it is not difficult to imagine his reaction to Gorbachev's proposal. In any event, on 7 December, Gorbachev told the world that the Soviet Union had decided to reduce its armed forces:

> In the next two years, . . . personnel will be decreased by 500,000 men, the volume of conventional weapons will be reduced considerably. These reductions will be carried in a unilateral fashion, outside the negotiations under the Vienna mandate.
>
> In agreement with our allies in the Warsaw Treaty, we took the decision to withdraw, by 1991, six tank divisions from the GDR, Czechoslovakia, and Hungary and disband them. From the groups of forces located in these countries, air assault and a series of other formations and units, including river-crossing units, will be withdrawn with their weapons and combat equipment. Soviet forces located in these countries will be reduced by 50,000 men, and in weaponry, by 5,000 tanks.
>
> All remaining Soviet divisions on the territory of our allies will be reorganized. They will be given a different structure from what they have today, which, after the enormous withdrawal of tanks from them, will become only defensive.
>
> At the same time, we will also reduce the number of personnel of our forces and the quantity of their weapons in the European part of the USSR.
>
> In all, on this part of our country and on the territory of our European allies, the Soviet Armed Forces will be reduced by 10,000 tanks, 8,500 artillery systems, and 800 combat aircraft.
>
> In these same two years we also will considerably reduce the grouping

of the Armed Forces in the Asian part of our country. In agreement with the Mongolian People's Republic, a significant part of the Soviet forces temporarily located there will return to the homeland.[94]

This announcement caused the international sensation Gorbachev expected. When he talked about the new military doctrine henceforth, about "reasonable and reliable sufficiency," as he did in this speech and frequently later on, it would be difficult to accuse him of strategic deception. The reductions in forces received all of the public attention at the time, but another point in the speech was equally important, especially for the economic advantages Gorbachev sought. The reduction in forces only took resources from the military, not the VPK. Thus Gorbachev added, immediately after enumerating the force reductions, that another important problem had to be addressed—the *"transition from an economy of armament to an economy of disarmament."*[95] "Is conversion of military production realistic?" "Yes," he said, adding that "the Soviet Union is ready:

to work out and present its own domestic conversion plan in the framework of economic reform;

to prepare plans, in the form of a qualitative experiment, for conversion of two to three defense plants in the course of 1989;

to publish the results of retraining specialists from military industry and also of using their tools, buildings, and facilities in civilian production.[96]

Here was the origin of what would later become the "military conversion plan." Little noticed at the time, it would become the center of policy and public attention in the next two years. The details of the military reductions were hastily put together in November, but this scheme of converting military-industrial firms to civilian production apparently was even more hastily developed. And it would prove far more intractable than force reductions.

The year had been difficult, and the outside observer at the time could easily conclude that perestroika was going nowhere, especially in the military sphere. The military seemed to be winning the game of cat and mouse by rendering the new defensive doctrine an empty slogan. With his U.N. speech, however, Gorbachev dragged the mouse out of the hole where the whole world could see whether or not it was following orders.

It was a threshold year, not just in military policy but in perestroika across the board. Gorbachev survived a political crisis, weakening the party without wholly destroying it, leaving it unable to help him but still able to hurt him. At the party conference in June he had compelled it to agree to political reforms that would dramatically widen the arena for military policy making. Also in 1988, glasnost began to bring heretofore concealed military issues into the public eye. The significance of this development must be traced in some detail.

EIGHT

Glasnost and the Public Debate

Without glasnost it would be ridiculous to talk about democratization.

V. I. LENIN

The INF treaty could have been fully implemented without significant change in overall Soviet force structure. Reducing manpower by 500,000 (from a total of about 5.2 million) personnel and cutting 10,000 tanks (from 53,000), 8,500 artillery systems (from 29,000), 800 combat aircraft (from about 4,880) was another matter, especially in light of the demobilization of six divisions in Eastern Europe and the withdrawal of 50,000 personnel.[1] The General Staff could no longer pretend that "new thinking" was only for Western consumption. It had to act.

Gorbachev counted on his political reforms to help force the military to respond to his new policies. Multicandidate elections for the Congress of People's Deputies in spring 1989 produced an entirely new political context. After the heavy fire of Nina Andreeva's letter sent them scurrying to their bunkers of self-censorship in the spring of 1988, editors and writers waited for several weeks and then returned to the parapets of glasnost to return her fire and expand their ranks beyond the captains of the intelligentsia to include foot soldiers from the ordinary citizenry. Interviews on television and letters to newspapers became the weapons of the wider public in the campaign for perestroika. Aleksandr Yakovlev, exercising his Politburo duty to oversee the media, was clearly behind this counterattack, and with Gorbachev's blessings. This wider glasnost campaign also involved a new legislature—the Supreme Soviet—and the popularly elected Congress of People's Deputies. Both offered an open political forum for debating military policy. But these new political institutions were created only in the summer of 1989; in the meantime, articulation of alternative military policies began in the media. Later, the civilian reformers, joined by a few young military officers, carried the struggle for military reform into the new legislature.

Beyond this fairly sophisticated debate, the broader public began to reveal its own views, sometimes offering specific solutions to particular military policy questions but more often expressing complaints and dissatisfaction with the Soviet military. Senior military officers and orthodox party officials responded with unconcealed anger. The variety of voices in this wider public defies easy categorization. Mothers, fathers, wives, and families of ordinary soldiers became vociferous, if not always harmoniously so. Privileged families in Moscow sought exemption from conscription for their children so that they could continue their education without interruption. Similar voices in the Baltic region and in the Transcaucasus began to articulate nationalist sentiments, becoming entangled with the larger issue of sovereignty in several of the union republics. Retired officers, veterans, Afghan veterans within the veterans' groups, and, finally, groups of serving officers added cacophony to the glasnost chorus. An explosion of this kind of public expression marked the last three years of Gorbachev's rule.[2]

Glasnost, of course, had already produced divisive commentary on military affairs before 1989, but in that year and through 1991, the debate revealed new force, surprising candor, and bitter acrimony. As Boldin noted, Gorbachev's "savage" anger over the Rust flight to Moscow foreshadowed his "feed[ing] the military" to the parliament, the media, and public opinion. Clearly this was part of his strategy for overcoming the military's obstinacy against "new thinking" and perestroika in its own ranks.

This chapter focuses only on one narrow part of glasnost: the role of the specialists and scholars in the several institutes in Moscow dedicated to the study of foreign affairs in general and security problems in particular. Most conspicuous among them were the Institute for World Economy and International Relations (IMEMO) and the Institute for the Study of the USA and Canada (ISKAN). Aleksandr Yakovlev was the director of IMEMO, and Georgii Arbatov was the director of ISKAN when Gorbachev became the general secretary. Yakovlev's influence on Gorbachev, of course, was strong. From Chernyaev's memoirs it is also clear that Arbatov had direct access to Gorbachev and frequently participated in discussions with him and his advisers. The Institute for the Economics of the World Socialist System, headed by Oleg Bogomolov and possessing a strong staff of scholars, also played an influential role, but more in economic and foreign policy than in military policy and strategy. Several other heads of institutes in the scholarly community also influenced Gorbachev on domestic policy, especially concerning the economy, but they were largely silent on military policy, though a few of their institute staff members offered important contributions.

The Yakovlev connection helps explain the role of the security and foreign policy specialists, particularly because he soon moved from IMEMO to the Central Committee and then joined the Politburo in early 1987. And it will be recalled that he was Gorbachev's front man when Ligachev and others tried to tone down the media's exploitation of glasnost. Arbatov struggled, with less success, for his own place among the influential. He had long competed with Anatolii Dobrynin, the Soviet ambassador in Washington, for primacy as the most informed voice on U.S. policy, but Dobrynin maintained the inside track until he was brought back to the Central Committee in March 1986 and then ousted in September 1988. Arbatov proved more adept at exploiting glasnost, for an obvious reason. His institute staff included some of the brightest and most articulate analysts, just as did Yakovlev's staff at IMEMO. Both produced the earliest attempts to put substance into the slogans of the new military doctrine.

Another group of participants in the debate included a few younger military officers. Lieutenant Colonel Aleksandr Savinkin, Major Vladimir Lopatin, and a number of others took a leading role. Precisely why they began to speak out is not clear. Poor conditions of life in the lower military ranks certainly justified it, but unless they were quietly encouraged by Central Committee officials working for Yakovlev, they risked their careers by joining the critics. The institutes probably encouraged them in order to gain allies within the military's own ranks. The institute staffs included several retired officers, but they needed a stronger base within the active military. In any event, Lopatin worked closely with some of the civilian reformers. A set of conservative younger officers also emerged to condemn the Lopatins and Savinkins. Colonel Viktor Alksnis was one of the more notorious "black colonels," as they were sometimes called.

A few senior officers also genuinely supported reform. Colonel General Dmitrii Volkogonov was the most senior and the most notable of these, but rather than making common cause with a particular group, he used his position as director of the MoD's Military History Institute to begin revising Soviet official history.[3]

Lack of authoritative information about the Soviet military handicapped all these critics and reformers. To make a case for major reductions and to propose alternative policies and strategies, they needed to know the size, structure, weaponry, fiscal outlays, and many other details. All such information was considered secret by the military. Even when Gorbachev forced the publication of fiscal outlays to defense in the spring of 1989, the military initially resisted, then released incomplete and confusing figures. Ironically, the civilian critics turned to Western sources, and not just for numbers of weapons, the budget, and the like, but also for analytic concepts and ideas about military force structure and strategy. As one member of the ISKAN staff put it, he and his colleagues had spent years learning to understand Western strategic and military viewpoints. Denied access to Soviet official military thinking and information, they resorted to Western data on Soviet forces and adapted Western concepts to the Soviet internal debate.[4] They could do this because scholars in IMEMO and ISKAN were essentially overt intelligence collectors, gathering all the information they could about U.S. and NATO military affairs and interpreting it for the Soviet government. Many of them had acquired great competency in thinking and talking in Western military categories. As glasnost gave them the opportunity, they employed that ability with impressive skill in the debate on Soviet military policy.

At first the defense ministry ignored them, especially in 1987–88. By 1988, its spokesmen began to respond, at first by dismissing these civilians as professionally incompetent in military affairs, later with more visceral language. They were, of course, defending the set of what we have seen were the interests and objectives pursued by Soviet grand strategy, although they never set forth either the goals or the strategy in such an explicit fashion. Understanding both, however, is essential for grasping just how radical the critics' challenges to them appeared to the defense ministry leadership. Although these public exchanges make up a fairly vast literature, elaboration of the main arguments in a selected few will expose the core issues and the way all sides dealt with them.

What Did the New Doctrine Mean?

The most general issue concerned the essence of "defensive defense," as the new doctrine was sometimes called. In writing their article on the World War II battle of Kursk, A. A. Kokoshin and retired Major General V. V. Larionov were borrowing the military's favorite laboratory for developing contemporary doctrine—the Great Fatherland War, as World War II was called in the Soviet Union.[5] Virtually every aspect of Soviet military doctrine, strategy, operations, and tactics was grounded in World War II experience—especially the last years of the war, when the Red Army was on the offensive, conducting large frontal operations, sometimes involving more than a hundred kilometers of depth in a single operation.[6] Thus Kokoshin and Larionov were speaking in terms very familiar to the General Staff. As pointed out earlier, Marshal Akhromeev's own comments in the United States were rooted in the experience of World War II. Akhromeev noted in his memoir that the Ministry of Defense and the General

Staff foresaw as early as 1986 what the consequences of the new doctrine would be for the Soviet Armed Forces. He and Marshal Sergei L. Sokolov, defense minister at that time, frequently discussed the possibility of the collapse of the Warsaw Pact security system and the ensuing impact on the entire structure of the Soviet military.[7] After Yazov replaced Sokolov as defense minister, Yazov and Akhromeev prepared a document outlining the implications for military redeployments, especially the social impact that they would have on military personnel, and presented it to Gorbachev. Although Gorbachev reviewed the report with his close advisers, he never shared his reaction with them.[8]

Thus it is not surprising that military authors did not pick up on the Kokoshin-Larionov concept. For the top military leaders the implications were too traumatic. Instead, their spokesmen struggled with reconciling Gorbachev's new formulas with their traditional formulas for explaining war and how to deal with it.[9] Political officers struggled with the abandonment of international class struggle and the primacy of "humankind interests" over "class interests." Some simply refused to try to deal with such ideological revisions.[10] For the most part, they paid lip service to Gorbachev's formulas but little more. While acknowledging that "preventing war" rather than "preparing to win a war" was the military's new task, they showed little comprehension of Gorbachev's "new thinking" about how this was to be done.

Rethinking Nuclear Weapons

Because Gorbachev made the nuclear weapons issue the centerpiece of his ideological revisions and foreign policy, it was the first topic addressed by the civilian analysts. Not only had he renounced the military's view that it had to be prepared to fight and win a nuclear war, but he also condemned Western deterrence strategy as equally unacceptable.[11] Both approaches assumed the political utility of nuclear weapons, an assumption that he flatly rejected. This kind of "new thinking" provided the civilian analysts with no principles or criteria—either of Soviet origin or from Western theories—for deciding an appropriate size and structure for Soviet nuclear forces (other than their total elimination). The military, meanwhile, not only stubbornly maintained its information monopoly to prevent "new thinking" about criteria but also adhered to an old criterion of the Brezhnev era, "equal security" through arms control agreements. Under that arrangement, Soviet nuclear weapons would be cut only in step with the United States, France, and Britain, a formula for a very slow-paced reduction. That simply left the field open for the civilian analysts who knew little about Soviet nuclear weapons doctrine but a lot about U.S. doctrine.

Some of them made a valiant attempt to understand the Soviet military's approach to nuclear weapons. Most notably, A. I. Bulanov and I. A. Krylova, in an article published in 1988, reviewed all the open Soviet literature on the topic.[12] They discovered that while a few voices, military and civilian, had argued that nuclear weapons could not be used to win a war, a so-called pre-nuclear viewpoint prevailed, treating nuclear weapons as usable to fight wars. They were new and powerful but not did change the nature of warfare. The authors discovered no specific indications of how nuclear weapons would be employed in support of wartime operations, however, only the military's conviction that they could be used to achieve victory. Not surprisingly, then, the civilian scholars turned to Western strategic thought for practical ideas about proper sizing and missions for nuclear forces.

A group of analysts in Institute for the Study of the USA and Canada (ISKAN)—Andrei Kokoshin, Aleksei Arbatov, and A. A. Vasiliev—had already taken this approach as early as 1984. They developed a computer-based model for nuclear exchanges that allowed them to test several variants, and in 1988, glasnost enabled Kokoskin to publish some of the results.[13] The researchers showed that stability could best be maintained by 50 percent reductions on both sides, but that increases in antiballistic missile defense (ABM) and antisubmarine warfare capabilities (ASW) by either side could upset this balance. At 75 percent reductions, ABM and ASW capabilities had a greater potential for disturbing the balance. At 95 percent reduction levels, the nuclear capabilities of third parties—Britain, France, and China—could not be left outside the arms control regime because even those small arsenals would become significant for the overall balance. This analysis apparently did not offend the Soviet military. It assumed mutual reductions at equal levels, something that the military had accepted in principle, and it emphasized the destabilizing effect of missile defenses, a view very much in line with the military's emotional reaction against President Reagan's Strategic Defense Initiative.

That changed in 1989 when Arbatov, whose father, Georgii, was the director of ISKAN, discussed the targets for nuclear weapons. He insisted that "counterforce" targeting—nuclear attacks aimed at the opponent's strategic nuclear forces for the purpose of reducing them and of "limiting damage" to one's own side—was nonsense. The only rational purpose for nuclear targeting was "countervalue"—destroying something of great value to the opponent with the aim of inflicting "unacceptable damage."[14] Here Arbatov was introducing three key Western concepts into the Soviet lexicon—counterforce, countervalue, and damage limitation—concepts that had been consistently rejected by the Soviet side during nearly two decades of arms control negotiations. Applying them to Soviet nuclear forces, Arbatov insisted that a 40–50 percent reduction in nuclear forces would leave an entirely adequate arsenal, though he complained that he could not be more precise because of the lack of information about the actual size of the Soviet nuclear forces. And he called for a reconsideration of the ABM system around Moscow, permitted under the 1972 treaty, suggesting that it might be scrapped to save money.

Other analysts also advanced arguments, basing them either implicitly or explicitly on Western concepts, but Arbatov was the most straightforward in calling for large cuts in nuclear forces. Throughout the next two years, the civilian critics repeatedly wielded these arguments in their relentless attack on the military.

The military's reaction came at two levels. The most senior officers responded obliquely and in general terms, remaining above this technical debate in 1988–90. The defense minister, General Dmitrii Yazov; the new chief of the General Staff, General Mikhail Moiseev; the General Staff's chief of arms control, Colonel General Nikolai Chervov; and the chief of the military science directorate, Colonel General Makhmut Gareev, merely hewed to Gorbachev's line about ridding the world of nuclear weapons. They left the direct attack on the civilian analysts to lower-ranking officers. Their point man, Colonel V. Strebkov, published an article about the same time as Arbatov's in which he criticized all criteria that yielded specific numbers of nuclear weapons. He wanted an open-ended measure allowing forces that would "not permit an unanswered nuclear attack on our country in any way, even in the most unfavorable conditions." Furthermore, he argued, geographical and other differences between the positions of the Soviet Union and the United States disallowed the use of the same sizing standard for nuclear forces.[15] Later Strebkov would attack Arbatov directly, ridiculing his use of such concepts as "unacceptable damage" and "countervalue" targeting.[16]

The senior military pronouncements in support of total elimination of nuclear weapons were actually closer to Gorbachev's own views than those of the civilian analysts. Unlike the generals, these civilians were accepting Western deterrence theory, which Gorbachev had explicitly rejected. Still, their arguments were of use to Gorbachev for pressuring the military to be specific about much smaller nuclear forces.

Defining Soviet Interests

"New thinking" radically transformed the issue of what constituted Soviet strategic interests and what threatened them. Surprisingly little attention was devoted to defining specific "threats" to Soviet security during the discussion on the new military doctrine in 1987 and 1988. The old threat, of course, the entire capitalist-imperialist world, had been summarily dismissed by Gorbachev in his ideological revisions. If the imperialists were no longer the primary danger to the Soviet Union, then who was? Military writers, as noted earlier, were attempting to hold on to the "international class struggle" as they incorporated "humankind interests" into their treatment of this issue. Senior officers continued to emphasize the growing military strength of NATO as evidence that it remained hostile in spite of Gorbachev's foreign policy.

One notable early attempt at redefining Soviet interests and threats to them was offered in January 1988 by three scholars in ISKAN.[17] They began with the postulate from Gorbachev's "new thinking" that security is indivisible and can no longer be sustained by military means: if one country has security, then all countries must be secure. Logically, therefore, thinking about Soviet security also had to take into account the security of all other states, especially imperialist countries. To make the security interests of the imperialist camp a concern for the Soviet military leaders was indeed a departure—and, as the authors recognized, not a congenial one. Yet it was imperative, given the premises of "new thinking." The old question of how the Soviet Union was to survive a hostile encirclement, they argued, was no longer relevant. The old answer to that question—considering virtually all foreign states as the enemy and building ever greater military power—had caused serious domestic policy errors that undermined security, compounded domestic difficulties, and mindlessly wasted resources.

But the authors did not go very far in specifying a new approach to defining and defending specific Soviet interests. They merely called for viewing the competition between socialism and capitalism in a "new complex of global problems" and warned against "absolutizing" past problems in the categories of the two-camp struggle. Still, for late 1987 and early 1988, they were presenting a fairly bold challenge to the General Staff's view of interests and the threats.

In 1989, such moderation gave way to candid specificity, as two analysts threw down the gauntlet. Georgii Kunadze and Sergei Blagovolin were both senior scholars in IMEMO, previously headed by Yakovlev, and although both undoubtedly shared many of his views, they were independent and original thinkers. Their ties to Yakovlev, though, makes their analyses of particular interest.[18]

Kunadze began by roundly criticizing the military for failing to define "defensive sufficiency" in practical terms.[19] Then he proceeded to lecture them on three central issues that he felt they did not understand but had to comprehend correctly before they could carry out perestroika in the armed forces.

The first concerned the way Soviet interests were defined. Ideological "stereotypical" thinking had to be abandoned. Until that was done, no "new thinking" would be possible in the Ministry of Defense. To help start thinking anew, he posited two categories of Soviet interests, those beyond Soviet borders and those within them. Very few Soviet interests abroad deserved to be defended by military means. The entire Third World merited no Soviet military commitments. In the past such commitments had always been justified by the imperatives of the international class struggle. Taking a sober, nonideological view of the Third World, he argued, would reveal not only that there were no Soviet security interests in those regions but also that Soviet involvement there had created a heavy economic burden while producing no gains. On this point the Soviet Navy drew Kunadze's biting criticism. Only Soviet ideological ambitions in the Third World justified its size. By dropping ideological lenses, one could see that the navy ought to be radically reduced. Only in Europe was there a Soviet interest beyond its borders deserving a military commitment. To meet it, Soviet conventional forces should be kept in balance with NATO forces, because failure to do so would prompt reliance on tactical nuclear weapons, something unacceptable in light of Gorbachev's goal of eliminating all nuclear weapons. With the exception of Europe, only domestic interests—the defense of Soviet territory—merited military forces.

Kunadze's second issue concerned "how" to defend Soviet territory. Should the whole country be defended uniformly, or should it be differentiated by regions? In his view, the Far East should be treated separately. Large military forces had been deployed there to counter U.S. military capabilities in northeast Asia and to support the Soviet foreign policy goal of expelling the U.S. presence from the region. This strategic reasoning made no sense at all because it failed to take into account that the U.S. presence was a stabilizing factor in northeast Asia. It prevented Japanese rearmament and war in Korea. To remove U.S. forces would create a vacuum and regional disorder. Would the Soviet Union really want to shoulder the economic, military, and political burden of filling the resulting vacuum? By shedding their ideological lenses, Soviet military leaders could see that the U.S. military presence objectively served Soviet security interests.

Chinese hostility had also been a reason for the huge Soviet military buildup in the Far East since the 1960s. Kunadze dismissed the Chinese threat as largely an illusion, based on a "vulnerability complex" in the minds of Soviet leaders and the public. In a stroke of his pen he justified a large reduction of Soviet forces in the Far East.

His third issue was the priority of domestic Soviet interests. The economy deserved first place, and that meant dismantling the military-industrial complex that had damaged the economy over many decades. Dismantling it also implied giving up the command economic system itself, because it benefited primarily the military-industrial sector.

This sweeping challenge to the military was new. Before 1989 no one dared be so candid in the open press. Yet Kunadze was reasoning quite logically from Gorbachev's "new thinking"—vague though it was—and drawing its inexorable conclusions. By dismissing the Third World from military concern, he was writing off the need for significant military forces along the whole of the southern Soviet border, as well as making a large part of the Navy's surface fleet obsolete. By understanding the objective role of U.S. military forces in the Far East and the subjective factor in Soviet fears of China, he was able to justify the reduction of perhaps a third of the Soviet conventional forces. Nuclear weapons had no lasting place in his scheme of dealing with military threats, so they too could be cut. With these drastic reductions in military requirements justified, he could logically go to the root of the economic problem—the military-industrial sector and the command economic system. But in making his recommendations for military cuts, he was not specific, beyond identifying the Navy for major reductions of its surface fleet.

Blagovolin delivered an equally sweeping and incisive critique, sharing Kunadze's points about Soviet interests, the international environment, and military threats to Soviet security.[20] At the same time, he added novel perspectives for his indoctrinated readers.

Major problems had arisen for Soviet military policy because it had long followed a course divorced from its original purpose, attaining strategic parity. No one had attacked the USSR even during the preparity period, yet once parity was reached, the old pace of military buildup continued. Blagovolin placed the blame not only on military leaders but also on party leaders who could not resist "military-technical thinking" about the race in tank production, artillery production, and so on.

Also unfortunate was their failure to understand what had become obvious to the economically advanced countries of the world: acquiring more territory did not necessarily increase state power. That was why territorial expansion had gone out of style among the leading states of the West. Increased power now came from rapid economic development based on economic interdependency through trade and on the development and exploitation of new technologies. Misreading these new dynamics had caused the Soviet Union to exclude itself from the benefits of modern economic development.

He also lectured Soviet military leaders for failing to understand the character of threat from the imperialist camp. He challenged them to explain this paradox: the larger and more impressive the Soviet military, the more cohesive were the political forces within the imperialist camp, allowing it to possess even greater military power. Soviet military leaders had contributed to that cohesion by continuing to view the world as if it were 1941, the eve of the German invasion of the Soviet Union. They had also failed to recognize a key reality in bourgeois democracies. Their public opinion and politically active social forces restrained leaders from aggressive foreign policies. Here, indeed, was a shocking insight for the Soviet military, one that was comprehensible only through nonideological "new thinking."

For Blagovolin, a proper reading of all these changes dictated Soviet foreign and military policies aimed at creating a "maximally favorable environment" in the world for the Soviet Union. Its military forces should no longer be directed against any particular state but kept only as a guarantee against an invasion of Soviet territory. Like Kunadze, he insisted that the Soviet military had to cease viewing the whole world as aligned against it and to recognize that in some instances, U.S. military power worked to its advantage. For an example, he cited the former Singapore leader Lee Kuan Yew's declaration that U.S. military power in Asia prevented Japanese rearmament, something very much in the Soviet interest.

Blagovolin differed with Kunadze primarily in his emphasis on the need for the Soviet Union to integrate its economy with the leading industrial states in order to share in their rapid growth and new technologies, the most important contemporary sources of state power. The foreign and military policy implications of their analyses, however, were generally the same. The Soviet Union had to cease frightening the world with military power, abandon old ideological formulas, and reduce its military forces to modest levels.

Like Kunadze, Blagovolin was harshly critical of the Soviet Navy, ridiculing in particular Admiral Gorshkov's naval doctrine of "global presence" and "force projection." Gorshkov's naval buildup had only given the U.S. Navy a reason to increase its capabilities, thereby obliging the Soviet economy to support a Soviet naval response. Air defense forces also struck Blagovolin as excessive, costing 15 percent of the budget and half a million troops. Hinting at the Rust flight, he suggested that they were not particularly effective in preventing "foreign intruders" from entering Soviet air space. Inefficiencies in military training programs also drew his ire. The Soviet military had five times as many tanks as the U.S. military, but Soviet tank crews received only one-tenth the training. With three times as many tactical aircraft as the U.S. military, Soviet pilots received only one-third of the training time given to U.S. pilots.

All of these points led Blagovolin to the economy. The military-industrial sector's "enclave" character was throttling scientific and technological advancement, something that ought to disturb the military because it was sacrificing future and more modern military potential. Moreover, no real progress in the civilian economy was possible without major reductions in the military sector.

Finally, anticipating the military's claim to special competence, he observed that no General Staff in the twentieth century had been able to predict accurately the forces actually required for war. Military power has no political function of its own and therefore cannot claim an autonomous place within overall state policy.

Some eight months later, in spring 1990, Blagovolin offered another penetrating analysis in the party's leading theoretical journal.[21] Driving home the economic realities for Soviet military power, he emphasized that the old ideologically based policy toward the advanced industrial world had rallied against the Soviet Union a coalition of states possessing seven or eight times the quantitative potential of the Soviet economy and a qualitative advantage that was beyond measurement. To say, as some military officers did, that the West was still building up its military power instead of responding to the new Soviet foreign policy was to overlook the facts. Noting West Germany's decision to reduce the Bundeswehr by 20 percent, and observing that U.S. defense spending was headed for a 2.6 percent drop in 1991 though it was already below the 1985 level, he challenged the accuracy of their assertions. What about new breakthroughs in military technology? Should they be feared? He thought not because the lengthy process required to field already existing technologies portended a fairly stable future, one without such surprises. Moreover, political and military collaboration with the United States could reduce the danger of technological breakthroughs, but that required abandonment of the old ideological view of the West.

Next he criticized the system of political control over the Soviet military. The Main Political Administration (MPA), with its political organs, amounted to "control over the military by the military," because the political officers had illusions that they were competent in professional military affairs though in fact their only competence was in ideological stereotypical thought. A new relation between society and the military in the Soviet Union had to be a major aim of perestroika, ridding the society of its excessive militarization and bringing the military under genuine civilian political control.

Most of these arguments can be found here and there in many other articles by civilian analysts, but Blagovolin and Kunadze mobilized them more comprehensively and effectively.[22] The sweep, depth, and cogency of their analyses were indeed impressive. But the many dimensions of the Soviet military establishment described in Chapters 1–5 made the political and bureaucratic obstacles to acting on their advice truly monumental, probably greater than either Blagovolin or Kunadze realized at the time, though Blagovolin perceived them more fully than most analysts.[23]

Not surprisingly, military spokesmen did not respond directly to these didactic articles. Indirectly, of course, they were rejecting them when they insisted that NATO was not matching Soviet unilateral reductions and that U.S. military programs were still going forward. Redefining Soviet interests and the threats to them fundamentally transformed the debate, leaving the military no cogent rebuttal. The defense minister, Yazov, and the chief of the General Staff, Moiseev, did admit, however, that defining the threat was a major question. Publishing major articles on military restructuring in leading newspapers in the spring of 1989, they placed that question in first place but offered no answers to it.[24]

Rethinking Conventional Forces

The INF treaty and progress toward a START treaty logically raised the issue of rethinking of the structure and missions for Soviet nuclear forces. Gorbachev's new defensive doctrine was intended to expand that rethinking to conventional forces as well, but it really began in a serious way only after his announcement of unilateral reductions. These cuts made restructuring imperative, and in principle, therefore, the MoD should have developed a rationale for the restructuring before the reductions were announced. In fact, the MoD had not done so, but it received considerable advice on the matter from the civilian analysts.

Although Kunadze and Blagovolin, to be sure, dealt with conventional forces in their calls for reductions, the debate was framed in a more technical fashion somewhat earlier, in mid-1988 by Kokoshin and Larionov, the authors who in 1987 had offered the Battle of Kursk as a basis for developing the military-technical side of the new military doctrine. This time they outlined four models for achieving a stable balance of conventional forces in Europe.[25] As a starting point, they took the Warsaw Pact's new doctrine that prevention of war is the main military task and noted that much thought had been given to criteria for strategic nuclear stability. The urgent problem at hand was translating the changes on the political side of the new doctrine into changes in the military-technical side for conventional forces as well. Thus they were presenting these four models as a step toward resolving precisely that problem:

- In the first variant, there would be no change from the way both sides had dealt with the conventional force balance in Europe for the previous several decades. The Soviet Union would maintain its plan for a major theater offensive from the beginning of a war. The drawbacks to this solution, of course, were obvious — the maintenance of traditional patterns of military thought, continuation of the arms race, and all the things Gorbachev sought to escape with this "new thinking" about military affairs.
- In the second variant, both sides would go on the defensive while trying to negotiate a peace for a few weeks, and if that failed, then they would take the counteroffensive at the strategic-operational level (as Akhromeev envisioned for an American audience), carrying through the conquest of Europe. The authors noted that they had envisioned this model in their earlier work on the Battle of Kursk. In their view, it had significant drawbacks. Each side would be seeking the initiative in a counteroffensive or be tempted to launch more limited spoiling attacks in anticipation of the other side's counteroffensive.
- The third model called for an initial defensive by both sides followed by counteroffensive operations at the army level (that is, the lowest operational level; the tactical level began with combat actions by division) to expel the invading forces and to reestablish prewar borders. Counterattacks might involve intrusions into the enemy's territory as part of the effort. As historical examples they cited Khalkhin Gol, a battle between Soviet and Japanese forces in Mongolia in 1939, and the Korean War during its last two years. Although this model offered several advantages, it also raised difficult questions about how far to carry counterattacks — only to restore the status quo ante border or to punish the aggressor by intrusions across the border, and if so, how far? How to determine "just compensation"? How much of the enemy's force to destroy — just the first echelons or his reserves as well?
- The fourth model called for defense initially, then counterattacks no greater than at the division or tactical level, to regain lost territory. The model would require that both sides structure their forces so that each could understand that neither had the capacity to counterattack at the strategic or operation level. In practice that would mean the elimination of several kinds of offensive weapons and forces, especially tactical air forces, rockets, and artillery capable of deep strikes, and also highly mobile ground forces capable of deep penetrations.

Although Kokoshin and Larionov offered these models for further study to develop practical criteria for the military-technical component of the new doctrine, they suggested that the political-military component of the Warsaw Pact's new doctrinal formula pointed toward the fourth variant. Strangely, no serious development or criticism of their models followed, although several civilian analysts cited one or more of them occasionally. Thus they became shorthand references in the public debate rather than the basis for additional analysis.

When Yazov and Moiseev published their views on military restructuring in the spring of 1989, without answering the civilian analysts or even acknowledging their commentaries, they simply presented their own highly general approach to the task—probably an effort to make the civilians' criticisms look unnecessary by asserting that all the necessary technical staff work was in progress to handle the problems of reform. They posed the problem as dealing with a set of questions.[26] Moiseev stated them first, and a month later Yazov essentially repeated them. The military-technical side of the new doctrine had to deal with "at least" four groups of questions: 1) an evaluation of the nature of the threat; 2) the composition of forces necessary to rebuff an aggressor; 3) establishment of training objectives for these forces; and 4) determination of how to use them. This, of course, made sense as a statement of the task, but it offered nothing concrete about accomplishing it. The unilateral reduction of forces, however, had to be carried out, and an accompanying major reorganization could not be dodged with rhetorical questions.

Somewhat earlier, in February, Yazov had actually provided some detail in *Izvestiya*, the official daily paper of the Soviet government, elaborating five points.[27] First, "combined arms formations"—that is, divisions and armies— would be converted to a new organizational structure, and as a result the number of divisions would be reduced almost by half. Second, tank regiments would be removed from all the motorized rifle divisions in Germany and Czechoslovakia, reducing the total number of tanks in each division by 40 percent, and tanks divisions would also lose a tank regiment, reducing their tank strength by more than 20 percent. Third, air-assault and river-crossing units would be withdrawn from both countries, reducing the capacity for offensive operations. Fourth, in the reorganization of divisions, there would be an increase in the numbers of antitank weapons, air defense systems, and combat engineer units that could lay mines, build obstacles, and provide camouflage, another step toward a purely defensive posture. Fifth, the troop level in the European part of the USSR would drop by two hundred thousand, and by sixty thousand in the southern part of the USSR. These personnel changes would also involve transforming a number of motorized rifle units into machine-gun and artillery units earmarked for defense only. Three-fourths of the troops in Mongolia would be withdrawn and their units disbanded, including the entire air force group deployed there.

These changes indicated significant restructuring. They prompted considerable speculation in the West about their implications, largely puzzlement over machine-gun units and new artillery formations. Still, they marked a substantial decrease in Soviet capabilities on the European central front. At the same time, the defense ministry provided no explanation of the goal of the changes—answers, that is, to the rhetorical questions posed by Moiseev and Yazov later that spring, particularly regarding a new definition of the threat. The civilian critics quickly discerned that although the defense ministry was beginning the unilateral reductions, it was not addressing the more comprehensive issues and proposals that the civilians were raising. Points raised by Kunadze and Blagovolin about the size and purpose of the navy and the air defense forces, for example, were ignored. Thus the critics stepped up their criticism.

Aleksei Arbatov, an analyst at ISKAN, took the lead in April, offering a detailed review of the whole Soviet force structure and calling for large and specific reductions—including not only types of forces but also, in some cases, even models of weapons. Like most of the critics, he began with deductions from Gorbachev's "new thinking" and then drew specific conclusions.[28] His case can be summed up as follows:

- The task of nuclear weapons was not to limit damage by the enemy but "to deliver a crushing blow to his life centers"—"countervalue" targeting. To achieve the destruction of 70 percent of U.S. industry would require no more than four hundred megaton-class weapons, or 10–15 percent of the then-current Soviet arsenal. The survival of that many weapons could be assured with a much smaller ICBM force backed up by a much smaller sea-based SSBN force. Building a strategic bomber force made no sense at all. The utility of Soviet air defenses was limited, and the Moscow ABM site was of questionable value; accordingly, both should be greatly reduced.
- The task of conventional forces was not to take the offensive in Europe and Asia but to defend and repel an enemy offensive. Moreover, war on two fronts was most improbable, and protracted conventional war was now impossible. In light of the number of NATO divisions, 30 active and 20 more in reserve status, only 20–30 Warsaw Pact divisions were needed to defend the central front and a few more on the flanks, or roughly one-third of the current Warsaw Pact divisional strength. The low probability of war in the Far East allowed major reductions in divisions there as well. Given that foreign sources estimated Soviet divisions to number at least 180, possibly 200 or more, a reduction by over one-half was feasible.

- No use should be made of Soviet forces in foreign conflicts or in the Third World. That removed the requirement for naval force projection, arms transfers, and sending Soviet military advisers abroad.
- Soviet force development had to be shifted from extensive to intensive means, meaning reductions in the quantity of forces. Moreover, Soviet forces should be built to meet tasks, not to match enemy forces, because that only fueled the arms race.
- Finally, disarmament negotiations were an opportunity to cut the burden of producing more weapons. Military industries were designing too many types of weapons, seeking a two-to-one advantage over the United States, and many of these weapons were of low quality, a waste of resources by any measure. Overall, military spending could be cut by 40–50 percent in the next five-year plan; otherwise, economic reform would be impossible.

Although some of his assertions would not bear close scrutiny—for example, the low probability of a two-front war, the impossibility of a long conventional war, and the fiscal savings to be gained from intensive rather than extensive force development—he scored a number of telling points. Also, his specificity about types and numbers of weapons and forces was a surprise to most Soviet readers, including many in the military. And the logic of his case reflected the strong influence of Western military thinking, most irritating to the Soviet military.

The military did not let Arbatov's piece go unchallenged. Apparently several military officers sought to answer it, but Major General Yurii Lyubimov was given the task. Beginning with a feigned tone of scholarly detachment, Lyubimov slowly broke into a scathing diatribe against Arbatov, making a few valid points but then giving way to ad hominem abuse, calling him an incompetent and likening him to one of Gogol's satirical characters who peddled "hairbrained schemes." [29] Arbatov replied, asking for a more objective discussion but sparing no ink in using Lyubimov's own text to show that he really offered no substantive arguments or information, that the defense ministry itself had produced patently contradictory figures from one year to the next at negotiations in Vienna, and that Lyubimov was posturing with tendentious arguments, leaving the reader to supply the logic and information necessary to render his views comprehensible.

Although he offered far more detail about weapons, force sizes, and recommended cuts, Arbatov's analysis was consistent with the views of Kunadze, Blagovolin, and others. Arbatov's piece was one of the high points in defining a new Soviet military force structure for both conventional and nuclear forces.

Just as Kokoshin and Larionov set the boundaries of the open debate regarding the use of conventional forces, Arbatov took the discussion of the required sizes and kinds of conventional and nuclear forces to its practical limit.

Parallel to this sophisticated technical debate, the mass media were publishing numerous pieces that attacked the military in a different fashion, appealing to a wider audience, caricaturing the military's penchant for secrecy, complaining about the terrible life of a soldier and senior officers' privileges, citing specific aspects of military practices that harmed the well-being of the society, and ripping apart military spokesmen's defense of the military establishment. Albert Plutnik, an accomplished satirist, provides one of the better examples, entitled "A Civilian's Polemical Notes on Restructuring in the Army."[30] The five hundred thousand–man reduction under way prompted him to ask how there could be surplus manpower in the military. In industry, surplus workers are common, but, he wondered, is the military just another ministry? Do many soldiers have nothing to do? A defense ministry spokesman said that "In the main those discharged from the army will be . . . ones who have stained the honor and dignity of an officer." Does this mean, Plutnik asked, that the army will rid itself only of those who should have been discharged anyway? Perhaps the military's manning levels are "more or less artificial." The military budget was to be cut by 14.2 percent. "The degree of accuracy is striking. Down to the last kopeck, so to speak. Yet none of us can name an accurate figure for our military expenditures." So no one can really figure out what that percentage means. "And some of our readers are worried. Are we not weakening our military might . . . in the face of world imperialism?" This fear might not be unfounded, he wrote, because veterans of the Afghan war, after being discharged, must "repay from their own pockets the damage done to their equipment during their years of service. . . . Yet for our illustrious paratroopers, it is no simple matter to obtain a new pair of boots to replace worn ones." Perhaps it was time to increase, not decrease the military budget, he suggested. Comparing the openness of U.S. military information with Soviet obsessive secrecy, Plutnik observed that Soviet citizens are not supposed to know which factories are military or where they are, but if one really wants to know, one needs only to ride a bus and wait until the bus driver stops and says, "Here is the secret factory." The generals say they are not obliged to inform the public of such information, but what about the Supreme Soviet? It, too, is kept in the dark.

Not all critics resorted to satire; more resorted to anger, but the message was the same. A common theme was the demand for less secrecy about Soviet military affairs, especially the defense budget and such personnel matters as the numbers of generals, their pay, and the overall strength of the armed forces.

As more information became public from individuals relating their own experiences and from other unofficial sources, the flood of such journalism grew.[31] The once inviolate military was rapidly becoming the object of bitter public outrage.

The Military Critics

Most of the younger officers in the debate did not deal with the large strategic picture as civilian scholars did. They addressed specific issues on which their experience made them knowledgeable. Initially challenging the system of universal conscription, they turned to the miserable conditions of life in the military, and finally to the economy. The nuclear weapons issue also troubled some of them. Although only a few got major attention in the media, the number of younger officers who welcomed military reform was quite large, perhaps even a majority in the beginning, when glasnost and perestroika enjoyed great popularity. A far smaller number worked actively for it in their active duty posts, but they were important as a sharp contrast to the generals who only paid lip service to reform or were outright hostile to it. The attitudes of all these officers are important to an understanding of why the military was far from single-minded toward Gorbachev and perestroika, and they help explain why the military found it increasingly difficult to act corporately as the political crisis deepened in 1989–91.

In November 1988, a short time before Gorbachev's announcement of unilateral cuts before the United Nations, Colonel Aleksandr Savinkin became the first active duty officer to call for military reform in the open press.[32] His timing and his recommendations were so appropriate for Gorbachev's announcement that one has to suspect that Yakovlev encouraged Savinkin's commentary. In a brief article he called for a small professional army in place of the large Soviet conscript army. Savinkin based his argument on the example of the Red Army's massive reduction in 1921–23, when it was cut from 5 or 6 million men to about 560,000 — that is, by 90 percent in just two years. This was Lenin's military policy, a wise one, and Stalin had been wrong to reverse it later in favor of universal conscription for a mass army.

After Savinkin's invocation of the Red Army's reform in the 1920s it became a frequent reference in the debate, used by civilian and military writers alike. S. Lipitskii exploited it in the spring of 1990 in the party's theoretical journal, making the case for contemporary radical reductions.[33] General Vladimir Lobov, together with the ISKAN scholar Andrei Kokoshin, wrote about General Aleksandr Svechin, a former tsarist officer who joined the Red Army and wrote a major book of strategy in the late 1920s, criticizing the younger Red Army theorists for their obsession with offense to the neglect of the defensive as form of warfare.[34] Lobov was less interested in genuine reform than in burnishing his academic credentials and improving his political standing with this historical reference to the importance of defense. But Kokoshin was a reformer, if a moderate one, careful and scholarly; he later became a deputy minister in the new Russian defense ministry, the first civilian in such a post.

In fall 1989, two young officers, Colonel Aleksandr Tsalko and Major Vladimir Lopatin, broke into the media, initially not as authors but in interviews with journalists.[35] Both were deputies in the Supreme Soviet, and were demanding military reform. Lopatin later became the object of vicious criticism from the Ministry of Defense, published his views in the West, and joined Boris Yeltsin's government in the Russian Soviet Federal Socialist Republic (RSFSR) in 1990.[36] He consistently called for reforms no less radical than those advocated by Aleksei Arbatov, and he pushed them in the new legislature in the fall of 1989.

Colonel General Volkogonov was the highest-ranking military critic, and a most unlikely one. A political officer who was for a long time at the Lenin Military Political Academy, he wrote some of the most diabolical tirades against the West, demonstrating great capacity as a propagandist. Then he became head of the Military History Institute, the defense ministry's center of serious military historical research. With access to classified party and military archives at both the Lenin Military Political Academy and the Military History Institute, he apparently took a serious look at the documents and underwent a transformation, becoming among the harshest critics of Stalin and even Lenin. His biography of Stalin, published in 1990, brought him international notoriety. Still, he had not clashed with the Ministry of Defense itself. That happened when he began editing a new history of World War II, planning to publish its first volume in 1991 on the fiftieth anniversary of the German attack on the Soviet Union. When he presented his draft to the military collegium of the defense ministry in March, he met an extremely hostile reception and was forced to abandon the entire project.[37] His military reviewers simply could not abide his candid treatment of the Nazi-Soviet Pact and Stalin's complicity in starting the war. If Stalin had been so incompetent, they wanted to know, then how did the Soviet Union win the war?[38]

Volkogonov later joined Yeltsin's Russian government as an adviser and aide, helping investigate the events of 19–23 August 1991 and devoting the remainder of his life to historical research in an effort to revise as much of the record of the Soviet period as he could.[39] He would probably have objected to being classified as one of the military critics, because he never joined the debate in the fashion of Lopatin, Tsalko, and Savinkin. Instead, he stood above it, occasionally speaking out for reform but directing most of his energies toward revising history, never entirely breaking his ties with his fellow generals.

A number of other officers worked for reform, but not by joining the public debate. Major General Aleksandr Vladimirov felt strongly about reform as early as 1988–89, and he used his contacts among the senior generals to try to persuade them of practical steps that could be taken, admittedly with no success.[40] A retired colonel, Vitalii Tsygichko, served from 1967 until his retirement in 1977 in an institute that supported the General Staff with computer-based modeling and analysis of conventional force balances and nuclear weapons. Moving to an institute in the Academy of Sciences in 1977, he continued to enjoy contact with Marshal Nikolai Ogarkov as a consultant until 1985. His disillusionment came from having his analysis consistently rejected when it did not conform to senior officers' preconceptions, particularly with regard to doctrinal changes in war plans they made for speeding up offensive operations and employment of tactical weapons. One analysis revealed that if both sides used only 25 percent of their tactical nuclear weapons in Europe, further prosecution of the war would be impossible because of the devastation; it was simply brushed aside.[41] Naval Captain Eduard Shevel'ev, who also served on the General Staff performing computer modeling, got into trouble for his independent views and lack of ideological enthusiasm but did not become an open dissident, continuing instead to work for reform from within the military. Like Tsygichko, he was increasingly disturbed by the gap between Soviet nuclear employment doctrine and what his models revealed.[42] Vladimirov, Tsygichko, and Shevel'ev, though exceptional, undoubtedly represented a significant number of field-grade officers quite well disposed to fundamental reforms, not willing to exploit glasnost fully, but willing to offer candid views to superiors as the public climate became more open.

A couple of other examples demonstrate another kind of reform attitude that was more widespread among younger officers. Colonel Aleksandr Lyakhovskii, who served in the General Staff's operations directorate and for several years in Afghanistan, began, while he was recovering from a serious wound in his leg, a study of the classified documents on the Soviet decision to invade Afghanistan. He published it as a book in 1995, remarkable for its inclusion of dozens of top-secret papers marking the trail of nearly a decade of decision making, bureaucratic politics, corruption, careerism, hardship, bravery, and combat operations.[43] Lyakhovskii remained strongly loyal to his army but spared little in criticizing the party leadership. Remaining on active duty, he became a major general in 1995. Colonel Aleksei Tsarev, a political officer in a strategic rocket regiment, developed his enthusiasm for reform in 1985 as a student at the Lenin Military Political Academy when he was sent to lecture to factory workers around Moscow. Later, seeing the conditions of military life again firsthand in a rocket regiment, he realized that young officers were so overworked and so abused by their careerist superiors that they could not provide proper leadership for their troops. Virtually all of them reacted to perestroika as a sign that at least this negative environment might be changed. Tsarev himself realized that the problems were not amenable to minor reforms and that the larger society and the economy as well as the army had to change.[44] He eventually retired and became an aide to the speaker of the Russian Duma in the mid-1990s. Lieutenant Aleksandr Rodin, a pilot, experienced a political radicalization while serving at the missile target range in Kamchatka. His tale of the brutal exploitation of soldiers' labor to enrich general officers has the mood of an episode from Dostoevsky's *Notes from the House of the Dead*. Managing to elude incarceration in a psychiatric hospital, he resigned from the military and became a radical reform deputy in the Leningrad Soviet in 1990.[45]

On the other side of the reform issue was a small group of younger officers voicing a mix of neo-Stalinist, populist, and fascist views. Most conspicuous among them stood Colonel Viktor Alksnis—ironically, the grandson of a former commander of the Soviet air forces who had been a victim of Stalin's purges. Elected as a deputy to the Congress of People's Deputies in 1989, he spoke out strongly against perestroika, concessions to the West, and the disorders that Gorbachev's policies were catalyzing. Directly to Gorbachev he shouted, "The army is no longer with you," during the leader's talk to a group of officers in November 1990.[46] Another example was Colonel Viktor Filatov, who became the editor of Ministry of Defense's *Military History Journal;* he transformed this prestigious academic journal into an organ of yellow journalism, publishing the protofascist rantings of the Soviet writer Karem Rash and serializing extracts from Hitler's *Mein Kampf*. The darling of the reactionary generals, he was promoted to major general a short time later but lost his post in the aftermath of the August 1991 political crisis.

These examples reveal at least four categories of quite different behavior among the field-grade ranks of the officer corps. First, a few broke with the generals and took the road of open political participation in support of fundamental military reform. Second, a far larger number sympathized with perestroika, recognizing the desperate need for reform; they had become personally disillusioned but remained politically passive. Third, a few retained their loyalty to the military but felt deep hostility toward the political leadership and the mess it had made in Afghanistan, the economy, social conditions, and the army itself. Finally, a few were more reactionary than most of the generals, becoming open political opponents of perestroika.

To be sure, answering all the critics of the military was not left to these reactionary junior officers. Dozens of senior officers, especially the defense minister and the chief of the General Staff, dealt with them, as we shall see. Glasnost and the public debate had forced the key issues on to the agenda— the character of the threat, the questions of force structure and doctrine related to nuclear weapons and conventional forces, the problems with the conscription system and morale in the military ranks, the military's place in the society and the political system, and the military-industrial sector's burden on the economy. Resolutions of these issues were no closer at hand, but the open and candid attention they were receiving marked a revolution in Soviet military policy making. It was no longer restricted to the secret circles of the Politburo, the Defense Council, the defense ministry, the General Staff, and the VPK.

The Exhaustion of Glasnost

The process that Gorbachev and Yakovlev had initiated—drawing the civilian academic community into a public debate with the military over defense policy —produced some of the results they intended. It certainly put the generals on the political defensive. Yet it failed to compel them to take seriously the systemic military reform demanded by "new thinking" and perestroika. Although the civilian scholars' pressure on the military continued, its importance was transcended by turmoil within the military during 1990–91. That upheaval turned the media's focus to more socially sensitive military issues, particularly to the conscription system, hardships confronting the troops and officers returning from Eastern Europe, and conversion of military industries. The larger policy issues of force structure and doctrine also shifted from the academic journals to the new parliament, where efforts were being made to write military reform into law.

What began as imaginative and pragmatic analysis in glasnost debate exhausted itself in acrimony. It is easy to sympathize with the insightful views of civilian analysts and to dismiss the military reactions as nasty, rigid, and irresponsible, as some of them were. These outside critics were justified in offering radical analysis and proposals because the military was headed for radical change which it could not prevent but refused to prepare to manage. At the same time, the military leaders understood what their critics did not: the practical difficulties in radical reforms. It was easy to call for a 50 percent reduction in the number of divisions and for scrapping most of the navy and much of the air defense forces. But to implement such reductions rapidly without throwing the entire military establishment into chaos was impossible. To believe that a 50 percent reduction in defense spending would easily translate large numbers of "guns" into equally large amounts of "butter" in a few years was indeed naïve.

Also lost on the civilian critics was the psychological impact on the generals as they watched the U.S. military develop its Air-Land Battle doctrine in the late 1970s, based on new technologies that made possible "smart weapons," better intelligence acquisition systems, and a new generation of tanks, artillery, infantry fighting vehicles, and combat aircraft.[47] By the early 1980s, several of these new weapons were being deployed in Europe. These developments threatened to undermine the modernization and restructuring of Soviet forces that had begun in 1978. Then came President Reagan's SDI, posing new uncertainties for the Soviet military, not just with its potential of revolutionizing ballistic missile defense but also with the prospect of space-based weapons that could be used against ground targets. The Soviet officers with access to intelligence on these U.S. programs were not disposed to see a benign international environment. In an interview in early 1990, Yazov was asked, "But sometimes quite authoritative authors are insistently claiming that today no danger of war exists, are they not?" He replied, "I am simply uncomfortable with such authors. The current political realities are so obvious that they cannot 'not be noticed.'"[48] He undoubtedly spoke with such intelligence information in mind.

Some of the civilian critics probably understood the technical military developments to some degree, but their choice was either to push hard for radical reductions while it was politically possible or to be worn down by foot-dragging military and military-industrial leaders. To understand the critics' attitudes, one has only to imagine their reaction as they watched a television interview with Colonel General Vladimir Lobov, deputy chief of the General Staff. Asked, "Then what is new in the new doctrine?" Lobov answered, "Well, there is a lot new. You understand, our new doctrine, as compared to the old doctrine, is a more offensive doctrine. Now this offensiveness is also not understood by some. . . . But the offensiveness of the doctrine lies in the fact that this doctrine is directed toward averting war." As the exchange continued, the interviewer finally asked, "Vladimir Nikolaevich, does it not bother you that, say, somebody in the West, after hearing our discussion, may say that the first deputy chief of the USSR Armed Forces General Staff has declared that the essence of the new military doctrine lies in its offensiveness when compared to the previous doctrine, which was defensive? Does this not embarrass you?" Lobov snapped back, "No, this does not embarrass me whatsoever."[49] Little wonder that Aleksei Arbatov, in his notorious article, criticized Lobov specifically for saying that Soviet forces needed to be reduced but refusing to specify by how much. Many civilian scholars and foreign ministry officials harbored deep resentment toward the military for refusing to engage in a serious discussion and also for repeatedly lying to them.[50]

The generals thought no better of the integrity and aims of their civilian critics. Marshal Akhromeev, for example, entered the fray in December 1989 with an "open letter" to the magazine *Ogonek*, taking it to task for all kinds of distortions, particularly for diminishing the foreign military threat.[51] The magazine's purpose, he concluded, was "discrediting the Armed Forces of the USSR." The marshal's outrage merely prompted the editors to point out in the same issue that he had exaggerated the size of the U.S. defense budget, the number of U.S. forces, and their readiness, and that he provided nothing specific about "defensive sufficiency" beyond the standard formula, to avert a war. In the same month, Georgii Arbatov made a biting speech to the Congress of People's Deputies, accusing the military of being the primary cause of the economic crisis, the stimulus for the Western military buildup, and the major impediment to perestroika.[52] The title of his speech — "An army for the country or a country for the army?" — was not exactly designed to cool military tempers. The military response was no less personal.[53] This crescendo of outbursts reached a new level at the Russian Party Conference in June 1990, when Colonel General Albert Makashov defended Marxist-Leninist orthodoxy, telling Gorbachev to his face that the army's communists would never accept "ideological surrender," then turning on the civilian critics and editors: "Citizens Arbatovs, Korotiches, Sobchaks, Yegor Yakovlevs, and company! Stand up and say it outright: we don't need an army. We can get by without the Armed Forces!"[54] Calls for Makashov's resignation followed in the media, but he remained in his post as commander of the Volga-Ural Military District and struck back, accusing his critics of violating the principles of glasnost and free speech and posing as a defender of pluralism.[55] In August, twenty-five marshals and generals, one admiral, and a party official signed a long statement in *Komsomolskaya Pravda*, expressing alarm that their critics were asking, "With whom will the army be in the event that a complex situation arises in the country? Where will it be led by generals who hold dear a power unlimited by law?" Why, they asked rhetorically, were such questions being constantly repeated in the media? "There is but one answer," the statement asserted, "to set the generals against society." Then it named several guilty newspapers, magazines, and televisions programs. Two former chiefs of the General Staff, Akhromeev and Ogarkov, were among the signatories.[56] During the next twelve months this hysterical glasnost raged on.

And so it was that the debate moved from the pages of stodgy academic journals into the newspapers and television and finally into shouting matches in the new parliament and in party meetings. Events countrywide contributed to its increasing shrillness—war in Nagorno-Karabakh between Armenia and Azerbaijan, separatist movements and violence in Tbilisi and Baku, separatist movements in the Baltic republics, and nationalist movements in Ukraine and Moldavia. Meanwhile, the MoD was implementing the unilateral reductions ordered by Gorbachev, but without a plan in line with where his "new thinking" was taking military policy.

NINE

Legislating Military Reform

Paper will put up with anything written on it.

OLD RUSSIAN PROVERB

G orbachev's political reforms in 1989 left unchanged all of the "executive branch" structures described earlier. Although he added a "presidency" to the executive a year later, his first and most significant change was in the legislative branch, where he replaced the old Supreme Soviet with a new one. It quickly became a forum for several political forces newly unleashed by glasnost and by genuine multicandidate, competitive elections that chose its members. Some members made valiant efforts to shape military policy, but they eventually failed, mainly because of the structural nature of the political reform, which reflected the ambiguities of Gorbachev's own tactics and goals. As one of his aides later realized, the very nature of the Soviet system raised doubts as to whether or not effective political reform was possible. These structural changes, therefore, must be appreciated in some detail because they provided the stage for the military reformers and allowed the creation of new public groups that both supported and opposed military reform.

The New Government Structures

Shakhnazarov, Chernyaev, and Yakovlev told Gorbachev repeatedly, beginning in early 1987, that the party would never carry through on reform because the purge of old cadres was not producing new people with the required commitment and organizational skills. The alternative was political reform that would allow Gorbachev to work around the party, an argument he finally accepted late that year. They were disappointed, however, that he did not use the Nineteenth Party Conference, where he pushed through political reform, to rout the opposition from both the Politburo and the Central Committee. His aides were also frustrated that Gorbachev refused to include a presidency for himself in the reform so that he would have an alternative political-organizational base to the party. Many of Yakovlev's slogans, particularly "a law-based society," thinly veiled the idea of transferring real power to state institutions and leaving the Communist Party diminished and forced to compete with other political parties. But Gorbachev still held a deep personal attachment to the party, and he did not share his aides' conviction that he had sufficient power to sweep out Ligachev and the more conservative members of the Politburo as well as to purge the large number of "dead souls" in the Central Committee—members who had been removed from top-level state and party posts but still retained Central Committee membership. Although Gorbachev shuffled the top leadership in September, he did not remove the seventy-five "dead souls" until the plenum in April 1989.[1]

In any event, the Nineteenth Party Conference approved his proposal for competitive elections to a Congress of People's Deputies, which would in turn elect a new Supreme Soviet as a permanent standing legislature, replacing the old Supreme Soviet with its semiannual rubber-stamp sessions. The following year, on 26 March 1989, elections were held to choose the 2,250 deputies. The congress in turn elected 542 deputies to the new Supreme Soviet, which chose Gorbachev as its chairman, but by a less than unanimous vote (87 deputies voted against him).

Although the elections of the congress's deputies were comparatively free, remarkably so by previous standards, the Communist Party set the rules to ensure the election of at least one hundred of its members. Those not on this list had to compete against at least one and, in some places, several other opponents. Stunningly, many high-ranking communists lost their elections. Thirty-four regional party secretaries failed to win a seat, including a candidate Politburo member, Yurii Solove'ev; several high-ranking military officers were dumped by their constituents, including General B. V. Snetkov, commander of the Group of Soviet Forces in Germany.[2] This was the kind of shake-up that Gorbachev sought.

When the Congress of People's Deputies opened on 25 May 1989, most of its proceedings were broadcast live on television, astonishing the Soviet public with the candor and theatrics of its proceedings as Gorbachev ruled at the gavel. Andrei Sakharov, the famous dissident and distinguished nuclear physicist, was among its first speakers. He raised all kinds of issues, like making the congress the permanent legislature and dropping the indirectly elected Supreme Soviet, but he finally supported Gorbachev because he saw no real alternative. For two weeks the congress dragged on, as a procession of speakers alternately attacked and defended government policies, the military, the KGB, the economic system, and other heretofore sacred institutions. Estonian deputies called for a commission to look into the Molotov-Ribbentrop Pact of 1939. The congress approved the motion, and Aleksandr Yakovlev was appointed to head the commission. Glasnost in the media, of course, had already introduced the Soviet public to this kind of debate, but witnessing it live in the congress on nationwide television marked a new phase of political openness for the ordinary citizen.

At this point most of the reform-minded intelligentsia supported Gorbachev. Sakharov's view was typical: there was no better alternative. The Supreme Soviet, the new parliament, was chosen and promptly went into session, following the congress's lead by electing Gorbachev its chairman as well. He had gotten what he wanted — two new state institutions for substantive political participation by a significant number of noncommunists. And, equally important, he was nominally in charge of both.[3]

The congress and the parliament were meant to facilitate the emergence of a "civil society" and to break the Communist Party's monopoly on power by providing a legitimate and effective political opposition. On the surface, it looked like an effective gambit for trimming the party's wings and putting Gorbachev beyond the reach of his party opponents. On closer examination, however, it was a flawed scheme based on a misreading of the political context, especially as it concerned control of resources.

He had replaced the old rubber-stamp Supreme Soviet with a new one, a genuine legislature, albeit complicated by the presence of the hybrid Congress of People's Deputies — a sort of "electoral college" for choosing the legislature that tried to share the legislative role as well. The executive branch, however, remained unchanged, in charge of the economy and all other executive tasks and still firmly in the grip of the Communist Party's personnel system. The judiciary also remained unchanged, entirely unprepared to deal with the plethora of disputes that were to arise between the executive branch and a legislature with real lawmaking power. Most important, the new parliament had no control over the budget and resources. The executive branch "owned" and ran the economy; thus it did not depend on the new parliament for its budget.

Chernyaev, Shakhnazarov, and Yakovlev continued to worry that Gorbachev had not moved far enough with these changes. As they asked, how was he to carry through a political reform in the executive to match the new legislative branch without creating a role for himself as a president or a prime minister? Chernyaev believed that to make the new system work, Gorbachev had to weaken the party far more and implement genuine market reforms. He would also have to recognize the emerging centrifugal political forces among the national republics, letting some of them secede and accepting a new union treaty for preserving even a rump Soviet Union.[4]

By the beginning of 1990, Gorbachev faced mounting problems that gave him second thoughts about failing to create a presidency as an alternative political base. In mid-January he visited Lithuania to try to dampen the separatist sentiment that had spread from the public into the top ranks of the Lithuanian communist leadership. He had to begin preparations for the Twenty-eighth Party Congress to be held that summer, knowing that Ligachev and others might well try to use it to unseat him. And he realized that conservative forces were blocking reform efforts in the parliament. Finally, he had to deal with the growing national minority sentiment for a new relation with Moscow—that is, a new union treaty. But once again he resorted to half-measures. Although he floated several far-reaching proposals for more sweeping political reform, his main goals included the creation of a presidency and the suspension of Article 6 of the constitution, which gave the Communist Party its "leading role"—a change introduced by Brezhnev in his 1977 revised constitution. With those aims accomplished, he believed he could confront the party congress with more ambitious initiatives in economic and military reform.[5]

At a Politburo meeting on 22 January, his proposals were discussed in connection with a new party platform to be approved by the Twenty-eighth Party Congress. Opinion was divided. Should Article 6 be suspended and a multiparty system allowed? That would destroy the party, but what else could be done? A federation or confederation treaty for the union? A confederation was unacceptable; some favored a federation, while others wanted to "let the process decide itself." Private property? Put so directly, it was unacceptable, but perhaps it could be called "private labor" or "individual property." An all-volunteer professional army? It was unacceptable, but how could it be prevented? As Chernyaev observed, the Politburo's belief in the effectiveness of subtle slogans was astounding. The approved resolutions were more artful in formulation than realistic about what had to be done.[6]

Chernyaev, Shakhnazarov, and Gorbachev's aide for economic affairs, Nikolai Petrakov, took Gorbachev's guidance from this meeting and closeted themselves to draft the platform. Yakovlev suddenly appeared at their evening working session, excitedly reporting an exchange he had just had with Gorbachev. The party leader was in distress, wondering what to do with national minorities and radical democrats besieging him on one side and defenders of socialism on the other. Yakovlev advised him to act decisively. He should make himself president, concentrate all power in his hands, pushing aside both the Politburo and the parliament; next he would appeal to the people directly on television and proclaim a program: give land to the peasants and then factories to the workers; grant genuine independence to the republics and a multiparty system in place of the Communist Party monopoly; slash the state apparatus and create private property; introduce a market and secure large Western loans; dispatch the generals, replacing them with colonels willing to carry out military reform. For economic reform, Yakovlev told Gorbachev that Slyunkov had a radical variant already in draft form and that it should be used.[7] Yakovlev insisted that Gorbachev had accepted most of these ideas, but the very next day, 29 January, at the Politburo meeting where Gorbachev was purportedly going to advance this strategy, he let the discussion wander as Ryzhkov and Ligachev disagreed over economic policy, finally directing Ryzhkov to use some points from Slyunkov's "variant." Everyone but Ligachev voted in favor of Gorbachev's proposal for a presidency, but not much else survived from Yakovlev's recommendations.[8] The February Central Committee plenum approved the creation of a presidency, but without any supporting staff structures.

Gorbachev was already wavering in his determination to transfer power from the party to the state, when an event occurred that made him hesitate about abandoning the party. The democratic forces in Moscow staged a demonstration specifically against Gorbachev and the party on 25 February, the anniversary of the first, the "democratic," revolution of 1917. Gorbachev had been losing the support of the democrats over the past several months. Now they came out with a manifesto condemning as cover for a dictatorship his proposal to create a presidency and calling for the end of the Communist Party and the KGB. As the Politburo assessed the demonstration at its meeting on 2 March, Gorbachev behaved, according to Chernyaev, more like a frightened party apparatchik than like the leader of perestroika.[9] Ryzhkov described it as a victory because the crowd was small. Vadim Bakatin, head of the MVD at the time, flatly disagreed: "What kind of victory? We frightened people. Most people did not come into the street out of fear. That is why a million did not gather."[10] Bakatin estimated the crowd at 250,000–300,000, not the 70,000–100,000 that KGB chairman Kryuchkov reported. Instead of frightening people, as his own police officers had done, he suggested that a political approach, talking to the demonstrators, made more sense. Gorbachev lost his temper at these suggestions for compromise, calling the demonstration pure political hooliganism and denying that it spoke for "the working class." According to Chernyaev, this affair drove Gorbachev right back into the party's embrace.

Just how far became apparent during General Valentin Varennikov's briefing on Lithuania to the Politburo on 22 March. Varennikov presented the military's plan for dispatching two regiments to Vilnius. They would isolate the independence-minded leadership and allow Lithuanian puppet leaders to call for the Soviet army to restore Moscow's control.[11] This so alarmed Chernyaev, reminding him of the events in Prague in 1968, that he appealed to Gorbachev the next day, warning that use of armed force in Lithuania would mean the end of all that Gorbachev had been struggling to achieve. Gorbachev brushed him off as "always frightened," told him that everything would work out all right, and directed him to mind his own business.

When the law creating a presidency was proposed to the Supreme Soviet, it met the spirit of the 25 February manifesto. Most of the new "democrats" voiced their fears that a president could become a dictator. Gorbachev nevertheless persuaded a simple majority to pass the law.[12] The next day, 15 March 1990, the Supreme Soviet elected him president after defeating a proposal to declare the earlier vote on the law null and void.[13]

Looking back at this juncture, Shakhnazarov doubted that Gorbachev could have achieved much more in any event.[14] Soviet society had begun to participate fairly vigorously in the political process, but it was far from being a "civil society" capable of moving the political center of gravity into the parliament.[15] Moreover, Gorbachev showed no real understanding of all the organizational changes necessary to give the presidency the capacity to govern, particularly with regard to the economy. In the old system, according to Shakhnazarov, the Council of Ministers managed the economy pretty much on its own, within general party guidance, but stayed out of foreign, military, and police affairs. When the council met, the foreign, defense, and interior ministries seldom attended. The party ran those ministries directly from the Central Committee apparatus. Thus an informal bifurcation of executive-branch management existed, leaving Gorbachev to follow his personal inclination to grow more detached from the tough management problems. He apparently did not realize that political reform would require that he take the management reins directly and would therefore need the organizational means to do so.

After a year and a half under the new system, Shakhnazarov observes, not one but three centers of power existed—the presidency, the Supreme Soviet, and the Council of Ministers. At the same time, at the regional and local levels of government, the old party-dominated centralized system remained unchanged.[16] Matters became all the more confusing at the center because the Council of Ministers was supposed to be responsible to both Gorbachev and the Supreme Soviet. The failure, in Shakhnazarov's judgment, lay in Gorbachev's reluctance to set up a genuine balance of power among the branches of government as well as to create new executive structures under the presidency which would displace the old Council of Ministers.[17] In addition, it was a mistake not to impose this reform on regional governments as well. At the lower levels the old system remained entirely unchanged, so that the reforms in Moscow disconnected the center from regional government, leaving them as merely a thin veneer over the old party-dominated local administrative system.

To deal with this fragmentation of power at the center after he became president in the spring of 1990, Gorbachev formed the Presidential Council outside the system, prompting jokes that he wanted "a kind of state Politburo."[18] The council was a collection of ministers, Central Committee officials, a few Politburo members, a journalist, a couple of writers, and the head of the Academy of Sciences—not exactly the people needed to run the executive branch of government, as Shakhnazarov sarcastically noted. It met a few times, and then Gorbachev lost interest in it.[19] He was again alone, dealing with the Council of Ministers as it tried to respond both to him and to the Supreme Soviet. And he still had to deal with opposition in the Politburo, a weakened Central Committee Secretariat, and the same old unresponsive regional party and state organs.

The Presidential Council did not please the defense ministry any more than it did other ministries and the parliament. General Moiseev, the chief of the General Staff, openly criticized it.[20] He favored a strong presidency and a clear chain of command based on the "rule-of-law principle," but not what was emerging. It had glaring deficiencies, he insisted, because military leaders were not allowed to speak during the debates over the council's role. First, the Defense Council was not even mentioned, though the president would need it in case of war. Was the Presidential Council to assume its functions? No one knew. Second, responsibilities for military issues within the presidency were poorly defined. Third, clarity about command authority over nuclear weapons needed to be established. Finally, the president's staff included no military experts. Moiseev did not worry long, however, because the Presidential Council was short-lived.

In late November 1990, Gorbachev sought to strengthen the presidency by asking the parliament to give it authority to issue decrees for solving "economic problems and the questions of preservation of law and order."[21] The authority would be temporary, however: five hundred days, while he carried through economic reforms.[22] At the same time, he abolished the Presidential Council and replaced it with a Council of the Federation, a National Security Council, and Special Service for Law and Order.[23] None of these became noticeably active.

All these changes, beginning with the May 1989 convocation of the Congress of People's Deputies, created a confusing new organizational context for making military policy. The Defense Council still existed. The Council of Ministers and the VPK remained as before. The Main Political Administration still had its "political organs" throughout the armed forces. The Politburo and the Central Committee were still active. At the same time, the defense ministry faced the new parliament's attempts to legislate military reform. Military policy would henceforth be worked out in the disorderly Supreme Soviet and the Congress of People's Deputies, in the old and decaying state institutions, in the faction-ridden Politburo, and also under media scrutiny.

Shakhnazarov's diagnosis of structural obstacles, although certainly accurate, focused only on the symptoms, not the disease. The system rested first of all on the command economy. Until private property had been instituted along with a market economy, the objective conditions for a civil society would be missing. Without private wealth, civil groups could not muster the means to compete effectively in the electoral process and certainly not in the lawmaking process. Yakovlev and Chernyaev were right about the need for early and radical economic reform. As long as the new parliament did not control the "power of the purse," its prospects for controlling the military were trivial.

Although Gorbachev was an avid student of Lenin—he often read aloud from Lenin's works to Chernyaev in the privacy of his office—he overlooked the most elementary aspect of Lenin's views: nationalizing all "the means of production" was the way to destroy parliamentary democracy. It followed, of course, that to create parliamentary democracy, private property and a market economy had to be restored. Yet Gorbachev approached market reforms cautiously and inconsistently right up to the fall of 1990, and even then he wrongly believed he could escape the dilemma posed by alternative approaches.[24] Moreover, his January 1990 trip to Lithuania and the 25 February anti-Gorbachev demonstration made him temporarily seek refuge in the party and socialism. Market reforms threatened both.[25]

Military Reform in the New Context

In winter 1988–89, the defense minister, General Yazov, and the chief of the General Staff, General Moiseev, were under pressure from at least four sources for major military restructuring. First, Gorbachev's unilateral reductions had to be implemented, no small challenge. Second, the civilian critics not only demanded reductions but also offered strong advice about what forces to reduce. Third, after more than two years of diplomatic maneuvering within the Conference on Security Cooperation in Europe (CSCE) forum, the long-enduring negotiations for mutual balanced force reductions (MBFR) were replaced with a new set of negotiations, centered on conventional forces in Europe (CFE). When these talks opened on 9 March 1989, it was clear to Soviet military leaders that Gorbachev intended much deeper cuts in conventional forces.[26] Fourth, the new parliament would undoubtedly add new voices to the chorus of military reformers.

The MoD Anticipates the Parliament

Yazov and Moiseev probably had all these things in mind when they published several articles in early 1989, announcing the MoD's restructuring plans and condemning their critics.[27] Their first articles, in February, detailed the unilateral cuts and proclaimed that their implementation was under way, but they added very little to what Gorbachev had said in his U.N. speech. The March and April articles spelled out a somewhat more comprehensive program of reorganization, and not surprisingly, they were highly duplicative of the earlier ones. All of them began with acknowledgement of Gorbachev's "new thinking." The arms race had to cease. The unilateral reductions announced at the United Nations were necessary. The Cold War was over. Nuclear weapons had to be banned because they have no political utility. Political measures were now decisive for preventing war. And the purpose of the Warsaw Pact's forces was to prevent war, not prepare for it. The buildup of military forces for security had reached a point where its continuation no longer made sense but only weakened the Soviet economy. The Soviet military sometimes mirrored the United States by building weapons it did not need. To this litany, the generals added some points of their own, not all of them consistent with "new thinking." The world was still dangerous. Local wars could still expand into a world war. The West had not only failed to reciprocate the Soviet reductions, but U.S. high-technology weapons programs, especially SDI, had not been stopped. In other words, Yazov and Moiseev accepted Gorbachev's policies but noted that their efficacy was still to be proven.

After such deference to "new thinking," what were they suggesting in practice? Yazov added some details to the standard figures on the unilateral reductions. The non-Soviet Warsaw Pact states would also make reductions — 56,000 troops, 1,900 tanks, 130 combat aircraft, and an average 13.6 percent reduction in defense budgets. This would bring the overall reductions in Eastern Europe to 296,300 troops, almost 12,000 tanks, and 930 combat aircraft.[28] The volume of arms production would decrease by almost 20 percent over the next two years; production of enriched uranium would cease in 1989–90. Defense industries would shift their output of civilian goods from 40 percent to 60 percent by 1995. And the personnel strength of the armed forces would drop from 4.2 million to 3.7 million. This meant that military science was also being "restructured" to work out a new theory of war and to publish new training manuals for such fundamental changes.

Yazov then balanced all the talk of reductions with an enumeration of continuing NATO military programs, the U.S. "competitive strategies" scheme for damaging the Soviet Union through the qualitative arms race, the new American Air-Land Battle doctrine, and NATO's "follow-on forces attack" (FOFA). Against this backdrop, he condemned the critics who advocated an all-volunteer army backed by a territorial militia, following the example of the Red Army in the 1920s. It would be too expensive, draw on too narrow a social base, fail to meet high-technology military requirements, and be unable to mobilize for a major war. He also flatly rejected the idea that half of the conventional forces could be cut, obviously alluding to Aleksei Arbatov's proposals.[29] In other words, he accepted nothing beyond the unilateral reductions.

Moiseev spoke of the General Staff's intensive work on reform. It was reevaluating the threat and deciding precisely what military forces were needed, efforts that created a "new approach to defining the makeup and structure of the Soviet military as a whole."[30] He emphasized the 14.2 percent cut in the defense budget and announced that several military districts and armies would be abolished and that almost 50 percent of the motorized rifle divisions would be eliminated. These changes were, he insisted, logically and systematically developed from the decision on a new military doctrine taken in 1985–86. Things were moving according to plan, and they had now reached a "new stage."[31] Like Yazov, he could not resist listing a number of threatening developments in Western military establishments, but his harshest criticism was against the proposal for an all-volunteer professional army backed by a territorial militia.

Both Yazov and Moiseev were trying to convey the impression that genuine military reform was beginning, based on careful professional planning. Indeed, implementation of the unilateral reductions was producing noteworthy changes. The elimination of the Central Asian Military District was announced in early June 1989.[32] Forces were withdrawing from Mongolia as well as from Eastern Europe. The General Staff completed its withdrawal of Soviet forces from Afghanistan in February 1989. Still, as the critics complained, the military leaders gave very little solid information by which to judge these changes. A reduction of the defense budget by 14.2 percent was meaningless unless one knew the actual size of the budget. It was left to Gorbachev to make the military budget figure public in May 1989—77.3 billion rubles. The generals were equally vague about changes in force structure, and they refused to define the precise shape and size that the military would eventually take. Thus they failed to convince the critics, among them, Gorbachev and his close supporters.

In the summer and fall of 1989, Gorbachev let the parliament step up the pressure for perestroika in the military. At the same time, he waved some olive branches at Yazov personally, expressed concern over the state of affairs in the military, and commended the MoD's work on reform. On 28 April he had promoted Yazov to Marshal of the Soviet Union, a title that he had earlier abolished, reserving it for wartime use only.[33] When Yazov was subjected to a withering barrage of criticism in the Supreme Soviet during his July confirmation hearing, Gorbachev personally stepped forward to defend him.

He praised Yazov as truly professional, candid in identifying problems, and responsive in carrying out decisions. As an example, Gorbachev said, "We have eliminated 101 divisions. Have you felt our army get weaker? No. They were feeding troughs." Admitting that Yazov had not always given the best answers to questions or made the best proposals, that at times he showed too much temper, as he had in answering the deputies' questions, and that he still was learning his job, Gorbachev declared that he nonetheless took "progressive" positions, and that he was definitely the man to head the defense ministry. With this mixed assessment, Gorbachev hastily demanded a vote, which confirmed Yazov.[34] The marshal was trapped. He had the president's public backing, but on the implicit promise that he would deliver more reductions in the future, and if he did not, he would be at the mercy of the parliament as well as Gorbachev. It was a salutary message not just for Yazov but for the military high command as a whole.

For the remainder of the year, Yazov had to deal with the accumulating problems in carrying out the unilateral reductions and withdrawals from Eastern Europe. At the same time he had to cope with pressure not just from Gorbachev but also from the parliament and the media. Thus he tried to convey the impression that MoD was implementing a well-planned scheme. Slogans are the coinage of such public-affairs markets, and predictably he proclaimed a "New Model of Security" in the pages of the party's theoretical journal.[35] In substance it differed little from what he had said in April, emphasizing the unilateral reductions, the cut in the budget and arms procurement, and plans for converting military industries to civilian production, but it provided more detailed figures on categories of budget reductions. During these same six months, however, the new Supreme Soviet was beginning to tackle military reform on its own—or, more accurately, on the part of some of its own young military deputies.

The Committee on Defense and Security

As the Supreme Soviet organized its system of committees, the one on "defense and security" took responsibility not just for the defense ministry but also for the MVD, the KGB, the VPK, and all agencies that dealt with military, police, and intelligence matters. Because Supreme Soviet deputies could also hold posts in the government and other organizations, many of them had little time for committee activities. Although the defense and security committee had among its forty-three members a few ordinary citizens—writers, metal workers, and scholars—the majority came from the defense establishment. Marshal Akhromeev himself was a member. Several weapons designers and factory directors from the VPK, a regional party secretary, and a chairman of the KGB for a union republic were in its membership. Major Vladimir Lopatin, the infamous young military critic, also belonged to it. All in all, almost 90 percent of its members had ties to the military and military-industrial establishment.[36]

The committee got off to a slow start. The chairman, V. I. Lapygin, who had a VPK background, offered passive leadership. The deputy chairman, V. N. Ochirov, was at the same time the commander of an air force regiment and firmly against reform. The three subcommittee chairmen included Ye. P. Velikhov, from the Academy of Sciences, of the armed forces subcommittee; M. P. Smirnov, a deputy aircraft designer within the VPK, of the VPK subcommittee; and G. P. Khrachenko, party first secretary of the Zaporozh'e Oblast, of the subcommittee on state security. Given their full-time posts elsewhere, they could only be part-time legislators—not to mention that their full-time posts little disposed them toward serious reform. This conflicted leadership spent endless hours trying to decide the committee's agenda and the scope of its powers, which were only vaguely defined by law. Authority over the military budget was limited to recommendations to the government on the overall state budget. Whether the committee had the authority to initiate legislation was not at first clear. A few members wanted to monitor the implementation of laws and policies by the ministries. The committee also sought review authority over arms control treaties and declarations of war.[37]

Even if these functions fell fully within the committee's authority, their execution would depend on its powers to oversee operations in the ministries.

Some of its members turned to the U.S. Congress's armed services committees for oversight techniques, visiting Washington to study the American system.[38] The members who genuinely favored military reform wanted to make the committee strong and active, much like its U.S. counterparts, but they quickly came up against strong opposition from two sources. First, the defense ministry and the VPK simply refused to provide the information necessary for effective oversight. Second, within the committee, those members from the military, the VPK, and the security services defended the ministries, insisting that the committee was competent to deal with the information it requested.

The reform-minded military deputies, not just committee members but also others, went to work on a "law on defense" that would define the place of the military establishment in the political system and provide a legal basis for the parliament's role in military policy making. What the reformers could not get the Defense and Security Committee to agree to informally, they now proposed to put into law. On 20 October 1989, they presented a draft bill to the Supreme Soviet.[39] It went nowhere.

Competing Reform Agendas

Reformers like Major Lopatin, Colonel Tsalko, Major Yevgenii Yerokhin, and others, however, were not so easily stopped. When the Second Congress of People's Deputies convened in December, a group of seventeen military deputies, mostly younger officers, prepared a reform concept paper and presented it to the congress.[40] The secretariat of the congress refused to make it public, but it stimulated action. At the next session of the Supreme Soviet in January 1990, the subcommittee on the armed forces created the Commission for the Preparation and Implementation of Military Reform in the USSR, chaired by Major Lopatin. Shortly thereafter the party got in the act at its February Central Committee plenum, approving language on military reform to be approved by the Twenty-eighth Party Congress in July. As one observer wrote, this language "soon enriched the military leaders' vocabulary" but produced no reform activity.[41] The military, however, had not waited to launch its own reform agenda. Already in late December 1989, an interdepartmental commission established under the leadership of the defense ministry began work on a "new law on defense" to be presented to the parliament by March 1990.[42]

The Radical Reform Agenda

Lopatin's commission reached out to seven institutes in the Academy of Sciences, as well as three military academies and four defense ministry institutes, for expert assistance because the defense ministry itself refused to provide either information or support.[43] In other words, it pulled together most of the scholars and analysts who had been engaged in the public debate over the previous two or three years and united them with the newly emerging group of younger officers who favored radical reform. Lopatin's final report consisted of more than two thousand pages in support of sweeping reform proposals.[44] Not surprisingly, it met criticism. Some of it was merited because the document contained internal inconsistencies, but most of it was emotional invective from senior officers in the MoD. Lopatin conducted the commission's work in complete openness, in contrast to the closeted conditions in which the government commission operated. From January until April its main themes were debated in the media. Defense military officials roundly ridiculed it while a number of newspapers and magazines defended it.[45] In early April, the parliamentary subcommittee on the armed forces approved the commission's work.

Getting to this point had not been easy. MoD opposition was only one obstacle to the Lopatin commission. The head of Main Political Administration tried to intimidate officers backing the commission report by warning that as communists they were acting as a "caste beyond reproach." Military deputies in the parliament were pressured by their military superiors to renounce their signatures on the report, and military deputies who did not support Lopatin took every opportunity to create difficulties for the reformers. In other words, the defense ministry engaged in behind-the-scenes arm twisting. The senior military made no effort to conceal its anger from the very beginning, when Lopatin and his colleagues had shared a draft of their ideas with the defense ministry in December 1989 in an effort to get its support. The defense ministry kept the affair secret, never admitting that it was invited to participate in the effort.[46]

The substance of the Lopatin commission's proposals makes clear why the defense ministry was upset. A large number of military policy issues surfaced in the public debate. As we have seen, the new defensive doctrine emerged first; then nuclear weapons took center stage in connection with arms control negotiations. Reductions of conventional forces followed, and that naturally spawned questions about manpower policy. The underlying purpose for all the proposals was to reduce the economic burdens of the huge military and its industrial establishment. All these issues remained largely academic. But the unilateral cuts that began in 1989 were another matter. They were large enough to require a significant redesign of the force structure. At the same time, the young officers pushing for reform were far better attuned to a multitude of problems within the lower military ranks. Having experienced them personally, they urgently wanted to go beyond glasnost and academic articles to impose radical but practical solutions. Accordingly, their proposals in the parliament were radical. They ignored the arid realms of nuclear weapons doctrine and schemes for achieving a balance of conventional forces in Europe, though they were concerned with an accurate appraisal of foreign military threats. Instead, they focused on life inside the military and ways to change it for the better.

Accordingly, the first and most critical issue was universal military conscription.[47] The Lopatin commission's draft proposed a gradual shift to a much smaller professional military, manned entirely by volunteers. Moreover, because a modern military required quality manpower before quantity, a professional military was imperative.

The origins of the thinking behind this proposal can be traced to the late summer of 1988. A roundtable discussion, including several civilians, a general, and a couple of field-grade officers, was broadcast on Moscow television. The participants were divided in their views but raised the heretofore forbidden idea of a small professional military in place of universal conscription. The Red Army's territorial militia system of the 1920s was also mentioned as a possible contemporary solution.[48] Colonel Savinkin soon thereafter published his views in support of a small professional army backed up by a militia, and the military conscription issue rapidly drew wide media attention. Over the next year, a few serving officers spoke out in favor of a professional army. Civilians, including several journalists and scholars, joined them. The generals reacted with alarm, condemning such ideas, and they drew support from a few journalists and senior party officials.[49]

The generals insisted that an all-volunteer military would cost far more than the present system, but Yazov, Moiseev, and Akhromeev each produced conflicting estimates of how much more, suggesting to the reformers that they were bluffing.[50] The militia concept drew especially sharp criticism as being neither appropriate for training troops to use high-technology weapons nor adequate for manning forces in remote locations. Even critics, however, noted that conscripts in the present system served too short a time to master newer and more complex weapons. The generals rightly insisted that a militia would exacerbate this problem. And they worried about how soldiers would be found to serve in the Far East, Central Siberia, and northern Russia, where large military and naval forces were deployed. The militia system would violate the principle of extraterritoriality—of sending every recruit far from his home to perform his military service. In several of the republics, where demands for national military formations were being voiced, the militia concept had special appeal. This prospect outraged the generals, who saw militia units as centers for anti-Soviet nationalist sentiment. Because nationalism was already becoming a major problem in a number of republics—Ukraine, Moldavia, the Baltic republics, and the Transcaucasus—this was not a theoretical issue. The generals also claimed that universal conscription afforded Soviet youth a basic political socialization that a professional military could not, thus risking a split between the army and society.

Touching virtually every family, the military conscription issue resonated widely. The intelligentsia hated conscription because it interfered with their sons' education. Less privileged parents harbored private fears about sending their sons for military service because they knew of the horrors of military life from returning veterans. Afghan veterans brought home more terrifying stories to reinforce the public mood against conscription. Separatist glasnost voices in the national minority republics began to exploit the conscription issue against Soviet rule. Conscription not only stirred the public against the generals but also caused disputes within the military and among the party leaders. Lieutenant General Vladimir Serebryannikov, a political officer, thundered against a professional military for a time but then switched to support reform, not just of the conscription system but of the military in general.[51] A few other officers changed to support reform as well. Many communist deputies in the parliament considered glasnost on military service a serious political mistake. Ligachev, Chebrikov, and other senior party leaders expressed similar judgments.

The generals were justly worried but miserably inept at articulating their case. Admittedly, the realities did not make it easy for them. They could only appeal to the Politburo to stop the public discussion. The Politburo, as Chernyaev noted, did not see how it could. Now, as Lopatin's commission proposed legislation for a professional army, the issue was moving from merely discussion to a showdown for action.

The second major objective of military reformers' draft was to bring the military bureaucracy under strong parliamentary oversight and to make its operations open to public scrutiny. Under the proposed arrangements, the defense ministry and the government would have to share the making of defense policy with the Congress of People's Deputies and the Supreme Soviet. This, of course, required the defense establishment, including the VPK, to provide freely the information demanded by the parliament and the congress. In the context of Gorbachev's political reform, there was no legitimate basis for objecting to Lopatin's proposals. The very purpose of the new parliament was to be a vital, substantive legislature in place of the old rubber-stamping Supreme Soviet. After six months of experience with conservative party, industrial, and military deputies struggling to make the new Supreme Soviet a rubber stamp as well, the reformers now were demanding that the legislature conduct business in the manner Gorbachev intended. The defense ministry found genuine parliamentary oversight preposterous and opposed it stubbornly, sometimes with outrage.

A third central feature of the draft was its approach to assessing threats to Soviet security. All the priorities for research and development, procurement, force levels, and force structure had to be based on a realistic assessment of threats and the doctrine of defensive sufficiency. The General Staff could argue that this was not new by citing the articles and media appearances over the past year in which Moiseev and Yazov had called for realistic threat assessments. Still, letting the parliament review the General Staff's threat assessments was unacceptable to the generals because they and the parliamentary reformers took radically different views of what constituted a threat. These young military deputies were closer to Kunadze and Blagovolin in their evaluation of the external world than to the General Staff. Lopatin in particular saw a benign international environment. They now considered the most powerful of the imperialist countries, the United States, a source of support for Soviet reform.[52]

A fourth key point of the draft concerned the budget. It had to be reduced significantly, and that meant large military cuts. The reformers offered a number of new ideas that had not previously appeared in the public debate. They called for eliminating large parts of the administrative and management bureaucracy throughout the defense establishment. A clear line was to be drawn between the functions of the MoD and the General Staff. (Here they were consciously following the American model.) Civilian specialists could be used in many posts, including minister of defense. The huge military educational establishment was also to be reduced. The nearly two hundred college-level commissioning schools, military academies, and specialized institutes simply were not needed. The training system drew attention, both for reductions and for improved effectiveness. Finally, the number of general officers was to be greatly reduced and their special privileges surrendered in the name of economy.

The MoD found it awkward to object to some of these proposals. More effective training made sense. Cutting military schools, however, also meant cutting many comfortable assignments for colonels and even generals who were commonly found on their faculties. The large number of generals and their special privileges touched a sensitive nerve because the MoD had been under fire from the media for more than a year on this issue. And to be sure, the idea of civilians running the MoD was anathema to the senior military.

Fifth, and related to these budget-cutting measures, the conditions of barracks life had to be improved, and social support for servicemen and their families needed to be increased. The generals never denied that life in the military was not what it should be; instead, they argued that the beastly behavior of soldiers and noncommissioned officers merely reflected the realities of the society in general. If the mores of the civilian society were improved, maladies would disappear from military life as well. Meanwhile, senior officers increasingly made social support for servicemen and families their own cause, especially as troop withdrawals began from Eastern Europe. Officers and families were coming home to find no housing or schools, and even troops faced inadequate barracks space.

Finally, the draft called for a sharp reduction of the Communist Party's influence on military affairs in favor of the parliament, putting political controls over the military on a legal basis and in the hands of democratically elected officials. The political organs would be reduced in number, removed from party control, and devoted not to ideological work but to troop morale and welfare. A number of the reformers were themselves political officers, including Lopatin. Thus they were keenly aware of the bogus character of the political organs.

This part of their proposal naturally won them the enmity of the Main Political Administration. The MPA took action on 26 April, a couple of weeks after the Lopatin commission presented its proposals, expelling Lopatin from the party, along with a fellow deputy, Lieutenant Nikolai Tutov.[53] The press cried foul play, defending Lopatin. The Central Committee's Party Control Commission reversed the MPA's decision a few days later, but the MPA initially refused to relent.[54] Tensions were sharpening.

The Lopatin commission's draft received a hearing only by the academician Ye. Velikhov's subcommittee of the Defense and State Security Committee, which sent it back for additional work.[55] Throughout the spring the MoD and its sympathizers subjected the draft to a barrage of press attacks.[56] Here was the kind of military reform program Gorbachev had sought for four years, but he lifted not a finger to support it. Chernyaev's inside account of his reaction to events in Lithuania and the anti-Gorbachev demonstration on 25 February makes clear that Gorbachev was on the political defensive through the Twenty-eighth Party Congress in July, but there were other reasons for his hands-off policy as well. Army units had been used to restore order in Baku in January. Just before the Red Army Day celebrations, 23 February, several senior officers openly criticized Gorbachev's reform, and they repeated their complaints around Victory Day on 8 May.[57] The MPA was organizing party conferences in military organizations in preparation for the party congress. Ligachev's supporters were actively opposing perestroika within the party. In this political climate Gorbachev would have had difficulty mustering political support in the parliament to take advantage of the Lopatin commission's work in any event, but when he drew back in fright at the 25 February manifesto and began contemplating military repression in Lithuania, it became impossible.

Lopatin's group and its sympathizers stepped up their public criticism of the MoD and the General Staff after they were defeated in the parliament.[58] Lieutenant General Serebryannikov, formerly an opponent of Lopatin's ideas, joined Lopatin publicly to condemn the conservative views of the MoD, arguing that it did not recognize that rapid change was imperative. A group of officers—students and faculty—at the General Staff Academy also voiced support for fundamental reform, made specific suggestions for force reductions, and criticized Moiseev's commission for working in secrecy. Lopatin himself blamed the Communist Party for blocking his efforts and called the MPA its tool for preventing all serious attempts at military reform.

The Military's Reform Agenda

As we have seen, General Moiseev's interdepartmental commission had begun work early in the year on a draft law on defense in cooperation with the legislature's Defense and Security Committee. The law also had to be tied to new legislation on ownership of property, independence of industrial firms, and regional economic autonomy.[59] In the wake of this public fanfare, the commission retreated into secrecy through the winter and spring, with only an occasional mention in the press. For example, Moiseev gave a brief interview to the military newspaper *Red Star*, complaining that no military official had been allowed to speak at the Central Committee plenum of 5–7 February and insisting if he had been, he would have outlined the MoD's concept of military reform embodied in the emerging draft law on defense, to be implemented in stages through the year 2000.[60] The law did not arrive in the parliament in March, however, as originally intended.

Only in early June was the substance of the government commission's work made public. Marshal Yazov did this in another lengthy article that made no mention of the "new model" proclaimed in his December article, a sign that it had been transcended.[61] He set forth five major areas of reform.

The first was a comprehensive restructuring of organizations and methods of work. It involved a "qualitative renewal" of personnel manning and force structure, of military-technical policy for production and procurement, and of all management systems. Staffs would be cut by more than 15 percent from the General Staff down to army level. General officers posts would be reduced by 30 percent. Initially all five branches of service would be retained, but civil defense troops and construction troops would be removed from the jurisdiction of the armed forces. All construction troop units working for civilian ministries were to be disbanded. The territorial-administrative system of military districts would be revised. These staff cuts, if carried out, would have been significant, and a number of them were.

The transfer of the civil defense troops and construction troops to non-military status was related to the CFE negotiations on conventional force reductions. Removing them from the armed forces allowed the defense ministry to lower the total numbers from which reductions would be mandated by the CFE treaty. Another motive was that the General Staff disliked the extent to which they were used for nonmilitary purposes. As Marshal Akhromeev put it, they were a "mechanism" used by civilian sector managers to profit at the expense of the MoD's resources.[62]

Smaller requirements for officers during the next ten years would allow the closing of 30–35 percent of all military educational institutions through consolidations and the elimination of 30–40 percent of the military departments in civilian educational institutions. Here Yazov was implicitly accepting one of the radical reformers' proposals.

Management changes also affected the relation between the MoD and the VPK. All weapons development questions would be transferred from the MoD to the General Staff, which would apply the competitive principle to weapons development, exploit the "modular" approach to building new systems, reduce the number of contractors in the VPK, and manage procurements strictly through financial contracts with VPK firms. These changes were in anticipation of economic reforms that Gorbachev would attempt in the fall.

The second sphere of reform concerned defensive doctrine. Here Yazov offered nothing new, simply noting that the doctrine required retaliatory military operations and that much work remained to revise training and planning in accordance with a purely defensive military posture. Acknowledging a limited role for the parliament, he said that the military should be used against only foreign threats based on decisions by the Congress of People's Deputies, the Supreme Soviet, and in certain cases, by the president. This limitation was an allusion to the growing discomfort that generals felt about using the army to repress domestic disorders, especially after the bloody episode in Tbilisi in April 1989. They were not squeamish, or at least not yet, but they hated the bad publicity such actions brought them.

Third, Yazov addressed the military conscription. While it had to be retained, he made some concessions for the future. In 1992 an experiment would begin with "contract" soldiers. Those who had completed their two-year obligation would be allowed to volunteer for additional service by signing a contract for a longer term at much better pay, a monthly salary of 150 rubles or more, compared with the five or six rubles a conscript received. Further change would depend on the results from this experiment. The feasibility of reducing the two-year service obligation to eighteen months was being studied, but "alternative service" to military duty was a premature idea, no matter that it was very popular. Finally, Yazov firmly rejected the national military formations sought by some of the republics, warning that they would only exacerbate interethnic tensions. Far from accepting the Lopatin commission's proposal for a professional force, Yazov was yielding modest ground on the issue.

Yazov's fourth point dealt with the MPA's political organs. They would be retained, but in the long run they had to distinguish between their educational and party functions. Yazov defined education to include political indoctrination as well as military, moral, and legal training. For party work he suggested an "all-army party commission" with the status of a Central Committee department. It would direct party work at each level in the military through a system of control commissions. Proposing to make the political organs into state instead of party structures was, of course, what the Lopatin draft had recommended. But the parliamentary reformers wanted party organizations entirely eliminated from the military establishment. On this point Yazov gave no ground.

Fifth, Yazov dealt with social support for servicemen and their families, repeating the litany of problems caused by withdrawals from Eastern Europe, the main one being a shortage of barracks, housing, and schools. Thousands of officers' families were homeless as they returned to their own country. His solution was twenty-four million square feet of new housing to be budgeted in the next five-year plan and another twenty-five million square feet in the following five years. Additionally, pensions were scheduled to increase by 15–20 percent.

The defense minister warned that all these reforms could not be accomplished quickly; no less than nine or ten years would be required. That was why the "comprehensive plan" envisioned phases, from 1991–95 through the year 2000. It would also require several new laws, which he expected the parliament to pass in a timely fashion. Most of the changes in the early 1990s involved the completion of the unilateral cuts and reductions mandated by arms control treaties. The major structural changes would come later in the decade.

Although no "law on defense" embodying this reform agenda was passed, the government took it as state policy. Yazov presented it for review by Gorbachev and the Defense Council in early September.[63] In November, General Moiseev explained that military reform was going forward based on work of his commission.[64] The collegium of the MoD had reviewed and approved it. Moiseev said, however, that in light of the issue of a new union treaty, it was premature to make it law. Moreover, negotiations in Vienna and Geneva over the previous six months had been producing arms reductions treaties that would have to be accommodated in the reform plan. (The CFE treaty, for example, had just been signed.) All this work on reform, he lamented, was being ignored by the press while it complained that nothing was being done.

Moiseev was right on some points. The radical reformers in the parliament had been stopped—at least temporarily—and to the extent that there was a military reform plan, it was the work of his government commission. As he admitted, the centrifugal forces of national sovereignty movements had indeed forced Gorbachev to consider a new union treaty, and that would dramatically change the conditions for military reform, not to mention complicate its implementation. The CFE and START treaties, of course, still posed uncertainties for force levels and deployments.

Lopatin's attempt to legislate military reform had failed, but it had had a strong impact by confronting the MoD and the General Staff with a radical alternative that the parliament might conceivably adopt in law. Although Yazov and Moiseev managed to prevent that eventuality, Major Lopatin and nearly a score of other military deputies had forced their issues onto the reform agenda. They had set the broad terms. Although Moiseev denied it, his commission had given ground on a number of reformers' demands. He later insisted that the public debate on military reform died down because Lopatin's group could not get beyond "general principles."[65] This was, of course, untrue. It died down because Gorbachev abandoned the parliamentary reformers in the spring and summer of 1990 under considerable party opposition over worsening political conditions among the national minorities.

Throughout the rest of 1990 and through the political crisis in late August 1991, the main lines of military reform were those outlined by Yazov in June and reiterated by Moiseev in November 1990. When Marshal of Aviation Yevgenii Shaposhnikov replaced Marshal Yazov as defense minister after the August 1991 crisis, he found the reform plans more or less as Yazov and Moiseev had described them a year earlier.[66] A lot of talk had transpired, but little progress had been made in practical implementation. As a result, vast social and political forces were overtaking the military's determination to proceed at a slow and deliberate pace.

Pressure Groups in the Struggle over Military Reform

The struggle over military reform catalyzed a number of public voluntary groups on both sides of the issue. Most of them included parliamentary deputies in their membership, giving them access to the legislative process. At the same time, they sought to broaden their membership and create sufficient organized political power to be taken seriously by both the parliament and the government. Although these particular groups appeared first in fall 1989, voluntary organizations for a variety of issues had been springing up by the hundreds since the previous winter.

Some of these so-called *neformal'ny* officially registered with the government according to Soviet laws for public organizations, but many did not. Many were too short-lived to be noticed. Others proved more durable. A few created branches in the republics and regional towns, but most had no existence beyond Moscow. Although most were founded on the initiative of private citizens, some were the creations of state authorities, often the KGB, as spoilers, troublemakers, and counterweights for groups and policies that some senior party officials did not like. A few of the voluntary groups concerned with military affairs proved quite vocal, even at times influential.

Shchit (Shield)

Among the most visible of such groups concerned with military policy was the Union for the Social Protection of Servicemen and Their Families, or Shield, as it was popularly called. In October 1989 its organizers managed to get time on television to explain their activities and goals.[67] They claimed to have about three hundred officers in their initiative group. Their purpose was to increase social support for soldiers, junior officers, and their families. As troop withdrawals from Eastern Europe proceeded apace, many officers and their families were coming back to inadequate or housing or none at all in the Soviet Union. Some were reported to be living in tents (a point the MoD flatly denied). Because the military command structure was not taking care of them, the Shield organizers declared that the officers and troops would have to take care of themselves. Thus they were founding an army "trade union." They took as their model a successful union created in 1956 by the West German military.

Under the leadership of Lieutenant Colonel V. G. Urazhtsev, recently expelled from the army for criticizing his immediate superior officer, Shield began demanding legislative action by the parliament. Toward the end of October, a group of Shield's military deputies submitted a draft law on social support. The

MPA reacted negatively to Shield's existence, while Andrei Sakharov's Inter-regional Group of deputies expressed support for it.[68] In November, Shield staged a small demonstration in Moscow to demand an end to Communist Party influence in the army and better pay for soldiers. Speeches by parents and members of families of soldiers about the horrible conditions of military service added to the group's image as a serious voice for rank-and-file military personnel.[69]

Just how large Shield became is not clear, but it remained visibly active, sometimes supporting Lopatin and his efforts, sending delegations to the United States to study the role of the U.S. Congress in military policy, and sponsoring programs in public education and information. The best evidence of its effectiveness is probably the military's continuing opposition to it. The following year, in December 1990, the parliament passed a law forbidding active-duty military personnel from joining unions. Liberal deputies opposed this law, but by that time, the conservatives had the upper hand in the Supreme Soviet, and Marshal Viktor Kulikov spoke in support of it.[70] That did not end Shield's existence, however, and it remained active after the end of the Soviet Union.

The Movement of Soldiers' Mothers

Mothers of Soviet soldiers first became politically active during the first Congress of People's Deputies, when three hundred women presented the deputies with a demand that their sons be discharged.[71] At the urging of the congress, those discharges were soon issued. That surprising success gave momentum to the so-called Committee for Soldiers' Mothers. According to Maria Kirba-sova, apparently the founder of a committee of soldiers' mothers in April 1989, groups of women also became active in the Baltic republics, in Georgia, Armenia, Uzbekistan, and Ukraine, and in regional Russian cities.[72] In January 1990, the committee staged demonstrations against sending Soviet troops to restore order in Baku.[73] In an effort to create an umbrella organization and strengthen their activities, they held an all-union committee of soldiers' mothers in Moscow's Gor'ki Park in mid-June, adopting a new name, Mother's Heart.[74] Thereafter the organization began to monitor cases of abuse and noncombat deaths, gathering statistics, calling for the removal of responsible commanders, and demanding laws from the parliament to improve soldiers' rights.

The potential political power of soldiers' mothers was evident. The senior military could hurl insults with impunity at radical junior officers in Shield and at Lopatin's group of military deputies after Gorbachev failed to support military reform in the spring of 1990. Mothers of soldiers were another matter. They gave the generals pause, even General A. D. Lizichev, the head of the MPA, who normally spared no critic of the military. Shield's leader, Urazhtsev, grasped the importance of this new movement and tried to seize control of it.

In early September 1990, the first All-Union Congress of Servicemen's Parents met in Moscow. Shield organized it with the assistance of another group, Mothers Against Force. The change from "mothers" to "parents" suggests Urazhtsev's determination to enlist the testimony of fathers as well as mothers on behalf of the cause. The congress listened to a parade of speakers describe how their sons were brutalized during military service, claim that fifteen thousand to twenty thousand soldiers had suffered noncombat deaths over the past four years, and demand that Gorbachev issue a decree protecting servicemen before the fall conscription call-up.[75]

In fact, Gorachev had just issued such a decree in response to pressure from Maria Kirbasova's Mother's Heart.[76] Urazhtsev was obviously trying to take the initiative away from the original organization for soldiers' mothers. Mothers Against Force had no previous record of notable activity. After the crisis of August 1991, when Marshal Shaposhnikov became defense minister, the mothers' movement put enormous pressure on him, and in his account of it, he describes a fight for its leadership. Colonel A. A. Alekseev and Lieutenant Colonel Urazhtsev persuaded Shaposhnikov to meet with all the movement's groups and factions, and he spoke to the All-Union Congress of Soldiers' Mothers, a crowd of more than two thousand. Alekseev, taking the lead as the organizer of the congress, excluded Urazhtsev's people entirely.[77] Shaposhnikov saw the whole thing as a petty struggle among ambitious officer-politicians who cared less about the plight of soldiers and their families than about their own fortunes.

This was also the case, of course, among most of the new political leaders at the time. The movement of soldiers' mothers became a powerful force, one that could persuade Gorbachev himself to issue a decree in response to its demands. Not surprisingly, the mothers' movement attracted ambitious and aggressive leaders. For disaffected field-grade officers like Urazhtsev and Alekseev, it presented a great political opportunity. Or, as Maria Kirbasova suspected, they may have been sent by the KGB to destroy the movement from within.[78]

Officers' Assemblies

In November 1989, "the officers' assembly" institution from Imperial Russian Army days was revived with encouragement from the MoD. In the nineteenth century, officers' assemblies normally existed in all regiments as social organizations that supported activities ranging from casinos and clubs to moral training and social support. In reviving them, the MoD was clearly trying to create a public organization that could work against Shield and the soldiers' mothers movement. In early December 1989, the first All-Army Officers' Assembly convened in Moscow.[79] Marshal Yazov spoke to the 1,500 delegates from all military districts, fleets, and groups of forces. Thereafter officers' assemblies began to attract considerable press attention. They could be counted on as a forum for criticism of the media's treatment of the military, for condemning the radical military reformers in the parliament, and for demanding better wages and social support for the military.

The attitude of the officers' assemblies toward the MPA was ambiguous. Their participation in moral education of officers seemed to put them on the MPA's bureaucratic turf, but there is no record of MPA complaints. Had the parliament passed a law eliminating the political organs, as was feared, political officers might well have simply moved into the officers' assemblies as their new place of duty. The more important role of this institution was political activism in the media and putting pressure on Gorbachev and the parliament in favor of the MoD. On the whole, however, they were not very effective beyond attracting occasional media attention.

Veterans Groups

A number of veterans groups existed. The All-Union Army and Labor Veterans' Organization was formed in 1985, headed by a former Politburo member, Kirill Mazurov. When he died in 1990, Marshal Ogarkov, former chief of the General Staff, became the organization's leader.[80] Another group, the All-Union Council of War Veterans, drew attention in September 1990 by calling for a traditional celebration of the anniversary of the Bolshevik seizure of power.[81] These two veterans groups were defenders of the traditional Soviet order. Veterans of the Afghan war, however, held mixed views about the Soviet system. Most felt that they had received too little attention and public respect. The Union of Democratic Afghan War Veterans was formed in honor of Andrei Sakharov and promised to devote its efforts to the "defense of democratic activities." [82] Although the veterans groups naturally expressed opinions on military affairs, they were not particularly active in the legislative struggle over military reform. Marshal Ogarkov offered a couple of public warnings about the direction of Gorbachev's military policy, and the Afghan veterans backed proposals for better social support for servicemen, but the veterans groups were not significant as pressure groups.[83]

Soyuz (Union)

Another small group worth mentioning is Union. It consisted of a group of reactionary deputies in the Supreme Soviet and the Congress of People's Deputies under the leadership of Colonel Viktor Alksnis. Alksnis had become notorious for telling Gorbachev at a public meeting in the fall of 1990 that the army was no longer with him. An ethnic Latvian, he nonetheless vigorously opposed national independence movements in the Baltic republics and the Transcaucasus. Reestablishing the old totalitarian system was his unabashed goal, and he even promised to support Gorbachev if he would attempt that.[84] Alksnis's Soyuz group had no broad following, and it was probably a creation of the KGB. Still, it was a factor within the parliament in defeating Lopatin's reform program.

In summary, the appearance of genuine interest groups trying to influence military policy was the direct result of Gorbachev's political reform. Like the reform, however, they remained a Moscow phenomenon without significant support or activity beyond the capital. They depended heavily on the media for influence. Kicking up a fuss and staging newsworthy events was their stock in trade. Because some of their members were deputies in the congress and the parliament, they had access to the legislative process, but they enjoyed no significant success either in fostering new laws or affecting government policy. The exception was the mothers' movement. It had a broad base of public support, a keen emotional appeal to virtually all parents with sons in the military or soon to be drafted. One convincing measure of its power was the bitter respect and anger it earned from the military leadership. Another was its continued existence in the late 1990s.

Throughout 1990 and early 1991, these groups kept up a torrent of media debate over the competing agendas for military reform. Instead of focusing on the overall reform objectives, however, they put most attention on the conscription system and social support for servicemen and the families. The more shrill this kind of public discourse grew, the wider the gaps became between Shield and the mothers' movement on the one side and the officers' assemblies and Soyuz on the other. It would be wrong to characterize any of them as winning the debate. They were merely a few of the organized voices as glasnost increased with regard to military policy. Serving officers, scholars, journalists, and many others offered more than a few words of advice publicly on military affairs during 1989–91.

Two individuals stand out among all these, however, for their leadership not just during 1989–91 but also long afterward. Major Lopatin was still a member of Russian State Duma in 1996 and still actively working for military reform. Maria Kirbasova was still heading the Russian Committee of Soldiers' Mothers in 1996, working to expand and strengthen her regional committees, advising parents of soldiers, and taking delegations of parents to the front in the war in Chechnya to entice their sons to desert the army. Urazhtsev, Alekseev, and others quickly disappeared.

One conclusion stands out above all others when this unprecedented struggle to legislate military reform is viewed as a whole: the opposing sides were talking past one another. The irreconcilable difference between the competing agendas was systemic versus nonsystemic reform. Lopatin and his colleagues insisted on systemic change. To abandon universal conscription in favor of a volunteer professional army, freed from the party's political organs, was to create a different kind of military establishment. It was to renounce more than sixty years of military institutional practice and its political foundations. Nor was the reform process to be dragged out. Lopatin's fellow deputies were seized with urgency. They rightly understood that the old military system obstructed perestroika's larger economic and political goals. Unless that obstruction could be overcome rapidly, perestroika would fail overall. And the reformers probably believed that the new parliament had given them a single opportunity that would either be seized or lost for good.

Senior military leaders proceeded from fundamentally different premises. Yazov and Moiseev sought to keep the Soviet military system intact. Forced to accommodate reductions, both unilateral and through arms control agreements, they cut a little here and little there while holding onto the system itself. The issue of universal military service was not the only one that exposed the senior military's opposition to systemic change. We have seen that during the early 1980s, when the General Staff had shifted its attention from gaining military equivalence with the United States at the strategic level to improving its capabilities for theater conventional force operations, a new command level — "high commands" — was created between the General Staff and fronts. One had been created in Chita in the Far East, another in Baku in the south. Two more, a western and a southwestern high command, were established to accommodate a much swifter offensive into Europe. When troop withdrawals from Eastern Europe began in 1989, according to Marshal Akhromeev, "some people" wanted to eliminate the new high commands. He and his colleagues in the defense ministry adamantly resisted what they saw as the destruction of a great achievement. Operational art at that level was not easily learned, as he argued, and to tear down something based on fifty years of experience and work was just not acceptable.[85] If Soviet military strategy was to emphasize the defensive, however, an excellent case for eliminating the high commands could be made. Akhromeev remained reluctant as late as 1991, clinging to the belief that a counteroffensive would still be required at the theater strategic level. Undoubtedly many senior officers in the defense ministry also shared his view right up until the end of the Soviet Union. Systemic change remained outside of their thinking about military reform.

Apparently, Yazov, Moiseev, and their assistants believed that waiting out the reformers while proclaiming to be reformers themselves was a viable strategy. Wrongly, they believed that time was on their side. It is easy to conclude that they were simply obtuse. But just as in the case of the public debate in 1988 and 1989, the military believed with some justification that the radical reformers did not appreciate the practical realities involved in implementing military reform.

A sense of the actual thinking among the senior military leaders on this point was left by Marshal Akhromeev in his memoir, probably written in early 1991.[86] He goes down the list of major proposals put forward by the radical reformers, pointing out the difficulties of carrying them out, conveying an appreciation that neither building up nor dismantling large, complex organizations is as easy as talking about it. His tone is one more of frustration than of anger, as he complains that the political leaders and the parliamentarians did not really want to discuss the difficulties candidly. The politicians, he was sure, were more interested in driving a wedge between the army and society than in dealing with the practical realities.

There was a degree of truth in Akhromeev's assessment. Yet this very attitude both justified and reinforced the militant attitude of the radical reformers, especially the younger officers. The generals stubbornly kept the traditional veil of Soviet secrecy over as much information about military affairs as possible while denouncing their critics as incompetent, ignorant, and ill-intentioned. The younger officers, of course, knew firsthand the serious problems inside the ranks of the army long ignored by the generals. And they had good reasons for their moral indignation over the refusal of the generals to take perestroika as an opportunity to improve the health of the army. Ignoring those realities, the generals believed that the younger officers ignored others.

A similar dual perception of reality inhibited the very foundations of Gorbachev's political reforms. The atmosphere in the new parliament conveys a sense of the surreal, make-believe legislation, halfway measures, and uncertainty and vacillation by Gorbachev and his Politburo colleagues about how far to let the process go. The new parliament had no chance to become a genuine legislature, primarily because it did not control the purse strings, but also because of the way Gorbachev treated it. When the subcommittee on defense actually produced draft legislation on military reform that should have pleased Gorbachev, he did not back it. Instead, he allowed a stalemate between the defense ministry and the parliamentary reformers.

TEN

The Intractable Party–
Military Connection

The army is that school where the party can instill its moral hardness,
self-sacrifice, and its discipline.

LEON TROTSKY

When Gorbachev took the path of political reform toward a "law-based society," it became necessary to remove the Communist Party from its "leading role" not only as the rule maker in the Soviet political system but also as the rule implementer. This involved breaking the grip of the party's regional and local committees and secretaries on all the state executive and judicial structures, both economic and noneconomic. Shakhnazarov, it will be recalled, noted the inconsistency of creating the presidency and the new legislature at the center while failing to make analogous organizational changes at the regional levels of government. Radical change at the center required parallel change at the local levels if the reform was to have the desired results.

Breaking the party's grip on the military was therefore not an independent endeavor but rather part of an overall loosening of the Communist Party's grip on the entire political system. For that reason, we must first place that measure within Gorbachev's scheme for removing the party from its leading role in the larger political system and then deal with the details of the MPA's fate. Finally, I offer a brief assessment of how well various Western theories of Soviet party-military relations explain their dynamics. Although an esoteric academic excursion, it relates directly to the Soviet military's role in the collapse of the Soviet state and contemporary Western misperceptions of it.

Organizational Implications

The party's organization for controlling most of the state executive bureaucracy was territorially based. Within each territorial administration—republic, oblast (roughly comparable to a state in the United States), krai (also comparable to a state), city, and district (comparable to a county or a city borough)—a party committee, the counterpart to the Central Committee apparatus in Moscow, asserted party control. As Jerry Hough has insightfully demonstrated, the regional party apparatus performed an integrating function somewhat analogous to the French system of prefectures.[1] Not all state structures, however, were organized congruently with the territorial-administrative boundaries of the Soviet Union. The railroads, for example, were organized on a functional basis without regard to local territorial divisions. The Armed Forces of the Soviet Union followed primarily the functional principle, although civil defense troops were an exception, being structured according to the territorial-administrative boundaries. The defense ministry also had its own territorial subdivisions—the military districts.

Where the functional principle applied to executive organization, it also applied to party organization. Thus the Main Political Administration (MPA), as we have seen, was functionally organized. Taking the regional party committees out of their "leading role" would not, therefore, remove the party's grip on the military. When Gorbachev belatedly decided to create a presidency in spring 1990, the issue of eliminating the party's leading role was also on the agenda. Gorbachev wanted to revoke Article 6, which institutionalized the party's leading role, in order to make a multiparty system possible. At the Central Committee plenum in February 1990, it was decided to amend the Soviet constitution, weakening but not removing Article 6.[2]

For the MoD (as well as other components of the armed forces—the KGB border troops and guards units, the MVD internal troops) this change threw the status of the MPA into question. The MPA, it will be recalled, enjoyed the status of a department in the Central Committee Secretariat. Should it continue to exist? What should happen to its vast network of political organs throughout the Armed Forces? Staffed entirely with officers, its personnel totaled about eighty thousand.[3] It had its own educational institutions, headed by the Lenin Military-Political Academy in Moscow. It had its own theoretical journal, *Kommunist vooruzhennykh sil* (Communist of the armed forces), which provided guidance and substantive materials for daily and weekly ideological indoctrination of all military personnel. Its officers dominated the armed forces' newspaper, *Krasnaya zvezda.*

The Size of the Political Challenge

Depoliticization of the Soviet military would not be easy. The MPA not only represented the parochial interests of its personnel, it also stood as a monument to the original integration of the Bolshevik Party with its fighting arm, the Red Army.[4] Its early chiefs were from the senior ranks of the Bolshevik party. I. T. Smigla was a Central Committee member in 1917; Sergei Gusev, Vladimir Antonov-Ovseenko, and Andrei Bubnov—heads of the MPA in the 1920s—were distinguished Bolsheviks. In the 1930s, Ian Gamarnik and Lev Mekhlis had lengthy experience in nonmilitary party posts as Stalinist apparatchiki. The early postwar chiefs of the MPA had experience in civilian party posts, and so did Aleksei Yepishev, who was head of the MPA from 1962 until his retirement at age seventy-seven in July 1985.[5] Aleksei Lizichev, apparently recommended by Yepishev to be his successor, was an exception.[6] He had no known nonmilitary party experience, only service in the field as a political officer, coming from the top MPA post in Soviet forces in Germany to head the MPA. The last head, Nikolai Shlyaga, was working in the Administrative Organs Department of the Central Committee when he was made deputy head of the MPA in January 1990.[7]

The MPA also had supporters in the ranks of the regular officers. That became publicly clear at the Russian Party Conference in June 1990, when the commander of the Volga-Ural Military District, Colonel General Albert Makashov, angrily told Gorbachev that the "army communists" would not surrender the party ideology. A number of younger officers, such as Colonel Alksnis, took this view to the extreme later in 1990, openly calling for Gorbachev to surrender the presidency as well as his party post.[8]

Before 1989, MPA spokesmen, primarily in their theoretical journal and in *Krasnaya zvezda,* voiced a mixed reaction toward perestroika and Gorbachev. Gorbachev's ideological revisions, after he clarified them in 1987, caused them consternation, but as we have seen, they did their best to support both "humankind interests" and the "international class struggle." As glasnost took hold in the media, however, their attitude changed. The severe criticism of the military in the press and proposals for an all-volunteer army provoked them to open anger. In his speech to the first Congress of People's Deputies in 1989, General Lizichev made no bones about his feelings on the idea of a fully volunteer army, accusing its proponents of giving "no thought to the consequences of such reasoning."[9] On the charges of mistreatment of soldiers and the miserable conditions of military life, he put the blame squarely on the civilian society. Low moral standards, drugs, alcohol, poor health, and the large numbers of ex-convicts among the youth were finding their way into the army's ranks. The army did not create these problems; society had. Soviet society in general was experiencing a mental and psychological decline among the youth because of television, radio, video games, and other electronic gadgetry.

Senior political officers more frequently voiced this line of public complaint from that time on. Yet it differed little, if at all, from the things that regular officers were saying. And it did not at first carry the anger that began to characterize the voices of senior regular officers. Marshal Akhromeev, it will be recalled, engaged in a vicious exchange with Georgii Arbatov and other civilian critics. Lizichev did not show his temper unrestrained in the media until an occasion on television in February 1990, when he condemned the waves of public criticism of the army, especially in the Baltic republics, and denounced "pacificism" in general.[10] By this time, however, such outcries were so common that he did not draw the reaction that Akhromeev had in 1989. Regular military officers voiced equally vehement defenses of the military in the same month, making Lizichev's remarks unexceptional. Moreover, General Moiseev directly named Gorbachev when he criticized the military aspects of the party platform being prepared for the upcoming Twenty-eighth Party Congress.[11] The only noticeable difference between the statements of Lizichev and of the regular officers was his concern with the KGB and other components of the armed forces as well as the party. That, of course, was indicative of his wider responsibilities. The regular officers were primarily concerned with the MoD's forces. Lizichev's MPA had political organs in the KGB and elsewhere.

The approach of the Twenty-eighth Party Congress prompted the military and the MPA leadership to mount a public offensive against Gorbachev's proposal to abolish the MPA outright. General Moiseev's concern about the party platform began to be repeated, and throughout the spring, the military's nervousness was no secret. Undoubtedly General Yazov's reports to his subordinates on the Politburo discussions in late January and February made them painfully aware that Gorbachev was planning to depoliticize the military. In typical fashion, Gorbachev and his allies made gestures to allay their fears and possibly to split the regular military from the MPA. On the eve of Red Army Day in February 1990, five full Politburo members attended the ceremonies, paying tribute to the army.[12] On 8 May, at a Victory Day ceremony in the Bolshoi Theater, Gorbachev addressed an audience of senior officers and veterans, praising the military for its heroism in World War II and admitting that Stalin had contributed to the victory. More important, he did not back the radical military reformers in the parliament during the spring and summer, the most critical time for them. At the same time, he was unyielding on perestroika, his foreign policy, and even the unification of Germany.

At a lower level in the military's ranks a quarrel over the MPA's political organs had surfaced publicly somewhat earlier, in fall 1989. Major Vladimir Lopatin and his colleagues, as part of their radical military reform, challenged the very existence of the MPA. The newly established institution of Officers' Assembly held an "all-army" meeting in Moscow in December 1989 at which Lopatin's supporters and Shield called for the abolition of the political organs. Conservatives staged the All-Army Officers' Assembly as a forum for endorsement of the MPA, but the opponents succeeded in making themselves heard. By the end of 1989 the future of the MPA was a public issue.

At the Twenty-eighth Party Congress, of course, Gorbachev faced more than a showdown with the military over the MPA and military reform. He was attempting to take away the very role that Lenin had conceived for the party as the vanguard of the working class, to introduce instead a multiparty system. Over the past year, not only had the party weakened, losing members in large numbers, but within its ranks factions were openly surfacing. Liberal party members were disillusioned with Gorbachev, sensing that he was drifting into the clutches of the party conservatives. Ligachev and Chebrikov were openly rallying the conservatives. In the middle Gorbachev had only a small following remaining.

A similar polarization occurred in the broad ranks of the officer corps, though it was not so conspicuous at the time. More and more officers were quitting the party in 1989 and 1990. Severe retributions against them were common but often ineffective. Lieutenant Colonel Aleksandr Rodin, for example, assigned to a missile impact range in Kamchatka, resigned from the party for reasons of conscience over the corruption he witnessed. He was incarcerated in a mental institution but gained release by threatening to create a public ruckus.[13] As the numbers rose, air force pilots were quitting the party at a higher rate than any other group. Shaposhnikov heard almost daily from Yazov, who asked him what measures he was taking to stop the exodus. Shaposhnikov says the matter became a family joke: "Yazov asks what measures are being taken against aviators leaving the party. Answer: none. Question: why? Answer: it is too late; they have all left. Question: and you? Answer: and I also. Only you remain in the party, and maybe the general secretary."[14]

Chernyaev's picture of Gorbachev throughout the spring and early summer shows him wrestling with alternative tactics for weakening the party. In directing Chernyaev to draft his speech for Lenin's birthday celebration, he said, "End the icon picture [of Lenin], respectfully move [him] into the ranks of other historical figures."[15] The reaction of Ligachev and his allies to the speech showed Chernyaev that Gorbachev had "ideologically and finally walled himself off from them."[16] Shortly before the congress, both Chernyaev and Shakhnazarov urged Gorbachev to take himself out of the struggle for control of the party, to abandon the post of general secretary. As they had done several times previously, they implored him to make the presidency and the state structures his main power base.

Ominous events in May and June convinced them that the opposition would defeat Gorbachev at the congress. The first occurred on May Day. The standard parade passed through Red Square as Gorbachev reviewed it from the Lenin Mausoleum, and then a second demonstration followed, organized by the so-called Moscow Voters' Clubs. Its slogans included "Down with Gorbachev," "Down with the CPSU, exploiter and robber of the people," "Down with socialism and the fascist red empire," "Freedom for Lithuania," and others. Gorbachev and the reviewing party stalked off the mausoleum. That provoked a chorus of catcalls and vicious insults from the crowd.[17] Such unprecedented behavior in Red Square against the top Soviet leaders was not only an embarrassment to Gorbachev but also a shock to the public, accustomed as it was to "seventy years of steel-like Soviet order," to borrow Chernyaev's phrase. These demonstrators, of course, were from the same circles that had produced the anti-Gorbachev manifesto and staged the affair on 25 February. Now they saw Gorbachev as the enemy, a symbol of the party bureaucrats and an impediment to perestroika.

The second event, the creation of a separate Russian Communist Party, was led by the forces who saw Gorbachev as the proponent of perestroika and a danger to the Soviet system.[18] Within the Russian Federation, unlike in other republics, there was no republic party structure. In a move to rally anti-Gorbachev forces, a Russian party conference was held in mid-June to establish a Russian Party Congress. The Leningrad party chief, Boris Gidaspov, took the lead, supported by many of the other regional party secretaries whose lives had been made both difficult and politically dangerous by Gorbachev's political reform, but Ligachev and Chebrikov were undoubtedly behind it as well. An antireformer, Ivan Polozkov, was elected by the Russian Party Congress as its first secretary in spite of Gorbachev's opposition. Several speakers openly hurled demeaning challenges at Gorbachev, who took them all in good temper. The real purpose of the event was hardly concealed. Afterward, Andrei Grachev, of the secretariat's International Department, characterized it as "preparation for a silent coup by the party officials against perestroika."[19]

Ligachev spoke approvingly of the Russian Party Congress and described the ill-considered nature of Gorbachev's policies. He anticipated victory at the upcoming Twenty-eighth Party Congress.[20]

Indeed, Gorbachev's aides had good reason to be concerned. Gorbachev himself admitted that the situation was dangerous, but he consistently refused their advice to leave the party in order to escape the showdown at the Twenty-eighth Party Congress. To Chernyaev's pleadings Gorbachev finally replied, "You know, Tolya, do you think I don't see? I see, and I read your memo. Arbatov, Shmelev . . . also say the same, they try to persuade me to abandon the general secretary post. But remember: that mangy mad dog can't be let off the leash. If I do that, the whole enormous thing will be against me." [21]

These remarks, if they are to be trusted, go far in revealing Gorbachev's tactics. If he left the party too early, before it was completely neutralized as a political organization, it could still defeat him, presidency or no presidency. Much could be said for the wisdom of this approach. At the congress he routed Ligachev and his allies from the Politburo. Had he left the party, its most reactionary forces would indeed have seized control. In the event, the attacks on Gorbachev were not even thinly veiled. The collapse of Soviet control in Eastern Europe, conditions in the economy, the crisis in the military, poor party administration, factionalism in the party, the party's declining public image, and other maladies were all laid at his feet. It looked as though he would be expelled from his party post until the last days of the congress, deserted, as he was by both the reform and antireform wings of the party.[22] Gorbachev's victory, however, was not really of his own making.

Boris Yeltsin—the man he had treated to a Stalin-style charade in fall 1987 and expelled from the Politburo and his post as head of the Moscow party organization (and shortly thereafter, from the Politburo as well)—would now rescue him. In making an unprecedented political comeback, Yeltsin was picking up two kinds of mutually reinforcing support during spring 1990—first, a significant number of the liberal democrats disillusioned with Gorbachev, and second, leaders of those republics bent on independence. In late May, the Russian Federation's Supreme Soviet elected Yeltsin its chairman. Thus he came to the Twenty-eighth Party Congress as the leader of a republic. And when he spoke at the congress, he announced that he was quitting the party, that is, doing precisely what Gorbachev's close aides had advised him to do in order to regain the support of the liberal democrats. Ironically, Yeltsin's speech saved Gorbachev from defeat. Attacking the conservatives as they sensed victory, Yeltsin bluntly told them that the party could not decide perestroika's fate, and that if the conservatives prevailed at the congress, they would face a struggle with the people over the "total nationalization of the party's power and property."[23] This was tough talk—an unambiguous threat to take away, by mass public action if necessary, the special stores, medical clinics, hotels, automobiles, dachas, apartment houses, and other property owned by the party and used most abundantly by the party nomenklatura and apparatchiki. Gorbachev adroitly seized the middle ground, surviving the attack against him, producing a compromise in the congress's resolutions, retaining his post as the general secretary, and ousting Ligachev and his supporters from the Politburo. Superficially it looked like a remarkable victory for Gorbachev after he had appeared so close to total defeat in the first days of the congress. In fact, it was Yeltsin's victory.

Not only did Yeltsin frighten the conservatives into compromises with Gorbachev, but he also gave nonparty liberal democrats and the party's more radical supporters of perestroika an alternative to Gorbachev, permanently destroying Gorbachev's support among the reform-minded intelligentsia and ensuring continued disintegration within the party. At the same time, Yeltsin was taking up the fight for the sovereignty of the Russian Republic. That gave the leaders of sovereignty movements in several of the national republics a new and powerful ally. For Lithuania and Georgia to challenge the legitimacy of Soviet rule was one thing; for Russia to challenge it was quite another. Once the national separatist movements could count on Russia to join them, the Soviet Union and its military were doomed. The very structure of Soviet politics changed during the summer of 1990. Henceforth Gorbachev would try to save the Soviet Union and to forestall the collapse of the party while Yeltsin worked relentlessly to destroy both.

A Task Uncompleted

That was the political context created by the Twenty-eighth Party Congress, the one in which the fate of the political organs in the military was to be decided. Beforehand, the MPA committed its considerable organizational capacity to helping the Ligachev wing of the party capture as many delegates to the congress as possible. As civilian party committees and their apparatus grew weaker under the forces of disintegration within the party, the MPA remained relatively unified, at least at the top. This led conservatives in the Central Committee Secretariat to use the MPA in some of its anti-Gorbachev activities in Moscow, bringing out demonstrators opposed to perestroika.[24] The MPA chief, General Lizichev, revealed his alliance with Ligachev by praising him to the press while the congress was in progress.[25] Still, the MPA had its own internal problems among the younger political officers. Major Lopatin himself was a political officer, and he and others like him fought for seats in the congress. Thus Lizichev needed to take special care in selecting the military delegation. His success was reflected in the number of flag officers in it, 170 of the 269 military delegates; of the remainder, 93 were "senior officers," meaning colonels, more likely to hew to the conservative line. Only one junior officer and two sergeants were included.[26] Thus the MPA produced a solidly conservative, anti-Gorbachev delegation that Ligachev and his allies could count on. A few reformers did manage to be included—for example, Colonel Aleksandr Tsalko, a proponent of ending the conscription system.

Although Gorbachev persuaded the congress to pass resolutions reaffirming support for his defensive military doctrine and a commitment to a system of contract soldiers to supplement conscription, he had to concede that the imperialist threat had not entirely receded. And he had to yield on abolishing the political organs.[27] They would be retained, but they would become state organs, no longer party organs. They would conduct educational, cultural, and administrative work, leaving command matters entirely to commanders. Although the MPA was no longer a department of the Central Committee, the party did not lose its preeminent position within the military.

In addition to the MPA, there had always been a party structure in the military analogous to party organization in all civilian state institutions. Party cells at the lowest level, managed by a hierarchy of party committees and conferences up to the all-union level, existed outside the political organs. This party structure would be retained. At its apex, there was to be an All-Army Party Conference that elected an All-Army Party Committee. This committee was to account directly to the Central Committee Secretariat for the party activities throughout the military.[28] To all appearances, the All-Army Party Committee was a new name for the MPA. The only substantive change was its loss of direct control over the old political organs and their transfer to the state. True, the political organs had also lost their authority to speak for the party within the military chain of command, but they were still in place, and so were the party cells and committees.

The result was hardly what Gorbachev sought, and it did little to reduce the power of the political organs. The formal changes, however, prompted a bitter public debate over the political organs and party's role in the army. Before the congress, Major Lopatin was among the conspicuous proponents of eliminating the political organs. Lieutenant Nikolai Tutov, who complained to the media that his unit's political organs had tried to stifle his outspokenness as a people's deputy, and Colonel Viktor Podziruk, whose skillful attacks on the political organs infuriated MPA leaders, also spoke for abolishing them.[29]

Not long before the party congress Colonel Podziruk got the opportunity to debate a political officer, Colonel Nikolai Petrushenko, in the pages of the MPA's journal, and thus to expose the political organs' activities.[30] Podziruk described political officers as incompetent, offering examples of how they wasted enormous resources on "socialist competition" exercises which could have better been used for genuine military training. He admitted that during the Russian civil war, when the Red Army depended heavily on ex-tsarist officers for military expertise, the commissar system had made sense. The political organs had also contributed to increasing literacy among the peasants in the army. But now they had outlived their usefulness. They were both superfluous and a nuisance to commanders. Podziruk insisted on genuine "unity of command"—a single commander in charge, and an end to the confusion created by political officers as deputies.

Surprisingly, Petrushenko agreed that the political organs were generally disliked in the army, but he rebutted the rest of Podziruk's points, beginning with a different interpretation of what Frunze had called for after the civil war. "Unity of command," he wrote, would soon turn into "unity of power." Without the counterweight of the political officer, a commander would soon be corrupted by his power. The denigration of the political organs could not be allowed, Petrushenko insisted; instead, they had to be improved. Perestroika demanded greater vigilance by the political organs because they were the "vanguard" in this process. Podziruk knifed back, expressing the hope that this did not mean a return to Stalinist methods, and exposing Petrushenko's example of effective work by a political officer as actually being his own personal case. The abyss between them was clearly unbridgeable.

The officers who proposed abolition of the political organs picked up some public support during the party congress. While it was in progress, forty-seven leading liberals signed a letter published in *Komsomolskaya pravda* on 4 July, expressing alarm over the tactics of the MPA leaders and expressing alarm that they might ally with other party conservatives to organize a coup. In the words of the signatories, "Joining forces with the reactionary part of the party apparatus, the party bosses in the military are bending every effort to keep their place in the army and the navy."[31] Lizichev's deputy, Colonel General Nikolai Shlyaga, stoutly denounced this charge to the press, insisting—falsely—that he spoke for the entire military delegation at the congress.[32] The deputy head of TASS (the official Soviet news agency) accused the generals at the congress of using the problems in the military to promote their own ambitions.[33] A member of the Democratic Platform, the reformist wing of the party, also spoke to the press, accusing the high command and the party apparatus of teaming up to defend their privileges and claiming that the younger officers in the parliament were becoming more radicalized in reaction.[34] As it turned out, inside the congress the MPA leaders were not alone in defending the political organs. Marshal Yazov himself argued against the depoliticization of the Armed Forces while also casting doubt on the wisdom of many other aspects of military reform.[35] And General Valentin Varennikov, commander of the ground forces, gave a press interview during the congress praising the political organs. Striking back when Yazov and Moiseev were nominated for election to the Central Committee, Colonel Tsalko openly objected, calling them opponents of perestroika, but he, Lopatin, Tutov, and other reformers had lost the fight.[36]

The opponents of the political organs did not give up after the congress. Perhaps they were encouraged when General Lizichev was relieved as head of the MPA a few days later, but Colonel General Shlyaga, his successor, gave them no cause to expect compromise.[37] Almost immediately he called efforts to depoliticize the armed forces "immoral," an attack on military capabilities. He insisted that the party still retained the most authoritative influence in the military.[38] Major Lopatin made the counter case, asserting that since the founding of the USSR the political organs had consistently undermined the professionalism of the army and jeopardized the state's security by using the military as an instrument of internal control.[39] The army had been used to impose collectivization of the peasants, to quell unrest, to Russify national minorities, and to help meet economic plans before World War II. Lopatin was disavowing official Soviet historiography that painted the Red Army as highly capable until Stalin killed off the officer corps in the late 1930s. Nor did the experience of World War II change things, Lopatin continued. The party once again turned officers into toadies of the party, fearing for their careers and promotions rather than seeking professional competence.

Lopatin, Tsalko, and their allies realized after the congress that they had no prospects of influencing military policy within the party or the parliament. Like the liberal democrats and the communists supporting the Democratic Platform, who had also failed at the congress, they joined Yeltsin, taking their causes into the political circles of the Russian Federation. When Yeltsin addressed the military policy of his government, instead of creating a Russian ministry of defense, he formed a national security committee. He left the chairmanship open until the fall of 1991, but he appointed Major Lopatin as the vice chairman in the fall of 1990. Henceforth, Lopatin and his allies — civilian and military — depended on Yeltsin and the Russian government as their base of official support.

The MPA in a New Guise

Not until the fall of 1990 did the changes approved by the Twenty-eighth Party Congress begin to be implemented. Yazov told an assembly of political officers in September that pluralism in the USSR meant that they had to strive harder to ensure that the Communist Party remained the leading force in the military.[40] He gave them no reason to suspect that their future existence was at stake. They would have to adapt to a different institutional basis, but they would survive. In early October, a major reorganization of the Central Committee apparatus abolished the MPA as a department, transferring control over the political organs to the office of the president and the parliament.[41] Toward the end of the month new "Instructions on the Work of the CPSU Organizations in the USSR Armed Forces" were issued, declaring that "CPSU organizations and their organs cannot interfere in the work of officials and military command organs."[42] Additionally, they designated "the All-Army Party Conference" as the "supreme leadership organ" of party organizations in the military, though it was not apparently established until five months later.

The "first" All-Army Party Conference convened on 29 March 1991, heralded as the instrument for the transformation of the political organs. Both Yazov and Gorbachev addressed the conference, but Colonel General Shlyaga, presumably out of a job since the MPA had been abolished, emerged as opening speaker.[43] Shlyaga followed the official line that the main goal of the transformation of the political organs was to make the party structures within the army independent from the state, and he insisted that that had been accomplished and that the separation of state and party functions was a success. Still, he could not resist venting against "activities by the ideological and political enemies of the CPSU, designed to create singularly negative relations between the society and the army."[44] Yazov also lashed out at "circles masquerading as democrats."[45] Behind the generals' show of anger was undoubtedly concern over the results of the mid-March referendum on whether or not to maintain the Soviet Union. Each mentioned it as an affirmation of the union, a considerable distortion of the results. In any event, their speeches set the mood at the conference.

Most speakers condemned the proponents of genuine change. Major General Mikhail Surkov, elected as the secretary of the All-Army Party Committee, stressed that "at present, some forces are seeking to use these calls [for reform] not only in order to undermine the influence of the Communist Party in the armed forces but also to reorient the army in their own interests." Moreover, he rejected the principle of separating state and party lines of authority when he asserted that "the armed forces should obey only one, ruling party" and that "now the Communist Party is the ruling one." With blatant hypocrisy, the antireform delegates postured as though they were defending the army from attack, insisting that the democrats and reformers wanted to destroy "unity of command" in the military.[46] The political organs and the MPA, of course, had always been a source of confusion about "unity of command." As long as the Soviet Union was committed to advancing the international class struggle and the demise of capitalism, the old fusion of the party with the officer corps made sense. For the last four years that had no longer been Soviet policy; thus the rationale for the party's deep organizational entanglement with the military also no longer existed. Gorbachev's political reforms implied control by parliament and the executive branch of the state over the military, not a single political party's control.

Dressed up after the first conference in its new garb as the All-Army Party Committee, the old MPA leadership surrendered little of substance to change. Colonel Viktor Kuznetsov, a political officer who had been dismissed from Lenin Military-Political Academy's faculty when he quit the party, stated publicly that the party retained control of the military command structure by simply ignoring laws on public organizations that applied to the party.[47] General Surkov told the press that the new party organization in the army "is not some newly created party. We are the same army communists . . . who organizationally used to be members of political organs."[48]

How effectively the MPA had withstood the assault on its existence became evident after the crisis in August 1991. When Marshal of Aviation Yevgenii Shaposhnikov replaced Yazov as minister of defense, one of the first issues on his mind was the elimination not just of the political organs but of all party activities in the military. In fact, the day before he was appointed, he suggested to the assembled MoD military collegium—as it advised Moiseev on what to tell Gorbachev now that the attempted coup was over—that "departyization" should be recommended. Moiseev agreed, but General Shlyaga, the former MPA chief, objected, rebuking Shaposhnikov, "You are a young man, still hot tempered."[49]

Shaposhnikov was not put off so easily. In casting his lot against the State Committee for a State of Emergency during the August crisis, he had also effectively cast his lot against the party. By his own account, his actions were not opportunistic but were, rather, based on growing feelings over the past few years that fundamental political change, including the end of the Communist Party's power monopoly, had to come.[50] The very next morning after this clash with Shlyaga, Shaposhnikov assembled the military council of his air force headquarters to announce his own decision to leave the party. All but one member supported him, and Shaposhnikov quit the party that day.

When Shaposhnikov went to work as defense minister, pulling out the military reform plans that Moiseev and Yazov had developed since January 1990, he quickly noticed that although the MPA was included for radical change, the transformation was only decorative. There had been no departyization or any effective plans for it.[51] A short time later, complete abolition of the political organs was a key part of the reform program he presented to the council of ministers. Although all of his program was approved by the council, implementing directives were never signed. He was told that they also had to be passed by the Supreme Soviet.[52] Gorbachev did issue a presidential decree forbidding political activities by any party or group within the MoD, KGB, and MVD in mid-September, and he also established a commission within the MoD to plan the dismantling of the residual political organs—now official "state organizations."[53] One member of the commission, Lieutenant General Aleksandr Lebed', describes it as such a mess that he refused to attend after the third meeting. Major Lopatin hounded General K. A. Kochetov, deputy minister of defense, out of the meeting. The chairman of the commission, Colonel General Eduard Vorob'ev, was continually insulted by a certain Colonel Dubrovskii, who wanted to bring the "nearly ninety-eight thousand" political officers to Moscow for a credentials review. This rough and impractical treatment struck Lebed' as ridiculous, so he quit the commission.[54] The self-righteous account by Lebed' should be taken with a grain of salt, but the clash he reports between the young reformers and the generals is entirely credible, and the commission achieved nothing.

Thus at the very moment when the defense minister was fully committed to the kind of reforms Gorbachev had long sought, the institutional structure for carrying them through was weak, fractured, and unable to respond. As Shaposhnikov discovered, quickly dispatching scores of thousands of political officers was not easy. Most of them survived the transition to the Russian military when it was created from the pieces of the Soviet military in the summer of 1992 because the political organs were retained as a state institution.

Shaposhnikov's personal views on the party and the military also reveal much about the nature of party-military relations. In his memoir he recalls his youthful attraction to the party's ideals and his enthusiasm for becoming a communist. He was undaunted by the realization that party membership was essential for any military career, for he saw no contradiction between the two. As an older officer he saw things differently. Hypocrisy dominated the party hierarchy, and senior officers groveled before party authority. There was no other choice. The Central Committee's Administrative Organs Department had the last word on all senior military appointments, beginning with division commanders. Shaposhnikov recounts that after he had vetted an officer for division command with his deputies, with the army commanders, and with the air forces military council, then finally personally interviewed and checked him for the tiniest flaw, the party review would begin in the secretariat at the lowest sub-sub department, working its way up. On occasion Shaposhnikov would receive a call from a former political officer, now working in the Administrative Organs Department. "Yevgenii Ivanovich," the caller would say, "the candidate is not appropriate," with no explanation, ending the matter abruptly. Shaposhnikov contained his fury on these occasions, but he never forgot them. Gorbachev's rise and the beginning of perestroika gave rise to new hope among officers that the party's hypocritical practices would be changed. They were not. Yeltsin's quitting the party, therefore, had a profound impact on Shaposhnikov and many other officers. Thereafter, the trickle of officers leaving the party became a flood.[55]

In an interview, I asked Shaposhnikov directly whether he had been a marshal first or a communist first.[56] Shaposhnikov laughed, recognizing the implications and insisting that it was a difficult question. He said that he could not really give an unambiguous answer; he could only explain his personal feelings over time. In his youth he had clearly been devoted to communism, but as he became older, being a pilot grew more important for him. It took him out of this world in a spiritual as well as a physical way. While flying he controlled his own fate. At the same time, the realities of being a party member increasingly troubled him. Still, playing the party role meant everything for his career. Finally, Shaposhnikov observed that the answer to this question would vary among different branches of military service. In the highly technical branches —the air force, navy, and strategic rocket forces—more officers looked at party membership largely as a career necessity, not as their primary commitment. In the ground forces, Shaposhnikov said, it was otherwise. Many officers were as firmly committed communists as they were military professionals.

Marshal Yazov and General Moiseev, of course, were ground force officers, and traditionally the military command structure was dominated by the so-called combined-arms officers from the ground forces. As a marshal of aviation, Shaposhnikov was not a combined-arms officer, and that meant that he could never command a front or a high command, or become chief of the General Staff. He was relegated to command of air force components only. During the August crisis, he said, he felt freer to express his objections to navy admirals and air force officers than to ground force officers precisely because of what he knew to be the stronger commitment to the party among the ground force officers. This evidence and similar comments by several field-grade officers tend to confirm the conclusion that in the more technical specialties, the party and the ideology had a much weaker grip on Soviet officers. In the main command lines and throughout the ground forces, however, the fusion of military professionalism with commitment as a communist was still quite strong right down to the end of the Soviet Union.

Theories of Party-Military Relations

Much of the foregoing story about the MPA, as well as the military's political behavior during Gorbachev's rule, was misunderstood at the time in the West, in part because the most widely accepted Western theories of party-military relations could neither anticipate nor account for it. Such theories may seen esoteric, but two are not. Their intellectual foundations are straightforward and popular American beliefs: military officers are inherently a danger to popular government, and civilian rulers are inherently nonmilitaristic and therefore more likely to favor democracy. Senior military officers and civilian politicians, therefore, are always in conflict, potentially, if not openly, and control of the military is therefore a fundamental problem for any political system. It is true that control of the means of violence is a universal and fundamental problem for most countries, but what is "military" and what is "civilian" in a political sense is not the same in all political systems. The Soviet system had several distinctive characteristics—Marxism-Leninism, which was essentially a theory of war; a revolutionary party, which was a "combat political organization" (as Philip Selznick called it); and a war mobilization economy—which made the civil-military boundary politically different from that boundary in Western political systems.[57]

Some scholars saw the Soviet case as manifesting an inexorable conflict between military professionalism and ideological considerations that undercut such professionalism, leading the regular officer corps to seek more autonomy vis-à-vis the party. Others saw Soviet civilian rulers using the MPA in a supportive role to commanders, helping with discipline and training, but with the potential for serious civil-military conflict ever present. The rivalry was quiescent because the party gave the military more or less what it wanted. Were it to do otherwise, the party would face a crisis as the military intervened politically to get what it wanted. A third interpretation was neither as popular as the first two nor based on their assumptions. Rather, it emphasized the remarkable similarity between the organizational ethos of a Leninist party (a disciplined group of "professional revolutionaries") and the ethos of a professional officer corps (a disciplined group of "professional managers of violence"). Both groups require their members to subordinate their lives to their assigned "missions." This theory also drew attention to several objective reasons for the party and the military to share Marxist-Leninist ideological values. The party was committed to revolution, which was a form of warfare, and the Red Army was the instrument that finally secured the revolution in at least one country. To spread it farther required a strong military capability. These distinctive realities meant that in the Soviet system, the military-party boundary was not the primary dividing line for policy conflicts. Conflicts always characterized Soviet military policy making, but civilian party leaders and military officers could be found on both sides. Moreover, officers were party members. Thus military policy conflicts were intraparty conflicts, not civilian-military or, more properly, party-military conflicts.

These three interpretations have been called, respectively, the "conflict model," offered by Roman Kolkowicz, the "control model" of Timothy Colton, and the "congruence model," which I have developed.[58] These labels are generally justified, although at the price of distortions, especially of the third interpretation. A number of other scholars have offered variants of these models.[59]

Kolkowicz's "conflict model" rests on the assumption that Soviet military professionalism and communist ideology are incompatible. Because the Communist Party sought more and more modern military power, it had to surrender increasing autonomy to military professionalism. In time, the military's accumulating professional autonomy would allow it to have concomitant political autonomy. The result would be inchoate institutional pluralism in the Soviet political system. This description of party-military relations fit nicely with the emerging view among Western students of Soviet politics that ideology was becoming less relevant and the system was in the early stages of a pluralist transformation.[60] Kolkowicz was writing in the late 1960s, and as events have since shown, such a transformation did not occur. Moreover, in twenty years following, evidence of a party-military conflict proved difficult to find, although evidence of intraparty conflict over military policy can be cogently inferred.

As a critic of Kolkowicz's thesis in 1973, I emphasized the congruence between the party's ideology and the military's own philosophy of war as well as the commonality between the sociological ethos of a Leninist party and a modern professional officer corps. Most of the evidence in this study vindicates that criticism, but not all of it. Shaposhnikov provides fairly strong evidence that professionalism in the technical branches of the Soviet military did increasingly alienate officers from the official ideology. Moreover, he cites his own experience of having his selection of senior air force commanders, based on their professional competence, arbitrarily overruled by the Central Committee Administrative Organs Department. Thus I must confess to underestimating the incipient conflict between military professionalism and the party's control apparatus in the military. Such conflict was there, especially in the 1980s, and as several Soviet officers testified (Colonel Podziruk, for example, as cited above), the political organs actually harmed military units' combat readiness by squandering their time on nonproductive activities. But this tension was largely the consequence of the erosion of ideological commitment and corruption within the party—the "hypocrisy" that Shaposhnikov saw—not something inherent in the ideology itself. Suppressed hostility toward the MPA and the party existed, but also strong commitment to the party, especially among the ground force officers.

There was something to Kolkowicz's focus on military-party conflict, but it did not become a basis for outright military-versus-party policy disputes. Nor did it yield the dynamic result Kolkowicz predicted although he had lots of impressive scholarly company in the 1970s claiming that institutional pluralism would emerge in the Soviet political system. Instead of inchoate pluralism, the system was experiencing bureaucratic stagnation, corruption, and degeneration.[61]

Colton's "control model" gained wide acceptance as a prudent middle ground, presumably more sensible and closer to the complex truths of Soviet politics. He recognized that Kolkowicz was wrong about historical party-military conflicts, but he explained the resolution differently. The party avoided conflict by paying off the military with the lion's share of the resources. According to the logic of his model, if that practice were to change, then a crisis in "civil-military relations" could be expected. Gorbachev's policies, of course, put this proposition to test; although the military did not like them, it did not revolt as Colton's model predicted. But as late as 1990, Thane Gustafson argued that Colton's model best explained Soviet "civil-military" relations.[62]

Gustafson's analysis and Colton's model contain two essential flaws. First, the issue was not "civil-military" relations. It was the character of "party-military" relations. Kolkowicz may have erred in his assumptions, but he was not confused on that point. Second, Gustafson realized that Colton's model encouraged the expectation of a political crisis between the party and the military. Yet he saw no compelling evidence of it. Thus he argued that a "new contract" in civil-military relations was being worked out which would avoid the impending crisis required by the logic of the control model. Had he used the congruence model instead, the lack of evidence of such a crisis would have made sense. In fact, a huge crisis was only a year or so away, but Gustafson was looking for a different kind of crisis, a "civil-military crisis"—one between civilian and military leaders—not the intraparty crisis that was emerging. The congruence model would have drawn his attention to Gorbachev's revisions of the ideology, evidence suggesting an impending legitimacy crisis for the party and the regime.

The congruence model, notwithstanding its underestimation of the role of military professionalism, stands up fairly well in explaining the dynamic of party-military relations. The MoD was highly displeased about force reductions, but it reluctantly accepted them. At the same time, it was politically active in alliances with conservative party leaders against perestroika. And like the party itself, the military was fracturing internally, with some officers opposed to Gorbachev, some willing to support him.

Another important way to see the source of the conceptual errors in the conflict and control models is to look at their intellectual roots. Each has its foundation in Samuel Huntington's theory of civil-military relations, specifically his definition of military professionalism.[63] The problem that arises for the conflict and control models is not in Huntington's theory itself but rather in its uncritical application to the Soviet case. The Soviet military only partially meets Huntington's three criteria for being "professional." As he put it, "The distinguishing characteristics of a profession as a special type of vocation are its expertise, responsibility, and corporateness."[64] The Soviet military was certainly corporate, and it demonstrated impressive expertise in managing violence during World War II, although not in Afghanistan. Its ethical responsibility is another matter. For Huntington the military's professional responsibility is to the "society" of a state, not to a class, not to revolution: to society "the officer corps alone is responsible for military security to the exclusion of all other ends."[65]

Here the Soviet military simply does not meet the definition, as Huntington was mindful when he pointed out the incompatibility of his concept of the military profession and Marxism.[66] Although his treatment of Marxism is not wrong, it overlooks significant compatibilities and adaptations made by Lenin and Soviet military theorists. Recalling Lenin's adaptation of Clausewitz's theory of war, he removed the state from Clausewitz's "paradoxical trinity" and replaced it with the international working class, transforming war from an interstate phenomenon to an interclass phenomenon. The Soviet military's ethical responsibility was to help achieve the eventual victory of the international socialist revolution—the eventual destruction of all bourgeois states. Securing the Soviet society was merely instrumental to the victory of socialism over capitalism, and not until the late 1930s, when Stalin declared that socialism was victorious in the Soviet Union, was the Red Army responsible to the whole of Soviet society. Before then, it helped with collectivization and other aspects of "class struggle" against "class aliens" in the country. As we have seen repeatedly, the Soviet officer corps, especially in its upper echelons, had deeply internalized this ideological basis for Soviet rule and expansion. It will be recalled that Marshal Akhromeev told Shakhnazarov that "socialist internationalism" was the reason why the Warsaw Pact countries should suffer the economic burden of large arms purchases from the Soviet Union. Ponomarev's understanding of the military component of "peaceful coexistence" in his argument with Chernyaev is evidence that party leaders understood the party-military connection in the same way. That Gorbachev felt he had to revise the ideology so radically where war and international class struggle were concerned is further evidence, as is the military's difficulty in accepting the revisions. Success in revolutionary activities, not the bourgeois ethic of security for the society of a bourgeois state, is the Marxist-Leninist ethical standard for both military officers and party members. Lenin had turned Clausewitz on his head: war is not the continuation of politics; politics is the waging of war through class struggle. The institutional implication for the Red Army was a basic blurring of civilian and military distinctions.

Thus the Soviet case simply falls outside Huntington's definition for military professionalism and outside his concept of civil-military relations as well. Of all Western theories of the Soviet case, only the congruence model takes these points into account.

Breaking the party-military connection was indeed imperative if the military was to be put on a purely legal footing in place of its ideological foundation. But Gorbachev failed to make more than token progress toward that goal. The MPA proved to be the most resilient sector of the party, and many regular officers, especially those in the combined-arms command positions, defended it against both Gorbachev's attempt to change it and the young military reformers' demand that it be abolished outright. Even after the dissolution of the Soviet Union, the MPA's political organs persisted as state bodies under a new name.

Party-military relations in the Soviet Union were not well understood in the West, a factor contributing to rather serious contemporary misreadings of key aspects of the Gorbachev's rule. A party-military crisis leading to a military coup was never a serious danger. A military-backed party faction ousting Gorbachev was. That almost happened at the Twenty-eighth Party Congress, but once Yeltsin reemerged on the scene in Moscow as the senior political leader in the RSFSR, that danger also receded as a much larger one loomed — the dissolution of the Soviet Union itself.

ELEVEN

The Intractable Military-
Industrial Sector

This country is not simply a military-industrial complex,
but a military-ideological complex.

ACADEMICIAN YURII RYZHOV

C utting back military forces, as Gorbachev knew, was difficult: reducing the military-industrial sector, he discovered, was close to impossible. The obstacles presented by the VPK in particular and the command economy in general have already been elaborated, but the three main impediments bear review: First, the military-industrial sector was very large, much larger than even the highest Western estimate. Second, ideological precepts gave both the military industrialists and the military consumers a powerful justification for first-priority claim on all economic resources as long as the worldwide victory of the working-class revolution was incomplete. Third, the command economy was essentially a permanent wartime mobilization system adjusted in peacetime to produce fewer weapons and more civilian goods.

These realities posed a basic question not fully understood by Gorbachev or anyone else in the Politburo. Could the command economic system actually reduce the military-industrial sector sufficiently and shift enough resources to the civilian sector to provide the kind of economic performance that the proponents of perestroika sought? To put the issue another way, using the elementary concept of the fungibility of "guns and butter," the Soviet economy was producing a large number of "guns" and a small amount of "butter" — goods for civilian consumption. Could the economy be moved to a new mix of guns and butter, where butter production was large and guns production small, without changing the very nature of the command system? The Politburo's answer to that question was, in principle, yes. Moreover, awareness of the question was not new. As we have seen, when industrial organization to support of the military sector was at issue in the 1920s, a frequent argument in favor of an early move to full central planning—"socialism in one country"—was that military industry could also produce civilian goods when not operating at full-time war production. A large part of military industry could maintain two lines of production, one military and one civilian. Central planners could easily change the mix by directives. This, Frunze and others claimed, was one of socialism's inherent advantages over a market system.

That argument, of course, overlooked a source of dynamism in market economies. As Joseph Schumpeter later argued, capitalism cannot be explained simply as a matter of market equilibrium.[1] It is also revolutionary, constantly bringing structural change because entrepreneurs introduce innovations to win a market advantage. This upsets rather than reinforces a market equilibrium. Entrepreneurs exploit new technologies to overcome the constraints of a competitive market and to create monopolies. In contrast, enterprise managers in a socialist economy prefer the maintenance of an equilibrium at a given level of technology.[2] That makes their planning and production tasks simpler. Adopting innovations brought by changing technology makes these tasks difficult.

The qualitative arms race with the West forced the VPK to introduce new technologies, but the rest of the economy was another matter. Steady technological change in the West did not have the same impact on the overall economy; thus Soviet industry accumulated an ever-larger stock of older industrial technology, creating an ever-widening technology gap. A major reason for the VPK's special administrative powers was to enable it to overcome resistance to innovation. It succeeded until the 1980s, though always lagging behind the Western military industry.

The civilian sector fell farther behind, disastrously behind in many areas. The reason is easy to see. Viewing the competition with the West as ultimately military, central planners had much weaker incentives to employ new technology in the production of consumer goods. The conditions of the Soviet economy in the mid-1980s therefore did not allow a purely administrative shift in the mix of production of guns and butter that would bring the kind of relief that Gorbachev sought. Neither the desired variety of consumer goods nor the advances in information-age technology could be attained by this approach.

Recalling figure 4 in Chapter 4, which compares planned, market, and mixed economies, we can see that by remaining on the X-Y plane, the Soviet economy missed out on the dynamic restructuring occurring in most economies on the X-Z plane during the postwar decades. At the same time, it created huge inefficient ministerial bureaucracies and accumulated large investments in increasingly obsolete technology, enormous obstacles to change. Moreover, the required labor mobility and new workforce skills posed further obstacles. Thus the notion that genuine economic relief was possible through a new, command-directed mix of guns and butter, increasing civilian production at the expense of weapons production, required considerable naïveté. Certainly some relief could be achieved, but this approach could hardly bring the Soviet economy up to the level of Western industrial economies. Only a considerable play of market forces for a long period could do that. The economic change Gorbachev wanted, therefore, was impossible without moving the Soviet economy off the X-Y plane—without subjecting it to more than trivial market forces.

This issue—how to overcome stagnation in the Soviet economy—could take us far afield from military policy, but a conceptual grasp of the underlying problems and choices is nevertheless critical to an understanding Gorbachev's ineffective military-industrial policies. It reveals the limits of Soviet leaders' understanding of their own problems. (It also raises questions about how well Western students of the Soviet economy appreciated the significance of the military sector.[3])

Leadership Perceptions of the Problem

As we have already seen, Soviet leaders during the initial years of Gorbachev's rule shared a strong consensus on both the nature of the economic problem and how to solve it. Ligachev, it will be recalled, admitted that military spending was ruining the economy and had to be reduced, though he differed with Gorbachev on how deeply to cut. He shared Gorbachev's conviction that mutual East-West arms control agreements would produce significant economic relief, but he insisted on maintaining rough military equivalence with the West.

Several military leaders shared this view of the economy's problems, as well as of the Gorbachev-Ligachev solution. In interviews and in their memoirs senior former Soviet military officers uniformly cited the burden of military spending as more than the Soviet economy could bear. Though reluctant about many aspects of arms control agreements, they said they favored mutual reductions that maintained the Soviet military's rough equivalence with the West. The same viewpoint emerged in interviews with a smaller number of former officers and civilians from the VPK arena.

Close aides to Gorbachev had a similar perception, but some were willing to give up military equivalence with the West. It will be remembered that Chernyaev was quite prepared to cut Soviet military spending unilaterally if large enough reductions could not be realized rapidly through arms control agreements. Still, he was initially convinced that the ailing economy could be significantly improved through the strategy of arms reductions and a shift of resource allocations within the command economy, though by 1990 he favored a rapid transition to a market economy. But in 1986 he was reflecting Gorbachev's conviction that there was an "organic connection" between domestic and foreign policy, and it was primarily in the impact of foreign policy on the economy. "Gorbachev saw that militarism devoured our science, without which he could not think of progress in perestroika."[4] After the INF treaty, however, Gorbachev realized that three years of his perestroika strategy had produced no visible economic relief. Yet nowhere at the time does Chernyaev mention either his own or Gorbachev's recognition that only market forces could make perestroika's "far-reaching intentions" a reality.

Shakhnazarov, as we have seen, likened the military establishment to a "Moloch," devouring the civilian economy. The vastly bigger U.S. economy, however, made the competition with the much smaller Soviet economy very lopsided. "In reality, although it is bitter to admit, were we in the position of the Moloch-people-eater, competing with the daughter of Vanderbilt. . . . At the time when the USA was spending a record 8 percent, our allocation reached a fifth of the social wealth created by the people."[5]

Other Gorbachev loyalists may not have matched Shakhnazarov's metaphors, but they shared his accurate perception of the realities. His perception of the systemic reasons for the economy's poor performance is another matter. He gave no sign of understanding them. Perhaps Yakovlev did, but he has left no record of it. He assembled Gorbachev's brain trust for the theoretical aspects of perestroika, and they included people like Abel Aganbegyan and Leonid Abalkin, who claimed expertise in economic affairs.[6] They in turn included among their own subordinates the earliest glasnost critics of the command economic system, like the sociologist Tatanya Zaslavskaya and the novelist Nikolai Smelev, both apparently self-taught and self-appointed economists.

Even if they did understand the economic problem as systemic, Gorbachev was not an easy pupil to educate. Gorbachev reportedly found economic issues very difficult to comprehend. In 1984–85, lengthy discussions were required to make him understand that even the Soviet economy had limited market sectors—for example, the labor and collective farmers' markets.[7] Boldin believes that at least through 1987 Gorbachev continued to believe that socialism was a superior economic system and that Soviet socialist achievements had to be retained, and Ligachev insisted that Gorbachev did not take market reforms seriously before 1989.[8] Some members of his brain trust, nonetheless, were advancing market reforms. That is obvious from the new law on the firm promulgated in July 1987, a law that would produce none of the fruits of a market reform and make life more complicated for central planners by giving firm managers some latitude in selling their products. The very nature of that law reflects the kind of faulty understanding of economics that Boldin attributes to Gorbachev. He came very slowly, if ever, to the conclusion that introducing market reforms offered the only solution, albeit not a quick one. Serious market reformers never had a strong sponsor, much less a member, in the Politburo right down through the fall of 1991. Nor were they to be found outside a small circle of experts in the academic institutes, not even in the ranks of the senior party apparatchiki.

The VPK System as Model for Reform

Systemic change had no place in Gorbachev's view of reform, certainly not initially. Because the VPK ministries were the best-performing and most technologically advanced sector of the economy, the idea of taking that system to other sectors came naturally. Moreover, people with VPK backgrounds were always prominent in the top leadership. Grigorii Romanov and Vladimir Dolgykh, both with military-industrial backgrounds, were party secretaries and members of the Politburo when Gorbachev took power, but they were not on Gorbachev's team. Like many others, they did not last long in the rapid turnover of personnel that Gorbachev forced on the Politburo and secretariat, but among the replacements, people with VPK experience were no less prominent. Lev Zaikov, picked by Gorbachev to become party secretary for the economic policy in 1986, had a strong VPK background. So did Oleg Baklanov, another new party secretary. Yurii Maslyukov, a new Politburo member, was chairman of the VPK. And Nikolai Ryzhkov, whom Gorbachev brought to the Politburo and appointed chairman of the Council of Ministers in 1985, had worked in military industry and dealt with it as first deputy chairman of GOSPLAN. Their thinking undoubtedly influenced economic reform policy making during the first three or four years of perestroika.

That was immediately evident. In 1985–86 six bureaus, following the organizational pattern of the VPK, were established under the Council of Ministers to manage entire sectors of the civilian economy.[9] The idea of applying the VPK management model to civilian sectors was not entirely new. It had earlier precedents and was much considered during Andropov's rule, but the scale of its application at this time was new. The bureau for agricultural industrial production (AGROPROM), which received considerable public acclaim, was based on the VPK model. If the VPK could make Soviet military industry world class, then why could not AGROPROM do the same for agricultural machinery? That, at least, was the logic.

This approach, of course, could produce no improvement. The VPK's success rested mainly on its first-priority claim on resources. Five other industrial sectors, or even one, could not have first priority if the VPK was to retain it. There was more to the VPK system's success than its management structure within the Council of Ministers. Predictably, none of the five bureaus produced significant positive results. AGROPROM got the most public attention, and notwithstanding its poor performance, it survived; in late 1989 it was still claiming a success that critics strongly disputed.[10] The performance of other bureaus also drew severe criticism, and not just from outside the government. The Council of Ministers, reacting to the report by a state commission directed to investigate bureaus in 1988, censured five military-industrial ministries that had failed to meet targets for equipping light industry.[11]

Along with this organizational scheme came a large transfer of top military industrial managers to the civilian sector. By late 1988, of the fifty-eight newly appointed ministers, about one-third had military-industrial backgrounds, and six of the thirteen deputy chairmen of the Council of Ministers also fell in this category. The significance of this change in personnel is difficult to assess. Julian Cooper saw it at the time as a calculated move to bring military-industrial expertise to the civilian sector based on the belief that these personnel were more competent.[12] That may be true, but it was more likely the work of patrons of the VPK at the Politburo and Secretariat level looking after the careers of their protégés. New career opportunities in the civilian sector were opening up with the creation of the several VPK-like bureaus. In any case, the VPK began seizing as much new bureaucratic turf as possible.

Another technique from the VPK was also applied in limited areas of the civilian machine-building industry. The system of voenpredy, or military representatives, it will be recalled, allowed the military to assess and approve the quality of military products before they were accepted as fulfilling the state plan. A limited trial of this system for a few civilian factories was made in 1985 and hailed as a success throughout 1986. The number of participating firms was then increased to include about 60 percent of all machine-building industry. This new institution, called Gospriemka, actually appears to have achieved positive results. In 1987 its agents accepted only 82–85 percent of final output.[13] The political backlash from managers and workers who lost their bonuses for failing to meet their plans, however, was too great, and Gospriemka lost its momentum thereafter.

The Decision to Attempt Military-Industrial Conversion

Gorbachev's frustrations over the lack of results from these and other attempts to achieve progress in the economy were mounting in early 1988. In the fall he decided on a more direct approach in dealing with the VPK. At a Politburo meeting on 3 November, the same one in which he pushed through approval of his decision to announce a unilateral force reduction at the upcoming United Nations meeting in December, Gorbachev also got a general agreement that military industry had to be reduced as well.[14] Accordingly, he added a mention to his U.N. speech of the Soviet Union's plan to begin experimenting with a military-industrial conversion program. This action also owed much to his belief that the VPK and the military were deceiving him about several of their activities, namely arms transfers, weapons upgrades in Soviet forces deployed in Eastern Europe, and development of bacteriological weapons.[15]

In 1989 Gorbachev continued to receive reports on the unauthorized arms transfers by the VPK to Cuba, Libya, and Eastern Europe. Shakhnazarov complained bitterly to Gorbachev that Baklanov and the VPK gave him a "classical 'flogging.' They did it all by the 'rules.'"[16] Possibly Gorbachev knew about these activities and approved them through other channels. Chernyaev acknowledges that Gorbachev kept him excluded in several other matters, handling them directly or through other staff aides, but he believed that on these occasions Gorbachev's reactions reflected genuine surprise.

These accounts of VPK behavior by Chernyaev and Shakhnazarov are corroborated and elaborated by another source with a wealth of firsthand experience. Aleksandr Lyakhovskii, a General Staff officer allowed to write a history of the Soviet intervention in Afghanistan and given extensive access to highly sensitive classified sources, describes a "mechanism" used for arms transfers not only to Afghanistan but generally to most client states.[17] The chiefs of Soviet military advisory missions abroad enjoyed as much prestige with their hosts in direct proportion to the weapons and technical supplies that they could "break loose from the USSR." Their hosts rewarded them handsomely with gifts, medals, and hard-currency shopping opportunities when they delivered weapons abundantly.

To take advantage of these opportunities, military advisers accumulated requests from their hosts and forwarded them to the General Staff through a variety of channels, each relatively small request having a comprehensive technical justification. The officers receiving the requests in the General Staff combined them into a single large requisition. Normally that order was then signed by top officials of the MoD, the Ministry of Foreign Affairs, KGB, Ministry of Foreign Trade, and the International Department of the Central Committee and forwarded to the Central Committee with a covering memorandum describing the rationale, details of delivery, and so on. The Central Committee Secretariat then added a draft Politburo approval document and draft directions to the Council of Ministers. These were forwarded to the Politburo, where they normally received pro forma approval. After that, everything in the implementation was automatic.[18] The incoming requests were too small to draw serious attention or objection, and when they were aggregated, they already had intermediate level General Staff approval. Staff aides in the other ministries and the Central Committee cooperated in the swindle by getting their senior officials to sign the supporting documents for the Politburo. Thus the Politburo was left with the impression that the General Staff and other agencies had reviewed the aggregate request from the policy viewpoint and found it compelling, when in fact they had not.

The staff-level personnel handling these requests in all the ministries and departments worked to make the process largely a formality because a number of interested officials profited personally from the sales. The terms of the sale were intentionally lax—25–75 percent not to be paid for—and ten years to pay with credit at 2 percent annually, terms usually causing a significant loss to the Soviet state budget. Officials from several of the conspiring agencies—for example, the MoD, the VPK, the foreign ministry—sometimes visited the recipient country a day or so before delivery to take credit for it and to share in the host's generous show of gratitude. VPK officials especially liked this "mechanism" because it allowed more military factories to produce at full capacity. At the other end of the line, the chief of a military mission supported it because his clout with his host was determined by his ability to exploit this "mechanism."[19]

Lyakhovskii's tale makes the anger expressed by Chernyaev and Shakhnazarov both more comprehensible and more credible. It also shows that the VPK was not only pushing products onto its domestic consumer but was also independently expanding its markets abroad. The U.S. Department of Defense estimated that Soviet arms sales to thirty countries in 1987 amounted to $21 billion.[20] Much of this sum was attributable to the "mechanism" that Lyakhovskii describes.

Gorbachev had abundant other reasons to be frustrated with the VPK. Instead of shifting resources to the civilian economy and improving its performance, military industrialists were exploiting his reform efforts to absorb more of civilian economy and producing weapons as if the Cold War were intensifying. When he announced the military-industrial conversion scheme at the

United Nations, it was based on little or no real planning. It was primarily a tactic to force the MoD and the VPK to take seriously arms production cuts. It had a major impact, but not the intended result.

Other Factors Affecting Military Conversion

"Military conversion," as it was popularly called, got off to a slow start. Over the next three years, an enormous amount was said and written about it, but remarkably little "conversion" was accomplished. At the same time, much changed—specifically, the old VPK system lost influence and began to disintegrate. This was due in part to the way military conversion was conceived and implemented. Other factors, however, contributed to the growing disorder within the command economy in general and the VPK in particular. Four of them in particular stand out. First, during the first three years of perestroika, the VPK had actually expanded. Second, the first real cut in the defense budget came in 1989. Third, the new law on the firm came into effect, increasing enterprises' discretion over sales of a portion of their production. Fourth, the new Congress of People's Deputies and Supreme Soviet brought additional participants into the military policy-making circle, weak but nonetheless vocal ones.

The expansion of the VPK was most prominent in its takeover of the light machine–building industry for agriculture and food processing. This put a large number of civilian firms under VPK management. Most of them were poorly equipped and in shoddy condition by VPK standards. Thus the VPK demanded capital credits to rebuild and reequip them.[21] The military conversion program was effectively a reversal of this earlier effort to involve the VPK in upgrading sectors of the civilian economy.

The second factor, the decision to cut the defense budget, does not seem to have been coordinated with the military conversion program. The decision must have been made in 1988 because in mid-January 1989, Gorbachev announced to the New York–based Trilateral Commission that the Soviet defense budget would be cut by 14.2 percent and arms procurement reduced by 19.5 percent. Still, the total expenditures for both budgets were secret, making it impossible to know what these figures meant in real terms. Gorbachev began to pull off the wraps of secrecy in May 1989 by announcing to the Congress of People's Deputies a figure for total 1989 defense spending of 77.3 billion rubles, causing an audible stir of disbelief among the deputies, who were accustomed to figures of about 20 billion rubles annually.[22] In September the finance minister, Valentin Pavlov, in presenting the state budget to the parliament, gave con-

Table 2   Soviet Defense Spending, 1989–90

	_1989_	_1990_	_% Change_
Procurement	32.6	31.0	−4.9
R&D	15.3	13.1	−14.4
Upkeep of the forces[a]	20.2	19.3	−4.5
Construction	4.6	3.7	−19.6
Pensions	2.3	2.4	+4.3
Other	2.3	1.3	−43.5
Total	77.3	70.1	−8.2

Sources: Kireev, "Konversiya v sovetskom izmepenii"; Yazov, "Novaya model' bezopasnosti i vooru-zhennye sily"; FBIS-SOV-89-116, "TASS Interviews Defense Minister Yazov," 19 June 1989, pp. 117–21.

Note: Variations of these data, to the third decimal place in some figures, were also published in _Pravda_, 10 June and 16 December 1989; _Izvestiya_, 16 December 1989; and _Pravitel'stvennyi vestnik_, no. 45, December 1989. Kireev's version is used in this table. His data do not add up precisely in all cases, but that can be partially explained by assuming that he rounded up or down to the closest tenths of billions of rubles.

[a] Operations, maintenance, and personnel.

siderable detail on spending in the defense sector.[23] And in December, Marshal Yazov published essentially the same figures for 1989–90 but in more detail, and a Central Committee official, Aleksei Kireev, did the same (see table 2).[24]

These data, however, met skeptical reactions both in the Soviet Union and in the West.[25] Although the new figures were welcomed, the critics pointed out that ruble prices for weapons and military pay were artificially low and in no way comparable to the figures in Western military budgets. This was of course true, but the very nature of the Soviet economy and its pricing system made it impossible to provide budget data that reflected the actual outlays to defense. Moreover, it was probably a bureaucratic feat to have aggregated the data in categories shown in table 2. That breakdown was undoubtedly designed to make them easier to compare with the main categories of U.S. defense budgeting—operations and maintenance (including personnel), research and development, procurement, and military construction. The figures did reveal, however, that the Soviet regime was at last serious about significant reductions in military spending.

What they meant for military conversion can also be inferred. The cut in weapons procurement implied large reductions in orders for the VPK ministries, leaving plenty of production capacity to be converted. At the same time, to the degree that genuine conversion of military industrial firms to civilian production was to occur, additional funds would be needed for retooling and workforce retraining. The potential for a clash between defense budget reductions and military conversion was therefore real.

Finally, this orderly approach to reducing the military budget, as reflected in present and projected figures in table 2, did not last. By 1991, those figures had lost all meaning. Both political and economic changes were occurring beyond the control of central planning, rendering such projections obsolete.

The third factor, implementing the new law on the firm, probably had an impact on military industries earlier than budget cuts. Precisely how it was applied to the military sector is unclear, and undoubtedly it was not uniformly implemented there. Research and development organizations, for example, were placed on the *khozraschet* (financial accounting) basis early in 1989. That excluded them from the state economic plan, making them no longer eligible for state credits and forcing them to meet their costs with revenues from selling their services to production enterprises. "Prosperity will depend on profit," a *Krasnaya zvezda* article asserted in announcing this change.[26]

In principle, both the new law on the firm and khozraschet were to apply to all defense enterprises.[27] The new law, however, giving enterprise managers discretion over production and sales of a portion of their output, created a special problem for defense enterprises because they had only one domestic customer, the state, and although they might use their new limited autonomy to sell the civilian products they produced, some of them had no civilian output. The khozraschet system also presented problems. As Aleksandr Isaev, an economist in a military-industrial institute, complained in the spring of 1989, that system was impossible to adopt in practice unless a number of other basic changes were instituted at the same time.[28] First, it required a competitive market environment. Because military industries were organized on a large monopoly basis, demonopolization into a much larger number of smaller firms would be required. The corresponding problem to the monopoly producer, of course, was the monopoly buyer. Because military industries sold only to the state, the buyer of military equipment also had to change its approach. Neither change had been made, but all military industries, according to Isaev, were put on a khozraschet basis in January 1989. Delivery prices to the state had always been kept considerably below actual production costs, the difference being made up by state credits. At these prices and without state credits, virtually all defense enterprises would be operating at a loss.

The way out of this predicament, Isaev argued, was to give enterprises the freedom to set their own wage rates, to deal directly in price negotiations with their suppliers, and to play a direct role in setting prices for their products.

On this last point, he insisted that military enterprises would have to be free to negotiate prices with the state for weapons and military equipment. Otherwise, they would never be able to meet their costs from sales at dictated state prices. Furthermore, to make such an arrangement work, the status of enterprise ownership had to be changed. Some would have to remain as wholly state-owned firms because of the narrow and special nature of their production, which was exempted from the law on the firm as well as khozraschet. All others could either become one of the two types of non-state ownership allowed under Soviet law—a collective (with the same status as collective farms) or a cooperative.

None of these changes was introduced. Instead, managers were left to fend for themselves, for their workforces, and for the large urban communities around them which traditionally depended on them to fund schools, housing, and many other social services. Isaev's analysis is particularly helpful for understanding the voluminous media reporting over the next two years about how military ministries and enterprises were reacting. Unemployment, delays in meeting workers' salaries, desperate attempts to find markets, illicit foreign sales of sensitive weapons systems, and the adaptation of military production machinery to civilian production were subjects of daily press accounts.[29] Although these difficulties appear to have been widespread, GOSPLAN, the State Bank, and the VPK kept many military enterprises operating on the old system. There was really no alternative unless the leadership was willing to see most military enterprises go bankrupt. It was not, and many VPK-controlled firms continued to operate as in the past.[30]

The fourth factor affecting the course of military conversion was the new parliament's Committee on Defense and Security and the Committee for Economic Reform. The former was packed with officials from the VPK, the military, and the police, making it initially more of a cheerleading group than an oversight committee. The latter included radical economic reformers who realized that the VPK was a major stumbling block to reform and, therefore, offered persistent criticism. Major Lopatin and the radical military reformers added a critical voice to the Committee on Defense and Security by the spring of 1990, however, and although their program focused primarily on the MoD, Lopatin leveled repeated charges that military conversion was not a serious program.[31] A parliamentary deputy, the academician Yurii Ryzhov, also carried on a personal crusade against the VPK, insisting that military conversion was entirely inadequate for reforming and reducing it. In the spring of 1989 he submitted a ten-page memorandum to Gorbachev, outlining the comprehensive dimensions of the military-industrial problem, and Gorbachev responded by establishing a commission of parliamentary deputies to develop these ideas into a new concept of "national security." After it submitted its report, the commission was told that Gorbachev was still reading it and that the commission's work was complete.[32]

These are typical of the more vigorous parliamentary efforts to influence military conversion. The nature of the new parliament's power, of course, was limited. It struggled ineffectively to get information on military and military-industrial matters, and its determined deputies were forced to use the media rather than legislation to influence Gorbachev and the government. As we have seen, they were successful in raising matters to public attention, but beyond that, their influence was negligible.

Finally, to grasp the public significance attached to military conversion and the hopes it was meant to inspire, one must keep in mind the sheer size of the military-industrial sector. Variously estimated to be not less than a fifth and perhaps more than 30 percent of the gross domestic product, it was a huge obstacle to economic reform. As several scholar critics pointed out with bitterness and scorn, breaking the influence of the VPK was the sine qua non for success in all other economic reform aims. The very essence of the Soviet economic system was its war mobilization character. Central planning was the war mobilization linchpin. More and more critics realized that moving to a market system was essential to break the grip of the VPK. They traced the origins of the problem to the period of War Communism and to the creation of the command economy in the First Five-Year Plan.[33] Thus nothing less than systemic change would make a genuine difference.

Trying to Implement Military Conversion

As already emphasized, before Gorbachev's brief U.N. announcement of military conversion, no serious plan for change had been worked out. Igor Belousov, chairman of the VPK, left little doubt on that point during an interview early in 1989.[34] When queried on the matter, he fell back on the figures Gorbachev had recently announced about cuts in the military budget. Before launching a program, he declared, military conversion had to be defined. Offering some vague thoughts about a definition, Belousov implied that conversion meant doing more of what the VPK was already doing to help in production of food-processing machinery and medical supplies. "But is this all still nothing more than plans for the future?" the interviewer asked. "No," Belousov insisted, noting that 345 defense firms were already involved in this work and accounted for one-fifth of the output of such products. Moreover, by 1995, the total output of all light industry would rise by 130 percent. Asked further whether this would not involve serious employment dislocations, Belousov shrugged off the question: "This problem is perfectly easy to solve in the conditions of our planned economy." When the interviewer noted that the U.S. Congress was cutting defense spending and asked about cooperation with the United States in cutting Soviet defense spending, Belousov went into a diatribe, declaring that U.S. military industrialists were resisting cuts and would probably succeed.

Belousov's comments reveal more than the absence of a military-industrial conversion plan. Obviously he had little enthusiasm for the very idea. The VPK was giving ground reluctantly. Belousov's mention of the production goals for 1995 gives another clue to the VPK's reaction. The Soviet economy was near the end of the twelfth five-year plan, and GOSPLAN was gearing up for the thirteenth, from 1991 through 1995. The VPK, as became clear over the next two years, tried to wrap military conversion into the new five-year plan and reduce it to the things that military enterprises had been doing for the previous year or so. The chairman of the Council of Ministers, Nikolai Ryzhkov, confirmed this at the end of 1989 while defending his approach to the thirteenth FYP before the Congress of People's Deputies. His assertion that "in 1990 the enterprises of the defense complex alone are to increase output of equipment for the food sectors by 37 percent" met the deputies' skepticism. He also reported that "a draft state conversion program has been drawn up." [35] It would cover the period to 1995 and would soon be discussed in Council of Ministers. The program was to involve more than 420 military enterprises that would shift from 5 percent to 100 percent of their production to civilian goods. A half-million workers would be shifted to civilian production in the process.

Frequently throughout 1989 and 1990, military and VPK spokesmen reminded the media that the VPK already dedicated 40 percent of its production to civilian goods. They also emphasized the large contribution that military industries already made to the civilian economy. Belousov's figures on this point were that all televisions and sewing machines, 97 percent of refrigerators, 70 percent of vacuum cleaners and washing machines, and 50 percent of motorcycles were already being manufactured by VPK firms. The goal of the military conversion plan was to dedicate 60 percent of VPK production to civilian goods by 1995.[36] The shift from the 40–60 ratio of civilian to military goods to 60–40 became a slogan for the conversion plan as interpreted by the VPK and military leadership. The limits of this scheme are readily apparent. While more television sets, refrigerators, sewing machines, vacuum cleaners, and motorcycles could probably be sold to Soviet consumers, these were not their primary demands. They wanted better clothing, more food, and more and better housing. The mix of civilian goods that could be obtained by merely shifting from 40 percent to 60 percent civilian output in the VPK was hardly a panacea for the Soviet consumer economy. As one critic observed, "Now there is a danger of producing a lot of goods no one wants."[37]

The VPK itself underwent a significant restructuring in July 1989—but not, as some observers believed at the time, in order to better manage military conversion.[38] Although it retained ten ministries, some ministries were renamed, branches were reallocated among ministries, and its new ministry of communications was provided with a "joint stock fund" by the USSR Industrial Construction Bank. The fund had a board of directors and eighty-six shareholders. The reorganization also seems to have involved moving more civilian enterprises into the VPK.[39] In retrospect, the reorganization looks less like a serious effort to manage military conversion than like the continuation of the earlier policy of trying to improve parts of civilian industry by bringing them under VPK management.

For all the talk of a "plan" for military conversion, none was ever adopted. As a local official in Novosibirsk explained in June 1990, conversion at the enterprise level began in an "uncontrolled way." Instead of a conversion plan, "relevant decisions were adopted within the existing Five Year Plan and the annual programs were ratified. This simplistic approach suggests that you can use the same equipment to produce weapons and consumer goods."[40] Obviously Ryzhkov's draft conversion plan of December 1989 had not been promulgated. In September 1990, the Presidential Council discussed the "draft" state conversion program, another indication that no plan had yet been adopted.[41] In late October, the parliament became involved, trying to produce a "law on conversion," but the parliamentary committee handling the legislation could not agree on its own draft, or on the drafts it had received from the Council of Ministers and the Academy of Sciences.[42]

In fall 1990, Gorbachev turned again to economic policy. A number of plans for a rapid shift to a market system had been worked by various circles in the Academy of Sciences. At Gorbachev's direction, the essence of Yavlinskii's so-called five hundred–day program was incorporated by the Shatalin group during the summer, and for a time it appeared to be destined for adoption. It contained a section on military conversion that said that there would be no early results from conversion, and for that reason, it put the emphasis on closing down large parts of military industry rather than converting them.[43] Rykhkov was also drafting a government variant of a new economic program in the Council of Ministers, far less radical, promising no fundamental change.

Gorbachev wavered in making a decision; the political climate shifted against radical change; and he finally produced what one analyst called a "veritable circus" by trying to meld the two programs.[44] The program adopted by the parliament in December 1990 was a list of platitudes devoid of substantive steps toward market reform. Thus military conversion was left in the same limbo in 1991 as it had been during 1989–90, waiting to be formalized in a plan.

The costs of conversion, as it was conceived, were not trivial. The basic purpose of conversion had been to save money and shift it to the civilian economy. Ryzhkov, however, in announcing that a draft conversion plan was ready in December 1989, said that about nine billion rubles would be needed to implement it. At the same time, the VPK's takeover of civilian light-industrial enterprises also required additional investment. In the spring of 1990, sixty-three billion rubles were allocated to the military conversion program in the new FYP, far more than had originally been anticipated, and this figure did not include construction costs.[45] Still, only thirteen billion of these rubles were apparently earmarked for actual conversion of military firms.[46] These figures give an indication of the VPK's resistance to the whole idea of conversion. It was using the occasion to place greater claims on the state budget and to continue the earlier program of taking over parts of civilian industry while dragging its feet on actual conversion of military firms. As the drafters of the Shatalin plan would recognize in mid-1990, a serious effort at conversion would be extremely costly and produce no significant early dividends. Retooling plants and retraining their management and labor force to deal with marketing in the private sector were not cheap undertakings.

Did Military Conversion Actually Occur?

Anecdotal press reporting on the military conversion experience throughout 1989–91 gave the impression that, notwithstanding the absence of a state plan and clear central guidance, military enterprises in most of the defense industrial ministries were in the throes of rapid change. The resulting dislocations in the labor force as well as dropping wages prompted the central council of the trade unions, jointly with the Academy of Sciences, to ask for a commission to focus on these problems.[47] A commission was created under the chairmanship of Vsevolod Avduevskii, and it quickly became a critic of many aspects of conversion endeavors over the next year, but it had no noticeable effect on government's conversion policy. Moreover, it was not clear that military conversion was the primary cause of the dislocations. The labor problems of 1989, especially the decline in wages, were probably more attributable to the impact of the new law on the firm and the imposition of khozraschet on managers at the firm level than to the conversion activities.

Neither conversion nor reductions in military procurement had a significant impact in 1989. A VPK official, commenting on this period several years later, observed that 1989 was the high point in the VPK's output of military goods.[48] Corroboration of that observation can be found in press reporting as well. In June 1990 a press account from Sverdlovsk, a major military-industrial center, noted that although talk about military conversion had been extensive for the past two years, only in 1990 had military orders begun to decline. Enterprise budgets were already so tight that a 10 percent reduction or even less would cause them to "burst at the seams."[49] The drop in military orders was beginning to do just that to many firms, displacing as many as thirty thousand workers in Sverdlovsk alone. To fill the gap, firms were receiving ministerial directions regarding what civilian goods they should produce, and in most instances, sale prices dictated for these products imposed large financial losses on the firms. GOSPLAN was stepping in to provide credits that offset the losses for the time being. According to the new FYP, this downward trend would reach a 30 percent reduction by 1995. The key point is that GOSPLAN and the State Bank were coming to the aid of many military firms. As the hard realities of military conversion became clear and local managers warned of the consequences, the central planners acted to stall them, putting off the day of reckoning by supplying additional credits.

Most of the problems confronting enterprise managers were predictable. Tied up in secrecy, accustomed to first priority on resources, they had difficulty finding civilian markets and new suppliers. Adapting their production lines was sometimes impossible. Their advanced technologies were not readily convertible to civilian production, and their designers and workers disliked giving up advanced military weapons production to manufacture baby carriages, lamps, and other simple consumer products. As these problems mounted and the VPK management failed to address them, conversion was often referred to as a "joke" or, as one journalist put it, "black humor."[50]

Equally predictable was the resistance to conversion within the VPK, especially at the ministerial and intermediate levels. At the firm level, however, ambivalence soon took hold. Initially opposed to the idea of conversion, many enterprise managers began to scramble to survive. They exploited their new discretion under the law on the firm, found outside markets, and enjoyed moderate success in adjusting to the civilian economy. As weapons procurement orders dropped precipitously in 1990–91, the pressures for adjustment increased, forcing managers to innovate. Those who succeeded began to enjoy their new autonomy, and as the strong central grip of the VPK relaxed, they were increasingly reluctant to see it reasserted.[51] By the fall of 1991, several military enterprises had moved quite far in trying to find not only new domestic markets but also foreign buyers.[52] Most military-industrial firms were not so successful.

The higher levels of the VPK saw growing enterprise autonomy as unacceptable and began to complain publicly about it. The high point came with a letter to *Pravda*, 6 September 1990, signed by all of the military-industrial ministers, several designers, scientists, and other high-level officials. It decried the "grave economic and social situation in the country whose negative consequences are increasingly gripping our enterprises." Enumerating all kinds of adverse developments over the previous year, the authors demanded that "central management of the enterprises must be retained." They called for a new law to ensure central control.[53] At the same time, a few critics within VPK circles complained that the shift to genuine market relations was far too modest, insisting that "destatization" of military enterprises should be increased to the point where state-owned military enterprises accounted for no more than 25 percent of the "national wealth." [54] The economist and director of the scientific research institute of the ministry of aviation, Aleksandr Isaev, led this group, consisting mostly of other economists in the VPK. These diametrically opposed views on how to proceed — retaining centralization versus much greater decentralization — reveal a split within the VPK itself on military conversion.

The MoD was ambivalent on military conversion; thus it did not come to the VPK's support. As the cut in the defense budget was approved for 1990, the deputy minister of defense for armaments procurement, General Vitalii Shabanov, admitted that he did not agree with it but could not prevent it.[55] A short time later, in February 1990, Marshal Yazov warned that defense costs would not go down because all the restructuring of forces was causing the operations and maintenance outlays to rise significantly.[56] Yazov's point helps explain the lack of sympathy for the VPK in the military. The MoD was facing huge new demands for social support to military personnel returning from Germany, as well as increased operational costs of these transfers and other restructuring efforts. Thus it had little enthusiasm for financing large procurement orders, preferring to put most of its shrinking budget into MoD operational expenditures. Moreover, the long-standing tensions between the VPK and the MoD began to surface more openly. During spring 1990, the chief of the General Staff sharply criticized the VPK, accusing it of overpricing weapons, failing to meet quality standards, and suffering from "bureaucratic egoism." The deputy commander of the strategic rocket forces also charged the VPK with arrogance and inattention to military needs. These and other critics called for an independent committee to investigate the VPK.[57]

For all the public talk about military conversion, the program never really took hold. No formal conversion plan was forthcoming. The VPK and the Council of Ministers did not really support it. Where factories actually attempted to convert to civilian production, the results were uneven at best, more often negative. At the same time, disruptive change was occurring at the enterprise level in several of the military-industrial ministries, but not as the consequence of the military conversion program. Rather, the new law on the firm, imposition of khozraschet, and cuts in the military budget were the primary causes.

Military production declined significantly in 1990–91. Precisely how much even the VPK probably did not know. The economic bureaucracy in Moscow was slowly losing control of its regional components, and the VPK was no exception. During these years, the union republics were seeking economic sovereignty, meaning much greater liberty in running all economic enterprises within their own borders. In 1990–91 Yeltsin began to make the same claim for the Russian republic. The drive toward economic sovereignty could not go far without becoming a drive for political sovereignty. As it did, Gorbachev found himself negotiating a new union treaty, a process that would provoke the August crisis in 1991 and his subsequent demise.

In summary, little military conversion occurred as Gorbachev conceived it. The top levels of the VPK and the Council of Ministers pretended to go along with it while dragging their feet. Instead of effective conversion, the program merely added to the growing disorder throughout the military-industrial sector. The VPK and GOSPLAN tried to mitigate this disorder with credits and other expedients. They saved the ministerial structures from collapse but increasingly lost control of those enterprises which could find alternative markets and adapt their production to meet them. Still, this number was not large. Nuclear weapons plants and many other highly specialized enterprises simply did not have that option.

Initial attempts to make the VPK part of the solution instead of the problem were based on fundamental misconceptions of the nature of the command economy. Even when Gorbachev came around to the idea of introducing limited market reforms, he apparently was never convinced that a basic systemic change was unavoidable if significant results were to be achieved. Perhaps Gorbachev's inability to understand this issue conceptually was actually a blessing.

Had he understood, he might have given up on perestroika. In the bliss of his ignorance, he remained determined to cut the military-industrial sector. The politics of reaching that goal were so difficult that the practical possibilities were nil. Still, Gorbachev persevered, and his eclectic tactics and erratic policies came together in unexpected and jolting ways that disoriented the military industrialists. Although the military conversion policy was publicly advertised as key to reducing the military-industrial sector, it played only a small role. The whole set of perestroika policies—foreign policy, arms control, loosening the bonds on the Warsaw Pact states, timid steps in economic reform, glasnost, and the political reform of the legislative branch of the Soviet state—slowly induced administrative and economic chaos that facilitated reductions. More by fortune than by calculation, Gorbachev paralyzed the VPK and then cut its resources.

In this political struggle, the MoD and the VPK failed to ally against perestroika policies—strangely, from some viewpoints. Julian Cooper, an authoritative student of the VPK, suggested in 1990 that a political clash between the party and an MoD-VPK alliance would produce a major crisis in "civil-military" relations.[58] Both the MoD and the VPK stood to lose a great deal from perestroika and therefore shared a strong objective interest in cooperating to stop it. "Rational choice" theorists would certainly approve of this logic, but no such alliance emerged. To be fair to Cooper, he did not predict that it would, only that in the context of Colton's "control model" of party-military relations such an alliance would produce a crisis if it were formed. Why was it not?

First of all, because Gorbachev's policies caused the VPK and the MoD to differ sharply over how to allocate the state military budget. As economic performance slowed in the 1970s, tensions rose between the MoD and VPK over the quality of weapons and equipment being produced. Tensions and quarrels were not new. They had existed since the First Five-Year Plan (1927–32) as the result of the MoD's system of voenpredy, which put the MoD in a position to demand high-quality products. GOSPLAN and the Chairman of the Council of Ministers refereed the MoD-VPK disputes, but the Politburo was the final arbiter. It always had members with strong ties to both bureaucracies, and the party's ideology rationalized the high-priority claim on resources by both.

When these relations are taken into account, the answer emerges. Although the VPK and the MoD were separate and sometimes competing claimants on resources, the party was not. It enveloped and penetrated both, and party leaders came from both. An MoD-VPK alliance against the party simply had no organizational or bureaucratic basis. MoD-VPK tensions were finally an intraparty policy affair, adjudicated within the Central Committee and the Politburo by senior officials from both bureaucracies.

Gorbachev's military policies therefore exacerbated tensions between the MoD and VPK instead of provoking them to ally against the party. Their only recourse against those policies was through the party, and that is why they looked to the conservatives in the party leadership for help. That is also why they backed Ligachev's faction at the Twenty-eighth Party Congress in 1990. And that is why both the minister of defense and the chairman of the VPK participated in the attempt to oust Gorbachev in August 1991. Failure to remove Gorbachev and reverse perestroika on both occasions left them caught in the inexorable dynamics of his policies. Senior military officers began openly voicing long-held feelings of ill will toward the VPK. As long as the Politburo exercised a strong hand and adhered to the official ideology, these feelings remained suppressed. Budget reductions, justified by ideological revisions, brought them to the surface. They were reinforced by the loss of VPK markets in Warsaw Pact countries as well as in Soviet client states elsewhere. Weapons piled up as buyers disappeared.

The full impact of this dynamic began to be felt only in 1990. The first five years of perestroika brought no basic structural change to the VPK. Its superstructure of ministers and bureaucracies survived. This point is important because the picture of chaos and decay within the military-industrial sector could leave the misimpression that Gorbachev effectively wrecked the VPK and cleared the way for a transition to a market economy after his departure from power. During his last couple of years of perestroika he shook up the VPK and loosened its grip on resources, but its structures survived to confront Russian economic reformers after the collapse of the Soviet Union.

TWELVE

The Army and Maintaining Domestic Order

Thus you find enemies in all those whom you injured by occupying that dominion, and you cannot maintain the friendship of those who have helped you to obtain this possession, as you will not be able to fulfill their expectations, . . . for which reason, however strong your armies may be, you will always need the favor of the inhabitants to take possession of a province.

NICCOLÒ MACHIAVELLI, *The Prince*

Of all the unhappy conditions to which princes or republics can be reduced, the most unhappy is that when they are unwilling to accept peace and incapable of sustaining war.

MACHIAVELLI, *The Discourses*

During the entire post-1945 period, the Soviet military conducted combat operations almost exclusively against peoples inside the socialist camp. True, Soviet pilots flew combat missions for Egypt, Soviet air force and air defense units fought in the Korean War, and Soviet military advisers participated in the war in Vietnam and a few other Third World conflicts. But the major deployments of Soviet military units in combat operations—some of them quite large—were dedicated to the maintenance of communist parties' rule in countries where they already held power. A massive Soviet military operation, in more than one hundred cities and towns, was hastily launched in East Germany after the 17 June 1953 workers' demonstrations against the new communist regime. The interventions in Hungary in 1956 and Czechoslovakia in 1968 are well known. Border skirmishes with Chinese forces were frequent in the 1960s, reaching their zenith with the fighting on Damansky Island in 1967. Finally, the dispatch of forces into Afghanistan in December 1979 had long been urged by its first victim, the Afghan communist party leader, Hafizullah Amin.

Throughout Soviet history, the Red Army and later the Soviet Army were used to put down domestic protests within the Soviet Union. The ministry of interior (MVD) had its own internal troops, several divisions strong, dedicated primarily to this role, but on some occasions they had to be reinforced by regular Soviet army units. The impact of these actions on the Soviet officer corps and their troops is not very well documented before the Gorbachev period; nor is the impact on public sentiments. The early operations, in the 1920s and 1930s, were unknown to Soviet citizens born after World War II, or were, at most, vague secondhand images, but this younger generation certainly knew of the bloody repression in Novocherkassk in southern Russia in 1962 and the repressions in Kaunas in Lithuania in 1972. Soviet army units participated in both. The military intervention in Hungary was widely known, but the invasion of Czechoslovakia seems to have had a much larger negative impact on the Soviet public mind. Many among the Soviet intelligentsia were deeply disturbed by the affair, and participating officers and troops brought home stories contradicting the official propaganda line about why it was necessary.

All these operations except Afghanistan were fairly short in duration and brought to apparently successful conclusions. That naturally limited their erosive effect on public support for the military. But the war in Afghanistan dragged on, eventually ending with a complete withdrawal in early 1989 and unofficial acknowledgment that it was a defeat for Soviet forces. Returning veterans, many of them permanently maimed by war wounds, brought home firsthand evidence to share with family and friends that was completely at odds with the media's image of what was happening in Afghanistan. Bodies of soldiers came home to be buried in sealed coffins, and the furtive manner in which the military handled these cases increased popular distrust of all official information on the war. Although Gorbachev easily gained the defense minister's support for pulling out of Afghanistan, he did not end the war rapidly. Its negative effects on public attitudes toward the Soviet military therefore continued unabated during his first three years in power.

At the same time, Gorbachev found himself increasingly turning to his military for maintaining order inside the Soviet Union. The most notable occasions were in Kazakhstan in December 1986, in Georgia in April 1989, in Azerbaijan in January 1990, and finally in Lithuania in January 1991. Soviet military units were directly involved in all of them and responsible for considerable carnage in every case. Conflicts between ethnic groups also began to arise: in Nagorno-Karabakh and Abkhazia in the Transcaucasus in 1988, in the Fergana Valley in Central Asia in 1989, and in Transdniestria and the region inhabited by the Gagauz in Moldavia in 1989.[1] Soviet military involvement in these conflicts varied from taking sides to trying to contain the violence while remaining neutral.

These events gradually became a serious political issue for Gorbachev and his senior military leaders. While struggling over foreign policy issues, arms control, withdrawals from Eastern Europe, cuts in military forces and the military budget, military-industrial conversion, and issues of military reform, they also had to deal with these traumatic episodes involving Soviet troops killing Soviet citizens. Glasnost allowed the media to cover them with fewer constraints, giving the public a clearer view of the facts than had ever been the case. The patriotic and self-sacrificing image that the media had persistently cultivated of the Soviet military in past decades received damaging blows from these events.

Using army units to enforce domestic order also exacerbated nationalist discontent. The victims in Kazakhstan, Georgia, Azerbaijan, Armenia, and Lithuania were primarily from the national minorities. Ethnic minorities within military units had always created tension, but by the late 1980s the problem was intensifying, undermining the reliability and combat effectiveness of many units.

Judging precisely the negative impact of all these factors on the Soviet military is impossible. Even deciding when it began is difficult. Impressionistic evidence suggests that the invasion of Czechoslovakia marked the beginning for a few officers.[2] The invasion of Afghanistan definitely had an effect, right from the beginning, among the most senior Soviet officers. Marshal Nikolai Ogarkov strongly opposed it, and so did most other senior officers around him.[3] By the time Gorbachev came to power, the negative influences of that war were fairly widespread in the general population. A further analytical challenge is separating the impact of that Afghan war and later uses of the military in the maintenance of domestic order from all the other forces unleashed by glasnost and Gorbachev's perestroika policies. There was obviously synergy among them. Surprisingly, Gorbachev and most of his party peers did not seem to understand the adverse consequences of using the military for police actions until it was too late. By the spring of 1989 the public reaction in a number of the republics had spilled over into attitudes toward military service. Massive resistance to military conscription began at that time in the Baltic republics and the Transcaucasus.

A closer look at some of these events helps explain why they were so destructive to the military. Of necessity the accounts that follow must be brief and tentative—brief because each would require a lengthy monograph to examine exhaustively, tentative because the available evidence on each is far from complete. Of primary importance here is a sense of the qualitative effects of these cases on the military itself.

The War in Afghanistan

The most significant effect of the war in Afghanistan was the loss of the Soviet military's image of invincibility. Earlier interventions in Eastern Europe had quickly restored communist rule. Almost ten years of fighting failed to achieve that in Afghanistan. No trick of propaganda could conceal this fact. Slowly but surely, the image of defeat etched itself in the Soviet public mind, especially in the minds of soldiers and officers who served in the war. As Gorbachev discovered when he raised the idea of withdrawal in the Politburo, most members were sick of it, ready to abandon Afghanistan to its fate, and inclined to absolve themselves of the responsibility by placing the blame on Brezhnev, Ustinov, Andropov, and Gromyko—all conveniently deceased but Gromyko.

Turning to the war itself, its adverse effects on the rank and file Soviet military were serious. Alexander Alexiev's study, based on interviews with thirty-five Soviet military veterans of the war, reveals their social and organizational manifestations.[4] Although longer and more detailed accounts of the war are available, they are consistent with Alexiev's succinct empirical findings.[5]

First, the lowest socioeconomic groups in Soviet society bore the main burden of service in Afghanistan. As word came back to the wider society about what duty in Afghanistan was really like, draft evasion began to spread, and bribing local voenkomat recruiting officials became a common way for a draft-age youth to avoid the war. Those families with more income and better social positions were better able to keep their sons from being sent to Afghanistan. The MoD and its voenkomat bureaucracy reacted to this adverse popular reaction by sending more conscripts from rural areas and fewer from urban areas because young men on collective farms had less opportunity and fewer means to evade conscription. The voenkomaty also turned to another vulnerable social group, the criminal element among the youth, sending large numbers of conscripts with criminal records to Afghanistan, either in lieu of jail terms or after they were released from jail.

Second, the same kind of selection of the worst possible candidates for duty in Afghanistan occurred within the military itself. Army units were occasionally transferred to Afghanistan as retribution for having poor discipline and training records. Officers who were demoted in rank for drunkenness were commonly reassigned to Afghanistan. Many poorly trained and short-handed units were filled out with Central Asian reservists and troops from construction battalions, notorious for their lack of training in combat skills.

Third, political officers often grossly misled soldiers when they indoctrinated them on the political situation in Afghanistan. Outright fabrications were common. They sometimes told soldiers that they would perform such humanitarian tasks as building houses, schools, and kindergartens. Or they told their units that they would be fighting against Chinese, Iranian, and American mercenaries. These falsehoods became transparent once the units arrived in Afghanistan, leaving the political officers with no credibility among the troops, undermining commanders' ability to maintain discipline and morale.

Fourth, discipline within units was nonexistent much of the time. Alexiev's interviewees convey a picture of brutal relations between officers and troops and among the troops themselves.[6] Officers physically beat soldiers, and soldiers occasionally retaliated by killing officers, attributing their deaths to operational causes. Hostile relations among ethnic groups, especially between Central Asians and Slavs, produced murders, riots, and occasional mutinies. Although Alexiev documents only a few examples of each of these behavior patterns, other sources confirm that ethnic conflict within military units was indeed widespread.[7] Soldiers of Central Asian ethnicity were especially disposed to fraternize with the Afghan rebels and to desert their units.

Also exacerbating interethnic problems was the notorious system of hazing of first-year conscripts by senior conscripts. The practice had so infested the enlisted ranks by 1980 that few units were free of this deviant behavior. Hazing led to widespread beatings, ethnic brawls, and physical injury to the point of death in many instances. Thus the Soviet Army took many of these problems with it when it went to Afghanistan. The war aggravated these worries and added new ones.

Drugs, for example—marijuana, hashish, and opium—were readily available. According to Alexiev's interviewees, about half of the troops regularly used drugs, especially the second-year conscripts. The reason: "You take drugs because when you smoke them you don't care about anything else at all. Life becomes easy for you."[8] Alcohol abuse had always been a problem in the Soviet military, and in Afghanistan it was more acute.

Health problems proved no less deadly than insurgents' attacks. Not only were medical units vastly overworked and poorly equipped, but laundry and bathing units were also lacking in many units, ensuring low hygiene standards. Casualties from disease and hygiene problems consistently remained higher than those from combat. As table 3 indicates, more than four hundred thou-

Table 3 Soviet Casualties in Afghanistan, 1979–89

Killed in combat	13,136
Noncombat deaths	2,676
Wounded in combat	23,258
Noncombat wounded	3,859
Traumatized/mutilated	22,939
Disease	404,414

Source: Lyakhovskii, appendix 14. Lyakhovskii used official data from the records of the General Staff for this appendix.

sand personnel contracted serious illnesses during the course of the entire war, about fifty thousand were wounded or injured, and more than fifteen thousand died. Aleksandr Lyakhovskii, whose account of the war is based largely on classified documents as well as his own service in Afghanistan, describes a mood of fear about disease and infected areas.[9] General Mikhail Zaitsev, for a time the commander of the 40th Army, was terrified of catching a local disease. Notorious among his subordinate commanders for meddling in their combat operations and causing them to fail, Zaitsev's presence was a constant matter of concern to them. They often caused him to cancel visits to their units by telling his staff aides that they were operating in disease-ridden areas.

Theft and corruption, also problems throughout the Soviet military, became more serious in Afghanistan.[10] Soldiers readily stole ammunition, weapons, vehicle parts, and just about everything else in the Soviet Army's inventory to barter with Afghanis. Some types of Western consumer goods could be obtained this way, but drugs were in greater demand. Officers proved impotent in their efforts to stop this thievery and barter—not surprisingly, in light of the strained relations between most junior officers and their troops.

Looting, plunder, and atrocities were widespread practices against the Afghani population, according to Alexiev's interviewees and corroborated by many Western media accounts during the war. Indiscriminate executions, rapes, mutilations of prisoners, arson, and crushing Afghanis under armored vehicles —the kinds of practices reported—are indicative of military units under weak and ineffective command. Moreover, such behavior undermines the discipline and morale of combat units, at least in the view of most Western professional officers. Soviet commanders apparently took a different view. I have asked many former Soviet officers and other former officials why such brutality is condoned. Uniformly they have replied that a human life is just not considered very valuable in Russia.

Lyakhovskii tries to paint a somewhat more positive picture of the Soviet officer corps' performance, but as the example of General Zaitsev indicates, even his picture is mixed. Although he strives to provide a heroic, though tragic, image of the army throughout the war, his book is filled with accounts of poor tactics and training, ignorance of local political circumstances, political officials vying with one another for personal advantage, corruption at high levels, and higher command levels interfering with more competent lower commanders. Other Soviet sources were sometimes highly derogatory. Documents from Afghanistan operations used as "lessons learned" at the Frunze Academy in Moscow, for example, convey a picture of gross incompetence in the conduct of tactical operations.[11]

From the very beginning of the Soviet army's deployment in Afghanistan, serious patterns of deviant and incompetent behavior emerged, and they became more widespread and more acute as the war continued. In fact, they provide a preview of the problems that surfaced sharply throughout the entire Soviet military during the last four years of its existence. Soviet forces took many of these problems with them into Afghanistan, but the environment there made matters worse. Veterans then carried the additional problems back to units in the Soviet Union, especially drug use, theft and sale of weapons and equipment, and increased violence against ethnic groups. Veterans also brought some of these problems back to civilian life, and that adversely affected public attitudes toward the military, especially those whom the war had hardened as criminals. In November 1989, eight months after the final withdrawal, the Supreme Soviet voted to grant amnesty to all former soldiers who committed crimes while serving in Afghanistan, including 2,540 soldiers already convicted.[12] Although one can only guess how many soldiers were guilty but never prosecuted, it was probably several times that number.

This line of analysis, to be sure, is qualitative, based mainly on impressionistic evidence. Was the scale at which these problems were recycled into Soviet society and into military units inside the Soviet Union sufficient to have a critical impact on the discipline, readiness, and morale of the whole Soviet Armed Forces? Probably not without the many other contributing factors. Still, it must have been more than a trivial contributing factor. Moreover, official propaganda policy of concealing this side of the Afghan war encourages an underestimation of its negative effects on the military as a whole.

Whatever the truth, at the Politburo meeting on 17 October 1985, when Gorbachev wanted a decision to withdraw from Afghanistan, it will be recalled that he read aloud several heart-rending letters from soldiers' mothers, complaining about the war. Summing up, he said that they all had the same leitmotiv: "International duty? In the name of what? Do the Afghanis themselves want it? Is it worth the lives of our children, who do not understand why they were sent there, what they are fighting for, killing old people and children? And you [the Soviet leaders] throw brand new soldiers against professional killers armed and trained with the best weapons, capable of opposing an entire brigade with ten of their own?" The message was clear: "The Politburo had made a mistake, and it had to be corrected, and soon—every day costs valuable lives."[13] To be sure, this was vintage Gorbachev, a theatrical performance staged for policy purposes; nevertheless, the circumstance that permitted such a performance says a great deal about the impact of the war on Soviet society.

"Nationalist Disturbances" in Alma-Ata

Among the early victims of Gorbachev's purge of the more senior party officials was Dinmukhamed Kunaev, first secretary of the party in Kazakhstan for more than twenty years and a Politburo member. At the December 1986 Central Committee plenum, Gorbachev replaced him with Gennadii Kolbin, an ethnic Russian, brought in from outside with no experience in Kazakhstan. Only his very close ties to Ligachev, Shevardnadze, and Gorbachev recommended him. He had a public reputation as a tough disciplinarian with great energy, and he reportedly had learned effective methods for cleaning up corruption under Shevardnadze's tutelage in Georgia in the 1970s.[14]

The appointment of an ethnic Russian to lead the Kazakh Communist Party provoked outrage in the Kazakh capital of Alma-Ata (renamed Almaty in 1992). Glasnost was not yet in full force in the fall of 1986, and for that reason official censorship allowed only a selective account of the events that followed.[15] Moreover, foreign correspondents were denied permission to visit Alma-Ata.

On the day Kolbin's appointment was announced, protesters gathered in the main square and remained there overnight. On the following day, 17 December, violence broke out when MVD troops tried to disperse the crowd with spades and attack dogs. The crowd began rioting in earnest at this point, and according to the British newspaper *The Guardian,* demonstrators numbered about ten thousand. They overwhelmed the party headquarters and broke into two prisons, releasing the inmates. Apparently army units were called in on the second day of rioting, after the MVD troops failed to control the situation. The army units came in armored vehicles and occupied the university, which reportedly supplied the demonstrators. This heavy-handed action soon ended most of the rioting.

The party launched a damage-control strategy at once, sending a Politburo member, Mikhail Solomentsev, and a host of party investigators from Moscow to the scene in Alma-Ata. The only detailed account of the disorder to appear in the Soviet press was on 19 December, and it depicted the events as nothing more than hooliganism provoked by national extremists.[16] The student demonstrators were said to be drunk and engaged in looting and vandalism — implying, of course, that they were not politically motivated. According to this official report, one policeman and one demonstrator were killed, but unofficial sources insisted that the numbers of dead were much higher.[17] Solomentsev made several public appearances during his stay in Alma-Ata, reasserting the party and state authority and emphasizing the need for better education in internationalism. Harsh judicial action followed. Two student demonstrators were sentenced to execution by firing squad, four were given fifteen-year prison terms, and one was given a fourteen-year term.[18]

Gorbachev and his Politburo colleagues apparently misjudged the depth of the nationalist sentiment revealed in this episode. Central Asian party leaders were notoriously corrupt. Sharaf Rashidov, head of the party in Uzbekistan, had been removed in 1984 after he and his clan had run that republic in the most corrupt manner imaginable for two decades. Apparently Gorbachev looked on the Central Asian republics as lacking genuine nationalist feelings in light of their Muslim cultural background and mixed ethnic makeup. And it may well have been that the demonstrators did not act spontaneously but rather at the urging of Kunaev supporters who realized that their privileged positions were about to vanish. Whatever the case, the party leadership in Moscow and in Alma-Ata acted swiftly and brought the affair to a quick conclusion. In no other subsequent episode of disorder among the national minorities did they act as effectively.

The situation required army units to restore order, but with virtually no press reporting on the bloody details, they had little impact beyond those who witnessed them directly. As long as the public was not complaining, the senior leaders in the defense ministry were prepared to accept the whole affair as a normal task. As glasnost widened, and when the outcry in the media became shrill against army commanders for their actions in restoring order or asserting Moscow's control, they reacted differently. In Alma-Ata in 1986, however, the generals took in stride the task of repressing unarmed civilians.

The Massacre in Tbilisi

Matters changed abruptly in spring 1989. Demonstrations began in Tbilisi, Georgia's capital, on 4 April, when members of the new National-Democratic Party started a hunger strike in front of a government building. By 7 April, the number of demonstrators grew to an estimated one hundred thousand. A strike also began on that day, including public transport workers, teachers, television employees, and workers in several factories. On 8 April, strikes and demonstrations continued.[19]

Dzumber Patiashvili, the first secretary of the Georgian Communist Party, his party colleagues, and the Georgian MVD chief, Shota Gorgodze, reacted by calling on Moscow to send additional MVD troops as well as army units. The Politburo in Moscow met twice, once on 7 April under Ligachev's chairmanship and again the next day under Chebrikov's chairmanship, to consider Patiashvili's requests. Gorbachev was in London until late on 7 April, thus missing the first meeting; why he failed to attend the second is not clear. The Politburo agreed to Patiashvili's requests. The defense minister, General Yazov, passed instructions to the Transcaucasus Military District Commander, Colonel General Igor Rodionov, and that same day army units arrived in Tbilisi. Yazov also sent a deputy minister of defense to Tbilisi, Colonel General Konstantin Kochetov. Based on a decision by the Georgian Politburo on 7 April, plans were hastily formulated for closing down the demonstration at 4:00 A.M. on 9 April. Forces were moved into place on 8 April, and Rodionov took control, directing Gorgodze and his MVD troops as well as the army forces. Rodionov and Kochetov reportedly assured Patiashvili and the Georgian Defense Council that the troops would be armed only with truncheons and shields for riot control, not with weapons and live ammunition, and that there should be no fatalities.[20] Thus the Politburo in Moscow seems to have left the decision to launch the operation to Patiashvili and his Georgian party colleagues, but Rodionov's enthusiasm for it suggests that he believed the Politburo actually desired it and had conveyed orders to carry it out through military channels.

MVD troops led the operation, reportedly using poison gas on the crowd, about eight thousand strong at this early hour. Army troops followed with truncheons and sharpened spades, attacking without warning. Although official reports put the number of dead at eighteen, including twelve young women, and the number of wounded civilians at 190, unofficial accounts are much higher.[21] The government at first tried to pass off the deaths as having resulted from the stampeding crowd, but eyewitnesses disputed that explanation, describing the crowd as calm and orderly. Most of the deaths were in fact caused by the army troops using their spades; others were attributed to the use of gas.[22]

On the day following the massacre, 10 April, a Politburo delegation of two, Eduard Shevardnadze and Georgii Razumovskii, arrived in Tbilisi to investigate the affair. On 14 April, Patiashvili resigned as party chief, to be replaced by Givi Gumbaridze. A number of dissidents were arrested, including Zviad Gamsakhurdia—later elected president of Georgia—and order was restored, at least temporarily. On 17 April, the Georgian Supreme Soviet appointed a commission to investigate the circumstances and to determine who was responsible for the actions taken in the early morning on 9 April.

Those, in brief, are the outlines of the Tbilisi massacre. The differences in the Politburo's handling of the events in Alma-Ata are at once apparent. The quick resort to the use of MVD and army units was the same, and the effort to control media reporting was similar but not nearly as successful. Glasnost was in full swing, and that allowed many of the gory details to become widely known. The image of Soviet soldiers clubbing unarmed Georgian women to death, needless to say, was emotionally explosive for the public, not just in Georgia but in most other non-Russian national republics.

Another major difference was the state of the official nationality policy. Nationalist groups in a number of the union republics were openly criticizing the policy by 1988. The dispute over Nagorno-Karabakh between the Armenians and the Azerbaijanis broke out in February 1988, when the Nagorno-Karabakh Oblast Soviet called for the region to reunite with Armenia.

In Georgia the local intelligentsia was waking up to the opportunities afforded by glasnost. By late 1988, Abkhazian separatism was an issue in Georgia, and during the fall, demonstrations in several Georgian towns cried out against Russification and in favor of greater Georgian autonomy. In November, nearly two hundred thousand people congregated in Tbilisi to demand changes in the USSR's constitution that would relax constraints on the rights of the republics.[23] In other words, the crisis in April 1989 was preceded by a long series of events revealing Georgian nationalist political and cultural sentiments against Soviet rule. The Politburo could hardly claim to have been surprised.

The biggest difference, however, was how the Politburo itself behaved. The political context was entirely different. The country was in the throes of the political reform approved the year before at the Nineteenth Party Conference. In spring 1989 multiple candidates were competing for positions as delegates to the new Congress of People's Deputies. Ligachev, Chebrikov, and others in the Politburo had grave reservations about this political reform. Moreover, Gorbachev was absent when the Politburo met to deal with Patiashvili's request for military forces to use against the demonstrators in Tbilisi. That allowed Gorbachev to deny approving the orders that allowed General Rodionov to order army units to repress the demonstrators. Shevardnadze was deeply angered by the episode, not only because of his sympathy for his fellow Georgians but also because, according to his own testimony, he was denied a chance to head it off.[24]

Gorbachev, he recollects, said on 7 April, "No matter what, the situation must be settled by political means. For that, if we need, we'll send Shevardnadze and Razumovskii."[25] Shevardnadze called Tbilisi at once and was told that the situation was in hand and that he was not needed. Thus the Politburo members, beginning with Gorbachev, were more concerned with avoiding responsibility than with dealing with the political crisis they had allowed, or perhaps encouraged, to develop in Georgia.

Gorbachev's personal evasions are described in Chernyaev's account of the 20 April Politburo meeting, which heard Shevardnadze's report after he and Razumovskii returned from Tbilisi.[26] Precisely what he reported Chernyaev does not say, but in his memoir Shevardnadze insists that no use of force was necessary and that the military could not have acted with approval from the MoD in Moscow.[27] Gorbachev listened to the report and then agreed with Shevardnadze that the affair had been ripening for some time. The blame, as Gorbachev saw it, lay with Patiashvili and the weakness of the party leadership in Tbilisi. They could not find common ground with the Georgian intelligentsia. He had, he insisted, frequently told Patiashvili to emphasize democratic methods in dealing with the awakening Georgian intelligentsia. As this episode showed, however, the Georgian party cadres knew only one method: force. Next Gorbachev complained about the lack of adequate and reliable information about the situation in Tbilisi. The secret cables between Moscow and Tbilisi, he said, had the handwriting of the GRU (Soviet military intelligence), KGB, MVD, and party organs all over them, each defending its own separate interests while ignoring the overall interest. On his arrival from London, Gorbachev complained, he was told that troops had been sent into Tbilisi, but only to guard certain sensitive installations, nothing more. Then martial law had been declared in Tbilisi, a "stupid" and "unnecessary" act in Gorbachev's words, and the Georgian Central Committee gathered in a bunker when its members should have been moving among the people calming them and explaining the measures. Meanwhile, the Politburo in Moscow had only limited information, wholly inadequate for making a proper decision.

Ryzhkov broke in at this point, asking, "And what did we know, sitting here in the Kremlin? The secretaries of the Central Committee knew something. But we—members of the Politburo, and I as head of the government—first learned about the events from the pages of *Pravda!* What is going on? How can the Politburo make decisions if the majority of its members don't know the facts?" Gorbachev tried to regain the floor, but Ryzhkov continued, "The army . . . what good is it when they throw the army against the people! Somebody gives the commander of the army in Georgia an order from Moscow, but the government—not a word or rumor is known to it about all this. And the military commander even addresses the Georgian Politburo, and we again learn about it in the newspapers? And Mikhail Sergeevich [Gorbachev] did not know, the chairman of the Defense Council, general secretary! How was that so? And if the army acts without informing the Politburo, that is worse."

Gorbachev turned to Yazov and addressed him sharply: "Dmitrii Timofeevich! Remember this forever, and issue an order today: henceforth without a Politburo decision the army is forbidden to participate in civil affairs."[28]

Gorbachev's performance on this occasion was poor theater, obviously intended to sidestep personal responsibility. Chernyaev, of course, admits his own bias in favor of Gorbachev's innocence. But even if he was not directly to blame, he had certainly initiated the policies that allowed the situation in Georgia to develop as it had. In his tactics of the moment, however, he was shifting the blame onto Ligachev, Chebrikov, and especially the military. Ryzhkov's comments have the sound of being prearranged, not only to absolve himself but also to suggest that someone in Moscow was usurping Gorbachev's power. Ligachev had chaired the Politburo meeting on 7 April, and in light of the sequence of events in Georgia, it was after that meeting that Patiashvili believed he had Moscow's green light, presumably from Ligachev. Moreover, General Rodionov and his army units were available at this point to back local MVD troops. Why did Gorbachev not attend the meeting on 8 April (chaired instead by Chebrikov), dig into matters, and put Rodionov's operation on hold? He admits that he was briefed on the Tbilisi situation immediately on his return to Moscow on the seventh—but inadequately. Was that true? Or did he know the main facts and choose to let Rodionov's operation proceed because he knew that Ligachev had already given the Politburo's permission, thereby relieving Gorbachev of the direct responsibility if things went badly? Chernyaev gives no answers to these obvious questions, and he essentially admits that in providing the details of the 20 April Politburo meeting, he is trying to demonstrate Gorbachev's innocence.

The Georgian commission's report on the affair—published in the Georgian press in October 1989—was full of contradictions but created the impression that Patiashvili was misled by Colonel General Rodionov's assurances that there would be no casualties. Patiashvili comes off badly, but Rodionov looks even worse. The report virtually ignored Gorbachev's role. It did, however, include testimony that Patiashvili spoke frequently to Politburo members in Moscow, including Gorbachev and Yazov, in the days just before the tragedy. Furthermore, Yazov testified that Gorbachev had spoken to Patiashvili immediately upon his return from Britain, the evening of 7 April.[29] If Yazov is to be believed, Gorbachev hardly gave the Politburo a valid picture of his own involvement.

Other testimony corroborates that impression. Saparmurat Niyazov, the first secretary of the Turkmenistan party at the time, tells a quite different story of Gorbachev's approach to politics in Georgia. According to this report, when Gorbachev learned of the massacre, he coldly replied, "The more blood they spill, the more they will come back and ask for our help." [30] Extremely disdainful of Gorbachev's nationality policy, Niyazov also quoted Gorbachev on an earlier occasion as saying that there was no real danger that the national republics would separate from the Soviet Union because they were so inextricably entangled with the Soviet economy that they could not survive if they tried. Moreover, if they did try to secede, they would soon return. Niyazov, of course, was hardly a disinterested observer of this affair.

Valery Boldin also gives an unflattering account of Gorbachev's role in the Tbilisi affair. He was with Gorbachev in London when news first came that events were getting out of control in Tbilisi. When they arrived back in Moscow, the Politburo members meeting them at the airport told Gorbachev that they had agreed that Shevardnadze should go immediately to Tbilisi on a peace-making mission; according to Boldin, the foreign minister did not go, apparently as a result of consulting with Gorbachev.[31] Patiashvili, who had a long history of strained relations with Shevardnadze, later told Boldin that Shevardnadze's trip had been delayed "because the conflict had already become irreversible, and that all the decisions had been agreed on, though he did not say by whom." [32] By implication, of course, Boldin is suggesting that it was Gorbachev. And he goes on to say that among all senior party leaders during the first Congress of People's Deputies (25 May–9 June 1989), the tendency to blame the military gained support. He also insists that he confronted Gorbachev directly for not taking the responsibility and for letting it fall on the military and a few subordinate party officials. Gorbachev gave no response, but Boldin sensed that his candor had touched a "raw nerve" with his boss.

Rodionov tried to defend himself at the Congress of People's Deputies, vehemently denying that any demonstrators had been clubbed to death by soldiers using shovels, and emphasizing the threatening political forces in Tbilisi that shielded themselves behind the demonstrators. Rodionov insisted that the episode had to be viewed in the overall political context, and the political opposition in Georgia was anything but peaceful. Thus it was actually a "provocation," not a "tragedy." [33] Following Rodionov's logic, of course, would lead back to Gorbachev's handling of the national problem in general as the root cause. No doubt Rodionov was as worried about what these events had done to the future of his career. (His worries proved groundless: he became the Russian minister of defense in 1996, though he was fired a year later.)

In the spring of 1989, Colonel Aleksandr Lebed' was the commander of an airborne division in Tula. His division was alerted on 8 April and flew to an airport near Tbilisi on 9 April.[34] He led a column of vehicles carrying his troops through Tbilisi on the night of 9 April, observing the evidence left from the clash earlier that day and the absence of people, even policemen, on the street. Although he did not arrive in time to witness Rodionov's early-morning action, he gives a vivid picture of the airborne regiment—the 345th—which carried it out.

This regiment was among the first units to enter Afghanistan in 1979 and one of the last units to leave in 1989. Its troops and officers had experienced extensive combat in the Bagram Valley and knew every kind of hardship. Deployed to Gyandzha (formerly Kirovabad) in Azerbaijan, it found no barracks, no motor parks, no apartments, and no money for dealing with these problems. Rather than a respite from war, the regiment had simply moved from one hot spot to another—the strife-ridden Transcaucasus. Alerted on 6 April, the regiment quickly traveled the 320-kilometer road distance to Tbilisi. Its soldiers had good fighting skills and knew how to kill ruthlessly, but in Tbilisi they saw no enemy, only demonstrators, and they had no training to deal with them. The demonstrators cursed the soldiers, baited them, and even hurled objects at them, but the airborne soldiers kept their peace. According to secondhand testimony from Lebed'—which is not very convincing at this point—the crowd gradually became so hostile that some decision had to be taken. It was taken, apparently by Rodionov, and the slaughter ensued.[35] And not surprisingly, given the psychological disposition of these troops as Lebed' describes it.

Lebed' held Rodionov in high regard, calling him one of the most "intelligent and educated" generals in the Soviet army. Rodionov had, Lebed' insists, strongly protested against Patiashvili's call for additional army troops but was overruled and not allowed to appeal to Moscow. As a result, no fewer than three airborne divisions arrived shortly in Tbilisi. The way Lebed' sees it, the massacre was the inevitable outcome of bringing in additional army units, especially these Afghan veterans. Rodionov, therefore, unjustly took most of the blame. "The general was guilty because he was a general," Lebed' laments, adding that Gorbachev and others indirectly acknowledged to Rodionov much later, after he had been relieved of command and made head of the General Staff Academy, that the accusations against him were absurd. In Tbilisi, meanwhile, signs remained publicly posted saying, "Rodionov is a murderer!" and "Death to the Murderer Rodionov!" Lebed' opines that had Rodionov demanded a trial of his case immediately following the episode, he would have been cleared, but the political leaders did not want that, and Rodionov was too "disciplined" to insist on it.[36]

The precise degree of Gorbachev's complicity in the Tbilisi massacre is less important here than the impact on the senior officers of the image that he and the Politburo were creating in connection with the affair. In the Alma-Ata affair, the Politburo and the military chain of command maintained the appearance of unity and unflinching determination to control the events. In the Tbilisi affair, the Politburo's indecisive and evasive behavior was soon brought into full public view, and the military chain of command appeared either to have broken down or to have acted without the Politburo's sanction. The members of the Politburo began pointing fingers at each other in the aftermath. At the same time they tried to push the blame onto the Georgian party leader, Patiashvili, and the military district commander, Colonel General Rodionov.

The reaction of Lebed' is instructive. He was little troubled by the bloody repression. In fact, he seems to believe that the provocative behavior of the demonstrators justified the lethal response. The generals were merely Gorbachev's scapegoats, according to Lebed', who was sure that most other generals probably shared his judgment. Moreover, he said, Yazov must have felt severely abused by Gorbachev's rebuke at the 20 April Politburo meeting after Ryzhkov suggested that the military had acted without authority in Georgia. Whether or not Yazov, Rodionov, and Lebed' had an accurate picture of the political situation in Tbilisi, they were convinced that the army had saved the party from political defeat in Georgia. Lebed' flatly says so. As a reward for this rescue, the generals were being portrayed in the media as murderers and butchers with the blood of unarmed young women on their hands. In Boldin's judgment, Gorbachev's behavior during the Tbilisi affair marked the total loss of his credibility with the military; thereafter, the widening gulf between them could not be closed.[37]

The account by Lebed' of the sentiments of soldiers just returning from Afghanistan makes more comprehensible their behavior toward demonstrators who taunted them.[38] Suppose, for example, that a regiment of U.S. troops had come straight back from heavy fighting in Vietnam to an army post in the United States without adequate housing and support facilities, and then imagine that it was dispatched to deal with antiwar demonstrators on a university campus. To say that the potential for violence would have been high is grim understatement. Who made the selection of units in the Tbilisi affair? Lebed' does not say, but he implies that Gorbachev was responsible. The General Staff undoubtedly decided, or at least approved the decision, that units from the battle front in Afghanistan would be sent to the unstable region of the Trans-caucasus. If Gorbachev cannot have it both ways in his view of this affair, neither can Lebed'.

Finally, the Tbilisi affair inspired a number of articles in the military's ideological journal critical of using the army to maintain domestic order.[39] Ironically, General Valentin Varennikov, commander of the ground forces, led off with a strong argument against it. He made his case on ideological grounds, citing Engels to the effect that armies may wage both internal and external wars, depending on where the enemy is. Since 1939, however, the Soviet Union had no internal enemies. Thus the army's mission could only be to prepare to repel external aggression. (This lofty reasoning did not still his thumping enthusiasm for using the army internally in Lithuania in 1990 and 1991 or in Moscow, Kiev, and elsewhere in the August crisis in 1991.) Two colonels reached the same conclusion but were less unqualified in rejecting a domestic function for the army. Finally, a retired colonel argued that only the internal use of the military had saved socialism in Eastern Europe on more than one occasion. Marshal Akhromeev offered a somewhat different view. For him the lesson from the Tbilisi intervention was that military commanders should take orders only from the government in Moscow, not from republican leaders.[40] This diverse theorizing and opinion hardly clarified the issue for political offi-cers who had to deal with it in political indoctrination classes for the troops.

Military Intervention in Baku

The next major crisis occurred in January 1990, in Baku, the capital of Azer-baijan. It was only one more episode, though an important one, in the long series of disorders in the region that had begun with the Nagorno-Karabakh conflict, which broke out in February 1988.

An autonomous oblast within the republic of Azerbaijan, Nagorno-Kara-bakh had a predominantly Armenian population and historical ties to Armenia. On 20 February 1988, the Armenian deputies to the oblast soviet called for Nagorno-Karabakh to be united with Armenia. The Politburo in Moscow re-jected the demand, and Gorbachev appealed for a reasonable solution. On 22 February, between fifty thousand and seventy thousand demonstrators took to the streets of the Armenian capital, Yerevan, in support of unification. Polit-buro members Anatolii Lukyanov and Vladimir Dolgykh arrived in Yerevan on the following day to investigate, but demonstrations and strikes continued, and violence occurred in Nagorno-Karabakh as a purge of the oblast party committee was implemented. Candidate members of the Politburo, Georgii

Razumovskii and Petr Demichev, appeared in the Nagorno-Karabakh capital, Stepanakert, on the day of the demonstration but apparently failed to control the situation—if indeed that was their intention. In Moscow a government press spokesman, Gennadii Gerasimov, declared that Gorbachev would allow no borders to be changed. By 27 February, disorders began to occur in Baku, and the following day in Sumgait, a city of more than two hundred thousand a short distance northeast of Baku, a pogrom occurred against resident Armenians. Twenty-six Armenians and six Azeris were reported killed.[41]

This is more or less the picture presented at the time by the Soviet media and generally accepted by the Western media, but it may have been highly distorted. It has been called a cover story for a Gorbachev-backed KGB scheme for stimulating the Nagorno-Karabakh conflict and inviting the violence in Sumgait that followed. From his examination of the media and chronology of events, Igor Nolyain makes a circumstantial case that Gorbachev, several of his Politburo colleagues, and the KGB were the perpetrators, pursuing a divide-and-rule strategy.[42] Looking at the media evidence, he asked how so-called criminals, recently released by jails, were able to travel about in buses and cars from various places in the Transcaucasus and to show up together to participate in pogroms against Armenians in Sumgait? Without the KGB's assistance, he insists, this would have been impossible. Equally suspicious was the sudden appearance of the USSR deputy procurator general, Aleksandr Katusev, in Baku, where he announced on the radio details of the violence. The procuracy and its officials traditionally remained out of the media during an investigation. Nolyain also quotes two credible sources, Yelena Bonner, Andrei Sakharov's wife, and Levon Ter-Petrossian, the president of Armenia, with a reputation as a liberal-democratic reformer, to the effect that nothing in the conflict had to do with ethnicity or religion. Nolyain, a Soviet émigré engineer living the United States, is hardly a detached observer, but he raises questions not easy to wave away. Nor are the judgments of Bonner and Ter-Petrossian to be dismissed easily. Whatever the truth, that a number of people in Moscow, Armenia, and Azerbaijan believed Gorbachev and the KGB initiated the strife in the Transcaucasus is a fact worth noting, particularly in light of even stronger evidence of later KGB manipulations in Baku.

Over the next two years, the dispute over Nagorno-Karabakh remained unresolved, and violence and disorders were periodic not only in the autonomous oblast but in other parts of Azerbaijan. Refugees began to move, both Armenians leaving Azerbaijan and Azeris leaving Armenia. Rather than impose a solution, Gorbachev tried to appear as the evenhanded mediator. At the same time, army units were assisting the MVD in maintaining order in both Armenia and Azerbaijan, but they too were attempting to avoid the public image of taking sides.[43] General Lebed' aptly characterizes Gorbachev's public handling of the Nagorno-Karabakh problem with a soldier's anecdote. As the story goes, a regimental commander and his chief of staff fell into a terrible quarrel. The regimental political officer was called in to referee the dispute. Having heard the commander's side of the argument, the political officer said, "You, the commander, are right." Next he listened to the chief of staff's argument and declared, "You, the chief of staff, are right." The local party secretary, who was also present, expressed his puzzlement. "The commander and chief of staff are both right? That can't be!" The agile political officer responded, "And you are also right!"[44]

That was the way it looked to many other generals as well as to Lebed', but for Gorbachev to have acted vigorously in Azerbaijan and Armenia, as he did in Alma-Ata in 1986, he would have undercut his own glasnost and perestroika policies in 1988 and 1989, especially in the eyes of the Western media. By that time, glasnost had allowed national separatist movements to emerge in both republics. Nationalism had long been highly developed among the Armenians, but their survival as a state surrounded by Muslim enemies inclined them since tsarist times to maintain strong ties to Moscow. Even an independent Armenia, therefore, would want strong ties to Moscow, and the Soviet leaders knew that. Azerbaijan was another matter. Azeri nationalism was nascent but weak when the Bolsheviks came to power. By 1989, however, it began to surface with the creation of the Popular Front of Azerbaijan as the political opposition to local communist rule. The Nagorno-Karabakh dispute provided impetus to this national awakening, a disturbing one to the Politburo because a nationalist separatist movement in Azerbaijan, unlike the one in Armenia, would have no hesitation about seeking a complete break from the Soviet Union.

In late 1989 the upheaval appeared to spiral out of control as mutually contradictory Soviet, Armenian, and Azeri legislative acts were promulgated.[45] The Supreme Soviet of the USSR passed a set of measures for bringing order to Nagorno-Karabakh on 28 November. The Armenian Supreme Soviet reacted with a decree for the unification of Nagorno-Karabakh with Armenia on 1 December, and on 4 December the Azerbaijan Supreme Soviet's presidium answered with a decree on normalization in Nagorno-Karabakh that contradicted the measures passed in Moscow. By late December the Popular Front of Azerbaijan was actively protesting Soviet rule in connection with restrictions in crossing the border with Iran. In Dzhalilabad, near the border, thousands stormed the party and police headquarters on 29 December. Rioting continued until 11 January 1990, when Popular Front members seized control of the party and municipal offices in Lenkoran, a city on the Caspian Sea.[46] On 13 January large demonstrations began in Baku against the republic's leadership, headed by Abdul-Rakhman Vezirov, the republican party's first secretary. The demonstrators reportedly demanded the removal of Vezirov and a referendum on secession from the USSR.

Part of the crowd, mostly Azeri refugees from Nagorno-Karabakh seeking revenge and apartments, embarked on a hunt for Armenians remaining in Baku, but of the more than two hundred thousand Armenians living there before February 1988, most had already departed by late 1989.[47] According to the chess master Gary Kasparov, who was living in Baku at the time, the Azeri refugees had received no assistance and housing from officials there who treated them wretchedly when they sought assistance. This gave rise to the popular suspicion that the KGB and the local communist officials were staging these anti-Armenian pogroms to undermine the Popular Front.[48] So, too, did the delay of the Soviet military intervention for the next several days, while the Popular Front and its angry followers continued to challenge Soviet rule not only in Baku but in Nakhichevan and other parts of the republic. Meanwhile, the Soviet official media stirred up a horrible picture of the Popular Front's behavior, describing Baku "as though a modern city had reverted to the Middle Ages." [49] Several sources, though, place the blame for the outbreak of violence and for the army's intervention squarely on Gorbachev and his lieutenants.[50]

So did the regime in Baku. A commission of the Supreme Soviet of Azerbaijan, assigned to investigate the whole affair long after it was over, concluded that "Gorbachev, Ye. Primakov, A. Girenko, D. Yazov, V. Kryuchkov, V. Bakatin, V. Varennikov, and other high-level people of the political and military organs of the former Union all carry the responsibility for criminal actions of the Soviet forces in Azerbaijan." [51] Here, of course, we have the general secretary and his top level MVD, KGB, and MoD aides. The commission added, however, that because it was denied access to the direct perpetrators of the actions in Azerbaijan, it could not establish a completely unbroken line of responsibility.

In December 1991 the commission learned from the minister of national security in Azerbaijan that throughout January 1990, two local KGB officials, V. Pirozhkov and G. Ageev, managed a series of covert actions aided by a group of collaborators sent from the KGB in Moscow. The former head of the KGB in Baku described things differently, reporting that immediately after the army intervened on 19 January, Kryuchkov called him and told him that the KGB had completely failed and that now everything in Azerbaijan would be decided by the MVD and the MoD of the USSR.[52] Although these two reports give contradictory views of the KGB's effectiveness, neither denies that it was vigorously trying to influence the situation.

Ekhtibar Mamedov, a member of the Popular Front leadership, testified that Primakov and Girenko called him to party headquarters in Baku shortly before the intervention and told him that military forces were needed to prevent Azerbaijan from separating from the Soviet Union, a secession that had to be prevented at any cost. They also told him that General Yazov had issued an order that if Soviet army units were not allowed to enter the city, they were to open a "tornado of fire on all resistance." Later the same day, the Baku garrison commander warned him that if the troops received the order, "they would spare neither children nor women." [53]

On 19–20 January, when the Soviet army arrived in Baku, its objective was apparently twofold — destruction of the Popular Front and a purge of the local leadership. The leadership purge began at once, but it did not go smoothly. On 20 January, Vezirov was removed from his post as first secretary of party and temporarily replaced by his deputy, and in Moscow, Gorbachev met with Ayaz Mutalibov, prime minister of Azerbaijan, to discuss conditions for withdrawal of Soviet troops from Baku. Gaidar Aliyev, the party boss of Azerbaijan during Brezhnev's time and until Gorbachev purged him in 1985, spoke out in Moscow against the army's intervention in Baku, and called for its withdrawal. The Supreme Soviet of Azerbaijan managed to meet on 22 January and demand immediate withdrawal of Soviet troops. Thus with Gorbachev's policy being challenged both in Moscow and Baku, the political situation remained unstable even under martial law.

Destruction of the Popular Front required several days but reached a somewhat more decisive outcome. Not only did the Popular Front offer armed resistance, but on 26 January, Soviet defense minister Yazov claimed that the Azerbaijan MVD was actually giving it aid and that some forty thousand armed militants were still on the lose.[54] Yazov was probably grossly exaggerating the size of the resistance, but for political purposes, he needed to make it look dangerous. The army's operations quickly extended beyond Baku to Dzhalilabad, Lenkoran, and elsewhere, putting pro-Soviet officials back in charge.

General Lebed' provides glimpses of the intervention at the operational level. His airborne division in Tula was alerted on 18 January and flew to the vicinity of Baku the next day. Other arriving forces included an airborne division from Pskov and "a mass of motor rifle units which were hastily brought to full strength with call-ups from Rostov Oblast, Krasnodar Krai, and Stavropol Krai." [55] Although Lebed' does not mention it, the Committee of Soldiers' Mothers swung into action in a number of localities as the motor rifle units were being mobilized, publicly protesting against their deployment to Azerbaijan. They received considerable media attention as a result, creating embarrassment for Gorbachev abroad as well as home.[56]

In light of all the media reporting on growing disorders in Azerbaijan, Lebed' says that his fellow officers were surprised that nothing was done on 12 January to nip the crisis in the bud: "How can this be? In Baku there is slaughter, and we are still in Tula." Apparently, after exhausting all arguments, Lebed speculates, Gorbachev "remembered the formula: VDV + VTA [airborne forces plus military transport aviation] = Soviet power in the Transcaucasus."[57] By 1990 Lebed' and all of his officers had enough experience of this sort to share a common opinion, which came to this: "The devil take all the party and state leaders. Instead of stopping a conflict in its infancy, they let it heat up, then become convinced of their own incompetence, and finally, as a rescue stick, put the airborne forces into action."[58]

Lebed' and his division landed about thirty kilometers from Baku late on 19 January. Trucks were waiting to carry his troops to Baku, but the scene around the airfield was not peaceful. Local resistance groups drove in vehicles around the perimeter of the airfield, firing small arms at incoming aircraft. Small groups were deployed to block his forces' movement onto the highway to Baku. After receiving clarification of this mission, he ordered combat engineers to cut the fence on one side of the airfield, allowing his column of trucks to evade the resistance groups, and off his division went to Baku, receiving periodic hostile small-arms fire along the highway and stopping several times to engage in brief firefights. It arrived in the city that night and successfully occupied its assigned sector.[59]

Looking into the ordinary soldier's psyche at this point, at least as he perceived it, Lebed' describes twenty-year-old youths who had been trained to shoot at targets on training ranges but still had no idea what it means "to kill people." What is more, they had been told that they were there to restore order among Azeris, who were Soviet citizens like themselves, not foreign enemies. They were confused, asking, "What are we? Policemen?" They arrived on the scene in a good-hearted mood, not at all disposed for combat. But they quickly changed to "fierce anger," cursing in the foulest fashion, characteristic of "airborne chauvinism." Survival became their primary concern. No longer smiling youths, they became "ferocious, well-trained wolves" once they saw a comrade fall. At the same time, they were filled with "black fear."[60] This may have been a fair description of airborne troops, but the motor rifle units, only recently mobilized, were hardly "well-trained wolves," though they surely shared the sense of "black fear" and probably matched the airborne soldiers' vocabulary of obscenities.

After a small skirmish on the waterfront in Baku, the troops of Lebed' knocked out the Popular Front's main command post and accomplished a few other assigned objectives. Just when they had earned a brief pause to eat breakfast Lebed' learned that a group of thirty-nine investigators of the USSR Procuracy, headed by a major general (whom Lebed' does not name), had arrived to investigate the actions of his division as well as others. In a meeting Lebed' was shown a stack of paper forms, all with the same heading: "Inventory of the crimes committed by the servicemen of the airborne forces on the territory of Baku, 19–20 January 1990." The crimes were already listed. They included the killing of hundreds of civilians, the wounding of thousands, and the theft of numerous cars, refrigerators, carpets, and large sums of money and valuables. The procurators' task was plainly defined: "to investigate immediately and to punish severely." The general in charge of the group demanded to speak with the officers of the two regiments that had been sent to Baku for this operation.[61]

The meeting took place at 5:00 P.M. that day. When the procurator general accused them of hiding criminals in their midst and threatened that if these culprits were not handed over, they would be taken by force, a short period of astonished silence followed. Some audible chuckling began, followed by a howl of laughter among the assembled officers. How, they asked, did the general propose to take them "by force"? Did the investigators believe they had the power to do that? The very idea struck the assembled officers as uproariously absurd.

Lebed', however, was not amused. He quietly ordered a colonel to remove the detail of soldiers providing security for the investigators. The general soon stalked out and drove away in a huff. The episode ended a short time later when one of the general's aides called Lebed' to beg for the security detail to be returned to protect his group from threatening local marauders. Lebed' refused unless the general himself called and offered a clear apology. He did, Lebed' reports, and in the most sniveling manner. The security detail promptly returned.[62]

Precisely what was behind this investigation Lebed' does not fully explain, but he believed at the time that it was to provide Gorbachev or some other high party official a basis for victimizing him as they had done to General Rodionov after the Tbilisi affair, if they felt the political need.[63]

Again, as in the Tbilisi affair, the evidence is mixed and incomplete, but instructive impressions stand out. In the first place, it must be remembered that the Baltic republics, particularly Lithuania, were threatening secession at this time. Chernyaev and Shakhnazarov were encouraging Gorbachev to let Lithuania go, but Gorbachev could not bring himself to make that decision. The Western media were also more sharply focused on Lithuania, making Gorbachev's actions there more critical for his relations with the West. At the same time, events in Azerbaijan were becoming serious. The local party leadership, which Gorbachev did not trust in any case, was losing control.

In this context it appears that Gorbachev decided, or was persuaded by the KGB and MVD chiefs, that covert measures were needed to keep matters in hand in Azerbaijan. Either they failed or they were intended to create the disorders that would justify sending the army to restore control. Just how spontaneous the Popular Front's violence really was is difficult to know, but considerable evidence suggests that the KGB was behind some of it with the aim of discrediting the Popular Front and justifying the army's intervention to destroy it. That the KGB, MVD, and MoD were operating on their own seems unlikely, though it cannot be ruled out. Thus Gorbachev's involvement is difficult to dismiss. Moreover, all of this scheming and stage-managing from Moscow is consistent with the assertion by the Turkmen party chief, Sapar-murat Niyazov, that Gorbachev viewed the spread of violence in Azerbaijan as having the effect of making the republic more dependent on Moscow.

From the account by Lebed', it is clear that he and many of his fellow officers viewed the affair with ambivalence. They were quite ready to act against separatists and troublemaking political elements in the Transcaucasus. What infuriated them was Gorbachev's failure to let them restore order early and rapidly rather than after the situation had seriously deteriorated. Even worse, Lebed' feared being made a scapegoat at the whim of Gorbachev or some other Politburo member if things went badly.

In this regard, his vignette about the arrival of the team of procuracy investigators is particularly revealing. If it is indeed true, as Gaidar Aliyev, Popular Front leaders, and the Azerbaijan commission testified, that the situation was not out of hand, there were possible grounds for criminal charges against the intervening army units. If these units were sent in to destroy the Popular Front, perhaps they began the shooting. Lebed', of course, attributes the initiation of hostile fire to the Popular Front, but his testimony is suspect in light of his attitude toward separatist political forces.[64] The alternative interpretation for the arrival of the procuracy group is that Gorbachev and his aides in Moscow hoped to have a case against Lebed' and other officers if things went as badly in Baku as they had in Tbilisi. If this was so, Lebed' spoiled their game by his rough treatment of the chief investigator.

Probably the most critical public damage from the intervention in Baku was the outrage of the soldiers' mothers movement against it. These demonstrations reflected the serious erosion of public support for the military. At the same time, officers' attitudes toward the party leadership, as reported by Lebed', were deteriorating dangerously. A couple of weeks later, in mid-

February, an army division in Tajikistan refused to move into the capital, Du-
shambe, to quell a crowd of rioters and looters estimated to be five thousand
strong. The commander and his officers said they refused because they did not
want to be blamed for the violence the operation would require, a further sign
of changing officer behavior.[65]

The Failed Intervention in Lithuania

Having more or less succeeded in repressing the separatist movement in Azerbaijan, Gorbachev faced a more serious challenge in Lithuania, Latvia, and
Estonia. Among these, Lithuania was the most assertive. On 11 March 1990,
the Lithuanian parliament declared the country's independence. The Congress
of People's Deputies in Moscow passed a resolution on 15 March calling the
Lithuanian action illegal. On 18 April, Gorbachev initiated an economic blockade of Lithuania. In July, Lithuania backed off a bit from its independence
stance by approving a hundred–day moratorium on its independence decision
as part of a tactic to begin negotiations with Moscow. After an opening meeting
between Soviet and Lithuanian delegations on 2 October, Gorbachev tough-
ened his position and the talks were broken off.[66]

Behind the scenes, President Bush and his aides exerted influence on both
sides to avoid a showdown because negotiations for German reunification were
in progress. Bush was backing German chancellor Helmut Kohl's goal of reunification within the year, and he was also seeking Gorbachev's concession
that a unified German state might remain in NATO. Bush feared that a bloody
affair in a Baltic republic might provoke a U.S. domestic backlash against Moscow that would ruin his delicate relationship with Gorbachev; U.S. diplomats
worked to prevent or at least postpone such a confrontation.[67] This episode of
diplomacy contrasts with the United States' inattention to the repressions in
Georgia and Azerbaijan. The U.S. media, the Congress, and the president implicitly drew a line between the Baltic republics and all the others when it came
to Gorbachev's domestic use of force, a point that could not have been lost
on him.

The fall call-up for the military went badly in several republics but especially in the Baltic region, and that became the pretext for staging an intervention in Lithuania. On 7 January 1991, the ministry of defense announced
that airborne troops would be used to enforce conscription in Baltic republics, Moldavia, Armenia, and Georgia, but Lithuania was the only republic to
which they were deployed.[68] On the same day the Baltic Military District commander, Colonel General Fedor Kuz'min, issued an ultimatum to the leaders

of all three Baltic countries not to interfere with intervening troops. He also told them that Marshal Yazov had given them until 13 January to enforce military conscription. This move fooled no one in the Baltic republics. They knew that they were facing the probable destruction of their nationalist regimes.

The next move occurred on 11 January by the furtive Lithuanian National Salvation Committee, with Juozas Jermalavicius as its spokesman. Refusing to name its members, Jermalavicius announced that the committee was seizing power.[69] The same day Soviet troops took over the press center and the National Defense Department in Vilnius, wounding several people in the process. The following day, the Vilnius garrison commander, Major General Vladimir Uskhopchik, told the press that these actions were all in accord with Gorbachev's directives.

Finally, on 13 January, the National Salvation Committee accused radio and television stations of broadcasting anti-Soviet propaganda and appealed to Uskhopchik to take action, which he did. Troops went to the Vilnius television tower, blaring the committee's pronouncements through loudspeakers. On arrival, the army units confronted an unarmed crowd surrounding the building. In the action that followed, Soviet troops killed sixteen unarmed Lithuanian civilians and wounded hundreds of others, events witnessed by Western reporters and captured on film.[70] This fiasco could not be denied or distorted as had been done in Baku.

The very next day, however, Gorbachev began backtracking, claiming that the violence was all at the initiative of the local commander. Yazov feebly tried to defend Uskhopchik by accusing the Lithuanian government of provoking him to the breaking point with its emotional anti-Soviet propaganda.[71] A delegation from the USSR Council of the Federation arrived in Vilnius to meet with members of the National Salvation Committee, but after one unidentified member met the delegation at the airport, he quickly disappeared and no more was heard of the ghostlike committee.[72]

Estonia escaped serious violence during this period, but Latvia did not. Notwithstanding the cessation of the intervention in Lithuania, on 20 January special MVD troops—so-called black berets, known also by their acronym, OMON, meaning "special purpose militia detachments"—stormed the MVD building in Riga.[73] They killed four people and wounded ten, mostly journalists and civilians.[74] This marked the end of a series of lesser episodes perpetrated by MVD units during the month.

Compared with the episodes in Alma-Ata, Tbilisi, and Baku, the intervention in Vilnius was a logical extension of the pattern that Lebed' so aptly described: a worsening situation, Gorbachev's vacillation, then fruitless use of the KGB and MVD, next dependence on the MoD's equation "VDV + VTA = Soviet power," and finally, in the wake of an unsuccessful or brutal military intervention, a policy of blaming local party and military officials. In Vilnius the MoD's equation failed for a number of reasons. First, the Lithuanian independence movement was far more advanced than in other republics where the strategy had been employed. Second, Western media attention to all three Baltic republics was much greater, and as a result, not just President Bush but several other Western leaders implored Gorbachev not to interfere with the new regimes there. Third, nobody believed that the hapless Major General Uskhopchik was acting on his own, and Gorbachev looked silly for accusing him of it. Fourth, the climate was changing within the ranks of the military. Some airborne unit commanders reportedly balked at orders to take their troops into the Baltic republics. Also, the troops in some instances were said to refuse to use their weapons against civilians.[75] Only special MVD units and a few KGB troops could still be counted on for operations against renegade political movements and public demonstrations.

Fifth, an ominous event occurred during this failed intervention. Heretofore, political leaders against whom interventions took place stood alone with no significant support from political figures in Moscow. Not so in the case of the Lithuanian independence movement. In January 1991, Boris Yeltsin not only visited the region but also used a radio address to appeal to Soviet soldiers in Lithuania not to support the intervention. He lectured them harshly: "Many of you think you are a Rambo—a hero who defends law and order. No! You are a pawn in a dirty game, a grain of sand in the Kremlin's building of an imperial sand castle. This year you will take off your uniform, demobilize, and tell your girlfriend, 'We bashed those Lithuanians.' Those memories will be the only security you can give her—neither freedom, nor good life—for you have blocked that path with your tanks."[76]

These were emotionally powerful words coming from the head of the Russian republic who had been a Politburo member only four years earlier. No one of his stature in Moscow was saying such things to Soviet soldiers in Tbilisi or Baku.

The use of the military to repress opposition to communist rule is a practice as old as the Soviet regime. Why did it seem to work effectively until the intervention in Afghanistan and then fail outright in the last years of the Soviet Union? One possible answer is that Gorbachev lost his political nerve. Through early and brutal measures he ended the crisis in Alma-Ata, but in dealings with the Transcaucasus, he was initially indecisive, then resorted to military repression but blamed others for it.

A second answer, compatible with the first, has been much emphasized in earlier chapters. The ideological revisions that Gorbachev made as a basis for launching perestroika erased the legitimacy of Soviet rule over non-Russian lands and peoples. Once international class struggle was pushed aside, troubling questions were inevitable. Why should Soviet troops control Afghanistan? Or the Warsaw Pact states? Without solid answers for such questions, they were soon bound to arise about Soviet rule in the Baltic republics, in Georgia, Azerbaijan, Central Asia, and even in Ukraine. Yeltsin was implicitly raising them as he condemned Gorbachev's military intervention in the Baltic republics.

Gorbachev had effectively denied himself the traditional means of last resort for keeping the Soviet empire together: military power. Yet he did not want to accept that reality. So he tried to have it both ways, continuing his "new thinking" in foreign and military policy and pursuing glasnost and perestroika in domestic policy. But that required an occasional resort to the use of the military for containing centrifugal political forces that glasnost was unleashing. In Afghanistan and Eastern Europe he accepted the implications, refusing to use the Soviet military to defend ruling communist parties when they were threatened by popular forces. In the Soviet Union, however, he rejected the implications and used military force. This contradiction in his policies could not be maintained indefinitely. In the Baltic republics he was left to choose between his perestroika policy and the remarkable popularity it had gained him in the West or the reversal of perestroika and the destruction of his image in the West.

The impact of all these episodes on the military was palpable. Although it cannot be said to have destroyed the army, it was certainly a contributing factor, especially to the demoralization of the officers in the most elite army units, the airborne forces.

Finally, the military and the nationality issue were fundamentally related, not just in the ethnic composition of the military but more importantly in the question of the stability of the empire. Without a military willing and able to repress national separatist forces, the durability of the empire would be thrown into serious doubt. The logic of a genuine transformation to democracy in the Soviet Union was inexorable: there could be liberal reform or there could be a multinational Soviet Union, but not both.

THIRTEEN

From Force Reductions to Disintegration

The army is a copy of society and suffers from all its diseases, usually at a higher temperature.

LEON TROTSKY

When the army of an empire can no longer recruit effectively, the regime itself is in danger. The Soviet empire crossed that threshold in 1989–91. As it broke apart, so did the Soviet Armed Forces. Only their Russian core managed to survive in a weakened and decayed state as the armed forces of the Russian Federation.

In 1985 the Soviet Armed Forces had about 5.3 million men under arms.[1] By 1990 the number had reportedly declined to 3.99 million.[2] With the dissolution of the Soviet Union, the residual Soviet Armed Forces belonging to the Russian Federation were 2.72 million strong.[3] Almost all of this drop occurred in three years, 1989 through 1991. Unlike previous postwar demobilizations— 1945–47 and 1955–58—this one took on a dynamic of its own as the political leadership became more divided on military policy and as the military leadership spent more energy opposing reductions than planning and managing them.

The disintegration was the result of three developments. Gorbachev initiated and sustained the first—huge force reductions—beginning with the unilateral reduction of Soviet military manpower by five hundred thousand, followed by his signing of the CFE treaty and finally his reluctance to stem the collapse of the Warsaw Pact, which compelled the complete withdrawal of Soviet forces from Eastern Europe. He precipitated the second—a bitter public reaction to military conscription and the realities of life in the military—by permitting glasnost on military policy. The third was unanticipated—a rapid spread of open resistance to conscription, which denied adequate replacements for the semiannual discharges of enlisted personnel. All three developments tended to reinforce one another, confronting the MoD and the General Staff with manpower problems they proved unable, and in many cases unwilling, to address effectively. At the same time, glasnost allowed more and more voices to demand particular solutions to each of these problems. By 1991, the disintegration of the Soviet military was reaching an advanced stage, and its political reliability was in doubt.

Force Reductions

After Gorbachev's announcement of a large unilateral force reduction in December 1988, the MoD began planning to carry it out. Of the five hundred thousand personnel to be discharged, fifty thousand were to come from Eastern Europe. Soviet forces in Mongolia were also to be reduced, an army with five divisions and seventy-five thousand troops.[4] The remainder was to come from units within the Soviet Union. Returning five hundred thousand men to Soviet civilian life, especially officers with families requiring housing and jobs, was not a simple matter. The MoD could not manage all these issues alone. The State Committee for Labor and Social Problems, therefore, was instructed to assist the Main Personnel Directorate of the MoD in solving them.[5] Personnel would be discharged through the voenkomaty or military commissariats in the districts from which they had entered military service. Implementation, however, raised a host of policy questions. What if discharged servicemen did not want to reside in those districts? Should they be allowed to move elsewhere? How would they find housing? How would they find jobs? Would there be training assistance to help them qualify for civilian employment?

Answering most of these questions was the responsibility of the city and district soviet executive committees (the lowest level of state territorial administration). The voenkomaty were instructed to provide the executive committees with information on the numbers of personnel being discharged, and using those figures, the executive committees were to arrange housing and jobs for returning officers and soldiers.[6] The deputy minister of defense for cadres, General Dmitrii Sukhorukov, explained the process to the press in March 1989, making it appear well planned but also admitting that there were significant obstacles.[7] Turning tank drivers into tractor drivers on collective farms and putting combat engineer officers in charge of rural construction teams would be the aim, but the lack of counterpart civilian jobs for many military specialties required retraining large numbers of officers, a task that would not be easy. Sukhorukov recalled that in the 1950s special commissions had been created under the local executive committees to find jobs for discharged military personnel, and "now, on the eve of major new reductions of the army, it is necessary to revive the commissions and step up their work." [8] Concerning officers and their families, he worried that city authorities, especially in Moscow, would be reluctant to issue residence permits because housing was already short. To alleviate this problem the MoD planned to build about eight hundred new apartments in Moscow over the next two years, but he admitted that this would meet only a part of the housing requirement.

Sukhorukov's fears proved well founded. Local authorities everywhere, especially in the Baltic republics, resisted the influx of retirees by controlling housing and contravening Soviet laws on support to former military personnel. The problem became so serious that Admiral V. P. Ivanov raised it at the second Congress of People's Deputies and demanded a number of actions, including the creation of an oversight committee, a commission, and a new legal status for MoD's conscription and discharge orders, measures intended to overcome the local resistance.[9]

The MoD, however, had difficulty managing its own internal affairs, not to mention coordination with local governments on requirements for family housing, schools, hospitals, and so on. Already by fall 1989, officer reassignments were chaotic. Some were discharged by mistake. Many arranged assignments in much desired posts in southern Russia, Ukraine, and the Black Sea region, leading to overstaffing and "doubles" — two officers assigned to the same job. Meanwhile, positions in units in Siberia and Central Asia went unfilled.[10]

By December 1989, 265,000 personnel had reportedly been discharged, as well as an additional 173,000 students who were allowed to leave the army early.[11] Thus the first year of implementation of the unilateral manpower reductions appeared to be proceeding according to schedule, but that was soon to change.

A month earlier, on 9 November, the Berlin Wall had come down, raising the prospect of German reunification. Political upheavals in Czechoslovakia, Hungary, and Poland followed almost immediately, and in Bulgaria and Romania before the year's end. These changes threw into question the very existence of the Warsaw Pact. That it would not survive long became apparent after its Political Consultative Committee (PCC) met in Moscow on 7 June 1990. The governments of East Germany, Poland, and Czechoslovakia formed a bloc, insisting on a transformed alliance serving "for a transitional period" while an all-European security system was institutionalized.[12] Although the organizational integrity of the Warsaw Pact was formally maintained on this occasion, the PCC authorized an intergovernmental commission to make it a treaty among truly sovereign states.

In bilateral relations, events moved even faster during the spring as the Soviet Union signed treaties with Czechoslovakia and Hungary for complete withdrawal of forces over the next couple of years.[13] These agreements added another 170,000 troops to be withdrawn in addition to the unilateral cut of 50,000. As negotiations for the reunification of Germany went forward in the summer of 1990, withdrawal of all Soviet forces from East Germany and Poland became inevitable. What had begun in 1989 as a relatively small withdrawal of 50,000 troops had snowballed into a massive movement of ten times that many as well a large number of officers' families. As one analyst put it, "About 650,000 Soviet citizens, including some 350,000 conscripts, 150,000 officers, and an estimated 150,000 family members, have been stranded in four Central and Eastern European states."[14] The withdrawal included thirty-one Soviet divisions organized as four "groups of forces," with all their technical support and logistics units.

The command and control structures of the Warsaw Pact surprisingly survived into 1991. At a PCC meeting in Budapest on 25 February, Gorbachev agreed to the Eastern European leaders' request to dissolve the pact's remaining institutions, and on 31 March they were abolished.[15] Maintaining the defunct military structures for an additional six or eight months was related to negotiations on conventional forces reductions being conducted in Vienna between the states of NATO and the Warsaw Pact. Gorbachev remained committed to his arms control strategy, and the U.S. and European leaders were anxious not to miss the chance for a major conventional arms control regime in the whole of Europe, especially in light of the swift reunification of Germany. The negotiations were predicated on NATO and the Warsaw Pact. The Warsaw Pact's premature disappearance, therefore, would alter the very basis of a treaty. Thus negotiators pressed ahead at unprecedented speed to complete the Conventional Forces in Europe (CFE) treaty in time for the Paris meeting of the Conference on Security and Cooperation in Europe (CSCE) in November.

CFE was a highly complex treaty involving a so-called central area, an expanded central area, an extended area, and two flank areas that would require sweeping repositioning of forces and weaponry (see map 6). On the Warsaw Pact side, the expanded central area included four military districts inside the Soviet Union—the Baltic, Belorussian, Carpathian, and Kiev MDs—and the extended area included the Moscow and Volga-Ural MDs. The northern flank area included the Leningrad military district (extending to the Arctic Ocean littoral), and the southern flank area included the Odessa, North Caucasus,

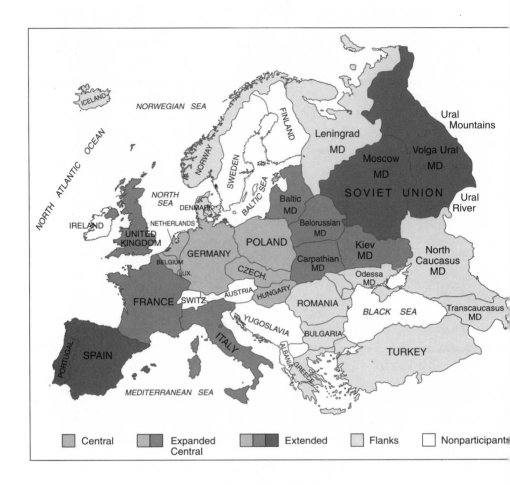

Central　　　Expanded　　　Extended　　　Flanks　　　Nonparticipants
　　　　　　　Central

Map 6. CFE treaty zones
(based on Daalder, *CFE Treaty*)

Table 4 CFE Arms Reductions

	July 1988 Level	Reduced Level	% Change
Tanks	41,580	13,150 (13,300)*	−68
Armored combat vehicles	57,800	20,000	−65
Artillery pieces	52,400	13,175 (13,700)*	−75
Combat aircraft	7,305	5,150	−30
Helicopters	1,330	1,500	+13

Sources: Daalder, *CFE Treaty;* Douglas L. Clarke, "The Conventional Armed Forces in Europe Treaty: Limits and Zones," *Report on Central Europe* 2 (11 January 1991): 34–39.
*Treaty maximum in parentheses; Warsaw Pact agreed on lower Soviet totals.

and Transcaucasus MDs. CFE specified reductions to be made within each of these areas within forty months from the date of the treaty's going into effect (see table 4). These reductions placed a huge additional burden on the MoD. Not only did they involve significant personnel dislocations, but they also committed the Soviet Union to an expensive program of weapons destruction, with cost estimates ranging upward from five billion dollars.[16] Moreover, they impinged on all the Soviet military districts west of the Urals, requiring significant force restructuring in each.

In the course of two years—from December 1988 to November 1990—Gorbachev committed his military to massive force reductions, first on a unilateral basis and then in accordance with the CFE multilateral treaty. To complicate matters, abolition of the Warsaw Pact's military structures also required additional cuts in headquarters in the Soviet Union. If the manpower reductions had concerned only conscripts, the challenge would have been considerably smaller. All but a few were unmarried, and those few were not allowed to have their wives and children with them. These young men wanted to leave the army as soon as possible. They could return home to their families or enter the labor force elsewhere in the country, much as they did twice each year when cohorts of conscripts were traditionally released. Removing all military formations, weapons, equipment, and infrastructure from Eastern Europe, including officers and their families, was far more complicated. Military units not to be disbanded required barracks and training areas in the Soviet Union, and those that were disbanded required storage depots for their weapons and equipment. Neither the barracks nor the storage facilities were available because the General Staff had never planned for a withdrawal from Europe, only the eventual occupation of all of Europe. Furthermore, many officers did not want to be discharged. With few skills that were in demand, they faced uncertain employment opportunities, and their families needed apartments, schools, nurseries, and other such community amenities, all in short supply in every city and town in the Soviet Union.

The magnitude of these tasks was staggering, but the General Staff's problems were not merely quantitative. Staff training at all levels was focused on preparation for a wartime high-speed offensive into Western Europe. The staff challenge of organizing a massive peacetime retrograde movement was beyond the training and experience of the General Staff as well as the staffs of the groups of forces and military districts. Nor were the many civilian agencies involved any better prepared to play their roles in this withdrawal. Predictably, it became chaotic in the extreme. Officers and their families had to absorb gross discomforts, and large numbers of weapons and vast stocks of equipment simply disappeared through theft, misappropriation, and the black market.

The housing problem proved especially acute. General Sukhorukov gave an indication of it in April 1989, when he told a television audience that 45,000 servicemen and their families were without apartments, while the construction of new housing would produce only 7,000–8,000 apartments in the next two years.[17] Almost a year later, in February 1990, Marshal Yazov told an interviewer, "Housing is the most acute problem today. . . . More than 173,000 families of officers and warrant officers do not have apartments."[18] At the same time another 74,000 apartments required upgrading.[19] These figures reflected the problems arising only from the unilateral reductions announced in 1988, not the exodus of Soviet forces from all countries in Eastern Europe that was soon to begin. General Moiseev put the numbers returning from Hungary and Czechoslovakia at 35,000 officers and 30,000 families.[20] Another 63,000 families, it was reported in September 1990, would be returning from Germany.[21] (In February 1991, this figure was raised to 77,000.[22]) Marshal Yazov gave an indication of the accumulating housing shortage in January 1991, when he noted that 10,500 officers in Moscow and 5,000 in Leningrad were without apartments.[23] MoD officials denied rumors that officers and their families were being housed in tents, but they admitted that troop barracks were being used as temporary family housing.

As these data show, housing became a serious problem in the spring of 1989, rapidly worsened, and was never solved. Inconsistencies in the various numbers announced by MoD spokesmen are obvious, and they may include exaggerations meant to incite public anger against Shevardnadze and Gorbachev for creating these woes for the military. The actual total is impossible to know, but the figure of 280,000 military families in need of apartments was cited in a letter to the Soviet leadership in July 1990, signed by forty-six "politicians, military, and scientists," most of whom were strong supporters of perestroika and radical military reform.[24]

The MoD might have been expected to undertake a crash housing construction program. Instead, senior officers initially resisted moving funds from other military construction commitments. Then in September 1990, Colonel General Nikolai Chekov, the deputy minister for military construction, disclosed a plan for building 436,000 apartments over the next five years.[25] That schedule would hardly meet the requirements. Moreover, Gorbachev had already cut the military construction budget for 1990. For relief, Moscow turned to Bonn. In response, the Federal Republic of Germany committed funds for construction of more than 45,000 apartments as part of the deal for the Soviet agreement to withdraw all its troops from Germany, but they would not be finished until 1995–96.[26] No near-term solution, therefore, was devised.

As General Sukhorukov indicated, the MoD depended heavily on local soviet executive committees to provide housing and jobs for returning troops and officers. Soviet law obliged them to do so. But because housing was always in short supply for all citizens, accommodating the rapid return of hundreds of thousands of officers' families was beyond local housing resources. The same was true of schools and other facilities.

Even before the withdrawal of all Soviet forces from Eastern Europe began, tension between the military and local governments was mounting. In early 1990, Marshal Yazov launched a tirade against local authorities, charging them with widespread attempts to deny housing, residence permits, jobs for officers' wives, and access to schools for their children. "There have been," as he put it, "instances of unequivocal threats, outright moral and physical attacks on Soviet servicemen, labeling them as 'occupiers,' and the creation of an unhealthy atmosphere around military camps of a number of military units in the Baltic region, Moldavia, and the Transcaucasus."[27]

As commitments to ever larger withdrawals from Eastern Europe were made in the spring of 1990, objections from local governments became louder and more widespread. In March the deputy chairman of the Moscow city executive committee threw doubt on the city's capacity to accept additional military personnel. Its military population had doubled over the past four years, causing many officers, "including generals," to live in crowded dormitories or rented "corners" of private rooms.[28] About the same time, the People's Front of Latvia objected to construction of new military housing near the city of Daugavpils for units returning from Czechoslovakia.[29] In April the Moldavian government suspended Soviet decrees requiring local authorities to provide housing for retired officers and discharged soldiers.[30]

In July a delegation representing the Committee on Defense and Security of the new Soviet parliament made an information-gathering trip to Eastern Europe. Astonished at what it found, it called on the government to develop a program to safeguard the social rights of returning servicemen. It also singled out the Baltic, Belorussian, Moscow, and Kiev military districts for special criticism.[31] In September a retired officer in Belorussia objected to plans for moving in additional military forces because the republic was already overburdened with nuclear weapons units; moreover, the Chernobyl nuclear power plant accident had made one-third of the republic uninhabitable.[32] In December, Yazov complained that the Latvian government had turned down residence permits for five thousand military personnel and twelve thousand members of their families, thus denying them a right to housing, jobs, and medical facilities. Throughout the Baltic region, he added, some local soviet executive committees had decided not to allocate food products to military residential areas and had cut off electricity, water, and telephone service.[33]

Resistance to resettling officers and their families in the Baltic republics and Moldavia was due in part to the political implications. The General Staff probably intended what the leaders in these republics accused them of—trying to influence their political climates with the presence of Soviet military units and Slavic officers and with their families, who would not sympathize with their separatist sentiments. On the whole, their resistance to an influx of units and families returning from Eastern Europe was more successful than might have been expected.

In light of the indignant mood these developments were causing in military circles, Shevardnadze's decision to resign as foreign minister in December 1990 is understandable. Not only had he done Gorbachev's bidding on the diplomatic front; he had also induced Gorbachev and the Politburo to make ever greater concessions in arms control, beginning with the INF treaty and concluding with the CFE treaty. Moreover, he was instrumental in bringing Gorbachev to accept the reunification of Germany within NATO.[34] Many officers, as they awoke to what had happened in Germany and Eastern Europe, blamed Shevardnadze as the primary culprit.

National Military Formations

As nationalist groups organized in the Baltic republics and in Georgia, Armenia, Azerbaijan, Moldavia, and Ukraine, the idea of national military formations also naturally arose. By late 1990, they were being created in all these republics. The Nagorno-Karabakh conflict catalyzed them in Armenia and Azerbaijan. Several informal national militias appeared in Georgia, allied with different political factions struggling for power.[35] Small national military formations appeared somewhat later in the Baltic region. In the summer of 1990, "home guards" emerged in all three republics.[36] Moldavia attempted to create both a national army and a new police force to deal with Gagauz and Transdniester separatists.[37] In Ukraine, the idea of a national military initially took hold in the western part of the country, around Lvov, where Ukrainian nationalism had strong roots. By summer 1990 the notion enjoyed wider support, reflected in the Ukrainian parliament's July declaration of sovereignty, which included a provision for a national army.[38]

These national formations reflected not only sentiment for political autonomy but also hostile feelings toward service in the Soviet military. Where they existed, local nationalist groups often tried to portray them as an alternative to the Soviet military for obligatory service. The MoD's assignment policy for draftees, "extraterritoriality," disallowing draftees from serving in their own home region, made alternative service in national formations especially attractive. The national minority populations, especially the non–Slavic ethnic groups, intensely disliked this extraterritoriality policy. National formations, if they could be part of a Soviet territorial militia system, therefore had appeal as a way to evade the extraterritoriality policy. Precisely for this reason opponents of a territorial militia system warned that it would encourage nationalism. Not surprisingly, Savinkin's scheme, a combination of a professional military backed by a territorial militia, drew little support from the MoD. Most of the proponents of radical military reform also ignored it, eschewing the national minority issue by emphasizing only a professional volunteer force.

In Moscow, some voices were heard in favor of national military formations, but opponents were far more vocal. Marshal Yazov criticized national formations sharply in late 1989.[39] Colonel General Grigorii Krivosheev condemned them on the day that the Ukrainian parliament voted in favor of its own army in July 1990, insisting that the deployment of Soviet forces could not be based on "demographics" but rather had to meet assigned missions and follow operational principles.[40] This was the military's strongest argument against a militia system and national formations, and it also explains the military's defense of the extraterritoriality policy. Units deployed in the far north, in the Far East, and in other remote areas could not otherwise be fully manned, as General Varennikov pointed out in a short history of Soviet experience with ethnic military units, written specifically to demonstrate their impracticality in contemporary circumstances, notwithstanding examples of their effective performance in World War II.[41]

In July 1990 Gorbachev issued a decree ordering all illegal armed groups to disband and turn over their weapons to the MVD within fifteen days.[42] Those that failed to do so were to be forcibly disarmed by local MVD authorities.

The General Staff announced that army units would assist local authorities in carrying out the decree if they desired such help.[43] Although the decree applied to all republics, its proximate cause was not the Ukrainian parliamentary action but rather the rise of armed groups in Armenia.[44] The Armenian parliament promptly voted to suspend the decree, insisting that it violated the Armenian constitution.[45] Nowhere was it implemented. By summer 1990 nationalist movements were too strong to disarm by a mere order to local MVD officials to collect their weapons.

An occasional voice in Moscow suggested that national militaries were not necessarily a bad thing. A couple of months after Gorbachev's feckless decree, Viktor Altaev argued that such groups offered an opportunity for reform. Because informal military detachments were growing in various republics "as the Soviet Union demilitarized," he believed the only solution was a federal structure. It could have a three-part military: 1) strategic forces subordinated to the center, 2) multinational federal units used to maintain order within the federation, and 3) territorial units subordinated to local governments.[46] In August 1990, when the military reform leader, Major Vladimir Lopatin, was asked whether national military formations weakened the state, he responded that although the 1922 USSR treaty assigned defense and security functions to the central government, the right to "one's own army formations was legislatively enshrined in the constitution right up to 1977."[47] All-union and republican armies were not, in his view, mutually exclusive. Much later, in June 1991, Valerii Semivolos made an economic case for national militaries. By his calculations, Ukraine contributed more to the overall Soviet military than the costs of an army adequate to its needs. Moreover, the republics in the Transcaucasus would actually need only very inexpensive militias.[48] To be sure, neither the generals nor Gorbachev found these views congenial.

The most fateful development in national military formations came in the Russian Federation (RSFSR) during the winter of 1990–91. Boris Yeltsin, now its leader, created a national security committee as a shadow Russian defense ministry, appointing Major Lopatin as its deputy chairman but leaving the chairmanship open. In November, Yeltsin threatened to create a professional army backed up by a militia system "if the initiatives and actions of the central authority affect the interests of Russia."[49] At the same time, the RSFSR's council of ministers began to look into social support for military personnel on the federation's territory and threatened to take control of the military commissariats as well.[50] After Yeltsin opposed the Soviet army's intervention in Lithuania in January 1991, his hints of creating a separate Russian military were taken more seriously. Gorbachev obliquely scolded him by warning that events in the Baltic republics were being used as a pretext for dismembering the Soviet Armed Forces, and Major General Leonid Ivashov, head of the MPA section in the minister of defense's office, made the charge directly, calling Yeltsin's actions a direct violation of the USSR constitution.[51] Although Yeltsin desisted from forming a Russian military, his national security committee proved an important link to senior Soviet officers during the coup attempt in August 1991.

Republican military formations were symptoms, not the problem. None was sufficiently armed, trained, and organized to confront the Soviet military effectively. That was evident when the Soviet military went into Baku in January 1990. Nationalist political forces were the real problem. Encouraging resistance to military conscription would provide them a far more effective means for destroying the Soviet military than would their national military formations.

The Conscription Crisis

The public debate over the conscription system inevitably raised questions about contemporary life in the Soviet military. Everyone knew it was horrible, and now glasnost allowed the media to report hundreds of stories about abuses and hazing in the barracks. This avalanche of public information inspired anti-conscription forces to organize and oppose military service outright. By the spring of 1989 they were gathering strength, and over the next two years they became quite powerful, effectively wrecking the conscription system as they created a sense of legitimacy for young men to evade military service.

The transformation of this amorphous popular sentiment into individual and group action is attributable to four sources of mobilizing activity. First, the intelligentsia in Moscow saw the opportunity to secure relief for their own sons. Second, editors gave opponents of conscription abundant voice and attention in the media. Third, Lopatin's military reform group and the soldiers' mothers movement took shape in the course of 1989. And fourth, informal groups in the national republics calling for sovereignty began openly encouraging draft resistance in the Baltic states and in the Transcaucasus. As news of their success spread to the Slavic republics, draft resistance began to increase there as well, but never on the scale as in the other republics. In Central Asia, neither glasnost nor perestroika kept pace with the rest of the country, leaving that region somewhat behind in these developments, but even there resistance was evident by 1990.[52]

Draft Deferments

Deferment of military service for postsecondary and university-level students became a troublesome issue in the early 1980s. By reducing the term of service from three to two years, the 1967 military service law required the induction of many more young men from each year's cohort. The law granted fairly generous deferments to students, but the drop in the 1961–69 birth rates was noticeably decreasing the pool of available draftees by 1980. In 1982, to make up the shortfall, students deferments were suspended until 1990.[53]

The urban intelligentsia hated the change. Most of their sons had access to a university or technical institute education, and they disliked seeing it interrupted by military service. Parents and sons alike were no less disturbed by conditions of life in the barracks. Many parents found illegal ways to help their sons avoid military service, but that was a nuisance, costly, and always risky.[54] They preferred legal postponement by student deferments. Moreover, few who received deferments were later forced to serve.

University officials also disliked the suspension of student deferments. As Viktor Sadovich, the first vice chancellor of the Moscow State University (MGU), explained, students of mathematics, physics, and chemistry have their most productive years between ages eighteen and twenty-two. "At this age, they frequently put forth original scientific ideas; therefore, for this category of students, a break in their studies can be an irreplaceable loss."[55] Where universities and college-level schools had a military faculty (department), students could take reserve officer-training courses and be allowed to finish their studies before serving two years as officers. But according to the vice chancellor, since 1984 the military commissariats had been drafting MGU students in the middle of their studies. In 1987, Sadovich and the dean of MGU, A. A. Logunov, wrote a letter to the Central Committee, complaining about the harm this policy was doing to the education of scientific cadres. The letter achieved limited results. MGU students in the departments of mechanical-mathematics, physics, and chemistry were thereafter allowed to complete their studies, but not students in other departments or in other schools.

Suspension of student deferments was a well-known sore point, even at the highest levels of the party. Chernyaev mentioned it specifically in a memorandum to Gorbachev in June 1987 as one of many reasons why the military needed reform.[56] He undoubtedly knew of the letter from MGU. The issue also received a surge of media attention in fall 1988, when MGU students demonstrated against mandatory officer training for veterans who had already completed military service before entering the university.[57] A number of journalists and television reporters took up their cause, as well as the larger issue of student deferments, pressing for a return to the liberal deferment policy.[58]

Surprisingly, they were successful. The MoD tried to block restoration of deferments by proposing that all students complete military service before they entered universities, but the proposal failed.[59] In April 1989 the presidium of the USSR Supreme Soviet issued a decree amending the law to grant all full-time students in universities and college-level institutions the right to a deferment until they completed their studies.[60] Where institutions of higher learning had military faculties, those deferred had to complete reserve officer training. Because only 2–4 percent of reserve officers were normally called to active duty, this allowed most students to avoid active service altogether.[61] Many provincial universities and institutes had no reserve officer training, but those in Moscow, Leningrad, Kiev, and a few other large cities did.

The journalists' success encouraged them to ask for more. Those students who had been drafted in 1986–88 were still serving. Under the new rule, they would not be serving. Why, therefore, should they not be discharged at once? The newly elected parliament responded on 11 July 1989 by authorizing their early release. Moscow television commentators gleefully announced, "This is our first victory, a victory for the USSR Supreme Soviet."[62] Colonel General Krivosheev, the General Staff's personnel chief, reacted bitterly to such gloating, reminding people that the 176,000 serving soldiers and junior officers affected by the decision would simply leave their positions unfilled because there was no one to replace them.[63] The resulting hardships would be borne by the less fortunate.

Obviously thousands of families celebrated the reinstatement of deferments. Indeed, they had scored a victory, a victory for the privileged at the expense of the underprivileged, as General Krivosheev rightly emphasized. It meant that the MoD was "having to draft all rural young people and those working young people who are not entitled to deferments." At the same time, many more students entering universities and institutes "are children from families of the intelligentsia, the managerial apparatus, or the services sphere, and far fewer are from workers' families."[64] He could have added that modern military technology was requiring better educated soldiers at the very time this policy change was shifting military service more heavily to the less well educated. The generals' anger over student deferments is understandable, but it did not cause them to reassess their opposition to a volunteer professional army, their only effective way out of their dilemma.

Life in the Military

The negative impact of the draft on science education in the universities was a legitimate motive for student deferments, but it was actually secondary to avoiding the demeaning and dangerous conditions of a Soviet soldier's life, an issue with much broader implications. The explosive political potential of those conditions seems to have been initially lost on party and military leaders alike. Conditions of barracks life in the Soviet military had always been depraved and brutal by comparison with conditions in Western militaries, but in the 1970s and 1980s, they became much worse as a result of a number of developments. The most important was a system of hazing called *dedovshchina*.

Military spokesmen explained dedovshchina variously, attributing it to a general decline in the moral quality of Soviet society caused by deficiencies in secondary education, single-parent homes, increasing crime, changing demographics, and the unwillingness of most commanders to confront it directly. Although there is some truth to most of these explanations, the catalyst for the emergence and stubborn persistence of dedovshchina was a change in the military draft system described earlier. A few military spokesmen acknowledged it in articles and public discussions but did not emphasize it adequately. During my interviews with several junior officers, however, it was salient in their explanations of the mechanisms of dedovshchina, though they did not put together the full picture.[65]

Before the 1967 law, a conscript served three years in all branches of service but the navy, which required four years. A single call-up of conscripts occurred each year, in the fall. Virtually no professional corps of noncommissioned officers (NCOs) existed. A very small number of "extended service" soldiers were promoted to the top NCO rank, *starshina*, and normally each company-sized unit had one such NCO. The platoon sergeants and squad leaders were draftees, selected from each annual conscription cohort. The military commissariats identified them during their last year of secondary school and also in courses conducted by DOSAAF. Upon arrival in their assigned military units, these soldiers were sent to a regimental NCO school for several weeks of training. Afterward they returned to line units as junior sergeants to occupy NCO positions vacated by soldiers recently discharged.

This system produced passable NCOs in the context of Soviet emphasis on a mass mobilization system. In the course of a year, they could achieve a modest competency in their jobs. That meant about two-thirds of the NCOs were reasonably experienced while the youngest third was still learning. The system compensated for this weak NCO structure by placing a very high ratio of officers to troops in tactical units, about twice as high as the ratio in most NATO armies. Lieutenants commanded platoons of fewer than twenty soldiers in motor rifle units, only eleven in tank platoons. Thus the proportion of company-grade officers was high enough in Soviet units to compensate partially for the absence of an experienced corps of NCOs.

The 1967 law reduced the term of service by one year, making most conscripts in most branches liable for only two years of active duty. The single annual call-up was replaced by two semiannual call-ups, one in the late spring, a second in the late fall. The semiannual call-ups put four cohorts of conscripts into each military unit. Every six months, the senior cohort was discharged as a new cohort arrived to replace it. The system of selecting and training NCOs remained basically the same except that regimental NCO schools began to die out as more premilitary training was provided in secondary schools and by DOSAAF. The extended-service NCOs, the starshiny, also began to decline in number when a new rank was created—*praporshchik* (*michman* in the navy)— between NCO and officer rank, roughly equivalent to "warrant officer" in the U.S. Army. Many starshiny were promoted to this new rank. Enjoying some of the privileges of officers, praporshchiki did not live with the troops as the starshiny had done, and that removed the influence of these senior NCOs from the barracks.

By the mid-1970s, the cohorts of conscripts were taking on a highly cohesive but perverse social character, much as classes in an American college. The "seniors"—that is, soldiers in the oldest cohort—became known as *stariki*, or the "old men." They had been around longer, and they knew the ropes. Not surprisingly, they began to dominate the barracks. They took charge of the younger soldiers. Each one acted as the *ded* (grandfather) for one or more new soldiers. In other words, each starik had his own "grandson" informally assigned to him and completely beholden to him as a personal servant.

The junior soldier washed the ded's laundry, cleaned his boots, washed his feet, cleaned his weapon, swept the barracks, cleaned toilets, and performed numerous other services for the ded. On work details, the stariki forced the younger soldiers to perform the heaviest and dirtiest tasks. To humiliate first-year soldiers, stariki gave them extremely obscene and demeaning nicknames. When junior soldiers received food packages and money from home, the stariki openly stole them. At mealtime, stariki frequently took a junior soldier's food for themselves. Homosexual rape was widespread. The slightest pretense of resistance by junior soldiers provoked beatings, commonly with belts and shovels, frequently causing serious physical injuries requiring hospitalization, sometimes leading to discharge with permanent physical disabilities.

Deaths and suicides became common. This was dedovshchina—loosely translated, "grandfather-rule."[66]

Dedovshchina destroyed the authority of most NCOs.[67] Because a few first-year soldiers became sergeants not long after arriving in a unit, they found themselves formally in charge of stariki privates. But in reality, the stariki were in charge. A new sergeant might have a ded who was formally his subordinate. Yet he could hardly give orders to his ded. It takes little imagination to grasp the mockery this made of the formal NCO rank structure.

Dedovshchina became deeply entrenched, displacing the authority not only of NCOs but also of the lieutenants and captains. When the officers departed at the end of the duty day, the stariki ruled the barracks. When the duty day began, if the officers tried to use the formal NCO command structure, it was unresponsive except when sergeants were also stariki.

Why did the officers allow the stariki to take control of the barracks?[68] After glasnost began, accounts appeared in the press of young officers who tried to discipline the stariki for brutal acts against younger soldiers, only to discover that their commanders would not support them. Such cases reinforced the legitimacy of dedovshchina not only in the eyes of the troops; junior officers also realized that they must accommodate the stariki. A group of military lawyers and sociologists conducted survey research on the dedovshchina phenomenon in the Moscow Air Defense District in 1988, seeking answers to its sources, patterns, and reasons for its persistence.[69] They discovered that most beatings took place at night when officers were not present, but some occurred during duty hours as officers stood by watching. More than one fourth of 289 officers questioned in the study said that to report incidents was to risk receiving a poor officer performance evaluation from one's superior because evaluations were commonly based on the number of disciplinary incidents in an officer's unit. Career considerations therefore also encouraged them to tolerate dedovshchina rather than to bring violators to account.

Before glasnost dedovshchina was a public secret. Soldiers took their stories home upon discharge and spread them widely. At the same time, official propaganda treatment of the military in the media and public ceremonies gave no hint of the horrors of hazing. Some veterans laughed off dedovshchina as something that "made men of them." Most junior soldiers accepted it, struggling to survive so that they could get revenge not against the stariki but against the incoming cohort of new soldiers.[70] During 1988 official pretenses began to meet open challenges. In late August an officer described it straightforwardly in a newspaper interview.[71] In that year Yurii Polyakov published a novella, *Sto dnei do prikaza*, in which dedovshchina was the main theme.[72] Sergei Kaledin also wrote a novella, published in 1989, about the practice in a construction battalion.[73] Both works portrayed dedovshchina with disturbing candor.

Dedovshchina was not the only problem in the barracks. Rather, it was a social matrix within which many other kinds of deviant behavior thrived. Soldiers drank excessively when alcohol was available, and when it was not, they drank all kinds of substitutes, even automotive brake fluid, often causing hospitalization and sometimes death. As we have seen, drug use became a serious problem in Afghanistan. By the mid-1980s, it had spread widely within the Soviet Union. A study conducted in 1987 estimated that five million youths experimented with drugs and another half-million were regular users. Of soldiers in the survey, 69 percent said that hashish was available; 22 percent of those serving in Afghanistan said that they could get heroin, and 11 percent said that LSD was available.[74] Ex-soldiers spread the drug culture to their civilian friends, reportedly accounting for most of the five and a half million.

Ethnic tensions, always a problem in the Soviet military, increased in the 1980s because declining birth rates among Slavs and increasing birth rates in the Muslim regions led to conscription of more soldiers from Central Asia and the Transcaucasus.[75] Soldiers from Muslim regions were most numerous in the construction troops, next in the ground forces and the air defense forces. The strategic rocket forces, the air forces, and the navy had far fewer Central Asians. This pattern is explained in part by the rarity of fluency in Russian among Central Asians. It was easier to accommodate them in the construction troops, next easiest in the ground forces, but lack of proficiency in Russian was a serious handicap in the more technical branches. Hazing of Central Asians was particularly brutal, and many groups from the Caucasus were treated little better. Slavic soldiers were highly creative in devising obscene ethnic slurs for Central Asians. Armenians, Georgians, Moldavians, and troops from the Baltic republics also stood apart from the Slavs, but they were not as despised as the Muslim ethnic groups. That did not spare them abusive attention, however, especially if they spoke poor Russian. Their lot was only marginally better than that of Central Asians.

Frequently the soldiers of minority ethnic groups in a regiment would band together informally in what was known as a *zemlyachestvo*—a group of soldiers from the same homeland.[76] A soldier might be the only Uzbek in his platoon, for example, but a zemlyachestvo tied him closely to all other Uzbeks in the regiment. If he felt that a Slavic starik had hazed him excessively, he might call on his zemlyachestvo to retaliate against the starik.[77] These brawls often produced serious physical injuries, sometimes riots, and occasionally deaths. Clashes sometimes broke out along religious lines, Muslims battling against "the Christians."[78] Not surprisingly, a political officer reported that 80 percent of all crimes committed in his unit in 1987 were dedovshchina-related. By 1989, Georgians, Armenians, Lithuanians, Latvians, and Estonians were complaining publicly about mistreatment by Russian soldiers and an increasing number of "mysterious deaths" in the barracks.[79]

Commanders' misuse of troop labor was also common in military life, sometimes reaching the scale of major scandals. In the 1970s a case in the Central Group of Forces in Czechoslovakia became so gross that Central Committee officials joined the investigation. Several general officers were providing large amounts of "free" troop labor to Czech collective farm managers, who reciprocated with abundant "gifts" to the generals.[80] Within the USSR this widespread corruption was generally tolerated. One common practice sustained the military's own agriculture. Regimental gardens and pigsties were standard in many garrisons. Commanders often sold part of the produce and pocketed the money. Use of troop labor to build dachas for officers, especially generals, was notorious. Schemes for exploiting troop labor could be extravagant, stretching from Moscow to the Far East. Troops at the missile impact range in Kamchatka, for example, harvested caviar from local streams; the caviar was packed in ten- and twenty-kilogram boxes, each labeled with a general's name, then flown across the Soviet Union and delivered to Moscow for the recipients' private disposal. Barrels of gasoline were sometimes included on the flights and delivered to general officers so they could avoid the price of fuel in Moscow for their private automobiles. To pacify the troops harvesting the caviar, the missile range commander supplied them with vodka.[81]

These practices understandably encouraged criminal behavior among the troops. If the generals could steal, the troops felt no inhibition to steal as well. Theft and sale of equipment, weapons, uniforms, gasoline, vehicle spare parts, and so on, already widespread, became rampant in the perestroika years. Troop criminality became especially acute in Afghanistan, where a total of 6,412 criminal charges against soldiers were recorded, including 714 murders, 2,840 weapons sales to Afghanis, and 524 drug trafficking cases.[82] Obviously these official figures do not reflect the full extent of criminal behavior in the ranks.

The junior officer's life was better than a soldier's, but it too involved hardships and tensions. Only three days of free time each month was standard in most units. Because many officers had families, this restriction placed great strain on familial relations. Field-grade officers and generals added to the pressures on junior officers by various types of intimidation. The most important event on the calendar for a young officer, especially for those serving in remote regions, was his annual month of leave. During the several weeks preceding their leaves, junior officers faced the threat of cancellation from higher commanders. Younger officers hated this widespread abuse.[83]

They equally detested the verbal indignities with which senior officers commonly treated them to emphasize their subordinate status. Caught between dedovshchina in the barracks and intimidation by superiors, they were an unhappy lot. Nonetheless, when comparing their situation — in particular, pay, housing — with their contemporaries in civilian life, they did not feel unprivileged until after Gorbachev initiated perestroika and glasnost.[84] With those reforms, the military profession began to lose the high social status it had enjoyed.

Another indication that junior officers felt abused and deprived of authority to perform their jobs was their initial attitude toward perestroika. Unlike the generals, junior officers initially welcomed it. They knew there were serious problems in the army, and they believed that perestroika would force them to be addressed. Not only might dedovshchina be eliminated, but younger officers would receive the personal dignity they deserved. Senior officers' demeaning terms of personal address in speaking to juniors were particularly rankling. As Colonel Aleksei Tsarev described the climate during the election campaign for the Congress of People's Deputies in spring 1989, the label "democrat" initially had a very narrow meaning to young officers, primarily a social meaning: politeness in interpersonal relations, specifically the use of the polite form of *you* — *Vy* in Russian — in place of *ty*, the personal form used to emphasize a person's inferior status, as landowners, for example, had addressed their peasants in tsarist Russia. To vote for "democrats" meant to vote in favor of improving senior officers' manners toward junior officers. This, according to Tsarev, accounts for the surprisingly radical vote within the military for the first Congress of People's Deputies. The junior officers wanted change, and their commanders could not control the way they voted in the spring elections of 1989.[85] As glasnost spread they often expressed their disdain for senior officers quite openly. A lieutenant colonel in Kaliningrad went on a monthlong hunger strike. Interviewed on Moscow television, he explained it as "a protest against the reactionary generals who are a brake on military reform."[86]

These generalizations have to be tempered with distinctions among the branches of service. Colonel Tsarev, Marshal Shaposhnikov, and other interviewees emphasized that officers in the navy, strategic rocket forces, and the air forces tended to be more widely read, more aware of world affairs, and distinctly more liberal in their social and political views than officers in air defense (PVO) and ground force units. Perestroika had support from junior officers in all forces, but those in the more technical forces were consistently more enthusiastic about it. Tsarev imputed uniformly base motives to the political views of senior officers. He considered them to be unprincipled careerists almost without exception. On the conscription issue, he felt that they got what they deserved for all-out opposition to a professional force. All the criticisms about military life were true; the generals did nothing to change it; and their defense of the conscription system, ostensibly argued in "professional" terms, was transparently a defense of their own personal interests in having a lot of slave labor at their disposal.

As the consequence of these various practices, the military became trifurcated—not a cohesive corporate entity but rather a hierarchy of three strata, each with its own internal dynamics and isolated from the others. The troops took over the barracks, brutalizing each other, making the company and battalion officers largely irrelevant for most activities other than managing combat operations. The junior officers nursed fear and veiled resentment toward senior officers. The generals, admirals, and marshals were predominantly corrupt careerists and opportunists, unprincipled, and without concern for the well-being of their subordinates—troops and officers alike. Certainly there were exceptions, but they were too few to overcome the trifurcation.

This sociological topography of the military helps explain why it could not act politically as a cohesive corporate structure. The party and KGB controls, to be sure, constrained its potential for political action. But they also contributed to its trifurcated character by encouraging mistrust and careerism. As they weakened during perestroika, the military lacked adequate cohesion to assume an independent political role. In a real sense, the party and KGB controls were its corporate spine, the ultimate source of effective sanctions to ensure discipline and order. When several senior officers—Marshal Yazov, General Moiseev, and Colonel General Boris Gromov of Afghan War fame, for example—expressed the gravest reservations about eliminating the MPA, they reflected a profound understanding of the military's sources of organizational cohesion and discipline.

The Conscription Revolt

Individual Soviet citizens obviously knew a lot about the realities of military life, but prohibition against all public discussion of the "closed zone," as the military was called by its critics, prevented them from having a comprehensive picture. The public debate over conscription changed this dynamic. The central media, beginning in mid-1988, focused intently on the negative features of military life. Senior military officials responded by condemning the media campaign as outright slander. But in 1989 the negative reactions toward the military spread far beyond media leaders to the ordinary citizens. They drew the practical conclusion: the best way for a young man to ensure his safety was to evade the draft.

The campaign for student deferments in the spring was the first small force contributing to what soon became an open conscription revolt. The MoD's concession on this issue probably helped blunt major draft resistance in Moscow, Leningrad, and other major Slavic cities in the 1989 spring call-up, but that effect proved temporary.

The soldiers' mothers movement was the second conspicuous force behind the revolt. Maria Kirbasova's Committee of Soldiers' Mothers, it will be recalled, proved enduring in spite of numerous attempts to split it and destroy it. Equally important, it had influence not just in Moscow but also in the Baltic republics, the Transcaucasus, and Ukraine. Its primary activity was gathering and publishing information about soldiers' deaths in an effort to hold commanders to account for them. The effect on the public was to provide moral justification for refusing to serve.

After the soldiers' mothers movement announced in June 1990 that some 15,000 soldiers had died over the preceding four or five years, figures on soldiers' deaths began coming from other sources as well. In August 1990 an Uzbek deputy to the Congress of People's Deputies disclosed that "in recent years," 190 recruits from Tashkent alone had been killed, and already in 1989, 430 Uzbek recruits had died.[87] To his request that the MoD look into the possibility of a campaign designed to kill Uzbek soldiers, a defense spokesman responded in November that only 167 Uzbek soldiers had been killed in the first nine months of 1989, and in the same period, 123 Russians, 25 Ukrainians, 15 Kazakhs, 13 Belorussians, 7 Georgians, and 7 Azeris had died, as well as some from other nationalities. This evidence, he added, showed that Uzbeks were not suffering disproportionately.[88] Needless to say, this disclosure of a smaller figure for Uzbek deaths did little to assure other ethnic groups, and it appeared to confirm initial Uzbek suspicions.

The data reported on soldiers' deaths were never consistent, but the available figures rose sharply in 1990. In December, Marshal Yazov told a closed meeting of officers that about 500 conscripts had committed suicide in 1990, while 69 officers and 32 NCOs had been murdered. On the same occasion, the MPA chief, Colonel General Nikolai Shlyaga, said that 2,000 soldiers had died in the first eleven months of 1990.[89] (This large figure probably included deaths from combat actions in Tajikistan and the Transcaucasus.) With a threatened hunger strike by soldiers' mothers looming, Gorbachev was prompted to create a special commission to look into these numbers.[90] In addition to procuracy and ministry of justice officials, the commission included republic-level legislators and members of the mothers' movement.[91] Within weeks the soldiers' mothers declared the investigation a sham and Gorbachev's decree a half-measure that failed to meet their demands for an alternative to military service and dissolution of the notoriously brutal construction troops.[92]

The third force behind the conscription revolt arose in the national republics. As the so-called *neformal'ny* (informal voluntary organizations allowed as part of perestroika) proliferated in 1988, national separatist leaders used them to build political support. The poor conditions of Soviet military life proved especially effective as an issue for mobilizing nationalist sentiment. The top political officer in the Baltic Military District, Major General Vladimir Sein, described the neformal'ny at work in Riga in the spring of 1989. As he approached the entrance to the Baltic military district headquarters one morning, he met crowds of young men and women in front of the building: "Judging by their determined and serious facial expressions, they were confident that they were acting for a 'just cause.' Many held placards with slogans that these young hotheads obviously did not 'dream up' by themselves: 'Be alert! The Stalinist plague still lives.' 'Forces of the USSR are occupiers in Latvia. Demand their removal.' 'Our Latvia is occupied by the Soviet Army, and therefore, according to international convention, our children cannot serve in such an army.' Such slogans affect unprepared young minds like a match in a powder box."[93]

Sein's anger was palpable as he spoke of the plethora of anti-Soviet organizations throughout Estonia, Latvia, and Lithuania, all attacking the Soviet military and imploring young men to avoid it. Worse yet, the local media were helping them, editorializing that "service in the armed forces is Hell" and characterizing military actions in Afghanistan as "one more sacrifice to the Stalinist monster." Sampling attitudes among draft-age youths, Sein observed, military commissariats discovered that 90 percent agreed with these antimilitary slogans. Sein admitted that his MPA apparatus was losing the struggle. It received little help from civilian party organizations. Although more political officers who could speak the local languages were needed, those of Baltic ethnic origin were asking to be transferred elsewhere to escape hostility from compatriots who considered them traitors. Finally, Sein declared, Soviet military leaders themselves were also culpable: "Being cheerfully certain that 'our nationality problem is solved,' we assiduously closed our eyes" to all the developments that created the situation.[94]

Sein was not exaggerating. Baltic nationalist movements were quite advanced by 1989. Moreover, public disclosure in 1988 of the secret protocol to the Nazi-Soviet Pact, in which Hitler ceded the Baltic states to Stalin, added to their indignation and determination.[95] Still, they had not yet—until 1990 and 1991—suffered violence from intervening military forces and local MVD and KGB units. In Armenia, Azerbaijan, and Georgia, however, violence was widespread by early 1989. The Tbilisi massacre and the role of Soviet army units in trying to control the Nagorno-Karabakh conflict had stimulated even stronger antagonisms toward military conscription.

The consequences were soon evident. The 1989 spring call-up proved a disaster in both regions. When it ended late May, only about 10 percent of draft quotas had been met in the Baltic republics, and less than 20 percent in Georgia and Armenia. The MoD reacted by extending conscription for another month and sending police and military officials to hunt down evaders. At the end of July, Colonel General Krivosheev insisted that the recruitment goal was more than 90 percent fulfilled in all republics, with one exception, Estonia, which had reached only 79.5 percent.[96] The 1989 fall call-up was again a disaster in Armenia, Georgia, and the Baltic republics. Kiev's military commissariat spokesman also reported about 2,000 evaders within the city.[97] Although percentages were not reported, a year later Colonel General Dmitrii Grinkevich gave the astounding figure of 400,000 for failures to appear. Most of these were apparently tracked down and inducted, however, because the military procurator's office cited 6,647 as the total number of draft evaders for 1989.[98] General Moiseev put the figure at 7,500.[99]

In spring 1990 draft evasion was even more widespread. Again the duration of the call-up had to be extended to reach 90 percent of the overall recruitment goal. This time, however, seven republics failed to meet it: Georgia (27.5 percent), Armenia (7.5), Lithuania (33.6), Latvia (54.2), Estonia (40.2), Uzbekistan (87.4), and Kirghizia (89.5).

Again in the fall of 1990, the reported figures were mostly lower, although some were up. Only 78.8 percent of the total recruitment goal was achieved. Georgia, Armenia, Lithuania, Latvia, Estonia, and Moldavia all fell below this level; no figure was given for Ukraine, but it reportedly had trouble reaching the goal in its western oblasts.[100] Although the Central Asian republics were still meeting the overall average, the Birlik political organization in Uzbekistan was encouraging young men to resist conscription and Tajikistan was beginning to experience difficulties.[101] Even within the Russian republic draft resistance was becoming significant, though not yet on such a large scale. That is evident from the USSR-wide figure, 78.8 percent achievement of the expected total.

For the spring call-up in 1991, the same kind of low but incomplete figures were reported: Armenia, Georgia, and Lithuania were all under 20 percent, Latvia and Estonia about 30 percent. Moscow city officials indicated that of all those eligible for conscription, only 50 percent were drafted; the remainder either received deferments, were in prison, or simply did not show up.[102] Colonel General Krivosheev again insisted that 90 percent of the overall recruitment goal had been achieved.[103] That claim seems dubious in light of Marshal Yazov's complaint at the end of June that the military was short by 353,000 conscripts because the republics made recruitment "practically impossible."[104]

One might object that because the available figures are fragmentary, often contradictory, mostly percentages rather than absolute numbers, and not easily comparable from year to year, they are of no use, or at best misleading. To be sure, they suffer these deficiencies and must be viewed cautiously, but they are not without utility. They convey a sense of both the size and the geographical disposition of the conscription revolt. No one, neither the anticonscription forces nor the senior military officials, denied the overall picture presented by these data: a conscription crisis that began in 1989 and continued through 1991 and into the post-Soviet period. It began in the Transcaucasus and the Baltic republics, later spreading to Moldavia, Ukraine, and Central Asia. The Russian republic and Belorussia experienced it less severely probably because student deferments relieved the pressures against conscription in the major cities, and in rural areas there was less political activism. Resistance appears to have leveled off in 1991, hitting a floor, if one judges by the available figures. That can be explained in part by the unilateral force reductions, the CFE treaty, and withdrawals from Eastern Europe which caused the total troop strength to drop. Thus the required number of conscripts declined each year through 1991.

The role of national separatist movements in the conscription revolt changed in 1990. In early 1989, nationalist opposition groups—the neformal'ny—took the lead while the republican governments remained generally passive. In late 1989 and throughout 1990, republican governments began to support draft resistance as well. Most of the republican executive organs or their supreme soviets took either policy or legislative measures to obstruct conscription, particularly the extraterritoriality policy for assignment of soldiers.

In summer 1989 the Georgian government demanded that its conscripts serve only in the European part of the USSR.[105] In the fall, Azerbaijan passed sovereignty legislation contravening service in the Soviet military.[106] In December 1989 the Estonian Supreme Soviet voted to allow Estonian conscripts to serve only on Estonian soil.[107] In February 1990 the Latvia Supreme Soviet passed an alternative service. Also in February, five thousand Lithuanian youths celebrated the country's 1918 independence anniversary by turning in their draft notices. In March the Lithuanian Supreme Soviet voted to exempt Lithuanian citizens from conscription, declaring that the 1967 military service law no longer applied to them.[108] By the summer, Lithuania's new defense minister was treating Soviet conscription as illegal.[109] The Uzbek Party first secretary, Islam Karimov, announced in March that if Uzbek conscripts were assigned to construction troop battalions, they should serve only on Uzbek soil; in September he made that decree Uzbek law and further ordered that all future conscription of Uzbeks be arranged by a treaty to be negotiated with Moscow.[110] The Armenian Supreme Soviet passed a resolution in May that all Armenian conscripts be allowed to engage in reconstruction work in the republic's earthquake damage zone.[111] The Ukrainian Supreme Soviet's declaration of Ukrainian sovereignty in June, as noted earlier, included the basis for a Ukrainian military, making the legality of Soviet conscription ambiguous. Moreover, the Lvov oblast took the sovereignty declaration as grounds for decreeing its military commissariats dissolved.[112] In September the Moldavian Supreme Soviet voted to suspend the obligation of its citizens to serve in the Soviet military until further notice; additionally, all Moldavian soldiers were to be returned to Moldavia to complete their service.[113] In October the Tajik Supreme Soviet passed a resolution requiring most conscripts to serve within the republic.[114] Finally, Yeltsin was threatening to take more control of military affairs on the Russian federation's territory, even to create a Russian defense ministry. Only four of the fifteen republics, Kazakhstan, Kirgizstan, Turkmenistan, and Belorussia, failed to take similar actions.

The conscription revolt gave national separatists not only a concrete issue, as they captured government positions in several republics; it also enjoyed broad and intense public support—broad because it touched the lives of virtually all families, intense because it was a life and death matter, as families contemplated their sons' military service.

The Contours of Disintegration

All three of these developments—force reductions and massive withdrawals from Eastern Europe and Mongolia, negative public reactions, and the resulting conscription revolt—were advanced by 1991. As a consequence, the Soviet Armed Forces rapidly fell into disorder, decay, and, especially in lower-level units, disintegration. Somewhat surprisingly, they did not collapse outright.

The major command structures proved fairly resilient. At the lower unit levels, however, "collapse" is an accurate description of what occurred in some cases. Many divisions and regiments in the ground forces, particularly in the

Transcaucasus, along the Chinese border, and in Central Asia, did collapse from a combination of "privatization"—that is, their officers sold off most of their matériel and weapons—plunder by local nationalist paramilitary groups, and lack of supplies and new conscripts. Many air force and air defense units became operationally ineffective, but they did not disappear outright. Naval forces deteriorated rapidly from lack of personnel and technical support. Ships rusted, and soon many were no longer seaworthy. The rocket forces suffered personnel shortages and other shortfalls, but apparently none of their operational units actually collapsed.

The construction troops, railroad troops, and civil defense troops, though affected by these developments, were more resistant to ruin than were the five branches of forces. Conscription shortfalls hurt construction units, but the urgency to build facilities and housing for redeployed forces kept many of them manned at reasonably full levels. The railroad and civil defense troops survived, though at reduced manning levels. As the General Staff struggled to meet personnel reduction goals, it proposed that all three of these branches be removed from the MoD, putting them under some other ministry. Their removal would then be counted as a deduction from the MoD total. This gambit failed, but after the dissolution of the Soviet Union the Russian defense minister was still trying to exclude them from the MoD.[115]

In addition to all the forces in the MoD, the KGB's border troops numbered about 250,000, and the MVD's internal troops, about 350,000 in 1985.[116] They remained in moderately good shape until the dissolution of the Soviet Union. Although they suffered many of the maladies of military life in other forces, they were better supplied and manned. By 1991, however, in sectors of the border in Far East, Central Asia, and the Transcaucasus, the border troops were suffering many of the ills afflicting regular military formations. After 1991 the new Russian Federation struggled to keep border troops on the former Soviet Union's external borders through bilateral agreements with members of the new Commonwealth of Independent States (CIS). The Baltic Republics, Ukraine, Moldavia, and Azerbaijan refused, but Kazakhstan, Kyrgyzstan (formerly Kirgizstan), Tajikistan, Turkmenistan, Armenia, Georgia, and Belarus (formerly Belorussia) accepted various arrangements, most commonly a heavy dependence on Russian officers and local conscripts.[117]

As several of the national republics asserted their independence, the implications for the Soviet Armed Forces began to trouble the General Staff and the commanders of the five branches of forces. To understand their particular concerns, one must recall the command and control structures described earlier. Each branch had its own peculiar structure. Some were easier to break into coherent separate parts than others, and each was deployed differently. These particularities defined the concerns of each commander of a branch of forces.

The ground forces were easiest to adapt to the dissolution of the USSR. Losing a few divisions in one republic or another would not paralyze the operational capabilities of the remaining forces. The command structure at the military district level and higher, however, was another matter, as was the logistics system.[118] Already in 1988–89 the ground forces were having trouble with command arrangements and logistics in Armenia, Azerbaijan, and Georgia; similar problems arose later in Moldavia and in the Central Asian republics, especially Tajikistan, where a civil war began not long after the dissolution of the Soviet Union. In Armenia, units of the 7th Army effectively became informal supply depots for Armenia armed groups that bought, stole, and sometimes forcibly took their weapons. The same practices were common in Georgia and Azerbaijan by 1989. The 14th Army in the Transdniester Autonomous Republic of Moldavia provided weapons to the local pro-Russian paramilitary organization when the Soviet Union broke up. In the Baltic republics and Tajikistan, weapons thefts and sales were rampant. By 1990–91, weapons, vehicles, and other equipment from ground forces units were spreading into civilian hands at an alarming rate. Regimental commanders in many cases resorted to selling anything in their possession, sometimes to get funds for feeding their troops, sometimes for personal gain. A large number of the ground forces' divisions were normally maintained at low manning levels, some at 10–15 percent, which meant that they had large amounts of equipment in storage that could be traded or sold without taking it from their troops. In the summer of 1989, Gorbachev told the parliament that Marshal Yazov had already demobilized 101 divisions, describing them as "feeding troughs."[119] Whether in fact that many divisions were demobilized at the time may be questioned, but Gorbachev was probably speaking of these partially manned units which were rapidly dissolving in any case.

Notwithstanding the ground forces' greater flexibility, the branch's most modern and important forces were in Eastern Europe, Belorussia, and Ukraine —that is, on the western and southwestern fronts. The fall of the Berlin Wall, the collapse of the Warsaw Pact, and Gorbachev's unilateral force reductions hit the ground forces the hardest. To be sure, the CFE treaty was also a staggering blow to them. Because the ground forces were more than two hundred divisions strong, they were a major target for force reductions. The more serious problem arose, however, with the creation of the CIS. Ground force units were deployed in every former Soviet republic, and nearly half of the major training areas were in Belorussia and Ukraine.[120] The ground forces had also stocked large numbers of weapons in Turkmenistan and left the weapons there after the creation of the CIS. Ownership was still a matter of dispute as late as 1997.[121]

The air defense forces were mainly affected by developments on the Soviet periphery—in the Baltic republics, Belorussia, Ukraine, the Transcaucasus, and Central Asia.[122] They operated on a district and sector basis, with first priority on the northern and northwestern approaches into the Soviet air space. They also had a southern district with its headquarters in Baku. In Kazakhstan and Tajikistan they had several R&D and special operational sites, including some for space activities. (Soviet "space forces" were included within the air defense forces, as was the ABM system around Moscow.) In addition to their military mission, the air defense forces also provided airspace control for the Soviet Union's civilian aviation. Both their military and civil aviation missions required them to see Soviet territorial space as one single entity. The same was true for the ABM early warning radars and control of space operations and testing. To break off part of it was to fracture the integrity of the entire system. This technical reality made serious degradation to the air defense forces unavoidable with the establishment of the CIS in 1992.

The Soviet Air Forces could be broken into separate and smaller formations where frontal aviation was concerned, but long range aviation (LRA), operating as a single entity, was particularly threatened by Ukrainian independence and to some degree by Baltic independence movements because LRA bases were located in both regions. Pilot training schools in Central Asia were also important to the air forces, especially the one in Kyrgyzstan. The creation of the CIS, therefore, dealt a serious blow to the air forces as well.[123]

The strategic rocket forces, also with a single operational focus, were deployed in four republics, mainly in the RSFSR but also in Belorussia, Ukraine, and Kazakhstan, where important test facilities were located, in addition to ICBM silos.[124] Their radar warning systems included sites in the Baltic region and in Belorussia. Before the breakup of the Soviet Union, therefore, Baltic and Ukrainian nationalists were probably the strategic rocket forces' main concern. Belorussia and Kazakhstan had no significant independence movements before 1992. But with the establishment of the CIS, the strategic rocket forces faced a crisis, which was eventually resolved in favor of turning all ICBMs and warheads over to the Russian Federation.

Of the navy's four fleets, two—the Northern and Pacific—were based entirely within the RSFSR.[125] The Baltic Fleet, however, included facilities in the Baltic republics, and the Black Sea Fleet was based in Crimea, part of Ukraine. The navy, therefore, had concerns as Baltic separatism arose fairly early. Although these fleets together were rather large, the Black Sea Fleet being by far the bigger of the two, their combat value against the U.S. Navy was not great.

The Soviet Navy's major combat potential was entirely based in the Northern and Pacific Fleets. That did not prevent the admirals from becoming extremely nervous about political developments in Ukraine and the Baltic republics. With the creation of the CIS, the navy reluctantly gave up its bases in the Baltic republics but held on to the Kaliningrad enclave between Poland and Lithuania. The Black Sea Fleet continued to deteriorate as it became a major issue of contention between Moscow and Kiev, more symbolic than substantive for naval power but of great political importance between the two countries.

The VPK also had grounds for worry as Gorbachev began to accede to demands for a new union treaty in late 1990. Although the largest part of military industries was in the RSFSR—estimates ranging from 60–80 percent of production firms and 90–100 percent of R&D institutes—key ancillary production and testing facilities were in other republics.[126] Belorussia and Ukraine held several major production facilities, and a large aircraft production firm was located in Tashkent, the capital of Uzbekistan. Among the most important nuclear weapons and rocket test facilities were those in Kazakhstan. So, too, were key sites for space launches and operations.

This is a simplified picture of the fragmentation of the Soviet military's forces and their industrial base, and it glosses over many related issues, like the military communications system, the central logistics system, the central personnel system, the officer schooling system, and the weapons procurement system. Still, it is sufficient to convey a clear picture of the major potential fault lines appearing by 1990 which would become sharply defined with the creation of the CIS in 1992. The picture is important for two reasons. First, it provides a more textured understanding of the practical meaning for force reductions followed by the dissolution of the Soviet Union. Second, it is roughly the picture the General Staff and all the senior military commanders must have held of what they were up against and what was happening to their forces. Little wonder they reacted viscerally against the radical military reformers and the liberal media. Their efforts to stretch out military reforms over a decade or more also become more comprehensible. Any military leadership anywhere would have boggled at the idea that such dramatic structural changes could be carried through quickly and in an orderly manner, especially in the conditions of the Soviet economy and society.

Additional Symptoms of Disintegration

The very character of barracks life was the best index of the degree of disintegration of the military. As draft resistance grew, the MoD compensated by accepting more conscripts with criminal records and members of minorities who spoke little or no Russian.[127] Not surprisingly, the crime rate in the military soared. In September 1990 the military procurator in Moscow reported a 40 percent crime increase over the past six months. Among more serious offenses, premeditated murders were up by 16.3 percent; serious bodily injury by 41.9 percent; and rape by 15.8 percent. Crimes committed by officers were up by 40 percent.[128] The leakage of weapons into private hands became rampant, especially in units in Eastern Europe and the Transcaucasus.[129] Both soldiers and officers engaged in the weapons trade, stealing weapons from their own units and also breaking into supply depots. General officers in Eastern Europe worked out commercial deals to divert shipments of arms and equipment to international arms merchants, pocketing large sums of foreign currencies. They also skimmed off some of the funds that the German government supplied to build housing in Russia for officers. These scandals surfaced in the media several years later when the Russian defense minister, General Pavel Grachev, and the former commander in Germany, General Matvei Burlakov, were exposed for their involvement. They were also accused of having military intelligence operatives assassinate a reporter, Dmitrii Kholodov, who had exposed their activities.[130]

Desertions increased, reaching as many as 500 a day in construction troop units in the Far East alone in 1990.[131] In some cases, several soldiers deserted together as a form of protest against mistreatment. Forty-four soldiers from a unit in Armenia managed to get media attention for their case.[132] An entire company of soldiers from a unit in Georgia ran away to Moscow, where they staged a demonstration in front of Moscow State University to protest their commander's sale of their labor to local collective farms for brandy.[133] After German reunification took place, desertions shot up in Soviet units still deployed there. Seven hundred soldiers had reportedly fled from these units by fall 1990.[134] Desertions sometimes involved violence. In Ukraine a group of three soldiers seized weapons and ammunition and went on a shooting spree, killing eight soldiers as they escaped.[135] The MoD's list of soldiers absent without leave reportedly included more than 2,500 by January 1991.[136] Given the deterioration of military district staffs and lower command levels and the unreliability of their reporting by this time, the actual figure was probably several times higher. Although not formally in the category of desertion, young men in premilitary service training in Leningrad's DOSAAF had dropped from two million to slightly over a million.[137]

Force reductions naturally required major redeployments of units within the Soviet Union as well as those from Eastern Europe. Sometimes redeployments met open resistance from families. In one notorious case in Zaporozh'e, a city in Ukraine, the officers' wives of an air defense unit staged a series of protests, including blocking a runway at the local airport, demanding that their husbands not be transferred to a post in Kazakhstan that was polluted and without family housing. They attracted sufficient media coverage to force the MoD to grant partial concessions to their demands.[138]

The navy suffered a surge of accidents on its nuclear-powered submarines in 1989. One sank off the Norwegian coast in April, and three more accidents followed, the last involving a missile-launch test in which "large damage was done to the surrounding water and territory."[139] The navy's readiness, never very high, declined even further as ships aged and rusted, and fewer patrols at sea were conducted. Deterioration of the Pacific Fleet noted by Japanese defense officials led them to downgrade significantly their estimate of its combat potential.[140]

As Western governments and observers began to express concern about the disposition and security of Soviet nuclear weapons, MoD officials announced that stockpiles of tactical nuclear weapons had already been removed from areas of unrest. In September 1990, General Moiseev gave the *Washington Post* assurances to that effect.[141] Other sources reported earlier that all nuclear weapons had been withdrawn from the Baltic republics and Azerbaijan.[142] Strategic nuclear weapons, however, remained in place in Belorussia, Ukraine, and Kazakhstan. The strategic rocket forces did not experience the same rapid deterioration characteristic of the other branches of forces, but they were by no means without problems common to other branches. Dedovshchina reigned in the barracks, and food shortages prompted soldiers in a rocket unit in the Urals to threaten to leave their duty posts.[143]

This admittedly impressionistic evidence conveys a compelling overall picture of disintegration on an ever-growing scale by 1991. The Soviet military was truly in a crisis that the generals showed little or no capacity to control.

Gorbachev initiated the unilateral force cuts to convince Western leaders that the Soviet Union was genuinely serious about even further decreases through arms control agreements. But the policy soon gave way to a general disintegration of the Soviet Armed Forces. Delay and resistance on the part of the generals left them ill prepared to deal with the unilateral force reductions. When the flood dike broke in Eastern Europe in late 1989, the wave of forced withdrawals overwhelmed the military's capacity to deal with it. The generals might have managed, albeit with difficulty, had they not also faced a conscription revolt. In fact, they deserved much of the blame for the conditions that inspired that revolt.

The senior military leadership was responsible for allowing the character of life in the barracks to become a countrywide scandal, and as the media made that a major issue, draft evasion lost its moral opprobrium in the eyes of most of society. Yet the generals were not the only culprits in this scandal. Party and KGB controls in the military contributed significantly to careerism and corruption in the senior ranks. And that in turn isolated and alienated the junior officers from the generals. The conscription system itself contributed to dedovshchina and the control of the barracks by the stariki. Had the officer corps been determined to do so, it could have brought discipline to the enlisted ranks. Such determination would have had to originate at the top, but hypocrisy and corruption at the top of the officer corps made effective campaign against dedovshchina most improbable. It could have been successful only if the MPA had also been strongly behind it, but the long Brezhnev era of relaxed party discipline and no purges had allowed the MPA to become even more corrupt and hypocritical.

On the nationality problem, the senior military leaders simply deceived themselves. The horrible patterns of barracks life not only revealed but also exacerbated enduring interethnic hostilities. As the conscription revolt broke out, no one should have been surprised that the national minority regions would lead it. Attempts to crush the emerging nationalist forces with the army both coincided with the conscription revolt and contributed to it.

Certainly the conscription revolt does not fully account for the dissolution of the Soviet Union, but its contribution was much greater than generally acknowledged. It was tied to most of the other factors that were coming together to make the once powerful Soviet military into a house of cards.

FOURTEEN

The August Crisis

Was there a "Kornilov plot" [in August 1917]? Almost certainly not. All the available evidence, rather, points to a "Kerensky plot" engineered to discredit the general [Kornilov].

RICHARD PIPES

The so-called State Committee for the State of Emergency in the USSR (GKChP) opened the last act in the drama of the disintegration of the Soviet Union. The generals might have saved it, but they did not. Failing to change the course of history by acting collectively to storm the White House, they changed the course of history by acting individually to open the doors of power to Yeltsin.

The Chronology of the August Crisis

On 18 August, Gennadii Yanaev, Valentin Pavlov, and Oleg Baklanov signed "The Statement by the Soviet Leadership," citing "the impossibility, owing to his state of health, of Mikhail Sergeevich Gorbachev fulfilling his duties as President of the USSR" and "overcoming the profound and all-round crisis of political, ethnic and civil confrontation, chaos and anarchy that are threatening . . . the citizens of the Soviet Union, the sovereignty, territorial integrity, freedom and independence of our Homeland" as the reasons for a state of emergency.[1] It also established the GKChP. The committee's membership included only one regular military officer, Marshal Yazov. Boris Pugo, head of the MVD, and Vladimir Kryuchkov, chairman of the KGB, also held general-officer rank and had armed troops under their command. Three of the other five were from the highest government positions—Yanaev, vice president of the USSR; Pavlov, prime minister of the USSR; Baklanov, first deputy chairman of the Defense Council. The last two members held lesser posts—Aleksandr

305

Tizyakov, president of the Association of State Industries, and Vasilii Starodubtsev, chairman of the Union of Peasants. Thus it was a essentially "the
government." Had Gorbachev joined it, it would have been "the government"
in fact. Its first resolution, issued on 18 August, declared a state of martial law
to begin the next day at 4:00 A.M. Moscow time—a declaration intended to
convey the committee's determination to brook no resistance.[2]

The main events of 18–22 August were as follows:[3]

Sunday, 18 August. Having left Moscow on 10 August for his Crimean vacation
house in Foros, Gorbachev finds his communications cut off some time between 4:00 and 5:50 P.M. At 4:50 a group of four emissaries from Moscow
arrives in Foros—Baklanov, from the GKChP; Boldin, Gorbachev's chief of
staff; General Valentin Varennikov, commander of the ground forces; and
Oleg Shenin, a party secretary and Politburo member. After meeting with
Gorbachev, they depart for Moscow at 6:00 P.M. without making public any
details of their meeting.

Monday, 19 August. Martial law takes effect as scheduled, and at the same time
a special KGB commando unit, known as Alpha, surrounds Yeltsin's dacha
in Arkhangel'skoe, near Moscow (map 7), but does not arrest him. Yeltsin
learns of the state of emergency shortly after 6:00 A.M., and most of the
top officials of his government, staying in dachas nearby, gather at Yeltsin's
dacha by 7:00 A.M. Anatolii Sobchak, the mayor of Leningrad, Colonel General Konstantin Kobets, and the deputy mayor of Moscow, Yurii Luzhkov,
join them by 7:30 A.M. After assessing the situation for a couple of hours
and drafting a declaration rejecting the GKChP, Yeltsin and his ministers
are persuaded by Kobets and Sobchak that they should make a dash for the
so-called White House, the building of the RSFSR's parliament in Moscow.
Yeltsin reaches the White House shortly before 10:00 A.M., and Sobchak flies
back to Leningrad. Yeltsin and his government issue their "Appeal to the
Citizens of Russia," condemning the GKChP as illegal, asking all citizens
not to obey it, and requesting their full support for the RSFSR government and its lawfully elected president. Telephone communications are not
entirely cut off, and the appeal reaches the media for immediate broadcast.
Yeltsin makes calls throughout the day to various government offices, establishing contact with military officers and members of the GKChP. About
noon, he comes out of the White House to make his famous appearance by
climbing onto a tank and delivering a spirited speech. During the rest of
the day, 250 deputies of the Russian parliament, journalists, and numerous
other people rally in the White House as several thousands gather outside
and build barricades against an attack on the building. Weapons are issued to

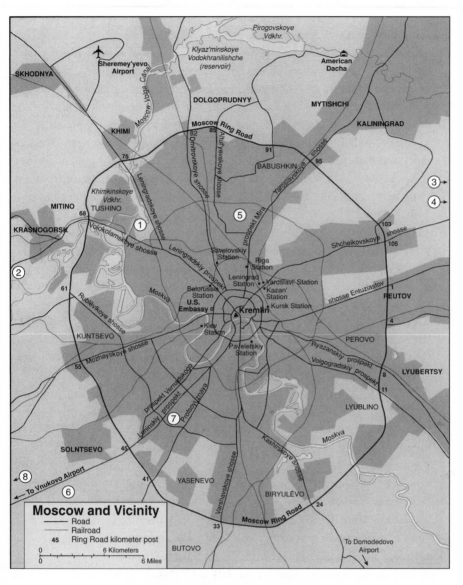

Map 7. Moscow and vicinity
(U.S. Government Printing Office)

Map Legend: **1.** Airborne headquarters vicinity   **2.** Arkhangel'skoe   **3.** Chkalovsk airfield
4. Medvezhi Ozera   **5.** Ostankino TV tower   **6.** Vnukovo airport   **7.** KGB "safe house"
vicinity   **8.** Kubinka airfield

volunteers, and a defensive perimeter is organized under General Kobets's guidance. Most of those inside the White House as well as some of the crowd outside will remain there, defending Yeltsin until the crisis dissolves on 21 August. Thus by the end of this first day, Yeltsin has established a rallying point for opposition to the GKChP, challenged its legitimacy, and fortified the White House sufficiently to prevent an easy arrest of his government.

The GKChP is surprised by Yeltsin's rapid consolidation of open resistance and makes no attempt to invade the White House on Monday. Rather, Kryuchkov speaks with Yeltsin by phone, offering various compromises. Only by evening does the GKChP realize that force will be required to deal with Yeltsin.

Tuesday, 20 August. Throughout the day meetings and preparations for an assault on the White House proceed in the GKChP, the MoD, the KGB, and the MVD. A few units move toward their positions around midnight, and according to some sources the operation actually starts, but that account will remain disputed. As armored vehicles engaged in implementing a curfew pass through an underpass on the Garden Ring (map 8) about midnight, they encounter a crowd that believes the vehicles to be headed to attack the White House. In the ensuing clash, three civilians are killed and one armored vehicle is set afire. In the event, no assault occurs.

On Tuesday morning the defenders of the White House are both exhausted and surprised to have survived the night. They spend the day improving their defenses, communicating with the media and foreign leaders, including President George Bush, and with officials in the MoD, MVD, and the Kremlin to learn all they can about the GKChP's intentions. Anxiety builds as they prepare for another tense night. Several times they are convinced that an assault has begun, but when a heavy rain begins to fall about 2:00 A.M., General Kobets reportedly rejoices because he believes that it stopped a helicopter movement, disrupting the anticipated assault.

Wednesday, 21 August. The GKChP begins unraveling in the early morning hours. Troop units are leaving the city by dawn. The crisis appears to be ending, but the GKChP has not surrendered. To the surprise of the White House, Kryuchkov with four other GKChP members and a senior party official fly off to Foros shortly after 2:00 P.M. Fearing their escape, Yeltsin calls the commander of the air forces to request that the plane be stopped, only to learn that it is under control of the General Staff, not the air forces, and that it can be stopped only by ordering fighters to shoot it down. Yeltsin declines that option and instead dispatches another plane with a delegation, headed by the Russian vice president, Aleksandr Rutskoi, in pursuit of Kryuch-

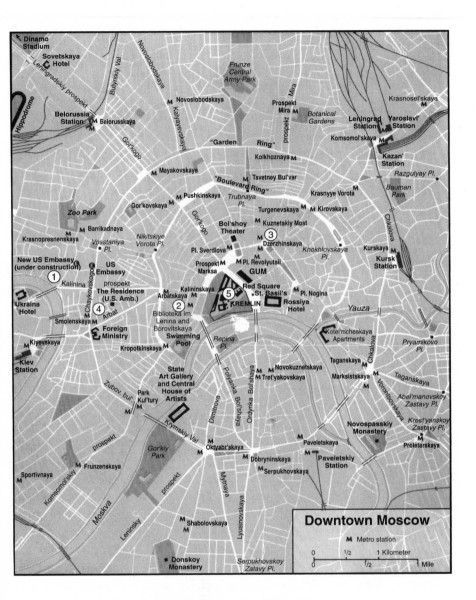

Map 8. Downtown Moscow

(U.S. Government Printing Office)

Map Legend: **1.** White House   **2.** Ministry of Defense and General Staff   **3.** KGB headquarters   **4.** Site where three civilians were killed   **5.** Kremlin—GKChP location

kov's group. Gorbachev will later claim that he initially refused to receive the GKChP members on their arrival in Foros, but eventually he meets two of them, Ivashko and Lukyanov. Pro-GKChP military forces at the nearby Bel'bek airport initially deny Rutskoi's plane permission to land but soon relent and disappear. Rutskoi's delegation finds the GKChP delegation at Gorbachev's dacha and arrests it. Shortly thereafter, Rutskoi's delegation, along with Gorbachev and Kryuchkov, board one plane, the GKChP prisoners board the other, and all fly back to Moscow, arriving at Vnukovo airport at 2:00 A.M. on 22 August. The GKChP group is taken into police custody at Vnukovo, marking the end of the crisis.

This truncated chronology obviously neglects not only important events transpiring elsewhere in the country but also gives short shrift to the role of the media, young people, the intelligentsia, and many other participants in Moscow. Their actions have been impressively examined elsewhere by John Dunlop, David Remnick, and others.[4] Here the main focus will be on the military's role.

The Creation of the GKChP

The USSR procurator general's investigation of the affair traces its origins to the referendum of 17 March 1991 on the restoration of statehood to the union republics.[5] Voters approved the right of the republics to self-determination and called for a new union treaty substantially altering the distribution of powers between the center and the republics. Recognizing the immediate threat to their own power, the plotters realized that only the reversal of perestroika would save them. Yeltsin's election as president of Russia increased their alarm. Their maneuvers at the spring Central Committee plenum and in the Supreme Soviet in June failed, prompting them to consider other ways to prevent the signing of the new union treaty, including martial law.

Thus Kryuchkov, Yazov, Pavlov (chairman of the Council of Ministers), Baklanov, Boldin, and Shenin began conspiring in the spring. Over the next three months the group expanded to include Anatolii Lyukanov (chairman of the Supreme Soviet), Pugo, two deputy ministers of defense—General Varennikov and Colonel General Viktor Achalov (deputy for airborne forces)—and six others.[6]

The plotters began meeting in a KGB "safe house" near Leninskii Prospekt (see map 8) on 5 August, the day after Gorbachev departed Moscow for Foros. Knowing that they had to act before he returned on 20 August, they focused on two tasks.[7] The first was dealing with Gorbachev. They would give him a choice: either declare martial law or resign. If he refused, they would declare him sick and let Vice President Yanaev act in his place. The second task was implementing martial law countrywide, including the arrest and detention of key democratic political leaders. KGB analysts were directed to estimate likely public reaction. The military's role in enforcing martial law was left vague, but the ground forces and the airborne divisions would obviously be required. Thus Varennikov, Achalov, and also Lieutenant General Grachev, commander of the airborne forces, were involved well before 18 August.[8]

Dividing the tasks with the MoD, the KGB was to isolate Gorbachev, detain Yeltsin and other potential troublemakers, monitor telephones, cut some phone lines, and provide special units where use of force was required. To the MoD fell the ill-defined mission of creating a sense of emergency and readiness to use force. For some of its tasks, however, the KGB required military assistance—holding detainees, moving aircraft with senior officials, and so on. MVD forces were given no specific tasks until 18 August.

By mid-August, the plotters had drafted resolutions, appeals, and declarations. The KGB was monitoring the telephones of most democratic political figures; a list of more than seventy people to be detained was compiled. The circle of conspirators was widened somewhat, and the plan for isolating Gorbachev was complete. On 17 August the plotters held a final meeting at the KGB safe house to confirm several final actions. The KGB and the military were to "detain and transfer" Yeltsin to Zavidovo, a party vacation compound several miles northwest of Moscow. A delegation was selected to fly to Foros to confront Gorbachev. One of its members, Varennikov, would meet afterward with local military commanders in the Crimea and then fly to Kiev to line up the three military district commanders in the Ukraine behind the plot. Finally, arrangements were made to detain key democratic leaders in a military installation at Medvezh'i Ozera (see map 7).[9] When Yazov demanded to know what KGB, MVD, and military units would make these arrests, what installations were to be guarded, and what actions each should take, Kryuchkov refused to answer. Because Pugo and the MVD were not yet informed, the details would have to be clarified the next day. Yazov, Varennikov, and Achalov stalked out in anger.[10]

To ready the MoD for action, Yazov convened several of his subordinates at 8:00 A.M. the next morning, described a deteriorating situation, warned that action could be required very soon, designated some Moscow military district and airborne units to be ready to move, but did not reveal the GKChP's existence. When Pugo finally arrived in Moscow in the afternoon, he and Kryuchkov came to Yazov's office about 4:00 P.M. to coordinate their joint actions.[11]

Nothing in the procurator's report suggests that the GKChP members expected popular resistance. On the contrary, they felt sure that announcing the emergency decree and bringing military units into the streets would ensure public acceptance of martial law.

The GKChP Launches Its Plan

About 8:00 P.M. on Sunday evening the GKChP convened in the Kremlin to await the return of the delegation from Foros. Kryuchkov shared what he had already learned by telephone: Gorbachev refused to cooperate. Kryuchkov, Yanaev, and Yazov insisted to the procurator that the meeting was very businesslike, but Achalov gave a different picture. Yanaev loudly denounced Gorbachev for refusing to cooperate. The others "were talking their heads off. . . . It was hard to understand who made decisions there, and none of those present showed any statesmanship."[12]

Anatolii Lukyanov, chairman of the parliament, testified to the procurator that he came to this meeting expecting to find Gorbachev. When he did not, he voiced doubts about the whole undertaking. Yazov remembered that Lukyanov asked whether the committee members had a plan. Yazov answered that they did not, but Kryuchkov insisted, "Why, we do have one."[13]

The mood worsened when the delegation from Foros arrived at about 10:00 P.M. According to Yazov, "They returned from Mikhail Sergeevich with long faces" and worry about their personal fates. The group was dismayed at Baklanov's report. Some cried out, "We've been set up. If we agree with that and break up the meeting, our heads will roll and you, you're clean. . . . We signed a death warrant."[14] According to Pavlov, someone shouted, "Don't think that if we flew [to Foros], you're clean. All here are in it. . . . I can say that for sure because I know the president well. We're all in it together."[15] Precisely who first tried to dodge responsibility is not certain, but two conclusions can be drawn.

First, several of the GKChP members expected Gorbachev to cooperate, either by supporting them or by stepping aside. Gorbachev admitted that Baklanov tried to persuade him to sign the emergency decree, and when he refused, Baklanov begged him to accept an alternative. "Mikhail Sergeevich, you are not expected to do anything at all, are you? All you have to do is just to stay here for some time, while we do all the dirty work for you, and afterwards, you'll come back."[16] Second, mutual suspicions immediately arose about who might try to save his own skin at the expense of the rest. For a time Yanaev's refusal to sign the emergency decree in Gorbachev's place threatened to halt the operation on the spot, but eventually he agreed.[17] When Pugo read the decree, his "hair stood on end." He warned that MVD troops alone could not implement it. Yanaev assured him that the military would help.[18] At this point, Yazov and Achalov left for the MoD to start troop movements.

The First Military Moves

Arriving at his office about 3:30 A.M., Yazov immediately summoned Colonel General N. V. Kalinin, Moscow military district commander; Colonel General Denisov, the chief of the main operations directorate of the General Staff; Colonel General Shlyaga of the MPA; and Achalov, telling them that Yanaev had assumed power because of Gorbachev's illness and signed the emergency decree. Kalinin and Achalov were to be ready at once to move troops into Moscow, and Kalinin was to plan for implementing a curfew if that became necessary. Yazov also told him to coordinate with non–Moscow MD units in the area—the airborne forces and military schools, for example—in order to avoid problems in movements. At 4:00 A.M. he called Kalinin and Grachev, ordering them to move their troops into Moscow. Kalinin was to bring units from the Tamanskaya and Kantemirovskaya divisions. Achalov was to assign an airborne unit to cordon off the Ostankino television station (see map 7), and Grachev was to bring in the airborne regiments from Tula, Kostroma, and Ryazan.[19] Achalov testified that he and a few others expressed strong reservations about moving troops into the city, but he is not very convincing.[20] An early participant in the plotting, he held intensely antiperestroika views.

Next Yazov convened the military collegium of the MoD at 6:00 A.M., explaining the situation and adding that the union treaty would not be signed, Gorbachev was ill, Yanaev was acting in his place, and an emergency decree had been signed. After listing the troop movements he had ordered, he told the acting chief of the General Staff, Colonel General Omelichev (Moiseev was on leave but appeared in the MoD later that day) to prepare an order to bring the entire armed forces from "regular" to "heightened" readiness level. Later that morning Yazov signed the order, completing his first round of actions.[21]

The warning meeting the day before had prepared unit commanders for movement orders, but Yazov was not specific about missions, nor could he be, given the vague instructions he got from the GKChP. Sending troops to surround the Ostankino television station was a last-minute improvisation, and he was soon improvising at every turn. Yazov later admitted to the procurator his misjudgment of the situation: "You understand . . . KGB troops, the KGB itself, the Army—all together. Who could resist them?"[22] He was convinced that the mere appearance of armed units in the streets of Moscow was enough to intimidate the population. In the event, of course, it was not.

Varennikov failed to intimidate Ukrainian party leaders but refused to admit it. Arriving in Kiev, he demanded a meeting with Leonid Kravchuk, the Ukrainian party secretary, at 9:00 A.M. Varennikov presented the emergency decree, but Kravchuk rejected the GKChP's instructions.[23] Varennikov threatened, but to no avail, then cabled Yazov, reassuring him that Ukraine was falling into line, though he had had to "sharpen the situation to some extent to let our comrades understand" that martial law was already operative.[24] A few hours later Varennikov followed up with reassuring cables about Ukraine but also with alarm about Yeltsin's pronouncements on the airwaves. "We all seriously request that you take measures on the liquidation of the adventurist Yeltsin group," he pleaded.[25]

Yeltsin's Escape to the White House

Kryuchkov assigned the KGB Alpha unit to detain Yeltsin as he flew into Moscow on the evening of 18 August. Although the unit knew Yeltsin's arrival time, it failed to meet him and lost track of him, eventually tracing him to his dacha in Arkhangel'skoe (see map 7) in the early morning hours. According to the procurator's report, Kryuchkov believed he could reach a compromise with Yeltsin and thus gave only conditional instructions to seize him.[26] Shortly after 3:00 A.M. Kryuchkov passed word to the Alpha unit commander, Major General Viktor Karpukhin, to move his personnel forward in Arkhangel'skoe in readiness to provide security for a meeting between Yeltsin and "government representatives." By 4:00 A.M. Karpukhin had deployed about sixty men either to provide security or to detain Yeltsin. At about 6:00 A.M., Karpukhin called KGB headquarters for permission to detain Yeltsin but was told to wait.[27] He was still waiting as the Alpha troops watched Yeltsin being driven off to the White House.

Although the White House defenders expected an assault on Monday night, the procurator's report provides no evidence that a raid was planned. Like Yazov, Kryuchkov expected the mere appearance of military forces on Moscow streets to prevent resistance. Less understandable, he also expected Yeltsin to compromise. Both seriously misjudged developments at the White House, and they launched no forces to break Yeltsin's defenses on 19 August.

Early on Tuesday, 20 August, Kryuchkov ordered KGB officers to plan an assault operation in cooperation with the MoD and the MVD. A two-stage meeting was to be held, the first at the KGB headquarters, the second at the

MoD (see map 8). Kryuchkov, Pugo, and Yazov had apparently conferred and agreed on these instructions some time before 9:00 A.M. [28]

The GKChP met from 9:00 A.M. until about noon. After hearing a report on the countrywide situation, it considered all kinds of proposals, from reducing consumer goods prices to censoring the media, but only one decision was made—to establish regional GKChPs. The discussion exasperated Yazov: "They had nothing but 'wishes.' They said it was necessary to take active measures. I asked Baklanov what he meant by 'take up active measures,' shall we shoot?" Baklanov replied, "I would never let you do that." "He was indignant," Yazov went on, "saying something like 'Do you think we started all of this to kill, to shoot? What for?' Then I added, 'Once we started it, we must be able to answer for it.'" [29] Yazov and Kryuchkov could see at that point that several GKChP members would not give advanced approval for an assault on the White House. They wanted the results without the responsibility for the decision.

The meeting later approved a curfew to begin in Moscow at 11:00 P.M. that day.[30] The aim was to clear the crowd from around the White House, making an assault operation less difficult. Yazov, it will be recalled, had ordered Kalinin to plan to enforce a curfew. When he received the order about noon, however, Kalinin reported that it could not be executed. Based on official curfew regulations, Kalinin's staff estimated that it would require 1.5 million passes and ten divisions of troops to man about two thousand checkpoints and thirty-three districts. Yazov waved off Kalinin's protests and ordered two airborne regiments flown in from the division at Bolgrad in the Odessa military district to assist him. Only reluctantly did Kalinin agree to announce the curfew on television at 10:00 P.M., and though armored vehicle columns began patrolling the streets, the MVD was not even informed. Not a single person was arrested.[31]

In the tunnel on Garden Ring road under Prospekt Kalinina, an armored column clashed with a crowd trying to stop its movement, causing the death of three civilians (see map 8). Witnesses at the White House and numerous press reports at the time claimed that these vehicles headed to assault the White House. The procurator's report identifies them as Kalinin's troops engaged in the feckless curfew effort, not part of an assault operation.[32]

The Military's Puzzling Behavior

The generals could no longer pretend. They were now forced to choose for or against Gorbachev, not collectively but individually, because the military was internally divided in its senior ranks. To better understand their individual decisions, we must address a series of questions about their collective action. Did they produce a plan for closing down Yeltsin's government by force? If so, was the plan feasible? And if it was, why did they fail to carry it out?

Did the Military Produce a Plan?

As already noted, no planning was ordered for an assault on Monday night.[33] Moreover, an airborne battalion and ten tanks from the Tamanskaya division were part of the White House defenses that night, and they would have complicated the task.[34] The procurator's report does, however, describe a plan hastily concocted at KGB headquarters about 6:30 P.M. on 18 August: fifty KGB officers were to take control of the White House in order to prevent the Russian parliament from assembling. For reasons not made clear, the officers in charge fell into a dispute among themselves, and the operation was not carried out.[35] Thus the first assault planning was begun two days later at the KGB, on orders from Kryuchkov, Yazov, and Pugo.

The Alpha unit's "A" group was to try to infiltrate the White House, and, if that failed, to blast its way in, followed by a second, or "B" group. The second group was to identify, bring out, and document those people detained. These groups totaled 260 men plus a reserve of 200. Additional KGB forces were assigned blocking roles. A MVD police unit was to help clear an approach path to the building for the KGB elements. The deputy minister of the MVD, Colonel General Boris Gromov, was to have MVD firefighting units available in case of a conflagration. Finally, airborne troops were to wall off the White House at some distance from its perimeter and also to prepare to break into the ground floor in the event that the Alpha unit failed or had trouble.[36] Because the procurator's account of this plan, code-named Thunder, is vague about how it would deal with the crowds around the White House, it is impossible to judge its feasibility. Nor is the report any clearer on the second stage of the planning that followed at the MoD, although it describes the meeting, names several of the key participants, and discusses the participation of the airborne units and MVD troops. It does, however, specify the execution time for the assault as 3:00 A.M. on 21 August.

At least two other sources, Lieutenant General Pavel Grachev and Major General Aleksandr Lebed', have also described the MoD meeting and, more important, have given a picture of how the plan was to work. Grachev elaborated it with extreme brevity.[37] Between 2:00 and 3:00 P.M. on the afternoon of Tuesday, 20 August, a meeting was held in General Achalov's office. Grachev says that Marshal Akhromeev, General Varennikov, Colonel General Kalinin,

Major General Karpukhin, several other officers, and some civilians unknown to him attended the meeting. The assembled group was told that the RSFSR government was opposing the GKChP and that negotiations had led to nothing. Next, "the mission was given: to occupy the parliament building." Grachev's use of passive voice makes it unclear precisely who specified that mission but implies that it was the GKChP. The assault was to begin at 3:00 A.M. on 21 August. The participating units would begin moving into position at midnight and be in place by 1:00 A.M. MVD troops were to deploy on Kutuzovskii Prospekt (apparently on and west of the bridge over the Moscow River, facing the front of the White House), the Alpha unit would deploy on the Naberezhnaya, the street along the river directly in front of the White House. The airborne units would deploy in the vicinity of the U.S. embassy west of the Garden Ring (see map 8). The MVD troops were to force a corridor through the crowd of defenders outside of the White House. The KGB Alpha unit would then move through the corridor and storm the building. How or when the MVD troops would cross the Moscow River from Kutuvsovskii Prospekt to confront the crowd, however, Grachev did not clarify.

The description by Lebed' differs in detail but is loosely compatible with Grachev's. Lebed' was in the MoD late on the afternoon of 20 August, reporting to Colonel General Achalov, who surprised him by asking how he would take the White House.[38] Lebed' asked what forces were available. Achalov listed the Dzerzhinskii division (MVD troops), the Alpha unit (KGB troops), the Tula airborne division, and a brigade of *spetsnaz* (army intelligence special operations forces). In broad strokes on a map, Lebed' assigned the MVD units of the Dzerzhinskii division to cover the front of the building and its right side. The Alpha unit was to take a position behind the Dzerzhinskii units, which would force a corridor through the mass of defenders to the building, allowing the Alpha unit to enter the White House. He placed airborne units covering the back of the building and its left side. Behind them he located the spetsnaz brigade, which, like the Alpha unit, would pass through a corridor opened by the airborne troops. Finally, he designated part of the airborne division as a reserve. Like Grachev, he made no mention of a helicopter assault, although White House sources, including General Kobets, insisted that one was organized. The procurator's report says that Varennikov ordered some assault helicopters to be ready to provide fire support for the ground assault, probably the source of Kobets's impression.

Grachev's version appeared in a short interview in a newspaper. This may explain his omission of the airborne forces to be deployed behind the White House and any mention of the spetsnaz brigade. Still, he placed the Alpha unit initially in front instead of behind the MVD troops who were to open a corridor through the defending crowd. The Lebed' version contains far greater detail.[39] Like Grachev, he describes a meeting of twenty to twenty-five senior officers in General Achalov's office in midafternoon; there he was asked to describe the situation at the White House and did so, concluding that an assault would inevitably produce many civilian casualties. General Varennikov reacted, "General, you are obliged to be an optimist. But you bring pessimism and uncertainty."[40] Marshal Akhromeev also pressed for an assault. Lebed' therefore got the impression that planning was in progress if not yet complete. To verify his "pessimistic" assessment, Lebed' was sent off with the Alpha unit commander and the deputy commander of the Moscow military district to reconnoiter the White House. Returning to confirm to Achalov what Lebed' previously described, they were then excused. Achalov, however, kept Lebed' behind, and there the episode just described took place. An astonished Lebed' outlined an assault concept. He was even more surprised that Achalov immediately accepted it without questions about coordination details and raced off, with Lebed' in tow, to General Gromov at the MVD. Gromov was with his chief of staff, Lieutenant General Dubinyak. Major General Chindarov, another deputy commander of the airborne troops, was also present. After Lebed' explained his scheme, Gromov uncharacteristically approved it as quickly as Achalov had. Recalling how both Achalov and Gromov in Afghanistan always demanded detail and care in operational planning, Lebed' found their behavior in this case especially strange. When he and Chindarov asked about coordination with MVD units—approach routes, signals, communications, and so on—Dubinyak waved them off, saying that the forces should move into position, then coordinate the details by telephone. Neither Gromov nor Achalov objected. As the only coordination details, the time of the assault was set, 3:00 A.M., and the time for units to be in position, 1:00 A.M. Thus there was a plan, albeit extremely rudimentary.

Was the Plan Feasible?

Testifying later before an investigative parliamentary commission that doubted the plan's feasibility, Lebed' claimed that he could easily have taken the White House by firing twenty to thirty antitank missiles through the windows of the building.[41] They would have set fire to the curtains and other inflammable materials, creating smoke that would have forced the defenders to flee. Then the assault forces would have had an easy time of it. In his outline to Achalov and Gromov, however, he had not mentioned this tactic, though airborne units had antitank guided missiles as standard equipment on their light armored vehicles. Was it an afterthought? Undoubtedly, and consistent with the general's love for shocking images. Even without using antitank missiles, however, the forces that Lebed' described should have been able to storm the building successfully if they were willing to spill blood.

Although feasible, the plan was extremely complicated because units from three different ministries were taking part. Each had its own command channels. Had the General Staff put an operational control group in charge, adequate coordination could have been established between the MoD, KGB, and MVD.

But the General Staff was not in control.[42] Yazov kept it uninformed in the days before the declaration of martial law, and he engaged it only partially thereafter. This fact makes far more credible the descriptions by Lebed' of the ad hoc and amateurish planning activities in the office of a deputy minister, with twenty to thirty high-ranking officers debating the operational issues. Normally these details would have been worked out by field-grade officers in the General Staff's main operations directorate, never by Achalov, a deputy minister.

All this notwithstanding, an aggressive and determined commander of either the MVD division or the airborne forces had adequate forces to seize the White House alone if he were truly determined and could count on his troops to follow orders. The conclusion must therefore be that the military did produce a feasible plan on 20 August, but a poorly developed one with virtually no coordinating arrangements.

Why No Assault?

The GKChP convened in the Kremlin at 8:00 P.M. on 20 August, only a few hours before the assault was scheduled to begin. All members were present but Pavlov, who was dead drunk. A few other people from the MoD, KGB, and the Central Committee also attended.[43] Instead of making a decision on the imminent planned assault, the group spent two hours reviewing the worsening situation in Moscow and countrywide reaction to it (which was mixed) and debating whether or not Yanaev should appear on television to deny that there would be an assault on the White House. (Kryuchkov insisted that it was too early to do that.) All agreed that Yanaev should signed a decree revoking Yeltsin's decrees. On these points testimony to the procurator was consistent, but not on the question of assaulting the White House.

Starodubtsev believed that either Kryuchkov or Pugo favored arresting

Yeltsin, no matter that blood would be shed, but he denied that a decision was taken. Tizyakov described a long debate in which Kryuchkov and Pugo favored the use of force.[44] The procurator's report concludes that there was no assault only because the officers in chain of command refused to carry out orders by Kryuchkov, Pugo, and Yazov, but it offers no testimony that any such orders were given, except to plan and deploy.[45]

The unavoidable impression emerges that those members who refused to approve an assault in advance truly wanted it to happen. When Baklanov and others who hesitated realized about 2:00 A.M. that the assault would not go forward, they condemned the military and the KGB in the vilest language for "getting cold feet" and having no courage.[46] They also pleaded with Yazov not to withdraw his forces from Moscow when they learned he had directed them to depart at first light that morning.[47]

Almost certainly the triumvirate of Kryuchkov, Pugo, and Yazov ordered the preparations for the assault on their own in face of evasions within the GKChP. As the moment of execution approached, with the GKChP still wavering, they flinched, each in his own way. The procurator general, Valentin Stepankov, claims in his book about the investigation that Yazov finally stopped the assault around 2:00 A.M.[48] Yet his own procuracy report credits lower-level officers with stopping the assault. He tries to finesse this contradiction by insisting that no order to stop the assault came before 3:00 A.M., by which time it was already clear that the units' commanders would not proceed in any case. He may be right, but the GKChP's refusal to express its mind clearly goes a long way toward explaining why no assault was made on the White House. Indecision permeated down the command lines in the MoD, KGB, and MVD.

The Military in Action

Would the commanders in charge have refused the order in any case, as Stepankov insists? Achalov and Gromov gave the impression that they were under great pressure to carry out an assault, and General Varennikov and Marshal Akhromeev strongly favored it. Most of the commanders of the operational units were under the impression that an order either had been or would be given to execute it. When the clock struck 1:00 A.M., however, none of the assault forces were fully in position, and when the time for the attack arrived, 3:00 A.M., no assault went forward. These facts suggest that numerous officers were reluctant and waiting to be pushed, or convinced that the operation was not seriously intended, or effectively undermining the operation.

When they testified after the event, several of them claimed that they personally blocked the plan's execution.[49] Karpukhin made that claim, but so, too, did two of his subordinate commanders. Because Yeltsin won the struggle, they all had strong incentives to prove that they had obstructed the GKChP and saved Yeltsin. A few, like Marshal Akhromeev (who committed suicide two days later), General Varennikov, and Marshal Yazov, made no excuses. Varennikov insisted that he had acted legally by supporting the GKChP, later demanding to be tried, went to trial two years later, and was acquitted by the court. Immediately after the event, however, most involved officers were stripped of the cover of collective military behavior and left to explain their individual choices. Not only were their careers at risk, but so was their freedom, perhaps even their lives. Thus they could hardly be expected to give objective accounts. Overcoming this bias will long be an obstacle for historians of the August crisis, but some accounts are more credible than others.

Yeltsin and his people naturally had their own opinions about which senior officers helped them. After the crisis, Shaposhnikov and Grachev received high-level appointments, compelling evidence that they had assisted the White House forces, and Lebed' received Yeltsin's praise as well. A look at Shaposhnikov's role is possible because he has written a detailed chronicle of his actions. Although Grachev has not, much about his role can be discerned from the account by Lebed' and a few other sources. Lebed' also turns out to have witnessed some of the most illuminating episodes in the military's operations. Admittedly, following the stories of these three officers provides an eclectic view, but together they yield a sense of the tension, conflicted loyalties, mistrust, and imponderables characterizing the officer corps during the crisis.

Did Marshal Shaposhnikov Save the Day?

Admiral Chernavin, commander of the navy, General Yurii Maksimov, commander of the rocket forces, and Marshal of Aviation Shaposhnikov (commander of the air forces) were inclined against the GKChP from the beginning, but only Shaposhnikov controlled forces that could affect events in Moscow — bombers and fighters in the Moscow military district and also the Military Transport Aviation (VTA) that provided lift for the airborne forces.[50] His use of them convinced Simon Kordonskii that he may have played the critical role in forcing the GKChP to capitulate.[51] Let us consider whether his own account confirms this judgment.

Shaposhnikov and his wife were scheduled to depart Moscow on 17 August for a vacation in her native Ossetia, a small republic in the northern Caucasus, but Yazov asked him to delay until the nineteenth. To his surprise, the MoD

military collegium was ordered to assemble at 6:00 A.M. on that date, disrupting his vacation plans once again.[52] Yazov told the collegium that martial law
had been declared and the armed forces had been ordered to "increased combat readiness."[53] He noted rising tensions in the country and the "negative
reactions" that a new union treaty would bring. Gorbachev was in a difficult
situation, he continued, unable to rule at the moment or to sign the treaty, and
for that reason it would not be signed. Then he named the members of the
GKChP and cited the constitution as the basis for Yanaev's taking over Gorbachev's duties. Adding that he did not want to see any blood spilled and that
confrontations should be avoided, he departed without taking questions.

Shaposhnikov reacted negatively as he recalled the army's recent operations in Tbilisi, Baku, and Vilnius, as well as in Czechoslovakia in 1968. He
decided that he could not "travel the road" with the GKChP. On returning
to his headquarters, he noted the wall display he had had installed to honor
all previous commanders of the air forces. Nine of them from the pre–World
War II period had become nonpersons, not even mentioned in the *Great Soviet
Encyclopedia* published in 1986. Six had been arrested and shot as "enemies of
the people," two had died in mysterious air crashes, and one had been put in
such unbearable circumstances that he died from physical and nervous exhaus-
tion. After the war, a tenth one had been dismissed and roughly treated. In all,
more than half of all previous air forces commanders had been shot or otherwise destroyed.[54]

A short time later he learned that General Achalov had called the air forces
command center, requesting aircraft to move airborne units to Moscow. When
Shaposhnikov called back to query his authority for the request, Achalov answered that Marshal Yazov had personally approved it. Next Shaposhnikov
called the VTA commander, General V. V. Yefanov, and told him to get ready
for the mission but to take no further actions.[55] This was his first obstructive
action.

His next step, somewhat impulsive, quickly threw suspicion on him. He
accepted a telephone call from a journalist who asked what was going on and
what he was doing about it. Shaposhnikov responded that the GKChP did not
deserve one drop of blood. When the journalist asked whether he could publish
that comment, Shaposhnikov agreed, but asked that his name be withheld.[56]

The next important development, establishing indirect contact with Yeltsin, was fortuitous. One of Shaposhnikov's subordinates, Colonel V. A. Burkov,
who had lost a leg in Afghanistan, came to his office and told him about the
state of affairs in the White House, explaining his own opposition views.[57] This

was Shaposhnikov's first knowledge of Yeltsin's stand against the GKChP. He assured Burkov that he also would not support the GKChP and that he believed other senior officers were with him. After this exchange, he felt much better because Yeltsin struck him as a man who could rally others like Burkov against this madness.

Trying to stay abreast of airborne troop movements and still suspicious of Achalov's authority to demand air movements, Shaposhnikov called him, asking for a progress report.[58] Achalov complained that the airborne units were ready but that the aircraft would not take off. Shaposhnikov reassured him that the VTA had orders to be ready and that poor weather might be the reason for their delay. Then he asked Achalov whether the defense minister knew about his movement plans. Achalov bristled, "And you are checking on me?" "Why not?" Shaposhnikov snapped. "He is my commander." Achalov hung up. The picture improved a bit when the VTA commander walked in right after this call. Yefanov had just been with Grachev, who was under pressure from Achalov to move troops to Moscow. Yefanov got the impression that Grachev was hesitating. To reassure Yefanov, Shaposhnikov told him that as long as Yazov was not pushing for movement, there was no need to hurry, but that he had to keep this conversation to himself. Shaposhnikov next called Grachev, who talked around the situation, saying that the troops were "stretching the rubber" to move and asking about the weather. Shaposhnikov, hinting at the "political weather," said it was not so good but that it might improve after a time. Grachev seemed to understand.[59] With this exchange and Yefanov's report, Shaposhnikov had a clearer picture of who was wavering. As his last act of the duty day, he called Burkov back to his office and gave him a message for Yeltsin: "The air forces will not act against the people."[60] Burkov excitedly raced off to deliver it.

In one day Shaposhnikov had traveled a long way. He awoke in the morning as a communist and the loyal commander of the VVS. By midmorning, he had made his "choice" (as he would entitle his memoir)—against the GKChP. He had not yet made a choice *for* anything or anyone. He had also taken very modest action against the GKChP by holding up the air movement of troop units. In the course of the day he gained some idea of how other senior officers stood. Achalov was for the GKChP; Grachev was wavering; and even Yazov, he remembered, had emphasized in his terse speech that he did not want to see blood spilled, a sign of reservation. By early evening, Shaposhnikov had made a second choice—for Yeltsin—by promising him the VVS's support. He was still formally a communist, but not for long.

At the regular morning conference with his own deputies the next day, 20 August, Shaposhnikov looked at them, wondering what they were thinking. Afterward, the three first deputies remained behind. He believed that two—Petr Deinekin and Anatolii Malyukov—shared his own views. The third, Gennadii Benov, harder to read, probably supported the GKChP. They discussed the previous day's events and began to exchange opinions on why no proclamations were coming from the Soviet parliament and the Central Committee. (Music from Swan Lake played on the office radio news station as they talked.) Shaposhnikov then abruptly expressed what had been crystallizing in his mind over the past several months. The army had to be divorced from the party. It could not be done now, he admitted, but it should be as soon as the crisis was over. "No matter how it comes out, I am leaving the party," he concluded. All three deputies fell quiet, "quiet in different ways." Deinekin and Malyukov, he realized, were with him, but Benov probably was not.[61]

By midday he would need all the support from his subordinates possible. Both his chat with the journalist the day before and the message he had sent to Yeltsin had been leaked. Rumors were afoot in the city that Shaposhnikov had been arrested for siding with Yeltsin, and foreign radios were reporting that the air forces opposed the GKChP. Anonymous phone calls from the KGB and the Council of Ministers began to come in, asking whether he had gone over to Yeltsin's side. Shaposhnikov simply declared that he had not heard the "voices" spreading that rumor and that he had nothing to deny. He was too busy at work to bother about it. He realized that he could not convince these callers, but to admit to the rumor would have brought his instant removal and arrest. He could only play for time.[62]

At 3:00 P.M. he received a call to report at once to Yazov.[63] He departed, telling Deinekin, Malyukov, and others not to bring shame on the air forces and to expect the worst—his arrest and probably theirs as well. He had every reason to expect to meet KGB arresting officers instead of the defense minister. When he arrived at the MoD, Yazov was away talking with Kryuchkov. While he waited, Shaposhnikov dropped in to see Moiseev, who was chatting with a subordinate. Obviously not welcome, he departed for Achalov's office. Absorbed in a pile of papers, Achalov made it clear that he was in no mood to talk.

Returning to wait for Yazov, he reflected on the man's character. In Shaposhnikov's judgment he was basically a good person thrown by chance into a job over his head after the Rust flight affair. To keep his subordinates under control, Yazov regularly abused them with foul language. He unfailingly turned every topic of conversation to discipline in the barracks, which he could not discuss calmly because all his efforts to eliminate dedovshchina and noncombat deaths brought no results. He simply "could not deal with democratization and glasnost or abandon his traditional views." [64]

Shaposhnikov was therefore astonished when Yazov received him warmly and asked, "What do you think I should do?" [65]

"You must stop this business, comrade minister of defense."

"How can it be stopped?" asked Yazov.

"Honorably for the authority of the armed forces. Revoke the increased combat readiness; take the troops out of Moscow; suspend martial law. Transfer power to the Supreme Soviet of the USSR."

"What must be done with the GKChP?" asked Yazov, speaking like a broken man.

"Disperse them. Declare them outside the law," demanded Shaposhnikov.

Yazov remained quiet for a time. Then Generals Moiseev, Achalov, and Kochetov walked in. Yazov immediately changed his expression, stood up as if Shaposhnikov had just arrived for a reprimand. Before Yazov could begin the telephone rang. He answered it, "Hello, Vadim Viktorovich," listened, then said that the idea of storming the White House was crazy and would not happen. Hanging up, he said that the caller was Bakatin, a former minister of the MVD, and repeated that "storming the White House is nonsense." Then Yazov turned back to Shaposhnikov, asking whether he knew why he had been summoned. Grasping Yazov's game of pretense, Shaposhnikov played along, answering, "No, I do not." Then Yazov upbraided him sharply and asked whether the rumors were true that the air forces had changed sides. Shaposhnikov flatly denied it, calling the rumors a provocation. Yazov shouted that there were too many "democrats in the air forces" and complained that Shaposhnikov was not in control of them. Shaposhnikov promised to assert control. Yazov abruptly dismissed him, ordering him to deal harshly with any "extremists" in his ranks. [66]

Shaposhnikov was naturally elated that Yazov had not revealed his anti-GKChP views to Moiseev, Achalov, and Kochetov, who, he was sure, had broken in expecting to witness Shaposhnikov's firing on the spot. Astonishingly, Yazov had protected him, apparently having some sympathy for his views. But Shaposhnikov may have misread Yazov's motives. Consider the situation as Shaposhnikov has described it. Yazov now knew where Shaposhnikov stood, and if Yazov had relieved him on the spot, the news would have spread in the MoD and soon arrived in the White House, prompting the defenders to be more alert and to improve their defenses. The phone call from Bakatin gave Yazov a way to convey the impression to Shaposhnikov that there would be no assault. He could be certain that Shaposhnikov would pass that word to Yeltsin, and if indeed an assault was planned, this disinformation might cause the White House defenders to relax. Speculative though it is, this line of inference is consistent with Shaposhnikov's account.

Upon returning to his headquarters, Shaposhnikov briefed Deinekin and Malyukov on what had transpired and directed Malyukov to lower all air force units from "increased combat readiness" to "constant combat readiness."[67] Next he telephoned each of his subordinate commanders, asking them to speak to him on a purely human basis and honestly about what they thought of the GKChP, the movement of troops into Moscow, and the likely future turn of events.[68] Shaposhnikov admits that he was asking them to risk extreme personal consequences. To his delight, all of them backed him. A few said that a crackdown should have occurred much earlier, but now it was too late. Shaposhnikov was euphoric now that he could be certain of his forces. He immediately had Malyukov revise his last order to lower the readiness level, adding that combat loads be removed from all aircraft, extra guard details cut back, and scheduled vacations to be reinstated. He now believed that no assault on the White House would occur, but if it did, his forces would oppose it.

Just as Yazov may have suspected, Shaposhnikov next passed word through Colonel Burkov to the White House that there would be no assault. Citing Yazov's warning about controlling extremists, he also told Burkov to warn the White House not to be trigger-happy. Burkov happily promised to convey these messages.[69]

At this point, late evening, Shaposhnikov went home for a rest. Shortly after he reached his apartment, however, Moscow television began to report troop movements toward the White House. (They were probably Kalinin's forces trying to implement the curfew.) Alarmed, he returned to his headquarters. No sooner had the duty officers briefed him than Colonel Burkov called from the White House, saying that all signs pointed to an assault. Shaposhnikov agreed with that assessment but declared that he knew no more than Burkov.[70] Then he tried to reach Yazov by telephone. Yazov's adjutant answered that the marshal was resting and could not be disturbed. Next he tried unsuccessfully to call Achalov. Finally he got Grachev on the line:

"Pavel Sergeevich, information is circulating here about storming the White House. Do you know anything?" Shaposhnikov asked.

Grachev responded, "Apparently something is being prepared. But there is no order. Maybe they're counting on somebody to get nervous and start the shooting anyway, and then they can blame it all on him."

"What are you thinking of doing?" Shaposhnikov asked.

"If they think they can count on the airborne troops to do this, then our nerves are strong. Let them even hint that I gave the order — I'll screw them," snapped back Grachev, apparently implying that his forces would storm the Kremlin rather than accept orders for an assault on the White House.

"Hold off on that, Pavel Sergeevich, wait. That's too easy. They'll just cross you out, and then what?" he asked.

Shaposhnikov believed that Grachev was at his breaking point. He tried to calm him down by recounting his meeting with Yazov and his conversations with his own commanders, then proposed that they think through all the alternatives. Based on what he knew, Shaposhnikov said he doubted that the airborne units would be ordered to storm the parliament building, but he had no information about the KGB and MVD units. Grachev then said that Gromov had told him that no MVD units would join the operation and that the MVD had apparently received no orders in any case.

Shaposhnikov concluded then, that if an order did come, it would be necessary to exert "strong influence on specific people," implying the GKChP. "How?" Grachev asked, adding that committee members were not even answering the telephone. Shaposhnikov suggested that Grachev go personally and demand that "these people" revoke the order. And if that did not work, then Shaposhnikov declared that he would launch a pair of aircraft as a warning, and give the "authors" an order, "Listen, if you do not revoke the order in fifteen minutes . . . aircraft will arrive and bomb you." Grachev called it a deal and promised to deliver the bombing threat if necessary.[71]

Somewhat later, Shaposhnikov was besieged with alarmed calls from the White House. He tried to calm the callers down, assuring them that there would be no assault either by airborne or MVD troops. At the same time, Shaposhnikov began contemplating how he would implement the bombing threat if that became necessary. Would helicopters be enough? What would be the political reaction and the practical result? He drafted an order, directing that two aircraft be ready to take off without armaments and fly over the Kremlin at a very low altitude as a warning. When Colonel Aleksandr Tsalko called from the White House, Shaposhnikov asked him to come at once to the headquarters.[72] He had known Tsalko as a pilot in Afghanistan and wanted him to hand-carry his order to the commander of the air forces in the Moscow military district for implementation. (Apparently Shaposhnikov did not trust his own communications, and Antoshin would surely want a written and signed order before taking such an extraordinary action.) After promising to come at once, Tsalko called back later to say that he could not get through the crowds. Burkov also called, describing crowds around the White House as growing, spirited, and able to stand off an assault. Burkov then held the phone in an open window so that Shaposhnikov could hear the crowds chanting their country's name, "Ros-si-ya! Ros-si-ya!"[73] Shaposhnikov scrapped his draft order for launching the aircraft. It was already 4:00 A.M. on 21 August and the dawn had fully broken.

The full impact of Shaposhnikov's actions that night is impossible to determine. But Stepankov, the procurator general, later confirmed that fighter-bomber aircraft were ready and expecting to take off.[74] What Grachev did after promising to deliver the threat is not known. The next scene for Shaposhnikov was the MoD military collegium at 9:00 A.M.

Meetings of the collegium had a fairly standard format, Shaposhnikov explains: first a report, next a speech setting an endorsing tone, then some "venting of steam" by a few deputies who did not like the report, followed by a concluding speech approving the initial report. It was, in his view, an empty ritual left over from Stalin's day. Officers spoke in order of seniority of rank. Shaposhnikov intended to break that rule and speak first, but Moiseev grabbed the floor, reporting on the status of regional commands until Yazov cut him off. Ignoring Yazov's nod to Shaposhnikov, General Kochetov seized the floor, talking about how the army had to reestablish itself with Gorbachev and regain his support. Yazov soon forced him to sit down in favor of "younger people," again motioning to Shaposhnikov. At last allowed to speak, he repeated what he told Yazov in his office the day before, only elaborating each point more fully. Yazov had to quit the GKChP at once and all his decisions had to be reported immediately to the media. Several other deputy ministers then spoke. Most endorsed Shaposhnikov's proposals, and General Maksimov, the commander of the rocket forces, and Admiral Chernavin, commander of the navy, did so emphatically. Yazov then took the floor, agreeing to most of what Shaposhnikov demanded, but he refused to quit the GKChP. He would not betray comrades whose opinions he shared. "That is my cross. I will carry it to the end," the marshal declared.[75] Shaposhnikov interrupted to urge that Yazov close the meeting and issue his orders so that the media would have them before the meeting of the Russian Supreme Soviet at 11:00 A.M. Yazov agreed, and the collegium adjourned. Unknown to Shaposhnikov at the time, Yazov headed back to the GKChP and joined Kryuchkov's group to fly immediately to Foros.

Shaposhnikov's work was not yet over. On television he watched the Russian Supreme Soviet meeting at 11:00 A.M., pleased that Yazov's latest orders were reported and well received by the deputies. Yeltsin spoke, saying it was necessary to send a delegation to Foros after Gorbachev. Shortly after the parliament adjourned, however, Yeltsin called Shaposhnikov to say that a GKChP delegation had flown out ahead of the plane he had sent to bring Gorbachev to Moscow.[76] No one knew where they were headed or what they intended to do. Was it possible, Yeltsin wanted to know, to stop the GKChP aircraft? Although Shaposhnikov said that the only option was to shoot it down, he tried to persuade General Moiseev to divert the plane, which was under the General Staff's control. Moiseev refused, declaring that Kryuchkov knew what he was doing. Shaposhnikov then tried to appeal to Moiseev through his deputy, General Deinekin, because they were General Staff Academy classmates, but Deinekin could not reach him. The GKChP aircraft flew to Foros, and its passengers were arrested, brought back to Moscow, and arrested again upon their arrival at Vnukovo airport at 1:00 A.M. on 22 August.

The story, as told here, is as close to Shaposhnikov's memoir as a summary can be. Did he play the pivotal role in blocking an assault on the White House, as Simon Kordonskii contends?[77] His own story suggests not, as does the procurator's report. Shaposhnikov pictures several other officers, even Yazov, as playing equally important roles. Some, like Admiral Chernavin and General Maksimov, had no chance to influence events directly, but their sympathy with Shaposhnikov's views certainly strengthened his resolve.

Can his story be believed? Although it has a number of factual errors — troop withdrawals from Moscow began several hours before Yazov's late-morning decision to order them on 21 August — it is basically confirmed in the procurator's report. It differs only in some minor details with an interview he gave to *Nezavisimaya gazeta* on 19 September.[78]

Grachev: Hero or Opportunist?

The most mysterious and perhaps the most critical actor in the top military ranks is Pavel Grachev. He has not written an account of his role, and in interviews immediately afterward he was brief and self-serving. Shaposhnikov's encounters with him have already provided a few clues, but they raise even more questions. The account by Lebed' offers more detail, including exposures of Grachev's double game between Yeltsin on the one hand and his MoD superiors on the other; it does not strip away all of the mystery, but a revealing picture emerges.

Grachev's connections with Yeltsin apparently began in February 1991. That is when Yeltsin's assistant Yurii Skokov said that he first met Grachev, after Yeltsin directed him to make contacts with the military.[79] During Yeltsin's presidential campaign in May, Grachev arranged for him to observe an airborne regiment drop by parachute into a training area near Tula. Yeltsin also spoke to the troops, promising to give the regiment five hundred additional apartments if he were elected president of Russia. Abundant vodka was served at lunch, and Grachev, seated next to Yeltsin, became one of his "warmest and sincerest friends," prompting a vintage Lebed' reaction: " 'Merriment in Russia is drinking'—the eternal formula for success." [80]

Grachev did indeed establish a personal relationship with Yeltsin during the spring, and it put him in a dangerous predicament during the crisis. Yeltsin telephoned him directly on the morning of 19 August, asking, "What is going on?" [81] Grachev told him all he knew about Yanaev's taking charge because Gorbachev could not carry out his duties. Yeltsin cursed, called the transfer of power a provocation, and asked Grachev to assign some of his people to guard the White House. Grachev promised that he would. The conversation probably determined all of Grachev's behavior thereafter, and he may have accepted Yeltsin's call before its dangerous implications dawned on him. It would almost certainly have been monitored by the KGB and reported to the GKChP and Yazov, marking Grachev as a Yeltsin supporter from the beginning, a position from which he could not extract himself thereafter.

Meanwhile, Lebed', who was then deputy commander of the airborne forces for training, was on vacation in Tula on 18 August. But he accompanied Colonel A. P. Kolmakov, commander of the Tula airborne division, as he marched his Tula regiment in its combat assault vehicles by road toward Moscow. The two other regiments, one from Ryazan, the other from Kostroma, also moved by road to the airborne headquarters in Tushino, fifteen to twenty kilometers northwest of central Moscow (see map 7). By 10:30 A.M. the Tula regiment had reached the Moscow outer ring road, and by noon it arrived at Tushino. There Lebed' received a call from Grachev's chief of staff, Lieutenant General Ye. A. Podkolzin, who directed him to go personally to the Russian parliament building, make contact with its security chief, and "organize the security and defense of the building" with the 2d battalion of the Ryazan regiment. [82] Lebed' asked for clarification—where was the 2d battalion and what communications could he use? Podkolzin told him to take no communications, to go in his "UAZ-chik" (as the Jeeplike military vehicle produced by the UAZ truck plant was called—pronounced Wazchik), and to expect the battalion to be approaching the parliament building at any time. Lebed' took with him a lieutenant colonel, a political officer, and departed just before 2:00 P.M. Arriving at the building, he had trouble finding the chief of security and was told by a suspicious police colonel that he ought to leave. He was first allowed to use the telephone to call Grachev and report his predicament. Grachev was angry, ordering him to go find the battalion. Lebed' set out to do that, passing with difficulty through the growing crowd and rising barricades.

At that point Lebed' began to wonder against whom was he to defend the building. He insists that he knew nothing yet of the GKChP, or Yeltsin's appeals, or anything else about the political situation. After more problems and a call to Podkolzin, asking where the battalion was located, he found it about three hundred meters southeast of the building. Its officers and troops were confused about the situation. Lebed' climbed onto a large concrete block so he could address all the assembled officers and troops. He briefly stated their mission and warned them to avoid all conflicts with the surrounding crowds. Then he asked the crowd of onlookers to go the White House and get a representative to come and clarify the situation. A veteran airborne officer immediately emerged from the crowd to introduce himself, offering his telephone in his nearby apartment to Lebed'. He accepted the offer, called the airborne headquarters, and received orders to settle the battalion for the night where it stood. Returning to the battalion, Lebed' found a delegation of five persons from the White House waiting for him. They took him to Skokov's office on the fourth floor of the White House, where he was shortly introduced to Yeltsin.

Yeltsin asked why he was there. "To organize the security and defense of the Supreme Soviet building with the forces of an airborne battalion," Lebed' answered.

"According to whose order?" Yeltsin asked.

"Commander of the airborne forces, Lieutenant General Grachev."

"To secure and defend against whom?" Yeltsin inquired.

Not knowing the answer, he gambled on an ambiguous reply, "Against whom does a guard post defend? Against any person or group of persons who encroach on the post or the sentry." This satisfied Yeltsin. He then expressed concern for Gorbachev's fate and asked about the mood of the troops commanded by Lebed'. The general said that his men knew nothing about what was going on, so they had no mood for or against anybody. Yeltsin was not pleased with this answer but he said that he trusted Lebed' and Grachev and that the battalion should be moved in at once.[83]

Getting the battalion through the crowd proved difficult. Colonel Tsalko, recognizing Lebed' as he departed through the barricades, approached him but was seized by a bodyguard assigned by Yeltsin's security chief and thrown into the crowd.[84] Tsalko began screaming to the crowd, "Provocation! Provocation!" and pointing to Lebed'. The bodyguards could not calm the excited crowd and had to take Lebed' back into the White House to work out another plan. Eventually, Lebed' was allowed to lead the battalion inside the barricades, where it deployed on the four corners of the building and settled down for the night. Lebed' had delivered, belatedly, what Grachev had promised Yeltsin much earlier that day.

Lebed' spent the remainder of the night with the Tula division commander, Kolmakov, checking other airborne deployments at Dynamo Stadium and Ostankino, arriving back at Tushino at 5:30 A.M. on the twentieth. Grachev called Lebed' at 5:50 A.M., asking where he had taken the battalion. Lebed' was perplexed. "What do you mean, where? To the Supreme Soviet building according to your order!" Grachev snapped back that Lebed' had not understood him correctly. Lebed' became angry, telling Grachev that his every order and instruction had been entered into the unit "journal record of combat operations" by three clerks. General Rodionov's experience in Tbilisi and his own in Baku had taught Lebed' to use this journal with three witnesses for every entry as protection against later attempts to deny the facts and make him a scapegoat. Grachev understood instantly and changed his approach. "Don't get mad," he said. "You spread stupidity all over the place. The chief is displeased." "What chief?" Lebed' demanded to know. "The minister," Grachev replied, adding, "Remember, you committed a stupidity. The chief is displeased. Go get the battalion and bring it out."[85]

Only then did Lebed' realize how Grachev was using him. Or so he insists. In Skokov's office in the White House he had learned about the GKChP membership with astonishment, thinking, "How can these people seize power? They were already the embodiment of authority!"[86] Angry though he claims he was at realizing that he was Grachev's "puppet," and without sleep for more than twenty-four hours, he set off for the White House. Arriving there about 8:00 A.M., he found the battalion eating breakfast and getting on famously with the civilian defenders. He ordered it into a march column, and by 11:00 A.M. it was moving away from the city's center on Leningradskii Prospekt toward Tushino.

Lebed' remained behind, trying to find his UAZ-chik outside the White House barricades. It had disappeared. A "testy, nasty, angry" group of journalists had gathered around him, asking why the battalion had departed. Suddenly an officer appeared to tell him that he was to report to General Staff by 1:45 P.M. Breaking away from this unwanted press conference, he found his UAZ-chik, raced to catch the battalion, gave it instructions, and then went to the General Staff building (see map 8).[87]

Grachev caught him as he arrived for a very brief and whispered exchange in Achalov's reception room. "Are you ready?"

"Ready for what?" asked Lebed'.

"Contain yourself!" Grachev warned as two aides approached and took Lebed' immediately to see Yazov.

Yazov simply stared at Lebed' in silence for a time, at last saying, "They told me you shot yourself."

"I do not see the grounds for that, comrade minister," Lebed' replied. Yazov then flew into a rage, using the foulest language to characterize the "intellects" of those who had given him that information. He dismissed Lebed', who walked off in puzzlement to Achalov's office. Later he learned that the media had reported on 19 August that Lebed' had deserted to Yeltsin, then the next day that he had committed suicide, and finally, on the twenty-first that he was a hostage in the White House.[88]

Returned to Achalov's office, he found himself in the planning meeting previously described. Soon after, he drafted his assault plan, went with Achalov to see Gromov at the MVD headquarters, and finally was allowed to return to Tushino before midnight, recounting everything to Grachev.

To Lebed', the world about him had become absurd. Generals he had known for years were behaving entirely out of character. He would have no more of it. He bluntly told Grachev that "the cards have been dealt" but that he was not going to play. "You know I am always ready to carry out any order, but I must understand its sense. I am not going to be manipulated like a puppet and entangled in the capital of the Union in a war I don't understand at all, a civil war." [89]

Grachev again surprised him, speaking in a fatherly tone, saying, "I did not waste my mentoring on you. I always trusted you, and remarkably, I was not wrong. We will do the following: You yourself, personally, go to the Supreme Soviet and find a way to get the word to the defenders that a blockade is feasible, that the storming will begin at 3:00 A.M. Then go to Medvezh'i Ozera and manage the arrival of two regiments of the Bolgrad division" (see map 7).[90]

"Drive to Chkalovsk airfield? Receive the regiments there?" Lebed' asked.

"No, you can manage from the office of the commander of the signal brigade [at Medvezh'i Ozera]," said Grachev.

This instruction did not please Lebed'. Having designed the assault plan, now he was to betray it to the other side. The whole thing was "an idiotic game." But off he drove in his UAZ-chik. To avoid recognition, he pulled off the license plate. He also took a "flexible" approach to his mission, not actually going to the White House but rather approaching it from three directions, chatting with people in the crowd on each approach to find some who seemed reliable, then giving them the warning information and asking them to make sure that it got to Skokov at once. Rather than 3:00 A.M., he gave 2:00 A.M. as the time of the assault. Next he raced to Medvezh'i Ozera. Chaos reigned at the detention center, where "no telling how many KGB officers were detaining . . . four people." In the brigade commander's office at Medvezh'i Ozera, Lebed' got on the telephone with officers at Chkalovsk and Kubinka airfields, soon realizing that the aircraft carrying the Bolgrad division had been directed to the wrong airfields. The division commander landed at Kubinka instead of Chkalovsk, out of position to control his forces. "Behind all of this disorder there was a strong organizational will," he felt compelled to conclude; it could not be purely by chance.[91] Nor was it. Shaposhnikov and his VTA commander, Yefanov, had imposed the confusion through their control of the airlift.

Shortly after midnight, Grachev called, ordering Lebed' to Tushino immediately. Once there he heard that Karpukhin was refusing to allow the Alpha unit to participate. The disposition of the MVD mechanized units was unclear. Grachev told him to call the Dzerzhinskii division command post and find them. The questions from Lebed' confused the duty officer, who said, "Vehicles? What vehicles? All the division vehicles are here; no one has gone anywhere." The Tula airborne units had not moved, and the spetsnaz had vanished. Elated, Grachev was energetic and talkative, but Lebed' gave way to fatigue and fell asleep on an office divan.

Grachev's own brief account is consistent with that of Lebed'.[92] On the evening of 20–21 August, his forces were prepared for the 3:00 A.M. assault, but shortly before midnight, he learned that the GKChP members had gone to sleep. He waited to see whether they would press for the assault. Karpukhin called to report that the Alpha unit would not attack. He called Gromov, who had no enthusiasm for the GKChP, and reported what Karpukhin had said. Gromov then declared that the MVD units would not move.

Grachev's interviewer asked him about Karpukhin's subordinate commanders, who had described Karpukhin as ready to assault and insisted that their own refusal actually stopped the Alpha unit. Grachev explained that Karpukhin was in a difficult position and could not be honest with his subordinates because any hint of his real feelings would have caused his immediate removal. Asked about the reproaches the airborne forces received in the media for leaving the White House, Grachev explained this puzzle as a result of the monitoring of his telephone conversations with Yeltsin. Yazov, he was sure, knew what he was doing, and for that reason the airborne battalion had to pull some "maneuvers" to confuse the minister and others. Yazov kept very quiet through it all, dealing very politely with Grachev. When Yazov ordered the movement of the Bolgrad airborne division to Moscow, Grachev called Shaposhnikov, who agreed to delay it under the pretense of bad flying weather. Yazov put so much pressure on, however, that the planes eventually took off. As they arrived in

Moscow, they were directed to land at the wrong airfields. That kept them from assembling in time for the 3:00 A.M. assault. To add confusion, he also sent one airborne regiment on a long march around the Moscow ring road, ordering it to turn toward Moscow on the Minsk highway and then stop.[93]

Grachev was asked to explain the behavior of one other division, the one located at Vitebsk, which had been transferred to the KGB. Reports were heard that it had also been called into Moscow. Grachev explained that this transfer was resisted by the division, that 150 officers refused to transfer to the KGB. When the GKChP appeared, it encountered hostility in the Vitebsk division, which simply would not move.[94]

Grachev's account better explains his strange reproach to Lebed' on the morning of 20 August and his order to withdraw the battalion from the White House. Grachev believed that he had been caught. Yazov was watching him. If Lebed' had spilled out the instructions that Grachev had given, Yazov might have pointed the finger openly at Grachev. If Yazov had transcripts of the Grachev-Lebed' telephone conversations on 19 and 20 August, he probably realized that Lebed' was confused and had not chosen Yeltsin's side.

Although Grachev is not clear that the GKChP gave an order to execute the assault, he speaks as though it did. Learning that its members had gone to sleep, he felt free to delay, waiting to see whether they would call and demand action. He makes no mention of Achalov passing Yazov's instruction around 1:00 A.M. to stop the operation—understandably so, because that would have given Yazov credit and lessened Grachev's own for stopping it. He also straddles the question of whether Karpukhin or his commanders stopped the Alpha unit.

All in all, Grachev tells a story that explains much of what happened and gives himself enormous credit for the outcome, but is he to be trusted? Lebed' wrote his account in 1995, at a time when he was openly hostile toward Grachev. He could have contradicted Grachev's September 1991 interview. Yet he does not, though he treats Grachev as having played a despicable double game. His testimony substantially confirms most of what Grachev has said publicly. Moreover, Grachev admits that he betrayed Yazov and the GKChP.

Was Grachev a hero or an opportunist? A very unattractive picture of Grachev emerges, not just from Lebed'. Shaposhnikov treats him gently but gives glimpses of his unsteadiness and his volatility. Moreover, if Yazov actually called off the assault, then the importance of Grachev's actions is somewhat diminished. From Yeltsin's viewpoint, Grachev was giving him heroic assistance. But to Lebed', Grachev was a duplicitous opportunist. Grachev may have answered impetuously, without thinking, when Yeltsin telephoned for help on the morning of 19 August. Belatedly realizing that his promise to send troops to defend the White House would be known to the KGB and Yazov, he was entrapped. He could never regain Yazov's confidence, and if the GKChP succeeded, he was finished. Cornered, he fought for his life, which meant fighting just as hard for Yeltsin's life. This, of course, is speculation, but it is consistent with the reports of Grachev's erratic mood, his disheveled appearance in the General Staff on 20 August, and his relentless exploitation of Lebed'.

Lebed': Puppet or Accomplice?

Lebed' makes himself look neutral throughout, standing above all the petty struggling among ambitious and frightened people, but according to Yeltsin's account, when Lebed' appeared at the White House, he advised Yeltsin to make himself commander of all military forces on Russian territory so that officers and soldiers would not be violating their oath in responding to his instructions. Yeltsin thanked him for the advice and followed it the next day, giving himself this new title.[95] Lebed' makes no mention of this.

Among the many vignettes that Lebed' relates, perhaps the most astounding is Achalov's invitation for him to draft an assault plan. At face value it seems incredible, either fiction or irresponsibility, but the procurator's report largely corroborates it.[96] When the context of their behavior is considered, however — the confusion, hesitation, and effort to dodge responsibility that characterized the GKChP and those around it — a dilatory pretense of following orders is not surprising in the senior military ranks. In this respect, Lebed' conveys a convincing picture.

His paranoia, however, leads him to flights of literary fancy. He explains the "theater of the absurd" in which he found himself as the creation of a "strong organizational will." But whose? U.S. President George Bush's! Everything was a huge "provocation" by Bush because Gorbachev had served his purpose. "He was expended material. By this time Bush was able to clarify to him that the architect of perestroika was he, Bush, and M. S. Gorbachev was only his slave."[97] Such a conspiracy theory reveals a sense of denial that was probably widely shared among the senior military officers as their world disintegrated before their eyes.

Yazov: Dunce or Tragic Figure?

By midyear 1998, the defense minister has left no personal account. All that is known of his role is from the procurator's report and the various testimonials about specific and short episodes. Shaposhnikov paints him as a tragic figure, intellectually and emotionally incapable of coping with the changing Soviet society, even unable to bring discipline to the ranks and eradicate the hazing and brutality among the troops. The portrait is consistent with the procurator's report. He seemed that way on the morning of 21 August at the military collegium, refusing to betray his GKChP colleagues but at the same time admitting that they had done the country great harm, affecting a redeeming nobility by accepting his fate instead of trying to worm out of it like General Kochetov, who demanded that the military try to ingratiate itself with Gorbachev on his return from Foros. Yeltsin tells of speaking on the telephone with Yazov during the crisis, finding him gloomy and depressed. Later Yeltsin learned that Yazov's wife, recently in an automobile accident, was so upset by the GKChP that she came to his office and rebuked him, saying, "Dima, who are these people you've gotten mixed up with here? Didn't you used to laugh at them? Call Gorbachev!"[98]

On the other hand, Yazov showed more determination to use force than did most of the GKChP members, even if that meant spilling blood. He truly wanted to reverse perestroika, and once the GKChP began scheming, he showed no hesitation to go forward and was frustrated with those who vacillated. At the same time, he strangely handicapped himself by excluding the General Staff from the planning and execution of the assault on the White House. Perhaps he feared that he could not trust more than a few of its officers, but more likely, based on his testimony in the procurator's report, he never believed that an operation like storming the White House would be required. In his words, "The unfortunate thing is that I didn't realize what had happened in the country, that we had different people already, and a lot of those people didn't share my political views, having their own views on everything. That was my mistake."[99]

Could he have acted in a way during the crisis that would have changed its outcome? Conceivably. Grachev believed that he was aware on 19 August that Shaposhnikov and Grachev were actively aiding Yeltsin. If he had relieved them at once, arrested and imprisoned them, perhaps even had them summarily tried and executed, would their replacements have continued to support Yeltsin? Would Gromov have dragged his feet? Would not Achalov and Moiseev have pushed ahead with storming the White House, bloody though it would have been? Yazov had options but did not make the choices that would most likely have galvanized action against the White House—unless KGB officers could no longer be found who were willing to arrest and shoot senior officials when so directed. If there were none, then the GKChP had virtually no chance of success.

The Military in the White House

That the military actually participated in the defense of the White House had less direct consequence than did its role in the MoD and the General Staff. Still, it contributed to the optimistic mood of the thousands of civilian defenders, inside and outside the barricades. Afghan veterans helped organize the defense on the streets. Field-grade officers like Tsalko and Burkov provided communications with the MoD and the General Staff. Burkov in particular seems to have had a catalyzing impact on Shaposhnikov. Generals were also present there.

Colonel General Konstantin Kobets publicly sided with Yeltsin in January 1991. In August he was at Yeltsin's side from early Monday morning at his dacha and throughout the three days at the White House. Yeltsin's ex-KGB security chief, Major General A. S. Korzhakov, was also there. So, too, was recently promoted Major General Aleksandr Rutskoi, Yeltsin's vice president. Kobets's rank, however, was a signal to the media and others about the lack of unity in the senior military. Furthermore, Kobets was an imposing figure, enormously thickset, with a strong voice and an authoritative manner.[100] His presence was clearly an asset for keeping up the morale and confidence among Yeltsin's supporters during the two nights of siege.

Can Kobets or any other officers in the White House be said to have played a critical role? In three ways the answer is yes. First, he and Sobchak were instrumental in getting Yeltsin and his ministers to stop dawdling at his dacha on the morning of 19 August and to make a break for the White House. Second, Kobets, Burkov, Tsalko, and probably a number of other field-grade officers seem to have been instrumental in opening and expanding the lines of communications with senior officers in the MoD and the General Staff. Third, this small group of officers helped create the appearance of an effective defense of the White House more quickly than otherwise would have been the case.

Their role was therefore important more for its contribution to the determined mood in the White House and the wavering convictions in the GKChP, KGB, MVD, and MoD than for any objective military capability. Lebed' was right when he scorned the claims of Russian parliamentary deputies that the White House's defenses could have withstood an attack. (In October 1993, two or three tanks firing at the building broke the defense of the barricaded parliament very quickly.) At the same time, that misguided faith is in itself evidence of the subjective contribution made by the military officers in the White House.

Why Did the Military Not Attempt a Coup?

Rumors of a military coup were rife from March through September 1990.[101] Some Western observers were convinced at the time that if Ligachev and others could not stop Gorbachev, then the generals would take power themselves and revoke perestroika.[102] Furthermore, a number of Western scholars believed that the military was politically quiescent in Soviet politics because it normally received most of what it asked for.[103] When Gorbachev began to deny it a great deal, the same logic suggested that the military would act assertively, causing a "crisis in civil-military relations."[104] If the military had acted a year or so earlier, according to one line of thinking, it would have not yet been afflicted with such mistrust among its senior officers that it could not act effectively. In the event, the idea of a purely military coup was apparently discussed within the MoD.

Lieutenant General Leonid Ivashov, an MPA officer, headed the political organ within the ministry of defense during the tenure of Ustinov, Sokolov, and Yazov. In 1995 I asked him why the generals let Gorbachev dismantle the military so quickly, destroying its superpower status in a half-dozen years, and, more pointedly, why they had not removed him and taken power themselves. "We tried," he responded, "but we had no leader. We begged Yazov to lead a coup, but he always asked, 'What will we do with the power if we take it?'" The idea of a military takeover did not stop there, according to Ivashov. After Yazov refused to lead a coup, discussion of alternatives began. One variant involved initiating it in one military district and then expanding it to others. But as Ivashov lamented, that plan went nowhere.[105]

If Ivashov is to believed, some officers did indeed contemplate a military coup, but by mid-1990 they were too divided and hesitant to act. The irony of all this for most Western theorists on Soviet civil-military relations is that Ivashov was a political officer whose job included preventing precisely what he encouraged, a military takeover. As a desperate communist, he obviously wanted the military to save the Soviet communist system. The generals who were not political officers—but who were equally desperate—wanted a Politburo faction to save the system. That was clear from the strong support that the military delegation gave Ligachev's faction when it tried to remove Gorbachev during the Twenty-eighth Party Congress in 1990. The Politburo conservatives lacked a leader as surely as did the military. Hypocrisy, mistrust, and careerism had crippled both party and the military leadership. Gorbachev's faction was no different in that he had undercut and weakened it as well. Chernyaev recounts Yakovlev's complaints about wavering support, and Cheryaev and Shakhnazarov, ultraloyalists, criticized him for it. They warned him throughout spring 1990 that the liberal intelligentsia was leaving him to join Yeltsin.

Not so conspicuously as with the Moscow intelligentsia, Yeltsin was also attracting some sympathy among the military. Major Lopatin, Colonel Tsalko, and other radical military reformers, of course, moved to Yeltsin's camp with the liberal intelligentsia. Kobets, deputy chief of the General Staff for communications, established an open relationship with Yeltsin in January 1991.[106] In February, Yeltsin began actively seeking more high-level contacts in the military, giving Yurii Skokov the task of finding them.[107] During his election campaign for the Russian presidency, Yeltsin became acquainted with General Grachev. Yeltsin chose the pilot and Afghan war hero Rutskoi as his vice presidential running mate. Yeltsin's political fortitude caused Marshal Shaposhnikov to admit, "The nonparty member Yeltsin turned out to be a very courageous man."[108]

Before the August crisis Yeltsin sought and won more support within the military than is generally realized. He made speeches to military groups, invoking a "Russian army," with only Russian soldiers.[109] He repeatedly blamed Gorbachev for the military's poor public image. The Central Committee records, presumably from KGB phone monitoring, list a surprisingly large number of telephone calls to senior officers during the August crisis, evidence of Yeltsin's success in building military contacts.[110]

Still, these contacts were hardly adequate to make Yeltsin confident that he could succeed in the August showdown. Other than Kobets, no general had publicly sided with Yeltsin's government before August, and the very few inclined to support him had not made up their minds before 19 August. Shaposhnikov entitled his memoirs *Choice* precisely because he realized on the morning of the nineteenth that he had to make up his mind.

Why the military itself did not try to take power should now be clear. Serious military policy issues were intraparty affairs. They did not set the military against the party. Moreover, by 1991 the party was too weak to control the military, as the GKChP discovered, and the military leadership was too corrupt, weak, careerist, and indecisive to act on its own. Most senior officers were either unwilling to take the risk or concerned only with their own careers, always ready to shift to the winning side in the larger political struggle for power. As lifelong communists, most of them behaved like other communists — as opportunists and careerists. The exceptions, like Shaposhnikov and some of the colonels who joined Yeltsin, were rejecting the communist system, not taking sides in a civil-military dispute. This view of August events raises fundamental questions about who the real coup makers were, the GKChP members or Yeltsin.

The Successful Coup

The media, Western and Soviet, pronounced the crisis of 18–21 August in Moscow a failed coup attempt, and scholars have done the same. This is puzzling in light of the outcome. Those accused of attempting to seize power by a coup occupied the most powerful posts in the regime when the crisis began. When it was over, a politician who had held no formal position in the central government had captured sufficient political power to begin the dissolution of the Soviet Union. Yeltsin was the coup maker, a successful one. The contrary view, that the coup failed, makes sense only if:

a) All previous Soviet leadership succession struggles are characterized as a series of coups, some failed, some successful.

b) Gorbachev can be fully absolved of complicity in creating the crisis.

c) The August crisis did not open the door to Yeltsin's seizure of power and subsequent dissolution of the Soviet Union.

If the first premise is accepted, then the August crisis is relegated to "politics as unusual" in the Soviet context, making it seem much less important than it was. The GKChP wanted to change the policies of the regime, not the regime itself. General Lebed' reacted to learning who the GKChP members were by wondering, "What kind of seizure of power could these people make? They were the embodiment of power, the vice president, the prime minister, the ministers of defense, security, and internal affairs!"[111] He grasped the essence of the situation. They wanted to save the regime. That was their quarrel with Gorbachev, not that he held the top position. They wanted him to change his mind, not to leave office, although they were prepared to remove him if he would not cooperate. The Soviet regime had no legal procedure for leadership succession. Every transition from one Soviet leader to the next had been a struggle unrestrained by laws. No one has ever called the Trotsky-Zinoviev-Kamenev "triumvirate" in 1920s a failed coup plot. Nor was the "antiparty group" affair in 1957 called a failed coup. Even Khrushchev's ouster in 1964 was most often called just that, his "ouster." For a faction within the top leadership to try to remove the party leader, therefore, was hardly an illegal act within a party that held itself entirely above the law. One may object that this is purely a distinction in semantics, but semantics can cause misleading historical interpretations.

The second premise goes beyond semantics. Gorbachev's complicity cannot be entirely discounted. His removal from power had long been expected by both Western and Soviet observers. According to Saparmurat Niyazov, a member of the Politburo at the time, a memorandum calling for Gorbachev's removal was circulated on the eve of the Central Committee Plenum in April 1991. When Niyazov asked him whether he had read the memorandum, already distributed to the Central Committee members, Gorbachev said he had not.[112] Thus alerted to it, he quashed this plot by convening the Politburo at once. Because no member would admit to supporting the proposal, it was dropped from the Central Committee agenda. (Niyazov failed to add that he still had a close call at the plenum, threatening to resign and provoking a rally in his favor.[113]) According to Niyazov, as soon as the plenum was over, Ligachev began gathering signatures on a similar memorandum for the next Central Committee Plenum. Niyazov also related that Yeltsin warned Gorbachev at the time of recurrent meetings in the offices of the KGB to plot his removal. Gorbachev replied that he was aware and asked, "And what will happen to you, Boris?" Yeltsin said he did not know but that "something worse would happen to you."[114] Gorbachev knew that his survival depended on remarkable cunning, not just in dealing with the Politburo but also with the national separatist forces. At the same time, when Gorbachev felt compelled to make concessions in negotiating a new union treaty with the republics (at the so-called Novo-Ogarevo process, begun on 22 April 1991), he knew that unless he could evade or considerably reduce their demands, the end of the Soviet state was imminent.

Gorbachev told Chernyaev more than once that he would not tolerate the idea of Lithuanian independence. As Chernyaev warned him, preventing it could mean siding with the worst enemies of perestroika, but he also knew Gorbachev's penchant for being unpredictable to his aides, as well as his skill in misleading his opponents. Boldin, of course, came to despise Gorbachev for his duplicity. Chernyaev and Shakhnazarov complained bitterly to Gorbachev about this on occasions, insisting that they could not do his bidding effectively if they were kept in the dark about his real intentions.[115] Still, Chernyaev insists that the policy results usually justified Gorbachev's cunning and deception — with one exception, the January 1991 crackdown in Lithuanian. Furious at being misled about it, Chernyaev wrote Gorbachev an unforgiving reproach.[116] But Chernyaev rejects insinuations that Gorbachev played a double game during the crisis of 18–21 August.[117] Nonetheless, Chernyaev's memoir reveals a cold, calculating, and brilliantly duplicitous Gorbachev, entirely capable of being behind the GKChP if that would block the republics' demand for autonomy approaching genuine independence. Shakhnazarov stood in awe of his skill in "political maneuver" but insists, not very convincingly, that he began to lose it by 1990.[118]

Other more distant observers saw the same kind of Gorbachev. Several of the members of the GKChP, as the procurator's report makes abundantly clear, were sure that Gorbachev was either already involved or would join them. Belief in his complicity was so strong in much of the testimony that the procurator is at pains to refute it. This picture of a duplicitous Gorbachev was shared beyond senior party circles. The account by General Lebed' of Gorbachev's role in the Tbilisi massacre and the army's intervention in Baku, admittedly based on limited evidence, portrays a man always playing a double game, always keeping a potential scapegoat at hand. And Niyazov's assertion that Gorbachev was playing a "dirty game" in Nagorno-Karabakh, Tbilisi, and Baku corroborates that judgment.

After the GKChP members were arrested, naturally Gorbachev's enemies wanted to implicate him as well. KGB sources certainly spread the impression that Gorbachev was involved. Amy Knight, distinguished for her scholarship on the KGB and its successors, takes this charge very seriously, concluding that the KGB may have been his scapegoat.[119] One might object that she has fallen victim to her excellent KGB sources on this point, but she is not alone in her suspicions. John Dunlop, whose comprehensive treatment of the August events is not likely to be surpassed for a while, also finds too many flaws in Gorbachev's story to absolve him.[120] They are on to something, but they underestimate Gorbachev. If the KGB had irrefutable evidence, it would have revealed it long ago.

A circumstantial case can be made, based on his record of repeated duplicitous tactics, that Gorbachev did intend to scapegoat the GKChP, but KGB post-facto rumor-mongering oversimplifies the matter. Gorbachev reacted negatively to Chernyaev's argument for letting the Baltic states go free, not once but several times. When Shakhnazarov pleaded the same point, Gorbachev flatly rejected the idea, saying, "I can't concede to them [the Lithuanians] . . . that will have to be without me."[121] But as the year went on, Gorbachev was forced to make concessions on the substance of the new union treaty. Yeltsin describes his behavior during the negotiations as struggling to escape the treaty's implications.[122] In other words, Gorbachev was no more enthusiastic about the new union treaty than were the GKChP members—who united, it will be recalled, largely in response to that treaty. Gorbachev did not differ with them on the principle of saving the Soviet Union; rather, he was more sensitive than they to the difficulty that the use of force would cause his relations with the West. He desperately needed a tactic for escaping the new union treaty and for saving his foreign policy at the same time—incompatible goals.

Well aware of the plotting against him over the previous six months, why did he not arrest some of the culprits? Pavlov, backed by Kryuchlov, Yazov, and Pugo, tried to convince the parliament in June to curb Gorbachev's powers. A manifesto, "A Word to the People," appeared in the press in late July, condemning perestroika as "an enormous . . . misfortune" and asking, "Why have crafty and pompous masters, clever and cunning apostates, and greedy and rich money-grubbers, sneering at us . . . seized power?" Its authors appealed to all social groups, proclaiming, "We are starting a national movement."[123] Two of its signatories, Starodubtsev and Tizyakov, became GKChP members. The U.S. ambassador, Jack Matlock, warned Gorbachev on 21 June that a plot was being hatched.[124] Gorbachev could not have missed all these signals. Does this mean that he was part of the conspiracy? Far from it; that would have been foolish. To keep his status in the West after a successful repression, he could not afford to have a surviving witness tie him to the plot.

If his opponents were ready to act, why not let them try to cancel the union treaty and repress the national separatists by force? Gorbachev must have realized that he was giving them an implicit invitation to act by departing for a vacation just before the treaty was to be signed. Leaving the dirty work to these plotters allowed Gorbachev to retain his options. If they succeeded, they would have to turn to him, precisely as Baklanov has suggested to him in Foros on 18 August. The West could not blame Gorbachev for their actions. Thus the plotters would need him to help them avoid the full wrath of the West. Would Western leaders give up the CFE and START treaties and the completion of the withdrawal of Soviet troops from Germany just to protest the reassertion of Soviet power within its own territories if Gorbachev were president? Was this gambit any more risky than ratifying the new union treaty and presiding over the breakup of the Soviet Union—a sure course to political oblivion for Gorbachev?

This reasoning may seem far-fetched, but if Gorbachev understood the implications of the new union treaty, then he also realized that his own political rope was short. In that situation, such reasoning is not so strange. It is vintage Gorbachev tactics. It remains, however, a hypothesis.

Either way, whether the GKChP really was a surprise for Gorbachev or whether he implicitly encouraged its creation, its actions were not really a coup but rather part of a power struggle among the party oligarchs, a periodic episode in Bolshevik politics even in Lenin's time and before his seizure of power.

One faction wanted to reverse perestroika; the other had to continue it to keep power. Moreover, Gorbachev was clearly disturbed about political trends. Yeltsin describes him as "sick of perestroika" by the winter of 1991.[125] But he was not sick of the West's fawning attention.[126] The leadership was in crisis, as one faction plotted to reverse the party's course, but it could hardly be called a coup.

The third premise, discounting Yeltsin's role, simply cannot stand scrutiny. Gorbachev and the GPChK unintentionally allowed Yeltsin to make a successful coup. The military could have blocked him, but it did not. Arresting the GKChP gave Yeltsin de facto political power. Rescuing Gorbachev and returning him to formal authority confronted Yeltsin with an awkward situation. The ever-inventive Yeltsin finally abolished Gorbachev's post by dissolving the Soviet Union, thereby eliminating the awkward formality. Again, the military could have blocked Yeltsin in November and December, but it did not act. By late August, Yeltsin held the real power, and by late December he had made it formal. The coup was complete.

Theorizing about the sources of the regime's stability, Shakhnazarov says there were two, "coercion and deceit," and that a wise dictator preferred more deceit and less coercion because it was a cheaper mix.[127] The August crisis revealed how much deceit had been eroded without a compensating increase in coercion. Moreover, the dictator no longer monopolized deceit. As it diffused in the top ranks of the army and the KGB, the regime's capacity to coerce evaporated. Neither KGB leaders nor generals could impose adequate corporate cohesion to spill blood. In August they had to choose sides as individuals because the illusions traditionally provided by the dictator's deceit no longer offered corporate refuge. The careerism and hypocrisy instilled by that refuge in the past now paralyzed most of them. Rather than act to save the system, they waited and watched, seeking to join the winning side. Although their individual accounts may intentionally distort the events, they inexorably yield a reliable picture of the consequences of their equivocating behavior.

Some of the few who did not equivocate chose Yeltsin's side. Others, who sided with the GKChP, could not find loyal subordinates to spill blood. Was the outcome, therefore, predetermined? One does not have to be a historical determinist to answer in the affirmative. Leaders' choices are constrained by social and structural realities, and it can be argued that by August 1991 they were such that no leader could have reversed perestroika. But was it too late? Exploring all the "might have beens" in the August crisis will fill many future history books, but one such speculative scenario seems to suggests itself above all others. What if Kryuchkov had ordered Yeltsin's detention in the early morning hours at Arkhangel'skoe? No defense of the White House would have been staged, at least not one with the strength that Yeltsin brought to it.

Perhaps some other rally point would have been created, perhaps several smaller ones. If one believes that the erosion of "coercion and deceit" had reached an irreversible stage by August, then various kinds of resistance would have succeeded without Yeltsin. Perhaps the crisis would have degenerated into civil war, as it did in 1918, but this seems doubtful. Psychological and moral disillusionment in the military's ranks make it difficult to see how two or more sides in a civil war could have maintained adequate discipline to sustain a conflict beyond an occasional bloody disorder. There were no new young "Bolsheviks" to organize and supply an army. And there were no old generals who could pull together remnants of the Soviet army and find foreign governments to support and supply them, as commanders of the White armies did in 1918–20.

But there is an instructive resemblance between the crisis of August 1991 and the Kornilov affair of August 1917. The head of the provisional government, Alexander Kerensky, fell into a misunderstanding with General Lavr Kornilov that prompted the general to move against the provisional government with the army. Kerensky initially invited Kornilov to provide support against the radical political forces in St. Petersburg, but then he became frightened of the conservative forces that might rally around Kornilov, declaring to his cabinet, "I will not give them the revolution."[128] His only way out was to ask leftist leaders in the Petrograd Soviet to defeat Kornilov's forces. They rose to the occasion, especially the Bolshevik military organization, confronted Kornilov's arriving troops, and caused them to melt away. That led to Trotsky's release from prison, allowing him to begin planning for the Bolshevik coup in November (October by the Julian calendar then in use in Russia).

Gorbachev's ever ambiguous and scheming behavior produced a similar misunderstanding between him and the conservatives in the party and the military, convincing at least some of them that he wanted them to save the union from the democratic and nationalist political forces. When they acted, however, he—like Kerensky when Kornilov acted—refused to join them to save the union. The democrats and nationalist-separatists (not just in the RSFSR but also in Ukraine) resisted and rescued Gorbachev—just as the Bolsheviks and other leftists rescued Kerensky. That opened the door to Yeltsin and his supporters, and by the end of December, their coup was complete.

FIFTEEN

Illusions of Another Chance

You, the military, take power into your own hands, install a government of your own liking, stabilize the situation, and then step aside.

GORBACHEV TO MARSHAL SHAPOSHNIKOV

The Soviet military would last only four more months. Its commands, staffs, formations, and other components would endure several months longer in an ambiguous status, but the Soviet military formally ceased to exist at the end of the last hour of the last day of 1991. On the first day of 1992, it was stateless, sure neither of its name nor to what political authority it owed allegiance. But in the days and weeks after the August crisis its leaders showed no awareness of its imminent demise.

Two parallel processes characterized life in the MoD and the General Staff during this brief interlude. The first was the change of personnel necessitated by the August crisis. The senior officers most closely allied with the GKChP were purged, and many more were supposed to be but avoided outright dismissal or forced retirement. The second was military reform. Troop withdrawals from Eastern Europe, budget reductions, the conscription revolt, and general deterioration of discipline and order in most military units desperately needed to be addressed. The deadlock between the radical military reformers and the generals had thus far prevented effective attention to this accumulating backlog of problems, but now there seemed to be a chance to address them.

Yeltsin's victory over the GKChP inspired new hope among the radical military reformers. They saw fall 1991 as an exceptional opportunity to sweep out the conservative senior officers and to replace them with strong proponents of systemic change. Success in the selection of new senior military officials was the precondition for effective military reform. Both, however, depended on changes in the political leadership and the resolution of the political stalemate that had produced the August crisis in the first place. The final act in this

347

stormy drama, therefore, was the playing out of all three processes: *a*) resolving the political struggle; *b*) purging the pro-GKChP personnel in the MoD; and *c*) implementing military reform.

Resolving the Post-August Political Stalemate

Since spring 1990, Yeltsin had been struggling to undermine Gorbachev's political position but not to take his place. Yeltsin had left the party, warning that if it tried to reverse perestroika, he would mobilize popular action to take away all the party's properties and privileges, and thereafter he took numerous measures to curb its powers in the RSFSR. During spring 1991, in the Novo-Ogarevo negotiation process, Yeltsin and the other heads of union republics chipped away at the powers of the Soviet state until the new union treaty left it largely a shell. It took more than a little pretense by all the participants at Novo-Ogarevo to deny that they were destroying the Soviet Union. Yet they pretended.

On 19 August, Yeltsin expected to be arrested. Three days later he arrested the GKChP. This extraordinary transition from outlaw to jailer was dizzying. Gorbachev held formal authority, but the power belonged entirely to Yeltsin. Yet both tried to act as if this had not happened.

Initially neither Gorbachev nor Yeltsin and his aides appeared to grasp the full dimensions of what had happened. Yeltsin's people fell into factional disputes among themselves and with the RSFSR parliament over reform issues in Russia alone.[1] Yeltsin insists that he remained committed to the new union treaty process, not set on the union's dissolution. When negotiations in Novo-Ogarevo were resumed in October, Yeltsin recounts, Gorbachev made many concessions that he would not consider earlier, but he insisted on retaining a strong center able to "determine matters of defense and some fiscal issues. A single president would remain to serve as guarantor for compliance with the treaty; he would also represent the Union of Sovereign States in dealing with other countries. The post of prime minister was retained in the central government, and a bicameral parliament would be convened in Moscow."[2] None of the republics found these points acceptable, Yeltsin reports, and one after another they began to drop out of the process, first the Baltic republics and then Georgia, Armenia, and Azerbaijan. Yeltsin naturally puts the blame on Gorbachev, suggesting that if he had been reasonable, agreement on a treaty would have been reached and a loose union preserved.

Yeltsin took a public stance in favor of saving the empire in the first couple of months after the August crisis, calling it a Union of Sovereign States which would preserve a common economic space, maintain the Soviet Union's military, create a commonwealth of sovereign states, and guarantee human rights over the whole of the Soviet territory.[3] Yet he fails to explain how this would be acceptable to the other republics if Gorbachev's concept was not. Moreover, Yeltsin's officials in the RSFSR government were rapidly stripping away the powers of the Soviet government, leaving it without the means to execute the very responsibilities his own conception assigned to the union center. In late September he said that the center would be allowed to keep only "defense, atomic energy, and railroads," hardly adequate for a "common economic space" and bound to bring clashes over defense policy.[4] On one point, however, Yeltsin left no ambiguity: he would not permit the center to retain enough power for Gorbachev to stage a comeback. Both Yeltsin's many statements and his government's plundering of the center's bureaucracies make clear that Gorbachev was not to be left with more than figurehead status.

Their struggle came to a head on 25 November in the Novo-Ogarevo negotiations. Just before the opening session, Gorbachev told the press that the heads of the republics had come to initial the treaty. Yeltsin was astounded. The treaty was not ready, and Ukrainian President Leonid Kravchuk and the Azeri leader, Ayaz Mutalibov, were not even present. Gorbachev's ploy merely angered the heads of the republics, prompting them to demand major changes in the treaty that shifted virtually all powers to the republics. Gorbachev refused to yield, lost his patience, and ran out of the room. At that point, Yeltsin declared, "We suddenly realized that it was over: we were meeting here for the last time."[5] At the end of the session, all the republican leaders refused to meet the waiting crowd of journalists, leaving Gorbachev to face them alone, but rather than admit what happened, he tried to sound optimistic, announcing that the meeting had been a success and that he hoped the treaty would be signed on 20 December.

Within a week, on 1 December, Ukraine voted in a referendum in favor of complete independence. This event, according to Yeltsin, left no public doubt about what had happened at the last Novo-Ogarevo meeting. "We had to find another way."[6] They found it at Belovezhskaya pushcha near Minsk, where Yeltsin, Kravchuk, and Stanislav Shushkevich, the chairman of the Belorussian Supreme Soviet, met secretly on 7–8 December and worked out the agreement to form the Commonwealth of Independent States (CIS), including Russia, Ukraine, and Belarus. The terms of the agreement were hastily drafted during a long night of debate and drinking, and not surprisingly, they were loosely defined on important issues, especially concerning the status of the Soviet military. On the morning of 8 December, Yeltsin called Marshal Shaposhnikov, the defense minister, to get his reaction to the agreement, having neglected to consult him in advance.[7] Shaposhnikov first inquired whether other republics could join, and Yeltsin said that they could. Shaposhnikov next asked Yeltsin to read specifically what the text stated about the armed forces. Yeltsin obliged, reading the paragraph that established the strategic forces under a single command. Then Shaposhnikov asked how Nursultan Nazarbayev, the head of Kazakhstan, felt about the agreement; Nazarbayev had great political authority within the Soviet Union, and a large segment of the strategic rocket forces were in Kazakhstan. Yeltsin replied that in a preliminary discussion Nazarbayev had reacted favorably. Shaposhnikov accepted this answer but had the impression—accurate, in fact—that Yeltsin had not kept Nazarbayev fully informed. Finally, Shaposhnikov asked whether the agreement said anything about conventional forces. Yeltsin admitted that it did not because differences of opinion were too great to allow quick settlement of the matter; he, though, firmly supported a unified command for conventional forces as well. The conversation continued for about twenty minutes or so, during which Shaposhnikov began to realize that a "new epoch" was opening. He posed no objections to Yeltsin and, instead, looked at the CIS as a possible solution for many of the problems he had been having with republican leaders over the previous two months. The Russian parliament ratified the CIS agreement on 12 December. Thereafter, events continued to move swiftly.

Nazarbayev was upset that he and the other Central Asian republics had neither been included nor seriously consulted. Knowing that Nazarbayev was arriving in Moscow to meet Gorbachev on 8 December, Yeltsin phoned him, urging him to come straight to Belovezhskaya pushcha instead, but Nazarbayev refused. He was afraid of being politically separated from the other Central Asian republics, and to avoid that, he arranged for the five Muslim republics to hold their own meeting on 13 December in Ashabad, the capital of Turkmenistan. There they announced their own commonwealth. Yeltsin had to scramble for a compromise, so he persuaded Nazarbayev to convene a meeting of the heads of eleven republics (the Baltic republics and Georgia refused to attend) on 21 December in Alma-Ata, where an enlarged CIS was agreed on, one open to all republics that wished to join.[8] The agreement took effect at midnight, 1 January 1992, and the Soviet Union ceased to be.

Marshal Shaposhnikov, reflecting on these events, argues that Gorbachev should have convened the Congress of People's Deputies immediately after his return from Foros and addressed it with a "self-critical analysis of both the situation in the country and his own personal performance," candidly confessing to his own failings.[9] Then he should have announced his resignation on the

Table 5   Dates of Republics' Declarations of Independence

Lithuania	11 March 1990
Latvia	4 May 1990
Georgia	9 April 1991
Estonia	20 August 1991
Ukraine	24 August 1991
Belarus	27 August 1991
Moldova	27 August 1991
Azerbaijan	30 August 1991
Uzbekistan	31 August 1991
Kyrgyzstan	31 August 1991
Tajikistan	9 September 1991
Armenia	23 September 1991
Turkmenistan	27 October 1991
Kazakhstan	16 December 1991
RSFSR (Russia)	Never formally declared

Source: Shaposhnikov, *Vybor* (1995), 138–39.

spot and proposed that the congress make Yeltsin president for three months while an election was prepared to choose Gorbachev's successor. Shaposhnikov admits that Yeltsin might have been reluctant to accept the presidency temporarily but believes that he could have been persuaded. Moreover, Shaposhnikov rightly observes that this exodus for Gorbachev would have preserved his dignity in a way that the actual events did not. The intriguing aspect of this scenario, of course, is that it would have harnessed Yeltsin's considerable political skills to preserving the union. Whether he could have struck a deal with the other heads of republics is a question Shaposhnikov does not try to answer, but it seems doubtful, given the momentum of the independence movement at the end of August.

Although several republics had previously asserted their "sovereignty," they had not declared a full and formal secession from the Soviet Union. Now they used the word *independence* to signify complete secession. Lithuania and Latvia had done so much earlier, in the spring of 1990, and Georgia followed suit in April 1991. Then in late August a deluge of declarations occurred followed by a trickle in the fall. The precise sequence is shown in table 5.

Conceivably Gorbachev could have convened the Congress of People's Deputies on 22 or 23 August, although even by then, four republics were on the record as declaring full independence of the Soviet Union. Gorbachev, of course, had not the slightest intention of yielding power voluntarily when he returned to Moscow. No doubt he would have flatly rejected such a scheme if it had been proposed to him, and that is the point of this speculation. By resigning and turning over his position to Yeltsin he certainly would have changed the course of events, but Gorbachev insisted on a fight he could not win and ensured that Yeltsin would oppose him. No matter what each claimed about trying to save the Soviet Union, neither was prepared to put its survival above his own personal ambitions. The final round of their four-year fight would end in a knockout blow against both Gorbachev and the Soviet Union.

Gorbachev at first tried to retain his power to make new appointments to replace the GKChP members and their supporters, but Yeltsin stepped in and reversed his decisions.[10] Yeltsin also compelled him to cooperate in persuading the Congress of People's Deputies to disband itself.[11] Gorbachev appealed to the remnants of the Communist Party, asserting his unwavering belief in Leninism, but the party was in no condition to help him. Immediately after the August crisis, Yeltsin's investigators rummaged through the party's files in the secretariat offices to gather evidence against the GKChP and its supporters, discovering in the process that the party had been egregiously misusing financial resources. Making this information public, Yeltsin's people branded the party as a criminal organization.[12] On the eve of the anniversary of the Bolshevik revolution, 6 November, Yeltsin decreed the Communist Party illegal on Russian soil although he did not aggressively enforce the edict.

All these actions were undermining Gorbachev's residual party political base at the same time that the RSFSR government was breaking up his presidential power base by colonizing parts of the Soviet executive branch and weakening others.[13] Gorbachev's reaffirmation of his commitment to Leninism and socialism surprised many observers at the time, but given his political predicament, falling back on the party, the military, and the police was his only hope. Clearly that is why he defended socialism and the continued existence of the party and why he tried to avoid a thoroughgoing purge of all the senior officials who had either supported the GKChP or failed to act against it. These were the only people who still opposed Yeltsin. Although playing a losing hand, Gorbachev acted with the same kind of assertive confidence and duplicity he had employed over the previous six years.

Dunlop argues that as Gorbachev's situation worsened in November, he began to encourage a conspiracy in the MoD and the KGB to seize power. Getting wind of it, Yeltsin reacted swiftly with Kravchuk and Shushkevich in early December to create the CIS, a step that dissolved Gorbachev's formal authority; he also decreed a pay raise for the military in an effort to cool its enthusiasm for a conspiracy.[14] Much of Dunlop's case is necessarily circumstantial, though he can point out that Sergei Belozertsev declared publicly in early December that a conspiracy was being planned. Whether or not the fiasco Gorbachev suffered at the Novo-Ogarevo meeting on 25 November was related to the conspiracy planning Dunlop does not say, but the timing suggests that it could have been used by the conspirators to justify their actions. The results of the Ukrainian referendum on 1 December certainly made a military takeover all the more urgent if that was the plan for saving the union. Alerted to the urgency of the situation, Yeltsin countered swiftly with the secret meeting at Belovezhskaya pushcha a week later. Dunlop reasons that Gorbachev was behind this "putsch" attempt because Kravchuk publicly accused him of dangerous steps toward bringing "nation against nation" and attempting to reestablish a "totalitarian state."[15] As evidence that Kravchuk was not entirely exaggerating, Dunlop points to the 10–11 December assembly of officers convened in Moscow at Gorbachev's request, apparently to rally the military leadership behind him in saving the union. Indeed, Gorbachev spoke to the meeting, making that case, but he met only expressions of scorn from the officers. When Yeltsin spoke to the assembly the next day, having promised a pay raise and now presenting his case for the CIS, he won them over, hijacking Gorbachev's last hope of escaping his political demise.

As compelling as it is, this hypothesis will probably remain inconclusive for lack of direct evidence, both of the actual conspiracy planning and Gorbachev's connection to it. There is, however, direct testimony that Gorbachev wanted the military to seize power, to prevent the union's breakup, and then to yield power. Shaposhnikov describes being suddenly called to the Kremlin one evening in early November. On arrival, Gorbachev met him alone, treating him with a politeness and warmth uncharacteristic of their previous meetings. After light conversation about family and personal matters calculated to put Shaposhnikov at ease, Gorbachev turned to his point of business. The union was approaching a breakup; all his efforts to prevent it had yielded no results; and it was necessary "to do something." This phrase caused Shaposhnikov to recall how many times over the past two months he had urged Gorbachev "to do something." It had been necessary "to do something" ever since 1985. Waking up to that reality at this late date struck Shaposhnikov as little short of absurd in light of all the republics that had already declared independence. Gorbachev continued, saying that he and Shaposhnikov had to consider all the "variants for escaping the crisis." The best of the variants, in his view, came to the following:

"You, the military, take power into your own hands, install a government of your own liking, stabilize the situation, and then step aside."

"And straight to prison *(Matrosskuyu tishiny)*, perhaps with a song," responded Shaposhnikov, adding, "Well, wasn't there something like that in August?"

"What do you mean, Zhenya," said Gorbachev, "I'm not proposing anything to you, I am simply outlining the variants, thinking aloud."

The mood cooled at once, and Shaposhnikov shortly departed. Some weeks later one of Gorbachev's aides told Shaposhnikov that Gorbachev had recently said of him, "He is not a bad man, but too intelligent for the post he occupies."[16]

This account, of course, cannot be confirmed by anyone but Gorbachev, who is hardly going to do so. Shaposhnikov omitted it from the first edition of his memoirs, and he told me that although he did not want to embarrass Gorbachev, he was induced by his editors to include it in the second edition. The story must be treated with caution but not dismissed because among the memoir literature Shaposhnikov's autobiography is reasonably accurate in the facts it presents. It is consistent with Dunlop's inference that Gorbachev was well disposed toward a military-KGB takeover. It also fits Dunlop's conclusion that a clique of officers, including the chief of the General Staff, General Vladimir Lobov, was attempting to overthrow Shaposhnikov by seeking to have the General Staff separated from the MoD and subordinated directly to the president. Shaposhnikov, however, puts that affair in a slightly different light.[17] Indeed Lobov did attempt to make the General Staff independent of the MoD, and Shaposhnikov allowed him to present his plan to the military collegium of the MoD, where it was thoroughly discussed and then voted down.[18] Lobov accepted the military collegium's decision but continued to agitate and scheme behind Shaposhnikov's back for his own plan's approval. Shaposhnikov confronted him for insubordination, but Lobov only feigned responsiveness. That convinced Shaposhnikov to seek his removal. How he arranged it, he does not say, but Yeltsin would have insisted on final say in the matter. It happened in early December, while Lobov was on a visit to London, at the very time Dunlop believes that Yeltsin and Kravchuk were awakening to the threat of a military takeover.

Lobov may well have been part of a conspiracy. If Gorbachev had tried but failed to persuade Shaposhnikov to lead one, the chief of the General Staff would have been the most logical alternative choice. Furthermore, Lobov's repeated insubordination suggests that he believed he had sponsors stronger than Shaposhnikov. In a two-hour interview with Lobov, I did not get the impression of a man who was, to borrow Gorbachev's words, "too intelligent for the post he occupied." On the contrary, he appeared as one who rose to high rank more through political cunning than professional competence. Whatever the case, Lobov was out, and Shaposhnikov remained in command, short-circuiting Gorbachev's preferred "variant," a military takeover.

Finally, the assembly of officers on 10–11 December was another critical juncture because both Gorbachev and Yeltsin made a bid before it for the military's support against the other. Yet it is not clear what difference it could have made. If a conspiracy had already been uncovered by Yeltsin's people, with Shaposhnikov in charge and the new chief of the General Staff, Colonel General V. N. Samsonov, loyal to Shaposhnikov (who described Samsonov very favorably several years later), all that a pro-Gorbachev reaction by the assembly could have achieved was media coverage on where they stood. In any event, Shaposhnikov describes Gorbachev's appeal as pitifully weak, without substance. He admitted that he had devoted too little attention to the military and asked to be forgiven for his neglect, prompting some officers to wonder why he had not resigned several years earlier.[19] One press report on the meeting gave three reasons for the officers' rejection of Gorbachev's appeal in favor of Yeltsin's. The first was national. Yeltsin emphasized a purely Slavic army, and many officers found the pan-Slavic idea attractive. Second, they could see little difference between Gorbachev's concept of a much weakened Soviet Union based on a new union treaty and Yeltsin's CIS with the promise of a unified armed forces. Third, one general said that the only thing that would really change would be the sign on the MoD building, especially because Yeltsin declared he had no intention of creating a Russian defense ministry.[20] The deep feelings of hostility toward Gorbachev among the senior officers were so strong by this time that the very idea of his winning them over was a bit far-fetched. His verbose speaking style especially irritated them, and when it was contrasted with Yeltsin's succinct, forceful, and authoritative style, Gorbachev hardly had a chance no matter what the facts. A few months later when the facts were clearer, however, some officers complained that if they had better understood the implications, they would never have supported the CIS.[21]

After the Belovezhsakya pushcha meeting, Gorbachev and Shakhnazarov turned the charge of a conspiracy against Yeltsin, calling his CIS agreement a "coup d'état."[22] In a sense they were right. They were wrong only about the timing; it happened not at Belovezhskaya pushcha but in Moscow, 19–21 August.

Yeltsin himself claimed in 1994 that the CIS agreement "was not a 'silent coup' but a lawful alteration of the existing order of things. It was a revision of the union treaty among three major republics of the Soviet Union." He admitted that the "myth" of a "sudden destruction" of the union would be hard to overcome, but "at that moment, the Commonwealth of Independent States was the only possible preservation of an integrated geographic region."[23] Objectively speaking, Yeltsin was right in this argument, but it was not a good defense against the charge of a coup d'état. He went on to make a better case: "I was convinced that Russia needed to rid itself of its imperial mission."[24] If he was indeed convinced of that, then he should have taken credit for a coup d'état against the empire instead of denying it.

Purging the GKChP Supporters

The political struggle throughout fall 1991 kept depending on the military and who controlled it. Control, at this point, had ceased being a matter of weakened party and KGB organizational mechanisms. Now it was primarily a matter of political leaders' appointing their own loyalists to the key posts while expelling those officers ill-disposed toward them. Both Gorbachev and Yeltsin understood this.

Accordingly, Yeltsin told Gorbachev as soon as he was back in Moscow that he should not make any appointments without Yeltsin's consent.[25] Gorbachev ignored him, appointing Moiseev as defense minister and Shebarshin as chairman of the KGB on the next day, 22 August. Learning of these choices that evening, Yeltsin objected to both appointees because of their connections—passive if not active—with the GKChP, and he immediately called Gorbachev, demanding that he rescind the appointments. But Gorbachev resisted reversing them, promising to think about how they could be changed later and insisting that it would be publicly embarrassing to change his mind so quickly. Yeltsin would not accept a delay. He told Gorbachev that he would be at his office the following morning to solve this problem at once.[26]

According to Yeltsin's account, Gorbachev continued to resist, admitting that he had made a mistake but seeking additional time to think about how to undo it. Some uncertainty existed as to Moiseev's complicity in supporting the GKChP, but Yeltsin insisted that if Moiseev had not taken a direct role in the plot, he had aided it passively, and he definitely had not acted to block it. Yeltsin's security people discovered the previous day that Moiseev had ordered a junior officer to burn all the documents in his office that connected him to the affair. Yeltsin insisted that Gorbachev call the lieutenant on the spot and ask him what he was doing. Reluctantly, he did. According to Yeltsin, the officer answered, "I received an order from Moiseev to burn all the coded messages concerning the August coup."[27]

Having made Gorbachev concede that a new minister of defense had to be appointed at once, Yeltsin proposed Marshal Shaposhnikov, who, it was well known, had resisted the GKChP from the beginning. As a new chairman of the KGB, Yeltsin suggested Vadim Bakatin, who had been minister of the MVD before the GKChP member Pugo had replaced him. Bakatin had a reputation as a reformer. Gorbachev agreed, giving up the struggle, and he also agreed that Shevardnadze should return to head the foreign ministry.[28]

Fortunately for Yeltsin, a meeting of the leaders of the republics was scheduled for 11:00 A.M. that morning in the Kremlin. He used that occasion to ask for their approval of the appointments that he had just forced on Gorbachev. They gave it without objections. That provided Yeltsin's heavy-handed dealing with Gorbachev additional political backing, but as Yeltsin noted in retrospect, just reversing three appointments had taken an enormous effort, and he realized that Gorbachev's concessions were merely temporary.[29]

Shaposhnikov's account of his own appointment, already partially described, is consistent with Yeltsin's, but it throws more light on Yeltsin's nervousness about his own situation at the time, 23 August. The day before, Shaposhnikov attended a meeting of the MoD military collegium, convened by the new defense minister, General Moiseev, to prepare an agenda of issues to raise with Gorbachev the next day. Shaposhnikov, it will be recalled, drew General Shlyaga's rebuke at this meeting for proposing the "de-partyization" of the military. Immediately afterward, he returned to the air forces headquarters determined to abandon his party membership. Because this would be a highly significant act in the eyes of his officers, he ordered his military council to convene the next day, 23 August, at 11:30 A.M., so that he could both announce and explain his decision. In the hour before it met, Shaposhnikov was organizing his speech. At 11:25 A.M., Moiseev called him from the Kremlin, telling him that Gorbachev wanted to see him at once. Moiseev had no idea why, but at the end of their conversation, Moiseev asked whether it was true that he had quit the party. Shaposhnikov admitted he had, and Moiseev seemed relieved, remarking, "That's in vain. Well, okay, come on anyway." Shaposhnikov delayed long enough to speak briefly to the military council at 11:30 A.M., announcing his decision but not taking time to explain why. The reaction surprised him. His words met a burst of approving applause and shouts of "Finally, hurrah!"[30]

Setting out for the Kremlin, Shaposhnikov was certain that Gorbachev wanted to upbraid him for leaving the party and probably force him to retire. Upon his arrival, shortly after noon, he found Moiseev nervously waiting in a reception room. After a few words with him, Shaposhnikov was led away to another reception room right in front of the entry to the main hall, where the leaders of the republics were meeting. After a few minutes, Yeltsin emerged from the hall. This was the first time Shaposhnikov had actually seen Yeltsin in person. Yeltsin greeted him only briefly with a handshake and then turned to a telephone, speaking to Ruslan Khasbulatov at the White House, telling him to verify some information and get back as soon as he had done so.[31] (Yeltsin's staunch ally in 1991, Khasbulatov led the White House against Yeltsin during the violence of October 1993.)

Curious about the substance of the phone conversation, Shaposhnikov tried to strike up a discussion with Yeltsin, offering him a drink of vodka from a bottle on the reception room table, but Yeltsin declined, remarking that there was no time for a drink; Khasbulatov had told him that the crisis was not over, that KGB elements were still planning to storm the White House. "We cannot let down our guard now," he admonished Shaposhnikov, and returned to the hall. Shaposhnikov immediately called his headquarters, issuing instructions that the Moscow military district air forces be put on "full combat readiness" and that plans be developed to make low-level flights over the city. Then he called Khasbulatov and told him of his actions.[32]

At this point, Shaposhnikov was called into the hall, where he faced the assembly of the "entire Novo-Ogarevo group" and Gorbachev. He was asked to recount his own actions during 18–21 August. He did that briefly, but before he could say that he had quit the party as well, Gorbachev cut him off, asking him what he thought about becoming minister of defense. Shaposhnikov at first demurred, suggesting that he be made a presidential adviser or, better, remain in his present post. Yeltsin interrupted, "Only minister of defense. The decree must be signed." Then Shaposhnikov realized that the issue had already been decided, but before accepting, he insisted on telling Gorbachev that he had quit the party, to which Gorbachev responded, "Well, that is not the worst thing." [33]

After signing the decree, Gorbachev asked Shaposhnikov's opinion of General Vladimir Lobov's serving as chief of the General Staff and Grachev as first deputy minister of defense. Shaposhnikov posed no objections, and Gorbachev asked for Moiseev to be brought in. Gorbachev told Moiseev to turn over his duties to Shaposhnikov and to install Lobov as chief of the General Staff and "to commit no stupidities." After a moment of astonishment, Moiseev's face immediately changed, as he announced in a firm voice, "You are doing this to me for no cause, Mikhail Sergeevich; I never did you any wrong."

"I know," answered Gorbachev, "but you did nothing to stop the events with which you had nothing to do. You know how I feel about you. This is the single thing I can promise: no injustices to you personally will be permitted." After a considerable silence, Moiseev responded, "I won't do anything stupid . . . and I'll never, as Shaposhnikov has, leave the party!" [34]

Yeltsin had acted none too soon by forcing Gorbachev to reverse his initial appointments to head the MoD and the KGB, but that was only the first step on a long road if all the important pro-GKChP officials were to be rooted out. Insofar as his political loyalty was concerned, Shaposhnikov was a wise selection on Yeltsin's part. He also was a good choice because he intended to move forward on the reforms that had been delayed for so long. The big question, of course, was whether Shaposhnikov could gain sufficient control of the MoD to put reliable and able supporters in all the key positions essential to implement reforms. Moreover, it was not at all clear that he could purge the senior ranks of all passive GKChP supporters. The challenge was more urgent in the MoD and the General Staff, but it also had to be faced in all the military districts countrywide. Shortly after the crisis, the commander of the Far Eastern military district said that his officers were about evenly split between support for Yeltsin and for the GKChP, but that most officers stood aside while only a few took a clear stand.[35] Failure to remove most of the pro-GKChP senior officers in their posts in the military districts and operational forces could therefore pose future difficulties for Yeltsin as well as Shaposhnikov.

Shaposhnikov was aware that he faced a huge battle; he knew that he had to overcome strong prejudices against himself, and not just because he was a pro-democratic reformer. He was an air forces officer and a pilot, not a combined arms officer. He had completed the same General Staff Academy course taken by all senior combined arms officers, who came entirely from the ground forces, but never before had anyone other than a combined arms officer been minister of defense. Breaking that tradition, he realized, would not go "smoothly, without a hitch."[36] It did not, and not only because he had broken that tradition.

Among the first problems he tackled was personnel, beginning at the very top. There were more than three thousand marshals, generals, and admirals on active duty, and seven hundred of them were over the mandatory retirement age of fifty-five. On discovering these figures in his new post, he recalled a meeting of the Defense Council in summer 1991, when Gorbachev asked Yazov how many flag officers there were. Now Shaposhnikov realized that Yazov had instantly lied, answering, "Nineteen hundred sixty-one!"[37] Gorbachev had ordered him to reduce that number, but obviously he had not. Realizing the magnitude of the needed reduction and the resistance it would meet, he took personal control of the matter. That may have been his first mistake. It offered a great opportunity to revitalize the top military ranks, but it also produced a wave of resentment against him, beginning among the oldest and highest-ranking officers.

The Group of Inspector Generals of the MoD had long been known as "heaven," a place where marshals and four-star generals and admirals could be assigned to serve until death. The sinecure was a scandal in the eyes of younger officers. Occasionally senior party functionaries were also put in the Group of Inspector Generals, with full privileges of a general officer. The legal basis for its existence and its authority within the MoD were ambiguous at best, as Shaposhnikov discovered on investigation. After asking Gorbachev and Yeltsin to back him, he took a decision to liquidate it. The outrage was thunderous. Attempting to calm the objections, Shaposhnikov promised he would retire on pension the day he reached sixty, a promise that prompted media commentary that Shaposhnikov had denied himself a "private airport" for the occasion of his own departure from the high-flying post of minister of defense.[38] He made the decision to abolish the Group of Inspector Generals stand, he insists, but a year or so later it still existed in the Russian MoD. From that point on, as he pushed through a number of personnel policy changes, including a mixed manning system of conscripts and volunteers, he realized that his subordinates were stalling and obstructing in order to defeat his policies.[39]

Shaposhnikov, in fact, puts it mildly in his account. He never really got control of the officer personnel mechanism. In September, Colonel General Kobets was put in charge of a commission to review how the military leadership behaved during the August crisis. According to Major Lopatin, the commission began to receive a large amount of unsolicited material from officers— reports of fellow officers who had supported the GKChP. On 26 October, when Lopatin, now a deputy in the Russian parliament, asked Kobets to convene the commission and invite representatives of parliamentary commissions also investigating the matter, Kobets reacted by sending Shaposhnikov a draft order to sign, disbanding the commission.[40] Lopatin was particularly angered for two reasons. First, he and other reformers had lobbied Gorbachev to appoint Kobets chairman of a committee for military reform on 23 September. Kobets expressed his gratitude by immediately taking a trip abroad and never convening the committee. Second, Kobets devoted all his energies to putting his own people into key positions in the MoD. The compromising material he obtained as head of the commission to investigate officers' behavior during the coup put him in a strong position to coerce the accusers and the accused alike to support him. Moreover, his protégé, Major General Yurii Rodionov, was promoted to lieutenant general and appointed head of the MoD main directorate for personnel.[41] (Kobets was arrested and jailed in 1997 for corruption and misuse of defense ministry funds.)

This small window into Kobets's machinations in personnel affairs gives a reasonably valid picture of how the purge of pro-GKChP officers was conducted. Lopatin is not far off the mark when he says that power and position became the primary goal of Kobets, Shaposhnikov, Lobov, and others, to the complete exclusion of military reform. Moreover, he explains Lobov's dismissal as the result of a temporary alliance between Kobets and Shaposhnikov. Curiously, Lopatin, who normally was well informed about such matters, makes no mention of General Grachev, first deputy minister of defense, in connection with these bureaucratic struggles.

It would be wrong to leave the impression that the purge of the pro-GKChP officers touched virtually none of the culprits. The major figures were dismissed—Yazov, Moiseev, Achalov, Varennikov, Tret'yak, and several others. Shaposhnikov puts the numbers as eight deputy ministers of defense, nine chiefs of main and central directorates, and seven commanders of military districts. That was a fairly significant decapitation of the senior military leadership. Still, it barely touched the large group of officers who either actively supported the GKChP or sympathized with it but sat on the fence waiting to see who would win. The number of senior officers who actively opposed the GKChP was fairly small. Many could claim not to have supported it, but they could not prove they were truly opposed to it. As Shaposhnikov undertook what he considered to be genuine military reforms, his support within the officer corps was thin, to say the least, and at the very top—in the MoD and General Staff—he faced determined opponents.

A Last Try at Reforms

For all the great hope and expectations for military reforms following the August crisis, little progress was made in the next four months. Most of the reasons should already be obvious from the political context, but it is well to summarize and sharpen them.

First, the political struggle between Yeltsin and Gorbachev virtually ensured that the government of the USSR would not act decisively on military issues. Any action that did not improve Gorbachev's political position was of little interest to him. He was desperate. Acting purely in the public interest was a luxury in which he would not indulge. Second, the politics of purging the pro-GKChP senior officers was not conducive to effective reform measures, especially those affecting personnel, and the most serious military reform issues had dramatic personnel ramifications.

The third reason proved the most decisive. As the story of Shaposhnikov's appointment as defense minister reveals, the heads of the republics began playing a role in military policy making. Movement on reform required strong and determined political backing. Gorbachev could not provide it from his lame-duck position. Yeltsin might have provided it. He certainly had the political power to back a number of planned changes in the MoD, but he would not focus on them even when they were brought to his attention. Initially unclear about whether to try to preserve something of the Soviet Union or to move swiftly to dissolve it, he was reluctant to spend his political capital on quick action within the MoD. Moreover, most of the republics had declared their independence by September, diluting Soviet political authority all the more.

The republics' independence raised a question which had received no serious thought, much less contingency planning, in the MoD: who would inherit what pieces of the Soviet military? Nor was Yeltsin thinking about that question. He went to Belovezhskaya pushcha to work out the CIS agreement with no serious preparation for dealing with the military aspects of it, and, as his call to Shaposhnikov on 8 December shows, he neither took a military adviser with him nor consulted with Shaposhnikov beforehand to establish basic criteria for deciding the military issues. He simply presented the defense minister with a fait accompli over the telephone, announcing that virtually no military details had been firmly worked out. Thereafter the republics would have a decisive say on virtually all military policy issues. Moreover, the republics were less interested in reforming the Soviet military than in dismembering it. Shaposhnikov, of course, had already discovered that early in the fall, long before the CIS agreement was signed.

A fourth reason, closely related to the third, concerned the military reformers in Moscow, those of Major Lopatin's inclination who had struggled to legislate military reform in 1989–90. Because most of them had moved to the Russian parliament, it was there in the fall of 1991 that they once again began pressuring the MoD and the General Staff for action and demanding to participate in the reform process, a demand that irritated the otherwise reform-minded new defense minister.

The political deck was so stacked against military reform in the last months of the Soviet Union that reform efforts could not be expected to achieve significant results. They deserve scrutiny not for what they accomplished but because they help answer two other important questions. First, why did a unified CIS armed forces fail to materialize? And second, what was the legacy of major unresolved issues bequeathed to the new Russian military?

Shaposhnikov the Reformer

Unlike his two predecessors under Gorbachev, Shaposhnikov was determined to implement reforms. Unlike them, he has also left his own written account of his efforts and key documents outlining his proposals for approval by the Soviet government. Keenly aware that the Soviet military was rapidly disintegrating, leaving him little time, Shaposhnikov filled his agenda with more issues than he could manage, but he did have a sense of direction and priority: restore stability within the military, preserve a unified Soviet Armed Forces, "departyize" the military, and rehabilitate its terrible public image. The minister of defense's job, as he saw it, was more political than purely military, requiring his attention to broader economic and social issues.[42]

The accumulation of public ill will toward the military, Shaposhnikov believed, had to be countered with an aggressive public affairs campaign. He had to convince the public that he would keep the military out of domestic politics and rid the barracks of dedovshchina and similar maladies. As a start, he used his confirmation appearance before the Supreme Soviet of the USSR to spell out the broad outlines of his concept of military reform. He also looked at polling data to discover that public confidence in the military was dropping—but not yet, in his view, beyond reversal. On the foreign front, he saw the probability of war as very low, thus permitting major military reforms without risk to the country's security.[43]

Playing the role of a genuine democrat and reformer, he at once made himself available to meet with all kinds of people, both MoD officers and ordinary citizens. To underscore his seriousness, he called the MoD the House of Open Doors. Endless meetings followed, involving as many as two hundred people in one day.[44] The soldiers' mothers movement quickly seized the opportunity to confront him with all of their complaints. Colonel A. A. Alekseev and Colonel V. G. Urazhtsev leaped to the fore, vying for control of the movement and each seeking to involve Shaposhnikov directly. He agreed to attend a meeting with all the committees connected to this movement, but as he spoke to its assembled leaders, he realized that the political ambitions of the two colonels stood in the way of addressing the actual problems of parents and soldiers. Thus within the MoD he formed a large staff of military lawyers, finance officers, and other staff officers to deal with individual cases. He wanted to establish a permanent committee in the MoD to deal with such cases, but Gorbachev would not approve it. Instead, Gorbachev created such a committee in his own office, but it was never active. In 1992 a similar committee was set up in the office of the Russian president, but it was equally feckless and soon abolished.[45] Nor was this burst of attention to parents and soldiers sustained.

Shaposhnikov quickly developed his ideas on military reform, beginning with a review of the planning that had been done under the leadership of Yazov and Moiseev since 1987. Its key components, as he saw them, were a) military doctrine, b) military art, c) organizational design and force structure, d) the system of arming and equipping the forces, *e*) the logistics system, *f*) manning and training, *g*) democratization of military life, and *h*) social and legal rights of military personnel and their families.[46] On the whole he judged this staff work as both sound and adequately comprehensive, but he found two "principal deficiencies." First, the reform of the MPA was only "decorative," leaving the essence of the old system in place. Second, a ten- to fifteen-year period was envisioned for the plan's implementation, a grossly unrealistic schedule in light of the political realities demanding rapid action.

Shaposhnikov was merely trying to implement much faster—within five years—the Yazov-Moiseev reform plan as it stood, with one exception. He was determined to deracinate the Communist Party's apparatus from the military. In fact, his memoir comes back again and again to the MPA, divulging an obsession with so-called "de-partyization" of the military. The elimination of article 6 of the Soviet constitution, the article that gave the party the "leading role" in the Soviet state, was especially important to him in this regard because it left all the prerogatives in military policy with state institutions, meaning that the military's organization and processes could now be put on a legal basis.[47] Hand in hand with his obsession about rooting out party controls, therefore, went an obsession with enshrining the MoD and its activities in laws, a goal he failed to achieve because the parliament would not oblige.

Shaposhnikov repeatedly claims that he was sensitive to the political changes occurring in the republics. He could not ignore their creation of ministries of defense—or national security committees—and their efforts to form their own military forces. Yet he would not yield on maintaining the unified military establishment in the face of strong opposition from key republics, especially Ukraine.[48] Thus he was quickly in a predicament analogous to Gorbachev's in the Novo-Ogarevo negotiations, defending the center against rapidly growing centrifugal forces. He recognized the hopelessness of Gorbachev's position. Why did he overlook it in his own? Laudable though it was, his explanation could not alter the power relations. Shaposhnikov understood the painful impact the dismemberment of the armed forces would have on the lives of several millions of servicemen and their families. This human factor became his banner in trying to persuade uncooperative officials in the republics. They simply did not believe him, assuming that his real motive was the restoration of Moscow's imperial power. They had a basis for their suspicions. He was always explicit about keeping a strong centrally controlled military even as he invited greater participation in military policy making by the republics.

That was clear on 6 September, when he briefly outlined his thoughts on military reform to the GOSSOVET, the State Council, a new body composed of the heads of the republics.[49] The first task, as he saw it, was to bring order and logistical support back to the armed forces. That required, first of all, working out an agreed concept of reform with all the republics. Thus he proposed that a commission directly under Gorbachev accomplish this quickly. Second, he envisioned a division of defense functions between the center and the republics, giving the republics control over civil defense troops, all the military faculties in civilian schools, and social support to military personnel and their families. Operational control of the forces, their training, and other purely military tasks would remain with the USSR ministry of defense.

He proposed two component parts for the armed forces. The first would consist of all strategic nuclear forces and conventional forces. The republics' national guards and militias would make up the second component. In peacetime, they would remain under the control of republican defense ministries or committees, but in wartime, they would come under the armed forces.

Implementation of all arms control treaties would continue, and that would involve significant reductions in total military manpower. In the process of making manpower reductions, the term of service should be reduced to eighteen months, and a mixed conscription-volunteer system of recruitment should be instituted, allowing conscripts to sign contracts after six to eight months' service for three to five years' additional service at significantly higher pay.

The armed forces had to be "democratized," and that included the elimination of the political organs in the military. All of these changes had to be enacted in law and also based on a treaty between the sovereign republics and the Soviet Union. All past draft evaders should be given amnesty, and penal battalions should be liquidated.

Finally, the most urgent issue was social support and legal protection for military personnel and their families, and that would require both enactment of laws and additional funding of housing construction.

No wonder the republics mistrusted Shaposhnikov. A mere glance at this outline shows that the republics would carry much of the training and support costs for the entire armed forces in exchange for their own trivial national guards and militias. Surprisingly, the GOSSOVET approved all of these proposals, but unsurprisingly, the draft decrees Shaposhnikov presented to implement them were not signed. Instead, he was told to present them to the Soviet parliament.[50] In the event, the parliament enacted only a few of the laws he desired. It endorsed minor provisions—amnesty for draft evaders, shorter terms of conscription, and contract soldiers, beginning in 1992—but little more. Other than a faster schedule for implementation and a strong emphasis on abolishing the party's organizations in the military, Shaposhnikov's reform concept was not very radical. It gave away nothing of importance to the re-publics while placing some costly responsibilities on them for maintenance of forces garrisoned on their territories.

Shaposhnikov did attempt to force through some significant changes, but they were not systemic reforms but rather reversal of bureaucratic decay that had accumulated over several years. For example, he attacked the corrupted system of military procurators. Officially they belonged to the Procuracy of the USSR, but they received all of their material support from the MoD. Because their reports on crime in military units were used as an index of commanders' performance, they could strike deals with commanders, promising to doctor their records in exchange for housing and other under-the-table resources. Shaposhnikov insists that he succeeded in making the military procurators organizationally independent, though the new system was not implemented until after the dissolution of the Soviet Union.[51]

Another of Shaposhnikov's reforms, already mentioned, was at least the temporary elimination of the Group of Inspector Generals in the MoD, along with the reduction of the ranks of general officers. He also talked about ending the practice of sending troops to help with the fall harvest on collective farms each year, but apparently he was unable to do so. He directed all military dis-trict commanders to inventory their weapons and property, but it is doubtful that his directive was implemented. The same is true of a directive he issued to city and district governments to provide housing and other logistical support to garrisons on their territories. The change he seems most proud of, eliminat-ing the political organs and party organizations from the military's ranks, was an illusory victory. They were renamed as training organs and removed from the chain of command, but they survived.[52]

Shaposhnikov admits more than once that the MoD bureaucracy was re-sisting most of his policies, and he expresses bitterness at the reluctance of several senior officers to help him save the armed forces by speeding up reform. As mentioned, he fell into a struggle with General Lobov over restructuring the MoD and the General Staff in mid-September, and he admits that much of the staff work he requested from Lobov in support of reform was carelessly done with the intention of blocking it.

Shaposhnikov confirms conclusions drawn earlier about the MoD budget for 1992, being prepared in the fall of 1991. When Gorbachev made pub-lic that the traditional annual military budget figure, about seventeen billion rubles, was only a small part of the actual defense burden, the MoD was forced to work out more realistic budget categories, which it did. Following essen-tially U.S. defense budgeting practice, they were: *a)* operations, training, and maintenance; *b*) procurement; *c*) research and development; *d*) military construction. As he faced the budget decisions that fall, Shaposhnikov shifted it heavily in favor of the first category, that is, toward personnel pay, support, and maintenance, and away from procurement. In the military construction category, he emphasized military housing.[53] His cuts in procurement angered the VPK, which Shaposhnikov intensely disliked, preferring a market economic system and a competitive contracting arrangement with military industries.[54] The military conversion plan was, in his words, not a plan but "a cavalry charge."[55] For all his talk about budget policies, however, it is not clear that they were followed by the government. In particular, every request he made for increased funding for personnel and military families' support was ignored by the finance ministry. Shaposhnikov's major problem, however, was elsewhere.

By mid-September he was sufficiently disturbed about military policy making by the republics that he wrote Gorbachev a memorandum, dated 22 September, requesting that four key issues be discussed urgently in a closed session of the GOSSOVET: *a*) the military policies of the republics, *b*) the status of forces on their territories; *c*) 1992 budget issues, and *d*) the fall conscription call-up.[56] Nothing apparently came of this request. Again on 3 October, Shaposhnikov addressed a memorandum to all members of the GOSSOVET, mentioning the actions of several republics as highly adverse for his reform program and requesting an urgent GOSSOVET discussion as well as decisions on what to do about these developments. Not until a month later, 4 November, was his list of issues put on the GOSSOVET agenda.[57]

Shaposhnikov took that belated occasion to spell out again his general approach to reform, warning of the dangers of letting the military situation get worse, and promising to push through his full reform program within five years. Gorbachev, Yeltsin, and "actually all of republican leaders participating" supported him.[58] A number of the republican leaders, of course, were not there. Again, as in early September, they told him that he would have to take all of his draft legislation to the Soviet parliament where he knew it would die. Indeed, no public record of such legislation exists.

Shaposhnikov's alarm was far from excessive in light of three different approaches he saw among the republics, which together seemed destined to cause the dismemberment of the armed forces. First, the Baltic republics made it plain that they were breaking all military relations with the Soviet Union, a policy that assumed the removal of Soviet forces from their territories. Second, Ukraine, Moldavia, and Azerbaijan were forming their own armies by nationalizing the Soviet forces deployed on their soil. Third, Russia, Belorussia, Kazakhstan, and the other Central Asian republics favored a combined armed forces. None of the republics accepted Shaposhnikov's own position, retention of the unified Soviet Armed Forces.[59]

His relations with the Baltic states became increasingly strained as he refused their demands for immediate Soviet troop withdrawals. In principle he acknowledged their right to make such demands, but he explained that he had to find facilities for the flood of Soviet forces returning from Eastern Europe before he could accommodate withdrawals from the Baltic region. Handling both withdrawals simultaneously simply was not possible. The Estonian and Latvian leaders dismissed this argument as a dodge, though the Lithuanian government was readier to compromise at the time. Shaposhnikov tried to appease Estonia and Latvia by offering them a "status of forces" treaty, guaranteeing noninterference in their internal affairs as well as technical assistance in forming their own armies, but they would have nothing to do with it. Gorbachev ignored Shaposhnikov's many requests for help, although he belatedly formed a commission, headed by Aleksandr Yakovlev and including Eduard Shevardnadze and Anatolii Sobchak, to negotiate with the Baltic republics. Yakovlev listened to Shaposhnikov's pleadings for action, but he never put the commission to work.[60]

Ukraine was key to saving a unified armed forces. Belorussia and Kazakhstan were reasonably cooperative, and if Ukraine would also cooperate, then something of Shaposhnikov's aim might be rescued. Thus he made numerous visits to Kiev, meeting with both military and civilian officials. Already in September, when he asked why Ukraine needed its own army, they reminded him that during the August crisis, General Varennikov had come to Kiev and ordered them to "stand at attention!" (Smirno!)—meaning obey the GKChP. They needed an army so that no future Varennikov could command, "Smirno!"[61] As this view hardened, Shaposhnikov's prospects for preserving a unified armed forces faded and most of his other reform plans remained stalled.

On one issue, however, he believed for a time that he had made some progress. The number of officers and families returning from Eastern Europe to find no housing awaiting them surged. By November it was more than 185,000. His desperate pleadings got the GOSSOVET to approve a cash allotment to officers adequate to rent housing on their own if the MoD could not provide it. This was to be enacted into law, but time ran out, and nothing came of it.

That was his tragedy. He was too late. His claims to be a reformer and a genuine democrat were convincing to a number of the most liberal-minded civilian politicians. Galina Starovoitova, for example, a future candidate for the Russian presidency and a leader of Democratic Russia movement, describes Shaposhnikov as honest, politically liberal, and extremely intelligent.[62] Shaposhnikov also had his critics among the democrats. Major Lopatin reproached him for not cooperating with the reformers in the parliament, and Shaposhnikov admits that he did not.[63] A couple of his fellow generals claim that he always had big ideas, started a lot of activity, but would not take firm decisions and carry them through.[64] They may be right, but as defense minister, Shaposhnikov had an impossible task, and whatever his failings, he did not allow the MoD to fall into the hands of reactionary generals during his tenure. This was not an insignificant achievement, because had he failed, or had he accepted Gorbachev's invitation to lead a military takeover, the country might well have drifted into civil war.

Other Reform Endeavors

Two other simultaneous military reform efforts were made in fall 1991, but neither had any significant impact on events. Lopatin and other military deputies in the Russian parliament tried to revive the essence of the proposals that Lopatin's commission had presented in spring 1990. As Lopatin complained, however, he was not allowed to organize a reform committee because, in his words, the "national patriots" and the "neo-Bolsheviks" were trying to seize control of the issue, and their policy was "the worse the better."[65]

Yeltsin himself initiated an independent military reform effort. Colonel General Dmitrii Volkogonov, a political officer who later was director of the Military History Institute, had become a Yeltsin adviser in the course of 1990–91. He headed a commission appointed by Yeltsin in fall 1991 to develop a reform program, but nothing came of it. A participant, Major General Viktor Ryabchuk, described Volkogonov as so absorbed in his relations with Yegor Gaidar and other civilian politicians that he neither took the effort seriously nor wanted to understand what it entailed.[66] Given that Volkogonov was a political officer and prolific writer of propaganda tracts, this is not surprising.

Thus as 1991 came to an end, military reform remained largely a matter of talk. The divided nature of the political leadership ensured that no serious reform would receive adequate political backing.

Passing the "Nuclear Button"

After the Belovezhskaya pushcha agreement and the Central Asian republics' subsequent agreement on a Muslim commonwealth, Yeltsin and Nazarbayev realized that they had to find a compromise. To that end they arranged a summit of republican leaders in Alma-Ata, the Kazakh capital, on 21 December, where the final terms for the dissolution of the Soviet Union were agreed. Shaposhnikov describes the climate at the meeting as unusually congenial, without the tensions of the Novo-Ogarevo process and with a genuine interest in a stable commonwealth.[67] This made possible the resolution of a few military issues, which looked like a major step in light of the virtual neglect of military issues at Belovezhskaya pushcha earlier in the month.

The most important concerned strategic nuclear forces. Agreement was reached that control of them would pass to Yeltsin and Shaposhnikov. Although several approaches were proposed, apparently a strong consensus emerged for keeping a unified strategic nuclear force with a centralized command system and also for preventing both the spread of nuclear weapons and competition for control over them.[68] Although Yeltsin would maintain the codes and communications means for approving the operational release of nuclear weapons, it was decided that he would not release them without first getting agreement from the leaders of Kazakhstan, Ukraine, and Belarus, the other republics on whose territory strategic nuclear forces were deployed.[69]

The summit meeting also addressed the issue of control of Soviet conventional forces, but here no solid agreement was reached. Shaposhnikov proposed a transition period, connected with reforms and with an emphasis on easing the hardships on officers and their families inexorably connected with redeployments and many other structural changes that had to be made. Although this gradual approach received majority support, it was not enough to provide the consensus needed to implement it.[70]

Finally, Yeltsin raised the issue of what to do with Shaposhnikov himself; the Soviet Union would cease to exist, but the ministry of defense would not. Yeltsin proposed that Shaposhnikov be confirmed as commander in chief of the Armed Forces of the CIS on the authority of all the heads of the member states in the new commonwealth. The proposal was accepted.[71] It left ambiguity about the role of the minister of defense, but Yeltsin envisioned that Shaposhnikov's new post as commander of the CIS Armed Forces would lift him above the old Soviet minister of defense post. Presumably, as the details of a unified CIS Armed Forces—nuclear and conventional—were worked out, then the old Soviet defense ministry apparatus and the General Staff would be converted to support Shaposhnikov's new command position. That is obviously how Shaposhnikov saw future developments.

Two of the major military issues—a unified strategic forces and Shaposhnikov's command of all CIS Armed Forces—appeared to be settled, but the agreements concealed more problems than they solved. A major quarrel soon broke out over what constituted the "strategic nuclear forces." Shaposhnikov

nikov took an expansive view, in line with Soviet traditional doctrine on the matter; Ukraine took a very narrow view, excluding most naval forces, some of the air forces' units, and most of the PVO and space units. The breadth of Shaposhnikov's authority as commander in chief of all CIS forces was soon equally disputed. That this would be a continuing issue was apparent from the failure to reach agreement on how to deal with the Soviet conventional forces. The function of the Soviet ministry of defense and the General Staff soon became a troublesome part of this issue. Although Shaposhnikov put the most optimistic face on the Alma-Ata decisions on military issues, he must have foreseen that little had actually been settled. For the moment, however, no one was challenging the decision to transfer control of strategic nuclear weapons to Yeltsin and Shaposhnikov because it meant taking control away from Gorbachev.

Immediately on their return to Moscow, Yeltsin and Shaposhnikov worked out with Gorbachev the formal procedures by which Gorbachev would transfer the "nuclear button" to Yeltsin on 25 December. The transfer would occur in the evening after Gorbachev's television appearance in which he would announce that he was giving up his position as president of the Soviet Union and commander of the Soviet Armed Forces. Shaposhnikov prepared the appropriate documents for the transfer, and Yeltsin signed them, but Gorbachev insisted that he would not sign them until after his television address. He agreed to meet with both Yeltsin and Shaposhnikov to effect the transfer of nuclear control immediately afterward.[72]

The procedure appeared to be finally agreed upon, but during Gorbachev's television speech, Yeltsin called Shaposhnikov, telling him to go see Gorbachev alone. Shaposhnikov protested, insisting that the situation was extremely delicate and that Yeltsin had to come for the transfer. Yeltsin would not be persuaded. If there were difficulties, then Shaposhnikov should call him and they would discuss how to proceed. Thus Shaposhnikov went to find Gorbachev still talking to journalists. After about ten minutes, Gorbachev received Shaposhnikov and learned that Yeltsin would not come. Because Yeltsin had already signed the documents, Gorbachev agreed to append his own signature and send them electronically to Yeltsin, who would call Gorbachev to confirm receipt. Then Gorbachev would turn over the codes and communication mechanism to Shaposhnikov, who would deliver them straight to Yeltsin. Shaposhnikov called Yeltsin and got his agreement.[73]

Gorbachev signed the documents and they were sent to Yeltsin. Shaposhnikov and Gorbachev chatted while waiting for Yeltsin's confirmation call. Gorbachev gave the appearance of being very positive and undisturbed by the magnitude of the occasion and about his own fate, but Shaposhnikov discerned that he was deeply troubled, "not himself at all."[74] After a few minutes, Yeltsin called to report that he had the documents. Gorbachev then said farewell to the technicians who had carried the codes and mechanism for him, thanking them for their support, and Shaposhnikov and the technicians went straight to Yeltsin.[75]

Yeltsin was subdued but focused fully on the equipment and how to use it. He received an extensive briefing on it and on all the details of how it would accompany him, where it would be located, and how he would have to adjust his daily routines in line with his new responsibility. Afterward, he and Shaposhnikov chatted for about an hour about problems they faced with the military before Shaposhnikov was allowed to leave.[76]

Shaposhnikov related this episode in great detail because he found such intense interest both within the Soviet Union and abroad about the transfer of control over nuclear weapons. Ambassadors, foreign ministers, defense ministers, scientists, and the media showered him with questions about it both before and afterward. They seemed unsatisfied with his answer to the question of just who in the CIS retained the political authority over nuclear weapons, but Shaposhnikov felt quite proud that the transfer had gone so quietly and that the temporarily shared political authority satisfied all the parties involved.

In retrospect, it was indeed a smooth transfer, although the personal tensions between Gorbachev and Yeltsin apparently were too much for Yeltsin at the last moment. In his autobiography, Yeltsin makes it seem as though he did show up for the nuclear control transfer, saying that "the press devoted enormous attention to our final summary meeting, because we performed the ritual of relaying the nuclear 'button.'"[77] Perhaps Yeltsin's ghostwriters simply made an error (as they clearly did on a number of factual points in the book), but Shaposhnikov's account gives grounds for believing that Yeltsin was not proud of his behavior in retrospect and wanted to purge it from the historical record.

It was, to say the least, a highly symbolic affair, marking Yeltsin's triumph and Gorbachev's humiliation — revenge for the humiliation Gorbachev had imposed on Yeltsin in October 1987 by subjecting him to vicious criticism and removing him from the Politburo. Yeltsin also had reasons to believe that Gorbachev had authorized the KGB to kill him because he was struggling to make a political comeback. No Soviet politician had ever survived dismissal from the Politburo and regained political power. Yeltsin had done so, and in the process he destroyed the Soviet Union. Perhaps being face to face with Gorbachev during the passing of control of such potentially destructive nuclear forces conveyed symbolism evoking more emotion than Yeltsin believed he could stand.

Or perhaps he believed that it was too much for Gorbachev and that he should spare him such humiliation.

Whatever the reasons for Yeltsin's behavior, this occasion, 25 December 1991, marked the end of the Soviet military and the beginning of what would soon become the Russian military. Formally the Soviet military existed for another week, through the end of the year, but its nuclear forces were subordinated to the Russian president on the twenty-fifth. Several weeks earlier, one behind-the-scenes episode concerning the nuclear forces had actually rattled Gorbachev. He summoned Shaposhnikov, telling him that he had received a telegram from "three colonels" who threatened to launch a nuclear weapon at each of the union republic's capitals unless he saved the Soviet Union. Gorbachev wanted to know whether this could be done. Shaposhnikov explained that it was not technically feasible unless Gorbachev granted the authority through the system of codes and computer controls in his possession. Obviously, the defense minister wanted the names of the colonels in order to track them down, but Gorbachev refused, convincing Shaposhnikov that they probably were not colonels but rather provocateurs in party circles engaging in desperate, belated schemes.

Now, during the last week of December, the Soviet military went quietly into "the dustbin of history," though a few "military patriots" were still sending word to Gorbachev that they would support his every effort to save the Soviet Union.[78] That the drama was exhausted was evident in anticlimatic headlines in the military's newspaper, *Krasnaya Zvezda:* ". . . The Army Awaits Decisions" (25 December); "The Nuclear Button Passes to B. N. Yeltsin" (26 December); "And So, the Union Turns Over Its Affairs . . ." (27 December); and ". . . Important Decisions for the Fate of the Army" (31 December). Inexplicably, a cartoonist managed to break this anesthetizing rhetoric in the last issue of the year, playing on Yeltsin's and others' assertions that the CIS would replace the Soviet Union as "a single strategic space" and "a single economic space." Belying the farce he pictured a soldier saluting as he reports to an officer,

"I serve a single economic space!"

"I declare my gratitude to you," the officer replies, returning the salute.

The fizzle and farce of the Soviet military's last days is not so strange, however, because the curtain had already risen on a new drama: what kind of armed forces would the CIS have? Yeltsin had left the question up in the air as the CIS agreements were signed on 8 December, and the Alma-Ata summit gave only vague answers. Shaposhnikov tried to get CIS military representatives to agree to answers in Moscow on 26–27 December, and again at the summit in Minsk on 30–31 December. Finished with "Soviet patriotism," the generals began scrambling for positions in the post-Soviet order, whatever it was to be. In Moscow a faction was trying to undermine Shaposhnikov's design. In Ukraine the new head of state and former party boss, Leonid Kravchuk, had gathered a group of officers to form a Ukrainian military. They quietly surrounded the three military district commanders in Ukraine and removed them on the first day of January. Plans to install a Ukrainian as commander of the Black Sea Fleet were developed, but Kravchuk would not approve it. In the event, Ukraine took control of all three military districts and all their subordinate units without significant resistance. In all the other republics similar dramas were occurring as all the newly independent states began to claim and tear off parts of the force structure.

The story of the formal demise of the Soviet military could be ended here, but its actual demise was not complete for some time. Let us, therefore, follow that process as it unfolded in early 1992 to see whether we have proclaimed its death prematurely. After all, some of those political groups that Trotsky condemned to "the dustbin of history" in 1917 resurfaced during perestroika and after. Whether or not an imperial army will be revived in Russia is a crucial but yet unanswered question.

SIXTEEN

The Illusion of the CIS Armed Forces

The Army Cannot Be Carved Up Alive

HEADLINE IN KRASNAYA ZVEZDA, 28 DECEMBER 1991

Pretenses that the Soviet Armed Forces would survive with only a change in name continued for another year and a half. President Yeltsin had promised that the CIS would have a unified military, and Marshal Shaposhnikov was determined to see that it did. By March 1992 most officers' illusions about this goal were rapidly evaporating, but Shaposhnikov maintained his own until mid-1993, when Yeltsin asked him to step down as the commander in chief of the CIS Armed Forces and take a position as secretary of the Russian Security Council.[1] By that time, a Russian ministry of defense had been formed, with General Grachev as the minister. Already facing insurmountable resistance from Ukraine and a number of other CIS members, Shaposhnikov's endeavor became transparently hopeless when the Russian defense minister openly refused to contribute resources to it.

Ironically and cynically, Grachev and his clique of generals schemed to prevent the Soviet military's resuscitation as the CIS Armed Forces. At the same time, they posed as "superpatriots," loudly resentful of the breakup of the Soviet Union but quietly stealing and selling off arms and equipment, building private dachas and buying luxury cars with the proceeds. They opposed the Russian foreign minister's pro-Western policy and worked to restore Russian control over the former Soviet Union, but their policies and operations in the former Soviet republics only intensified hostility toward Moscow.[2] One could argue that they merely followed the example set by their political leaders in the destruction of the Soviet Union. General Grachev was no less determined to unseat Marshal Shaposhnikov than Yeltsin and his supporters were to destroy Gorbachev's political position. And just as Yeltsin was prepared to dissolve the

Soviet Union to achieve his goal, Grachev was willing to undermine the creation of the CIS Armed Forces.

This is not to say that Grachev could have saved the Soviet Armed Forces by cooperating with Shaposhnikov any more than Yeltsin could have saved the Soviet Union by cooperating with Gorbachev. Ukrainian opposition in both cases would have been extremely difficult to overcome, not to mention the separatist movements in the Baltic and Transcaucasus republics. Rather, General Grachev's conduct underscores the hypocrisy that masked personal ambitions with pretenses of patriotism and indignation over the loss of the empire. Here the story of these events will be told only as a summary account of the losing struggle by Marshal Shaposhnikov to transform, at least temporarily, the Soviet Armed Forces into a CIS Armed Forces.

The Paradox of the CIS Armed Forces

The cartoon portraying the soldier who "serve[d] a single economic space" captured the paradox of the CIS Armed Forces.[3] Establishing such a force was impossible without the restoration of the empire. An army without a clear political authority over it must either cease to exist or become its own political authority, creating its own state. For the first few months of 1992, however, pretenses were kept up that a compromise solution to this paradox was attainable. Shaposhnikov claims that he sought only a transition period of five years to ease the travails of officers and their families, although he hoped it might also allow the republics to discover shared interests in some form of joint CIS forces.[4] At least this is the argument he says he made to the Officers' Assembly in Moscow on 17 January 1992, when it accused him of destroying the Soviet Armed Forces and demanded his removal.[5] He threatened to resign and argued that the only way to have saved the Soviet military was through wider and bloodier repressions than the officer corps had already recoiled against in Tbilisi, Baku, Lithuania, and Moscow. This prospect was sufficient to dampen the demand for his removal. Yet Shaposhnikov had not completely given up on restoring a new union. Watching the leaders of the republics in the Novo-Ogarevo negotiations convinced him that they wanted to oust Gorbachev more than to destroy the Soviet Union.[6] By that logic, once Gorbachev was removed, it should be possible to maintain most of the former Soviet Union as a single political entity. The Alma-Ata summit on 21 December 1991, however, should have disabused him of that illusion.

Although Shaposhnikov put a good face on the meeting, the fundamental issues were not resolved but only postponed until the CIS summit in Minsk on

30–31 December 1991. This was his last chance to get these issues addressed effectively. To secure as much agreement in advance as possible, he convened a committee of republican defense representatives on 26–27 December. (The committee, which he had established in early September, continued under the CIS as the Council of Defense Ministers.[7]) Here Shaposhnikov tried to sell his concept for the CIS military (fig. 8). He envisioned the political authority as vested in all the presidents of CIS states collectively. The forces themselves would be subordinate to a single supreme commander, who would report to the CIS Defense Council under the CIS presidents. Although each CIS state would have its own armed forces, ultimately they all came under the control of supreme commander of the CIS Armed Forces.

Ukraine and several other states rejected it outright. This scheme was essentially the one Shaposhnikov had been urging since early September when he outlined it to the GOSSOVET. In fact, the collective of CIS presidents was the same set of people as those in the GOSSOVET, the heads of the republics.

His plan was even less attractive to them now, especially to Ukraine, which was, in Shaposhnikov's words, "the initiator and motor of the processes of disassociation in the defense sphere."[8] Yet he stuck to his old arguments. If one cared about the fate of all the military personnel, then one had to support keeping the Soviet military's centralized systems for logistics, personnel, procurement, and technical support. Otherwise, taking care of the personnel would be impossible. Nor could the traumatic implications of dividing up the Soviet military be ignored. Not only was it impossible to break most of them into operationally coherent pieces parceled out to each CIS state in a short time, but it would also be enormously expensive, and it would radically reduce CIS military capabilities, making parts of them virtually unusable for combat operations for several years. Implementing the recently signed arms control treaties — CFE and START — would also become more difficult, a point Shaposhnikov periodically raised. Finally, dividing the nuclear forces was something that Russia would not accept and the rest of the world would find extremely undesirable.

These technical considerations were real but difficult for civilian politicians to understand. The Soviet military's obsession with secrecy meant that virtually no civilian understood the structure of the USSR-wide PVO system of radar, air control systems, centralized communications, and control networks. They were like a "public good," in that for one republic to have the PVO system, it also had to be able to defend all the others. Dividing it would virtually destroy the system. The space program and the early warning system against missile attacks were also in this category. Parts of the navy and the rocket forces

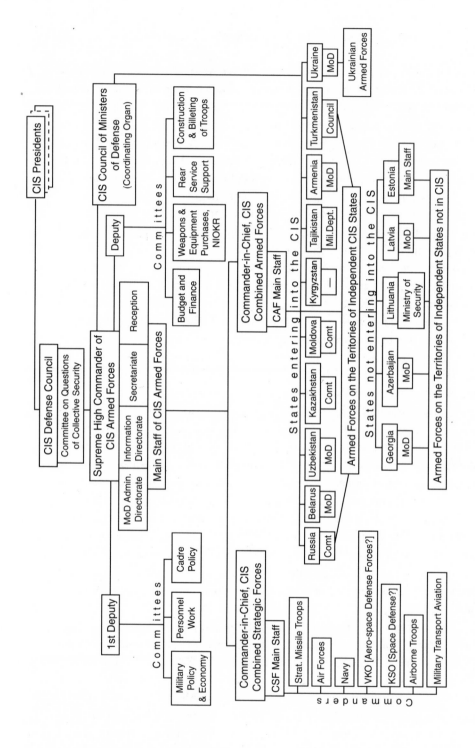

Figure 8. Ministry of Defense plan for CIS AF

had an all-or-nothing character. When logistics, military industries, and military research and development were included, the implications of fragmenting the Soviet military were all the more disruptive.

One might argue that the solution was to demobilize most of the armed forces and simply give up all these capabilities. Indeed, this was the most logical alternative. Moreover, it had already been happening during the previous two years of disintegration in the military. Still, such a large demobilization could not be completed in a couple of months, or even in a year. In the meantime, military personnel had to be fed, paid, and housed, and that required maintenance of the systems for central finance and logistics. Equipment and weapons had to be stored, and that required the central technical supply and support systems. Shaposhnikov had created an MoD commercial organization to sell off as much excess equipment as possible, but he soon regretted it because corrupt business deals quickly made it more of a problem than a solution.[9] There was no short-term solution, no matter that one was politically imperative.

The more one digs into the technical realities that dividing up the Soviet military entailed, the easier it is to appreciate why Shaposhnikov could remain so insistent about keeping a unified military, at least through a transition period. His arguments did not persuade the committee of republican defense officials at their 26–27 December meeting, however, as they underscored the political implications of his plan. All but Russia would be left without an army, and Russia would still have most of the old Soviet army deployed throughout the other republics. Having come this close to genuine independence, most of them were unwilling to risk Shaposhnikov's proposed arrangements. Even if they trusted Shaposhnikov—which the Ukrainians did not—they could not be sure that another General Varennikov might not arise, come to their capitals, and say "Smirno!"

An alternative plan was put to the meeting by Colonel General Kobets (fig. 9). How he was able to do so is not clear, but statements by Major Lopatin suggest that Kobets developed his plan not within the General Staff but in the reform group he headed that fall for the Russian government. The republican defense chiefs preferred the Kobets plan primarily because it put their own armed forces directly under the control of their heads of state. Another less obvious difference was also important. Kobets's design called for a "combined," *(ob'edinennye)* not a "unified" *(edinye)* CIS Armed Forces, as Shaposhnikov's did. The plural connotation of *combined* contrasted with the central connotation of *unified,* but this was not just semantics. Shaposhnikov never tried to conceal the centralized character of his scheme. For all the technical reasons just reviewed, that was essential, at least through several years of transition. He

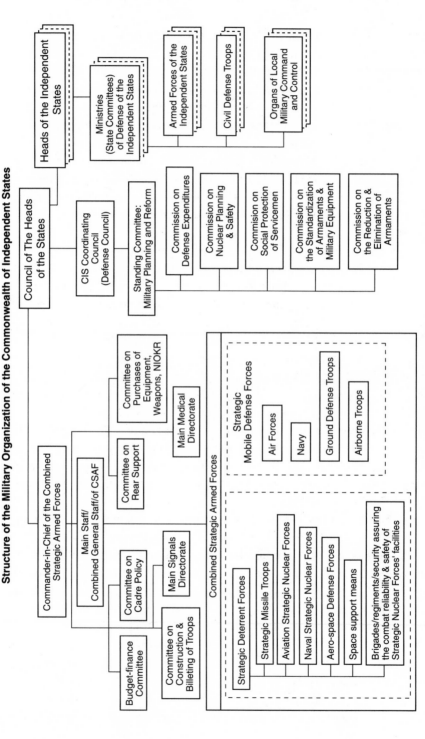

Structure of the Military Organization of the Commonwealth of Independent States

Figure 9. Kobets plan for CIS AF

was fully prepared to put plural political bodies over the unified CIS Armed Forces—the CIS Presidents, the CIS Defense Council, and the Council of Defense Ministers—but the supreme commander had to retain central control to execute the policy guidance from these plural bodies, and all the staff functions remained under the supreme commander as well. In the Kobets design, not only was military command split among the CIS states, but several of the staff functions were placed in commissions not responsible to the commander of the CIS Armed Forces.

Although the meeting expressed its preference for the Kobets design, some of its features were still unacceptable. The combined CIS Armed Forces, in Kobets's scheme, were to be divided into two new categories, strategic deterrent forces and strategic mobile defense forces. These two components effectively included all of the old Soviet military, less civil defense troops and a few other small elements. Ukraine, Georgia, Azerbaijan, and Armenia were already "nationalizing" some of the conventional forces to be included in the strategic mobile defense forces and had no intention of giving them back.

The concept of strategic deterrent forces also posed serious differences between Ukraine and Moscow. The Soviet military had never drawn the clear line between nuclear "deterrent" forces and all others as the U.S. Department of Defense did, not least because it never accepted, or really understood, the U.S. concept of nuclear deterrence. Forces that could achieve "strategic" objectives as opposed to "operational" and "tactical" objectives were considered strategic forces. They included the bulk of Soviet nuclear forces, but they also included other forces centrally controlled by the General Staff, not allocated to fronts, groups of forces, and military districts. Most of the PVO, the space program, and large parts of the navy were also considered strategic components. Not surprisingly, Ukraine, Kazakhstan, and to a lesser degree Belarus were inclined to the U.S. definition of what constituted strategic forces because it left fewer forces under Moscow's control.

This dispute and how it was eventually settled—with considerable direct U.S. involvement as an arbiter and supplier of funds and technical resources— is a story unto itself, deserving its own separate history. In short, the residual Soviet command structure moved tactical nuclear weapons onto Russian territory before they became a major issue of dispute. The nuclear weapons in the navy were almost entirely deployed in the Pacific and Northern fleets, both based in Russian ports, so they were removed from the dispute. The silo-based ballistic missile forces and parts of the long range aviation could not be quickly redeployed from Ukraine, Kazakhstan, and Belarus. Nor could all the space program facilities and nuclear testing ranges in Kazakhstan be either moved or disbanded quickly. Belarus and Kazakhstan proved cooperative in yielding control of all of these forces and installations to Russia under a lengthy schedule of redeployment and, in the case of test facilities in Kazakhstan, bilateral agreements for their continued use by Russia. Ukraine was not so easily appeased. Only with urging and financial aid from the United States did Ukraine eventually agree to removal of these installations from its territory. And the Black Sea Fleet, which Moscow initially tried to define as part of the strategic forces, remained a neuralgic point in Ukrainian-Russian relations until 1997, when the fleet was finally divided and Moscow agreed to lease the Sevastopol port in the Crimea for twenty years.

Overlapping these issues was the task of implementing both the START and CFE treaties. Once Ukraine agreed to the removal of all strategic missile units, Belarus and Kazakhstan already having done so, START implementation became a U.S.-Russian issue only. CFE was another matter. It left Ukraine with a considerable advantage because the most modern ground forces were located in the western military districts. Belarus had the same advantage but took a highly cooperative attitude toward Moscow. The Baltic states insisted on complete withdrawal, because they stood outside the CIS. Later Russia policies in the Transcaucasus would lead the Russian military to violate CFE limits on that flank of the CFE zones, posing yet another troublesome issue that would require additional negotiations for revising these limits in 1996–97.

Such disputes over strategic forces and arms control implementation issues were too complex to resolve in the few days near the end of 1991 before the CIS became a reality. One additional issue highlighted by the Shaposhnikov and Kobets approaches deserves attention because it goes to the heart of the paradox that both men faced.

Once Shaposhnikov's concept of a truly unified CIS Armed Forces was compromised, it was difficult to find a stopping point for yielding direct control over military forces to the republics where they were deployed. Sovereignty and independence, as understood in international law, gave the strongest arguments to the republics. By accepting the concept of combined forces, as his design did, Kobets was implicitly giving them the legal basis for an interstate collective security arrangement, precisely what NATO is. In the course of the spring, the Warsaw Pact and NATO models became part of the vocabulary in the debate. Shaposhnikov's approach and Kobets's for the most part were closer to the Warsaw Pact model. Ukraine and others wanted something closer to the NATO model. The practical obstacles, however, were enormous. The CIS states first had to establish their full independence from Moscow, set up their own armies, and then voluntarily reenter a collective security arrangement as an international organization, not a political union. They had to be sure that Russian imperialism was no longer a threat. These requirements could not be met overnight, and even if they were, all the problems of dividing up the Soviet Armed Forces that troubled Shaposhnikov still had to be confronted.

Toward the CIS Collective Security Treaty

The Minsk summit on 30–31 December 1991 had no chance to resolve all these disputes, and it did not. A follow-up summit was therefore convened in Moscow on 16 January 1992. In the intervening two weeks, Shaposhnikov fell into a bitter dispute with Ukraine over the military oath.[10] It seemed a trivial matter, but it was symbolic of the paradox confronting the CIS Armed Forces. Officers normally take an oath to the political authority they serve. Ukraine insisted that all officers in its new armed forces take an oath of allegiance to Ukraine. Shaposhnikov insisted that any new oath should be to the peoples of the CIS, but he had to yield.

Of much greater substantive significance, Ukrainian officials moved quickly to ensure their control over military forces on their territory. In accord with the Minsk agreements, Shaposhnikov sent an order on 3 January 1992, formally transferring authority over conventional forces to Ukraine. President Kravchuk then approved the firing of the three military district commanders (the Ukrainian, Odessa, and Carpathian military districts were all within Ukrainian borders). On 7–8 January each was removed, none of them resisting because within their headquarters Kravchuk's people had quietly created a network of officers loyal to his government.[11] With the air poisoned by both this episode and the dispute over the officers' oath, no real progress was made at the Moscow summit.

Another attempt was made at a summit in Minsk on 14 February 1992. On the surface, this meeting could point to progress. The following agreements were reached:

- Strategic Forces Agreement, signed by all but Moldova (the new name for Moldavia).
- General Purpose Forces Agreement, signed by eight states but not Ukraine, Moldova, or Azerbaijan.
- Appointment of Marshal Shaposhnikov as commander in chief of the CIS Armed Forces.
- Agreement on Supplying the Armed Forces, signed by seven states but not by Ukraine, Kazakhstan, Azerbaijan, or Russia.

- Agreement on Safeguards for Servicemen, signed by all but Moldova.
- Decision to establish a Defense Ministers' Council, signed only by five: Russia, Armenia, Tajikistan, Uzbekistan, and Kazakhstan.
- Protocol on Military Issues, an instruction to the defense ministers to prepare the next block of agreements for the next summit.[12]

Although these agreements were significant, the number of states that refused to sign them is a better indication of the limited results. More important, none of the agreements concerned central financing. Shortly after the meeting Shaposhnikov seemed close to achieving agreement on a central budget, but Georgia would not sign it and Ukraine accepted it only for strategic forces.[13] Thus he was forced to try again to make progress on both central budgeting and logistics at the next summit in Kiev, on 20 March. In the event he did not.[14] Although the Kiev summit appointed his deputy commanders and revised some of the language in the Minsk agreements, it remained stalemated on fundamental issues.[15]

No summit was held in April, and in Moscow, Yeltsin began to speak candidly about the impossibility of creating a CIS Armed Forces. Moreover, the Russian military representatives were resisting some of the agreements Shaposhnikov proposed. Privately they were agitating for the creation of a Russian defense ministry, the very thing Yeltsin had promised not to establish.

The next summit convened in Tashkent on 15–16 May 1992 to address an agenda of nearly thirty issues. Shaposhnikov spoke beforehand about "a search for a civilized way to divide up the arms, equipment, and property of the former Soviet army, to create national armed forces, and form a unified defense budget."[16] The Russian military delegation stole the show, however, by proposing a collective security treaty that would put the CIS on a path toward the NATO model. It was accepted, though only six states signed it at the summit. Others could sign later if they desired.[17]

The Russian delegation's motives for proposing this treaty were more concerned with creating favorable circumstances for founding a new Russian defense ministry and an independent Russian military than with bringing the NATO model to the CIS. It would also release Yeltsin from his promise not to create a Russian defense ministry. It would cut the ground from under Shaposhnikov's command position. And it would recognize the realities of disagreements at all the previous CIS summits on military matters. General Grachev and his clique of combined armed officers, mostly veterans of the Afghan war, had found a happy coincidence between their dislike of Shaposhnikov and the other republics' objections to his concept of a unified armed forces. For Grachev personally, it offered a way to destroy Shaposhnikov's position.

Grachev, of course, had hardly created the objective conditions that allowed him to undo Shaposhnikov. Shaposhnikov himself recognized them in the address to the Congress of People's Deputies in early April 1992. They were his theme, embodied in the title of his speech: "An Army Without a State is Not an Army, a State without an Army is Not a State."[18] Still, he pleaded for help in reversing them rather than coming to terms with them.

Although Shaposhnikov would persevere for another year in trying to create something of a CIS Armed Forces, his efforts were doomed to failure after the Tashkent summit and the creation of a Russian defense ministry. He was probably destined to fail from 1 January 1992, given the underlying political paradox, but Yeltsin kept up the pretense for nearly three months.

The Russian Ministry of Defense

Speaking to the same Congress of People's Deputies as Shaposhnikov had in April, Yeltsin turned briefly to military issues: "About the army: you know that for a long time Russia made no decision about setting up its own army, trying to preserve the unified Commonwealth Army. Well, that did not work. A state commission has now been set up . . . under Colonel General Volkogonov to carry out the primary work on establishing a Russian Army and Navy."[19] With the creation of the CIS, the Soviet MoD was formally abolished. Its departments and the General Staff, however, remained as Shaposhnikov's apparatus in his endeavor to establish a unified CIS Armed Forces. Yeltsin had retained the RSFSR's national security committee, however, renaming it the Defense Committee, and General Grachev became its chairman. This met his promise not to create a Russian defense ministry. In mid-March, right after the Kiev summit of the CIS, Yeltsin issued a decree, appointing himself Russian minister of defense and Grachev as deputy minister, along with a civilian, Andrei Kokoshin, as a second deputy minister. Yeltsin's announcement to the Congress of Deputies, therefore, was merely reporting a step he had already formally taken.

According to Shaposhnikov, Yeltsin was irritated that most of the CIS states had defense ministers but Russia did not. He finally insisted that Russia have one as well, but by appointing himself to the post, he created the awkward situation of having to sit as a member of the CIS Council of Defense Ministers under Shaposhnikov's chairmanship. Yeltsin more than once remarked about it to Shaposhnikov, who felt that Yeltsin was pushing him to become the Russian defense minister. In April 1992, Shaposhnikov once again made his case for patience in creating the organizational mechanisms for the CIS Armed Forces but also endorsed the idea that Yeltsin become the Russian defense minister, implicitly rejecting Yeltsin's hint that he, Shaposhnikov, ought to hold that post.[20]

Shortly after the congress, tensions between Yeltsin and its deputies increased sharply. Grachev convened all the military district commanders and let them know they were expected to support Yeltsin if a crisis arose with the congress and the parliament. Shaposhnikov considered Grachev's actions wholly inappropriate because they risked embroiling the military once again in politics, as had happened in 1991. A few weeks later, Shaposhnikov had another unpleasant experience while traveling with Yeltsin and his aide, Yurii Skokov, to several provincial Russian cities. During a flight, Skokov reported to Yeltsin the substance of the evening television news from Moscow, making it appear that Yegor Gaidar, the prime minister, had upstaged and slighted Yeltsin. This kind of personal intrigue angered Shaposhnikov and alerted him to scheming between Skokov and Rutskoi as well, who were backing Grachev for Russian defense minister.[21]

At the beginning of May, Grachev approached Shaposhnikov. Grachev said that Yeltsin had not defined either his or Kokoshin's duties as the two deputy defense ministers and that he was going to see Yeltsin that day to propose that Shaposhnikov be appointed defense minister to overcome this confusion. Shaposhnikov recognized his disingenuous pose at once, understanding that the decision had already been made in favor of Grachev. Thus he told Grachev to tell Yeltsin that he did not want to be minister of defense for two reasons. First, he had not lost faith in eventual success with the CIS Armed Forces, and second, he had come to know too well a couple of people in Yeltsin's entourage, and he did not want to become part of a circle of their kind. That evening Grachev's appointment as Russian defense minister was announced on television.[22]

Obviously this account is Shaposhnikov's biased view. It may not be the whole story, but in part it rings true. Grachev, Skokov, and Rutskoi were all schemers, and Shaposhnikov's picture of Grachev's behavior fits everything else known about him.

The End of the CIS Armed Forces

The creation of the Russian defense ministry completed the practical dissolution of the Soviet military, which had been formal since 31 December 1991. Henceforth there could be no more illusions that the Soviet MoD might merely change the sign on its doors. Shaposhnikov and a skeletal staff to support his role as commander of the CIS Armed Forces were evicted from the MoD and General Staff buildings and given offices in the former offices of the Warsaw

Pact headquarters on the northern outskirts of Moscow.[23] The symbolism was palpable: the quiet, pompous Warsaw Pact buildings, isolated in a grove of large trees, conveyed the feeling of a rural environment rather than the bustling urban setting that surrounded the MoD and the General Staff buildings in central Moscow. Shaposhnikov had almost literally been put out to pasture. Still, he would continue his struggle to give the CIS Armed Forces organizational substance for another year. In June 1993 the Russian defense ministry vetoed his last attempt, complaining that it could not afford funds for the CIS armed forces. He resigned his post that month, ending all illusions about the Soviet military reincarnated as the CIS Armed Forces.

Conclusion

To revive Russia without the army or apart from the army is impossible. The army —
this is not these or those generals, no matter how great their services. . . . The army —
this is the live personification of the official being of Russia.

PETER STRUVE

I n the opening pages of this study, two questions were posed to guide us
through the saga of the Soviet military's demise — how and why did it
happen? A prior question had to be answered before starting on that jour-
ney — what *was* the Soviet military? More specifically, what was distinctive or
unique about it, compared with Western militaries defending against it? Answers to all three questions should now be apparent. Some critical summing
up, nevertheless, is necessary, not only to bring those answers into sharper
focus and prevent them from being lost in the vast details of the story, but also
as a basis for taking a much larger perspective on the central significance of the
military for both Russian and Soviet political development. The perspective
throws light on why Russia has heretofore failed to find its way onto the path
of liberal political and economic development, a question of utmost importance
for contemporary Russian politics.

Understanding What the Soviet Military Was

When Tsar Nicholas II abdicated his throne to Grand Duke Michael in March
1917, he addressed his abdication manifesto not to the Duma and its Provisional
Committee, which were demanding it, but to the chief of staff of the Russian
army. According to the eminent historian Richard Pipes, this little-noted detail
has great significance because "in Nicholas's eyes the army command was the
one remaining bearer of sovereignty."[1] He is right, and he could have said more.

388

The army was the creator as well as embodiment of the stability and legitimacy of the Russian Empire in the eyes of all of Nicholas's predecessors as well.

The Soviet military, as a component of the Communist Party, was also the embodiment of the creation, sovereignty, and stability of the Soviet Empire. Like the Russian military, the Soviet "Workers' and Peasants' Red Army" conquered and sustained the Soviet Empire. The unfinished international working class revolution depended on the Red Army to secure "socialism in one country" and to confront the capitalist camp in the event of a military showdown. With its new name, Soviet Armed Forces, it extended communist rule into the very center of Europe after World War II and repressed uprisings against Soviet rule. Until its failure in Afghanistan, the Soviet military had been the most dependable means of expanding the Soviet empire.

In a word, Soviet military power cannot be understood apart from Soviet political and economic power. That should now be clear from several distinctive institutional realities that have been underscored throughout this study, several of them quite at odds with widely accepted understandings of the Soviet system during its last couple of decades. They need not all be recapitulated here, but a few major ones should be highlighted.

First, the role of the official ideology was critically important for the military's own justifications and claims on resources. Certainly it changed over time, especially in the post-Stalin period, but it was not becoming irrelevant, as sometimes believed. Rather it was increasingly internalized. Hypocrisy and corruption certainly endangered it, but that was true in Stalin's time. The most significant change was the disappearance of ruthless purges that Stalin had used to revitalize the ideology and hide hypocrisy.

Second, the military dimensions of the command economy were far larger and more deeply rooted than generally appreciated. Soviet secrecy partly explains this misperception, but not entirely. Another factor was the Western subconscious inclination to see "socialism" in Fabian or West European Social Democratic terms, that is, an economic system primarily concerned with economic equity and social justice. Soviet socialism retained its Marxist revolutionary foundation, giving pursuit of the international class struggle priority over social and economic welfare until the worldwide socialist revolution was complete. Thus Soviet socialism required a permanent war economy.

Third, the military was an integral part of the Communist Party. This reality set the Soviet case outside the Western theories of civil-military relations for modern professional armies. Both the party's and the military's "professional ethic" was to ensure progress in the international class struggle, eventually overthrowing the bourgeois international order, not merely to ensure the security of the Soviet state within that order. Soviet political and economic organization reflected this shared ethic. Anticipation that the military as an autonomous entity would intervene in Soviet politics therefore had no basis either in political values or in institutional arrangements. There may be a wider lesson here for understanding civil-military relations in Western advanced industrial and postindustrial states. Are not the interdependencies of their militaries with the rest of the society and economy so complex that autonomous political action by the military has become impractical? Perhaps military coups are only characteristic of political systems in earlier stages of development or of systems on quite different paths of development.

Fourth, the Soviet military's approach to nuclear weapons and arms control has been fundamentally misunderstood by many in the West. To have adopted deterrence theory and its concepts of what constitutes military stability would have required Soviet leaders to abandon the ideological foundations of their state's legitimacy and purpose. Gorbachev, Yakovlev, Shevardnadze, and several of their aides understood this, and that is why Gorbachev revised the ideology. The destabilizing consequences for the Soviet regime show why Western expectations that mutually shared U.S. and Soviet views of nuclear weapons and arms control could not lead to a shared political stability. Ligachev, Marshal Akhromeev, and several other of Gorbachev's opponents understood this too well but too late to stop Gorbachev.

Was the Soviet Military a Paper Tiger?

The question of the threat actually posed by the Soviet military, not entirely new, naturally arises in light of the military's rapid demise. The picture of corruption in the senior officer ranks, brutality in barracks, and disaffection in the junior officer ranks—all of which contributed to the military's disintegration— encourages the view that in the event of a NATO–Warsaw Pact conflict, the Soviet military would have fallen apart. Do the findings of this study really support that conclusion? An unambiguous answer in the absence of such a conflict is impossible, but there are compelling reasons to doubt it.

The particular design of Soviet forces, their command and control arrangements, the manning and training systems, and the operational concept of echelonment reflect impressive competence on the part of the Soviet military leaders in exploiting inherent strengths and mitigating weaknesses of the Soviet state, society, and economy. Manpower was cheap but of low quality. Weaponry was abundant though not always state of the art. The command and control system ensured "tactical rigidity"—that is, simple offensive tactical patterns and decision procedures—combined with "operational and strategic flexibility"—that is, the ability to allocate and shift reserves and deep fire support to exploit major opportunities across the whole of the front against NATO. Army, division, and lower-level units might be chewed up as they arrived at the front to face agile NATO tactical units, but the Soviet quantitative advantage compensated for that possibility. At the same time, the General Staff's direct control of all Warsaw Pact armies, second-echelon fronts, and deep fire support by rockets and aviation provided flexibility in pushing large amounts of combat power through any major gaps emerging in NATO's defense. Moreover, Warsaw Pact forces had devoted far more attention to operating on a nuclear battlefield in Europe, and a decision to use nuclear weapons could be made quickly in Moscow, without consultation among the Warsaw Pact states. NATO, by comparison, had great flexibility at the tactical level—division and lower-level units. But at the operational level, especially above corps in the multinational army groups and higher commands, NATO was comparatively rigid. Shared political authority on a multinational basis introduced procedures and criteria that could have slowed decision making with disastrous results, particularly a decision to use nuclear weapons. Soviet awareness of this reality is reflected in the response to Air-Land Battle with the concept of the theater strategic operation, which dramatically accelerated the pace of offensive in an effort to overwhelm the NATO operational-level decision-making cycle.

But would Soviet troops, victimized by dedovshchina and ethnic tensions, have performed effectively? Would the junior officers have demonstrated sufficient initiative? KGB and MPA controls provided powerful means of compelling unwilling officers and troops to fight. More important, the outbreak of war would have sublimated many of the social and political problems within the military's ranks. What the Soviet military could not endure was continuing peace combined with the bleeding sore of an unwinnable political and military struggle in Afghanistan. War in Central Europe could have been its salvation.

This is not to argue that the Warsaw Pact would have prevailed in such a war. Rather, it is to explain why its military units would not necessarily have collapsed and why they might have achieved considerable offensive success initially. It is simply illogical to infer from the disintegration of the Soviet military in 1989–91 that it had little or no capacity to wage effective war in Central Europe. That judgment requires different kinds of evidence which only a war could have provided. Equally unconvincing is the argument that NATO countries, primarily the United States, really did not need to spend as much as they did on military forces to defend against the Soviet Union. The evidence from this study encourages precisely the opposite conclusion: the military competition, both in the qualitative arms race and in U.S. reaction to Soviet tactics and operational doctrine, contributed enormously to the economic and political climate that allowed Gorbachev to follow the new course he did.

How and Why the Soviet Military Collapsed

"How" the Soviet military collapsed needs no further explanation. The story has been told, but "why" is another matter. The simple answer is that Gorbachev made it collapse. He undermined it with his policies, sometimes intentionally, sometimes unwittingly. A more elaborate assessment must begin with a point made several times in this study about the role of leaders in explaining the dynamics of politics. Leaders have a degree of choice in making policies. Depending on their skill and intelligence in seeing real alternatives, they can increase that discretion, but they are constrained by structural conditions and reactive decisions by subordinates and other people affected by their choices. Interactions of policies, conditions, and reactions create the dynamics of politics (and of military operations in both peace and war). And the top policy maker's choices are often decisive in the creation of a particular dynamic between policy and its impact on structural conditions and reactive choices by all of those people affected. Certainly that was the case with Gorbachev's choices, not just in military policy but in his foreign and domestic policies as well. Let us review them in their bare essentials from this analytic viewpoint.

Convinced that fundamental changes were essential to overcome sluggish economic performance, Gorbachev looked for fiscal relief that would allow significant changes in capital allocations. The Soviet Union produced too many "guns" but not enough "butter." Fiscal relief, he believed, could be obtained by cutting the production of guns and shifting the savings to butter production. All his aides, advisers, Politburo colleagues, and even generals agreed with this strategy.

They began to disagree only when Gorbachev resorted to means for reducing the "production of guns" that Ligachev and others saw as undermining the system itself. Gorbachev viewed arms control agreements as the primary means for military reductions. To get the large cuts he deemed necessary, he had to convince Western leaders that they could safely risk such agreements. The first two years of his rule, therefore, brought a radically new foreign policy. Gorbachev went abroad to sell himself to Western leaders as a man they could trust, and he succeeded dramatically. Meanwhile, his domestic policies began with two main thrusts. During his first two years he implemented a sweeping turnover of senior party officials—an administrative purge on a scale not seen since the 1950s, and in the senior military ranks, not since the 1930s. The other thrust was economic, and it was no more novel than his party cadre policy. Called acceleration, it employed traditional bureaucratic methods for trying to squeeze better performance from the command economy. The new departure was the attempt to employ the VPK and its methods in selected sectors of the civilian economy. Thus Gorbachev's radical foreign policy was not matched by radical domestic policies until 1988, when the new laws on the economic firm took effect and glasnost was encouraged.

He also began tinkering with the official ideology and military doctrine, and by 1987 he had promulgated revisions in the official ideology that effectively destroyed the traditional method of defining the Soviet Union's main adversaries. Domestic backlash set in. Over the next two years, Gorbachev sparred with Ligachev and other conservatives who recognized the deadly implications of his ideological revisions, the political awakening among the national minorities, and his glasnost policy. Alternately advancing and retreating, Gorbachev kept surprising his opponents by inviting more popular forces to participate in the political struggle. By late 1989, the party was losing control, the military leadership was alienated, and the armed forces began to show signs of disintegration.

There was no way to retreat and no clear way to go forward without yielding to the centrifugal forces emerging in the national republics. By the time Yeltsin had made his comeback as leader of the RSFSR, Russian separatism was on the agenda. Gorbachev had lost the democratic forces as well as the regional party apparatus and the senior military, leaving himself with virtually no domestic political base. He had unleashed the public against the military, the junior officers against the generals, and mothers against conscription of their sons. He was destroying what Nicholas II knew was the embodiment of the empire.

This analysis shows why the debate about whether the Soviet Union collapsed from internal factors or from Western military and political pressures is a false issue. Both sides are right about some of the reasons for the collapse of the Soviet Union and both are wrong in claiming to have the complete answer. More important, however, they both miss the critical precipitating factor: political voluntarism, the role of leadership. To ignore Gorbachev's choice making is a fundamental error. The Soviet Union was doomed to an eventual breakdown, but it could have been delayed for several years, perhaps decades. Several totalitarian systems in much worse economic shape—North Korea,

Cuba, Vietnam—have outlasted the Soviet Union. Gorbachev's role, therefore, is necessary for explaining the timing and manner of the Soviet system's collapse, the "how" as well as the "why."

Gorbachev was not the only consequential political actor. Why did neither top military officers nor his Politburo colleagues stop him from destroying the Soviet Union? They understood where he was taking them. They knew that by mid-1987, Ligachev was saying so publicly in 1988, and Marshal Akhromeev insists that he saw the implications for the Warsaw Pact quite early. Three major reasons explain why.

First, no single general or clique of generals could stop Gorbachev so long as he was the party leader and unopposed by a Politburo faction able to oust him. The military's entanglement with the party, its internalization of the party's ideology, and the party's control of promotions made it so much a part of the party that it could not act as a corporate force against the party. It could only follow an anti-Gorbachev faction in the party, which it did at the Twenty-eighth Party Congress in 1990. So to ask why the military by itself did not stop Gorbachev is a nonsense question.

Second, Gorbachev combined uncommon cunning and duplicity with a fatally flawed understanding of the Soviet system. This combination gave him a remarkable advantage over his opponents. He consistently surprised them because, as they would say afterward, he had no deep convictions. He insisted that he retained his commitment to Leninism while effectively destroying the ideology. He methodically weakened the party but would not leave it. He detested the military but depended on it to repress national separatist movements. Most consequential for his policy making, however, was his flawed understanding of the Soviet political system, especially how it coped with the nationality problem. This ignorance kept him from understanding that his tactic of expanding political participation would eventually destroy the Soviet Union. At the same time, the tactic consistently constrained his opponents and confronted them with forces they could not contain, much less overcome.

Only Ligachev among the Politburo members had the stature and the control over cadre assignments necessary to unseat Gorbachev. He tried, but too late and always too timidly. His fatal handicap, however, was that he understood why Gorbachev's policies would destroy the Soviet system. That left him unable to expand his political base outside the party as Gorbachev was doing. Neo-Stalinism was the only viable strategy for him, but he apparently had neither the skills nor the stomach for it.

Shevardnadze and Yakovlev, it will be recalled, said they knew that they were destroying the Soviet Union. They understood what Ligachev did, but they did not share his goals. Their personal contributions to the dissolution of the Soviet Union and its armed forces were only slightly less critical than Gorbachev's, but without Gorbachev and his flawed understanding of what kept the Soviet Union stable, they could not have succeeded.

Yeltsin's decisions were also critical to the course of events. After he recovered from the shock of his expulsion from the Politburo in 1987, he eventually defeated Gorbachev precisely because he was willing to destroy the Soviet Union. He beat Gorbachev at his own game of appealing to a wider popular base of political support, adding the national separatist movements to the democratic forces in Moscow, which he stole from Gorbachev. Here Gorbachev faced the ultimate limit to his tactics. He would not (and could not, without losing power) compete with Yeltsin for the support of national separatists. That precluded him from doing to Yeltsin what he had done to Ligachev and others—widen popular participation in order to gain support for his own policies while leaving his opponents no choice but to fall back on the traditional means of political repression. Thus he eventually found himself in the same predicament, depending more and more on the party-KGB-military base against national separatists, but now this base was too weak to save him—the ironic consequence of his own policies.

The third reason no one could overthrow Gorbachev is related to the second. The cumulative effect of Gorbachev's scheming and duplicitous tactics was to intensify the efforts of all his opponents to match him. Dealing, double-dealing, and double-double-dealing simply got out of hand. That was apparent after the Tbilisi massacre, when Shevardnadze became enraged about the duplicity and double games causing bloodshed in his native republic. There was no less scheming in Stalin's day, but periodically Stalin physically eliminated his opponents, thereby reinspiring discipline and responsiveness to his orders by the police, the party, and the military. Gorbachev did not destroy his opponents politically, much less physically, and that soon made the KGB, the party apparatus, and the military leery about taking sides, because they could not be sure who would eventually come out on top. For a time, their tentativeness differed from past practice only in degree, not in kind. But after the scheming had gone on for three or four years without decisive showdowns, even second- and third-level party, police, and military officials began to keep open their options because they were not compelled to take sides unambiguously. After a couple of years of this behavior, the apparatus was hopelessly unresponsive to Politburo direction.

At some point during last couple of years of the Gorbachev period, the forces of dissolution began to outweigh the forces of centralization. Perhaps

Dunlop is right that the GKChP, if it had stormed the White House, could have saved the Soviet Union. No doubt it could have gained control of Moscow, but reversing all the centrifugal forces in the republics and the far-flung regions of the RSFSR would not have been easy. The bureaucracies that held the Soviet Union together for so long were no longer effective—particularly the military, which was the last line of defense, the "embodiment" of the sovereignty and stability of empire. Had the GKChP been victorious against the White House, it might have postponed the dissolution of the Soviet Union for awhile, but not for long.

The military had become so entangled in the scheming and plotting among the top party leaders that it could no longer be forced to respond effectively to a single command authority. Careerism and opportunism made them too vulnerable to bribes and promises of promotions from competing party leaders. In a struggle to reimpose strong central control, the members of the GKChP would soon have fallen out, and the "outs" probably could have found generals to support them by undercutting military commanders supporting the "ins." At the same time, local military commanders would have made alliances with regional political leaders who could promise food and housing to their troops. Moreover, the disruptions in the MoD's central logistics and finance system were already forcing many local commanders to fend for themselves.

Once the combination of ideological élan and fear of physical retribution that Lenin, Stalin, and even Khrushchev had used to sustain Bolshevik discipline had eroded, saving the empire was impossible. Moreover, there was no one among the GKChP members with the strength of personality and mind and also with the character required to imprison hundreds of thousands of people and to execute many of them and work to death the rest. A Bolshevik regime requires special leaders. Lenin and Stalin, Mao, Ho Chi Minh, Castro, and Kim Il-sung are examples. No such people were to be found in the Soviet politburo in the 1980s.

To sum up, a set of structural conditions provided the Soviet empire's stability, and key among them, the last defense against destabilizing forces, was the military. The combination of external pressures and internal problems, especially declining economic performance, convinced most of the elites that a radically new course was necessary to overcome what they called "the period of stagnation." Gorbachev needed that mood among the elites to allow him to launch perestroika, but he did not have to launch it. For more than two years his policies looked more like a variant of neo-Stalinism—a party purge coupled with a bureaucratic campaign within the command economic apparatus—than it did a break with the past. But when Gorbachev added glasnost, took halfway measures with the 1987 new economic laws on the firm, reversed military doctrine, and revised the ideology, he was indeed taking a new course that inexorably led to the collapse of the system.

How could a man who could rise to become general secretary of the Communist Party of the Soviet Union be so oblivious to the requisites for the system's stability? He obviously failed to grasp the force of nationalism in several of the republics. That he never held a party leadership position in a non-Russian republic has been widely noted to explain this blind spot. That he never served in uniform has received less attention, but none of his predecessors had so little experience with the Soviet military or so little personal contact with senior officers. The Russian civil war and World War II had socialized his predecessors in military affairs and left them with close contacts in the officer ranks. If his chief of staff, Boldin, is to be believed, Gorbachev loathed the military, especially after the Rust incident. That psychological disposition made it extremely difficult for him to understand, much less acknowledge, what a much less intelligent Russian leader, Nicholas II, instinctively understood: the army command was the embodiment of the regime's sovereignty and stability. No less puzzling is Gorbachev's naïve view of economic affairs. Boldin comments on his weak knowledge of economics. Shakhnazarov declares that Gorbachev was uninterested in the economy to the point of boredom. He left the economy to the Council of Ministers while he and the Politburo dealt with politics — party affairs and foreign policy.

With this answer to why the Soviet military, along with the Soviet Union, collapsed, it is possible to assess the larger political significance of the central place the military held, not only in the Soviet system but also in the Imperial Russian regime.

Three Structural Variables

Two elements of Gorbachev's strategy for perestroika stand out clearly. First, its primary goal was to overcome economic stagnation. Political liberalization was not the goal. It was not even an initial consideration. Some of Gorbachev's advisers desired it, but he did not; nor did Ligachev. The economic crisis catalyzed the Politburo consensus for new policy departures. Second, the economic crisis was to be solved by reducing the military spending burden. In the simplest terms, the essence of perestroika was changing the relation between two variables, the economy and the military.

Shakhnazarov tells us that during Andropov's rule, this relation was much discussed and debated. He suggested to Andropov that political reform was necessary before effective economic reform was possible, but Andropov insisted that economic improvement had to precede political change. Gorbachev initially proceeded on Andropov's assumption. Only when he became frustrated at the party's and economic bureaucracies' resistance to economic reform and the lack of result did he turn to political reform, and then it was not a goal but a means. Unable to convert guns into butter, he resorted to mobilizing new political forces against the bureaucrats.

Once so-called political reform began—it was not actually political reform but more accurately an invitation for heretofore repressed political forces to check and block Gorbachev's opponents—it inexorably allowed the nationalist separatist forces to emerge. By the end of 1988, they were making surprising gains in the Baltic republics and in the Transcaucasus, and they were gathering strength in western Ukraine.

At this point, perestroika involved not just two but three variables: 1) the economy, 2) the military, and 3) the nationality problem. Liberal political ideas, market economic principles, a free media, new relations with the West, arms control, and all of the other matters that captured the political stage in the Soviet Union were only reflections of the dynamics of these three variables, not the basic issues or driving forces. They were the modalities for the intensifying political struggle. Gorbachev was not a liberal democrat. He saw himself as a true Leninist who could adapt the ideology and the party to escape the dead end toward which Brezhnev had been taking the country. Chernyaev more than once remarks on Gorbachev's penchant for reading from Lenin's works, sometimes quoting aloud in the privacy of his office to Chernyaev. The Brest-Litovsk peace that Lenin signed with the Germans in 1918 against the wishes of most of his Central Committee colleagues was an example of Lenin's remarkable capacity to make huge concessions and then turn them into a strategic victory. Mikhail Shatrov made the episode the subject of a play he wrote and staged, *Brestskii mir* (The Brest Peace), in Moscow in 1987–88. Gorbachev found the intended analogy between Lenin's strategy and his own so flattering that he sent Shatrov as part of his advance party to Washington for a summit meeting.

The reason for drawing out the key variables underlying perestroika is to reveal a set of three structural conditions that had long trapped Russia in a dynamic vicious circle. They can be traced back to the late fifteenth and early sixteenth centuries, when the Muscovite princes had subdued all other Russian principalities, changed their title from *prince of all Russias* to *tsar*—literally *caesar*—and accepted the doctrine of Moscow the Third Rome, a myth cooked up by inventive clerics after the fall of the Byzantine Empire to link the tsar directly to the founders of the Roman Empire, giving him claim on its legitimacy.

At the same time this imperial political ideology was taking root in Moscow, its boyars were beginning to expand beyond Russian ethnic territories. Ivan III's twenty-year war with Lithuania left Moscow in control of some Lithuanian territory. More important, Moscow finally broke the Tatar Yoke and no longer had to pay taxes to the khans. In the sixteenth century, Moscow would conquer Kazan and other Tatar strongholds, bringing Tatars under its rule. Moscow was on the imperial path which it would follow right down to Gorbachev's rule.

Muscovite statecraft owed far more to the Tatars than to Byzantium, and nothing to Rome.[2] The Moscow princes proved extremely effective tax collectors because they learned the Tatar methods. The khans had increasingly favored Moscow over other Russian principalities precisely because it had met its tax burdens. As the various princely clans feuded and fought, the Tatars preferred to see Moscow win because its princes were better tax collectors. The consequences for the peasantry and the agrarian economy were devastating.[3]

Moscow's exceptional skill in extracting wealth from an impoverished peasantry gave it other advantages. Armies are expensive. As Peter the Great once remarked, "Money is the artery of war."[4] At the same time, as Peter created an iron industry and brought other Western industrial technologies to Russia, the state's dominating role in directing both private and state firms proved highly inefficient.[5] But Moscow was able to support its army as it devoured more and more territory. The resulting rapid imperial expansion reinforced this taxation pattern because larger and more widespread military forces were required to rule the growing imperial territories. The expansion naturally alarmed Russia's neighbors, ensuring their hostility and reinforcing Moscow's sense of being surrounded by enemies. Eliminating those enemies by force, however, increased the burdens of imperial rule and created new enemies on the periphery.

During the eighteenth and early nineteenth centuries this pattern continued unabated, but in the course of the nineteenth century a new political factor arose to increase centrifugal political forces in the non-Russian territories, especially in the European parts of the empire: nationalism. This new idea inspired mass support, previously unavailable to local political elites, among non-Russian ethnic groups for separatism from Moscow. Poland rose up in arms against Russian rule twice in the nineteenth century. Finnish, Lithuanian, Latvian, and Estonian nationalisms were outwardly quiescent but inwardly germinating. Ukrainian nationalism was nourished by the influence of Ukrainian literary figures and the Uniate Church, which recognized papal authority although it retained the Orthodox rites.

The Russian regime reacted by reinforcing the old pattern. It could not risk letting market forces take hold and move Russia into the industrial revolution that was occurring in Western Europe, because accompanying political liberalism was incompatible with Russian autocracy. Still, Russia needed an industrial base for modern military power, prompting the state to sponsor and control industrialization, an approach that ensured slow progress and inefficient capital allocations.[6] At the same time, the military budget remained the largest item in the state budget throughout the century, reflecting the continuing imperialist expansion—especially in the latter half of the century—but it was never adequate to keep up with changing military technology. As Dietrich Geyer observes, "In Russia, expansion was an expression of economic weakness, not exuberant strength."[7]

As the Russian intelligentsia reacted to all these modernizing forces and Western political thought, they increasingly focused on the so-called peasant question—that is, how to develop an economy that was almost entirely based on peasant agriculture. The radical left wing of the intelligentsia devoted little attention to the military question or the nationality question, leaving them mainly to the regime. Financing and staffing the military remained the central issue for the regime throughout the century.[8] In fact, the Great Reforms in the 1860s and 1870s, including the emancipation of the peasantry, were catalyzed by defeat in the Crimean War, the first war of any consequence that Russia had lost since the seventeenth century. An army of illiterate peasants could not match the literate Western armies.

The only other issue that rivaled the military question for the tsar's attention right down to World War II was the nationality question. The Polish uprisings signaled to the tsar the power of this new force. Count S. S. Uvarov, minister of education under Nicholas I, concocted a slogan for the regime's legitimacy—Autocracy, Orthodoxy, and Patriotism.[9] This vague assertion of the primacy of the monarch, the church, and the people serving the tsar, without any ethnic or national distinctions among them, was as potent a justification of the regime as was ever articulated before its collapse in 1917. The conservative wing of the intelligentsia also attempted to find a principle of legitimacy for the regime that could compete with nationalism.[10] Its candidate was Slavophilism, but ruling out non-Slavs was a formula for breaking up the empire. Orthodoxy was another candidate, based on adherence to the Russian Orthodox faith, but it ruled out the Catholic Slavs. Although sympathetic with the Slavophiles, the tsar and his advisers, sensitive to the danger of giving various elements in the empire justification to secede, refrained from officially embracing either Slavophilism or Othodoxy. By the turn of the twentieth century, some conservatives were becoming reactionary, turning to anti-Semitism and encouraging pogroms, attitudes and actions that would later characterize modern fascism. (Hitler's ideologist, Alfred Rosenberg, was a Baltic German who was educated at Moscow State University.) Left without a legitimacy principle that could meet the political challenges unleashed by the French Revolution, the tsar could only look to the Russian army as the state's guarantor.

The left wing of the Russian intelligentsia also spawned its radicals, first populists, then Marxists.[11] The Marxists began to confront the nationality question toward the end of the nineteenth century. The Jewish Bund, a Marxist political organization that also belonged to the Russian Social Democratic movement, put the issue on the agenda, but Marxism provided no easy formulas other than the Second International's call for international working-class solidarity.[12] With the outbreak of World War I, however, that formula collapsed, as most European Marxists supported their national governments in the war. Lenin, of course, did not, seeing nationalism as a weapon for the revolutionaries in Russia.

Of all Lenin's slogans in 1917, two of the most important were "Bread, Peace, and Land" and "National Self-Determination." Together they provided solutions to the three big questions. "Peace" was a policy for abolishing the army. "Land" to the peasants was a policy for breaking state control over most of the economy through the landed nobility. "Self-determination" would crack the empire.

Lenin implicitly grasped the essence of the interrelated structural foundations on which the Russian Empire rested. To destroy the regime, one had to break them. His slogans took direct aim at the heart of each foundation. Once the empire collapsed, of course, he began reversing all three policies, first his nationality policy, then his military policy. The Red Army was created and most of the national separatist movements were defeated. He had to leave it to Stalin to reverse his peasant policy with the First Five-Year Plan. When that was done, the Soviet Union had restored and intensified the old vicious circle, and most important, provided a new legitimacy principle—Marxist-Leninist internationalism—for opposing both liberalism and nationalism.

When Gorbachev undertook his perestroika policy, he was up against these long-standing structural conditions. He recognized two of them, the old peasant question—the economy—and the military question. He correctly understood that the military question had to have a new answer, but beyond arms reductions through arms control agreements, he had no clear strategy. And he had a far more limited appreciation of the kind of answer needed for the economic question. He did not, however, take the Soviet nationality question into his calculations. He naïvely assumed that they could not break away because of their economic entanglements with the Soviet Union. He did, however, recognize the nationality question within the larger Soviet empire: the Warsaw Pact states of Eastern Europe. Making no bones about letting them go, he cut loose their ruling communist parties to maintain power as best they could without the support of the Soviet military.

As Gorbachev's radical new course became apparent to the West in 1987–88, the question most frequently asked was whether or not he could succeed. Seldom did anyone ask, "Succeed at what?" The evidence available about his thinking (as well as of the thinking of several other Politburo members and several of Gorbachev's close aides) suggests that Gorbachev himself was not very clear about his own answer to that question. Undoubtedly he wanted to put the economy on a level with those of the most advanced Western economies. Whether or not he truly wanted political liberalization remains unclear. Shakhnazarov's analysis suggests that he did not understand what that would involve institutionally when he decided on political reform.

Gorbachev could not overcome the inexorable logic of the age-old structural conditions that stabilized both the Russian and Soviet empires, but he began tinkering with two of them, the military and the economy. Weakening and greatly reducing the military and introducing very limited market reforms would inevitably break the stabilizing interrelations of the economy, the military, and the nationalities. As Gorbachev persevered on his course to reduce the military and to raise expectations of market reforms, he broke the stabilizing vicious circle, and the Soviet Union collapsed.

The question of whether or not Gorbachev could "succeed" needed a predicate: at what? If the predicate was liberalizing the Soviet Union to include introducing a market economy and radically reducing the military without dissolving the Soviet Union, the answer was clearly no. If the predicate was carrying his perestroika policy to its logical conclusion, then the answer was yes. He did succeed at that, but he certainly did not intend that success.

Was there an alternative strategy open to Gorbachev? Let us suppose that he recognized the three old questions and their interrelations. Would he have started with the military question? In retrospect it is easy to say that he should not have, but by doing so he did break the vicious circle. Some of his critics in the West and in the Soviet Union, looking at the Chinese example, believed he should have started with the economic question by abolishing collectivized agriculture, but this would have met huge resistance within the party bureaucracy. Alternatively, he might have started with the nationality question. Off-loading the nationalities was the essential precondition for reducing the military. Considering the larger Soviet empire, including its satrapies in the Warsaw Pact, Gorbachev showed no qualms in letting them go. In fact, he proved both willing and effective in withdrawing Soviet military forces from Eastern Europe. The burden of the Transcaucasus, the Baltic republics, Moldavia, and Ukraine, however, was another matter. Chernyaev, Shakhnazarov, and Yakovlev urged him to abandon the Baltic republics, and Shevardnadze would certainly have helped him disengage peacefully from the Transcaucasus. Gorbachev, however, would not hear of it, even in the Baltic republics.

It would be left to Yeltsin to grasp this ultimate logic of the old vicious circle. The nationalities had to be freed, including the Russians. How far to let this devolution process go, however, was not clear to anyone, including Yeltsin. Should it include Tatarstan? And the Muslim region of the northern Caucasus? In the case of Chechnya, we know Yeltsin's initial answer. Even scholarly detachment does not allow one to see the best answer to this question. But it seems fairly clear that the process must go far enough to allow most of the military burden to be dropped. Otherwise, the domestic peace and security necessary for a successful transition to a market system cannot be secured.

This historiographical reflection not only shows the fundamental importance of the Soviet military to the course of events in 1985–89 but also suggests that the future of Russian political development will depend critically on whether or not Moscow has finally left the imperial path. If it returns to that path, liberal political and economic development will be imperiled by new military requirements and the repressive political measures necessary to meet them in face of popular opposition to them. The danger remains real—as demonstrated by the war in Chechnya, the Russian military's role in Tajikistan, Russian military activities in Georgia, Armenia, Azerbaijan, and the Transdniester Republic, the struggle with Ukraine over the Black Sea Fleet, Sevastopol, and the Crimea, and Moscow's periodic threats against Estonia, Latvia, and Lithuania.

At the end of part one of *Dead Souls,* Gogol asks, "And thou, Russia, art thou, too, rushing headlong like the fastest troika that is not to be outdistanced? . . . Russia, whither art thou speeding? . . . She gives no answer. The jingle bells pour forth their wonderful peal, the air, torn to shreds, thunders and runs to the wind. Everything on earth is flying past, and other nations and states, eyeing her askance, make way for her and draw aside." Several decades later, Dostoevskii answered Gogol through the voice of the prosecutor in *The Brothers Karamazov.* Speaking of other nations drawing aside from the speeding Russian troika, the prosecutor says, "But they will cease one day to do so and will form a firm wall confronting the hurrying aberration and will check the frenzied rush of our lawlessness for sake of their own safety, enlightenment, and civilization." The prosecutor's prediction has come to pass, and surprisingly, the Russian nation also ceased standing aside in 1991. That broke the vicious circle and opened a new path to Russia.

Haltingly and unhappily, Russia has begun to follow it. Whether it remains on that path will be indicated by the role and character of the new Russian military. If it again becomes a substitute for law and the foundation of Russia's sovereignty and stability, the three old structural conditions will reassert themselves. If it becomes the guardian of a constitutional state based on a market economy, popular political participation, and guaranteed individual rights, then Russia will have at last answered not only Gogol's question but Peter Chaadaev's, who pondered Russia's destiny in 1829: "We are one of those nations which does not appear to be an integral part of the human race, but exist only in order to teach some great lesson to the world. Surely the lesson we are destined to teach will not be wasted, but who knows when we shall rejoin the rest of mankind, and how much misery we must suffer before accomplishing our destiny?"[13]

Chronology

1985

11 March	Gorbachev becomes general secretary of the CPSU.
March	U.S.-Soviet arms control negotiations resume in Geneva after a two-year cessation.
1–2 July	Shevardnadze promoted from nonvoting to full member of the Politburo and appointed minister of foreign affairs; Romanov removed from the Politburo; Gromyko relieved as foreign minister, appointed as chairman of the Supreme Soviet; Yeltsin made a party secretary.
29 July	Gorbachev announces unilateral suspension of nuclear testing.
2–5 October	Gorbachev visits France, mentions "reasonable sufficiency."
17 October	Gorbachev reports to the Politburo that he has told Afghan leader Babrak Karmal that the Soviet Union will begin disengaging from the war in Afghanistan; the Politburo approves.
19–21 November	Gorbachev and Reagan meet in Geneva.
24 December	Yeltsin becomes secretary of the Moscow party organization.

1986

15 January	Gorbachev makes speech proposing to eliminate all nuclear weapons by 2000.
25 February–6 March	Twenty-seventh Party Congress takes place.
26 April	Chernobyl nuclear power plant accident occurs.
10–11 June	Gorbachev emphasizes arms control to the Warsaw Pact PCC meeting in Budapest.

405

10 July	Gorbachev meets with military officers in Minsk, tells them not to expect more resources for defense.
11–12 October	Gorbachev and Reagan meet in Reykjavik, Iceland.
16–18 December	Riots break out in Alma-Ata, Kazakhstan, after Kunaev is replaced as first secretary of the Kazakh CP.
19 December	Sakharov is told that he can return from exile in Gor'ki to his apartment in Moscow.

1987

27 January	Central Committee plenum focuses on political reform.
28 March–1 April	British Prime Minister Thatcher visits Gorbachev in Moscow.
28–29 May	Gorbachev compels the Warsaw Pact PCC meeting in Berlin to adopt a new military doctrine aimed at "preventing war," not preparing to fight a war, giving the Warsaw Pact doctrine a new, more "defensive" cast.
28 May	Mathias Rust lands near Red Square in a small Cessna aircraft after eluding Soviet air defenses.
25–26 June	Central Committee plenum; Yakovlev elected to the Politburo.
30 June	"New Law on the Firm" promulgated as a step toward market reforms.
23 August	Demonstrations in the Baltic republics staged on the anniversary of the Nazi-Soviet Pact of 1939.
11 November	At Gorbachev's urging, Moscow party committee ousts Yeltsin as its secretary.
7–10 December 1987	Gorbachev visits Washington and signs the INF treaty.

1988

8 February	Gorbachev announces publicly his intent to withdraw Soviet troops from Afghanistan.
13 February	Riots break out in Nagorno-Karabakh.
17–18 February	Central Committee plenum; Yeltsin removed from the Politburo.
24 February	Large demonstration organized in Estonia to commemorate the seventieth anniversary of Estonian independence.
28 February	Pogroms against Armenians occur in Sumgait, Azerbaijan.

13 March	Nina Andreeva publishes a letter in *Sovetskaya Rossiya*, offering a Stalinist critique of perestroika.
14 April	Terms for Soviet withdrawal from Afghanistan signed in Geneva.
23 May	Central Committee plenum approves theses for Nineteenth Party Conference.
29 May–1 June	Reagan meets Gorbachev in Moscow.
13 June	Azerbaijan Supreme Soviet rejects request from Nagorno-Karabakh Soviet to transfer the territory to Armenia.
14 June	Demonstrations held in capitals of all three Baltic republics, commemorating Stalin's deportations in 1940–41.
15 June	Armenian Supreme Soviet approves annexation of Nagorno-Karabakh.
28 June–1 July	Nineteenth Party Conference approves political reforms.
June–July	Marshal Akhromeev visits the United States and tours U.S. military installations as the guest of the chairman of the Joint Chiefs of Staff.
23 July	Demonstrations in the Baltic republics protest annexation to the Soviet Union.
5 August	Ligachev condemns "humankind interests" and the downgrading of "class struggle" to an audience in Gor'ki.
21 September	State of emergency declared in Nagorno-Karabakh following disorders.
30 September	Gorbachev announces a major shakeup in the leadership and restructuring of the Secretariat to the Central Committee plenum.
22 November	Anti-Armenian riots occur in Baku.
1 December	Supreme Soviet approves new election law permitting contested elections and secret ballots.
7 December	At the United Nations, Gorbachev announces that the Soviet military will be reduced unilaterally.

1989

15 February	Soviet troop withdrawal from Afghanistan completed.
9 March	Negotiations begin on Conventional Forces in Europe (CFE) treaty.
26 March	Elections held for the Congress of People's Deputies.
9 April	The Tbilisi massacre in Georgia: army troops kill several civilians while repressing a demonstration.

25 April	Seventy-five Central Committee members are retired at the plenum.
	Soviet troops begin withdrawal from Hungary as part of the unilateral reductions.
28 April	Yazov promoted to marshal of the Soviet Union.
April–May	Evasion of the spring call-up of military service reaches such high levels that the call-up is repeated in June–July.
25 May–9 June	Congress of People's Deputies: TV coverage of open and free debate in the congress astonishes the Soviet public.
10 June–4 August	First session of the newly elected Supreme Soviet (parliament).
3 July	Yazov confirmed as defense minister by the new parliament.
6–7 July	Warsaw Pact PCC meeting in Bucharest.
27 October	Warsaw Pact foreign ministers renounce the Brezhnev doctrine.
November–December	Military service call-up again fails to reach its quotas.
9 November	The Berlin Wall comes down.
19 November	Georgian Supreme Soviet declares sovereignty.
2–3 December	Gorbachev and Bush meet on Malta.
12 December	Second session of the new Supreme Soviet convenes.
25–26 December	Central Committee plenum rejects Lithuanian CP's withdrawal from the CPSU a week earlier.
Late December	The Congress of People's Deputies approves Lopatin commission to develop a plan for military reform; about the same time, the MoD is directed to lead a government commission to draft "law on defense" for military reform.

1990

11–13 January	Gorbachev visits Lithuania, experiences negative public reactions.
13 January	Pogroms against Armenians take place in Baku.
19 January	Army troops enter Baku and oust the Azerbaijan National Front.
4 February	Mass demonstration of democratic reformers in Moscow, ostensibly supporting Gorbachev.
5–7 February	Central Committee plenum approves Gorbachev's proposal to create a presidency of the USSR.

25 February	Second mass demonstration by democratic reformers in Moscow, this time openly hostile to Gorbachev.
11 March	Lithuania declares independence.
13–14 March	Congress of People's Deputies amends the constitution to create a presidency and revises Article 6 on the "leading role" of the CPSU; elects Gorbachev as president.
13 April	Parliamentary Committee of Defense and Security sub-committee discusses Lopatin commission's reform proposals but does not adopt them.
1 May	Red Square demonstration taunts Gorbachev; he leaves in anger.
4 May	Latvia declares independence.
29 May	Yeltsin is elected chairman of the Supreme Soviet of the RSFSR.
30 May–4 June	Gorbachev visits Washington to meet with Reagan.
3 June	Yazov publishes article on military reform proposal worked out by the MoD-led government commission.
7 June	Gorbachev calls for reform of the Warsaw Pact at its Moscow meeting of the PCC.
8 June	RSFSR Supreme Soviet declares sovereignty; declares its laws take precedence over laws of the USSR.
19–22 June	RSFSR Communist Party created at its conference; Polozkov elected first secretary.
2–13 July	Twenty-eighth Party Congress held; Yeltsin speaks, quits the party; Gorbachev survives as general secretary; Ligachev removed from the much-enlarged Politburo.
22 August	Turkmenistan declares sovereignty.
25 August	Tajikistan declares sovereignty.
9 September	Bush and Gorbachev meet in Helsinki.
3 October	Reunification of Germany takes place after "two plus four" negotiation over the previous months.
9 October	Supreme Soviet passes a law authorizing a multiparty system.
25 October	Kazakhstan declares sovereignty.
28 October	Ukrainian political movement, Rukh, makes "independence" its goal.
30 October	Kyrgyzstan declares sovereignty.
19 November	CFE treaty on reductions in conventional forces signed in Paris.

| 20 December | Shevardnadze resigns his post as foreign minister and warns of coming dictatorship. |
| 27 December | Congress of People's Deputies elects Yanaev as vice president of the USSR. |

1991

13 January	Army and KGB units take repressive actions in Lithuania, killing several civilians in the process.
14 January	Valentin Pavlov becomes chairman of the Council of Ministers of the USSR.
30 January	Central Committee plenum sharply criticizes Gorbachev.
9 February	Referendum in Lithuania shows that 90 percent of voters favor independence.
3 March	Referenda in Latvia and Estonia show large majorities in favor of independence.
17 March	USSR referendum shows a majority favors a "voluntary union," although voting was not conducted in some places, and the measure does not return a majority in some areas.
30–31 March	All-Army Party Conference held; All-Army Party Committee created to replace the MPA.
31 March	Warsaw Pact officially dissolved.
9 April	Georgia declares independence.
23 April	Nine republics enter negotiations with Gorbachev on a new union treaty, the so-called Novo-Ogarevo process.
12 June	Yeltsin elected president of the RSFSR by popular vote.
17 June	Pavlov, supported by Yazov, Kryuchkov, and Pugo, asks the Supreme Soviet to limit Gorbachev's powers but fails to receive approval.
5 August	Plotters meet in a KGB safe house to make plans for establishing a state of emergency.
18–21 August	State Committee for an Emergency in the USSR (GKChP) isolates Gorbachev in the Crimea and seeks to reverse perestroika but fails. Members of the GKChP are arrested.
20 August	Estonia declares independence.
21 August	Gorbachev returns to Moscow.
23 August	Marshal Shaposhnikov is appointed minister of defense, and General Lobov is made chief of the General Staff.

24 August	Gorbachev resigns as general secretary of the CPSU.
24 August	Ukraine declares independence.
27 August	Belorussia and Moldova declare independence.
30 August	Azerbaijan declares independence.
31 August	Uzbekistan and Kyrgyzstan declare independence.
6 September	USSR "GOSSOVET" recognizes the independence of Lithuania, Latvia, and Estonia.
9 September	Tajikistan declares independence.
23 September	Armenia declares independence.
3 October	Marshal Shaposhnikov sends appeal for approval of military reform to the GOSSOVET, but it is not discussed in this body until 4 November.
27 October	Turkmenistan declares independence.
6 November	Yeltsin bans the CPSU and the Russian CP.
Early November	Gorbachev invites Marshal Shaposhnikov to the Kremlin and suggests that the Soviet military take political power to save the Soviet Union from dissolution.
25 November	Gorbachev announces that the new union treaty will be signed as the heads of the republics gather at Novo-Ogarevo, but they refuse.
5 December	Ukraine revokes the 1922 treaty that made it a member of the USSR.
7 December	General Lobov relieved as chief of the General Staff.
7–8 December	Yeltsin, Kravchuk, and Shushkevich meet secretly in a Belovezhskaya pushcha in Belorussia and agree to form the Commonwealth of Independent States (CIS), including Russia, Belarus, and Ukraine.
9 December	Yeltsin calls Shaposhnikov to get his support for the CIS.
10–11 December	Gorbachev and Yeltsin each appeal to an assembly of senior military officers in Moscow for support.
11 December	The RSFSR parliament approves the CIS agreement.
16 December	Kazakhstan declares independence.
22 December	Heads of eleven republics meet in Alma-Ata and sign an agreement for a much enlarged CIS, including all union republics except for the three in the Baltic region and Georgia.
25 December	Gorbachev resigns. The Russian flag is raised over the Kremlin.

26–27 December   Shaposhnikov convenes a meeting of the defense representatives from all the CIS states in Moscow to prepare proposals.

30–31 December   CIS summit meeting in Minsk.

31 December   The USSR formally ceases to exist.

1992

16 January   CIS summit meeting in Moscow.

14 February   CIS summit meeting in Minsk.

20 March   CIS summit meeting in Kiev.

6 May   General Pavel Grachev appointed Russian minister of defense.

20–21 May   CIS summit meeting in Tashkent; collective security treaty signed.

1993

June   Shaposhnikov resigns as commander in chief of the CIS Armed Forces.

Biographical Reference

Akhromeev, Sergei. Marshal of the Soviet Union, chief of the General Staff, 1984–88; special adviser to Gorbachev, 1988–91; supported GKChP in the August crisis of 1991, then committed suicide.

Alekseev, A. A. Colonel; active in trying to seize control of the movement of soldiers' mothers in 1990–91.

Alksnis, Viktor. Colonel; outspoken opponent of military reformers in the Congress of People's Deputies and the parliament; active in the Officers' Assemblies movement.

Andreeva, Nina. Schoolteacher in Leningrad whose letter condemning glasnost, perestroika, and most of Gorbachev's policies was published in *Sovetskaya Rossiya* in April 1988 with Ligachev's support.

Andropov, Yurii. General secretary of the CPSU, 1983–84; sponsored Gorbachev's rapid rise in the party apparatus.

Arbatov, Aleksei. Scholar and analyst in ISKAN who strongly supported radical military reform; son of Georgii Arbatov, director of ISKAN.

Arbatov, Georgii. Director of ISKAN; specialist on U.S. affairs; adviser to Gorbachev and supporter of perestroika.

Bakatin, Vadim. Chief of MVD, 1988–90; chairman of the Federal Security Agency (successor to the KGB), October 1991.

Baklanov, Oleg. Party secretary for defense industries from 1988; first deputy chairman of the Defense Council; leader in the GKChP plot of August 1991.

Belousov, Igor. First deputy chairman of the Council of Ministers and chairman VPK, 1988–91.

Benov, Gennadii. Lieutenant general; deputy commander of the air forces during the August 1991 crisis, sympathetic to the GKChP.

Bizhan, Ivan. Lieutenant general; deputy chief of the operations directorate of the General Staff during the crisis of August 1991, then moved to become a colonel general and deputy minister of defense in Ukraine in fall of 1991.

Blagovolin, Sergei. Professor in IMEMO and proponent of "new thinking" in foreign policy and radical military reform; had close ties to Aleksandr Yakovlev in the Central Committee and the Politburo.

Bogomolov, Oleg. Director of the Institute of Economy and World Socialist Systems; deputy in the Congress of People's Deputies; early leader in democratic movement.

Boldin, Valery. Personal chief of staff to Gorbachev; supported the plotters in the GKChP in August 1991.

Brezhnev, Leonid. General secretary of the CPSU, 1964–83.

Burkov, V. A. Colonel on Marshal Shaposhnikov's air forces staff, sympathizer with Yeltsin's forces during 19–21 August 1991.

Burlakov, Matvei. Colonel general; commander of Soviet forces in Germany and involved in corruption scandals with General Pavel Grachev.

Chebrikov, Viktor. Chairman of the KGB, 1982–88; Politburo member, 1983–89; became opponent of perestroika in 1988–89.

Chernavin, V. M. Admiral; deputy minister of defense and commander of the navy, 1987–91.

Chernenko, Konstantin. General secretary of the CPSU, 1984–85.

Chernyaev, Anatolii. Professional party worker; specialist in foreign affairs; worked in the Central Committee International Department in 1970s and 1980s; accompanied Gorbachev to Belgium in 1972 to visit the Belgian Communist Party leadership; Gorbachev's special assistant on foreign policy, February 1986–December 1991.

Chervov, Nikolai. Colonel general; General Staff's representative in arms control affairs during last years of Gorbachev's rule.

Demichev, Petr. Party secretary, 1971–85; nonvoting Politburo member, 1971–88; minister of culture; retired in September 1988.

Deneikin, Petr. Lieutenant general; deputy commander of the air forces during August 1991 crisis; supported Marshal Shaposhnikov's actions against the GKChP.

Detinov, Nikolai. Colonel general; career engineer in the VPK; worked in the Central Committee Defense Industries Department in the early 1980s; served as a member of the so-called Little Five; backstopped arms control negotiations, 1969–91.

Dobrynin, Anatolii. Ambassador to the United States, 1962–86; party secretary, 1986–88.

Dolgykh, Vladimir. Party secretary, 1978–85; nonvoting Politburo member, 1982–88; retired in September 1988.

Falin, Valentin. Career diplomat, ambassador to Germany; chief of the Central Committee International Relations Department, 1990–91.

Filatov, Viktor. Major general; reactionary editor of the General Staff's *Military History Journal*, 1986–91.

Frunze, Mikhail. Red commander in the Russian Civil War; commissar of military and naval affairs, 1924–25; theorist on a Marxist military doctrine; died as a result of an operation he was forced by Stalin to undergo in 1925.

Gareev, Makhmut. Colonel general; chief of the directorate of military science of the General Staff.

Gorbachev, Mikhail S. General secretary of the CPSU, 1985–91; president of the USSR, 1990–91.

Gorshkov, Sergei. Admiral; commander of the navy until 1987.

Grechko, Andrei. Marshal of the Soviet Union; minister of defense, 1972–76; Politburo member, 1973–76.

Gribokov, Anatolii. General; deputy chief of the General Staff and chief of staff of the Warsaw Pact Armed Forces.

Grinkevich, Dmitrii. Colonel general; involved with personnel policy in the MoD, 1985–91.

Gromyko, Andrei. Politburo member, 1973–88; foreign minister until summer 1985, when Shevardnadze replaced him; chairman of the Supreme Soviet, 1986–88.

Isaev, Aleksandr. Economist in a VPK institute; vocal on impact of economic reforms on military industries.

Ivashov, Leonid. Lieutenant general; political officer in charge of the MPA organ in the office of the minister of defense under Ustinov, Sokolov, and Yazov.

Kalinin, N. V. Colonel general; commander of the Moscow military district during the crisis in 1991.

Karimov, Islam. First secretary of the Uzbekistan Communist Party, 1989–91.

Khrushchev, Nikita. First secretary of the CPSU, 1953–64.

Kirbasova, Maria. Founder and leader of the committee of soldiers' mothers movement in April 1989; the movement was variously named during 1989–91 and after, but she remained at its center in spite of numerous efforts to oust her and dilute the movement.

Kirshin, Yurii. Major general, deputy director of the Military History Institute.

Kochetov, Konstantin. Colonel general, first deputy minister of defense, 1987–91; Yazov's emissary to Georgia in connection with Tbilisi massacre, April 1989; inclined toward the GKChP in August 1991.

Kokoshin, Andrei. Scholar, analyst on strategic and military affairs in ISKAN; frequent contributor to the public debate over military doctrine.

Kolmakov, A. P. Colonel; commander of the Tula airborne division during the crisis of August 1991.

Kornienko, Georgii. Diplomat and in charge of U.S. affairs in the foreign ministry; involved in the Little Five backstopping arms control negotiations; dubious about Gorbachev's foreign policy; close associate of Marshal Akhromeev.

Krivosheev, Grigorii. Colonel general; head of the directorate for personnel on the General Staff.

Kryuchkov, Vladimir. Chairman of KGB, 1988–91; Politburo member, 1989–91; key figure and leader in the GKChP plot of August 1991.

Kulikov, Viktor. Marshal of the Soviet Union; commander of the Warsaw Pact forces until 1987.

Kunadze, Georgii. Scholar and analyst on foreign and military policy in IMEMO; frequent contributor to the public debate over military and foreign policy from 1988 onward.

Kunaev, Dinmukhamed. First secretary of the Kazakhstan Communist Party; removed by Gorbachev in 1986.

Kuz'min, Fedor. Colonel general; commander of Baltic military district, 1990–91.

Kuznetsov, Viktor. Colonel; political officer and instructor at Lenin Military-Political Academy; relieved from his duties for active support of military reform.

Larionov, Valentin. Major general; long retired and working as an analyst in ISKAN during Gorbachev's rule; participant in the public debate over military doctrine.

Lebed', Aleksandr. Colonel in 1990, major general in 1991, and later lieutenant general; commander of the airborne division at Tula, 1989–91; deputy commander of the airborne forces for training in 1991; deeply involved in the events of crisis of August 1991. Presidential candidate in 1996.

Ligachev, Yegor K. Party secretary, 1983–90; Politburo member, 1985–90; initially a strong ally of Gorbachev but shifted into opposition; expelled from the Politburo in July 1990.

Lizichev, Aleksei D. General; chief of the MPA; relieved from his post after the Twenty-eighth Party Congress in July 1990, where he backed Ligachev's effort to oust Gorbachev. Strongly opposed to military reform in the military and all efforts to dissolve the MPA.

Lobov, Vladimir. Colonel general; deputy chief of the General Staff until after the crisis of August 1991, then chief of the General Staff until he was ousted in early December for opposition to defense minister Marshal Shaposhnikov.

Lopatin, Vladimir. Major; a political officer elected as a deputy to the Congress of People's Deputies in 1989; prominent leader among the young officers in favor of radical military reform; appointed deputy chairman of Yeltsin's RSFSR National Security Committee in fall of 1990.

Luk'yanov, Anatolii. Nonvoting Politburo member, 1988–91; first deputy chairman of the Supreme Soviet, 1989–91; involved but not a member of the GKChP in the crisis in August 1991.

Lyakhovskii, Aleksandr. Colonel; veteran of the war in Afghanistan; served on the General Staff; sponsored by General Varennikov in writing a book indicting the political leadership for the war in Afghanistan.

Makashov, Albert. Colonel general; commander of the Volga-Ural military district; outspoken opponent of Gorbachev's policies and strong defender of Marxism-Leninism and the Soviet system.

Maksimov, Yurii. General, deputy minister of defense and commander of the rocket forces; did not sympathize with the GKChP plot in August 1991.

Malenkov, Georgii. Chairman, USSR Council of Ministers, 1953–56.

Maslyukov, Anatolii. Lieutenant general; deputy commander of the air forces during August 1991 crisis; supported Marshal Shaposhnikov's opposition to the GKChP.

Medvedev, Vadim. Party secretary from March 1986 in charge of ideology; Politburo member, 1988; member of Gorbachev's Presidential Council, 1990.

Mikhail Moiseev. General, Chief of the General Staff from December 1988, when Marshal Akhromeev resigned, until immediately after the August crisis in 1991, when he was forcibly retired. Remarkably inexperienced as a newly appointed chief of the General Staff, he was beholden to Gorbachev initially but gradually became an opponent of perestroika in the armed forces.

Nazarbayev, Nursultan. First secretary of the Communist Party of Kazakhstan and Politburo member, 1989–91.

Niyazov, Saparmurat. First secretary of the Communist Party of Turkmenistan and Politburo member, 1990–91.

Ogarkov, Nikolai. Marshal of the Soviet Union; relieved as chief of the General Staff in late 1984; had a reputation for intelligence, outspokenness, and innovation; headed veterans' organization during Gorbachev's rule and occasionally expressed publicly his doubts about perestroika.

Patiashvili, Dzumber. First secretary of the Communist Party of Georgia during the Tbilisi massacre, 9 April 1989; blamed for that event by Gorbachev and replaced shortly thereafter.

Pavlov, Valentin. Minister of finance, 1989–91; chairman, Council of Ministers of the USSR, 1991; member of the GKChP in the crisis of August 1991.

Petrakov, Nikolai. Special assistant to Gorbachev on economic matters.

Petrov, Ivan. General who conducted nuclear weapons testing in early 1950s.

Plutnik, Albert. Journalist who exploited glasnost to satirize the military's resistance to reform.

Podkolzin, Yevgenii. Lieutenant general; chief of staff of the airborne forces during the crisis of August 1991.

Podziruk, Viktor. Colonel; strong critic of the MPA, 1990–91, calling for its dissolution.

Polozkov, Ivan. First secretary of the Communist Party of Russia when it was organized in June 1990; allied against Gorbachev before and during the Twenty-eighth Party Congress.

Ponomarev, Boris. Longtime chief of the Central Committee International Department; resisted Gorbachev's foreign policy.

Pugo, Boris. Nonvoting member of the Politburo, 1989–91; head of the MVD, 1990–91; early career in the KGB; member of the GKChP in August 1991; committed suicide as the GKChP fell apart.

Rashidov, Sharaf. First secretary of the Communist Party of Uzbekistan and nonvoting member of the Politburo when Gorbachev came to power; notoriously corrupt; purged in 1985.

Rodin, Aleksandr. Lieutenant colonel; pilot; resigned from the party while serving in Kamchatka because of the hypocrisy and corruption he witnessed among senior officers; threatened with incarceration in a mental institution but managed to resign from the military to return and become active in politics in Leningrad, where he won a seat in the Leningrad Soviet in 1989.

Rodionov, Igor. Colonel general, commander of the Transcaucasus military district during the Tbilisi massacre of April 1989; relieved and appointed chief of the General Staff Academy; served as Russian minister of defense, 1996–97.

Romanov, Grigorii. Party secretary for defense industries and Politburo member who rivaled Gorbachev as a candidate for general secretary when Chernenko died. Gorbachev removed him from both posts a few months later in 1985.

Rust, Mathias. Young West German who flew a small Cessna aircraft to Moscow, evading Soviet air defenses and landing near Red Square, 28 May 1987; tried and imprisoned by Soviet authorities but eventually released to German authorities.

Ryzhkov, Nikolai. Chairman of the Council of Ministers, 1985–90; Politburo member, 1985–90.

Ryzhov, Yurii. Director of the Ordzhonikidze Aviation Institute; headed a commission on conversion of military industries in 1989–90 as a proreformer.

Sakharov, Andrei. Nuclear physicist who invented the Soviet hydrogen bomb; member of the Academy of Sciences; liberal-minded dissident from the late 1960s; exiled to the city of Gor'ki in the 1970s; allowed to return to Moscow by Gorbachev in December 1986; elected a deputy to the Congress of People's Deputies; died shortly after the second Congress of People's Deputies in December 1989.

Savinkin, Aleksandr. Lieutenant colonel; first voice to call publicly for ending universal military conscription in 1988; supported radical military reform endeavors in the parliament, 1989–91.

Serebryannikov, Vladimir. Lieutenant general; political officer who initially attacked proposals for ending conscription; later changed his mind and supported the young military reformers calling for an end to conscription.

Shabanov, Vitalii. General, deputy minister of defense for armaments; one of only two senior deputy ministers to survive the purge of the MoD after the Rust flight to Red Square in May 1987.

Shakhnazarov, Georgii. Professional party worker for many years in the Central Committee International Department; spent a couple of years with Andropov when he was chairman of the KGB; special assistant to Gorbachev, February 1988–December 1991.

Shaposhnikov, Yevgenii I. Marshal of aviation, deputy minister of defense and commander of the air forces, 1989–91; opposed the GKChP in August 1991; appointed defense minister immediately after the crisis in place of Marshal Yazov; upon creation of the CIS, appointed commander of the CIS Armed Forces; retired from that post in June 1993.

Shatalin, Stanislav. Economist and member of the Academy of Sciences; leader of a team of economic reformers that produced the so-called Shatalin Plan in the fall of 1990.

Shenin, Oleg. Party secretary, 1990–91; involved in the plotting to oust Gorbachev in August 1991.

Shevardnadze, Eduard. Foreign minister and Politburo member, 1985–1990; first secretary of the Communist Party of Georgia, 1973–85; nonvoting Politburo member, 1978–85.

Shevel'ev, Eduard. Captain in the navy; worked on nuclear weapons issues in the General Staff in the late 1970s, early 1980s; career ruined in early 1980s when he criticized the party.

Shlyaga, Nikolai. Colonel general; political officer; replaced General Lizichev as head of the MPA after the Twenty-eighth Party Congress in July 1990; very hostile to Gorbachev's attempts to dismantle the MPA.

Skokov, Yurii. Assistant to Yeltsin when he became chairman of the RSFSR Supreme Soviet in 1990; assigned by Yeltsin in February 1990 to seek out contacts and potential supporters among the senior military leadership; involved in the defense of the White House during the crisis of August 1991.

Slipchenko, Vladimir. Major general, served on the General Staff through 1987; thereafter an instructor at the General Staff Academy.

Slyunkov, Nilolai. Party secretary for economic affairs, 1987–90; Politburo member, 1987–90; first secretary of the Communist Party of Belorussia, 1983–87.

Smirnov, Leonid. First deputy chairman, Council of Ministers and chairman of the VPK from the 1970s until shortly after Gorbachev came to power.

Sobchak, Anatolii. Law professor; elected to the Congress of People's Deputies in 1989; among founders of the democratic movement and the "interregional group of deputies" headed by Andrei Sakharov; elected mayor of Leningrad in 1991; supported Yeltsin during the crisis of August 1991, openly resisting the authority of the Leningrad military district commander on 19–20 August.

Sokolov, Sergei. Marshal of the Soviet Union; minister of defense, 1984–87; relieved of his duties as defense minister as a result of the Rust flight to Moscow, May 1987.

Sokolovskii, Vasilii D. Marshal of the Soviet Union; chief of the General Staff, 1952–60; lead author of the collective that wrote *Military Strategy* (1962), giving the first major authoritative Soviet military views on war in the nuclear age.

Solomentsev, Mikhail. Chairman of the Party Control Commission, 1983–88; nonvoting Politburo member, 1971–83; full Politburo member, 1983–88.

Starodubtsev, Vasilii. Chairman of the Union of Peasants; included in the membership of the GKChP in August 1991 to broaden its political base.

Stepankov, Valentin. Procurator general of the USSR who investigated the GKChP's activities and all involved in the August plot.

Stepanov, Andrei. Special assistant to Shevardnadze while he was foreign minister; together with Sergei Tarasenko, one of Shevardnadze's closest staff aides.

Strebkov, V. Colonel; spokesman for the MoD's views on military doctrine, nuclear forces, and related issues in the public debate over Gorbachev's defensive military doctrine.

Sukhorukov, Dmitrii. Colonel general, deputy minister of defense for cadres.

Tarasenko, Sergei. Special assistant to foreign minister Eduard Shevardnadze; together with Andrei Stepanov, one of Shevardnadze's closest staff aides.

Tizyakov, Aleksandr. President of the Association of State Industries; included in the GKChP in August 1991 to broaden its political base.

Tsalko, Aleksandr. Colonel; pilot and veteran of the war in Afghanistan; elected to the Congress of People's Deputies in 1989; strong supporter of radical military reform; active in the defense of Yeltsin at the White House in August 1991.

Tsarev, Aleksei. Colonel; political officer who served as deputy commander for political affairs in regiment of the rocket forces; became a supporter of radical military reform in 1989–91 because he was disillusioned with hypocrisy in the party and senior military ranks and the brutality in enlisted ranks.

Tsygichko, Vitalii. Colonel; served on the General Staff performing analysis of estimated effects of nuclear weapons employment during an offensive into Europe; his findings were rejected, causing him to move to a civilian research institute to continue his modeling of nuclear weapons use in military operations; had some contact with Marshal Ogarkov when he was chief of the General Staff in the early 1980s.

Tukhachevskii, Mikhail. Marshal of the Soviet Union; outstanding commander during the civil war; military theorist and head of the military modernization program in the late 1920s and early 1930s; executed in 1937.

Tutov, Nikolai. Lieutenant; served in the rocket forces; elected to the Congress of People's Deputies in 1989; party delegate to the Twenty-eighth Party Congress, 1990; radical military reformer.

Urazhtsev, V. G. Colonel; organizer of the military union Shield, in 1989; appeared to be a radical military reformer but tried to take over the soldiers' mothers movement; although he had a reputation for opposing the party, some of the proponents of military reform considered him a KGB agent provocateur.

Uskhopchik, Vladimir. Major general, garrison commander in Vilnius, January 1991, when KGB and army units took repressive measures; Gorbachev blamed him for this action.

Ustinov, Dmitrii. Marshal of the Soviet Union; minister of defense, 1976–84; party secretary, 1965–76, Politburo member, 1976–84; early career was in military industries, including commissar of armaments, 1941–45; minister of armaments, 1946–53; minister of defense industries, 1953–57; chairman of the VPK, 1957–65.

Varennikov, Valentin. General; deputy minister of defense and commander of the ground forces, 1987–91; fired from these posts for supporting the GKChP during the crisis of August 1991; first deputy chief of the General Staff and head of the operational group managing the war in Afghanistan, 1979–87.

Vladimir, Aleksandr. Major general; supported military reform as an insider in the MoD during Gorbachev's rule; shifted to Yeltsin's side during the crisis of August 1991 and continued as a proponent of military reform in 1991–93.

Volkogonov, Dmitrii. Colonel general; political officer and author of many propagandistic tracts at the Lenin Military-Political Academy; as director of the Military History Institute, clashed with the ministry of defense collegium over a new history of World War II for the fiftieth anniversary of the German invasion of 1941; wrote a scathing biography of Stalin, Lenin, and Trotsky; became strong supporter of Yeltsin; headed a commission to create a Russian ministry of defense in spring 1992.

Voroshilov, Klimentii. Marshal of the Soviet Union, Red Army commander during the civil war and close associate of Stalin; commissar of military and naval affairs, 1925–34; commissar of defense, 1934–45; Politburo member from the 1920s until 1957, when Khrushchev dismissed him as one of the "antiparty group."

Yakovlev, Aleksandr. Ambassador to Canada, 1973–83; director of IMEMO, 1983–85;

party secretary, 1986–90; Politburo member, 1987–90; considered one of the main sources of ideas for Gorbachev's perestroika and glasnost policies; used by Gorbachev as the main protagonist against Ligachev and the Politburo conservatives from 1987 onward.

Yanaev, Gennadii. Deputy president of the USSR, December 1990–August 1991; member of the GKChP during the crisis of August 1991 who assumed Gorbachev's powers as president of the USSR.

Yavlinskii, Grigorii. Economist, member of the State Committee on Economic Reform, 1989–90; deputy chairman of the RSFSR council of Ministers from 1990.

Yazov, Dmitrii. Marshal of the Soviet Union; appointed minister of defense in the wake of the Rust flight incident in May 1990; became acquainted with Gorbachev in 1985, when he was commander of the Far Eastern military district; supported Gorbachev's policies until 1989, when he was increasingly caught between the conservatives in the MoD and the radical military reformers in the parliament and the media; joined the plot that established the GKChP during the crisis of August 1991; arrested and dismissed on 21 August 1991.

Yefanov, V. V. General, commander of military transport aviation; supported Marshal Shaposhnikov's efforts to thwart the GKChP during the crisis of August 1991.

Yeltsin, Boris N. First secretary of Moscow party, 1985–87; candidate member, Politburo 1986–88; elected chairman of the RSFSR Supreme Soviet in 1990; elected president of the RSFSR in 1991; humiliating dismissal from post as the Moscow party boss in October 1987 prompted him to launch an unprecedented political comeback over the next three years; became the freely elected president of the Russian republic (RSFSR) in spring 1991; joining with other heads of union republics in the fall of 1990, helped catalyze the national separatist movements that eventually allowed them to dissolve the Soviet Union in December 1991.

Yerokhin, Yevgenii. Major; radical military reformer in the parliament in 1989–91.

Zaikov, Lev. Party secretary, 1985–87; Politburo member, 1986–91; first secretary of the Moscow Communist Party, 1987–89; headed the revitalized Big Five in the Politburo backstopping arms control negotiations, 1985–87, leading to the INF treaty; early career was in military industries in Leningrad, then as first secretary of the Leningrad Communist Party.

Zaitsev, Mikhail. General, commander in Afghanistan, 1985–86, given two years to end the war by Gorbachev.

Notes

Introduction

    1. Paret, *Understanding War*, 10.

Chapter 1. The Soviet Philosophy of War

    1. Odom, "Why Does the Soviet Union Build Such Large Military Forces?"

    2. N. N. Sukhotin, *Voina v istorii russkogo mira* (St. Petersburg, 1898), 113–14, providing a report to the tsar from the Imperial General Staff, observed that between 1700 and 1870, Russia was at war 106 years. I am indebted to Richard Pipes for pointing out this source to me. He quotes it in his *Survival Is Not Enough: Soviet Realities and America's Future* (New York: Simon and Shuster, 1984), 36, 286. Its special importance is that it shows that Russian military elites themselves certainly did not believe that Russia was the victim of frequent foreign invasions. In fact, the only serious invasions of Russian territory since the Swedish campaigns against Peter the Great were Napoleon's campaign in 1812, the Crimean War in 1854–55, and Hitler's invasion in 1941. Toward the end of World War I, of course, German forces pressed into Russian territory against no Bolshevik resistance, but the war began in 1914 with a large Russian offensive into East Prussia. Notwithstanding the actual record of Russia's habit of frequently invading its neighbors, the popular image remains strong in Russia that it has always and frequently been the victim, not the perpetrator of wars.

    3. See Karl Marx and Frederick Engels, *The German Ideology* (New York: International Publishers, 1947), especially 24–69.

    4. Karl Marx, *The Civil War in France* (New York: International Publishers, 1940).

    5. V. I. Lenin, *Two Tactics of Social Democracy in the Democratic Revolution* (New York: International Publishers, 1935).

    6. In *The Lenin Anthology*, 204–74.

    7. Social Democracy was the popular term for Marxism, synonomous with it until 1919, when Lenin created the Communist International or the "Third International," signifying that he meant it to take the legitimate mantle of Marxism and European Social Democracy away from the Second International of Social Democratic parties. Here I use "Social Democracy" as it was used at the time, to mean organized Marxism on both national and international levels. The origins of organized Social Democracy in Europe, of course, are found in Ferdinand Lassalles's founding of the German Social Democratic Party (SPD) in 1863. Marx was involved in this party at its inception, and today it survives as the

contemporary German SPD, albeit with radically revised Marxist ideology. The First International, linking other Marxist parties in Europe, was founded in the 1860s concurrently with the German SPD. It failed to survive, but the Second International, founded in 1881, had more success in developing a sense of solidarity among all the Social Democratic parties of Europe. Lenin's creation of the Bolshevik faction within the Russian Social Democratic Labor Party did not initially involve a break with the Second International. That came with Lenin's anger over the support for World War I espoused by most member parties.

8. In *The Lenin Anthology*, 13–114.

9. Marx and Engels, *Communist Manifesto*, 22.

10. They were published in the USSR as "Vypuski i zamechaniia na knigu Klauzevitsa 'O voine i vedenii voin'," *Leninski sbornik* 12 (1931): 387–452. For a recent treatment of Clausewitz's influence on Lenin, see Jacob W. Kipp, "Lenin and Clausewitz: The Militarization of Marxism, 1915–1921," in Frank and Gillette, *Soviet Military Doctrine*, 63–84.

11. See Gat, *Development of Military Thought: The Nineteenth Century*, 22–48, for an excellent examination of the intellectual influence of Clausewitz on Marx and Engels (there was not much) and on Lenin (there was a lot). Gat is one of the few scholars who correctly notes that Hegel's influence on both Marx and Clausewitz was an important connection for Lenin, who recognized it and used it to enhance his own reading of Clausewitz. Gat is also informative on the political climate in which Lenin studied Clausewitz in 1915.

12. Clausewitz, *On War* (Howard and Peret), book I, chapter 1, section 28, p. 89.

13. Ibid., p. 124. Gat's account of French military thinkers reviewing and reevaluating Clausewitz's theory of war in the 1880s reveals how they had come to see that Jomini's heavy dependence on "geometric and geographic" concepts left out far too much in his theory of war.

14. This interpretation derives more from my own inferences than from explicit acknowledgment by Lenin in anything he has written. Not surprisingly. Lenin was hardly steeped in knowledge of either physics or mathematics; nor was he likely aware that Newton was not the last word in physics. Looking back, however, we can see the analogy in alternative conceptual approaches in physics and mathematics to Lenin's mix of material determinism and political voluntarism. The same is true of Clausewitz, whose choice of the meteorological metaphor fog can hardly be explained by his knowledge of modern meteorological science. Still, the contemporary analogy provides insight into how both Lenin and Clausewitz were conceptualizing the political and military realities they were studying.

15. In Tucker, *Lenin Anthology*, 550–625.

16. Heinrich Dietrich von Buelow, for example, insisted that Napoleon's secret to success could be explained by two lines of attack converging at 90 degrees on the objective. See Paret, *Understanding War*, 81, who elaborates this point in a comparison of Clausewitz's views with Buelow's in assessing Napoleon as an enemy.

17. Rapaport, in an introductory essay for his edition of *On War*, 32, underscores Lenin's shift from interstate to interclass war in his adaptation of Clausewitz but does not draw the connection to Clausewitz's trinity.

18. *Marxism-Leninism on War and the Army*, 7; italics in the original. The citation is from the translation of *Marksizm-Leninizm o voine i armii* (Moscow, 5th ed., 1968), published under the auspices of the United States Air Force, U.S. Government Printing Office, Washington, D.C., 1972. The first Soviet edition was published in 1957 by a collective of fourteen authors.

19. Howard, *War and the Liberal Conscience*. In this context the term invokes European political liberalism and its intellectual antecedents from the Enlightenment onward.

20. In June and July 1995, I interviewed a number of high-ranking former Soviet officers, including the last Soviet minister of defense, Marshal Yevgenii Shaposhnikov, as well as several field-grade officers, asking them all how the official ideology affected their views on military affairs and warfare. A few explicitly understood the point made here about the role of ideology on Soviet military affairs. Others initially dismissed it, but in the course of the interview, it was apparent that they had internalized, perhaps unconsciously, most of the ideological baggage of Marxism-Leninism on war.

21. See Roberts, "Prelude to Catastrophe." Roberts skillfully criticizes the literature that dismisses the ideological basis of Stalin's foreign and military policies. She also provides an exhaustive review of international relations theory and organization theory, showing that they fail miserably as explanations for Stalin's policies unless ideological calculations are included as playing a central role. She shows compellingly that such calculations as often as not led to disastrous policy results.

22. Borkenau, *World Communism*, remains the best single history of the Comintern. For evidence from the Comintern's archives on its control over a foreign communist party and its close cooperation with Soviet foreign intelligence operations, see Klehr, Haynes, and Firsov, *Secret World of American Communism*.

23. I have Professor Leon Lipson of Yale University to thank for pointing out that Lenin never used the term "peaceful coexistence" *(mirnoe sosushchustvovanie)* but spoke, rather, of "peaceful cohabitation *(mirnoe sozhitel'stvo)*. My student Dominique Corbett found for me at least one early use of "peaceful coexistence." In June 1920, G. V. Chicherin, commissar of foreign affairs, wrote in a report to the Soviet government, "Our slogan was and remains one and the same: peaceful coexistence with foreign governments, no matter what kind they are." *Dokumenty vneshnei politiki SSSR* 2 (1 January 1919–30 June 1920) (Moscow: Gosizdat politicheskoi literaturi, 1958), 639. Nation, *Black Earth, Red Star*, 38, apparently errs in making Lenin the author of the peaceful coexistence slogan. This volume on Soviet strategy and foreign policy is one of the few attempting to include military policy in a review of the entire Soviet period. While not a wholly revisionist interpretation, it tilts clearly to the side of the 1960s and 1970s American revisionist history of the East-West relations.

24. Roberts, "Prelude to Catastrophe," offers an impressive argument, based in part on recent access to Soviet archives, that the Nazi-Soviet Pact appealed to Stalin mainly because of his ideological calculations. See also Dominque N. Corbett, "Peaceful Coexistence: From Lenin to Gorbachev," M.S. thesis, Yale University, 1990, 27–31.

25. The secondary literature on this period is large, but Ulam, *Expansion and Coexistence*, still offers the best survey of Soviet foreign policy. Kaplan, *Diplomacy of Power*, adds the military component. Rubinstein, *Moscow's Third World Strategy*, is the best overall treatment of the strategy of peaceful coexistence applied in the Third World. Ellison, *Soviet Policy Toward Western Europe*, offers a solid perspective on Soviet strategy in Europe. Finally, Brzezinski, *The Soviet Bloc*, remains the best treatment of Moscow's relations with foreign ruling communist parties.

26. Sokolovskii, *Voennaya strategiya*.

27. See, for example, Warner, *Military in Contemporary Soviet Politics*.

28. Sukhotin, *Voina v istorii russkogo mira*.

29. Victor Chernov, "Lenin," in *The American Encounter: The United States and the Making of the Modern World*, ed. James F. Hodge Jr. and Fareed Zajaria (New York: Basic, 1997), 50. This is a compendium of articles from *Foreign Affairs* on the journal's seventy-fifth anniversary.

Chapter 2. Party, State, and Military Structure

1. A vast literature exists on this party-state distinction in the Soviet system. Barghoorn and Remington, *Politics in the USSR*, 489–519, provides an excellent set of organizational charts, clarifying the structure, in addition to their excellent textual treatment of it.

2. Almquist, *Red Forge*, 137, lists and describes each of the nine.

3. Although no single text offers the full story of the origins and evolution of this body, Holloway, "Innovation in the Defence Sector," 297–300, provides enlightening details of its interwar predecessors. Almquist, *Red Forge*, 23–24, gives a brief description of its postwar character.

4. Odom, "Who Controls Whom in Moscow?"

5. Suleiman, *Tyl i snabzhenie deistvuyushchei armii*, part 2, 170. Citing the decree establishing the STO at the end of 1919, Suleiman describes it as a "permanently operating interdepartmental commission of the SNK (Council of People's Commissars) which had the final decision power on all questions concerning defense of the republic.

6. Studenikin and Taranenko, "Vvidu chrezvychainogo polozheniia," provides details of the GKO's establishment and purpose on its forty-fifth anniversary.

7. Holloway, "Innovation in the Defence Sector," 297.

8. The Council of Commissars was the forerunner of the postwar Council of Ministers. Upon seizure of power in 1917, the Bolsheviks threw out the term *minister* because it had a bourgeois connotation and replaced it with what Trotsky thought sounded more revolutionary, *commissar*. Ministries, accordingly, became commissariats.

9. This information comes from an interview, 30 June 1995, with Colonel General Nikolai Detinov, who served for a time in the 1980s in the Central Committee Secretariat Defense Industries Department, a position that allows him to speak with authority about the Defense Council.

10. Yevgenii Volk, interview, 27 June 1995.

11. Ibid.

12. Colton, *Commissars, Commanders, and Civil Authority*, offers the best history and analysis of the MPA.

13. Sergei Tarasenko, a close aide to Shevardnadze, described the Foreign Ministry's relation with the International Department as periodically competitive, interview, 26 June 1995.

14. Shakhnazarov, *Tseny svobody*, 90, expressed thinly veiled anger at the level of corruption among Soviet generals.

15. According to Soviet doctrine for the use of military forces, there are three levels of employment — tactical, operational, and strategic. The dividing lines were sometime blurred and overlapping, but roughly speaking, tactics included division-level ground operations, while operations involved actions from army-level up to the front level. Above that, at high commands and finally at the General Staff, actions were viewed as strategic.

16. See especially Shaposhnikov, *Vybor*, 9–99, for a number of accounts of collegium meetings that give considerable insight into the concept.

17. Shaposhnikov, *Vybor*, describes the military collegium's handling of the crisis of 19–23 August 1991, when the attempt to impose martial law failed, and also details how the collegium dealt with manpower, resource, and reorganization issues throughout that fall. Major General V. I. Filatov, editor of the MoD's military history journal, told me of Marshal Yazov's convening a meeting of the military collegium in the summer of 1991 to discuss a handwritten note from Gorbachev and to complain about Filatov's publication of a couple of

items that Gorbachev found offensive. This episode demonstrates that the collegium occasionally dealt with rather trivial issues.

18. *Voennyi Entsiklopedicheskii Slovar'* (Moscow: Voenizdat, 1984), 136.

19. As documents emerge from the Soviet archives, they provide such evidence. See, for example, Zubok, "Nuclear Weapons After Stalin's Death." Holloway, "Innovation in the Defence Sector," offers glimpses into the military industrialists' role as well. Holloway, *Stalin and the Bomb*, provides the story of the Soviet nuclear weapons program. Vernon V. Aspaturian, "The Stalinist Legacy in Soviet National Security Decisionmaking," in Valenta and Potter, *Soviet Decisionmaking for National Security*, 23–73, shows how Stalin dealt with scientists and engineers in the policy process. Colton and Gustafson, *Soldiers and the Soviet State*, includes a number of contributions which try to sort out the degree of policy influence exercised by the military-industrial sector. A much larger literature exists, but most of it rests on inferences from fairly limited evidence, mainly from memoirs written by retired Soviet military industrialists themselves.

20. See Hintze, "The Origins of the Modern Ministerial System," in *Historical Essays*, 216–66.

21. Huntington, *Soldier and the State*, is the classic work on the emergence of modern military professionalism and its political implications. It has been challenged on this particular point, some students arguing that professionalism in military affairs has earlier roots. Even if that is the case, a new kind of professionalism appeared in the nineteenth century.

22. Bayer, *Evolution of the Soviet General Staff*, provides an account of why Lenin and Stalin initially disallowed the General Staff and of factors leading Stalin to establish it in 1935.

23. The exact process of compiling and prioritizing military resource requirements has always been largely a mystery in the West because it was kept so secret. Lieutenant General M. S. Vinogradov, who served in the Organization and Mobilization Directorate of the General Staff, described it briefly to the author in an interview on 13 March 1996. Based on intelligence analysis of adversaries' capabilities, performed by the Intelligence Directorate, and on war plans developed in the Operations Directorate, and the tactical and operational doctrine developed by the five military services under General Staff management, each of the five services compiled annual and five-year resource requirements and presented them to the Organization and Mobilization Directorate. This directorate, based on the chief of the General Staff's guidance, cut them back and fitted them into the overall allocation levels approved by the Politburo. Then they went forward to the minister of defense, who normally accepted them as presented and took them to the Politburo for final approval. Considerable bureaucratic politicking accompanied the work of the Organization and Mobilization Directorate's cuts and prioritization, but normally it had the final say unless the chief of the General Staff insisted on changes, which he sometimes did.

24. The Soviet Ground Forces, or *Sukhoputnye voiska*, included what western military establishments call the army, with a much larger aviation component. The army, in Soviet parlance, had the connotation of virtually all the armed forces but the navy.

25. SAF is the traditional NATO acronym for the Soviet Air Forces; in Russian, the acronym was VVS, derived from *Voenno-vozhdunaya sily* — literally "military air forces."

26. William Burr, "Soviet Cold War Military Strategy: Using Declassified History," *Bulletin: Cold War International History Project* 4 (Fall 1994), 10. The Russian name for the service was *Protivo-vozhdushnaya oborony strany;* the acronym PVO did not include a letter for *strany*, literally "of the country."

27. SRF is the NATO acronym for strategic rocket forces, as the service was called in

the west. In Russian it is called *Raketnnye voiska strategicheskogo naznacheniya,* or RVSN. I will refer to it as rocket forces or strategic rocket forces.

28. General Anatolii I. Gribkov asserted on 27 March 1995 in a meeting of former U.S. and Soviet officials discussing the Carter-Brezhnev years in Fort Lauderdale, Florida, that because rough equivalence with the United States in strategic forces would be reached in 1979, already in 1978 the military leadership decided to shift the emphasis to improving capabilities for war at the theater level, especially command and control, including Soviet control over Warsaw Pact forces.

29. *Military Balance, 1985–1986,* p. 30.

30. Ibid.

31. Ibid.

32. Little Western attention has been given to this KGB apparatus in the military. For an early exception, see Brzezinski, *Political Controls in the Soviet Army.* This pamphlet includes interviews with former Soviet officers after World War II in which they describe the special sections and how they worked. See also Colton, *Commissars, Commanders, and Civilian Authority,* for another exception, probably the only additional one.

33. The Soviet acronym was GPU, for *Glavnoe politicheskoe upravlenie.* Colton, *Commissars, Commanders, and Civilian Authority,* is the classic work on the MPA.

34. Garthoff, *Soviet Military Doctrine,* 241, sums up the political officers as "a combination of deputy commander, chaplain, special services recreations officer, welfare officer, personnel officer, censor, and local newspaper editor." This description, written when American Soviet studies were in their infancy, holds up well after four decades and a fair amount of academic quarreling over the character of the political officer.

35. Shaposhnikov, *Vybor,* 98–99, describes the level of competence possessed by political officers for handling military operational matters. He was determined to close down the political organs precisely because they lacked such competence.

36. Colonel Aleksei Tsarev, interview, 29 June 1995. Tsarev was a political officer in a strategic rocket unit. He went into detail to explain why young officers were less concerned by their party records than senior officers, who increasingly became more communist than professional officers in order to secure promotions and assignments.

Chapter 3. How the Military Was Manned

1. The most textured revelations of the earliest Bolshevik concerns with the quality of their military personnel are provided by Leon Trotsky. See his *Kak vooruzhilas' revolutsiya,* 3 vols. (Moscow, 1923–25). Erickson, *Soviet High Command;* Odom, *Soviet Volunteers;* Fedotoff White, *Growth of the Red Army;* and von Hagen, *Soldiers in the Proletariatian Dictatorship,* treat many aspects of the military manpower problems and policies in the interwar period. Jones, *Red Army and Society,* is the best and most comprehensive treatment of postwar manpower policy. Goldhammer, *Soviet Soldier,* and Gabriel, *New Red Legions,* offer more specialized treatments of the postwar period.

2. *Military Balance, 1985–1986,* 21. This source gives the figure as 5,300,000, excluding 600,000 KGB and MVD uniformed personnel.

3. This figure was taken from the author's unclassified briefing on Soviet military capabilities while he served in the Department of Army in 1981–85.

4. See Odom, *Soviet Volunteers,* 23–32, for a brief exposition of the Social Democratic military policy and the problem it created for Lenin and Trotsky with the military opposition at the Seventh and Eighth Party Congresses in 1918 and 1919, respectively.

5. Ibid., 42–57.

6. Kozlov et al., *O Sovetskoi voennoi nauke,* 201–2. Different figures can be found in different Soviet sources. For example, Fedotoff White, *Growth of the Red Army,* 183–88, cites Trotsky's report to the RSFSR Sixth Congress of Soviets as setting the highest level during the civil war at 5.3 million men. The 1923 figure that I use here, 520,000, is taken from Fedotoff White's carefully documented account, but 560,000 is often used in later Soviet sources. The other figures are all from Kozlov et al., *O Sovetskoi voennoi nauke.* Accounting for actual numbers of personnel was undoubtedly subject to significant inaccuracies in the early years of the Red Army; discrepancies among sources are therefore not surprising. The Soviet penchant for secrecy also probably accounts for misleading and different later numbers in Soviet secondary sources. These inaccuracies, however, are not important here because they do not contradict the overall trends of expansion and contraction of manpower levels.

7. *Military Balance, 1985–1986,* 21.

8. The Russian defense minister, General Pavel Grachev, reported in 1993 that the ratio of flag officers, other officers, and enlisted personnel in 1978 was 1:169:530. See FBIS-SOV-93-024, 8 February 1993, "Grachev Says Defense Ministry May Become Demilitarized," 22. During the glasnost years and even after the abolition of the Soviet Union, Soviet and Russian military spokesmen have been consistently cryptic in reporting the numbers of flag officers and officers. The breakdown derived from Grachev's ratio is probably off the mark a bit, but it is a rough approximation.

9. Figure provided by the U.S. Department of Defense.

10. Odom, *Soviet Volunteers,* 3–58. As this study shows, the Bolsheviks, acutely aware of the Soviet citizenry's general unfamiliarity with motor vehicles, aircraft, radios, and more complex weapons, launched all kinds of intensive programs to wipe out this technical and cultural lag behind Western industrial societies.

11. Fedotoff White, *Growth of the Red Army,* provides the best detail on emerging new Red officer corps.

12. Odom, "Militarization of Soviet Society."

13. Jones, *Red Army and Society,* 81.

14. Cross, "Soviet Higher Educational System," 4.

15. Odom, "Militarization of Soviet Society," 37–38.

16. Shaposhnikov, *Vybor,* 85.

17. Shakhnazarov, *Tseny svobody,* 90. As an official of the Central Committee Secretariat, Shakhnazarov helped investigate a case in the 1970s involving generals with Soviet forces in Eastern Europe.

18. Shaposhnikov, *Vybor,* 84–89, reveals the breadth of petty corruption in the form of dachas and privileges and gives the impression that it was known and generally tolerated.

19. Colonel Aleksei Tsarev, interview, 28 June 1995.

20. See Graham, "Soviet Military Commissariats," for details on the voenkomaty (military commissariats). These organizations have received almost no scholarly attention, though they played an important role in the lives of all men in Soviet society from their teenage years until their late forties.

21. Odom, "Militarization of Soviet Society," 41–50. For details of the preservice training programs and their content, see Jones, *Red Army and Society,* 63–73.

22. Jones, *Red Army and Society,* 39, provides the categories and age groups for the reserve obligations.

23. Ibid., 95–98, 105.

24. Ibid.

25. Ibid., 53–57.

26. Various figures can be found, from five to seven rubles a month; at the old official exchange rate during the Soviet period, this was the equivalent of six to eight U.S. dollars, although the actual purchasing power was less, especially in choice of consumer goods. See Seaton and Seaton, *Soviet Army*, 182, who give the figure as eight dollars.

27. See, for examples, F. Saushin, "Vovremya upravlenie prodovol'stvennogo snab-zheniya Mo. SSSR," *Tyl i snabzhenie* no. 8 (August 1973): 56–61; A. Stizhkov, "Iz pavil'onov BDNKh—na polya voennykh sovkhozov, *Tyl i snabzhenie* no. 9 (September 1973): 63–65; and the announcement in *Krasnaya zvezda*, 25 January 1974. The agricultural enterprises of the Soviet military have received no Western attention of note, but they were rather exten-sive.

28. Rakowska-Harmstone, "Nationalities and the Soviet Military," 83.

29. Ibid. Rakowska-Harmstone reports that émigrés firmly believe this to be a major consideration in the policy of allowing no soldier to serve in his home region.

30. Keep, *Last of the Empires*, 92–93.

31. Ibid., 72–94, for an excellent summary of the nationalities problem in the Soviet military, including some statistical data on numbers and distribution of ethnic minority per-sonnel.

32. See General Varennikov, "Iz istorii sozdaniya I podgotovki etnicheskykh voennykh chastei," for a fairly detailed account for the history of national formations in the Soviet mili-tary. Varennikov's motive for this unusual exposition on the topic was to oppose some of the reformers' demands that national military units be revived as part of military perestroika.

33. Jones, *Red Army and Society*, 180–207, for example, in her otherwise excellent study of the sociology of the Soviet military, concluded that the integration of national mi-norities in the military did contribute to a Soviet consciousness at the expense of national minority identification. From 1989 onward, overwhelming evidence to the contrary emerged in the Soviet press.

34. I. Rodionov, "Kogda perestanut glumit'sya nad armei I dezhavoi?" *Molodaya gvar-diya* no. 9 (1990): 3–9.

35. Colonel General Bizhan, deputy minister of defense in Ukraine, recounted this story of his awakening to Ukrainian nationalism to a few other Americans and me near Kiev on 12 October 1996.

36. Jones, *Red Army and Society*, 188–202. Jones rightly dismissed the notion that these concerns threatened the Soviet military with a manpower crisis, but they did create prob-lems.

37. See Feshbach and Friendly, *Ecocide in the USSR*, especially chapter 8, for health conditions in the military and the medical problems that affected conscription.

38. Odom, "Militarization of Soviet Society," 43.

39. Ibid., 41–44.

40. As a serving U.S. officer at the time, I heard this explanation repeatedly from intelligence officials and also from university scholars studying Soviet political and military affairs.

41. See Sokolovskii, *Voennaya strategiya*, especially the last edition. Sokolovskii him-self did not write the book but headed the collective of writers who contributed to it.

42. See Odom, "Militarization of Soviet Society," for a fuller explanation of the con-nection between military preservice training and the 1967 military service law.

43. Jones, *Red Army and Society*, 38–42, draws a connection between the requirements

of nuclear war and the mobilization base, but she does not suggest that this consideration may have inspired the 1967 Law on Universal Military Service.

44. Aleksei Tsarev, a former colonel and political officer in an SS-18 missile unit, explained this barracks dynamic to me, interview, 28 June 1995. He emphasized especially the reaction of hazed soldiers, who sought not to change the system but to get revenge on the next group of new soldiers. Fighting over food and petty thievery fueled the strife between junior and senior cohorts. Officers tried to control the barracks at times, but they were not backed up by higher commanders. The troops quickly recognized the junior officers' lack of authority and took firm control of life in the barracks. The situation, in Tsarev's view, was simply beyond the control of the best platoon leaders and company commanders.

45. Ibid. Tsarev gave several examples of senior soldiers effectively taking charge of daily tasks and carrying them through when directed by their officers, or rather forcing junior soldiers to perform them at the demand of senior soldiers. A number of other interviewees offered similar stories and generalizations, with many saying that the junior officers became dependent on the senior enlisted cohort to get almost anything done by their troops.

46. Ibid. Again, Colonel Tsarev offered extensive detail on the existence of ethnic group behavior in military units. He was particularly concerned with conveying the impossible predicament confronting junior officers in dealing both with their troops and their abusive superiors.

47. Rakowska-Harmstone, "Nationalities and the Soviet Military," 72–74, also provides considerable detail and evidence on the strife among ethnic groups in the Soviet military.

48. In Russian, *ded'* means "grandfather." The *-shchina* ending connotes a general social or political phenomenon, usually negative. Thus *dedovshchina* meant the practice of second-year soldiers exercising their parental, or "grandfather," rights to demand the obedience and subservience of first-year conscripts.

Chapter 4. The Permanent War Economy

1. Shakhnazarov, *Tsena svobody,* 42, says military expenditures approached 40 percent of the national income. Elsewhere he puts weapons procurement at 16 percent and the KGB and MVD at 4 percent, totaling 20 percent, "The highest military expenditures in the world" (49). Presumably this second figure includes only the procurement budget of the MoD. In fact, neither Shakhnazarov nor other high-level officials with full access to official data could determine the total Soviet outlays to defense because of the arbitrary pricing and accounting system, as well as many nonbudgetary contributions to the military.

Western assessments include Bergson, "On the Measurement of Soviet Real Defense Outlays," and Becker, *Burden of Soviet Defense.* Bergson and Becker have long been associated with the CIA's estimates, though each has his reservations about some aspects of the CIA's methodology. Cohn, "The Economic Burden of Soviet Defense Outlays," offers a figure of 6–8 percent for Soviet military spending, a figure close to the CIA figure at the time, 6–9 percent, and generally accepted in the academic community. William T. Lee is an analyst who worked for both DIA and CIA and who has been the most vocal critic of the low estimates made by Becker, CIA, and others. But his highest estimate—in the 16–18 percent range *(Estimation of Soviet Defense Expenditures)*—looks much too low in retrospect. Birman, *Secret Incomes,* attempts to uncover large and hidden parts of the state budget that go to defense spending; see also his "Economic Situation in the USSR," in which he argues that the CIA estimate of the Soviet GNP was twice its real size, and therefore, the CIA's estimate of military expenditures as a percentage of GNP was far below the mark. Rosefielde, "Soviet Defence Spending," continues his previously strong criticism of the low Western estimates; although he has offered no detailed accounting that produced a definite figure, his general line of reasoning has been considerably vindicated by emerging evidence. Rowen and Wolf, *Impoverished Superpower,* offer a collection of essays most of which cogently attempt to correct the traditionally low estimates of mainstream Western analysis. See Odom, "Riddle of Soviet Defense Spending," for my summary of the debate and ranges of estimates, and for my conclusion that the figure was at least 20 percent and probably higher. All in all, the Western debate was more heated than enlightening, punctuated with strongly emotional exchanges.

2. See Frederick C. Barghoorn and Thomas F. Remington, *Politics in the USSR,* 3d ed. (Boston: Little, Brown, 1986), 511–13, for the list of all ministries in 1983. Between forty-five and fifty-five ministries were involved in the industrial and commercial sectors, depending on how ambiguous cases are categorized.

3. Colonel General N. N. Detinov, interview, March 1996.

4. See Stone, "Red Army and Stalin's Revolution," for extensive archival evidence on this point.

5. Aircraft construction was an exception. It remained outside the narrow military-industrial grouping because air transport was considered a dual-use sector, and civil and military aircraft were kept to a common design to the extent possible. The chemical industry was also apart from the military sector but considered of great military importance for the production of poison gases, which had made their appearance on the battlefield in World War I. See Odom, *Soviet Volunteers,* especially 58–88.

6. See, for example, Dobb, *Soviet Economic Development;* Nove, *Economic History of the USSR;* Erlich, *Soviet Industrialization Debate;* Bergson, *Economics of Soviet Planning;* and Gregory and Stuart, *Soviet Economic Structure and Performance,* 3d ed. None of these more than cursorily acknowledges the existence of a military-industrial sector, and none deals with military considerations in Soviet economic policy—a rather astounding fact in light of the primacy of military industries in the system. An exception is Holloway, "Innovation in the Defence Sector," who looks at the early structural developments of the system and the management of technology before and after World War II. Almquist, *Red Forge,* offers a look at the structure and process of Soviet military-industrial system but still fails, as late as 1990, to emphasize the dominance and enormity of the military sector. The best work is Stone's "The Red Army and Stalin's Revolution," which has opened up this question with remarkably illuminating evidence from Soviet archives. It should cause considerable revision of our understanding of the factor in Soviet rapid industrialization.

7. Richard E. Ericson, "The Soviet Statistical Debate: Khanin Versus TsSU," in Rowen and Wolf, *Impoverished Superpower,* 63–92, reviewing the work of the Soviet economist Grigorii Khanin's dramatically low estimate of the Soviet GNP and the large share in the defense sector, is one of the few Western economists to concede the problem: "The implications of the K-S results and the debate they have spurred are dramatic, for they call on us to reevaluate our understanding of the nature and consequences of a Soviet-type economic system, as well as the strength and position of the Soviet Union" (90). Rowen and Wolf, also economists, by publishing their volume of edited essays, were pressing for such a reevaluation, one they have long insisted was needed.

8. Stone, "The Red Army and Stalin's Revolution," provided the best account of this episode. Also see Bayer, *Evolution of the Soviet General Staff,* 107–8. The plan called for the

production of 1,100 tanks by 1932. A plan for 1924–29 had also been developed, but it was concerned more centrally with the structure of the Red Army and less with the procurement of modern weaponry; moreover, it produced no significant results in the military-industrial sector. See "O sostanyanii oborony SSSR," *KPSS o vooruzhennykh silakh Sovetskogo Soyuza* (Moscow: Voenizdat, 1969), 264–66. See also Habeck, "Imagining War," for the problems this plan faced, especially in tank design and production, and the secret cooperation in tank development between the Red Army and the German army during the first FYP.

9. David Stone, in a colloquium at Yale University, 16 February 1994, reporting on his research in the Red Army archive (TsGASA) on military industries during the first FYP, emphasized that the 1926–27 war scare whipped up in the Soviet press was not matched by a surge in military production. Rather it was used to justify rapid industrialization. Stalin responded differently to the Far East crisis of 1931, when Japan invaded Manchuria; then he made no fuss in the press but pushed the fledgling military-industrial sector to step up weapons production. Tukhachevskii's desire for early rearmament is well known, but Voroshilov, who played it down at the Fifteenth Party Congress in 1927, has been generally believed to have shared Stalin's reluctance to put rearming the Red Army ahead of the broader industrialization task. Stone found Voroshilov's handwritten note to Ordzhonikidze, head of the party's auditing commission, in which he went on to say that if someone later tried to blame him for this defense fiasco, he would wash his hands of it and ask for relief "from responsibility for preparation of the army." As Stone noted, this Voroshilov is quite different from the public Voroshilov, who always appeared to defer in every way to Stalin.

10. Odom, *Soviet Volunteers*, 40–57. Frunze was more aggressive about rapid military modernization, but as he replaced Trotsky as head of the Red Army, he became a strong defender of reducing the military budget in order to support economic reconstruction.

11. I am grateful to David Stone for showing me his findings in the Red Army archive on the *Kommissiya oborony*, including its membership, meetings, kinds of decisions, and central role in dictating military-industrial and procurement policy. Also, Holloway, "Innovation in the Defence Sector," provides considerable detail on the institutional developments in the mid- and late 1930s.

12. Kliment E. Voroshilov, *Stat'i i rechi* (Moscow: Voenizdat, 1937), 196, announced to the Fifteenth Party Congress that "at last a special apparatus has been created in the bowels . . . of GOSPLAN" to coordinate military mobilization and industrial work.

13. In some ways, this commission looks like the State Defense Committee (GKO) of World War II, but that body's antecedent is the Council for Labor and Defense (STO), which lasted until 1937. Its detailed involvement in military procurement and R&D affairs and its formal location below the STO makes it look more like the antecedent to the Defense Committee of the late 1930s and the VPK in the postwar period. The party general secretary did not normally participate in VPK proceedings as he did in the Defense Commission, but that change reflects not so much its VPK-like function as it does the postwar technical industrial complexities and subsequent routinization that limited his capacity to be involved.

14. Almquist, *Red Forge*, 56–57, provides a description of how the voenpredy operated in the postwar period.

15. Holloway, "Innovation in the Defence Sector," provides evidence on a number of these changes in the 1930s.

16. See Kravchenko, *Voennaya ekonomika SSSR*, especially 14–20, for an accounting of military production as a portion of the national income during World War II. He puts it in the range of 50–60 percent.

17. Frunze, "Front i tyl v voine budushchego," in *Izbrannie proizvedeniya*, 133–43.

Frunze enjoyed considerable prestige for his civil war leadership as a "Red Commander"—that is, he was not one of the "military specialists" from the Russian Imperial Army recruited to provide expertise to the Red Army. From June 1921, when he published a short essay, "The Unified Military Doctrine and the Red Army," making a case for a unique Marxist military science and doctrine, he insisted that the ex-imperial professional officers, lacking a Marxist grounding, could not possibly provide the leadership for post–civil war Red Army, something the new Red Commanders feared Trotsky would allow. Stalin probably had a hand in Frunze's rapid emergence as the leader of the Red Commanders, as well as a part in his death under the knife of surgeons who performed a stomach operation on him at the party's orders and against Frunze's wishes in late 1925. Frunze's views on military affairs, however, clearly appealed to Stalin more than just for tactical political reasons. When Stalin's crony Voroshilov succeeded Frunze in 1925, he continued Frunze's programs and doctrine. See Fedotoff White, *Growth of the Red Army,* 158–82.

18. Frunze, "Front i tyl v voine budushchego," 141.

19. Here I shall assume virtually no market-price formation in the Soviet system, only prices established by the state bureaucracy, GOSTsEN. Clearly the Soviet labor market affected wages, but wages were not allowed more than occasional or trivial impact on the price of goods and services. There was also a food market for the produce from the private plots of collective farmers. Although those goods sold at market prices, state food stores provided most of the same products at fixed prices, irrespective of supply and demand. Notwithstanding these exceptions, from a macro perspective, it is fair to say that the Soviet economic system effectively denied market pricing any significant effect on patterns of investments and industrial production. This, of course, overlooks the so-called "second economy"—the large black market that emerged in the 1970s and 1980s—but neither was that market allowed to affect state prices and major investment patterns. Central planners, of course, gave way to bureaucratic political pressures for some investments, especially construction, but that phenomenon contributed no relative scarcity information to Soviet official prices. They remained "planners' prices."

20. For some of the points elucidated here, I am indebted to Wladyslaw W. Jermakowicz, who for many years conducted research in Poland on economic organization, performance, and reform in the Soviet and other Eastern European economies. However, I have gone somewhat beyond his presentation, and he is not responsible for any of the flaws that critics may discover. See his "Foundations and Prospects."

21. Jermakowicz, "Foundations and Prospects." Professor Jermakowicz told me that all of the research of his institute in Poland on economic reforms in the Soviet Union and Eastern Europe showed that reforms did not correlate with economic performance at all but rather with leadership changes. Shifting toward P2 allowed large purges of officials. Both the political interests of the party leaders and the bureaucratic interests of the ministries in reasserting lost controls soon pushed the economy back toward P1.

22. For a couple of examples that make the case in largely nontechnical terms, see Kornai, *Road to a Free Economy,* and Prybyla, *Market and Plan Under Socialism.* Some readers may conclude that I believe that the debate between socialists and capitalists is over and that capitalists have won. The debate itself has always had a "ships passing in the night" quality because no unambiguous empirical measures for either system have been identified or agreed on. To the extent that the debate has been about the long-term performance of central planning encompassing the whole of an economy without consumers registering preferences through market pricing, I have never understood why anyone thought such a system would not soon slow down and decay from massive inefficiencies measured by either

consumers' or planners' preferences. The information problem is simply too large for any bureaucracy to manage, even one with vast computer power. Seen from this viewpoint, the Soviet economic experiment was doomed from its inception, and some Soviet officials knew it. Academician Viktor Glushkov conveyed vividly the information-overload problem when he estimated in the mid-1960s that at the contemporary rate of the expansion of the planning bureaucracy, the entire Soviet population would be employed in it by the year 2000. This aspect of the question seems to have been resolved by the Soviet experience. The issue of what kind of state involvement in the economy and how much of it a state can usefully accept while avoiding stagnation and even regression or collapse, however, is far from decided. Technological change, social structure, and political and cultural factors make any apparently good answer temporary at best.

23. On the issue of explaining differing long-term economic performances, see North, *Structure and Change* and *Institutions, Institutional Change, and Economic Performance*. North's sweeping and highly innovative theories would seem particularly appropriate for explaining the Soviet case. Rejecting the neoclassical theories for explaining institutional efficiency, he argues in example historical cases that "rulers devised property rights in their own interests and transaction costs resulted in typically inefficient property rights prevailing." (*Institutions, Institutional Change, and Economic Performance*, 7). Olson, *Rise and Decline of Nations*, applying neoclassical economic theory with some innovative additions, seems to encourage a similar expectation of the poor performance and decline of the Soviet system. But North has a more textured treatment of institutions and therefore a more persuasive case. This is not to say that Olson is wrong; on the contrary, his approach, applied to the Soviet case, suggests the same answer as North's. Neither approach, however, has been applied to the Soviet case, as far as I am aware.

24. Stone, "The Red Army and Stalin's Revolution."

25. See *Soviet Acquisition of Militarily Significant Technology*. No author or publisher is mentioned in this document, but it was produced and distributed by the CIA as an unclassified booklet. Although the Soviet report on which it is based probably was biased to make the KGB's efforts appear in the best light, the scope of espionage successes remains impressive, even when significantly discounted for the bias.

Chapter 5. Military Strategy

1. General Vitalii Gribkov commented at a meeting in Fort Lauderdale, Florida, 27 March 1995, about Soviet military planning in 1978. He said that the Soviet military leaders had concluded in 1978 that by 1979 they would enjoy full strategic parity with the United States and that they decided to shift their emphasis to theater war planning and armaments. This included changing the command arrangements within the Warsaw Pact so that the transition to war could be carried out more swiftly, giving the General Staff operational control of all Warsaw Pact forces. In addition to this change, exercises and other activities were devoted to theater operational improvements. Gribkov's remarks confirm my impression of Soviet military activities in this period, an impression derived while serving both in the White House (NSC Staff) and as a senior officer in the U.S. intelligence community.

2. U.S. theorists in this camp are too numerous to list, but the pioneers of its logic included Brodie, *Strategy in the Missile Age*, and Schelling, *Strategy of Conflict*. They did not, however, deal with precisely what Soviet nuclear strategy was; rather, they insisted that the nature of nuclear weapons had imparted a new reality for warfare that invalidated the traditional logic of military strategy. Effective "defense" was no longer possible in light of

the destructiveness of such weapons; thus a new strategic logic was henceforth operative, based on both sides having virtually unlimited power to destroy each other but no defense. As the Soviet nuclear forces grew, this group had to begin to take account of Soviet strategic thinking on the matter. For an account of the development of this line of Western theory and strategy for nuclear forces up to the 1980s, see Freedman, *Evolution of Nuclear Strategy,* who pays some attention to Soviet published thinking on the matter but tends to dismiss it as perhaps explaining some Soviet weapons programs but not a rejection by the top leadership of the Brodie-Schelling logic. The views of this first group of U.S. theorists also took official sway at the top levels of the U.S. Department of Defense during Robert McNamara's tenure as secretary of defense. Most of his successors retained key aspects of this view, but James Schlesinger, the incumbent for a time during the Nixon administration, implemented a policy of developing "limited nuclear options" that might be used to control the escalation of a nuclear war if it broke. Harold Brown, President Carter's secretary of defense, held a fairly orthodox version of this view, but watching Soviet programs and exercises seems to have convinced him that Soviet leaders, especially military leaders, did not share his perception. Thus he supported another change in U.S. nuclear employment doctrine, articulated in Presidential Directive 59 in 1980, which publicly took his "counterveiling strategy" label. Caspar Weinberger, Brown's successor, saw little or no reason to assume that Soviet leaders shared the U.S. concept of mutual destruction. These judgments are based on my observations and direct dealings with all of them but McNamara while they were in office. Those scholars and think-tank analysts who held with the basic idea of mutual vulnerability of the U.S. and the USSR to virtual total destruction tended to take it without reservations, as inexorable, inescapable for either side. Incumbents in posts responsible for implementing U.S. military strategy were sometimes, but not always, inclined to consider what would happen if nuclear deterrence strategy failed and what should be done to cope with that event. These different positions can stimulate quite different thinking and approaches to nuclear weapons.

3. Again, the U.S. theorists in this camp are too numerous to name, but the first serious rebuttals to Brodie and Schelling were advanced by Wohlstetter, "The Delicate Balance of Terror," and Kahn, *On Thermonuclear War.* They, too, more or less ignored Soviet thinking while finding flaws in logic of mutual vulnerability and Brodie's and Schelling's prescriptions about what constituted rational behavior in the nuclear age. Garthoff, *Soviet Strategy in the Nuclear Age,* provided an assessment of Soviet thought, insofar as sources allowed, revealing a picture of preparation and willingness to fight a nuclear war guided by somewhat modified traditional military strategic thought. Garthoff, however, later seems to have rejected his own early characterization of the Soviet view, consistently siding with the first group and U.S. deterrence theory. For a later work by a distinguished member of this second group, one that emphasizes the Soviet side as sensibly rejecting the logic of U.S. deterrence theory outright, see Gray, *War, Peace, and Victory.* For a post–Cold War critical review of deterrence theory, see Payne, *Deterrence in the Second Nuclear Age.*

4. For my own position in this debate, see Odom, "The Soviet Approach to Nuclear Weapons." I was closer to the second group in judging the evidence from the Soviet side.

5. Holloway, *Stalin and the Bomb,* especially 224–72, sheds remarkable new light on this period and Stalin's views and policies. In as much secrecy as possible he pushed nuclear weapons development, and the Soviet military was compelled to test them in tactical exercises in order to gain empirical experience which could be used for developing organization and doctrine for their use in war. Holloway learned from interviews with former Soviet officials involved with Stalin and these tests that they never doubted that atomic bombs could be used in war. On the contrary, they assumed that they would be.

6. Ibid., 241–42.

7. Ibid., 253–72, 320–45. Holloway's chapter 12 explains Stalin's "war of nerves" and chapter 15 recounts how Malenkov, Khrushchev, and others backed away from Stalin's approach as they came to appreciate the nature of nuclear explosions.

8. See Odom, "The Soviet Approach to Nuclear Weapons," for a short summary of the Soviet-Chinese debate over nuclear war and the formula the Soviet side used to hedge the issue. Holloway, *Stalin and the Bomb*, 320–45, provides an excellent treatment of Khrushchev's difficulties with fitting nuclear weapons into the official ideology, as he was challenged not only by Chinese critics but by internal critics as well.

9. Odom, "The Soviet Approach to Nuclear Weapons," 124.

10. Holloway, *Stalin and the Bomb*, provides evidence of these factors, concerning both Soviet and U.S. capabilities and war plans in the 1950s.

11. A paradox characterized U.S. declaratory nuclear weapons strategy and actual force development and war planning. While Secretary of State John Foster Dulles was proclaiming his "massive retaliation" policy in the 1950s, tactical nuclear capabilities were being deployed in Germany. In the 1960s, while proclaiming "flexible response," presumably meaning graduated military operational responses in the event of war in Europe, Secretary of Defense Robert McNamara was building strategic nuclear forces for "assured destruction" and mutual vulnerability while letting tactical nuclear doctrine and war planning languish. As the Soviet side reached nuclear parity with the U.S. side in the 1970s, Henry Kissinger proclaimed the unwinnability of nuclear war and tried to substitute strategic arms control for nuclear strategy. Only late in the Carter and Reagan administrations was the heavy emphasis on arms control paralleled by serious efforts to design a workable nuclear strategy that went beyond a simple acceptance of its hopelessness, namely Presidential Directive 59 and National Security Directive 13.

12. Sokolovskii, *Voennaya strategiya*. This volume, published in 1962 and revised in 1963 and 1968, was a compendium of works by unnamed authors. Sokolovskii himself had been involved closely with the Soviet nuclear program from Stalin's last years.

13. The "principle of the objective" in U.S. military parlance is the first of nine such principles, and it states that the objective in war is the destruction of the enemy's forces, not the conquering of terrain or cities, or any other goal that does not contribute significantly to destruction of the enemy's military. While the nine principles of war as articulated by the U.S. military were not accepted in the Soviet Union, the central idea of the objective was deeply ingrained in Soviet military thought, and most of the other principles had Soviet equivalents. See Sokolovskii, *Voennaya strategiya*, 229 (1962 edition).

14. Surprise is also one of the nine principles of war in the U.S. military lexicon.

15. Paul Warnke, *SALT II: Toward a More Secure World* (Washington, D.C.: Arms Control and Disarmament Agency, 1978), 17.

16. Holloway, *Stalin and the Bomb*.

17. Gribkov, in discussion in Fort Lauderdale, Florida, 26–27 March 1995.

18. Gribkov made this point in response to American participants who were trying to draw out from him Soviet views on nuclear use.

19. Meyer, "Soviet Theatre Nuclear Forces," provides an especially insightful analysis of Soviet calculations of nuclear weapons target requirements for the theater campaign in Europe. See also Gromley, "New Dimension to Soviet Theater War"; Trulock, "Soviet Perspectives on Limited Nuclear War"; and Gromley, "Emerging Attack Options."

20. Timothy Aepel, "Trove of Documents Proves NATO's Fears Were Well Founded," *Wall Street Journal*, 13 June 1991, describes initial reports from a review of 250,000 mili-

tary documents taken by West German authorities. East German war plans envisioned that nuclear weapons would be used on the second day after the outbreak of hostilities; chemical weapons would also be included in a mix of nuclear and conventional-weapons attacks. According to these plans, about forty tactical nuclear weapons were to be directed at Hamburg and its vicinity. Moreover, exercises involving this kind of operation were being conducted as late as June 1990, six months after the fall of the Berlin Wall.

21. Igor Shmeshko, interview, June 1995. Shmeshko also said that Western concepts of deterrence theory and the unwinnability of nuclear war were wholly unknown to him and his fellow officers.

22. Rodionov, "Voennaya nauka."

23. Major General V. V. Larionov, "Bezopasnost'," *Nezavisimaya gazeta*, 19 December 1992, p. 2.

24. Bulanov and Krylova, "Sootnoshenie politiki i yadernoi voiny."

25. Savel'yev and Detinov, *The Big Five*, 2–13. Savel'yev, a civilian military policy specialist, assisted Detinov in writing this account of how the Soviet side saw the arms control process and how it developed its positions and negotiating tactics. Detinov's point about why the ABM treaty was accepted suggests that the treaty actually accelerated the buildup of offensive nuclear forces. Detinov, while holding general officer rank, is an engineer whose career was in military industries. Intimately involved with the key five Politburo members handling the Soviet side of the negotiations, he makes his statements based on two decades of frequent contact with these leaders when they were explicitly or implicitly making their views on nuclear war known. Deterrence theory and concepts of stability were never part of Soviet thinking in these circles, although he and some of his colleagues came to comprehend U.S. thinking based on them. Equality with the U.S. arsenal, superiority if possible, was the goal in the minds of his superiors, Detinov reports. Quite elderly now, Detinov struck me as remarkably detached and analytical compared with other former Soviet officials. He seemed to have no particular personal scores to settle and was very admiring of Paul Nitze, who wrote an introduction for his book. Thus his testimony is among the most credible available.

26. L. I. Brezhnev, "Vydayushchiisya podvig zashchitnikov Tuly," *Pravda*, 19 January 1977. For an example of the way Brezhnev's so-called Tula line was interpreted and developed in Western scholarly circles, see Roeder, *Red Sunset*, 202–6. In fairness to Roeder, he also concludes that the military did not accept the views in Brezhnev's Tula speech and eventually prevailed with him. This, of course, rests on the questionable assumption that Brezhnev really had to be persuaded. Roeder is hardly alone in his views, taking them primarily from analysts focused on Soviet military and security affairs.

27. In U.S. testing in the 1950s, medium tanks proved safe havens for their crews at a distance of eight hundred meters from ground-zero of a twenty-kiloton explosion. As a student in the U.S. Army's tactical nuclear targeting course in 1960, I was taught that a ten-kiloton weapon dropped on a Soviet tank battalion in march column would destroy only seven or eight tanks, not a high return from such a troublesome weapon, given the residual radiation and other problems it would create.

28. The results of these programs are documented in the annual issues of *Military Balance* from the 1960s to 1988. *Soviet Military Power* (Washington, D.C.: U.S. Government Printing Office, 1985, 1986, and 1987), produced by the U.S. Department of Defense from intelligence sources, includes similar and additional information as well as pictures of the weaponry and equipment.

29. The dynamism of this buildup is difficult to convey accurately, but it was impressive. As an officer in the U.S. Military Liaison Mission to Soviet Forces in Germany,

1964–66, I observed much of this new material and the new weapons as they came into units and were employed in training exercises. In Moscow from 1972 to 1974 I observed new models of weapons appearing in Red Square at the 7 November demonstration. And in February 1978 I was allowed to witness additional weapons and units in an exercise, "Berezina," conducted near Minsk. The impression was one of dynamic military matériel and processes of force development, with almost every year offering new models of weapons and modifications in organization, training, and operational doctrine.

30. The Kama River truck plant, which was modernized with U.S. automotive technology, played a key role in helping the Soviet military to overcome its shortfalls in motor transport.

31. Professor John Erickson pointed out this fact to me sometime in the late 1960s. I believe he was the first person in the West to grasp it.

32. See Starry, "Extending the Battlefield," for the basic thinking that underpinned Air-Land Battle. Officially promulgated as U.S. Army doctrine in 1982 in U.S. Army FM 100-5, *Operations,* and revised in FM 100-5, 1986.

33. See Ogarkov, *Vsegda v gotovnosti k zashchite otechestva,* for his most comprehensive statement on these issues. Also see Odom, "Soviet Force Posture." In this piece, I describe the basic outlines of the 1980s revisions in strategy for war in Europe, its emphasis on conventional operations without nuclear weapons and its basic concepts of a much higher-speed offensive.

34. See *Soviet Military Power,* 113.

35. Ibid., 119, and *Military Balance, 1987–1988,* 27. Also see Odom, "Soviet Force Posture," for a general description of these changes and their rationale.

36. See MccGwire, *Military Objectives in Soviet Foreign Policy,* 117–212, for the best open source treatment of Soviet war plans for all TVDs. MccGwire's conclusion that the Soviet military made a major decision to give emphasis to conventional war planning in 1967, however, is too precise for such a change. Furthermore, it does not square with any of the testimony from former Soviet generals and other officials, or even with most of the published Soviet writings. Notwithstanding this most dubious point, his assessment of Soviet operational objectives and schedules for achieving them in the event of a global war are in general accord with most U.S. intelligence holdings at the time. He offers the only open source analysis that conveys the enormity of the force requirements for those plans, and it is highly recommended to readers who want to get a much more textured view than is possible to offer here.

37. Holloway, *Stalin and the Bomb,* 241, reports this decision and resulting naval programs.

38. Tritten, *Soviet Naval Forces and Nuclear Warfare,* 12, cites some of the more detailed efforts of this sort.

39. Ibid., 1–9, rightly attributes this view to Michael MccGwire.

40. See *Military Balance, 1987–1988,* 33, 37–38, for details on numbers and types of Soviet naval vessels.

41. Tritten, *Soviet Naval Forces and Nuclear Warfare,* generally comes to this same conclusion, differing with many other Western students of the Soviet Navy. Writing in the 1980s, however, he had both the advantage of a late view of the shape the Soviet fleet was actually taking and more information about Soviet naval doctrine.

42. "Bibliografiya: Voina 19. goda Gen. Dzhulio Due," *Vestnik vozdushnogo flota* no. 4 (April 1931): 13–16.

43. Panico, "Rise and Fall of the Heavy Bomber," 97. For general studies of the Soviet

air forces, see Kilmarx, *History of Soviet Air Power,* and Boyd, *Soviet Airforce.* Panico offers a critical review of these and other Western sources. He also finds the roots of Soviet heavy bomber development in Imperial Russia during World War I, and traces the largely ignored emergence of the world's first all-metal strategic bomber fleet until its demise, after Soviet views on the proper role of air power were significantly modified as a result of the Spanish Civil War. He also points out that by the outbreak of World War II, however, Soviet heavy bombers were already becoming obsolete compared to German, British, and later U.S. design and technology. Thus Stalin's development strategy for air power suffered from a number of serious misjudgments.

44. Holloway, *Stalin and the Bomb,* 234–50.

45. See *Soviet Military Power, 1988,* 50–53.

46. See Savel'yev and Detinov, *The Big Five,* 48.

47. *Soviet Military Power, 1988,* 15.

48. In about one month's time, more than a Cuban motor rifle division was put into Ethiopia. Parts of it came by sea, but airlifts directly from the Soviet Union provided much of the equipment.

49. For the best study of Soviet force projection into the Third World, See Porter, *USSR in Third World Conflicts.*

50. See Odom, *On Internal War,* for an assessment of the opposing U.S. and Soviet strategies. For comprehensive studies of Soviet Third World strategy, see Rubinstein, *Moscow's Third World Strategy,* and Kaplan, *Diplomacy of Power.*

51. Lyakhovskii, *Tragediya i doblest' Afgana,* 80–82, explains how officers and diplomats exploited the bureaucratic decision-making process in Moscow to take personal advantage of weapons and equipment transfers to these Third World Soviet military missions. Military industrialists, staff officers on the General Staff, and foreign mission chiefs all knew how to milk the system for greater weapons transfers and to gain personally from a number of sources, including foreign leaders and military commanders who rewarded such behavior by their Soviet advisers.

52. See MacFarlane, *Superpower Rivalry and the Third World Radicalism.*

53. Of all the Soviet efforts to use so-called national liberation movements to undermine the European and American centers of "imperialism," in line with Lenin's thinking about them, the Vietnam case was the most successful. U.S. involvement in the war there was, in Marxist-Leninist categories, "objectively" undercutting the "imperialist camp" and helping the "socialist camp." Curiously, within the anti-Vietnam war movement in the United States, no one made this obvious argument—that President Johnson and his advisers were "objective allies" of Moscow. In a discussion in Moscow, November 1991, with Colonel General Danilevskii (for twenty-one years the special assistant to the chief of the General Staff), I asked whether he and his fellow officers in the General Staff had viewed the war in Vietnam in this light. At first he was a bit puzzled but soon grasped the point, breaking into a sustained chuckle, saying that while he never really thought of it that way, it was certainly true.

54. Lyakhovskii, *Tragediya i doblest' Afgana,* 63–67.

55. Savel'yev and Detinov, *The Big Five,* 7.

56. Ibid., 9.

57. Ibid., 66.

58. For examples, see Garthoff, *Deterrence;* van Oudenaren, "Deterrence, War-Fighting, and Soviet Military Doctrine"; Blacker, *Hostage to Revolution;* Laird and Herspring,

Soviet Union and Strategic Arms Control; Holden, *Soviet Military Reform;* Michael Krepon, *Arms Control in the Reagan Administration* (Washington, D.C.: University Press of America, 1989).

59. Gray, *War, Peace, and Victory;* Rowny, *U.S. and Soviet Approaches to Arms Control;* and Richard Pipes, *Survival Is Not Enough* (New York: Simon and Schuster, 1984). For a number of essays relevant to this issue, also see Hoffman, Wohlstetter, and Yost, *Swords and Shields.*

Chapter 6. Deciding to Change Course

1. Author's notes from Marshal Akhromeev's account to a Council on Foreign Relations meeting in New York City, 11 July, 1988.

2. Chernyaev, *Shest' let s Gorbachevym,* 10–64, recounts numerous episodes behind the scenes in the Central Committee Secretariat, the Politburo, and in public that reveal the disgust with which Chernyaev and many of his peers viewed Brezhnev, Chernenko, Gromyko, Ustinov, Grishin, Ponomarev, and others of the senior party leaders. Andropov, according to Chernyaev, shared some their views. Chernyaev worked for a long time in the International Department of the Secretariat, and beginning in February 1986 he spent the next six years as a special assistant working directly for Gorbachev, a position that makes this memoir of special value as a source.

3. Shakhnazarov, *Tsena svobody,* 11.

4. Ibid.

5. I asked Shevardnadze in December 1993 whether he understood from the beginning that Gorbachev's reforms might require the collapse of the Soviet Union and the Soviet system. He answered yes without hesitation, but then added that the union fell apart more quickly than he anticipated. He believed that it could be maintained for three to five more years while economic and political reforms were pushed through and republican leaders adjusted to handling greater autonomy, avoiding the chaos of an early breakup. On that judgment he confessed that he had been wrong. When I asked him whether Gorbachev had shared this understanding, he said no. Gorbachev, in his view, remained convinced that perestroika could be carried out within the Soviet system. In particular, he never understood the fragmenting potential of the nationality issue. Asked whether any other Politburo member had understood that perestroika would destroy the Soviet system, Shevardnadze answered, "Yes, probably Yakovlev," then added that he doubted whether any others had understood at the beginning. In June 1994, I put the same questions to Yakovlev during a dinner chat. He replied that indeed he had realized that they were destroying the old regime, adding with a certain glee, "and we did it before our opponents woke up in time to prevent it!" Shevardnadze, he believed, understood what they were doing, but Gorbachev did not.

6. Yakovlev, *Fate of Marxism in Russia.* Yakovlev's special responsibility in the Central Committee at times was ideology; the irony of his writing this bitter diatribe against Marxism is difficult to exaggerate.

7. Ligachev, *Inside Gorbachev's Kremlin,* 16, observes that in 1983, "I, like many other provincial Party secretaries, was impatient for change, uncomfortably aware that the country was headed for social and economic disaster." Chernyaev, *Shest' let s Gorbachevym,* 10–64, quotes liberally from his diary in 1984–85, expressing the same impatience for change among many of the second level officials in Party Secretariat.

8. Ligachev, *Inside Gorbachev's Kremlin,* 17–26.

9. Chernyaev, *Shest' let s Gorbachevym*, 30–31, 43, 46–47. Watching the purge from his post in the International Department during 1985, Chernyaev was alternately encouraged and discouraged—discouraged that the purge was not sweeping enough.

10. Not only were Gorbachev's new antialcohol measures extremely unpopular, but they caused a huge loss in tax revenue by cutting sales in half between 1984 and 1986. The population reacted by making *samogon* (the Russian equivalent of moonshine) on such a large scale that it created a sugar shortage. The antialcohol campaign had become both an economic disaster and a political embarrassment by 1987, forcing Gorbachev to abandon it. See Parker, *Kremlin in Transition*, 26–27.

11. I would add that he also confused himself in the process. See Odom, "How Far Can Soviet Reform Go?" See especially p. 17, "The paradox remains, nonetheless, that great central control is required to achieve a great decentralization of economic control and power. If Gorbachev succeeds, he will lose his centralized power to forces that could cause the breakup of the empire."

12. Interviews, June and July 1995.

13. Ligachev, *Inside Gorbachev's Kremlin*, 329.

14. Ibid.

15. For a much fuller treatment of cooperation and conflict between Gorbachev and Ligachev, see Parker, *Kremlin in Transition*, vol. 2, especially pp. 151–239. Parker provides an excellent and textured account of the clique politics in the Politburo and Central Committee, based on open sources and his observations while serving in the U.S. embassy in Moscow, tracing the initial Gorbachev-Ligachev cooperative ties, their breakdown, and Ligachev's efforts to gather his own support, especially from Chebrikov.

16. Ibid., 66–82.

17. Shakhnazarov, *Tsena svobody*, 40–41. For Ligachev's version of this issue, see *Inside Gorbachev's Kremlin*, 50–52. He says that he was in favor of revoking Chernenko's decree on cadre assignments to the central apparatus but makes no mention of selecting people without regional party experience. He simply says that he sought people who moved around from region to region and also got some experience at the center, evading Shakhnazarov's point.

18. Ligachev, *Inside Gorbachev's Kremlin*, 82–117, 329–31.

19. Ligachev made these points during a faculty dinner discussion at Yale University on 11 November 1991, where I was among guests who questioned him on many aspects of perestroika.

20. Ligachev, *Inside Gorbachev's Kremlin*. Throughout his memoir, Ligachev details Yakovlev's duplicity in outflanking him on glasnost and media policy. Gorbachev is made to look duped and eventually wholly misguided by Yakovlev's scheming.

21. Chernyaev, *Shest' let s Gorbachevym*, 62.

22. Boldin, *Ten Years That Shook the World*, 172.

23. Shakhnazarov, *Tsena svobody*, 20, for the quotation (italics in the original), and 20–34, for conversations with Andropov.

24. Ibid., 14–15.

25. Ibid., 15.

26. Ibid., 18–21.

27. For the speech and his answers to questions, see Mikhail S. Gorbachev, *Selected Speeches and Articles* (Moscow: Progress, 1985), 338–54.

28. Chernyaev, *Shest' let s Gorbachevym*, 57.

29. Ibid., 59–60.

30. Ibid., 61.

31. Ibid., 67.

32. Ibid., 67–68.

33. Shakhnazarov, *Tsena svobody*, 38–45, offers examples.

34. Ligachev, *Inside Gorbachev's Kremlin*, 47.

35. Shakhnazarov, *Tsena svobody*, 41.

36. Conversation with Shevardnadze in Tbilisi, December 1993.

37. Shevardnadze was noted for his ruthless purges during his tenure as head of the Georgian MVD from 1965 to 1972. In December 1972, Brezhnev removed V. P. Mzhavanadze from the post of first secretary in the Georgian Communist Party and replaced him with Shevardnadze. Mzhavanadze's corrupt rule in that republic apparently exceeded even Brezhnev's norms. Amid reports of instability in Georgia, Shevardnadze took control and implemented a local purge. I was serving in the U.S. embassy, 1972–74, and was sent to Tbilisi a month after Shevardnadze took charge to look for any visible signs of the rumored disorders that were believed by the diplomatic community to be occurring as a result of his actions. No evidence of them was discovered, but Shevardnadze's reputation as a hard line local satrap was widely acknowledged. See Rakowska-Harmstone, "Dialectics of Nationalism," for a summary of the Mzhavanadze case. For more detail, see Ronald Grigor Suny, *The Making of the Georgian Nation* (Bloomington: Indiana University Press, 1988), 305–13.

38. Tarasenko showed me a copy of this memorandum, dated 1 April 1985.

39. I possess this memorandum, which bears Shevardnadze's handwritten reaction.

40. Sergei Tarasenko, interview, 26 June 1995.

41. In our December 1993 conversation, Shevardnadze told me that he understood nothing of the details at this first meeting and was concerned about the Politburo's reaction to the minutes of the meeting. He coped by announcing to the U.S. negotiators that regardless of their seeming to have all the best arguments, which he could not refute, they were wrong and his position was right. That ended the session. When the Politburo gave him a "bravo" for this performance, he knew he had won room for maneuver and time to master the issues.

42. Tarasenko Interview, 26 June 1995.

43. Ibid. Tarasenko and Stepanov devoted constant attention to developing these tactics, and they often got ahead of Shevardnadze, who decided the timing.

44. Ibid. Tarasenko said that he repeatedly challenged the General Staff to elaborate a position and a strategy for arms control based on its own policies for reform. Never once, he said, did it offer a single written paper in response. It acted as though arms control had no bearing on its policy or any relevance that it had to acknowledge or accommodate.

45. For an account of Shevardnadze's tactics and cooperation with his U.S. counterparts, see Zelikow and Rice, *Germany Unifed and Europe Transformed*, especially 149–50, 244–45, 260, 285, 293–300, for Tarasenko's role.

46. See Leonov, *Likholet'e*, 323–29, for a former KGB officer's account of the angry reactions from the military, KGB, and VPK at "Little Five" sessions in Moscow as Shevardnadze rolled over them in setting Soviet positions in arms control negotiations with the United States.

47. Boldin, *Ten Years That Shook the World*, 172–73.

48. Chernyaev, *Shest' let s Gorbachevym*, 37.

49. Lyakhovskii, *Tragediya i doblest' Afgana* (Moscow: GPI Iskona, 1995), 284, provides a copy of this secret report. This book is an insider's account of the entire Afghan war, beginning with the Politburo's handling of Taraki's seizure of power in the spring of 1978 to the 1990s. Lyakhovskii both fought in Afghanistan and served on the General Staff after

being seriously wounded. During his convalescence, he was allowed access to many classified military, KGB, Central Committee, and Politburo materials for writing his history of the war. Obviously he had high-level backing, and his equally obvious purpose is to expose the top party leaders and reveal the bureaucratic realities in the Central Committee, VPK, foreign ministry, and the General Staff, as well as to emphasize the misuse of patriotic soldiers and officers, rescuing their honor and dignity from the mix of personal and political motives among the party and military elites that perpetrated the disaster. This bias produces considerable important factual evidence and objective analysis.

50. Ibid., 289–91, for the text of his secret report.

51. Ibid., 291, 294. Lyakhovskii is scathing in his assessment of General Mikhail Zaitsev's incompetence, but he also reports poor performance and inability to adapt, to learn the insurgents' tricks, and to develop shrewd tactics in response on the part of company, battalion, and regimental commanders. He also cites several outstanding exceptions, but they were just that, exceptions.

52. Ibid., 293.

53. Ibid., 293, 295.

54. Ibid., 295–98.

55. Ibid.

56. Lyakhovskii, *Tragediya i doblest' Afgana*, 535.

57. Shakhnazarov, *Tsena svobody*, 41–42.

58. Ibid., 80. Shakhnazarov knows his Milton, who wrote in *Paradise Lost* of the ancient Semitic god to whom children were sacrificed, "Moloch, horrid king, besmear'd with blood, Of human sacrifice and parents' tears." "Adorning the Moloch" is the title of his chapter on the military.

59. Ibid., 42, 83–84. Shakhnazarov gives different estimates of the size of Soviet military expenditures at different places in this book. On p. 42 he says it was 40 percent of the national income, on p. 83 only 17 percent, and in other places roughly a fifth. He probably did not know, for two reasons. First, the pricing and accounting methods were severely biased to make the official figure lower than it would have been if it had been calculated in market prices. Second, on pp. 52–53 he complains that accurate data on military spending were not released until 1990. My treatment of Soviet military spending in Chapter 5 above, of course, has already explained why Soviet officials had no precise idea of what was actually spent on defense, only that it was a lot.

60. Ibid., 84.

61. Ibid., 81.

62. Ibid., 85–86.

63. Ibid., 86.

64. Ibid., 87.

65. Cited by Raymond L. Garthoff, "New Thinking and Soviet Military Doctrine," in Frank and Gillette, *Soviet Military Doctrine*, 200. No text of these remarks by Gorbachev was published.

66. It was printed as a "declaration," in *Kommunist* 2 (1986): 3–11.

67. Parker, *Kremlin in Transition*, 2: 83, is the only observer, to my knowledge, to pick up this point on deterrence theory at the time.

68. Ibid.

69. Boldin, *Ten Years That Shook the World*, 160.

70. Major General I. Sidelnikov, *Krasnaya zvezda*, 25 December 1985.

71. Parker, *Kremlin in Transition*, 2: 84.

72. Boldin, *Ten Years That Shook the World*, 166–68.

73. Ibid. Boldin offers his account as seen from Gorbachev's chief of staff position, and Chernyaev, *Shest' let s Gorbachevym*, 156–61, offers another view, consistent with Boldin's but with additional insights. Both sources are the primary bases for the account here.

74. Boldin, *Ten Years That Shook the World*, 167.

75. Chernyaev, *Shest' let s Gorbachevym*, 156. Boldin said that Gorbachev and Chernyaev "were like twins." Boldin, *Ten Years That Shook the World*, 111.

76. Chernyaev, *Shest' let s Gorbachevym*, 156–57.

77. Chernyaev's knowledge of Russian and Soviet military reforms is obviously faulty. Three reforms occurred between the 1820s and the early 1900s. In the Soviet period, three periods of peacetime reform can be identified, as well as the constant reform from the beginning throughout World War II. Still, the kind of reform Chernyaev had in mind had, as he noted, occurred only twice—in the 1920s and on the eve of World War II. Such periodization, of course, is always a matter of debate.

78. Chernyaev, *Shest' let s Gorbachevym*, 158.

79. Ibid., 160.

80. Major General V. Slipchenko, interview, 29 June 1995. He was involved with air defense matters on the General Staff at the time, and he insists that the VPK was allowed to escape all blame when in fact it was among the seriously guilty.

81. Colonel Igor Smeshko, interview, 22 June 1995.

82. Chernyaev, *Shest' let s Gorbachevym*, 160.

83. Linda Brewer, "The Soviet Military Elite Under Gorbachev," unpublished paper by the U.S. Air Force Intelligence Agency, 22 August 1989.

84. Gorbachev, *Perestroika*, published simultaneously in 1987 in Russian and English. The Russian version is the source for page citations hereafter. Most of them can be found on pp. 139–49 of the English translation.

85. Quoted in Chernyaev, *Shest' let s Gorbachevym*, 168–69.

86. Ibid. 168.

87. Gorbachev, *Perestroika*, 150–51.

88. Ibid., 147–48.

89. Ibid., 151 (emphasis added).

90. Ibid., 145.

91. Gorbachev's language at the time drew little Western attention on this point, but it bore significant implications for a lot of Western analysis on Soviet views on nuclear war. For example, Brezhnev's Tula speech in 1977 was widely believed to have reflected an official Soviet rejection of the winnability of nuclear war. Yet in 1987, Gorbachev took pains to say that the change occurred only in 1986 at the Twenty-seventh Party Congress, and even then the official language was ambiguous. According to several former senior Soviet officers whom I interviewed in June and July 1995, it did not change in reality even then because they still believed that like Brezhnev, Gorbachev was merely trying to mislead the imperialist Western powers. Still in the early 1990s Western scholars could be found making their analysis of Soviet foreign and military policy on their earlier inference from Brezhnev's Tula speech and other such leadership statements. See, for examples, Blacker, *Hostage to Revolution*, 26–30; Garthoff, *Detente and Confrontation*, 36–68; and Roeder, *Red Sunset*, 201–9.

92. Only a year earlier, Major General S. A. Tyushkevich, in editing a book for "scientific workers, teachers, propagandists, and all those interested in the questions of war and peace," asserted that "nuclear war being prepared by imperialism is impermissible as a rational continuation of politics, as a means for achieving its political aims. This conclusion does

not contradict the proposition of Marxism-Leninism on the mutual relation of war and politics, that any war is the continuation of the policy of defined classes and states by forceful means" (*Voina i sovremennost'*, 91). Throughout the book's chapter on "world nuclear war," emphasis is on the continuing validity of Marx, Lenin, and Clausewitz in the nuclear age, warning about the destructive nature of nuclear war but in no sense admitting that it could not be fought for political ends. This general formula, of course, had been standard in military publications since the late 1960s, and it is obviously what Gorbachev was disavowing.

93. Lieutenant General Leonid Ivashov, interview, 5 July 1995.

94. For a few examples, see Usachev, "Vseobshchie i klassovye osnovy v mirovoi politike"; Zagladin, *Vneshnepoliticheshaya straregiya KPSS*, 11–21, 145–46, 330 (a party textbook); and Tabunov, "Dialektika klassogo I obshchechelovechstva." General Tabunov does his very best to salvage something from "class analysis" while accepting the primacy of humankind interests.

95. Chernyaev, *Shest' let s Gorbachevym*, 230. Ligachev's remarks were published as "Za delo—bez raskachki," *Pravda*, 6 August 1988.

96. Chernyaev, *Shest' let s Gorbachevym*, 230–35.

97. As one of those skeptics, I woke up to Gorbachev's ideological revisions only when Secretary of State George Shultz asked me in late 1987 whether I had read Gorbachev's book, *Perestroika*. I had not, but immediately did, and was profoundly struck by Gorbachev's virtual abandonment of "class interests" and the "international class struggle." Having just published an article, "How Far Can Soviet Reform Go?" in which I concluded that Gorbachev would destroy the Soviet empire if he continued on his present course but doubted that he would do so, I was all the more puzzled, because his ideological revisions seemed to indicate that indeed he was determined to continue that course. I am especially grateful to Secretary Shultz for prompting me to read Gorbachev's book at the time.

98. Marshal Yevgenii Shaposhnikov, interview 29 June 1995. Shaposhnikov was present at the meeting in Warsaw when Yazov made these remarks.

99. Shakhnazarov, *Tsena svobody*, 87.

Chapter 7. Defensive Doctrine and Arms Reductions

1. The cat-and-mouse metaphor is from Shakhnazarov, *Tsena svobody*, 88.

2. Chernyaev, *Shest' let s Gorbachevym*, 253, stresses this aspect of Gorbachev's thinking in connection with the U.N. speech in December 1988, but he also repeats the same point throughout his memoir.

3. Western students of the Soviet military did not understand this very well at the time, but toward the end of Gorbachev's rule, a better appreciation was emerging. See Colton and Gustafson, *Soldiers and the Soviet State*, chapters 4, 5, 6, and 9. Robert Campbell, Julian Cooper, and Thane Gustafson are the authors of these chapters dealing with what Cooper and Gustafson see as a triangular relationship between the VPK, the uniformed military, and the Communist Party. On the face of it, this seems sensible, but it makes the party look more like a separate and segregated institution than the integrating institution it was, embracing both the VPK and the Ministry of Defense. And it fails to emphasize the split within the party that Gorbachev's military policies provoked.

4. Numerous texts and monographs in the Soviet military literature provide the same standard definition, and it can be traced to Mikhail Frunze, the Commissar of Military and Naval Affairs in 1924–25, who led the struggle against Trotsky to create a "unified military doctrine" based on Marxism. See Gareev, *M. V. Frunze*, 105–57.

5. See M. V. Frunze, *Izbrannye proizvedeniya* (Moscow: Voenizdat, 1957), 2: 7, for the original elaboration of these two components.

6. This was made explicit in the "Statement of the Meeting of Representatives of the Communist and Workers' Parties," held in 1960 in Moscow. For the text, see *The Struggle for Peace, Democracy, and Socialism* (Moscow, 1961), especially p. 73: "The Communist Parties, which guide themselves by Marxist-Leninist doctrine, have always been against the export of revolution."

7. As articulated in the Soviet officers' textbook by a collective of fourteen authors, *Marxism-Leninism on War and the Army*, "Thus, the need to defend the socialist gains against all attacks by international imperialist reaction, the armed defence of the socialist countries, is one of the general laws of the transition from capitalism to socialism, one applying to all the countries making this transition while the world imperialist system and the constant threat of military attacks by the imperialists against the socialist countries continues to exist" (127). And "Thus by defending the peaceful construction of socialism and communism, and by ensuring the security of the socialist countries, the Soviet socialist state, together with other socialist states, defends the peace and security of all peoples" (128).

8. See *Soveshchanie politicheskogo konsul'tativnogo kometita gosudarstv*, 13–35.

9. See Meyer, "Sources and Prospects of Gorbachev's New Political Thinking," for one of the more penetrating analyses at the time.

10. Notes taken by the author at this meeting.

11. Shakhnazarov, *Tsena svobody*, 89.

12. Ibid.

13. Ibid., 89–90.

14. Ibid.

15. See, for examples, Kosarev, "Doktrina obespecheniya mira"; V. Gulin and I. Kondyrev, "Vypolnyaya resheniia XXVII S'ezd KPSS: Oboronnitel'noe napravlenie sovetskoi voennoi doktriny," *Morskoi sbornik* 6 (February 1988): 8–13; Semeyko, "Vmesto gor oruzhiya."; Zhurkin, Karagonov, and Kortunov, "Reasonable Sufficiency"; Tatarnikov, "Do urovnei razumnoi dostatochnosti"; Ponomarev, "Kriterii dostatochnosti"; Bogdanov and Lokshin, "Razumnaya znachit dostatochnost'."

16. On this reaction in Soviet military circles, see Mary C. FitzGerald, "The Dilemma in Moscow's Defensive Force Posture," in Frank and Gillette, *Soviet Military Doctrine*, 347–62.

17. Yazov, *Na strazhe sotsializma i mira*, 33.

18. Kokoshin and Larionov, "Kurskaya bitva v svete sovremennoi doktriny."

19. Aleksandr G. Savel'yev and Nikolai N. Detinov, *The Big Five: Arms Control Decision-Making in the Soviet Union* (Westport, Conn.: Praeger, 1995). Savel'yev, a younger man, a civilian scholar and specialist in defense affairs, assisted Detinov in preparing this memoir of his observations of two decades of U.S.-Soviet arms control negotiations. Although Detinov holds the rank of colonel general, he is an engineer who made his early career in the VPK. He served on its staff and also in the Defense Industries Department of the Central Committee Secretariat at different times. Detinov takes a remarkably scholarly and detached viewpoint in his account, and he emphasizes that he is reporting only what he knows from direct experience, offering the historical record as accurate a description and interpretation as he can. In an interview with him in Moscow, 30 June 1995, I was impressed by his objectivity and candor. The memoir is a very uneven account, neither well edited nor well translated, but what it offers—a great deal—has the ring of authenticity.

20. Ibid., 16–20.

21. *Voennyi Entsiklopedicheskii Slovar'* (Moscow: Voenizdat, 1984), 769.

22. Ibid., 84.

23. Ibid., 18, 28, 33.

24. Ibid., 19.

25. Ibid., 32, 64.

26. See Garthoff, *Great Transition,* 84–141, for an account of the breakdown in negotiations that places most of the responsibility on the U.S. side.

27. Savel'yev and Detinov, *The Big Five,* 114.

28. Ibid., 114–15.

29. Ibid., 112, 120–21.

30. Ibid., 83–91.

31. Blacker, *Hostage to Revolution,* 98–100.

32. Ibid., 92.

33. Ibid., 92–93.

34. Ibid., 95–109, gives a comprehensive account of how the decision to locate this radar in Krasnoyarsk occurred, how the Soviet side tried to evade U.S. charges of a violation of the ABM treaty, and why it finally conceded the violation.

35. For examples, see Blacker, *Hostage to Revolution,* 103–12, and Garthoff, *Great Transition,* 291.

36. Chernyaev, *Shest' let s Gorbachevym,* 75.

37. Ibid., 78.

38. Ibid., 80.

39. Ibid., 85–88.

40. Ibid., 97–100.

41. Ibid., 102.

42. Ibid., 103–4.

43. Ibid., 105.

44. Ibid., 106–7.

45. Ibid., 107–9.

46. Ibid., 111.

47. Ibid., 111–12.

48. Garthoff, *Great Transition,* 285–92, for example.

49. Ibid., 115.

50. Savel'yev and Detinov, *The Big Five,* 119–20.

51. Ibid., 127–28.

52. Ibid., 131–32.

53. Ibid.

54. Ibid., 133–35.

55. Ibid., 138.

56. Chernyaev, *Shest' let s Gorbachevym,* 187–89.

57. Several U.S. officers who participated in on-site inspections told me of the astonishment they repeatedly met among Soviet military and industrial officials. Having "imperialists" in their midst, peeking into the installations and monitoring the factories' output, was extremely difficult for them to accept at the local levels where inspections were occurring.

58. Ibid., 191.

59. Quoted ibid., 253–54.

60. Ibid., 254–55.

61. Shakhnazarov, *Tsena svobody,* 41–42.

62. Ibid., 44. Shakhnazarov emphasizes that perestroika was entirely reversible at this time, and only after the Congress of People's Deputies and a new Supreme Soviet (parliament) were convened had the point of no return been reached.

63. Discussion with Ligachev at Yale University, 11 November 1991. Ligachev insisted that the Politburo never considered introducing a market system until 1989.

64. Aslund, *Gorbchev's Struggle for Economic Reform*, 107–12.

65. Ibid., 208.

66. See Odom, "How Far Can Soviet Reform Go?" 26, for this assessment: "Nonetheless, the paradox remains that great centralization of power is required to achieve decentralization of economic control and power. If Gorbachev succeeds, he will lose his centralized power to forces that could undercut the political authority of the regime to a degree that could lead to the breakup of the empire."

67. Shakhnazarov, *Tsena svobody*, 35–50. Shakhnazarov explains his own views as well as Gorbachev's insofar as he could infer them.

68. Boldin, *Ten Years That Shook the World*, 168.

69. Chernyaev, *Shest' let s Gorbachevym*, 203–8, 210–13, gives an account of the Politburo discussions and the negative impact of the letter on many party organizations.

70. Ibid., 200.

71. Ibid., 210. Chernyaev recalls Gorbachev airing the idea of becoming president as well as remaining general secretary while on vacation in January 1988.

72. Ibid., 208–10.

73. Ibid., 213.

74. Shakhnazarov, *Tsena svobody*, 46. In Shakhnazarov's judgment this reconsideration was a serious mistake. Gorbachev still enjoyed the kind of authority at the time, Shakhnazarov argues, that would have allowed him to carry the conference against Ligachev, Chebrikov, and the other dissenters in one sweep.

75. Ibid., 48.

76. Ibid., 47.

77. Ibid.

78. Ligachev, *Inside Gorbachev's Kremlin*, 94–114.

79. His remarks were published in *Pravda*, 6 August 1988.

80. See Chernyaev, *Shest' let s Gorbachevym*, 230–39, for Gorbachev's negative reaction. According to Chernyaev, Gorbachev's anger was restrained but deep.

81. Ibid., 234–37.

82. Ibid., 240. Chernyaev reported to Gorbachev that this was how Western journalists were characterizing the affair.

83. Ibid., 240–41; Shakhnazarov, *Tsena svobody*, 46–50.

84. Ligachev offered this characterization of Gorbachev in a discussion at Yale University, 11 November 1991.

85. Chernyaev, *Shest' let s Gorbachevym*, 255–57.

86. Akhromeev and Kornienko, *Glazami marshala i diplomata*, 72–73.

87. *Pravda*, 26 July 1988.

88. Eduard Shevardnadze, "Towards a Safe World," *International Affairs* 10 (1988), 13–25.

89. *Pravda*, 1 November 1988.

90. Chernyaev, *Shest' let s Gorbachevym*.

91. As described in Chapter 6, Sergei Tarasenko, Shevardnadze's personal assistant, wrote him a memo in 1985 suggesting a fundamental change in Soviet relations with the

Warsaw Pact states, making them more like the United States' relations with its NATO allies. Among the specific points he suggested was "a deep analysis of our very military presence in brotherly socialist countries." Shevardnadze noted in pen on the memo, "We will return to this question later." They did, in the fall of 1988, three years later. Tarasenko provided this memo to the author.

92. Chernyaev, *Shest' let s Gorbachevym*, 257–59. See also Garthoff, *Great Transition*, 317–18.

93. Chernyaev, *Shest' let s Gorbachevym*, 257–60. Chernyaev includes Shevardnadze's protest letter in full text and also provides one of his own memos and one by Shakhnazarov to Gorbachev in mid-1989, complaining about arms sales continuing to Eastern Europe and VPK construction of unauthorized new naval combatants and MIG-29 transfers abroad. They both convey a picture of the VPK and the Ministry of Defense proceeding on their own course as if "new thinking" and perestroika concerned them not in the least.

94. Gorbachev, *Izbrannye rechi i stat'I*, 198–99.

95. Ibid., 199–200 (italics in the original).

96. Ibid., 200.

Chapter 8. Glasnost and the Public Debate

1. See Chapter 4 for these weapons totals.

2. See Gorshkov and Zhuravlev, *Nesokrusmimaya i legendarnaya*, for more than five hundred pages of excerpts from the public debate over military affairs during and after Gorbachev's rule. Four additional scholars helped compile this large compendium, scoring the crescendo of ever more emotional and even hysterical voices in this chorus.

3. D. A. Volkogonov, *Triumf i tragediya: politicheskii portret I. V. Stalina*, 2 vols., rev. ed. (Moscow: Novosti, 1990). This highly unflattering portrait of Stalin, while offering little new to Western historians, provided far more information about him to the Soviet public than had been seen in official print before. Later, after the end of the Soviet Union, Volkogonov wrote biographies of Trotsky and Lenin.

4. Andrei Kortunov, interview, 3 July 1995.

5. Kokoshin and Larionov, "Kurskaya bitva v svete sovremennoi oboronnitel'noi doktriny."

6. See Glantz, *Soviet Conduct of Tactical Maneuver*, for an excellent study of the Soviet military's use of World War II experience for developing its contemporary military doctrine.

7. Akhromeev and Kornienko, *Glazami marshala i diplomata*, 69.

8. Ibid.

9. For examples, see Kirshin, Popov, and Savushkin, *Politicheskoe soderzhanie sovremennoi voiny* (Kirshin was deputy director of the Military History Institute and a political officer, as were his coauthors); Krupchenko, "K semidesyatoi godovshchine velikogo Oktyagtrya"; *XXVII S'ezd KPSS o Sovetskoi voennoi doktrine* (no author given for this officers' textbook); Savushkin, "Istok i razvitie sovetskoi voennoi doktriny"; and Yaremko, "Vozrozhdenie taktiki." The first three, published in 1987, acknowledge Gorbachev's line about "preventing war" as being the most important military task and admit that nuclear weapons are no longer usable for pursuit of policy, especially Western "nuclear deterrence," but then go on to describe an increasingly dangerous world based on class struggle. The fourth, published in early 1988, cites the Soviet experience of the 1920s, when military reductions were huge, insisting that "preventing war" was the main task at that time, so, by implication, there was nothing so radical about the new doctrine. Finally, the fifth piece, a newspaper article

published in 1989, simply pokes fun at the emphasis on defense, noting that in the "period of stagnation," Brezhnev's time, any high-level statement was taken as "scientific truth," even if it was voluntaristic and ignorant. The same was true, the ridicule continued, in Khrushchev's era concerning reducing artillery and aviation; today, the same pattern is seen in all the talk about "defense." Between May 1987 and September 1989, the author went on, there were twenty-seven articles on defense and one on offense in the classified military journal *Voennaya mysl'*. His candor was on the mark about the military's sentiments: that Gorbachev's ideological revisions were ignorant assertions being taken as scientific truths.

10. For examples, see Usachev, "Vseobshchie i klassovie osnovy mirovoi politiki"; Tabunov, "Dialektiki klassovogo i obshchechelovecheskogo"; and "Mirnoe sosushchestvovanie v svete novogo politicheskogo myshleniya," *Kommunist vooruzhennykh sil* 4 (1989): 85–88. The last piece, comprising letters from readers, was harshly critical of Gorbachev's abandonment of the Leninist substance of "peaceful coexistence" as a "specific form of the international class struggle."

11. For those who had missed Gorbachev's declaration on this point in his book, *Perestroika*, his spokesman V. V. Zagladin told the press, Soviet and foreign, at the Nineteenth Party Conference in June 1988 that "rejecting nuclear war, and leading the struggle to prevent it, we abandoned the possibility of victory in it." This was an admission, of course, that heretofore, they had held that victory in nuclear war was possible.

12. Bulanov and Krylova, "Sootnoshenie politiki i yadernoi voiny."

13. Kokoshin, Arbatov, and Vasilev, "Sokrashenie yadernykh vooruzhenii i strategicheskaya stabil'nost'."

14. Arbatov, "How Much Defense Is Sufficient?"

15. Strebkov, "Kriterii voenno-strategicheskogo pariteta."

16. Dmitriev and Strebkov, "Ustarevshaya kontseptsiya."

17. Zhurkin, Karagonov, and Kortunov, "Vyzovy bezopasnosti."

18. In several conversations, Blagovolin told me of his close ties to Yakovlev, observing that he had prepared numerous policy papers for Yakovlev to use in discussions with Gorbachev and in the Politburo.

19. Kunadze, "Ob oboronnitel'noi dostatochnosti voennogo potentsiala SSSR."

20. Blagovolin, "Voennaya moshch': skol'ko, kakaya, zachem."

21. Blagovolin, "Geopoliticheskie aspekty oboronnitel'noi dostatochnosti."

22. For another good example, see Pozdnyakov, "Natsional'noe i internatsional'noe v vneshnei politike." Pozdnyakov develops a new look at "interests" through ideological revisions and a review of the distortions of them since the Bolsheviks took power. For a fascinating piece that also takes the argument back to mistaken policies of the 1920s and 1930s, see Alimurzaev, "Shchit ili mech?" For emphasis on economic interests, see Shashkov, "Skol'ko stoit besopasnost'?"

23. I am indebted to Blagovolin for elaborating, during several discussions in Moscow and Washington between 1991 and 1994, some of the obstacles the military establishment presented.

24. Moiseev, "Sovetskaya voennaya doktrina," and Yazov, "Na osnove novogo myshleniya."

25. Kokoshin and Larionov, "Protivostoyanie sil obshchego naznacheniya."

26. Yazov, "Na osnove novogo myshleniya," and Moiseev, "Sovetskaya voennaya doktrina."

27. Yazov, "V interesakh vseobshchei bezopasnosti i mira."

28. Arbatov, "How Much Defense Is Sufficient?"

29. Lyubimov, "O oboronnitel'noi dostatochnosti." The Gogol allusion was undoubtedly to Chichikov in Gogol's novel *Dead Souls,* who paid a pittance for dead peasants, allowing the seller to avoid tax on them in the year they died; he could then borrow money, using the deeds for the peasants as collateral.

30. Plutnik, "Voennyi urok."

31. For a noteworthy example that makes more telling points than most and exploits information about the U.S. military for comparisons, see Kononov and Borisov, "Silna li armiya?"

32. Savinkin, "Kakaya armiya nam nuzhna?"

33. Lipitskii, "Voennaya reforma 1924–25 godov."

34. See Foye, "Military Debates of the 1920s," for commentary on the Lobov-Kokoshin article and others devoted to the Red Army's experiences in the 1920s.

35. Foye, "Radical Military Reform," elaborates on their activities in the fall of 1989.

36. See Lopatin, "The Army and the Economy."

37. The stenographic report of the military collegium's response was published in *Nezavisimaya gazeta,* 16 June 1991. V. Arsenev interviewed Volkogonov on the affair in *Izvestiya,* 24 June 1991.

38. Major General Viktor Filatov, editor of *Voenno-istoricheskii zhurnal* before he was forced out after the crisis of 19–23 August 1991, told me the substance of the complaints against Volkogonov at the military collegium session in March 1991, in which Filatov participated.

39. Volkogonov died in late 1995.

40. Major General Vladimirov, interview, April 1995.

41. Memorandum of conversation, 27 June 1990, by Colonel Andrew F. Krepinevich, U.S. Army.

42. Captain Eduard Shevel'ev, interview, 29 June 1995.

43. Lyakhovskii, *Tragediya i doblest' Afgana.*

44. Colonel Aleksei Tsarev, interview, 28 June 1995.

45. Lieutenant Aleksandr Rodin, interview, 7 July 1995.

46. *RFE/RL Daily Report* no. 220, 19 November 1990; Stephen Foye, "Gorbachev, the Army, and the Soviet Union," RFE/RL research paper, 28 November 1990.

47. See FitzGerald, "Advanced Conventional Munitions," for insight into the Soviet reactions to the new weapons systems. Also see Odom, "Soviet Force Posture," and Petersen and Hines, "Conventional Offensive," for operational changes being made in Soviet war planning in the 1980s in an effort to counter the U.S. developments.

48. This interview was published in *Pravitel'stvennyi vestnik* 6 (February 1990): 1, 8–9.

49. JPRS-UMA-88-025, Moscow Television, 21 October 1988, p. 4.

50. More than one civilian defense analyst and foreign ministry official told me during interviews—but not for personal attribution—that they were repeatedly lied to by senior military officials. Their visceral disdain for the Soviet officer corps, especially the generals, was palpable. A former foreign ministry official recounted numerous misleading briefings to the Politburo commission on Afghanistan by General Varennikov. One defense analyst remarked that he was actually delighted when he was viciously attacked by military writers in the press, because they had ignored his criticism for more than a year. Their anger proved that at last they were acknowledging his arguments.

51. *Ogonek* 50 (1989): 6–8.

52. An edited version of Georgii Arbatov's speech appeared in *Ogonek* 5 (1990).

53. Major General G. Kirilenko, "What to Consider Reasonable, What to Consider Sufficient?" *Literaturnaya Rossiya* 12 (23 March 1990): 17.

54. FBIS-SOV-90-120, Moscow Television, 21 June 1990, pp. 92–93.

55. Letter to the editor, *Izvestiya*, 7 July 1990. V. Nedein, "Tsel' Generala Makashova," *Izvestiya*, 21 June 1990, had demanded the general's resignation.

56. *Komsomolskaya pravda*, 4 August 1990.

Chapter 9. Legislating Military Reform

1. Parker, *Kremlin in Transition*, 317.

2. Ibid., 309, 316–17.

3. Keep, *Last of the Empires*, 359–60.

4. Chernyaev, *Shest' let s Gorbachevym*, 279–84.

5. Ibid., 326–28.

6. Ibid., 327.

7. Ibid., 330–32.

8. Ibid., 332–33.

9. Ibid., 334.

10. Ibid., 335.

11. Ibid., 337–38.

12. *Izvestiya*, 16 March 1990, published the new law.

13. FBIS-SOV-90-052, "Presidential Powers Bill Survives Postponement," 16 March 1990, p. 44.

14. Shakhnazarov, *Tsena svobody* (1993), 139.

15. The term "civil society" came into use in 1988–89 in the Soviet Union in connection with Gorbachev's idea of a law-based state. Civil society, of course, was the term Tocqueville used in describing the nature of American society in his book *Democracy in America*, and it has remained in the Western political science lexicon to describe societies with strong social and political groups initiated by private citizens and used to control government and policy making in addition to their immediate and more direct purposes.

16. Shakhnazarov, *Tsena svobody*, 136.

17. Ibid., 136–37. Shakhnazarov reports that the British, French, and U.S. models of government were all considered and that Gorbachev was presented with several alternatives, all more radical than the compromise he finally decided on his own.

18. Ibid., 138. In the West at the time, the Presidential Council was thought by many analysts in the U.S. government to be a successor to the Defense Council because it included most of the Defense Council participants—the defense minister, the foreign minister, the chairman of the VPK, and the chairman of the KGB. Shakhnazarov's account makes clear that this was a mistaken interpretation. Moreover, it turned out that the Defense Council still existed. I also made this erroneous inference at the time.

19. Ibid., 138–44. As the Presidential Council withered, it became the object of jokes —for example, What is a member of the Presidential Council? An unemployed person with a presidential salary.

20. Interview with M. A. Moiseev, "Vazhnyi shag v voennostroitel'stve," *Krasnaya zvezda*, 16 March 1990.

21. *RFE/RL Daily Report* no. 183, 25 September 1990.

22. In the summer of 1990, Gorbachev at last became serious about economic reform, and from then until the late fall he considered a number of variants taken from the so-called Shatalin Plan, Yavlinskii's four hundred–day plan, and the Abalkin Plan. Always the compromiser, he finally chose a hastily developed version which took elements of all of them but had no real prospects for causing a transition to a market economy. See Aslund, *Gorbachev's Struggle for Economic Reform*, 203–24.

23. FBIS-SOV-90-223, "Gorbachev Addresses Supreme Soviet," 19 November 1990, p. 26–27.

24. Aslund, *Gorbachev's Struggle for Economic Reform*.

25. Chernyaev recounts many occasions when these emotional dimensions of Gorbachev's personality seemed to take over his better judgment, not just in the spring of 1990.

26. Daalder, *CFE Treaty*, 5.

27. See Yazov, "O voennoi reforme," *Pravda*, 9 February 1989; "V interesakh vseoshchei bezopasnosti i mir," *Izvestiya*, 28 February 1989; and "Na osnove novogo myshleniya," *Krasnaya zvezda*, 13 April 1989; as well as Moiseev, "S pozitsii oboronnitel'noi doktriny," *Krasnaya zvezda*, 10 February 1989; "Sovetskaya voennaya doktrina," *Pravda*, 13 March 1989; "Istoki napryazhennosti," *Krasnaya zvezda*, 4 May 1989.

28. Yazov, "O voennoi reforme."

29. Yazov, "Na osnove novogo myshleniya."

30. Moiseev, "Sovetskaya voennaya doktrina."

31. Moiseev, "S pozitsii oboronnitel'noi doktriny."

32. "V ministerstve oborony SSSR, *Izvestiya*, 3 June 1989.

33. For the decree promoting Yazov, see *Krasnaya Zvezda*, 29 April 1989.

34. FBIS-SOV-89-127, "Gorbachev Speech Supports Yazov," 5 July 1989, pp. 48–50.

35. Yazov, "Novaya model bezopasnosti I vooruzhunnie sily."

36. Sturua, "Komitet o vosprosakh oborony i bezopasnosti."

37. Ibid.

38. Major Vladimir Lopatin made several visits during which I met with him and his colleagues twice, gaining the impression that they fully grasped that the U.S. Congress's power rested primarily with its unchallenged control of the purse strings. Their committee's weakness, as they readily admitted, derived from its lack of such fiscal controls.

39. *RFE/RL Daily Report* no. 201, 23 October 1989.

40. Sturua, "Peripetii voennoi reformy."

41. Ibid.

42. FBIS-SOV-90-003, "Chief of Staff Outlines Draft Law on Defense," 4 January 1990, p. 91; and FBIS-SOV-90-003, "USSR Law on Defense: What Should It Be Like?," 4 January 1990, p. 104.

43. Lopatin, "Proekt voennoi reformy."

44. Sturua, "Peripetii voennoi reformy."

45. See *RFE/RL Daily Reports* no. 57, 21 March 1990; no. 63, 29 March 1990; and no. 67, 4 April 1990.

46. See Foye, "Radical Military Reform," for an excellent account of the defense ministry's struggle against Lopatin and his supporters.

47. An overview of the immense set of papers, more than two thousand, that composed the commission's work, can be found in "Proekt semnadtsati," *Komsomolskaya pravda*, 11 February 1990. The author is using a typescript version given him by Major Lopatin as well as Foye, "Radical Military Reform."

48. "Armiya i obshchestvo," *XX vek i mir* 9 (1988): 18–20.

NOTES TO PAGES 187–96

49. For an analysis of this early debate over the conscription versus a professional military, see Arnett and FitzGerald, "Restructuring the Armed Forces."

50. Ibid., 206.

51. See Foye, "Radicalization of a Defense Establishment Theorist," for an examination of Serebryannikov's metamorphosis.

52. Lopatin expressed this view to me in the summers of 1990 and 1991 while he was visiting Washington, D.C., seeking help in carrying through Soviet military reform.

53. *RFE/RL Daily Report* no. 83, 30 April 1990.

54. *RFE/RL Daily Reports* no. 85, 3 May 1990; no. 91, 11 May 1990; and no. 94, 16 May 1990. When Lopatin went to Vologda, the northern provincial city from which he had been elected, local officials tried to prevent him from speaking to the May Day demonstration, but the crowd forced them to relent. Lopatin went public back in Moscow, reporting in a radio interview that the MPA was delaying the return of his party membership so that he could not be a delegate to the upcoming party congress. A number of military party organizations in the Moscow Military District offered him membership as an alternative.

55. "Voennaya reforma—pervoe priblizhenie," *Krasnaya zvezda*, 7 April 1990.

56. For examples, see *RFE/RL Daily Report* no. 78, 4 April 1990; Kirshin, "Za chem nuzhna voennaya reforma?" and FBIS-SOV-90-078, "Army General A. D. Lizichev on Anti-Army Sentiments," 24 April 1990, p. 71.

57. For the February criticisms see *RFE/RL Daily Reports* no. 30, 12 February 1990; and no. 39, 23 February 1990.

58. See *RFE/RL Daily Reports* no. 93, 15 May 1990; no. 104, 31 May 1990; and no. 162, 27 August 1990.

59. FBIS-SOV-90-003, "Chief of Staff Outlines Draft Law on Defense," 4 January 1990, p. 91; and *RFE/RL Daily Report* no. 3, 4 January 1990.

60. M. A. Moiseev, "Zadachi u nas odni," *Krasnaya zvezda*, 10 February 1990.

61. Yazov, "Voennaya reforma."

62. Akhromeev and Kornienko, *Glazami marshala I diplomata*, 188–90.

63. FBIS-SOV-90-171, "Yazov Discusses Reform Before the Defense Council," 4 September 1990, p. 65–69.

64. "Nachal'nk generalnogo shtaba o voennoi reforme," *Krasnaya zvezda*, 21 November 1990.

65. Interview with M. A. Moiseev, *Krasnaya zvezda*, 12 June 1991.

66. Shaposhnikov, *Vybor*, 74. Although critical of the lengthy time envisioned for carrying it out, Shaposhnikov considered the main elements of this plan to be sound and comprehensive. His predecessor, however, had failed to grasp the essence of the changing political climate and the urgency of implementing the entire reform scheme in less than five years.

67. *RFE/RL Daily Report* no. 198, 18 October 1989.

68. *RFE/RL Daily Report* no. 201, 23 October 1989.

69. *RFE/RL Daily Report* no. 224, 27 November 1989.

70. *RFE/RL Daily Report* no. 232, 7 December 1990.

71. Shreeves, "Mothers Against the Draft."

72. Maria Kirbasova, still heading the Russian Committee of Soldiers' Mothers in 1996, told me in an interview on 11 March 1996 that she had founded the committee in April 1989 and that eventually her organization had cooperating mothers' groups in all these republics and regions. Kirbasova's son was killed while serving as a soldier, and she has since dedicated her life to improving the conditions of military service.

73. *RFE/RL Daily Report* no. 229, 4 December 1990.

74. *RFE/RL Daily Report* no. 124, 2 July 1990.

75. *RFE/RL Daily Report* no. 172, 10 September 1990.

76. *RFE/RL Daily Report* no. 174, 12 September 1990.

77. Shaposhnikov, *Vybor*, 77–78.

78. Maria Kirbasova, in the interview cited above, told me that Urazhtsev was a suspicious character and that he was actually trying to destroy the movement. Whose word is to be believed about these organizational fights is impossible to know, but Urazhtsev's actions tend to corroborate Kirbasova's accusation.

79. *RFE/RL Daily Report* no. 218, 15 November 1989.

80. *RFE/RL Daily Report* no. 55, 19 March 1990.

81. *RFE/RL Daily Report* no. 179, 19 September 1990.

82. *RFE/RL Daily Report* no. 67, 4 April 1990.

83. For Ogarkov's warnings see *RFE/RL Daily Report* no. 92, 14 May 1990.

84. FBIS-SOV-90-227, 26 November 1990, "Alksnis Airs Criticisms of Gorbachev," 75–78.

85. Akhromeev and Kornienko, *Glazami marshala i diplomata*, 295.

86. Ibid., 288–304. Akhromeev, it will be recalled, committed suicide shortly after the crisis in August 1991. His coauthor, Georgii Kornienko, completed their joint manuscript and published it a year later. Akhromeev's own accounts, however, are clearly marked as his own in most places.

Chapter 10. The Intractable Party-Military Connection

1. Jerry Hough, *The Soviet Prefects: The Local Party Organs and Industrial Decision-Making* (Cambridge: Harvard University Press, 1969).

2. See Dunlop, *The Rise of Russia*, 19, 93–97. Matlock, *Autopsy on an Empire*, 331–33, provides a sense of the climate in dealing with Article 6 at the time.

3. Shaposhnikov, *Vybor*, 76.

4. For a history of the MPA, see Timothy J. Colton, *Commissars, Commanders, and Civilian Authority*.

5. Ibid., 96–100.

6. For Yepishev's recommendation of Lizichev, see *RFE/RL Daily Report* no. 45, 5 March 1990.

7. *RFE/RL Daily Report* no. 3, 4 January 1990.

8. Alksnis, "Armiyu ne otdelits' ot naroda"; V. Litvin, "Vyiti iz nokdauna," *Sovetskaya Rossiya*, 21 November 1990.

9. FBIS-SOV-89-152, "Stenographic Record of the Congress of People's Deputies," 9 August 1989, pp. 21–24.

10. *RFE/RL Daily Report* no. 40, 26 February 1990.

11. *RFE/RL Daily Report* no. 30, 12 February 1990.

12. *RFE/RL Daily Report* no. 39, 23 February 1990.

13. Lieutenant Colonel Aleksandr Rodin, interview, 7 July 1995. Rodin managed to gain release from the mental institution and to resign his commission. This was in 1988–89. By 1990, the flood of officers leaving the party made such punitive tactics impractical. Rodin returned to his home in Leningrad and was elected to the city soviet for a term. In 1995 he was campaigning against inhumane treatment of juvenile delinquents in St. Petersburg pris-

ons, who slept three or four to a single bed, suffered physical abuse, including broken arms, and often had all their belongings stolen. Ironically, former MPA officers were employed to manage and operate these juvenile detention centers.

14. Shaposhnikov, *Vybor,* 59–60.

15. Chernyaev, *Shest' let s Gorbachevym,* 342.

16. Ibid., 343.

17. Ibid., 344.

18. Dunlop, *The Rise of Russia,* 18–21.

19. Chiesa, "28th Congress of the CPSU."

20. Ibid.

21. Chernyaev, *Shest' let s Gorbachevym,* 356.

22. A translation of the proceedings of the public sessions of the Twenty-eighth Party Congress can be found in six supplementary volumes, FBIS-SOV-90-127S, 128S, 130S, 132S, 135S, and 136S, dated, respectively, 2, 3, 6, 10, 13, and 16 July 1990. Chiesa, "The 28th Congress," offers an interpretation of the event.

23. Quoted by Chiesa, "The 28th Congress," 33. Chiesa's interpretation of Yeltsin's role at the congress at the time was soon vindicated by events, and he was one of the few observers to realize how fundamentally Yeltsin's actions in the spring and summer of 1990 had restructured the political struggle in the Soviet Union.

24. A well-informed American, who wishes to remain anonymous, told me that printed materials for these demonstrations had telltale signs of having come from the military printing house and that several other support activities for them also revealed MPA assistance. Asking Russians about this MPA help, he learned that the central party apparatus could not, or would not provide it. The MPA stepped in to help.

25. *RFE/RL Daily Report* no. 132, 13 July 1990.

26. *RFE/RL Daily Report* no. 148, 6 August 1990.

27. *Documents and Materials,* 102–4.

28. FBIS-SOV-90-211, "Instructions on Armed Forces' Party Activities," 31 October 1990, pp. 51–54.

29. Foye, "Rumblings in the Soviet Armed Forces."

30. Plugatarev, "Pered litsom ili po puti otritsaniya?"

31. *RFE/RL Daily Report* no. 127, 6 July 1990.

32. *RFE/RL Daily Report* no. 126, 5 July 1990.

33. *RFE/RL Daily Report* no. 127, 6 July 1990.

34. *RFE/RL Daily Report* no. 131, 12 July 1990.

35. *RFE/RL Daily Report* no. 126, 5 July 1990.

36. For Tsalko's objection see *RFE/RL Daily Report* no. 132, 13 July 1990.

37. For the dismissal of Lizichev see *RFE/RL Daily Report* no. 133, 16 July 1990.

38. *RFE/RL Daily Report* no. 136, 19 July 1990.

39. Lopatin, "Armiya i politika."

40. FBIS-SOV-90-171, "Yazov Addresses Assembly of Ideological Workers," 4 September 1990, pp. 34–35; and *RFE/RL Daily Report* no. 170, 6 September 1990.

41. *RFE/RL Daily Report* no. 193, 10 October 1990.

42. *Krasnaya Zvezda,* 25 October 1990, published the full text of these new instructions.

43. For their respective speeches see Yazov, "Na perelomnom etape," Gorbachev, "Zadachi obshchenarodnoi bazhnosti."

44. Shlyaga, "Splachivat' partiinie ryady."

45. Yazov, "Na perelomnom etape."

46. TASS, 3 April 1991.

47. *RFE/RL Daily Report* no. 45, 5 March 1991.

48. Surkov, "Za pravdu nado stoyat'."

49. Shaposhnikov, *Vybor,* 54–55.

50. Ibid. The whole of Shaposhnikov's memoir can be read as a justification for his actions in helping stop the attempt to overthrow Gorbachev, or at least to reverse his policies. Because these actions vaulted him to the position of minister of defense, they could also be interpreted as careerist opportunism. We do not need to decide here which were his true motives. His evidence about the events and the policy processes remains useful and generally reliable no matter what his motives were. At least one democratic reformer, however, Galina Starovoitova, a leader in Democratic Russia, told me that she and several of her fellow democrats considered Shaposhnikov to be a remarkably principled man in the context of these events.

51. Ibid., 74.

52. Ibid., 82–83.

53. "Soobshschenie," *Krasnaya Zvezda,* 14 September 1991.

54. Lebed', *Za derzhavu obidno,* 416–17. In 1996 Lebed' ran for the presidency of Russia.

55. Shaposhnikov, *Vybor,* 55–59.

56. Marshal Yevgenii I. Shaposhnikov, interview, 29 June 1995.

57. For Selznick's terminology see Selznick, *Organizational Weapon.*

58. See Herspring and Volgyes, *Civilian-Military Relations,* chapters 1–4, for all three viewpoints.

59. For example, see Rice, "The Party, the Military, and Decision Authority," who describes a "loose coupling" between the General Staff and the Politburo, a description that is not really at odds with the congruence model but by implication leaves open the prospect of a decoupling in line with the control model. Nichols, *Sacred Cause,* argues that the military was excessively ideological while the party was pragmatic, which is really a perversion of the congruence model and curiously at odds with the party's inability to be sufficiently pragmatic to preserve itself. The muddles in Nichols's analysis are foreshadowed by the category mistakes in the book's title. "Civil-military" relations is a flawed concept for the Soviet case; and the Soviet Union, a multinational empire, could hardly have a "national" security policy. Zhong, "Transformation of the Soviet Military," misreads the August crisis as a "military coup" attempt in the context of all three models—conflict, congruence, and control. Lepingwell, "Soviet Civil-Military Relations," recognizes that according to Colton's model, the military's influence should have increased during perestroika but did not; yet he sticks to that model. Kaufman, "Organizational Politics," treats party-military relations as analogous to civil-military relations in any state and "tests" a couple of theories of international relations, trying to explain the General Staff's strategy for war in Europe and the acceptance of the ABM treaty. Neither explanation is consistent with the evidence I have presented in Chapter 5. All of these works published since 1992 confuse the political-military dynamics even more than those published earlier, owing both to the models they use and the unreliability of much of the evidence they cite. For example, Lepingwell's assertion that the military opposed use of their forces for maintaining internal order is based on their articles to that effect. As I shall show, they lost their enthusiasm for such missions because Gorbachev would not back them when they massacred civilians, not because they really had

qualms about it. By 1990–91, however, that was becoming a problem, but the source was Gorbachev's political tactics, scapegoating the generals who carried out repressions.

60. See H. Gordon Skilling and Franklyn Griffiths, eds., *Interest Groups in Soviet Politics* (Princeton, N.J.: Princeton University Press, 1971). This volume is the classic and initial attempt to try to apply group theory to Soviet politics. See Odom, "Dissenting View," for my critique and rejection of group theory for interpreting Soviet politics.

61. See Odom, "Soviet Politics and After," for a critique of this scholarship and an alternative explanation of the dynamic behavior of the Soviet system, more accurately characterized by S. P. Huntington's concept of "political decay" than as a "political transformation." See p. 96.

62. See Colton and Gustafson, *Soldiers and the Soviet State*, especially Gustafson's chapter at the end and his concluding section of this book, where he makes this case.

63. Huntington, *Soldier and the State*, 8.

64. Ibid., 8.

65. Ibid., 15.

66. Ibid., 92–93.

Chapter 11. The Intractable Military-Industrial Sector

1. Schumpeter, *Capitalism, Socialism, and Democracy*, 81–86.

2. Prybyla, *Market and Plan Under Socialism*, 65–66, 134–54, and 175. Kornai, *Socialist System*, also is useful on this point.

3. Neglect of the military-industrial sector and the military rationale in much of the central-planning system is characteristic of most Western analysis of the early five-year plans. Dobb, *Soviet Economic Development*, 13, 18, notes that military factors "partly dictated" the pace of industrialization in the 1930s but otherwise ignores them. Nove, *Soviet Economy*, 155, wholly ignoring the ideological grounds for great military industrial power, observes that "the Soviet authorities took for [a] given that rapid industrialization is the overriding aim of public policy." Three trivial references to defense spending constitute his apparent sense of its importance. Harry Schwartz, *Russia's Soviet Economy* (Englewood Cliffs, N.J.: Prentice-Hall, 1954), in an early textbook, hardly mentions military industry. Spulber, *Soviet Economy*, in another textbook, wholly ignores the military-industrial sector. Erlich, *Soviet Industrialization Debate*, 28–29, 37, 51, 167–68, 180, notes that military factors played a role in deciding for rapid industrialization but develops them only marginally, lamenting on p. 180 that Stalin's faction reflected two basic characteristics, "a sense of irreducible bipolarity in the world coupled with a supreme readiness to eradicate everything that cannot be readily controlled." Erlich obviously overlooked the participation in the industrialization debate by Frunze and other military officials. Carr and Davies, *Foundations of a Planned Economy*, and Bergson, *Economics of Soviet Planning*, might have been expected to deal with the war mobilization character of the economic system, but they did not. Awakening to the impact of the military sector was surprisingly slow, even late in the postwar period. For an example, see Gregory and Stuart, *Soviet Economic Structure and Performance*, 4th ed. The four editions of this text, which present what might be called the "mainstream" Western interpretation of the Soviet economic system, begin by essentially ignoring the military-industrial factor and later puzzling over it as a disturbing afterthought. These and virtually all other studies of the Soviet economy simply do not take seriously the Marxist-Leninist theory of war as an ideological factor that guided the design of the command economic system from its inception. Luke, *Ideology and Soviet Industrialization*, in light of his focus on

the role of ideology, might have been expected to stumble onto the military implications of "international class struggle," but neither "war" nor "defense" nor "military" appears as an entry in his index. Even with the advent of perestroika and the deluge of information on the significance of the military-industrial sector, the military factor in the Soviet economy was still ignored. See Gregory, *Restructuring the Soviet Economic Bureaucracy*, and Dyker, *Restructuring the Soviet Economy*.

A few exceptions can be found. Cooper, *Soviet Defence Industry*, is one, and his work includes numerous other insightful pieces on the issue. Holloway, "Innovation in the Defence Sector," is another exception, especially for tracing some of the prewar institutional arrangements for the military-industrial sector and postwar weapons programs. Harrison, *Soviet Planning in Peace and War*, shows awareness of the leadership's thinking about war and the economy in the 1920s and 1930s but never gives it the primacy it deserves. A fairly extensive literature from think tanks, such as the RAND Corporation, dealt with various aspects of the military-industrial sector, but by and large they appear not to have influenced the university community of students of the Soviet economy. Nor did this literature, produced mostly for the Department of Defense, effectively pull the whole picture together or emphasize the role of ideology and institutional structure dating from the late 1920s.

4. Chernyaev, *Shest' let s Gorbachevym*, 254.

5. Shakhnazarov, *Tsena svobody*, 83-84.

6. Boldin, *Ten Years that Shook the World*, 73.

7. Ibid., 23.

8. Ibid., 73-74; Yegor K. Ligachev, informal conversation, 11 November 1991.

9. Aslund, *Gorbachev's Struggle for Economic Reform*, 117.

10. Dudorov, "Konversiya dlya agro-promyshlennosti."

11. *Pravda*, 21 July 1988.

12. Julian Cooper, "The Defense Industry and Civil Military Relations," in Colton and Gustafson, *Soldiers and the Soviet State*, 177-79.

13. Aslund, *Gorbachev's Struggle for Economic Reform*, 81-84.

14. Chernyaev, *Shest' let s Gorbachevym*, 257.

15. Ibid., 258. The British and American ambassadors provided Chernyaev with fresh evidence that the USSR was violating the convention prohibiting such weapons. Gorbachev immediately instructed Shevardnadze, Baklanov, and Yazov to prepare an answer. Their response was merely to propose an exchange of experts with the United States and Britain, leading Chernyaev to conclude that indeed the VPK was developing such weapons.

16. Ibid., 257-58.

17. Lyakhovskii, *Tragediya i doblest' Afgana*, 80-82. Lyakhovskii served both in Afghanistan and on the General Staff handling Afghan affairs. He was wounded badly in the leg, and during the year while he was recovering, he was permitted to search through Politburo, secretariat, General Staff, and other extremely secret documents for writing his history. Many of his brief explanations of the "bureaucratic mechanisms" that were regularly exploited to get decisions desired by subordinate levels of the military, VPK, and party organizations provide remarkable insights into how policies of some types were actually made and implemented. A colonel until 1994, he was promoted to major general in the Russian army.

18. Ibid.

19. Ibid.

20. *Soviet Military Power* (Washington, D.C.: Government Printing Office, 1988), 138. For details about Soviet arms sales by regions and countries, also see 22-31.

21. FBIS-SOV-89, "Minister Interviewed on Defense Industry Conversion," 22 June 1989, pp. 74–78. L. Ryabev, minister of medium machine building, describes his ministry's experience in dealing with ten such firms. Even the buildings of some had to be torn down and rebuilt, and four hundred types of machinery had to be redesigned or substantially modernized.

22. "Soviet Military Budget: A $128 Billion Bombshell," *New York Times*, 31 May 1989. The figure caused a stir in the U.S. Congress.

23. *RFE/RL Daily Report* no. 183, 26 September 1989; FBIS-SOV-89-183, "Report of 1985–88 Budget Secrets Published," 22 September 1989, pp. 83–85.

24. Yazov, "Novaya model' bezopasnosti i vooruzhennye sily."

25. See Weickhardt, "Recent Discussion of Defense Economics."

26. JPRS-UMA-89-009, "MOD R&D Organizations Switch to Khozraschet," 20 April 1989, p. 72.

27. Isaev, "Reforma i oboronnye otrasli."

28. Ibid.

29. See *RFE/RL Daily Report* no. 24, 2 February 1990, for the case of three ministers in VPK being caught trying to sell weapons to Western buyers for hard currency.

30. Vitalii Vitebskii, interview, 13 March 1996. Vitebskii was a design engineer in the firm that produced SS-18 rockets.

31. *RFE/RL Daily Report* no. 107, 6 June 1990. Lopatin told the newspaper *Izvestiya* that military conversion was "a fairy tale." He also circulated a manuscript in typescript, "Armiya I ekonomika," in which he made a rather comprehensive case that the military sector of the economy was the logical and stifling product of the earliest developments in the creation of the Soviet state.

32. See interview with Yurii Ryzhov, "In Place of an Epilogue," *Moscow News* (in English) no. 8 (3 March 1991): 9.

33. Three excellent examples of this line of thinking are Kireev, "Konversiya v sovetskom izmerenii"; V. Saitgareev, "Ekonomicheskie korni sovetskoi voennoi byurokratii"; and Kuznetsov and Shirokov, "Naukoemkye proizvodstva i konversiya oboronnoi promyshlennosti."

34. FBIS-SOV-89-028, "Belousov Queried on Defense Industrial Conversion," 13 February 1989, pp. 82–83.

35. FBIS-SOV-89-249, "Ryzhkov Interviewed on Economic Program," 29 December 1989, pp. 39–46.

36. FBIS-SOV-89-164, "Defense Industrial Chief Welcomes Glasnost," 25 August 1989, pp. 70–72; and FBIS-SOV-171, "Belousov Outlines Defense Industries Conversion," 6 September 1989, pp. 79–85.

37. Kireev, "Konversiya v sovetskom izmerenii," 104.

38. See Tedstrom, "Managing the Conversion."

39. Ibid.

40. FBIS-SOV-90-120,"Novosibirsk 'Council' Oversees Conversion Problems," 21 June 1990, p. 56.

41. FBIS-SOV-90-190, "Conversion Program Detailed," 1 October 1990, p. 43.

42. FBIS-SOV-90-213, "Defense Committee Examines Conversion Bill," 2 November 1990, pp. 27–28.

43. Tedstrom, "Shatalin Plan."

44. Aslund, *Gorbachev's Struggle for Economic Reform*, 208–11.

45. Ibid. 102.

46. *RFE/RL Daily Report* no. 107, 6 June 1990.

47. *RFE/RL Daily Report* no. 204, 26 October 1989.

48. Vitalii Vitebskii, interview, 13 March 1996.

49. FBIS-SOV-90-112, "Problems of Economic Conversion Discussed," 11 June 1990, pp. 59–60.

50. FBIS-SOV-90-184, "Defense Plant to Produce Agricultural Equipment," 21 September 1990, pp. 38–39. See also Smart, "Amid the Ruins," for an account of the characterization by an official in Leningrad of military conversion as a joke.

51. See Smart, "Amid the Ruins," 349–64, for an excellent account of the military conversion program in general and the reaction of enterprise managers in particular, based on interviews with managers in Kiev, Moscow, and Leningrad in 1991.

52. When I visited a military electronics firm near Moscow in November 1991, the manager provided a sales talk and a review of his several efforts to attract Western firms to buy components that his plant was producing for the Soviet space industry. The manager noted that he alone was in charge now. A year earlier, a party official and the trade union leader would have been in the office with him, sharing control of the firm. Now the responsibility was entirely his, and not just for the firm but also the surrounding small town, where all of his workforce lived. Housing, schools, and public facilities depended largely on the firm for fiscal support.

53. FBIS-SOV-90-175, "Letter from Defense Industry Deplores Disarray," 10 September 1990, pp. 68–69.

54. *RFE/RL Daily Report* no. 187, 1 October 1990.

55. FBIS-SVO-90-003, "Reaction to 8.2% Cut in Defense Budget," 4 January 1990, p. 103.

56. FBIS-SOV-90-037, "Yazov Interview," 23 February 1990, p. 84.

57. *RFE/RL Daily Report* no. 55, 19 March 1990. This report summarizes three press accounts and a roundtable discussion in February and March 1990.

58. Cooper, "The Defense Industry and Civil-Military Relations," 190–91.

Chapter 12. The Army and Maintaining Domestic Order

1. See Martha Brill Olcott, "The Slide into Disunion," *Current History* 90 (October 1991): 338–39, for an excellent summary and analysis of these events.

2. Lieutenant Colonel Alexander Rodin, interview, 7 July 1995, said that the 1968 invasion of Czechoslovakia undercut his trust of the regime. He also insisted that he was not alone in this regard. Marshal of Aviation Yevgenii Shaposhnikov also told me in an interview on 29 June 1995 that he had always been troubled by the invasion.

3. See Lyakhovskii, *Tragediya i doblest' Afgana*, 10–89. Lyakhovskii's book, based on access to many Politburo, Central Committee, KGB, and General Staff classified documents, provides compelling evidence that Ogarkov and his assistants were flatly overruled when they opposed the invasion. The effect was a serious loss of confidence in Brezhnev, Ustinov, and most of the other Politburo members. Colonel General Anatolii Gribkov, at the time a deputy chief of the General Staff, told me in March 1995 that shortly before the invasion he had gone to see Ogarkov to register his strong objections to it, only to be told by Ogarkov that Ustinov had "decided" already and he could not be turned around. These officers, of course, have a strong interest in placing the blame wholly on the Politburo in order to absolve themselves, but much evidence does suggest that they opposed the idea from the be-

ginning. It is not true, however, that they were all so eager to withdraw. General Varennikov, for example, regularly gave overly optimistic briefings to the Politburo Commission which Gorbachev appointed to oversee the withdrawal. According to Sergei Tarasenko, a regular attendee of its meetings, Varennikov did all that he could to head off a complete pullout. Interview, 12 March 1996.

4. Alexiev, *Inside the Soviet Army in Afghanistan.*

5. Amstutz, *Afghanistan,* especially 127–97, offers a summary assessment of all forces in the war, Soviet, the Moscow-backed government, and the insurgents. This book is also an excellent assessment of political, economic, and international factors during the first five years of the war. The author, a U.S. foreign service officer, served as deputy chief of mission at the U.S. embassy in Kabul during and after the Soviet invasion, allowing him to provide a lot of firsthand evidence. Lyakhovskii, *Tragediya I doblest' Afgana,* tells the story from the Soviet side, also as a participant with much firsthand evidence as well.

6. Alexiev, *Inside the Soviet Army in Afghanistan* 35–44.

7. Daugherty, "Bear and the Scimitar." Daugherty reports that problems were so acute with Central Asian ethnic groups in Soviet units that these soldiers were largely withdrawn after the first several months of the war, being replaced with Slavs and other non–Central Asian ethnic groups.

8. Alexiev, *Inside the Soviet Army in Afghanistan,* 50.

9. Lyakhovskii, *Tragediya I doblest' Afgana,* 293–95.

10. Alexiev, *Inside the Soviet Army in Afghanistan,* 50–54.

11. See Grau, "Bear Went Over the Mountain." Grau includes translations of three chapters of a study of combat actions in Afghanistan used at the Frunze Academy for training field-grade officers. His editorial comments take the gloss off the Frunze Academy evaluations.

12. *RFE/RL Daily Report* no. 226, 29 November 1989.

13. Chernyaev, *Shest' let s Gorbachevym,* 57–58.

14. Elizabeth Teague, "Russian Appointed to Top Party Post in Kazakhstan," *Radio Liberty Report 465/86,* 16 December 1986.

15. For reporting on the affair at the time, see Olcott, "The Slide into Disunion"; Martin Walker, "Gorbachev Ignores Sakharov Rights Plea," *The Manchester Guardian,* 22 December 1986; and Sheehy, "Alma-Ata Riots." Olcott, *The Kazakhs,* provides excellent background.

16. TASS, 19 December 1986.

17. Ann Sheehy, "The Alma-Ata Riots and Their Aftermath."

18. FBIS-SOV-87-112, "Students Sentenced in Alma-Ata," 17 June 1987, p. 78.

19. Fuller and Ouratadze, "Georgian Leadership Changes."

20. Fuller, "Official and Unofficial Investigations." This brief article is an excellent and detailed account of the Tbilisi affair, based on a critical review of the report of the commission set up by the Georgian Supreme Soviet to investigate the matter. According to some sources, the decision to stop the demonstration came from the Georgian Defense Council on 8 April.

21. Fuller and Ouratadze, "Georgian Leadership Changes," 30.

22. Fuller, "Official and Unofficial Investigations," 28.

23. Fuller and Ouratadze, "Georgian Leadership Changes," 29.

24. Shevardnadze, *The Future Belongs to Freedom,* 192–95.

25. Ibid., 193.

26. Chernyaev, *Shest' let s Gorbachevym,* 284–87.

27. Shevardnadze, *The Future Belongs to Freedom*, 194.

28. Chernyaev, *Shest' let s Gorbachevym*, 286–87.

29. Fuller, "Official and Unofficial Investigations," 28.

30. Memorandum of conversation with Niyazov in Ashgabat, 27 May 1996. I participated with Z. K. Brzezinski and Paul Wolfowitz in this meeting with President Niyazov, who spoke at length about Gorbachev, calling him a "liar" whom the West wrongly saw as a "saint." Niyazov declared that he was present when Gorbachev made this remark, and that on hearing it, "something broke in me, and I felt that I could no longer support communist rule." He said that Gorbachev's reaction to events in Baku in January 1990 was equally cold-blooded. Niyazov, of course, has his own ax to grind, but he chose these examples, as well as Nagorno-Karabakh and the Transdniester Autonomous Republic, to demonstrate that Gorbachev was "narrow-minded" and rigid on nationality policy.

31. Boldin, *Ten Years That Shook the World*, 222–23.

32. Ibid.

33. I. Rodionov, "Tragediya . . . ili provokatsiya?" in Gorshkov and V. V. Zhuralev, *Nesokrushimaya i legendarnaya*, 57–58.

34. Lebed', *Za derzhavu obidno*, 281–82.

35. Ibid., 279–82.

36. Ibid., 282.

37. Boldin, *Ten Years That Shook the World*, 224.

38. Lebed', *Za derzhavu obidno*, 278–86.

39. Varennikov, "Prednaznacheniie Sovetskykh Vooruzhennykh Sil"; Vorob'ev, "Mera kraine nezhelatel'naya"; Belkov, "Armiya dolzhna delat' svow delo"; and Skorodenko, "V tselyakh zashchity sotsializma."

40. *RFE/RL Daily Report* No. 213, 8 November 1989.

41. For accounts of these events, see Tolz, "Developments in Dispute"; Fuller, "Preliminary Chronology"; Sheehy, "Soviet Media Coverage."

42. Igor Nolyain, an engineer living in Newark, N.J., in 1996, sent me an unsolicited manuscript, "Moscow's Secret Initiation of the Azeri-Armenian Conflict," in which he analyzes the Soviet media coverage, not just of the Nagorno-Karabakh conflict but also in the Fergana Valley, in Alma-Ata, Latvia, and numerous other outbreaks of so-called ethnic conflict. The polemical document would not qualify as a scholarly work, and the English prose is sometimes difficult to follow, but it offers more than diatribe. Nolyain makes no secret of his hostility toward Gorbachev and other Soviet leaders.

43. Lebed', *Za derzhavu obidno*, 218, says that in March 1988, when he took command of the airborne division stationed in Tula, one of his regiments, the 137th from Ryazan, had already been deployed in Sumgait for a month. The 7th Army of the Transcaucasus Military District, located in Armenia, found itself involved in helping to keep order there and in Nagorno-Karabakh. Western press reporting on Soviet army units keeping order in both republics, however, was limited in 1988–90, and for that reason, their role was not nearly as well known in the West as were the activities of army units in Tbilisi and in the Baltic states during this period.

44. Ibid., 287.

45. Zabrodin, "Chto 'vysvetila' tragediya v Zakavkaz'e?" This account is clearly biased in assigning blame, but it provides a chronology of the crisis and generally accurate details on the growing tensions in the months before Soviet troops intervened in Baku.

46. Fuller, "Gorbachev's Dilemma in Azerbaijan."

47. Fuller and Deich, "Interview with Gary Kasparov."

48. Ibid. Kasparov, the world chess champion, was convinced by what he observed in late 1989 and early 1990 that party and KGB officials were abetting the anti-Armenian sentiments among these refugees, who were provincial, uneducated, and nasty. He reported that Armenians fleeing Baku were told by Azeris who packed and shipped their personal belongings that no shipping containers could be dispatched after 12 January. Kasparov took this as evidence that these Azeris knew in advance that the pogroms would begin on 13 January, that they were not at all spontaneous. Moreover, the Azeri refugees were more interested in taking the apartments and homes of the Armenians than in physical attacks on them, and many of the refugees moved in to abandoned housing on the spot.

49. Quoted by Fuller, "Gorbachev's Dilemma in Azerbaijan," 14. Also see Elizabeth Fuller, "Will Azerbaijan Be the Next 'Domino'?" for additional analysis of the Soviet media's disinformation campaign at the time.

50. Nolyain, "Moscow's Secret Initiation," lists several; also, President Niyazov of Turkmenistan, in a conversation cited above, hints strongly at Gorbachev's complicity.

51. V. Vyzhutovich and V. Samedov, "Vvod voisk v Baku sanktsioniroval Gorbachev," in Gorshkov and Zhuralev, *Nesokrushimaya i legendarnaya*, 108–11. This piece, first published in *Izvestiya*, 13 February 1992, right after the abolition of the Soviet Union, is an investigative effort to pull together as complete a retrospective view on the intervention in Baku as possible two years after the event.

52. Ibid.

53. Ibid.

54. Melanie Newton, "Events in Azerbaijan," *Report on the USSR* 2, no. 5 (2 February 1990): 23–24.

55. Lebed', *Za derzhavu obidno*, 292.

56. *RFE/RL Daily Report* no. 20, 29 January 1990.

57. Lebed', *Za derzhavu obidno*, 287.

58. Ibid., 288.

59. Ibid., 289–93.

60. Ibid., 291–92.

61. Ibid., 298–300.

62. Ibid., 300–302.

63. Ibid., 297.

64. Ibid., 289–93.

65. *RFE/RL Daily Report* no. 33, 15 February 1990.

66. Girnius, "Lithuania's Struggle with the USSR," provides a succinct but thorough account of these developments.

67. Zelikow and Rice, *Germany Unified and Europe Transformed*, 257.

68. Ibid.

69. Girnius, "Lithuania's National Salvation Committee."

70. Kusin, "Patterns of Intervention."

71. Foye, "Gorbachev Denies Responsibility."

72. Craig Whitney, "Soviet Leader Rebukes Separatist Movements," *New York Times*, 15 January 1991.

73. In Russian, OMON stands for *Otryady militsii osobovogo naznacheniya*.

74. Bungs, "Black Berets Storm Latvian Interior Ministry."

75. Yasmann, "Did Paratroopers Refuse to Shoot?" In addition to this published re-

port, rumors were afloat in Moscow and U.S. government circles that one battalion commander refused to move his unit to Lithuania and also that the Baltic Military District commander gave all three republics' leaders advanced warnings about the plan for intervention.

76. Translated by Michael Rywkin in "Analysis of Current Events," year 2, no. 2 (February, 1991), published by the Association for Study of the Nationalities at City College of New York. The recording of Yeltsin's radio address was reportedly made by Radio Liberty.

Chapter 13. From Force Reductions to Disintegration

1. *The Military Balance, 1985–1986* (London: International Institute for Strategic Studies, 1985), 21.

2. Interview with Marshal D. T. Yazov, *Pravda*, 23 February 1990.

3. *The Military Balance, 1992–1993* (London: International Institute for Strategic Studies, 1992), 92.

4. *The Military Balance, 1985–1986*, 29. Eventually this entire force was withdrawn.

5. FBIS-SOV-89-032, "Help for Discharged Soldiers Discussed," 17 February 1989, p. 91.

6. Ibid.

7. FBIS-SOV-89-046, "General on Problems of Released Army Personnel," 10 March 1989, pp. 101–3.

8. Ibid.

9. FBIS-SOV-90-006, "Treatment of Servicemen in Baltics Deplored," 9 January 1990, pp. 59–60.

10. I. Varfolomeev, " 'Dvoie' na dolzhnostyakh," *Krasnaya zvezda*, 12 November 1989.

11. FBIS-SOV-89-241, "Chervov Says 265,000 Discharged from Armed Forces," 18 December 1989, p. 122.

12. Clarke, "Warsaw Pact."

13. Clarke, "Soviet Troop Withdrawals."

14. Kusin, "Soviet Troops."

15. Kusin, "Gorbachev Agrees to Warsaw Pact Meeting"; and Kusin, "Yet Another End."

16. Daalder, *CFE Treaty*, 27.

17. FBIS-SOV-074, "Roundtable on Servicemen's Problems," 19 April 1989, pp. 50–52.

18. Yazov, interview.

19. Foye, "Soviet Armed Forces Face Housing Crisis."

20. Ibid., 6.

21. *RFE/RL Daily Report* no. 182, 24 September 1990.

22. FBIS-SOV-91-032, "Defense Ministry Spokesman on Housing Problem," 15 February 1991, p. 58.

23. Serge Schmemann, "Soviet Rightists See a Nation Run Amok," *New York Times*, 27 January 1991.

24. "Pis'mo rukovodstvu o problemakh armii," *Komsomolskaya pravda*, 4 July 1990.

25. *RFE/RL Daily Report* no. 182, 24 September 1990.

26. *OMRI* 1, no. 151, 4 August 1995. Thirty-eight thousand had been finished in August 1995.

27. FBIS-SOV-90-037, "Yazov Interview in *Pravda*," 23 February 1990, p. 83.

28. *RFE/RL Daily Report* no. 50, 12 March 1990.

29. *RFE/RL Daily Report* no. 56, 21 March 1990.

30. *RFE/RL Daily Report* no. 68, 5 April 1990.

31. *RFE/RL Daily Report* no. 134, 17 July 1990.

32. *RFE/RL Daily Report* no. 172, 10 September 1990.

33. FBIS-SOV-90-232, "Army Official on Protecting Servicemen," 3 December 1990, p. 74.

34. See Zelikow and Rice, *Germany Unified and Europe Transformed*, especially chapters 7–9, for the most comprehensive picture of Gorbachev's and Shevardnadze's role in this outcome. Chernyaev, *Shest' let s Gorbachevym*, 346–48, takes part of the credit (or blame) but reports that Shevardnadze's support of his position was critical in bringing Gorbachev to accept it. For a Western diplomat-participant's account, see Matlock, *Autopsy on an Empire*, 382–88.

35. For the Transcaucasus, see Fuller, "Paramilitary Formations in Armenia," and Fuller, "Georgia's National Guard."

36. For the Baltic republics, see *RFE/RL Daily Report* no. 35, 19 February 1990; *RFE/RL Daily Report* no. 96, 18 May 1990; *RFE/RL Daily Report* no. 162, 27 August 1990.

37. For Moldavia, see *RFE/RL Daily Report* no. 171, 7 September 1990; *RFE/RL Daily Report* no. 177, 17 September 1990; Vladimir Socor, "Gorbachev and Moldavia," *Report on the USSR* 2 (21 December 1990): 11–14.

38. For Ukraine, see *RFE/RL Daily Report* no. 141, 26 July 1990; Mihalisko, "Ukrainians Ponder Creation of National Army"; Valerii Semivolos, "Should Ukraine Have Its Own Army?" *Novoe vremya* no. 26 (June 1991): 35, translated in FBIS-SOV-91-139, "Economic Case for Republic Army," 19 July 1991, 82–83.

39. Yazov, interview.

40. *RFE/RL Daily Report* no. 141, 26 July 1990.

41. JPRS-UMT-90-002-L, "From the History of Creation and Training of Ethnic Military Units," 28 January 1990, pp. 1–7. Varennikov's article appeared in *Voennaya mysl'* no. 2 (1990): 3–13.

42. *RFE/RL Daily Report* no. 141, 26 July 1990.

43. *RFE/RL Daily Report* no. 142, 27 July 1990.

44. *RFE/RL Daily Report* no. 147, 3 August 1990.

45. *RFE/RL Daily Report* no. 143, 30 July 1990.

46. *RFE/RL Daily Report* no. 171, 7 September 1990. Altaev's article appeared in *XX Vek i mir* no. 6 (1990).

47. FBIS-SOV-90-162, "More Good and Varied Armies," 21 August 1990, p. 61.

48. Semivolos, "Should Ukraine Have Its Own Army?"

49. FBIS-SOV-90-226, "Yeltsin Considering Establishing Russian Army," 23 November 1990, p. 59.

50. FBIS-SOV-90-225, "RSFSR Resolution Adopted on Armed Forces," 21 November 1990, p. 78.

51. FBIS-SOV-91-035, "Official Assesses Moves for Republican Armies," 21 February 1991, pp. 68–69; interview with Major General Ivashov and Major Yu. Rubtsov, *Krasnaya zvezda*, 2 February 1991.

52. *RFE/RL Daily Report* no. 102, 29 May 1990; *RFE/RL Daily Report* No. 124, 2 July 1990; *RFE/RL Daily Report* no. 209, 2 November 1990.

53. Krivosheev, "Ob vseobshchei voennoi sluzhbe."

54. JPRS-UMA-89-013, "Trial Reveals Malfeasance in Military Commissariat in Vilnius," 26 May 1989, pp. 18–20. This account, published in the newspaper *Trud*, 4 April

1989, gives a number of examples of how parents got their sons illegally exempted from conscription.

55. Interview with Viktor Sadovich, FBIS-SOV-89-072, "University Official on Student Draft Deferments," 17 April 1989, pp. 107–8.

56. Chernyaev, *Shest' let s Gorbachevym,* 156–58.

57. Sadovich, interview.

58. Krivosheev, "Ob vseobshchei voennoi sluzhbe."

59. Ibid.

60. "Studenty i armiya," *Izvestiya,* 14 April 1989.

61. R. Makushin, "Kak budet prokhodit's prizyv," *Krasnaya zvezda,* 11 April 1989.

62. Krivosheev, "Ob vseobshchei voennoi sluzhbe."

63. Ibid. Although Krivosheev uses the figure 173,000, Chervov gave it as 176,000 after the students had been released. Both figures appeared in several other sources. Which is closer to the truth is impossible to determine.

64. Ibid.

65. Colonel Aleksei Tsarev and Lieutenant Colonel Aleksandr Rodin provided the best insights, but I had to draw them out because they had no basis for comparing the Soviet system with Western military practices. The explanation offered here is primarily mine, based on observing the Soviet army in East Germany, 1964–66, and in Moscow, 1972–74, and piecing together the stories of many former Soviet citizens about their life as conscripts. It is consistent with most of the published Soviet commentary as well, but it puts far more emphasis on the paramechanistic effect of the change to a two-year service term based on semiannual call-ups.

66. For a very brief, chilling, but effective description of dedovshchina, see the testimonial by a former soldier, A. Terekhov, "Strakh pered morozom," *Ogonek* no. 19 (1988): 19.

67. See JPRS-UMA-89-015, "Response to Readers on Nature of Dedovshchina," 15 June 1989, pp. 15–18. This article, from *Krasnaya zvezda,* 22 April 1989, gives a rare but keen insight into the impact of the dedovshchina on first-year NCOs and on the ineffective methods of the military commissariats in selecting them.

68. Ibid. The author of the article asked why "officers calmly fight an armed foe, but they retreat and even flee from an enemy named 'dedovshchina.'"

69. Interview with the researchers, "'Dedovshchina' na vesakh zakona," *Kommunist vooruzhennykh sil* 24 (1989): 50–58.

70. Terekhov, "Strakh pered morozom," makes this point.

71. Interview with military sociologist Yu. Deryugin, *Argumenty I fakty,* 27 August–2 September 1988.

72. Yurii Polyakov, *Sto dnei do prikaza* (Moscow: Molodaya gvardiya, 1988).

73. Kaledin, "Stroibat." It later appeared as a book, *Stroibat* (Moscow: Kvadrat, 1994).

74. *RFE/RL Daily Report* no. 20, 9 February 1990.

75. Rakowska-Harmstone, "Nationalities and the Soviet Military."

76. See Baranets, Rumyantsev, and Lukashenya, "Nadezhnost' internatsional'nogo zakala," for a discussion of ethnic relations in the military based on sociological research as well as officers' experience. It treats zemlyachestvo in some detail.

77. Ibid., 36, offers a case similar to this hypothetical one.

78. For example, a battalion-size unit was quartered for a day in a six-floor building near Leningrad during transit. The officers were billeted on the top floor, the troops on the lower floors. During the evening, the officers heard a furor below, and when they investigated, they found the Muslim Central Asian soldiers fighting the Christians, mostly Slavs.

Instead of breaking up the fight, the officers joined the Christians. The melee was eventually broken up but not reported to higher authorities, and the unit moved on the next day to its destination with no disciplinary action taken. Interview with Russian officers by a U.S. Army sergeant, Rachel Kavarsky, during a Partnership for Peace exercise in 1995, related to me in March 1996. The terms "Muslims" and "Christians" were used by the Russian officers. They also insisted that Muslim-Christian splits of this sort were not exceptional.

79. Crowe, "Soviet Conscripts Fall Victim."

80. Shakhnazarov, *Tsena svobody*, 90.

81. Lieutenant Colonel Aleksandr Rodin, interview, 7 July 1995. Rodin was a pilot who flew the caviar to Moscow.

82. *RFE/RL Daily Report* no. 76, 19 April 1990. The newspaper *Rabochaya gazeta*, 6 April 1990, reported these figures.

83. Colonel Aleksei Tsarev, a former political officer, related these details and generalizations in an interview in Moscow, 28 June 1995. Tsarev served as the political officer for an SS-18 ICBM regiment, as well as in several other operational units, and he is a graduate of the Lenin Military-Political Academy who left the army to become a staff aide to the speaker of the State Duma in 1994.

84. Ibid.

85. Ibid.

86. FBIS-SOV-90-178, "Officer Stages Hunger Strike Against Generals," 13 September 1990, p. 67.

87. *RFE/RL Daily Report* no. 152, 10 August 1990.

88. *RFE/RL Daily Report* no. 226, 29 November 1989.

89. *RFE/RL Daily Report* no. 232, 7 December 1990.

90. *RFE/RL Daily Report* no. 134, 17 August 1990.

91. *RFE/RL Daily Report* no. 219, 16 November 1990.

92. *RFE/RL Daily Report* no. 222, 23 November 1990.

93. Sein, "Sfera osobogo vnimaniya," 19.

94. Ibid., 19-24.

95. FBIS-SOV-88-164, "Izvestiya Carries Report," 24 August 1988, pp. 24-25. See also Yu. Afanasyev, "'Deystvovat' dostoyno nashego vremeni," *Sovetskaya Estoniya*, 29 September 1988.

96. *RFE/RL Daily Report* no. 134, 17 July 1990. Krasnaya zevzda, 12 July 1990, gave comparative figures for the spring calls up in both 1989 and 1990.

97. *RFE/RL Daily Report* no. 76, 19 April 1990.

98. See "Tochka zreniya: vesennii prizyv," *Pravda*, 16 May 1990.

99. *RFE/RL Daily Report* no. 243, 22 December 1989.

100. FBIS-SOV-91-012, "Press Chief on Rounding Up Draft Evaders," 17 January 1991, p. 54.

101. *RFE/RL Daily Report* no. 124, 2 July 1990; *RFE/RL Daily Report* no. 209, 2 November 1990.

102. FBIS-SOV-91-141, "Abolition of Student Deferment," 23 July 1991, pp. 51-52.

103. Ibid.

104. Schemann, "Soviet Rightists."

105. Fuller, "Georgians Win Concessions."

106. *RFE/RL Daily Report* no. 216, 13 November 1990.

107. *RFE/RL Daily Report* no. 233, 8 December 1989.

108. *RFE/RL Daily Report* no. 52, 14 March 1990.

109. *RFE/RL Daily Report* no. 35, 19 February 1990.

110. *RFE/RL Daily Report* no. 49, 9 March 1990; *RFE/RL Daily Report* no. 170, 6 September 1990.

111. *RFE/RL Daily Report* no 87, 7 May 1990.

112. *RFE/RL Daily Report* no. 175, 13 September 1990.

113. *RFE/RL Daily Report* no. 169, 5 September 1990.

114. *RFE/RL Daily Report* no. 209, 2 November 1990.

115. Odom and Dujarric, *Commonwealth or Empire?* 157.

116. *The Military Balance, 1985–1986,* 30.

117. Knight, *Spies Without Cloaks,* 138–63. While all the CIS countries established their own security services and border control system, the KGB kept bilateral relations with most of them. Each case varied considerably from all others. Knight is the best source on the details.

118. See Odom and Dujarric, *Commonwealth or Empire?* 153–57, for readjustments in the ground forces after the dissolution of the USSR.

119. FBIS-SOV-89-127, "Gorbachev Defends Yazov," 5 July 1989, p. 49.

120. Odom and Dujarric, *Commonwealth or Empire?* 153–56.

121. Turkmen President Saparmurat Niyazov, interview, Ashagat, 27 May 1996.

122. Odom and Dujarric, *Commonwealth or Empire?* 152.

123. Ibid., 152–53.

124. Ibid., 151–52.

125. Ibid., 150–51.

126. Ibid., 139.

127. *RFE/RL Daily Report* no. 77, 20 April 1990.

128. *RFE/RL Daily Report* no. 181, 21 September 1990.

129. *RFE/RL Daily Report* no. 136, 19 July 1990; *RFE/RL Daily Report* no. 151, 9 August 1990; *RFE/RL Daily Report* no. 191, 8 October 1990;

130. Kholodov worked for *Komsomolskaya pravda,* which carried several of his stories about Grachev, Burlakov, and other generals involved in shady financial dealings. In fall 1994 he reported that the military procurator in Germany had discovered that $6.7 million had been stolen, apparently by Burlakov, the commander of the Western Group of Forces there. Grachev was suspected of sharing in this money. *Komsomolskaya pravda,* 20 October 1994, published evidence that Grachev ordered two Mercedes cars purchased from housing funds from Bonn and then shipped them to Moscow for his use. Grachev and Burlakov got the military procurator to press charges of slander against *Komsomolskaya pravda* the next day. Kholodov was killed by a suitcase bomb shortly thereafter, and military intelligence operatives were widely believed to have been the perpetrators. Ignoring all this uproar for a time, Yeltsin finally removed Burlakov from his post pending an investigation for corruption. He did nothing to Grachev, but the defense minister became known in the press as "Pasha Mercedes." He was forced to admit that the autos were purchased with German housing funds, but he insisted that Yeltsin had granted advanced approval. See also *RFE/RL Daily Report* no. 202, 24 October 1994; *RFE/RL Daily Report* no. 208, 2 November 1994; and *RFE/RL Daily Report* no. 212, 8 November, 1994.

131. *RFE/RL Daily Report* no. 73, 12 April 1990.

132. *RFE/RL Daily Report* no. 28, 8 February 1990.

133. *RFE/RL Daily Report* no. 26, 6 February 1990.

134. *RFE/RL Daily Report* no. 219, 16 November 1990.

135. *RFE/RL Daily Report* no. 194, 11 October 1990.

136. JPRS-UMA-91-001, "Military Procurator on AWOL Problem," 2 January 1991, pp. 51–52.

137. JPRS-UMA-91-001, "Massive Decline in Leningrad DOSAAF Membership," 2 January 1991, p. 53.

138. *RFE/RL Daily Report* no. 229, 4 December 1990.

139. *RFE/RL Daily Report* no. 29, 9 February 1990.

140. *RFE/RL Daily Report* no. 109, 8 June 1990.

141. *RFE/RL Daily Report* no. 186, 28 September 1990.

142. *RFE/RL Daily Report* no. 57, 21 March 1990; *RFE/RL Daily Report* no. 48, 8 March 1990.

143. FBIS-SOV-90-211, "Rocket Unit Threatens Walkout Over Food Shortage," 21 November 1990, p. 49; Tsarev, interview.

Chapter 14. The August Crisis

1. Translated in *Putsch*, 17. This is a complete collection of all the information issued by the Russian Information Agency (RIA), 19–21 August 1991.

2. Ibid.

3. The information in this scenario is documented in the remainder of this chapter. Dunlop, *The Rise of Russia*, 186–255, provides much the same scenario, and so does Knight, *Spies Without Cloaks*, 17–24, though the version presented here differs from these two sources on a few points where the author found more compelling alternative evidence. Remnick, *Lenin's Tomb*, 431–90, also offers an excellent mix of the context and details of the events of 18–21 August.

4. Dunlop, *The Rise of Russia;* Remnick, *Lenin's Tomb.*

5. *The August Coup,* 1: 1. This is a rough English translation of the investigation by the USSR procurator general, V. Stepankov, a copy of which I possess. It was informally obtained by a U.S. business organization that intended to use it in the production of a film about the events of the August crisis. It consists of six typescript volumes rather poorly translated but comprehensible if a reader knows Russian and therefore can recognize the Russian translator's probable reasons for poor choices of English terms and errors in grammar and syntax.

6. Ibid. 1: 2.

7. Ibid. A safe house is an apartment or house where intelligence operatives meet clandestinely with their agents. The KGB has scores of them throughout Moscow.

8. Ibid., 1: 3–4.

9. Ibid., 1: 4–5.

10. Ibid., 1: 74.

11. Ibid., 2: 256–57.

12. Ibid., 2: 260–61.

13. Ibid., 2: 262.

14. Ibid., 2: 266.

15. Ibid.

16. Ibid., 1: 132.

17. Ibid., 2: 286.

18. Ibid.

19. Ibid., 2: 291–93.

20. Ibid. 2: 299.

21. Ibid. 2: 292–94.

22. Ibid., 1: 17.

23. Ibid., 3: 448–53.

24. Ibid., 3: 453.

25. Ibid., 3: 454.

26. Ibid., 6: 843–54.

27. Ibid., 6: 852–55.

28. Ibid., 6: 854, 858.

29. Ibid., 4: 503–7.

30. Ibid.

31. Ibid., 4: 519–27.

32. Ibid., 4: 531–43.

33. Dunlop, *The Rise of Russia*, 239, suspects there was such a plan. He cites Karpukhin's interview in which he described a KGB-MVD operation planned for Monday evening, 19 August, to have been executed by his Alpha unit and MVD forces, together totaling about fifteen thousand troops. Karpukhin also mentioned a planning meeting on 19 August which General Lebed' attended and after which they went together to reconnoiter the White House. According to Lebed', he could not possibly have been there on the nineteenth because he was busy trying to deliver an airborne battalion to the White House to help in its security and defense, as Grachev had ordered him to do. Moreover, Lebed' recounts the meeting Karpukhin describes as occurring on 20 August, with the same senior figures present and also followed by his and Karpukhin's reconnoitering of the White House. Grachev also places the meeting on the twentieth. Both sources are consistent with the procurator's report. Possibly Dunlop has confused the dates.

34. Ibid., 240. The procurator report also describes the defection of the Tamanskaya unit to the White House.

35. *The August Coup*, 6: 866–67.

36. Ibid., 6: 861–64.

37. N. Burbyga, "My na storone Rossii," *Izvestiya*, 4 September 1991. Burbyga interviewed Grachev for this piece, giving the general a chance to explain his own role and to answer several other questions.

38. Lebed', *Za derzhavu obidno*, 401.

39. Ibid., 399–402.

40. Ibid., 399.

41. Ibid., 400–401.

42. Major General Vladimir Slipchenko and Major General Viktor Ryabchuk, interview, 20 September 1996. Both officers were in Moscow at the time, one at the General Staff Academy and one at the Frunze Academy, and they insist that the orders for bringing military units into Moscow on 19 August were informal and oral, directly from Yazov, and that the General Staff was effectively cut out. Colonel General Ivan Bizhan, deputy minister of defense in Ukraine, told me on 12 October 1996 that during the August crisis he was deputy head of the General Staff's Operations Directorate and that indeed his directorate, which would have handled the planning and drafting of orders, was not involved at all. Yazov and some of his deputies handled these matters informally in their own offices.

43. *The August Coup*, 4: 610–22.

44. Ibid.

45. Ibid., 6: 811, and elsewhere.

46. Ibid., 6: 929.

47. Ibid., 6: 930.

48. Valentin Stepankov and Yevgenii Lisov, *Kremlevskii zagovor* (Moscow: Ogonek, 1992), 82, quotes Achalov as saying that Yazov told him to call off the assault about an hour before it was to begin. Stepankov, it should be noted, reveals three strong biases. First, he refuses to consider Gorbachev as anything but innocent; second, he is determined to prove that Lukyanov was involved, though he was not a GKChP member; and third, he is convinced that the GKChP was really of one mind in favoring the assault.

49. Dunlop, *The Rise of Russia,* 239–40.

50. On the resistance of Chernavin, Maksimov, and Shaposhnikov, ibid., 247–48. Dunlop cites an interview of Korotkevich in *Literaturnaya gazeta,* 2 October 1991, in which Korotkevich reports impressions he gained from speaking to Admiral Chernavin on the first day of the crisis. Chernavin was opposed to the GKChP and indicated that Maksimov (commander of the rocket forces) and Shaposhnikov were as well.

51. Ibid. 248.

52. The collegium included the minister, all the deputy ministers, and a number of other officers. The concept of such collegia, sometimes called councils, dates back to the earliest days of the Red Army. It reviewed major issues and decisions, providing a forum for exchanging views among the top military leaders. Sometimes it dealt with trivia, other times it addressed the most critical issues.

53. The Soviet system of increasing the readiness for war of its forces had three levels, "constant combat readiness," "increased combat readiness," and "full combat readiness for war." Although they differed in many details, they roughly paralleled the U.S. military's three "defense conditions"—DEFCON 3, DEFCON 2, and DEFCON 1—the last being the highest level.

54. Shaposhnikov, *Vybor,* 20–22.

55. Ibid., 22.

56. Ibid., 22–23.

57. Ibid., 23–24.

58. Ibid., 25.

59. Ibid., 27.

60. Ibid.

61. Ibid., 28–29.

62. Ibid., 29–30.

63. Ibid., 30.

64. Ibid., 32–33.

65. Ibid., 34–35.

66. Ibid., 35–36.

67. Ibid., 38.

68. Ibid., 37–38.

69. Ibid., 38.

70. Ibid., 38–39.

71. Ibid., 39–40.

72. Ibid., 40.

73. Ibid.

74. Dunlop, *The Rise of Russia,* 248. Dunlop cites a statement by Stepankov in a press interview in Moscow.

75. Shaposhnikov, *Zybor,* 46.

76. Ibid., 47–49.

77. See Dunlop, *The Rise of Russia*, 238, for a direct quotation from Kordonskii to this effect.

78. FBIS-SOV-91-180, "Shaposhnikov Interview Recounts Coup Attempt," 17 September 1991, 28-30.

79. Yurii Skokov, quoted in Gorshkov and Zhuravlev, *Nesokrushimaya i legendarnaya*, 239, from documents of the postcrisis criminal investigation, said, "I have been acquainted with Grachev since February 1991, after Yeltsin directed me to find contacts with the army."

80. Lebed', *Za derzhavu obidno*, 380-81. Lebed' is quoting from the earliest Russian chronicle, *Povest' vremennykh let*, where Prince Vladimir rejects the Muslim religion because it disallows drinking alcoholic beverages. In an old Slavonic Russian, "Veselie Rusi est' piti." That is, "Merriment in Russia is drinking."

81. Burbyga, "My na storone Rossii."

82. Lebed', *Za derzhavu obidno*, 385.

83. Ibid., 389-91.

84. Ibid., 394-95,

85. Ibid., 396-97.

86. Ibid., 390.

87. Ibid.

88. Ibid., 398-99.

89. Ibid., 403.

90. Ibid.

91. Ibid., 403-4.

92. Burbyga, "My na storone Rossii."

93. Ibid.

94. Ibid.

95. Yeltsin, *Struggle for Russia*, 87.

96. See *The August Coup*, 6: 923-29 in particular.

97. Ibid., 6: 408.

98. Yeltsin, *Struggle for Russia*, 80. This story circulated widely in Moscow, probably as a result of its inclusion in Stepankov and Lisov, *Kremlevskii zagovor*, 86.

99. *The August Coup*, 1: 17.

100. I spent an hour with Kobets and five other Americans in his General Staff office three months after the crisis, in November 1991. He was a bear of a man, considerably overweight but stout and broad, with a square, hard face, reddish, probably from abundant alcohol consumption, very threatening in demeanor. But as he spoke, his mood rapidly alternated between aggressiveness and extreme politeness; he listened to questions and responded astutely as he measured his audience's reaction. He engendered my respect but also my skepticism about his veracity. In this regard, he was typical of Soviet senior officers, able to pipe any tune and to change tunes instantly without the slightest trace of embarrassment.

101. General Boris Gromov denied that a coup was possible in March; see *RFE/RL Daily Report* no. 61, 27 March 1990. Marshal Viktor Kulikov denied rumors of a coup in May; see *RFE/RL Daily Report* no. 104, 31 May 1990. Gromov denied them again in June; see *RFE/RL Daily Report* no. 106, 4 June 1990. In September, as airborne units moved into the vicinity of Moscow, rumors were rampant and the parliament was in an uproar over them; see FBIS-SOV-90-187, "More Details of Troop Movements Near Moscow," 26 September 1990, p. 67, and FBIS-SOV-90-188, "Army Issue Disrupts Session" and "Pravda Describes Coup Rumors," 27 September 1990, p. 40; "Yazov Explains Troop Movements

to Supreme Soviet," ibid., 39-40, and "Vasiliev Chairs Debate Over Coup Speculations," ibid., 67-68.

102. Several journalists, scholars, and government analysts in Washington expressed this belief to me at the time.

103. Colton and Gustafson, *Soldiers and the Soviet State*, is based on Colton's "control model" of party-military relations in the Soviet Union, which asserts this assumption. Most of the essays, written in 1989, were trying to find an explanation for why a crisis in party-military relations, which Colton's thesis certainly predicted, had not already occurred or would not soon occur.

104. Ibid., especially Gustafson's concluding chapter.

105. Ivashov, interview, 5 July 1995.

106. Yeltsin appointed him to the RSFSR state committee on defense and security matters. *RFE/RL Daily Report* no. 23, 1 February 1991. He also made Colonel General Dmitrii Volkogonov his adviser at the same time.

107. Yurii Skokov, quoted in Gorshkov and Zhuravlev, *Nesokrushimaya i legendarnaya*, 239.

108. Dunlop, *The Rise of Russia*, 249. Dunlop quotes Yeltsin from USSR Central Television, 29 August 1991.

109. Lebed, *Za derzhavu obidno*, 380. A major, the political officer of a battalion, listening to Yeltsin's demand that Russia have its own army and realizing that the RSFSR was not ethnically homogeneous, spoke up, asking what would he do if the battalion commander was Ukrainian, the deputy commander a Belorussian, he—the political officer—a Russian, and the deputy for armaments a German. Yeltsin waved off the question, saying, "We will look into it," and then talked about providing the division with five hundred new family apartments.

110. Boris Pugachev, a professor who was appointed to a small group to review the Central Committee documents immediately after the August crisis for evidence of involvement with the GKChP, told a small seminar at Yale University in December 1991 of the large number of phone calls Yeltsin had made to high-ranking military officers during 19-21 August.

111. Lebed', *Za derzhavu obidno*, 390.

112. Niyazov recounted this episode to me and to others in Ashgabat, Turkmenistan, on 27 May 1996.

113. See Matlock, *Autopsy on an Empire*, 513-15, for details on Gorbachev's close call during the plenum. His account does not refute Niyazov's tale, but it shows that there was more to it than a quick Politburo meeting to remove the proposal for his dismissal from the agenda the next day.

114. Niyazov, oral account.

115. See for example, Chernyaev, *Shest' let s Gorbachevym*, 428-29, for a memo signed by Chernyaev and Shakhnazarov.

116. Ibid., 408-11.

117. Ibid., 477-88, gives his eyewitness account of events at Foros.

118. Shakhnazarov, *Tsena svobody*, 16.

119. Knight, *Spies Without Cloaks*, 19-28. Knight gives considerable credence to the view that Gorbachev was not the innocent victim of the GPChK.

120. Dunlop, *The Rise of Russia*, 186-255.

121. Shakhnazarov, *Tsena svobody*, 94.

122. Yeltsin, *Struggle for Russia*, 16–39.

123. "Slovo narodu," *Sovetskaya Rossiya*, 23 July 1991. Twelve people signed this appeal. Besides Starodubtsev and Tizyakov, General Varennikov, commander of the ground forces, was later tried for his complicity. General Gromov, deputy minister of interior, escaped trial but was involved in the planning to assault the White House. Aleksandr Plekhanov, a journalist, was a poison-pen reactionary. Valentin Rasputin was a populist-nationalist writer, and Gennadii Zyuganov led the Communist Party of the Russian Federation after the collapse of the Soviet Union.

124. Matlock, *Autopsy on an Empire*, 541–46. Matlock received his information from Gavril Popov, the mayor of Moscow, and was instructed to tell Gorbachev that the U.S. government had information, more than rumor but less than hard evidence, of a plot to remove him from office. Gorbachev laughed it off. President Bush also telephoned to warn him, giving him the source, Popov. When Popov later read Matlock's account, he claimed that he meant for Matlock to warn Yeltsin, who was in the United States at the time, not Gorbachev, whom he could have easily reached directly in Moscow.

125. Yeltsin, *Struggle for Russia*, 16.

126. Chernyaev, *Shest' let s Gorbachevym*, 379–429. Chernyaev describes Gorbachev's speeches, while he basked in the praise he was receiving during foreign trips in fall 1990 and spring 1991, as increasingly filled with circular and unrealistic logic about his situation at home. The narcotic of lionization by foreign leaders and journalists was warping his thinking in an increasingly visible way.

127. Shakhnazarov, *Tsena svobody*, 50.

128. Quoted by Pipes, *Russian Revolution*, 457. Pipes convincingly argues that Kornilov did not attempt a military putsch but rather Kerensky misled him, provoking him to understandable anger and indignation, and then unleashed the radical political forces to destroy him.

Chapter 15. Illusions of Another Chance

1. Dunlop, *The Rise of Russia*, 260–71.

2. Yeltsin, *The Struggle for Russia*, 109.

3. Ann Sheehy, "The RSFSR and a Future Union," *Report on the USSR* 3 (11 October 1991): 3–4.

4. Quoted by Dunlop, *The Rise of Russia*, 269.

5. Yeltsin, *The Struggle for Russia*, 110.

6. Ibid., 111.

7. Shaposhnikov, *Vybor*, 126–27.

8. Dunlop, *The Rise of Russia*, 271–73.

9. Shaposhnikov, *Vybor*, 138–39.

10. Yeltsin, *The Struggle for Russia*, 106.

11. Ibid., 109.

12. Dunlop, *The Rise of Russia*, 256.

13. Ibid., 256–84. Dunlop's account of both developments provides both extensive details and several fascinating interpretations of their dynamics and significance.

14. Ibid., 271–74.

15. Ibid., 274–75.

16. Shaposhnikov, *Vybor*, 137–38.

17. Ibid., 115–16.

18. Shaposhnikov does not give a date for this military collegium meeting, but Vladimir Lopatin places it on 17 September 1991. See FBIS-SOV-015, "Lopatin Views Status of Army Reform," 23 January 1992, p. 50.

19. Shaposhnikov, *Vybor*, 137.

20. FBIS-SOV-91-239, "Significant Proportion for Yeltsin," 12 December 1991, p. 25.

21. Sergei Rogor et al., *Commonwealth Defense Arrangements and International Security*, joint paper by the Institute of USA and Canada (Moscow) and the Center for Naval Analysis (Alexandria, Va.), June 1992, pp. 3–4.

22. Dunlop, *The Rise of Russia*, 272, 275.

23. Yeltsin, *The Struggle for Russia*, 113–14.

24. Ibid., 115.

25. Ibid., 106.

26. Ibid.

27. Ibid., 107.

28. Ibid.

29. Ibid., 108.

30. Shaposhnikov, *Vybor*, 60–61.

31. Ibid., 62.

32. Ibid., 62–63.

33. Ibid.

34. Ibid.,64.

35. FBIS-SOV-91-173, "General Says Half of Army Backed Coup," 6 September 1995, pp. 59–60.

36. Shaposhnikov, *Vybor*, 67.

37. Ibid., 84.

38. Ibid., 87.

39. Ibid., 89.

40. FBIS-SOV-92-015, "Lopatin Views Status of Army Reform," 23 January 1992, p. 51.

41. Ibid. and FBIS-SOV-91-179, "Gorbachev Dismisses Defense Officials," 16 September 1991, p. 46.

42. Shaposhnikov, *Vybor*, 65.

43. Ibid., 66–72.

44. Ibid., 76–78.

45. Ibid., 78–79.

46. Ibid., 74.

47. Ibid., 75.

48. Ibid., 79.

49. Ibid., 79–82.

50. Ibid., 82.

51. Ibid., 86.

52. Ibid., 97–98.

53. Ibid., 91–93.

54. Yevgenii I. Shaposhnikov, interview, June 1995. Shaposhnikov said his experiences with the VPK were extremely frustrating. He could not prevail on one design bureau to accept the pilot ejection seat from another design bureau. Rather it designed a new one from scratch at huge cost and with poorer performance standards.

55. Shaposhnikov, *Vybor*, 92.

56. Ibid., 90–91, for the text of the memorandum.

57. Ibid., 109–12, for the text of the memorandum.

58. Ibid., 113.

59. Ibid., 116.

60. Ibid., 118.

61. Ibid., 103–4.

62. Starovoitova told me this during her stay at Brown University in 1995.

63. Shaposhnikov, *Vybor*, 108.

64. Major General Vladimir Slipchenko and Major General Viktor Ryabchuk, interview, 20 September 1996.

65. FBIS-SOV-92-015, "Lopatin Views Status of Army Reform," 23 January 1992, pp. 50–51. This is an interview Lopatin gave to *Nezavisimaya gazeta* on 7 January, analyzing why no serious reform progress had occurred over the past one and half years.

66. Major General Viktor Ryabchuk, interview, 20 September 1996. Ryabchuk said that Volkogonov was constantly on the telephone with Gaidar and other civilian politicians during the commission's session, and he offered a number of instances of Volkogonov's general ignorance of how the MoD worked. Moreover, Ryabchuk said, Volkogonov did not want to be bothered with learning enough to make sense of the reform issues.

67. Shaposhnikov, *Vybor*, 134.

68. Ibid., 134–35.

69. Ibid., 140–41.

70. Ibid., 134–35.

71. Ibid.

72. Ibid., 135–36.

73. Ibid.

74. Ibid.

75. Ibid., 140.

76. Ibid.

77. Yeltsin, *The Struggle for Russia*, 122.

78. Shakhnazarov, *Tsena svobody*, 307, says that offers from military officers poured in during the last week of 1991 when it was far too late.

Chapter 16. The Illusion of the CIS Armed Forces

1. Shaposhnikov, *Vybor*, 246–48.

2. Odom and Dujarric, *Commonwealth or Empire?* 114–25, elaborates the struggle between the Russian foreign and defense ministries over the primary direction of foreign policy. The foreign minister, Andrei Kozyrev, favored Russia's integration with the West; General Grachev, backed by Vice President Aleksandr Rutskoi, gave first priority to the restoration of Russian hegemony over the former Soviet Union with the eventual goal of reintegration of the former Soviet republics into one state.

3. *Krasnaya Zvezda*, 31 December 1991.

4. Shaposhnikov, *Vybor*, 135. He insisted on a five-year transition period at the summit in Alma-Ata, 21 December 1991, and he basically adhered to it thereafter.

5. Ibid., 148.

6. Ibid., 127.

7. Ibid., 105. Shaposhnikov actually began convening meetings of the equivalents of the ministers of defense of the republics on 10 September 1991 as a forum for trying to work

out interrepublican military issues. The forum remained active through the fall and became the Council of Defense Ministers of the CIS after 31 December 1991.

8. Ibid., 144.

9. Ibid., 163. In his speech to the Congress of People's Deputies, April 1992, Shaposhnikov explained how military commercial ventures had attracted all kinds of outside circles to begin selling off equipment and property on a wide scale, far beyond what was envisioned.

10. FBIS-SOV-91-251, "Further Reportage on Minsk Commonwealth Summit," 30 December 1991, pp. 15–20. See Shaposhnikov, *Vybor*, 144–45, for his version of the dispute.

11. Colonel General Ivan Bizhan, deputy minister of defense in Ukraine, related this episode to me and others on 12 October 1996. It was proposed to Kravchuk to relieve the commander of the Black Sea Fleet at the same time, and a group was ready to board a plane for Sevastopol to do that, but Kravchuk refused to allow it. According to Bizhan, the Ukrainian military and political leaders believed that these rapid moves in early January were critical for Ukraine's ability to hold on to its independence. Had any of the three military district commanders resisted relief, they were to be arrested.

12. FBIS-SOV-92-032, "Minsk Summit Agreements," 18 February 1992, pp. 18–27.

13. JPRS-UMA-92-008, "Agreement on a Single Budget," 4 March 1992, pp. 15–16.

14. FBIS-SOV-92-055, "Agreements Signed," 20 March 1992, p. 17.

15. Ibid., 17–18.

16. Odom and Dujarric, *Commonwealth or Empire?* 24.

17. "Military and Security Notes," *RFE/RL Research Report* 1, no. 22 (29 May 1992): 55–56. This piece summarizes the Tashkent summit results.

18. See Shaposhnikov, *Vybor*, 158–66, for the full text of the address.

19. FBIS-SOV-92-068, "Yeltsin Reports on Economic Reform to Sixth Congress of People's Deputies," 8 April 1992, p. 27.

20. Shaposhnikov, *Vybor*, 154–55.

21. Ibid., 166–67.

22. Ibid., 167–68.

23. The Warsaw Pact headquarters are several kilometers north of the center of Moscow on Prospekt Mira, in a large building complex set back in a grove of trees. When the author visited the site in June 1995, it possessed a tomb-like quiet highly symbolic of the lack of vitality in the CIS military structure. The psychological impact of the move there for Shaposhnikov and his staff must have been traumatic. The pomposity of the place notwithstanding, its sense of remoteness from the center of activity in downtown Moscow is at once conspicuous.

Conclusion

1. Pipes, *Russian Revolution*, 316.

2. Dominic Lieven, *Nicholas II* (New York: St. Martin's, 1993), 2, sums up the Muscovite political system in the following illuminating way: "Moscow politics had something of the Al Capone air. To outwit rival princely gangs in northeastern Russia, not to mention the Tatars, it was vital for Moscow's rulers to stick together and for the prince's absolute authority to be recognized. Life was unpleasant for any lieutenant who aroused the boss's ire. On the other hand the princely boss could not rule without his lieutenants. The rewards of unity and ruthlessness were enormous. In six centuries the tiny principality of Moscow expanded to cover one-sixth of the world's land surface. . . . On the brilliantly successful

example of gangster politics the Orthodox Church put a religious and patriotic stamp of approval and nineteenth century nationalist historians scattered phrases about Russia's unity, power and world-historical destiny."

3. Blum, *Lord and Peasant,* provides evidence of the tax cadastres of Muscovy in the fifteenth and sixteenth centuries that indicate the devastating degree of resource extraction accomplished by the Moscow princes.

4. Quoted in Florinsky, *Russia,* 1: 357.

5. Ibid., 1: 390–93.

6. Geyer, *Russian Imperialism,* 186–219, examines Count Witte's effort to expedite Russian industrialization, its connection to imperial expansion, and its overall failure. Imperial Russia, to be sure, was experiencing fairly rapid economic growth during its last two decades, but among Witte's economic policies, his support for territorial expansion contributed little or nothing to it.

7. Ibid., 205.

8. See Menning, *Bayonets Before Bullets,* especially 30–33, 104–8, 217–21, 231–34. This excellent monograph is the best available on the relatively neglected subject of the Russian military in the century before the Russian Revolution.

9. Florinsky, *Russia: An Interpretation,* 2: 754. Florinsky uses *nationality* instead of *patriotism.* The Russian word, *narodnost',* literally means "peopleness" or populism, and it certainly was not intended to mean nationalism. As Florinsky makes clear in his text, Uvarov was trying to capture Nicholas I's words, "the entire life of a man must be regarded merely as service, for everyone has to serve." *Narodnost'* might therefore be translated in this case as "service," though patriotism certainly implies service. "Populism" is a more accurate translation, but the revolutionaries appropriated *narodnost'* later in the century, not the association Uvarov had in mind.

10. See Thaden, *Conservative Nationalism,* for a study of the right wing of the Russian intelligentsia.

11. See Keep, *Rise of Social Democracy,* for a study of the left wing of the Russian intelligentsia, primarily its Marxist factions.

12. See Szporluk, *Communism and Nationalism,* 229–30, on this point specifically, the entire book for the larger issue of nationalism and Marxism.

13. Peter Chaadaev, "First Philosophical Letter," in Marc Raeff, *Russian Intellectual History: An Anthology* (New York: Harcourt, Brace, and World, 1966), 160.

Bibliography

A Note on Sources

Two types of sources—interviews and memoirs of senior Soviet military and party officials—provided important evidence for this study. Some of the interviews were actually conversations and discussions, and they are so indicated in the notes. The choice of interviewees was somewhat arbitrary, based on their willingness to be interviewed, their probable knowledge of relevant issues and events, and their availability. What they were willing to divulge varied, and in some cases, important questions simply had to be dropped and lines of investigation abandoned. With three or four exceptions the interview results at the time seemed of little value, but in the course of writing the study, I found them more fruitful, and in a few cases highly illuminating.

Memoirs, especially by Anatolii Chernyaev, Georgii Shakhnazarov, Marshal Yevgenii Shaposhnikov, and Lieutenant General Aleksandr Lebed', proved extremely useful in providing not only a large amount of detail but also a strong sense of seeing the Soviet policy-making process from the inside. Memoirists, to be sure, tend to have stronger personal biases and agendas than most authors. Where these factors appeared to make factual accuracy questionable even though the content was important, I have tried to make that clear. That an individual involved in the events wrote an account and asserted it to be the truth is revealing in itself. I do not believe that any of the study's major conclusions rest on such "truths" alone, and one major conclusion—that deception and mistrust were rife among both military and political leaders—is based on skepticism about such testimonial evidence.

The bulk of the evidence, of course, came from published materials. The deluge of newspaper and journal articles on military affairs during Gorbachev's rule, caused by the relaxation of censorship under the glasnost policy, presents a serious problem of volume. To sort through these sources, I have relied heavily, but not exclusively, on the *Foreign Broadcast Information Service* (FBIS), as well as the Radio Liberty reporting. The *RFE/RL Daily Reports* and the weekly *Report on the USSR* have been equally helpful in tracking and documenting the record of public events. In many cases, however, I used the original Russian version of journal articles and the more consequential newspaper articles. Many of the very important ones were not translated, and others seemed too critical in their content to rely on translations.

The wealth of secondary literature in both English and Russian on Soviet military affairs, especially for 1985 and earlier, is vast and varied in quality and reliability. The books and articles included in the bibliography that follows are a small sampling, selected to provide a wide range of coverage, both in time and subject matter. Most of them deal only with the pre-1985 period. For the 1985–91 period, the literature in English is understandably still limited, often overtaken by events. Books, journal articles, and newspaper pieces in Russian for this short period are voluminous, but also often overtaken by events. Thus I have included only a sampling of articles and books that cover the central issues at that time.

Finally, in selecting this bibliography I have tried to provide a range of literature that will support graduate-level courses devoted to the study of Soviet military and foreign policy, including examples of strongly opposed interpretations of Soviet military policy and politics that held currency in the West during the Cold War.

English-Language Sources

Alexander, Arthur J. "Decisionmaking in Soviet Weapons Procurement." *Adelphi Papers* no. 147/8. International Institute for Strategic Studies, 1978–79.

Alexiev, Alexander. *Inside the Soviet Army in Afghanistan.* Santa Monica, Calif.: RAND Corporation, 1988.

Alexiev, Alexander, and A. Ross Johnson. *East European Military Reliability: An Emigre-Based Assessment.* Santa Monica, Calif.: RAND Corporation, 1986.

Allison, Roy, ed. *Radical Reform in Soviet Defence Policy.* New York: St. Martin's, 1992.

Almquist, Peter. *Red Forge: Soviet Military Industry Since 1965.* New York: Columbia University Press, 1990.

Amann, Ronald, and Julian Cooper, eds. *Industrial Innovation in the Soviet Union.* New Haven: Yale University Press, 1982.

Amstutz, J. Bruce. *Afghanistan: The First Five Years of Soviet Occupation.* Washington, D.C.: National Defense University Press, 1986.

Arbatov, Alexei G. "How Much Defense Is Sufficient?" *International Affairs* 4 (1989): 31–44.

———. *Lethal Frontiers: A Soviet View of Nuclear Strategy, Weapons, and Negotiations.* New York: Praeger, 1988.

Arnett, Robert, and Mary C. Fitzgerald. "Restructuring the Armed Forces: The Current Soviet Debate." *The Journal of Soviet Military Studies* 3 (June 1990): 193–220.

———. "A Volunteer Red Army?" *Orbis* 34, no. 2 (1990): 398–402.

Aslund, Anders. *Gorbachev's Struggle for Economic Reform.* Updated and rev. ed. Ithaca, N.Y.: Cornell University Press, 1991.

Aspaturian, Vernon V. "Continuity and Change in Soviet Party-Military Relations." In Simon and Trond Gilberg, *Security Implications of Nationalism in Eastern Europe,* 217–67. Boulder, Colo.: Westview, 1985.

———. "The Soviet Military-Industrial Complex: Does It Exist?" *Journal of International Affairs* 26, no. 1 (1972): 1–29.

Ball, Nicole, and Milton Leitenberg, eds. *The Structure of the Defense Industry.* New York: St. Martin's, 1983.

Barghoorn, Frederick C., and Thomas F. Remington. *Politics in the USSR.* 3d ed. Boston: Little, Brown, 1986.

Barylski, Robert V. "The Soviet Military Before and After the August Coup: Departyization and Decentralization." *Armed Forces and Society* 19, no. 1 (1992): 27–45.

Bayer, Philip A. *The Evolution of the Soviet General Staff, 1917–1941.* New York: Garland, 1987.

Bayev, Pavel, Vitalii Zhurkin, Sergei Karagonov, and Viktor Shein. *Tactical Nuclear Weapons in Europe: The Problems of Reductions and Elimination.* Moscow: Novosti Press Agency, 1990.

Becker, Abraham. *The Burden of Soviet Defense: A Political-Economic Essay*. Santa Monica, Calif.: RAND, 1981.

Bellamy, Chris. *Red God and War: Soviet Artillery and Rocket Forces*. London: Brassey's Defence, 1986.

Bergson, Abram. *The Economics of Soviet Planning*. New Haven: Yale University Press, 1964.

———. "On the Measurement of Soviet Real Defense Outlays." In *Marxism, Central Planning, and the Soviet Economy: Economic Essays in Honor of Alexander Erlich*, ed. Padma Desai, 65–92. Cambridge: MIT Press, 1983.

Berman, Robert P. *Soviet Air Power in Transition*. Washington, D.C.: Brookings Institution, 1978.

Bialer, Seweryn, ed. *Stalin and His Generals: Soviet Military Memoirs of World War II*. New York: Pegasus, 1969.

Birman, Igor. "The Economic Situation in the USSR." *Russia* no. 2 (1981): 13–28.

———. *Secret Incomes of the Soviet State Budget*. Boston: Nijhoff, 1981.

Blacker, Coit D. *Hostage to Revolution: Gorbachev and Soviet Security Policy, 1985–1991*. New York: Council on Foreign Relations Press, 1993.

Blank, Stephen J., and Jacob W. Kipp, eds. *The Soviet Military and the Future*. Westport, Conn.: Greenwood, 1992.

Blum, Jerome. *Lord and Peasant in Russia*. Princeton, N.J.: Princeton University Press, 1961.

Bluth, Christopher. "The Evolution of Soviet Military Doctrine." *Survival* 30 (1988): 149–62.

Boldin, Valery. *Ten Years That Shook the World: The Gorbachev Era as Witnessed by His Chief of Staff*. Trans. Evelyn Rossite. New York: Basic, 1994.

Borkenau, Franz. *World Communism*. Ann Arbor: University of Michigan Press, 1962.

Boyd, Alexander. *The Soviet Airforce Since 1918*. New York: Stein and Day, 1977.

Brodie, Bernard. *Strategy in the Missile Age*. Princeton, N.J.: Princeton University Press, 1959.

Brzezinski, Zbigniew K. *The Soviet Bloc: Unity and Conflict*. Rev. and enlarged ed. Cambridge: Harvard University Press, 1967.

———, ed. *Political Controls in the Soviet Army*. New York: Research Program on the USSR, 1954.

Bungs, Dzintra. "Black Berets Storm Latvian Interior Ministry." *Report on the USSR* 3, no. 5 (1 February 1991): 19.

Burin, Frederic S. "The Communist Doctrine of the Inevitability of War." *American Political Science Review* 58, no. 2 (1964): 334–58.

Carr, E. H., and R. W. Davies. *Foundations of a Planned Economy*. New York: Macmillan, 1972.

Cassen, Robert, ed. *Soviet Interests in the Third World*. London: Sage, 1985.

Checinski, Michael. *The Military Industrial Complex in the USSR: Its Influence on R&D and Industrial Planning and on International Trade*. SWP-A22302, Fo. P1. III. 20–81. Ebenhausen, Germany: Stiftung für Wissenschaft und Politik, 1981.

———. "The Soviet War-Economic Doctrine in the Years of Technological Challenge (1946–1983): An Overview." *Crossroads* no. 12 (1984): 23–51.

Chiesa, Giulietto. "The 28th Congress of the CPSU." *Problems of Communism* 39 (July–August, 1990): 27.

Clark, Alan. *Barbarossa: The German Conflict, 1941–45*. New York: Quill, 1965.

Clark, Susan L., ed. *Soviet Military Power in a Changing World*. Boulder, Colo.: Westview, 1991.

Clarke, Douglas L. "Soviet Troop Withdrawals from Eastern Europe." *Report on Eastern Europe* 1 (30 March 1990): 43–44.

———. "Warsaw Pact: The Transformation Begins." *Report on Eastern Europe* 1 (22 June 1990): 34–37.

Clausewitz, Carl von. *On War.* Trans. and ed. Michael Howard and Peter Peret. Princeton, N.J.: Princeton University Press, 1976.

———. *On War.* Ed. Anatol Rapaport. Middlesex, England: Penguin, 1968.

Cohn, Stanley H. "The Economic Burden of Soviet Defense Outlays." In *Economic Performance and the Military Burden in the Soviet Union,* 33–37. Washington, D.C.: U.S. Government Printing Office, 1970.

Colton, Timothy J. *Commissars, Commanders, and Civilian Authority: The Structure of Soviet Military Politics.* Cambridge: Harvard University Press, 1979.

Colton, Timothy J., and Thane Gustafson, eds. *Soldiers and the Soviet State: Civil-Military Relations from Brezhnev to Gorbachev.* Princeton, N.J.: Princeton University Press, 1990.

Cooper, Julian. *The Soviet Defence Industry: Conversion and Economic Reform.* New York: RIIA/Council on Foreign Relations Press, 1991.

Cross, Jack L. "The Soviet Higher Educational System." *College Station Papers* no. 4. Texas A&M University, 1984.

Crowe, Suzanne. "Soviet Conscripts Fall Victim to Ethnic Violence." *Report on the USSR* 1 (October 1989): 8–9.

Daalder, Ivo. *The CFE Treaty: An Overview and an Assessment.* Washington, D.C.: Johns Hopkins Foreign Policy Institute, 1991.

Danilovich, A. A. "On New Military Doctrine of the CIS and Russia." *Journal of Slavic Military Studies* 5, no. 4 (1992): 517–38.

Daugherty, Leo J. "The Bear and the Scimitar: Soviet Central Asians and the War in Afghanistan." *Journal of Slavic Military Studies* 8 (March 1995): 73–96.

Dinerstein, Herbert S. *War and the Soviet Union.* New York: Praeger, 1962.

Dobb, Maurice. *Soviet Economic Development Since 1917.* New York: International Publishers, 1948. Rev. ed. 1966.

Dobrynin, Anatoly. *In Confidence: Moscow's Ambassador to America's Six Cold War Presidents, 1962–1986.* New York: Random House, 1995.

Documents and Materials: 28th Party Congress of the Communist Party of the Soviet Union. Moscow: Novosti, 1990.

Douglass, Joseph D., Jr., and Amoretta Hoeber. *Soviet Strategy for Nuclear War.* Stanford, Calif.: Hoover Institution Press, 1979.

Dunlop, John B. *The Rise of Russia and the Fall of the Soviet Empire.* Princeton, N.J.: Princeton University Press, 1993.

Dunn, Walter S., Jr. *Hitler's Nemesis: The Red Army, 1935–1945.* Westport, Conn.: Praeger, 1994.

Dyker, David A. *Restructuring the Soviet Economy.* London: Routledge, 1992.

Ellison, Herbert J., ed. *Soviet Policy Toward Western Europe.* Seattle: University of Washington Press, 1983.

Erickson, John. *The Military Technical Revolution.* New York: Praeger, 1966.

———. "The Origins of the Red Army." In *Revolutionary Russia,* ed. Richard Pipes, 224–58. Cambridge: Harvard University Press, 1968.

———. *The Road to Stalingrad: Stalin's War with Germany,* vol. 1. New York: Harper and Row, 1975.

———. *The Soviet High Command: A Military-Political History, 1918–1941.* London: Macmillan, 1962.

———. "Soviet Military Manpower Policy." *Armed Forces and Society* 1, no. 1 (1974): 29–48.

Erickson, John, Lynn Hansen, and William Schneider. *Soviet Ground Forces: An Operational Assessment.* Boulder, Colo.: Westview, 1986.

Erlich, Alexander. *The Soviet Industrialization Debate, 1924–1928.* Cambridge: Harvard University Press, 1960.

Evangelista, M. A. "Stalin's Postwar Army Reappraised." *International Security* 7, no. 3 (1982–83): 110–39.

Fare, Diane. "After Afghanistan: The Decline of Soviet Military Prestige." *Washington Quarterly* 13, no. 2 (1990): 5–16.

Fedotoff White, Dmitri. *The Growth of the Red Army.* Princeton, N.J.: Princeton University Press, 1944.

———. "Soviet Philosophy of War." *Political Science Quarterly* 51 (1936): 321–53.

Feshbach, Murray, and Alfred Friendly Jr. *Ecocide in the USSR.* New York: Basic, 1992.

FitzGerald, Mary C. "Advanced Conventional Munitions and Moscow's Defensive Force Posture." *Defence Analysis* 6, no. 2 (1990): 167–91.

———. *Changing Soviet Doctrine on Nuclear War.* Dalhousie, New Brunswick: Dalhousie University Centre for Foreign Policy Studies, 1988.

———. "Marshal Ogarkov on the Modern Theater Operation." *Naval War College Review* 30, no. 1 (1986): 6–25.

———. *Soviet Views on SDI.* Pittsburgh: University of Pittsburgh, Carl Beck Papers no. 601, 1987.

Florinsky, Michael T. *Russia: An Interpretation.* 2 vols. New York: Macmillan, 1960.

Foye, Stephen. "Gorbachev Denies Responsibility for Crackdown." *Report on the USSR* 3, no. 4 (25 January 1991): 1–3.

———. "Military Debates of the 1920s and Contemporary Defense Policies." *Report on the USSR* 2 (6 April 1990): 9–12.

———. "The Radicalization of a Defense Establishment Theorist: Vladmir Serebryannikov, 1985–90." *Report on the USSR* 2 (22 June 1990): 2–6.

———. "Radical Military Reform and 'The Young Turks.'" *Report on the USSR* 2 (13 April 1990): 8–10.

———. "Rumblings in the Soviet Armed Forces." *Report on the USSR* 2 (16 March 1990): 2–3.

———. "Soviet Armed Forces Face Housing Crisis." *Report on the USSR* 1 (15 March 1990): 5.

Frank, Willard C., Jr., and Philip S. Gillette, eds. *Soviet Military Doctrine from Lenin to Gorbachev, 1915–1991.* Westport, Conn.: Greenwood, 1992.

Freedman, Lawrence. *The Evolution of Nuclear Strategy.* New York: St. Martin's, 1981.

Fukuyama, Francis. *Moscow's Post-Brezhnev Reassessment of the Third World.* Santa Monica, Calif.: RAND Corporation, 1986.

Fuller, Elizabeth. "Georgia's National Guard." *Report on the USSR* 3 (15 February 1991): 18–19.

———. "Georgians Win Concessions on Military Service." *Report on the USSR* 1 (27 July 1989): 4–5.

———. "Gorbachev's Dilemma in Azerbaijan." *Report on the USSR* 2, no. 5 (2 February 1990): 14.

———. "Official and Unofficial Investigations into Tbilisi Massacre Yield Contradictory Results." *Report on the USSR* 1 (3 November 1989): 26–31.

———. "Paramilitary Formations in Armenia." *Report on the USSR* 2 (3 August 1990): 20–23.

———. "A Preliminary Chronology of Recent Events in Armenia and Azerbaijan." *Radio Liberty* 101/88 (15 March 1988).

———. "Will Azerbaijan Be the Next 'Domino'?" *Report on the USSR* 2, no. 2 (12 January 1990): 17–18.

Fuller, Elizabeth, and Mark Deich. "Interview with Gary Kasparov." *Report on the USSR* 2, no. 5 (2 February 1990): 18–22.

Fuller, Elizabeth, and Goulnara Ouratadze. "Georgian Leadership Changes in Aftermath of Demonstrators' Deaths." *Report on the USSR* 1 (21 April 1989): 28–31.

Gabriel, Richard A. *The New Red Legions.* Westport, Conn.: Greenwood, 1980.

Gallagher, Matthew P. "Military Manpower: A Case Study." *Problems of Communism* 13, no. 3 (1964): 12–20.

———. *The Soviet History of World War II.* New York: Praeger, 1962.

Gallagher, Matthew P., and Karl F. Spielmann Jr. *Soviet Decision-Making for Defense.* New York: Praeger, 1972.

Gareev, Makhmut A. "On Military Doctrine and Military Reform in Russia." *Journal of Slavic Military Studies* 5, no. 4 (1992): 539–51.

Garthoff, Raymond L. *Detente and Confrontation: American-Soviet Relations from Nixon to Reagan.* Washington, D.C.: Brookings Institution, 1985.

———. *Deterrence and the Revolution in Soviet Military Doctrine.* Washington, D.C.: Brookings Institution, 1990.

———. *The Great Transition: American-Soviet Relations and the End of the Cold War.* Washington, D.C.: Brookings Institution, 1994.

———. *Soviet Military Doctrine.* Glencoe, Ill.: Free Press, 1953.

———. *Soviet Military Policy.* New York: Praeger, 1966.

———. *Soviet Strategy in the Nuclear Age.* New York: Praeger, 1958.

Gat, Azar. *The Development of Military Thought: The Nineteenth Century.* Oxford: Clarendon, 1992.

Gatzke, Hans W. "Russo-German Military Collaboration During the Weimar Republic." *American Historical Review* 63, no. 3 (1958): 565–97.

Geyer, Dietrich. *Russian Imperialism: The Interaction of Domestic and Foreign Policy, 1860–1914.* New Haven: Yale University Press, 1987.

Girnius, Saulius. "Lithuania's National Salvation Committee." *Report on the USSR* 3, no. 4 (25 January 1991): 6–7.

———. "Lithuania's Struggle with the USSR." *Report on the USSR* 3, no. 5 (1 February 1991): 1–3.

Glantz, David M. *From the Don to the Dnepr: Soviet Offensive Operations, December 1942–August 1943.* London: Frank Cass, 1991.

———. *A History of Soviet Airborne Forces.* London: Frank Cass, 1994.

———. *The Initial Period of War on the Eastern Front: 22 June–August 1941.* London: Frank Cass, 1993.

———. *The Military Strategy of the Soviet Union.* London: Frank Cass, 1993.

———. *The Soviet Conduct of Tactical Maneuver: Spearhead of the Offensive.* London: Frank Cass, 1991.

———. *Soviet Military Deception in the Second World War*. London: Frank Cass, 1989.

———. *Soviet Military Intelligence in War*. London: Frank Cass, 1990.

———. *Soviet Military Operational Art*. London: Frank Cass, 1991.

Glantz, David M., and Jonathan M. House. *When the Titans Clashed: How the Red Army Stopped Hitler*. Lawrence: University Press of Kansas, 1987.

Glantz, Mary E. "The Origins and Development of Soviet and Russian Military Doctrine." *Journal of Slavic Military Studies* 7, no. 3 (1994): 443–80.

Golan, Galia. *The Soviet Union and National Liberation Movements in the Third World*. Boston: Unwin Hyman, 1988.

Goldhammer, Herbert. *The Soviet Soldier: Soviet Military Management at the Troop Level*. New York: Crane, Russak, 1975.

Gorbachev, Mikhail S. *Perestroika: New Thinking of Our Country and the World*. New York: Harper and Row, 1987.

———. *Selected Speeches and Articles*. Moscow: Progress, 1985.

Gormley, Dennis M. "A New Dimension to Soviet Theater Strategy." *Orbis* 29, no. 4 (1985): 537–69.

Goure, Leon. *Civil Defense in the Soviet Union*. Berkeley: University of California Press, 1962.

———. *The Military Indoctrination of Soviet Youth*. New York: National Strategy Information Center, 1973.

———. *War Survival in Soviet Strategy: Civil Defense*. Miami, Fla.: Center for Advanced International Studies, University of Miami, 1976.

Graham, Albert E., Jr. "Soviet Military Commissariats: History, Organization and Function." M.A. thesis, Georgetown University, 1970.

Grau, Lester W. "The Bear Went Over the Mountain: Soviet Tactics and Tactical Lessons Learned During Their War in Afghanistan." *Journal of Slavic Military Studies* 8 (March 1995): 97–163.

Gray, Colin. *War, Peace, and Victory*. New York: Simon and Schuster, 1990.

Green, William C. *Soviet Nuclear Weapons Policy: A Research and Bibliographic Guide*. Boulder, Colo.: Westview, 1987.

Green, William C., and Theodore Karasik, eds. *Gorbachev and His Generals: The Reform of Soviet Military Doctrine*. Boulder, Colo.: Westview, 1990.

Gregory, Paul R. "Economic Growth, U.S. Defence Expenditures and the Soviet Defence Budget: A Suggested Model." *Soviet Studies* 26, no. 1 (1974): 72–80.

———. *Restructuring the Soviet Economic Bureaucracy*. New York: Cambridge University Press, 1990.

Gregory, Paul R., and Robert C. Stuart. *Soviet Economic Structure and Performance*. New York: Harper and Row, 3d ed. 1986, 4th ed. 1990.

Gromley, Dennis. "A New Dimension to Soviet Theater War." *Orbis* 29 (Fall 1985): 537–69.

———. "Emerging Attack Options in Soviet Theater Strategy." In Hoffman, Wohlstetter, and Yost, *Swords and Shields*, 87–122.

Guertner, Gary L. "Three Images of Soviet Arms Control Compliance." *Political Science Quarterly* 103, no. 2 (1988): 321–46.

Habeck, Mary. "Imagining War: The Development of Armored Doctrine in Germany and the Soviet Union, 1919–1939." Ph.D. diss., Yale University, 1996.

Hansen, James H. *Correlation of Forces: Four Decades of Soviet Military Development*. New York: Praeger, 1987.

Harrison, Mark. *Soviet Planning in Peace and War, 1938–1945.* London: Cambridge University Press, 1985.

Hemsley, John. *Soviet Troop Control: The Role of Command Technology in the Soviet Military System.* New York: Brassey's, 1982.

Herspring, Dale R. *The Soviet High Command, 1967–89.* Princeton, N.J.: Princeton University Press, 1990.

Herspring, Dale R., and Ivan Volgyes, eds. *Civil-Military Relations in Communist Systems.* Boulder, Colo.: Westview, 1978.

Heuser, Beatrice. "Warsaw Pact Military Doctrines in the 1970s and 1980s: Findings in the East German Archives." *Comparative Strategy* 12, no. 4 (1993).

Hintze, Otto. *The Historical Essays of Otto Hintze.* Ed. Felix Gilbert. New York: Oxford University Press, 1975.

Hoffman, Fred S., Albert Wohlstetter, and David S. Yost, eds. *Swords and Shields: NATO, the USSR, and New Choices for Long-Range Offense and Defense.* Lexington, Mass.: D. C. Heath, 1987.

Holden, Gerard. *Soviet Military Reform: Conventional Disarmament and the Crisis of Militarized Socialism.* London: Pluto, 1991.

Holloway, David. "Battle Tanks and ICBMs." In Amann and Cooper, *Industrial Innovation,* 368–414.

———. "Innovation in the Defence Sector." In Amann and Cooper, *Industrial Innovation,* 277–367.

———. *The Soviet Union and the Arms Race.* New Haven: Yale University Press, 1983.

———. *Stalin and the Bomb: The Soviet Union and Atomic Energy 1939–1956.* New Haven: Yale University Press, 1994.

———. "State, Society, and the Military Under Gorbachev." *International Security* 14, no. 3 (1989–90): 5–24.

Holloway, David, and Jane M. O. Sharp. *The Warsaw Pact: Alliance in Transition?* Ithaca, N.Y.: Cornell University Press, 1984.

Hooker, Mark T. *The Military Uses of Literature: Fiction and the Armed Forces in the Soviet Union.* Westport, Conn.: Praeger, 1996.

Howard, Michael. *War and the Liberal Conscience.* New Brunswick, N.J.: Rutgers University Press, 1978.

Hudson, George E. "Soviet Naval Doctrine and Soviet Politics, 1953–1975." *World Politics* 46, no. 3 (1994):355–83.

———, ed. *Soviet National Security Policy Under Perestroika.* Boston: Unwin Hyman, 1990.

Huntington, Samuel. *The Soldier and the State: The Theory and Politics of Civil-Military Relations.* Cambridge: Harvard University Press, 1957.

Ivanov, D. A., V. P. Savel'yev, and P. V. Shemanskii. *Fundamentals of Tactical Command and Control.* Moscow: Voenizdat, 1977.

Jermakowicz, Wladyslaw W. "Foundations and Prospects for Soviet Economic Reforms: 1949 to 1987." In *Gorbachev's New Thinking,* ed. Ronald D. Liebowitz, 111–46. Cambridge, Mass.: Ballinger, 1988.

Johnson, A. Ross, R. W. Dean, and Alexander Alexiev. *East European Military Establishments: The Warsaw Pact Northern Tier.* New York: Crane Russak, 1980.

Jones, Christopher D. *Soviet Influence in Eastern Europe: Political Autonomy and the Warsaw Pact.* New York: Praeger, 1980.

Jones, Ellen. *Red Army and Society: A Sociology of the Soviet Military.* Boston: Allen and Unwin, 1985.

Kahn, Herman. *On Thermonuclear War*. Princeton, N.J.: Princeton University Press, 1960.

Kaplan, Stephen S. *Diplomacy of Power: Soviet Armed Forces as a Political Instrument*. Washington, D.C.: Brookings Institution, 1981.

Katz, Mark N. *The Third World in Soviet Military Thought*. Baltimore: Johns Hopkins University Press, 1982.

Kaufman, Stuart. "Organizational Politics and Change in Soviet Military Policy." *World Politics* 46 (April 1994): 355–83.

Keep, John. *Last of the Empires: A History of the Soviet Union, 1945–1991*. New York: Oxford University Press, 1995.

———. *The Rise of Social Democracy in Russia*. Oxford: Clarendon, 1963.

Kilmarx, Robert A. *A History of Soviet Air Power*. New York: Praeger, 1962.

Kintner, William R., and Harriet Fast Scott, eds. *The Nuclear Revolution in Soviet Military Affairs*. Norman: University of Oklahoma Press, 1968.

Klehr, Harvey, John Earl Haynes, and Fridrikh I. Firsov. *The Secret World of American Communism*. New Haven: Yale University Press, 1995.

Knight, Amy. *Spies Without Cloaks: The KGB's Successors*. Princeton, N.J.: Princeton University Press, 1996.

Kolkowicz, Roman. *The Soviet Military and the Communist Party*. Princeton, N.J.: Princeton University Press, 1967.

Kornai, Janos. *The Road to a Free Economy*. New York: Norton, 1990.

———. *The Socialist System: The Political Economy of Communism*. Princeton, N.J.: Princeton University Press, 1992.

Kramer, Mark. "The 'Lessons' of the Cuban Missile Crisis for Warsaw Pact Nuclear Operations." *Bulletin: Cold War International History Project* issue 5 (1995): 59, 110–15, 160.

Krepon, Michael. "A Navy to Match National Purposes." *Foreign Affairs* 55 (1977): 355–67.

Kusin, Vladimir. "Gorbachev Agrees to Warsaw Pact Meeting on Military Structures." *Report on Eastern Europe* 2 (22 February 1991): 43–45.

———. "Patterns of Intervention: Budapest, Prague, Vilnius, and Riga." *Report on the USSR* 3, no. 4 (25 January 1991): 3–6.

———. "The Soviet Troops: Mission Abandoned." *Report on Eastern Europe* 1 (7 September 1990): 37–38.

———. "Yet Another End for the Warsaw Pact." *Report on Eastern Europe* 2 (15 March 1991): 34.

Laird, Robbin F., and Dale R. Herspring. *The Soviet Union and Strategic Arms*. Boulder, Colo.: Westview, 1984.

Lambeth, Benjamin S., and Kevin Lewis. *The Strategic Defense Initiative in Soviet Planning and Policy*. Santa Monica, Calif.: Rand Corporation, 1988.

Lebow, Richard Ned. "The Soviet Offensive in Europe: The Schifflen Plan Revisited?" *International Security* 9, no. 1 (1985).

Lee, William T. *The Estimation of Soviet Defense Expenditures, 1955–75: An Unconventional Approach*. New York: Praeger, 1977.

Lee, William T., and Richard F. Starr. *Soviet Military Policy Since World War II*. Stanford, Calif.: Hoover Institution Press, 1986.

Leebaert, Derek, and Timothy Dickson, eds. *Soviet Strategy and New Military Thinking*. New York: Cambridge University Press, 1992.

Leites, Nathan. *Soviet Style in War*. New York: Crane Russak, 1982.

Lenin, Vladimir I. *The Lenin Anthology*. Ed. Robert C. Tucker (New York: W. W. Norton, 1975).

Lepingwell, John. "Soviet Civil-Military Relations and the August Coup." *World Politics* 44, no. 4 (1992): 539–72.

Liddell Hart, B. H., ed. *The Red Army.* New York: Harcourt, Brace, 1956.

Ligachev, Yegor K. *Inside Gorbachev's Kremlin.* New York: Pantheon, 1993.

Lopatin, Vladimir. "The Army and the Economy: Aspects of Soviet Military Reform." *Global Affairs* 6, no. 1 (1991): 1–22.

Luke, Timothy W. *Ideology and Soviet Industrialization.* Westport, Conn.: Greenwood, 1985.

MacFarlane, S. Neil. *Superpower Rivalry and the Third World Radicalism: The Idea of National Liberation.* Baltimore: Johns Hopkins University Press, 1985.

Macgregor, Douglas A. "Uncertain Allies: East European Forces in the Warsaw Pact." *Soviet Studies* 38 (1986): 207–26.

Mackintosh, Malcolm. *Juggernaut: A History of the Soviet Armed Forces.* New York: Macmillan, 1967.

Mahoney, Shane E. "Defensive Doctrine: The Crisis in Soviet Military Thought." *Slavic Review* 49, no. 3 (1990): 398–408.

Malle, Silvana. *The Economic Organization of War Communism, 1918–1921.* New York: Cambridge University Press, 1985.

Marx, Karl, and Friedrich Engels. *The Communist Manifesto.* New York: International Publishers, 1948.

Marxism-Leninism on War and the Army. Moscow: Progress Publishers, 1972. Published under the auspices of USAF, USGPO. Trans. of *Marksizm-Leninizm o voine i armii.* Author collective, fourteen Soviet authors. Moscow, 5th ed., 1968.

Matiunin, Sergiusz. "The Cossack Revival." *Uncaptive Minds* 7, nos. 1–2 (1994–95): 105–18.

Matlock, Jack F., Jr. *Autopsy on an Empire: The American Ambassador's Account of the Collapse of the Soviet Union.* New York: Random House, 1995.

MccGwire, Michael. *Military Objectives in Soviet Foreign Policy.* Washington, D.C.: Brookings Institution, 1987.

MccGwire, Michael, Ken Booth, and John McDonnell, eds. *Soviet Naval Policy: Objectives and Constraints.* New York: Praeger, 1975.

Mendelson, Sarah E. "Internal Battles, External Wars: Politics, Learning, and the Soviet Withdrawal from Afghanistan." *World Politics* 45, no. 3 (1993): 327–60.

Menning, Bruce W. *Bayonets Before Bullets: The Imperial Russian Army, 1861–1914.* Bloomington: Indiana University Press, 1992.

Meyer, Stephen M. "How the Threat (and the Coup) Collapsed." *International Security* 16, no. 3 (1991–92): 5–38.

———. "The Sources and Prospects of Gorbachev's New Political Thinking on Security." *International Security* 13, no. 2 (1988): 124–63.

———. "Soviet Theatre Nuclear Forces." *Adelphi Papers* no. 187, parts 1 and 2. International Institute for Strategic Studies, 1983–84.

Mihalisko, Kathleen. "Ukrainians Ponder Creation of National Army." *Report on the USSR* 3 (22 February 1991): 16–18.

The Military Balance, 1985–1986. London: International Institute for Strategic Studies, 1985.

The Military Balance, 1987–1988. London: International Institute for Strategic Studies, 1987.

Nation, R. Craig. *Black Earth, Red Star: A History of Soviet Security Policy, 1917–1991.* Ithaca, N.Y.: Cornell University Press, 1993.

Neely, Theodore A., and Stephen F. Kime. "Perestroika, Doctrinal Change, and the Soviet Navy." *Strategic Review* 16 (1988): 45–55.

Nelson, Ronald R. "A New Soviet Military? The Next Generation." *Orbis* 33, no. 2 (1989): 195–207.

Nichols, Thomas M. *The Sacred Cause: Civil-Military Conflict Over Soviet National Security Policy, 1917–1992.* Ithaca, N.Y.: Cornell University Press, 1993.

North, Douglass C. *Institutions, Institutional Change, and Economic Performance.* New York: Cambridge University Press, 1990.

———. *Structure and Change in Economic History.* New York: Norton, 1981.

Nove, Alec. *An Economic History of the USSR.* Harmondsworth, Middlesex, England: Penguin, 1982.

———. *The Soviet Economy.* New York: Praeger, 1966.

Odom, William E. "A Dissenting View on the Group Approach to Soviet Politics." *World Politics* 28 (July 1976): 542–67.

———. "How Far Can Soviet Reform Go?" *Problems of Communism* 36 (November-December, 1987): 12–24.

———. "The Implications of Active Defense of NATO for Soviet Military Strategy." In Hoffman, Wohlstetter, and Yost, *Swords and Shields,* 159–74.

———. "The Militarization of Soviet Society." *Problems of Communism* 25, no. 5 (1976): 34–51.

———. *On Internal War: American and Soviet Approaches to Third World Clients and Insurgencies.* Durham, N.C.: Duke University Press, 1993.

———. "The Riddle of Soviet Defense Spending." *Russia* no. 2 (1981): 53–58.

———. "Smashing an Icon." *National Interest* no. 21 (1990): 62–74.

———. "The Soviet Approach to Nuclear Weapons: A Historical Review." *ANNALS* 469 (1983): 117–35.

———. "Soviet Force Posture." *Problems of Communism* 34 (July–August 1985): 1–14.

———. "The Soviet Military: The Party Connection." *Problems of Communism* 22, no. 5 (1973): 12–26.

———. "The Soviet Military in Transition." *Problems of Communism* 39, no. 3 (1990): 51–71.

———. "Soviet Politics and After." *World Politics* 45 (October 1992): 66–98.

———. *The Soviet Volunteers: Modernization and Bureaucracy in a Public Mass Organization.* Princeton, N.J.: Princeton University Press, 1973.

———. *Unreasonable Sufficiency? Assessing the New Soviet Strategy.* London: Institute for European and Defence Studies, 1990.

———. "Who Controls Whom in Moscow?" *Foreign Policy* no. 19 (1975): 109–22.

———. "Why Does the Soviet Union Build Such Large Military Forces?" In *On Not Confusing Ourselves,* ed. Andrew Marsall, J. J. Martin, and Henry S. Rowen, 114–46. Boulder, Colo.: Westview, 1991.

Odom, William E., and Robert Dujarric. *Commonwealth or Empire? Russia, Central Asia, and the Transcaucasus.* Indianapolis: Hudson Institute, 1995.

Olcott, Martha Brill. *The Kazakhs.* Stanford, Calif.: Hoover Institution Press, 1987.

Olson, Mancur. *The Rise and Decline of Nations.* New Haven: Yale University Press, 1982.

Panico, Christopher J. "The Rise and Fall of the Heavy Bomber: The Soviet Union and Strategic Bombing, 1925–1940." M.A. thesis, Yale University, 1991.

Paret, Peter. *Understanding War: Essays on Clausewitz and the History of Military Power.* Princeton, N.J.: Princeton University Press, 1992.

Parker, John W. *Kremlin in Transition.* Vol. 2, *Gorbachev, 1985–1989.* Boston: Unwin Hyman, 1991.

Parrott, Bruce. *The Soviet Union and Ballistic Missile Defense.* Boulder, Colo.: Westview, 1987.

Payne, Keith. *Deterrence in the Second Nuclear Age.* Lexington: University of Kentucky Press, 1996.

———. *Nuclear Deterrence in U.S.-Soviet Relations.* Boulder, Colo.: Westview, 1982.

Petersen, Philip A., and John G. Hines. "The Conventional Offensive in Soviet Theater Strategy." *Orbis* 37 (Fall 1983): 695–739.

Pipes, Richard. *The Russian Revolution.* New York: Vintage Books, 1991.

Porter, Bruce. *The USSR in Third World Conflicts: Soviet Arms and Diplomacy in Local Wars, 1945–1980.* New York: Cambridge University Press, 1984.

Prybyla, Jan. *Market and Plan Under Socialism: The Bird in the Cage.* Stanford, Calif.: Hoover Institution Press, 1987.

Putsch: The Diary, Three Days That Collapsed the Empire. Oakville, N.Y.: Mosaic, 1992.

Rakowska-Harmstone, Teresa. "The Dialectics of Nationalism in the USSR." *Problems of Communism* 23 (July–August 1974): 13.

———. "Nationalities and the Soviet Military." In *The Nationalities Factor in Soviet Politics and Society,* ed. Lubomyr Hajda and Mark Beissinger, 72–94. Boulder, Colo.: Westview, 1990.

Remnick, David. *Lenin's Tomb.* New York: Random House, 1993.

Rice, Condoleeza. "The Party, the Military, and Decision Authority." *World Politics* 60, no. 1 (1987): 55–81.

Roberts, Cynthia A. "Prelude to Catastrophe: Soviet Security Policy Between the World Wars." Ph.D. diss., Columbia University, 1995.

Roeder, Philip G. *Red Sunset: The Failure of Soviet Politics.* Princeton, N.J.: Princeton University Press, 1993.

Rosefielde, Steven. "Soviet Defence Spending: The Contribution of the New Accountancy." *Soviet Studies* 42 (January 1990): 59–80.

Rowen, Henry S., and Charles Wolf Jr., eds. *The Impoverished Superpower: Perestroika and the Military Burden.* San Francisco: ICS, 1990.

Rowny, Edward. *U.S. and Soviet Approaches to Arms Control.* Washington, D.C.: Department of State, 1986.

Rubinstein, Alvin Z. *Moscow's Third World Strategy.* Princeton, N.J.: Princeton University Press, 1989.

Ruehl, Lothar. "Offensive Defense in the Warsaw Pact." *Survival* 33 (1991): 442–50.

Rush, Myron. "Guns Over Butter in Soviet Policy." *International Security* 7, no. 3 (1982–83): 167–97.

Sadykiewicz, Michael. *Organizing for Coalition Warfare.* Santa Monica, Calif.: Rand Corporation, 1988.

———. *The Warsaw Pact Command Structure in Peace and War.* Santa Monica, Calif.: Rand Corporation, 1988.

Samuelson, Lennart. *Soviet Defence Industry Planning: Tukhachevskii and Military Mobilization, 1926–37.* Stockholm: Stockholm School of Economics, 1996.

Savel'yev, Aleksandr G., and Nikolai N. Detinov. *The Big Five: Arms Control Decision-Making in the Soviet Union.* Westport, Conn.: Praeger, 1995.

Schelling, Thomas. *The Strategy of Conflict.* New York: Oxford University Press, 1960.

Schumpeter, Joseph. *Capitalism, Socialism, and Democracy.* New York: Harper and Row, 1947, 81–86.

Scott, Harriet Fast, and William F. Scott. *The Armed Forces of the USSR.* 3d. rev. ed. Boulder, Colo.: Westview, 1984.

Seaton, Albert, and Joan Seaton. *The Soviet Army: 1918 to the Present.* New York: New American Library, 1987.

Selznick, Philip. *The Organizational Weapon: A Study of Bolshevik Strategy and Tactics.* Glencoe, Ill: Free Press, 1960.

Sheehy, Ann. "The Alma-Ata Riots and Their Aftermath." *Radio Liberty* 3/87 (23 December 1986).

———. "Soviet Media Coverage of Recent Events in Armenia and Azerbaijan." *Radio Liberty* 109/88 (14 March 1988).

Sheer, Alan B. *The Other Side of Arms Control: Soviet Objectives in the Soviet Era.* Boston: Unwin Hyman, 1988.

Shevardnadze, Eduard. *The Future Belongs to Freedom.* New York: Free Press, 1991.

Shreeves, Rosamund. "Mothers Against the Draft: Women's Activism in the USSR." *Report on the USSR* 2 (21 September 1990): 3–7.

Simon, Jeffrey. *Warsaw Pact Forces: Problems in Command and Control.* Boulder, Colo.: Westview, 1985.

Simon, Jeffrey, and Trond Gilberg, eds. *Security Implications of Nationalism in Eastern Europe.* Boulder, Colo.: Westview, 1985.

Simpkin, Richard, with John Erickson. *Deep Battle: The Brainchild of Marshal Tukhachevskii.* London: Brassey's, 1987.

Smart, Christopher. "Amid the Ruins, Arms Makers Raise New Threats." *Orbis* 36 (Summer 1992): 353.

Snel, Gerard. *From the Atlantic to the Urals: The Reorientation of Soviet Military Strategy, 1981–1990.* Amsterdam: VU University Press, 1996.

Sokolov, Boris V. "The Role of Lend-Lease in Soviet Military Efforts, 1941–45." *Journal of Slavic Military Studies* 7, no. 3 (1994): 567–86.

Soviet Acquisition of Militarily Significant Technology: An Update. 1985.

Soviet Military Power: An Assessment of the Threat, 1988. Washington, D.C.: Government Printing Office, 1988.

Spahr, William J. *Zhukov: The Rise and Fall of a Great Captain.* Novato, Calif.: Presidio, 1993.

Spulber, Nicolas. *The Soviet Economy: Structure, Principles, Problems.* New York: Norton, 1962.

Starry, Don. "Extending the Battlefield." *Military Review,* March 1981, 28–42.

Stepankov, V., ed. *The August Coup.* 6 vols. Moscow: 1991. [Rough English translation of Procurator General Stepankov's official report.]

Stevens, Sayre. "The Soviet BMD Program." In *Ballistic Missile Defense,* ed. Ashton B. Carter and David N. Schwartz, 182–220. Washington, D.C.: Brookings Institution, 1984.

Stone, David R. "The Red Army and Stalin's Revolution: Defense Industry and the Transformation of the Soviet Economy, 1926–33." Ph.D. diss., Yale University, 1997.

Sutton, Anthony C. *Western Technology and Soviet Economic Development 1945–1965.* Stanford, Calif.: Hoover Institution Press, 1973.

Szporluk, Roman. *Communism and Nationalism.* New York: Oxford University Press, 1988.

Tarasulo, Isaac J., ed. *Perils of Perestroika: Viewpoints from the Soviet Press, 1989–1991.* Wilmington, Del.: SR, 1992.

Tedstrom, John. "Managing the Conversion of Defense Industries." *Report on the USSR* 2 (16 February 1990): 11–18.

———. "The Shatalin Plan and Industrial Conversion." *Report on the USSR* 2 (16 November 1990): 8–10.

Thaden, Edward C. *Conservative Nationalism in Nineteenth Century Russia.* Seattle: University of Washington Press, 1964.

Tolz, Vera. "Developments in Dispute over Nagorno-Karabakh," *Radio Liberty* 99/88 (4 March 1988).

Tritten, James J. *Soviet Naval Forces and Nuclear Warfare: Weapons, Employment, and Policy.* Boulder, Colo.: Westview, 1986.

Trulock, Notra, III. "Soviet Perspectives on Limited Nuclear War." In Hoffman, Wohlstetter, and Yost, *Swords and Shields,* 53–86.

Tsypkin, Mikhail. "The Soviet Military: Glasnost' Against Secrecy." *Problems of Communism* 40, no. 3 (1991): 51–66.

Ulam, Adam. *Expansion and Coexistence: The History of Soviet Foreign Policy, 1917–1967.* New York: Praeger, 1968.

Valenta, Jiri, and William C. Potter, eds. *Soviet Decisionmaking for National Security.* London: Allen and Unwin, 1984.

Van Cleave, William R. *Fortress USSR: The Soviet Strategic Defense Initiative and the U.S. Strategic Defense Response.* Stanford, Calif.: Hoover Institution Press, 1986.

van Oudenaren, John. "Deterrence, War-Fighting, and Soviet Military Doctrine." *Adelphi Papers* no. 210. International Institute for Strategic Studies, 1986.

Volgyes, Ivan. *The Political Reliability of the Warsaw Pact Armies: The Southern Tier.* Durham, N.C.: Duke University Press, 1982.

von Hagen, Mark. *Soldiers in the Proletariatian Dictatorship: The Army and the Socialist State, 1917–1930.* Ithaca, N.Y.: Cornell University Press, 1990.

Waller, J. Michael. *Secret Empire: The KGB in Russia Today.* Boulder, Colo.: Westview, 1984.

Warner, Edward L., III. *The Military in Contemporary Soviet Politics: An Institutional Analysis.* New York: Praeger, 1977.

Watson, Bruce W., and Peter M. Dunn, eds. *The Future of the Soviet Navy: An Assessment to the Year 2000.* Boulder, Colo.: Westview, 1986.

Weickhardt, George G. "Recent Discussion of Defense Economics." *Report on the USSR* 2 (9 March 1990): 9–13.

Wetting, Gerhard. "New Thinking on Security and East-West Relations." *Problems of Communism* 37, no. 2 (1988): 1–19.

Whiting, Kenneth R. *Soviet Air Power.* Boulder, Colo.: Westview, 1986.

Wilkson, Spencer. *The Brain of the Army: A Popular Account of the German General Staff.* New ed. Westminster: Archibald Constable, 1895.

Wimbush, S. Enders, ed. *Soviet Nationalities in Strategic Perspective.* New York: St. Martin's, 1985.

Wohlstetter, Albert. "The Delicate Balance of Terror." *Foreign Affairs* 37, no. 2 (1959): 211–34.

Wolfe, Thomas W. "Political Primacy Vs. Professional Elan." *Problems of Communism* 13, no. 3 (1964): 14–22.

———. "Soviet Approaches to SALT." *Problems of Communism* 19, no. 5 (1970): 1–10.

———. *Soviet Strategy at the Crossroads.* Cambridge: Harvard University Press, 1964.

Wollenberg, Eric. *The Red Army.* London: Secker and Warburg, 1938.

Yakovlev, Alexander. *The Fate of Marxism in Russia*. New Haven: Yale University Press, 1993.

Yasmann, Victor. "Did Paratroopers Refuse to Shoot?" *Report on the USSR* 3, no. 5 (1 February 1991): 18.

Yeltsin, Boris N. *Against the Grain*. New York: Summit, 1990.

———. *The Struggle for Russia*. New York: Random House, 1994.

Yost, David S. *Soviet Ballistic Missile Defense and the Western Alliance*. New York: Cambridge University Press, 1988.

Zelikow, Philip, and Condoleeza Rice. *Germany Unified and Europe Transformed: A Study in Statecraft*. Cambridge: Harvard University Press, 1995.

Zhong, Yang. "The Transformation of the Soviet Military and the August Coup." *Armed Forces and Society* 19, no. 1 (1992): 47–70.

Zhurkin, V., S. Karagonov, and A. Kortunov. "Reasonable Sufficiency: Or How to Break the Vicious Circle." *New Times* 40 (12 October 1987): 13–15.

Zisk, Kimberly Marten. *Engaging the Enemy: Organization Theory and Soviet Military Innovation, 1955–1991*. Princeton, N.J.: Princeton University Press, 1993.

Zubok, Vlad. "Nuclear Weapons After Stalin's Death: Moscow Enters the H-Bomb Age." *Bulletin: Cold War International History Project* 4 (Fall 1994): 14–18.

Non-English-Language Sources

Akhromeev, Sergei F., and Georgii M. Kornienko. *Glazami marshala i diplomata*. Moscow: MO, 1992.

Alimurzaev, G. "Shchit ili mech? K istorii Sovietskoi voennoi doktriny." *Mezhdunarodnaya Zhizn'* no. 4 (1989): 112–22.

Alksnis, Viktor. "Armiyu ne otdelits' ot naroda." *Krasnaya zevzda*, 15 November 1990.

Arbatov, A. G., A. A. Vasilev, and A. A. Kokoshin. "Yadernye oruzhiya i strategicheskaya stabil'nost." *SShA: Ekonomika, ideologiya, politika*, nos. 9–10 (1987): 3–13, 17–24.

Babakov, A. A. *Vooruzhennye sily SSSR posle voiny, 1945–1986 Gg*. Moscow: Voenizdat, 1987.

Baranets, B., N. Rumyantsev, and Ye. Lukashenya. "Nadezhnost' internatsional'nogo zakala." *Kommunist vooruzhennykh sil* 8 (1989): 35–44.

Belkov, O. "Armiya dolzhna delat' svow delo." *Kommunist vooruzhennykh sil* 19 (October 1989): 14–19.

Blagovolin, Sergei E. "Geopoliticheskie aspekty oboronitel'noi dostatochnosti." *Kommunist* no. 4 (1990): 114–23.

———. "Voennaya moshch': skol'ko, kakaya, zachem." *Mirovaya ekonomika i mezhdunarodnye otnosheniya*, August 1989, pp. 5–19.

Bogdanov, V., and G. Lokshin. "Razumnaya znachit dostatochnost'." *XX vek i mir* 12 (December 1988): 2–9.

Bulanov, A. I., and Krylova I. A. "Sootnoshenie politiki i yadernoi voiny." *Voprosy filosofi* no. 5 (1988): 110–24.

Chernyaev, Anatolii S. *Shest' let s Gorbachevym*. Moscow: Izdatel'skaya gruppa Progress-Kultura, 1993.

Danchenko, A. M., and I. F. Vydrin, eds. *Voennaya pedagogiya*. Moscow: Voenizdat, 1973.

Danilevskii, A. F. "Tverdaya liniya." *Voenno-istoricheskii zhurnal* no. 4 (1989): 14–21.

Dmitriev, V., and V. Strebkov. "Ustarevshaya kontseptsiya." *Krasnaya zvezda*, 10 April 1990.

Dudorov, N. "Konversiya dlya agro-promyshlennosti." *Ekonomicheskaya gazeta* no. 46 (November 1989): 10.

Frunze, M. V. *Izbrannie proizvedeniya.* Moscow: Voenizdat, 1957.

Gareev, Makhmut A. *M. V. Frunze: Voennyi teoretik.* Moscow: Voenizdat,1985.

Gorbachev, Mikhail S. *Izbrannye rechi i stat'i.* Vol. 7. Moscow: Izdatel'stvo politicheskoi literatury, 1990.

————. *Perestroika i novoe myshlenie dlya nashei strany i dlya vsego mira.* Moscow: Politizdat, 1987.

————. "Zadachi obshchenarodnoi bazhnosti." *Krasnaya zvezda,* 2 April 1991.

Gorbatschow, Michial. *Erinnerungen.* Berlin: Siedler Verlag, 1995.

Gorshkov, M. K., and V. V. Zhuralev, eds. *Nesokrushimaya i legendarnaya: v ogne politicheskiyh batalii.* Moscow: Terra, 1994.

Grechko, Andrei A. *Vooruzhennye sily sovetskogo soyuza.* Moscow: Voenizdat, 1975.

Gribkov, Anatolii I. *Im dienste der Sowjetunion: erinnerungen eines armeegenerals.* Berlin: q Velag, 1992.

Isaev, A. S. "Reforma i oboronnye otrasli." *Kommunist* no. 5 (1989): 24–30.

Izyumov, A., and A. Kortunov. "Sovetskii soyuz v menyayushchemsya mire." *Mezhdunarodnaya zhizn'* no. 7 (1988): 53–64.

Kaledin, Sergei. "Stroibat." *Novyi mir* 4 (1989): 68–89.

Khalipov, Vyacheslav F. *Voena politika KPSS.* Moscow: Voenizdat, 1988.

Kireev, A. "Konversiya v sovetskom izmerenii." *Mezhdunarodnaya zhizn'* no. 4 (1990): 99–110.

Kirshin, Yurii. "Za chem nuzhna voennaya reforma?" *Novoe vremya* no. 12, 20–26 March 1990, pp. 30–31.

Kirshin, Yu. Ya., V. M. Popov, and R. A. Savushkin. *Politicheskoe soderzhanie sovremennoi voiny.* Moscow: Nauka, 1987.

Kokoshin, A. A., A. G. Arbatov, and A. A. Vasilev. "Sokrashenie yadernykh vooruzhenii i strategicheskaya stabil'nost'." *SShA: ekonomika, politika, ideologiya* 2 (1988): 3–12.

Kokoshin, A. A., and V. V. Larionov. *Doktriny, konseptsii, perspektivy.* Moscow: Progress, 1990.

————. "Kurskaya bitva v svete sovremennoi doktriny." *Mirovaya ekonomika I mezhdunarodnaya otnosheniya,* August 1987, pp. 32–40.

————. "Protivostoyanie sil obschlego naznacheniya v knotekste obespecheniya strategicheskoistabil'nosti." *Mirovaya ekonomika i mezhdunarodnye otnosheniya,* June 1988, pp. 23–31.

Kononov, Igor, and Yurii Borisov. "Silna li armiia?" *Smena* 18 (September 1989): 6–8, 18.

Korichnevii putch krasnykh. Moscow: Tekst, 1991.

Kornienko, Georgii M. *Kholodnaya voina: svidatel'stvo ee uchastnika.* Moscow: Mezhdunarodnye otnosheniya, 1994.

Kosarev, V. "Doktrina obespecheniya mira." *Krasnaya zvezda,* 29 September 1987. Interview with General A. I. Gribkov, chief of staff of the Warsaw Pact forces.

Kozlov, M. M., leader of author collective. *Akademiya general'nogo shtaba.* Moscow: Voenizdat. 1987.

Kozlov, S. N., M. V. Smirnov, I. S. Vaz', and P. A. Sidorov, *O Sovetskoi voennoi nauke.* 2d ed. Moscow: Voenizdat, 1964.

Kravchenko, G. S. *Voennaya ekonomika SSSR v gody Velikoi Otechestvennoi Voiny, 1941–1945.* Moscow: Voenizdat, 1970.

Krivosheev, G. F. "Ob vseobshchei voennoi sluzhbe." *Krasnaya zvezda,* 31 August 1989.

————, ed. *Grif sekretnosti snyat: poteri vooruzhennykh sil SSSR v voinakh, boevych desitviyakh i voennykh konfliktakh.* Moscow: Voenizdat, 1993.

Krupchenko, I. Ye. "K semidesyatoi godovshchine velikogo Oktyagtrya." *Voenno-istoricheskii zhurnal* 10 (October 1987): 3–10.

Kunadze, Georgii F., "Ob oboronnitel'noi dostatochnosti voennogo potentsiala SSSR." *Mirovaya ekonomika i mezhdunarodnye otnosheniya,* October 1989, pp. 68–83.

Kuznetsov, E. N., and V. Shirokov. "Naukoemkye prioizodstva i konversiya oboroni promyshlennosti." *Kommunist* no. 10 (1989): 15–22.

Lebed', Aleksandr. *Za derzhavu obidno . . .* Moscow: Moskovskaya Pravda, 1995.

Leonov, N. S. *Likholet'e.* Moscow: Mezhdunarodnye otnoshenyia, 1995.

Lipitskii, S. "Voennaya reforma 1924–25 godov." *Kommunist* 4 (1990): 102–9.

Lizichev, A. D. *Put' peremen, vremya deistvii.* Moscow: Voenizdat, 1989.

Lobov, Vladimir N. *Voennaya reforma: svyaz' vremen.* Moscow: Aviar, 1991.

Lomov, N. A., ed. *Nauchno-tekhnicheskii progress i revolyutsiya v voennom dele.* Moscow: Voenizdat, 1973.

Lopatin, V. "Armiya i politika." *Znamya* 7 (1990): 147–59.

————. "Proekt voennoi reformy." *Izvestiya,* 11 April 1990.

Lyakhovskii, Aleksandr. *Tragediya i doblest' Afgana.* Moscow: GPI Iskona, 1995.

Lyubimov, Yurii. "Ob oboronitel'noi dostatochnosti i nekhvatka kompetentnosti." *Kommunist Vooruzhennykh Sil* no. 16 (1989): 21–26.

Milovidov, A. S., ed. *Vonno-teoreticheskoe nasledie V. I. Lenina i problemy sovremennoi voiny.* Moscow: Voenizdat, 1987.

Milovidov, A. S., and V. G. Kozlov, eds. *Folosofskoe nasledie V. I. Lenina i voprosy sovremennoi voiny.* Moscow: Voenizdat, 1972.

Moiseev, M. A. "Istoki napryazhennosti." *Krasnaya zvezda,* 4 May 1989.

————. "Sovetskaya voennaya doktrina." *Pravda,* 13 March 1989.

————. "S pozitsii oboronitel'noi doktriny." *Kraznaya zvezda,* 10 February 1989.

————. "Zadachi u nas odni." *Krasnaya zvezda,* 10 February 1990.

Ogarkov, N. V. *Vsegda v gotovnosti k zashchite otechestva.* Moscow: Voenizdat, 1982.

Plugatarev, I. "Pered litsom ili po puti otritsaniya?" *Kommunist vooruzhennykh sil* 7 (1990): 29–38.

Plutnik, Albert. "Voennyi urok." *Izvestiya,* 21 March 1989.

Ponomarev, Manki. "Kriterii dostatochnosti: dva podkhoda." *Krasnaya zvezda,* 11 December 1988.

Portugal'skii, R. M. "K voprosu o perekhode ot oborony k nastupleniyu." *Voennaya mysl'* no. 6 (1990): 15–22.

Pozdnyakov, Ye. "Natsional'noe i internatsional'noe v vneshnei politike." *Mezhdunarodnaya zhizn'* no. 5 (1989): 3–14.

Rodin, B. N., ed. *Razvitie tyla sovetskykh vooruzhennykh sil, 1918–1988.* Moscow: Voenizdat, 1989.

Rodionov, Igor. "Voennaya nauka." *Krasnaya zvezda,* 2 December 1992, pp. 2–3.

Saitgareev, V. "Ekonomicheskie korni sovetskoi voennoi byurokratii." *Voprosy Ekonomiki* no. 10 (1990): 31–39.

Savinkin, A. "Kakaya armiya nam nuzhna?" *Moskovskie novosti* no. 45 (1988): 6.

Savkin, V. E. *Osnovnye printsipy operativnogo isskustva i takti.* Moscow: Voenizdat, 1972.

Savushkin, R. A. "Istok i razvitie sovetskoi voennoi doktriny." *Voenno-istoricheskii zhurnal* 2 (February 1988): 19–26.

Sein, V. "Sfera osobogo vnimaniya." *Kommunist vooruzhennykh sil* 11 (1989): 19–24.

Semeyko, L. "Vmesto gor oruzhiya.: o printsipe razumnoi dostatochnosti." *Izvestiya*, 13 August 1987.

Shakhnazarov, Georgii. *Tsena svobody: reformatsiya Gorbacheva glazami ego pomoshchnika.* Moscow: Rossika-Zevs, 1993.

Shaposhnikov, Yevgenii. *Vybor.* 2d rev. and expanded ed. Moscow: Nezavisimoe izdatel'stvo PIK, 1995.

Shashkov, E. "Skol'ko stoit besopasnost'?" *Kommunist* 4 (1989): 110–17.

Shlyaga, N. "Splachivat' partiinie ryady." *Krasnaya zvezda*, 30 March 1991.

Shtemenko, S. M. *Novyi zakon i voinskaya sluzhba.* Moscow: Voenizdat, 1968.

Skorodenko, S. "V tselyakh zashchity sotsializma." *Kommunist vooruzhennykh sil* 19 (October 1989): 19–20.

Sokolovskii, Vladimir D. *Voennaya strategiya.* Moscow: Voenizdat, 1962. Rev. eds. 1963, 1968.

Soveshchanie politicheskogo konsul'tativnogo kometita gosudarstv—uchastnikov Varshavskogo Dogovora. Moscow: Izdatel'stvo politicheskoi literatury, 1986.

Stepankov V., and Ye. Lisov. *Kremlevskii zagovor.* Moscow: 1992.

Strebkov, V. "Kriterii voenno-strategicheskogo pariteta." *Kommunist Vooruzhennykh Sil* no. 4 (1989): 18–24.

Studenikin, Petr, and Ivan Taranenko. "Vvidu chrezvychainogo polozheniia . . ." *Pravda*, 30 June 1986.

Sturua, G. M. "Komitet o vosprosakh oborony i bezopasnosti." *Mirovaya ekonomika i mezhdunarodnye otnosheniya*, January 1990, pp. 79–85.

———. "Peripetii voennoi reformy." *Mirovaya ekonomika i mezhdunarodnye otnosheniya*, July 1990, pp. 87–92.

Suleiman, N. *Tyl i snabzhenie deistvuyushchei armii.* Moscow: Gosizdat, 1927.

Surkov, Mikhail. "Za pravdu nado stoyat'." *Sovetskaya Rossiya*, 6 April 1991.

Tabunov, N. "Dialektika klassogo i obshchechelovechstva." *Kommunist vooruzhennykh sil* 8 (1989): 17–24.

Tatarnikov, V. "Do urovni razumnoi dostatochnosti." *Krasnaya zvezda*, 5 January 1988.

Trotsky, Leon. *Kak vooruzhilas' revolutsiya.* 3 vols. (Moscow, 1923–25).

XXVII S'ezd KPSS o Sovetskoi voennoi doktrine. Moscow: Voenizdat, 1989.

Tyushkevich, S. A. *Kritika burzhuaznykh kontseptsii po voprosam sovetskogo voennogo stroitel'stva.* Moscow: Voenizdat, 1987.

———, ed. *Voina i sovremennost'.* Moscow: Nauka, 1986.

Usachev, I. G. "Vseobshchie i klassovye osnovy v mirovoi politike." *Kommunist* 11 (1988): 10–18.

Varennikov, V. I. "Iz istorii sozdaniya I podgotovki etnicheskykh voennykh chastei." *Voennaya mysl* no. 2 (February 1990): 3–13.

———. "Prednaznacheniie Sovetskykh Vooruzhennykh Sil." *Kommunist vooruzhennikh sil* 18 (September 1989); 22–25.

Vorob'ev, K. "Mera kraine nezhelatel'naya." *Kommunist vooruzhennikh sil* 18 (September 1989): 25–27.

Voroshilov, Kliment E. *Stat'i i rechi.* Moscow: Voenizdat, 1937.

Yaremko, V. "Vozrozhdenie taktiki." *Krasnaya zvezda*, 25 October 1989.

Yazov, D. T. "Na osnove novogo myshleniya." *Krasnaya Zvezda*, 13 April 1989.

———. "Na perelomnom etape." *Krasnaya zvezda*, 2 April 1991.

———. *Na strazhe sotsializma i mira.* Moscow: Voenizdat, 1987.

————. "Novaya model' bezopasnosti i vooruzhennye sily." *Kommunist* no. 18 (1989): 61–72.

————. "O voennoi reforme." *Pravda*, 9 February 1989.

————. *Verny otchizne.* Moscow: Voenizdat, 1988.

————. "V interesakh vseobshchei bezopasnosti i mira." *Izvestiya*, 28 February 1989.

————. "Voennaya reforma." *Krasnaya zvezda*, 5 June 1990.

Yegorov, P. T., I. A. Shlyakov, and N. I. Alabin. *Grazhdanskaya oborona.* Moscow: Vyshaya shkola, 1970.

Zabrodin, V. "Chto 'vysvetila' tragediya v Zakavkaz'e?" *Kommunist vooruzhennykh sil* 6 (1990): 11–12.

Zagladin, N. V., ed. *Vneshnepoliticheshaya straregiya KPSS I novoe politicheskoe myshlenie.* Moscow: Politizdat, 1988.

Zakharov, Matvei V. *General'nii shtab v predvoennye gody.* Moscow: Voenizdat, 1989.

Zhurkin, V., S. Karagonov, and A. Kortunov. "Vyzovy bezopasnosti—Starye i novye." *Kommunist* no. 1 (1988): 42–50.

Index

DATE DUE
